SCIENCE
in the Elementary and Middle School

Dennis W. Sunal

The University of Alabama

Cynthia Szymanski Sunal

The University of Alabama

Merrill
Prentice Hall

Upper Saddle River, New Jersey
Columbus, Ohio

Library of Congress Cataloging-in-Publication Data

Sunal, Dennis W.
   Science in the elementary and middle school/Dennis W. Sunal, Cynthia Szymanski Sunal.
     p.cm.
   Includes bibliographical references and index.
   ISBN 0-13-028342-8
     1. Science-Study and teaching (Elementary) 2. Science-Study and teaching (Middle
school) I. Sunal, Cynthia S. II. Title.

LB1585 .S863 2003
507.1'2—dc21

2001059135

Vice President and Publisher: Jeffery W. Johnston
Editor: Linda Ashe Montgomery
Editorial Assistant: Evelyn Olson
Development Editor: Hope Madden
Production Editor: Linda Hillis Bayma
Production Coordination: Amy Gehl, Carlisle Publishers Services
Design Coordinator: Diane C. Lorenzo
Cover Designer: Ceri Fitzgerald
Cover Photo: SuperStock
Production Manager: Pamela D. Bennett
Director of Marketing: Ann Castel Davis
Marketing Manager: Krista Groshong
Marketing Services Coordinator: Tyra Cooper

This book was set in Berkeley by Carlisle Communications, Ltd. It was printed and bound by Courier Kendallville, Inc.
The cover was printed by The Lehigh Press, Inc.

Photo Credits: Dennis W. Sunal, pp. 2, 6, 11, 16, 26, 29, 33, 34, 36, 60, 81, 106, 123, 145, 153, 158, 166, 175, 215, 228, 236, 239, 250, 260, 278, 311, 322, 348, 361, 376, 388, 397, 412, 416, 446, 449; Cynthia Szymanski Sunal, pp. 52, 70, 96, 140, 190, 202, 329; Luz Carime Bersh, pp. 134, 184; Nancy Swanek Szymanski, pp. 266, 273, 424; Cheryl Sundberg, p. 335.

Pearson Education Ltd.
Pearson Education Australia Pty. Limited
Pearson Education Singapore Ptd. Ltd.
Pearson Education North Asia Ltd.
Pearson Education Canada, Ltd.
Pearson Educación de Mexico, S.A. de C.V.
Pearson Education—Japan
Pearson Education Malaysia Pte. Ltd.
Pearson Education, *Upper Saddle River, New Jersey*

10 9 8 7 6 5 4 3 2 1
ISBN: 0-13-028342-8

Preface

Science in the Elementary and Middle School views science literacy as a vital part of the knowledge of all students and adults in the 21st century. Meaningful learning of science content, skills, and values enables students to fully participate in modern society.

Drawing upon many years of elementary and middle school teaching experience, higher education, supervising, and research, we have written this textbook to illustrate: (1) strategies for teaching relevant science for full understanding; (2) the use of an inquiry approach that empowers students to more fully comprehend their world; and (3) theory and research supporting best practices in the teaching of science.

Our text focuses on *meaningful learning of essential science knowledge that has its foundation in the national science standards*. It is built upon recognizing that students construct knowledge in their own minds so that it has meaning for them. The research literature in science education and in constructivism contributed heavily to the approach taken in this book. As we have worked with the research literature, conducted our own research, and developed and taught science lessons, we have used the theories and strategies discussed in this book. Based in the broader areas of inquiry teaching and learning, we find that the learning cycle approach to structuring lessons and units provides teachers and learners with flexibility, assuring the inclusion of the best aspects of the major theories describing how students learn. We have applied the learning cycle of Exploration, Invention, and Expansion in teaching science concepts, generalizations, skills, and dispositions.

CHAPTER FEATURES

This book is rich in examples and illustrations of how to teach science. Each chapter is organized so that it reflects the nature of inquiry learning through the learning cycle.

Exploration

Each chapter begins with an Exploration activity that helps the readers recall their prior knowledge and use it to solve a specific science teaching and learning problem. *Classroom Scenes* features bring readers into the lessons. The chapter sequence also enables readers to test and check their prior ideas.

Invention

Readers then work with explanations that develop more appropriate and usable ideas related to the teaching and learning area that makes up the focus of the chapter. Each chapter involves an active learning process. Opportunities for reflecting on the reading, checking ideas based on classroom experiences, and interacting with others appear throughout the chapter. These activities help readers reflect on their practice with the new ideas.

Lesson plans for the range of grade levels, from kindergarten through middle school, move the readers from *Classrooms Scenes* and exploratory activities to the planning that results in meaningful science teaching. Lesson plans and *Classroom Scenes* are found throughout the book.

Opportunities for application of and reflection on this book's ideas are found in the *Applying What You Know* activities. Readers will benefit most from these sections if they are used as they are encountered in the book, and if shared with others. Instructors may use these as discussion starters.

Expansion

The latter parts of each chapter focus on the application and extension of the teaching and learning area that makes up the focus of the chapter. These are accomplished through additional scenarios, sample lesson plans, and *Applying What You Know* activities.

ORGANIZATION OF THIS TEXT

Chapters 1 through 6 focus on student learning, inquiry teaching, and setting appropriate science goals. Critical elements for teaching science are dealt with in detail in the remaining chapters. Examples of these include assessment through fully involving diverse learners, integrated teaching across subject areas, classroom management, unit development, incorporating technology, safety, and facility and resource planning. Major curriculum movements, such as multicultural education and the full involvement of diverse learners in the classroom, are discussed in detail and integrated throughout the many science topics considered.

Chapters 12 through 15 tie the book's discussions together by providing a comprehensive approach with starting points for teaching physical sciences, biological sciences, and Earth sciences. These last chapters help the reader anticipate the prior knowledge students may bring to each of these three major science areas. They identify the content and appropriate strategies that can be utilized in teaching each of these areas. These last four chapters can be used as a resource for many of the earlier chapters as those are being read and reflected upon.

SUPPLEMENTS

This textbook and its accompanying materials serve as a comprehensive reference for those who are teaching and developing the science education curriculum.

Companion Website

This text-integrated supplement at *www.prenhall.com/sunal* provides readers with access to Internet links for resources supporting and extending this book's discussion of meaningful science instruction and curriculum through research, meaningful activities, self-assessments, chat areas, and a threaded message board. For the professor, the Syllabus Manager™ allows online creation and management of course syllabi.

Instructor's Manual

This useful tool provides additional support for instructors, including test questions and online integration.

ACKNOWLEDGMENTS

We wish to thank our editors, Hope Madden, Linda Montgomery, and Linda Bayma, for their encouragement and for keeping us on task.

The suggestions and comments of the reviewers challenged us to think in new directions. The extensive amount of time each reviewer devoted to reviewing the manuscript for this book is much appreciated. We would like to thank Sylven S. Beck, George Washington University; William L. Boone, Indiana University; John R. Cannon, University of Nevada; Michael O'Dell, University of Idaho; J. Preston Prather, University of Tennessee; and Robert D. Sweetland, Wayne State College.

Discover the Companion Website Accompanying This Book

THE PRENTICE HALL COMPANION WEBSITE: A VIRTUAL LEARNING ENVIRONMENT

Technology is a constantly growing and changing aspect of our field that is creating a need for content and resources. To address this emerging need, Prentice Hall has developed an online learning environment for students and professors alike—Companion Websites— to support our textbooks.

In creating a Companion Website, our goal is to build on and enhance what the textbook already offers. For this reason, the content for each user-friendly website is organized by chapter and provides the professor and student with a variety of meaningful resources.

For the Professor—

Every Companion Website integrates **Syllabus Manager™**, an online syllabus creation and management utility.

- **Syllabus Manager™** provides you, the instructor, with an easy, step-by-step process to create and revise syllabi, with direct links into the Companion Website and other online content without having to learn HTML.

- Students may log on to your syllabus during any study session. All they need to know is the web address for the Companion Website and the password you've assigned to your syllabus.

- After you have created a syllabus using **Syllabus Manager™**, students may enter the syllabus for their course section from any point in the Companion Website.

- Clicking on a date, the student is shown the list of activities for the assignment. The activities for each assignment are linked directly to actual content, saving time for students.

- Adding assignments consists of clicking on the desired due date, then filling in the details of the assignment—name of the assignment, instructions, and whether it is a one-time or repeating assignment.

- In addition, links to other activities can be created easily. If the activity is online, a URL can be entered in the space provided, and it will be linked automatically in the final syllabus.

- Your completed syllabus is hosted on our servers, allowing convenient updates from any computer on the Internet. Changes you make to your syllabus are immediately available to your students at their next logon.

For the Student—

- **Chapter Objectives**—outline key concepts from the text.
- **Interactive Self-quizzes**—complete with hints and automatic grading that provide immediate feedback for students.

  After students submit their answers for the interactive self-quizzes, the Companion Website **Results Reporter** computes a percentage grade, provides a graphic representation of how many questions were answered correctly and incorrectly, and gives a question-by-question analysis of the quiz. Students are given the option to send their quiz to up to four e-mail addresses (professor, teaching assistant, study partner, and so on).
- **Web Destinations**—links to www sites that relate to chapter content.
- **Message Board**—serves as a virtual bulletin board to post—or respond to—questions or comments to/from a national audience.
- **Chat**—real-time chat with anyone who is using the text anywhere in the country—ideal for discussion and study groups, class projects, and so on.

To take advantage of the many available resources, please visit the *Science in the Elementary and Middle School* Companion Website at

www.prenhall.com/sunal

Brief Contents

Contents

CHAPTER 14

CHAPTER 15

NOTE: Every effort has been made to provide accurate and current Internet information in this book. However, the Internet and information posted on it are constantly changing, so it is inevitable that some of the Internet addresses listed in this textbook will change.

SCIENCE

in the Elementary
and Middle School

1

What Is Effective Science Teaching?

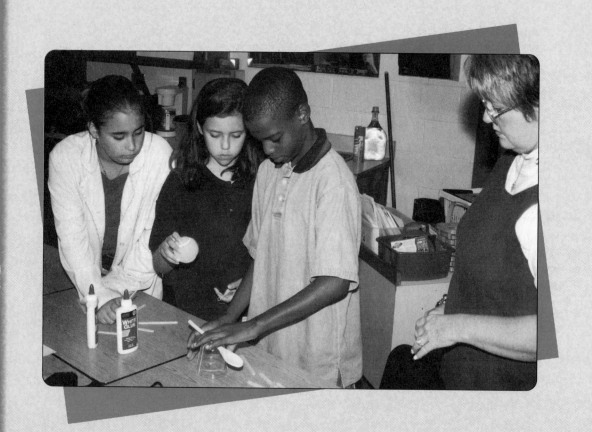

▼△▼ EXPLORING YOUR IDEAS ▽△▽△▽△▽△▽△▽△▽

What image do your students have of science and scientists? What image do *you* have of science and scientists? Draw a quick sketch of a "scientist" at work *before you read on*. Describe the meaning of the drawing in a brief narrative.

When asked to draw such a sketch, many people draw a picture that features a Caucasian male scientist, wearing a white lab coat with a pocket full of pens and pencils. He is middle-aged, wears glasses, is unkempt in appearance, and is partially bald. Flasks, test tubes, filing cabinets, books, and electronic equipment surround him. The science he performs may be harmful to people (Kahle, 1989; Mead & Metraux, 1957).

Look at your drawing. How many of these features did your drawing have? If you were given a chance to add in any of these items, which ones would you add in now?

When people talk about their pictures, their comments suggest that the scientist is antisocial or poorly adjusted, but very busy with his experiments (Kahle, 1989). In 1957, for example, students were asked to draw a sketch of a scientist at work. The comments accompanying their sketches included:

"The scientist is a brain."

"He spends his days indoors sitting in a laboratory."

"He is so involved in his work that he does not know what is going on in the world."

"He has no other interests and neglects his body for his mind."

"He can only talk, eat, breathe, and sleep science." (Mead & Metraux, 1957)

Which of these comments, if any, do you agree with? If you are similar to most people, your sketch will have many of the characteristics identified from previous studies. You are also likely to agree with many of the student comments.

The descriptions of scientists reveal something about people's attitudes toward science, most notably that they have changed little over the 30 years separating the two research studies reported by Mead and Metraux (1957) and Kahle (1989). The image of scientists, and by extension of science, built by these sketches and comments is inaccurate, negative, and likely to make students anxious about science, discouraging them from considering a career in science as either interesting or welcome.

People around the world, from primary school students to undergraduate pre-service teachers, hold stereotypic views of science and scientists (Driver, Leach, Millar, & Scott, 1996; Kahle, 1989). In particular, most elementary and middle school students consider scientists to be male. This masculine image of both science and scientists probably detracts from a girl's interest and self-confidence in science. Kahle (1989) found that attitudes could be changed. After a yearlong intervention program, more middle school boys and girls drew female scientists, and most students' depictions became less stereotypical. The drawings often showed a person with a neat, attractive appearance. These results suggest that stereotypes can be reduced. It is important that teachers recognize the stereotypes they personally hold. Stereotypes are subtly transmitted in communication and behavior. Once stereotypes are recognized, action can be taken to reduce and limit the possibility that we perpetuate these stereotypes with our students.

Chapter Objectives

1. Identify and describe differences between classrooms where teachers have different views or beliefs about science.
2. Describe science in terms of the construction of knowledge.
3. Relate important elements of scientific literacy in a web diagram.
4. Describe why science is an essential part of the elementary and middle school program.
5. Identify the characteristics of effective science teaching.

DIFFERING VIEWS OF SCIENCE IN THE ELEMENTARY AND MIDDLE SCHOOL

Since many students probably hold a stereotypical view of science, teaching science involves helping students find out what science really is. There is no single, simple view of science for people of all ages. This chapter began with the views people hold of science and scientists. The chapter continues by describing differing views of elementary and middle school students' science experiences in classrooms. This investigation of classroom science will lead to a discussion of the meaning of science and scientific literacy in our everyday lives. Several important characteristics of effective science teaching will be explored. The chapter will conclude with a consideration of the key processes in effective science teaching in the elementary and middle school classroom.

Watching young children in a park can be enlightening. They sense, play, and explore, all without being "taught." They ask questions like: "What do birds do at night?" "Where do animals get their fur?" "When do trees eat?" "How are rocks made?" This natural exploration of learning science begins at birth and continues as the "tools" of observation, language, reading, and mathematics are learned and used. The exploration involves us in understanding ourselves and interpreting what happens in the environment around us.

Applying What You Know

How Does Science Learning Take Place in the Classroom?

The previous activity in *Exploring Your Ideas* represented a reflection that can help you develop a deeper understanding of the key ideas in teaching science. Other reflection activities can also help develop such an understanding. As a reader, you will find that reflection activities involve you in comparing your own knowledge with the new ideas being presented. Such activities will help you reflect on, and more fully understand, effective science teaching. Complete the *Applying What You Know* activity below before reading on.

Draw a "web" showing your understanding of how science learning takes place in a classroom. Start with a brief list of terms, the elements essential for science learning to take place with students. Connect the terms with arrows to show how the parts of the classroom learning process interact. Compare your web with others to see differences in your perception of science teaching and learning. Discuss the results of this comparison with a peer group.

Considering the interaction between oneself and the world; relating aspects of the environment to each other; and connecting the physical environment to the cultural, social, and inner world of the child is called *science for children*. Science happens every time a child purposely steps into a puddle or asks a question about the night sky. Our discussion of science in the elementary and middle school begins with the origins of children's knowledge and with a look at a classroom. As we look into the classrooms below, try to determine what these teachers think science is.

CLASSROOM SCENES

Classroom A: *Tuesday, October 12.*

Sue Baldwin, a third-grade teacher for the past three years, reminded her class,

> "We will have to hurry if we are going to finish the chapter before the busses come. Don't you want to go home today? Remember, it's about 'What are living things made of?'"

Then she instructed, "Open your books to page 183. Tom, begin reading to us at the top of the page."

Tom read,

> "All living things are made of cells. A plant has many thousands of cells. People have even more cells. A skin-like covering called a cell membrane (mem-brayn) surrounds the cell. Next to the cell membrane is a thicker covering. It is called the cell wall."

The lesson continued, with Debra and Johnny reading, for two more pages. Ms. Baldwin wrote new vocabulary words and their definitions on the board.

> "Since we didn't finish today, tomorrow I will have group leaders go to the library to find a book with a drawing of a cell. During free time tomorrow I want all members of the group to copy the new words into their journal and draw and color a cell. Next week's science lesson will be on, 'How living things grow.'"

Classroom B: *Tuesday, October 12.*

Harris and his partners, Shukila and Louis, were part of a new activity that Ms. Brown, a third-grade teacher for the past three years, had wanted to try for some time. The activity related to a science textbook chapter on "What are living things made of?" Ms. Brown took the 24 students outside to two large trees near their classroom window. She asked several of the students to "touch the trees and say one thing about them." She knew that the students played near the trees daily during recess, and wanted to use something familiar to them. Harris said, "They have bark." Shukila noted, "One is rough and the other is smooth." Others reported the trees: "are tall," "have leaves," "are green and brown," and "are small enough to put my arms around."

Next, Ms. Brown asked, "What is inside the trees? What is in the parts of the tree you can't see?" After waiting a short while to give the students time to construct their own ideas, Ms. Brown called on Louis. "The trees are hollow inside, I saw one once in the woods," he reported. It was an unexpected response. She decided not to comment on it. Additional responses were: "trees are solid inside," "birds and ants live inside," "it is made of soft stuff inside," and "it is made of sticky, gluey stuff inside." Only two students said, "I don't know what's inside." Ms. Brown concluded that most of the students already had an idea of the tree's structure, although it was only a partial and incomplete concept.

Back in the classroom the students, in small groups, drew their view of the inside of a tree. Ms. Brown asked them to think about: "What happens inside of a tree?" and "How does what's inside of a tree help it live and grow?" while they were drawing. In order to have the students confront each other with their ideas, she also asked groups of students to talk to each other about their drawings during this time. Next, the students were asked to pick up three pieces of tree cross-sections out of a box and examine them using magnifying glasses and rulers. After drawing the cross-sections, the students discussed what they had drawn with each other. Ms. Brown continued the lesson, using the text as a resource for information in a group discussion, and concluded by describing key ideas in the lesson. This was followed by an art activity where students drew the inside of a tree and wrote a story describing what they had found.

What does Ms. Baldwin think science is? What does Ms. Brown think science is? Which teacher probably holds the more stereotypical view of science and scientists? Which teacher probably fosters a more stereotypical view among her students?

Modern science in the elementary and middle school years focuses on how students learn, what teachers can do to facilitate student learning, and how the classroom environment creates opportunities for rich student experience. Within this framework, science is seen as an active process occurring in the student and influenced as much by the student as by the teacher. Science learning depends on how the student perceives events, what information is encountered, and the student's prior knowledge. Science learning is the student's construction of meaning (Kalchman, 1998; Saunders, 1992). In this view, science is a construction of knowledge from sensed information that is interpreted in terms of a student's prior knowledge.

In this classroom lesson, observable data are processed.

WHAT IS SCIENCE IN ELEMENTARY AND MIDDLE SCHOOL CLASSROOMS?

Science is defined as a way of constructing meaning that systematically uses particular ways of observing, thinking, investigating, and communicating to develop interconnected ideas about the physical and biological world. The ideas are not only developed in the individual but also in a community of learners. These ideas have enabled people to develop an increasingly comprehensive and reliable understanding of humanity and its environment (American Association for the Advancement of Science, 1990, 1993a).

For further information, see *Benchmarks for Science Literacy*, American Association for the Advancement of Science (AAAS).

What does the view that students construct their own knowledge imply for the classroom? Students must have something to act on—evidence developed through their own experience that can be related to the science idea or skill to be taught. Students collect this evidence using all their senses as they make observations of materials they are working with and experiences they are involved in. They need to work with this perceived information in their minds, relating it to their prior experiences, prior knowledge, and ways of thinking. Predictions should be made and discrepancies encountered. It is through challenges to our present way of thinking that we understand new ideas.

Students need to classify and describe the observed objects, experiences, and/or information. Using these and higher-order thought processes are natural, but often students are not good at it. Students are only ready to see patterns in the world around them and draw conclusions about those patterns after activities challenge them and make them think. Science in the elementary and middle school years is a construction process that goes on in students' minds. It starts and ends in students' hands-on activity and personal or shared interaction with the world (see Figure 1–1).

Science in the classroom is experienced as a verb, not a noun. If a classroom lesson involves these essential components, it is defined as science teaching. Leaving out any

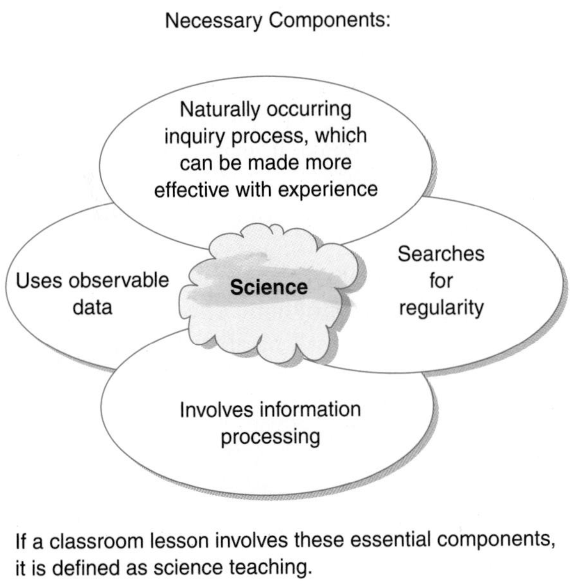

Necessary Components:

FIGURE 1-1 *What is science in the elementary and middle school classroom?*

If a classroom lesson involves these essential components, it is defined as science teaching.

single component creates learning based on rote memory rather than understanding through meaningful learning (Driver, Leach, Millar, & Scott, 1996; Sunal & Sunal, 1991b).

The two classroom anecdotes described in *Classroom Scenes* typify the controversy in elementary and middle school science teaching today. The lessons taking place in many classrooms do not use, or poorly involve, the ideas and materials research studies have found to be effective and the state and national standards have provided as guidelines. In many classrooms, the dominant format is teaching directly from the textbook with little or no additional activities other than fact-oriented worksheets, media presentations, or lectures (Aldridge, 1994; Riley, 1999; Yager, 1988). The priority is to cover most of the textbook in the time available for science (usually less than one hour per week in many elementary classrooms) and to place the responsibility for learning the content on the students (Madrazo & Rhoton, 1999; Tressel, 1988). The content to be learned typically consists of memorizing terms, their spelling, and definitions (National Research Council, 1996; Tobin, 1988). This type of teaching does not really teach science nor does it produce scientifically literate citizens.

What Is Scientific Literacy?

Science literacy can be defined in a number of ways. A general goal for **scientific literacy** in schools is an awareness, appreciation, and understanding of the key scientific concepts and processes required for personal decision making, participation in civic and cultural affairs, and economic productivity (National Research Council, 1996). The need for a scientifically literate populace, and the widening gap between expectations and reality in our schools, was increasingly brought to our attention during the 1980s and 1990s. The problem is reported as urgent in the 21st century. Being scientifically literate means that a student can ask, find, or determine answers to questions from everyday life about the environment in which he or she lives.

This process of awareness, appreciation, and understanding of the environment is not learned through any other school subject. Technological and environmental concerns require decision making from citizens who have basic scientific literacy in the physical, life, and earth sciences (Laubenthal, 1999; Rutherford & Ahlgren, 1990). Being literate involves the ability to read with understanding labels, warnings, and instructions on consumer products, foods, and practices. In these areas the American science education program is viewed as having failed to create meaningful science learning in students (Carnegie Commission, 1991; National Research Council, 1996). These are serious problems in a complex society where citizens are expected to make informed decisions.

WHY IS SCIENCE LITERACY ESSENTIAL FOR STUDENTS?

Why should we be concerned about the state of scientific literacy among elementary and middle grade students? Is science an essential part of the program? The answer is, "Yes, science plays a critical role in all our lives." The decision making all citizens frequently do involves scientific knowledge. In classroom science, students make meaningful use of basic tools such as mathematics, reading, writing, and technology. These tools are used for learning. They have a purpose. Science provides experiences through which students can develop the thinking skills that are the foundation of reading, writing, mathematics, and technology.

When science is considered to be memorizing facts, reading textbooks, watching a demonstration, answering questions, and illustrating knowledge students already know, its impact on students' learning is minimal. It deserves no more than an hour a week of time in the curriculum. However, the impact on a student's perception and attitude toward science leads to views of science as authoritarian, unattainable, and a body of facts to be memorized.

When science is considered an integral part of the intellectual development of students and a relevant set of experiences in which students naturally bring in all areas of the school curriculum and everyday life experiences, it then becomes an essential part of the school program. When confronted with an interesting problem related to their environment, it is natural for students to observe, then to ask questions, seek help in books, draw what they see, make measurements, and write about the problem. This is what science is about and what reading, writing, and mathematics provide tools to do. When students "do" science they use thinking skills and knowledge from the entire school curriculum. Rather than being "something to do when there is time," science is instead a fundamental aspect of curriculum today.

Applying What You Know

What Teaching-Learning Processes Happen in a Science Lesson?

What teaching-learning process occurs when students are involved in a classroom science lesson? Draw a web with lines connecting the terms that follow: *scientific literacy, knowledge, meaningful learning, exploration, gathering evidence, everyday experience, science,* and *students.* Compare your results with others. Later, compare your web to Figure 1–2 and discuss the results of this comparison with others. The definition of science in Figure 1–2 integrates all the elements you were asked to relate in the web above. Consider the web that would typify Ms. Baldwin and Ms. Brown. How would their webs be similar and different?

WHAT ARE THE CHARACTERISTICS OF EFFECTIVE SCIENCE TEACHING?

To understand effective science teaching, what should we look for while visiting a classroom where students are engaged in learning science in a meaningful way? To begin with, we need to look at general characteristics of the classroom environment and roles played by the teacher and students.

Classroom Environment

When asked about improving the teaching of science in the elementary and middle school, most teachers say time and resources are the critical factors. However, in studies of effective science teaching these factors did not show up as important in creating higher levels of learning in students (Gallagher, 1989; Sunal & Burry, 1992). If these are not critical factors, what classroom characteristics are related to student understanding, especially to changes in students' conceptions of science?

The "back to basics" emphasis in schools in the 1970s suggested that drill activities and an emphasis on lower-level understandings were important factors in improving science teaching. While researchers reported positive effects, national science achievement scores actually plummeted during this time. The time spent on drill and lower-level understandings also was found to be detrimental to students' higher-level understandings,

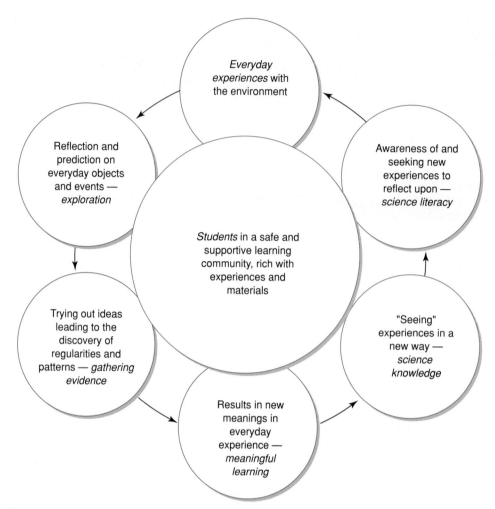

FIGURE 1-2   *Effective science teaching and learning in elementary and middle school*

use of thinking skills related to science, and experience with problem-solving strategies used in science (Martens, 1992).

Teachers who want to increase science literacy must pay careful attention to what they say and do in the classroom and to the kind of classroom climate they establish. The classroom environment must foster higher-level thinking skills in a safe and motivating climate if science is to be meaningful to students.

Exemplary Teachers

A great deal of effort has been devoted to identifying teachers who create meaningful learning; that is, understanding as opposed to the memorization of science. The characteristics associated with these teachers include reliance on supplemental materials, use of a variety of action-oriented instructional strategies beyond lecture and reading, use of hands-on materials in an investigative approach, use of groups as in cooperative learning settings, peer tutoring, integration of teaching and learning aids such as simulation and database com-

Can you identify characteristics of effective science teaching in this classroom?

puter software, assessment of higher levels of thinking, and student projects (Bianchini, 1998; National Research Council, 1996; Roueche, Sorensen, & Roueche, 1988; Tobin, 1988). Others report that exemplary teachers of science ask higher-order questions and allow students time and opportunities to apply the content to be learned in new contexts. They assess students' prior knowledge and challenge their naive concepts about the world (Daisey & Shroyer, 1995; Sunal & Burry, 1992; Tobin & Fraser, 1987). Effective teachers of science have been characterized as able to create student motivation for activities both in and out of the classroom (Daisey & Shroyer, 1995; Yager, Hidayat, & Penick, 1988).

Student Actions

Several key processes are important in student science learning. These are observation; gathering and communicating evidence; involvement in hands-on, minds-on science experiences; and inquiry. Also, an appropriate classroom climate and teacher action are required to foster students' use of these processes.

Observation

The fundamental process is observation. **Observation** starts by using the senses to gather information from the environment. As students gain experience, their observation skills become more useful and complex. Those skills which develop include using all appropriate senses in each observation, distinguishing inferences from observations, using both qualitative and quantitative descriptions in observations, and observing changes as well as the beginning and ending states of an event. More advanced development of the skill of observation includes ordering one's observations, being proficient at using measuring and other devices to extend the range of one's observations, and recording information using drawings, tables, narratives, computers, and other communication tools.

A concern about helping students make observations is one of perception. People observe the real world using what they already know (their prior knowledge). New information is likewise sensed only in terms of what they know. The existing ideas students bring to an activity should not be regarded as a problem that inhibits seeing and knowing, but as the means by which they are able to make sense of new ideas (Millar & Driver, 1987; Sunal, 1994). Tasting hoummous (mashed chickpeas flavored with lemon juice and olive oil) from Egypt, octopus in a Thai soup, or borscht (a type of beet soup) from Russia for the first time will be interpreted by what we already know. Hoummous might be new to our sense of taste and different in consistency and flavor from our usual foods. The soups from Thailand and Russia may be sensed as an unpleasant taste because of the strangeness of the food. However, the unpleasantness may not be related to actual taste but to the un- usual seafood shapes in the octopus soup or to the dark purplish color of the borscht soup.

Observation for elementary and middle school students should focus not only on the direct sensing but also on the use of language, evidence, and ideas that students bring to the observation. Only through repeated student discussions and observations, in which the new information is related to their prior knowledge, will meaning become possible. As another example, young students using a microscope to observe onion skin at first do not see cells and parts of cells. They see blurry images, lines, and blobs. Only through drawing and discussing what they see over several sessions does understanding of the pat- terns representing the onion skin's cell structure begin to grow.

Gathering and Communicating Evidence

Knowledge comes from the students' own construction of it using evidence. *Evidence* is developed from information gathered through observation. It is also the result of infer- ences made from the information gathered. Many thinking skills are used to form a body of evidence from which students construct knowledge.

Students do not construct science knowledge from hearing an authority tell them some information. The more the teacher presents information or the science textbook is used to teach a topic, the less opportunity students have to construct knowledge they un- derstand. Students should not be presented with "ready-made" knowledge—science con- cepts or generalizations to be memorized. They will not understand the meaning of these concepts and generalizations because they were constructed by someone else (Driver, Leach, Millar, & Scott, 1996). It is important that the teacher provides students with the experiences and materials through which they can construct science knowledge.

Evidence gathered through making observations should be diverse. It should vary de- pending on the developmental level of the student. For example, drawing and other forms of artwork are natural ways to record observations among younger students. Crayons, col- ored chalk, yarn of different textures, and different types of paper are among the art ma- terials students should be regularly using. Observations of a leaf or a sound relate to the students' perception of texture, color variations, and loudness. Comparisons can be made of different students' observations. Both qualitative and quantitative information can be a part of even young students' observations. For older students, in addition to the use of art, narratives involving poems, journals, and even short stories can be used to commu- nicate the evidence discovered through their observations. Technology can help students quickly record observations using word processing, still pictures, and video recording. Technology can be used as a tool to communicate, translate, and analyze their observa- tions on tables, bar graphs, and charts.

Involvement in Hands-On, Minds-On Science Experiences

The phrase *hands-on science* has come to be identified by many teachers as the one and only method for teaching science. However, this is an incomplete view of how students learn sci- ence. Asking students to work with materials relating to a science topic is not sufficient by itself for meaningful learning to take place. For example, asking students to complete a task using step-by-step directions such as putting a magnet to paper clips and counting how many paper clips are picked up or observing seeds germinate over a two-week period is not enough. What is needed besides hands-on science is *minds-on science.* In minds-on science, activities are structured so students interactively experience them. Students have an effect on the materials and also are affected by them. The activity poses problems and creates conditions that change students' approaches to the activity. It is only through interactive experience producing conflict, confrontation, or confusion that students are challenged to create meaning from an activity. A group of second-, third-, and fourth-grade teachers using a hands-on, minds-on approach have said the following about this approach:

> "We found teaching that includes student action and thinking very motivating for students. They liked coming up with their own ideas and testing them out."

> "Investigating their own ideas makes students clarify their own thinking. They are more willing to change their old way of thinking about an event."

> "They are more likely to use the ideas introduced in class in their daily lives."

Inquiry

Inquiry has been a popular term used in science teaching for the past 25 years. It has had many interpretations, some of which included an approach to teaching through discovery and the use of the scientific method. These interpretations have been limited, focusing on only part of the total inquiry process. **Inquiry** is the method by which students construct meaning as they learn science. New meaning is constructed only by asking questions about events that do not fit with students' present thinking, making predictions about events related to these questions, testing the predictions, and checking to see if the results of these tests answer the original questions better than the students' prior knowledge answered them. Effective science teaching for elementary and middle grade students has all of these aspects.

CLASSROOM SCENES

A fifth-grade teacher wanted to introduce her students to the concept of gravitational force. To begin the lesson she asked two sets of questions: First, what happens when you hold out and release a ball and a piece of paper in the classroom? Why? Second, what happens when you hold out and release a ball and a piece of paper on the moon? Why?

The teacher next divided the class into small groups, assigned roles, and asked them to discuss their ideas about the questions. They were also asked to present any conclusions they reached.

For the first question set, most groups found it difficult to see that there was a significant problem to explain. They knew that "the ball would fall when you let go of it. It isn't lightweight, so it will fall fast." One group further stated that "the ball falls because of air" while another group said "the ball falls because gravity pushes it down."

The second question set caused greater discussion. The students seemed to have less confidence in their explanations. One group concluded "the ball will fall slowly when released." Another group said "the ball will float away because there is no gravity." A third group decided "the ball will fall when released because there is air in the structure that serves as the moon station. If you were outside the moon station structure, the ball would stay still because there is no air."

The lesson continued with the teacher asking the students to get evidence for their conclusions. She provided them with balls, timers, a video camera for recording what occurred, and a videotape of objects falling in a vacuum container on Earth and astronauts on the moon releasing various types of objects. Later in the lesson students were encouraged to use the Internet and the library to check their conclusions. Finally, they were asked to predict what would happen if a ball were dropped by an astronaut on Mars.

Applying What You Know

What Parts Can You Identify in a Science Lesson?

As a concluding activity, examine the lesson web in Figure 1–3. What is the topic of this lesson? At what grade level(s) might it be taught? The web represents a definition of science as discussed in the chapter. Notice the part of the lesson that involves each of these ideas: science literacy, knowledge, meaningful learning, exploration, gathering evidence, everyday experience, and students. Compare your answers with your peer group. Discuss the results of this comparison with others.

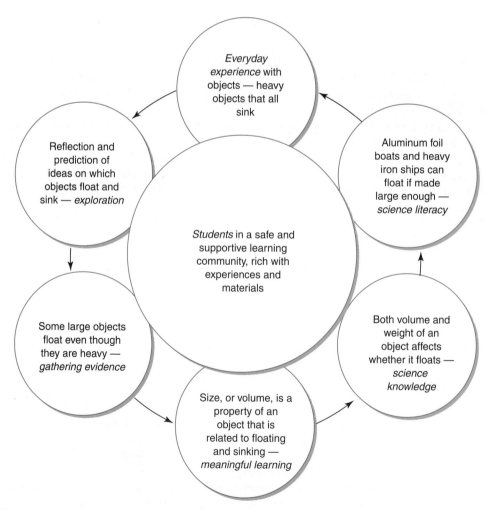

FIGURE 1-3   *Science lesson on sinking and floating for fourth grade*

SUMMARY

Living in today's world requires new skills and knowledge. And yet the pace of change is still accelerating. Helping each student develop his abilities in the 21st century is a complex and challenging task. Science is a process that facilitates our construction of knowledge and successful interaction with the world.

Scientific literacy is an important goal in the development of every student. A scientifically literate individual has an awareness, appreciation, and basic understanding of the key scientific concepts and processes required for personal decision making, participation in civic and cultural affairs, and economic productivity.

Science in the elementary and middle school is a natural process that begins with students' own experiences, involves reflection and discovery, and results in new meaning.

- Science *begins* with observations of everyday experiences. It involves information about everyday objects and events and is supported by information reported by others.
- Science *involves* reflection, including observing, gathering and communicating evidence, and inquiry in a series of hands-on/minds-on experiences.
- Science *continues* with the discovery of regularities and patterns in the evidence as a result of the processing that occurred earlier.
- Science *results* in the students' construction of *new meaning* and the associated *thinking skills* involved in creating scientific knowledge.

When this process is applied in everyday life, a student is said to be science literate. The context in which the student constructs meaning influences the result. Thus, the characteristics of the classroom and the teacher influence student attitudes and are a part of the meaning that is constructed.

Teachers in elementary and middle school classrooms have found that effective science learning for students consists of an action and an interaction, not facts to be memorized. Effective science teaching involves students in activities that confront them with situations they cannot adequately work with using only their prior knowledge. To accomplish this, effective teachers of science encourage observation, gathering and communicating evidence, and inquiry about the environment. They foster interaction between students and action with materials that result both in hands-on science and in minds-on science.

chapter 2

Students' Conceptions of the World: The Origin of Science Ideas

▼▲▼ Exploring Your Ideas ▼▲▼▲▼▲▼▲▼▲▼▲▼

Where does our scientific knowledge come from? To help you develop an answer to this question, consider another question: What are two experiences young children might have had with magnetism before beginning kindergarten? Next, identify the scientific knowledge you think students bring into the classroom based on these two experiences. Then describe two additional experiences the same student is likely to have had with magnetism by the time he begins middle school. Next, identify the scientific knowledge the student brings to the middle school classroom based on these experiences. Finally, answer the question with which this activity began: *Where does our scientific knowledge come from?*

Chapter Objectives

1. Explain the importance of science learning that is meaningful to students.
2. Explain how rote memorization differs from other forms of science learning.
3. Describe the relationship of students' experiences to their science ideas.
4. Describe the effect of prior knowledge on learning new scientific knowledge.
5. Explain the importance of teachers understanding their students' prior knowledge about a scientific idea before introducing it to them.
6. List strategies that facilitate students' understanding of scientific ideas.

WHAT IS MEANINGFUL LEARNING IN SCIENCE?

Science knowledge does not simply exist out in the universe waiting to be discovered. On the contrary, knowledge of science is found in the minds and bodies of thinking beings (Johnson, 1987; Nelson, 1999). **Learning** is defined as the process of constructing knowledge as sensory data are given meaning in the context of an individual's prior knowledge.

Learning and teaching are closely connected, though the connection is not a direct one. One can have meaningful learning with or without teaching, although teachers strive to increase meaningful learning. This chapter focuses on the meaningful learning of science (see Figure 2–1). Meaningful learning is learning with understanding which involves creating knowledge of the environment that makes it possible to have an awareness, appreciation, or ability to make decisions and successfully participate in everyday life (National Research Council, 1996). This kind of learning is very different from rote memorization.

Meaning can only be formed in students' minds by their own active efforts (Guy & Wilcox, 1998; Saunders, 1992). It cannot be created by someone else. As a result, students cannot be passive during science learning. The meaning of concepts such as "evaporation" or "a liquid," the process of identifying types of trees, the understanding of why it rains, or the effect of doubling the number of bulbs in a circuit are examples of ideas for which students must develop their own meaning. Students must wrestle with an idea in their own minds until it becomes meaningful to them. Teachers facilitate meaningful learning by planning and using experiences in science that engage students to work with ideas in their own minds (Miller, Steiner, & Larson, 1996).

Meaningful science learning is an active construction process, creating a network of experiences and ideas we call **knowledge.** Beginning early in life, students use their experiences to begin building many networks of science knowledge. The experiences students have, and the connections they make between those experiences, help them develop their ideas about the world. As students have more experiences and opportunities to connect them to various ideas, the networks of science knowledge grow more complex. Figure 2–2 shows an example of a network that has led to one current science idea in a very young student's mind. Meaningful science learning is a process of integrating and building many types of science ideas by:

- Adding, modifying, and connecting relationships between ideas.
- Identifying reasons for these relationships.
- Finding ways to use ideas to explain and predict natural phenomena.
- Finding ways to apply the ideas to many events. (National Research Council, 1996)

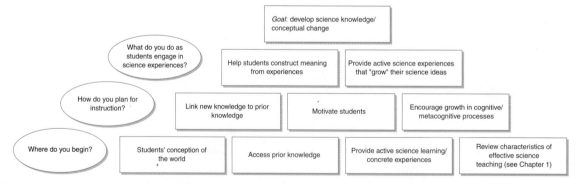

FIGURE 2–1   *The "building blocks" for developing students' conceptions of the world*

For further information, see the Companion Website at *http://www.prenhall.com/sunal* for a link to the National Science Education Standards.

Learning science meaningfully involves and depends upon the *background knowledge* the learner brings to a situation, whether the learner's *attention is focused* on the ideas being presented, and the *mental and physical actions* of the learner as she and her peers interact with objects and events during the process.

Teaching in order to stimulate active learning differs from traditional and behavioristic orientations to science teaching. Traditional science teaching is supported by a transmission learning model. This model holds that knowledge is transmitted through a funnel or speaking device. The teacher asks questions or gives assignments in order to determine if the students have received the message.

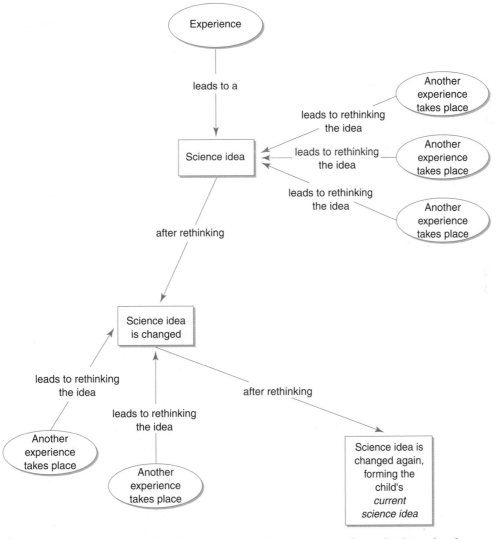

FIGURE 2-2 *The network of experiences and opportunities for rethinking that have led to one science idea in a very young child's mind*

What Is the Transmission Model of Science Teaching?

Science teaching according to the transmission model begins with the teacher, or text-book, presenting summarized information the student will be expected to "recite" at a later time. This "telling" is sometimes followed by a demonstration or teacher-guided "ex-periment" designed to show the "truth" of the information. Telling students that evapo-ration is the escape of molecules from a wet surface, asking them to repeat the definition, and then asking them to explain what happens to the wetness on the surface of their skin when they get out of the bath are examples of the transmission teaching model.

The transmission model views the science curriculum as a list of things to be trans-mitted and memorized as a catalog of facts. Traditional science teaching may involve tech-niques that enhance memorization and recall, including frequent repetition and the use of punishment to enhance learning. By themselves, memorization strategies are not neces-sarily ineffective teaching. Students often enjoy memorizing facts they view as useful, and they appreciate a strategy that helps them memorize. The issue is whether such learning is the goal of the science program rather than meaningful learning. A traditional science pro-gram centered around memorizing a catalog of facts does not help students find meaning in what they are learning. In addition, much of the teacher's energy is devoted to student motivation and discipline because of the passive and abstract approach of traditional sci-ence teaching. Science taught in this way leads to low interest and apathetic responses from many students by the time they reach middle school (Glynn & Duit, 1995).

How Are Behavioristic Strategies Used in the Transmission Model of Science Teaching?

Sometimes used as a supporting strategy for traditional science teaching, behavioristic teaching techniques focus on quick reinforcement of student responses to an event or stimulus. For example, students are asked to read a chapter on heat and temperature and write answers to questions asking them to recall what was written in the chapter. Students are then rewarded for correct answers. In this type of teaching, the emphasis is on low-order learning, memorization, and recall.

Memorization of scientific concepts results in learning without meaning, and without an understanding of what is being taught. Memorized scientific concepts provide students with an arsenal of facts such as "the maple leaf has points" or "the name of one dinosaur is Diplodocus." However, students often do not understand the meaning of those facts and are unable to relate them to the larger picture. For example, "the maple leaf has points" will mean little to a student who has never seen a maple leaf, or to a student who has seen a maple leaf but who has not had the chance to compare it with other tree leaves, noticing that some have rounded edges, some have a single point, and so on. Unless our experiences with real leaves allow us to relate the maple leaf and its points to other tree leaves, that bit of factual knowledge does not lead anywhere. Moreover, a new idea taught in this way is not connected to what a student already knows about the world (see Figure 2–3).

It is sometimes thought that learning centered on a hands-on approach is useful. Ex-amples of hands-on approaches include a learning station where students are asked to put three different liquids on their hands and describe the effect without a follow-up or dis-cussion, or telling students that "evaporation is the escape of molecules from a wet sur-face" followed by having the students dip their hands in water to feel the cooling effect. The problem with this hands-on approach is that it does not create meaningful learning. More is needed. While the student has had some related personal experience, the learn-ing cannot be recalled easily because the new idea is not connected to what the student knows about the world (see Figure 2–3). Thus, the approach is similar to memorization.

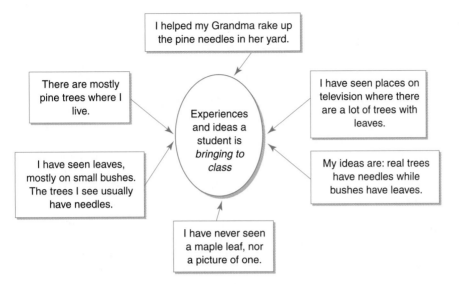

How well will the school experiences below connect into the knowledge network this student is bringing to class?

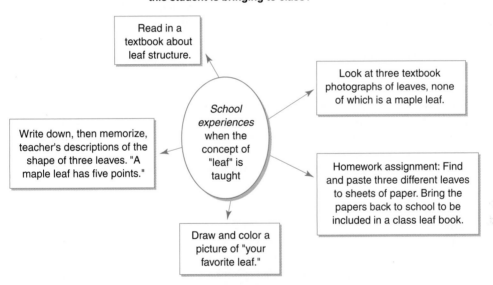

FIGURE 2-3   *How well will school experiences connect into a student's knowledge network?*

What Is Direct Instruction in Science?

Another aspect of traditional science teaching is that it often uses direct instruction targeting a narrow learning objective. Direct science instruction typically limits science learning to a particular solution. Frequently, the learner is focused on the memorization of the science idea or skill. Since the student does not have to search her long-term memory to replace inadequate ideas, these old ideas remain and are likely to be applied uncritically to the next problem they seem to fit. The new directly taught solution is usually forgotten, or the learner is unable to recall it unless the exact classroom conditions are reproduced. Memorization is encouraged by direct instruction. Science learned by rote memorization does not address how, when, or under what conditions facts can be summarized, the useful meaning of a concept, or the meaning or use of generalizations that allow predictions.

Traditional teaching can be appropriate for low-order learning goals that depend on rote memory such as spelling science words, repeating the names of dinosaurs, and listing the names of the planets in order from the sun. It may also be helpful for learning routine tasks such as using a balance to accurately weigh an object or putting materials back on shelves in the appropriate locations after a science activity. While traditional teaching may be appropriate, it generally results in learning with little meaning and deserves only a small portion of the students' and teachers' time and effort.

What Is the Learning of Science through the Construction of Meaning?

The learning of science knowledge begins when the learner actively works with objects and events found in everyday, or classroom, experiences. These experiences result in a *new construction* of sensory information from the world in the learner's mind, and a *reconstruction* of previous knowledge. This is the process of learning science more effectively.

For active learning to occur, classroom experiences are first perceived by the student. Then, the student mentally reconstructs this perception in his mind. This reconstruction is his representation of the classroom experience. This representation is transformed to fit the student's current background, or prior, knowledge. It is not an exact duplicate of what the teacher or another student perceives about the same experience. Once the student fits the classroom experience into what is already known in his mind, the perception of the experience is complete and the idea is connected to the student's prior knowledge. The student has constructed personal meaning out of the experience. Because the experience has been given meaning, the student is able to apply the new knowledge in situations different from the one in which it was learned. Figure 2–4 displays this process of meaningful learning. Compare this sequence to the definition of classroom science shown in Chapter 1, Figure 1–2.

Why Should We Question Teaching Strategies?

Changing conditions in society, science, and our educational system make it important to question teaching strategies. In previous times, society valued the reproduction of information rather than the understanding and use of knowledge. "Lectures" transmitted information orally because there were few or no textbooks. "Recitation" involved students repeating facts memorized from the lecture notes, which was useful because it was thought that information existed to be reproduced, rather than examined, by students. Students learned to give specific answers to specific questions found in the text or asked in a lecture. For example, when asked to "Name the dinosaurs" or "What are dinosaurs?" students might have been expected to recall a definition or give the names "Stegosaurus," "Diplodocus," and "Tyrannosaurus Rex." If another dinosaur had been discovered and identified, but had not been mentioned in the lecture, the students were not expected to name it, even if they had heard about the discovery outside of school. Today, science is changing so rapidly that scientific knowledge doubles every two years. No one can know all scientific facts: there are simply too many, and the number continues to grow. Therefore, educational goals for scientific literacy in the 21st century must focus on higher-level knowledge. Learning through active mental and physical involvement is appropriate for higher-level goals of science learning, those beyond rote memorization and recall. Higher-level science knowledge goals include: (1) understanding concepts, (2) understanding generalizations, (3) developing higher-level thinking skills, and (4) developing attitudes and dispositions about the physical world (see Figure 2–5). These should be the goals of an elementary and middle school science program.

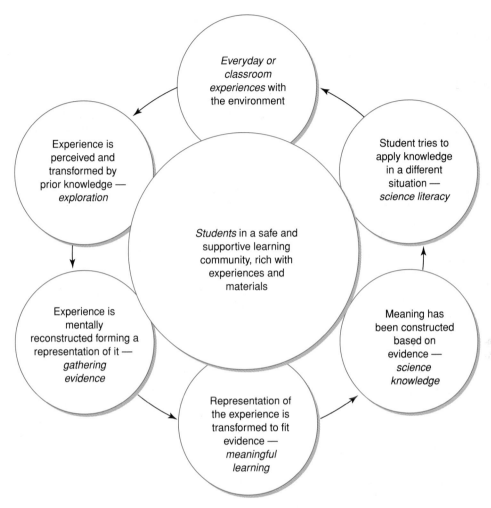

FIGURE 2-4   *The process of meaningful learning in science*

1. *understanding concepts* (e.g., heat can be transported or stored in an object)
2. *understanding generalizations* (e.g., predicting relationships between how fast heat travels and the type of material within which the heat is traveling)
3. *developing higher-level thinking skills* (e.g., science process skills such as classifying rock crystals based on previous knowledge of geometric shapes and skills such as critical thinking, decision making, and problem solving)
4. *developing attitudes and dispositions about the physical world* (e.g., willingness to suspend judgment about a problem until a sufficient amount of evidence is available to form a reasonable conclusion)

FIGURE 2-5   *Higher-level science knowledge goals*

HOW IS SCIENCE KNOWLEDGE DEVELOPED THROUGH CONCEPTUAL CHANGE?

Building relationships between science experiences and ideas gives meaning to those experiences. Groups of experiences and ideas form concepts, thinking skills, or dispositions. Concepts are then grouped to form generalizations. Together, a group of experiences and the ideas and dispositions developed from those experiences form a **knowledge schema**. Figure 2–6 gives an example of the knowledge schema built by an individual for the concept "pond ecosystem." The knowledge schema began in experiences the individual had

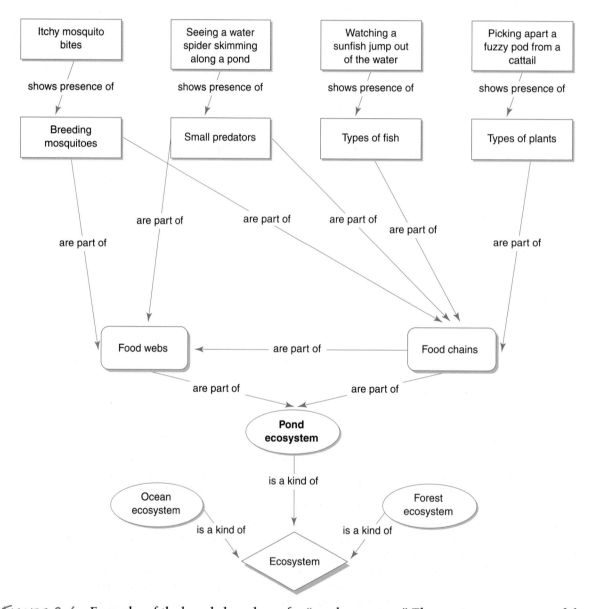

FIGURE 2–6   *Examples of the knowledge schema for "pond ecosystem." The arrows suggest some of the relationships found in this knowledge schema. Every part of the structure is related to every other part in some way*

around a pond, such as seeing a water spider skimming along the pond and picking apart a fuzzy pod from a cattail found at the edge of the pond. Other experiences included watching a sunfish jump out of the water and scratching mosquito bites inflicted by some of the many mosquitoes living near the pond. These experiences led to ideas that included "types of fish" and "breeding mosquitoes." The individual was then building a knowledge schema connecting personal experiences to ideas. Eventually, the individual realized the breeding mosquitoes and different types of fish are part of food webs and food chains found in a pond ecosystem. Later, the concept of the pond ecosystem was connected to the bigger idea of an "ecosystem" and to the ideas of "forest" and "ocean." The knowledge schema then was quite complicated, linking experiences to several kinds of ideas.

The important aspect of a knowledge schema, such as the "pond ecosystem" in Figure 2–6, is that once any element in the structure is activated, the entire structure can be searched, recalled, and brought to bear when creating understanding of a new experience. The mention of mosquitoes in a unit or chapter dealing with food webs may lead a student to think about a fish eating the mosquito and other types of insects common to the habitat of the pond. If a student has no experiences with a fact, but just memorizes it, there are no connections that can lead to ideas or to remembering related experiences. Throughout life we have additional experiences, rethink our ideas, and reorganize our knowledge schemas. Elementary and middle school students need many experiences which they discuss and think about in order to build knowledge schemas that represent accurate and useful science knowledge. Teachers have an important role in helping students change and further develop their knowledge schemas.

The process of learning that involves making changes in students' knowledge schemas is termed **conceptual change** (Driver, Leach, Millar, & Scott, 1996). Conceptual change is part of a process where three events occur:

First, specific sensory data are taken into short-term memory from sensory memory.

Second, conceptual change takes place in science knowledge schemas through thought processes taking place in the short-term memory.

Third, the knowledge is stabilized through its application to a variety of tasks. *Stabilization* means the new process is stored in long-term memory and we are able to retrieve it.

Conceptual change goes on all the time. When the required changes are not too great, the individual is likely to reorganize a knowledge schema into a more appropriate one. For example, an individual may notice that there are fewer mosquitoes around a pond in late summer than there were in early summer. Other observations might be that her shoes are not sinking into the mud like they did earlier in the summer, many of the plants around the pond have brown leaves, and bushes that were in the water earlier are now on dry land. After some reflection, these observations and experiences are connected into the knowledge schema. The schema is changed to include the conclusion that the pond ecosystem shows many changes over several months and the generalization that weather, such as less rain in late summer, causes the changes observed in the pond ecosystem.

When the needed conceptual change is great, a person can be helped by peers, teachers, or parents who involve the person in helpful experiences, guide the person to make observations of important factors in those experiences, suggest different ways of organizing the information from the experiences, and discuss confusing aspects of the experiences (Harlen, 1985b). Each science knowledge schema is related to other knowledge schema, just as the parts of a specific schema are related to each other. Thus, a student's scientific knowledge is made up of many interconnected schemas. When one science schema changes, its relationship to other knowledge schemas also changes. For example,

*What connections must be made
with these students' prior
knowledge for a science lesson
you are planning?*

when the individual's "pond ecosystem" schema changes after visiting the pond in late summer, his ideas may affect his schemas for ecosystems connected with other kinds of bodies of water.

To help students learn, teachers must understand that their short-term goals involve helping students create meaningful relationships between ideas and experiences. However, this is not the only type of learning toward which science teaching aims. If middle school students are to develop more advanced science knowledge schemas than the ones they had as young students entering elementary school, teachers need to realize they are working toward the longer-term goal of changing science knowledge schemas, or conceptual change. The elementary science curriculum, for example, should not focus only on expanding experiences of simple concepts regarding magnets, heat, or ecosystems, but work instead toward exploring the more numerous and complex relationships within and between these concepts. Classroom experiences should help students move from working with representations of real objects to communicating their observations in a variety of ways. To develop more abstract concepts, students have to learn to link ideas and apply them in situations that are not directly observable. Finally, teachers must understand that all this development leads to the ultimate goal of science teaching: changes in cognitive development, the knowledge framework in the mind of the student.

WHAT IS THE ROLE OF PRIOR KNOWLEDGE IN LEARNING SCIENCE?

While some learning consists of acquiring totally new knowledge, most learning, even in young students, either:

- *fits with* what we already know, or
- *changes* what we already know. (American Association for the Advancement of Science, 1993a)

For further information, see the Companion Website at *http://www.prenhall.com/sunal* for a link to the National Science Education Standards.

Acquiring new knowledge directly from experience is not possible without some prior knowledge within which to interpret the new experience. If connections are not made to the students' prior knowledge, the new experience may be confusing or might not be perceived. As suggested in Chapter 1, when looking at a piece of onion skin through a microscope for the first time, young students see blurry images, lines, and blobs. It is only through repeated observations and discussions of the onion skin's cellular structure over several sessions that an understanding begins to grow regarding the patterns they see.

Topics that are a typical part of the elementary and middle school curriculum and textbooks include matter, magnets, magnetic fields, plants, photosynthesis, how living things grow, water habitats, and forests. These are studied every one or two years in a spiral fashion. Each time the concepts are studied, they are broadened and expanded to wider and deeper contexts. The student's prior knowledge is used (see Figure 2–1). Even at the kindergarten level, objects and events involved with any of these topics call up some prior knowledge schema containing experiences and ideas that are already interrelated.

If a student has played with a magnet, such as a flat refrigerator magnet, she will relate her prior knowledge of magnets to the way she expects a bar magnet to act. She will also relate it to the explanation she has personally constructed of why she expects the magnet to act in a certain way in the present classroom setting. Generally, this prior knowledge includes the idea that "magnets stick to things that are metal." The concepts of poles, repelling actions, and connections with electricity may not be part of her knowledge structure because these require more organized activities with magnets not usually experienced by young students.

If the student has not had any experiences with magnets, the classroom observations are likely to be incorporated into those experiences. Perhaps the student will relate the magnet experiences to "things that stick together," glue, or stickiness. Perhaps the student will relate the magnet experiences to "dirty" and "bad" values associated with sticky foods on hands and clothes, spilling sticky liquids on floors and furniture, sap on trees, and sticky soil and mud. These beliefs about the way the world works are called **alternative conceptions** (Helm & Novak, 1992; Layman, 1996). The students would not have prior knowledge of magnets related to metals or to more specific aspects of magnetism, but would try to fit the new experience into a knowledge schema that seemed relevant, thus forming an alternative conception. An alternative conception generally is an incomplete or inaccurate view of how the world works. Whether or not students have had experiences with magnets, teaching about magnets for meaningful learning does not just involve the presentation of new concepts. Instead, the teacher helps students change prior knowledge networks by adding new concepts that fit with more effective explanations of the physical events and processes with which they are involved.

Effective science teaching starts with, and expands upon, old knowledge networks and relates new information to what is already known. Also, existing knowledge can interfere with the development of new ways of viewing the world. Students sometimes find it difficult to drop an old way of viewing things and adopt a new one based on a few minutes of contradictory experience. Supportive classroom strategies used over a longer period of time are needed. Because teaching key ideas takes time, the total number of science ideas taught throughout the year should be reduced to provide enough time to teach key ideas well.

For a listing of common alternative conceptions that students bring to the classroom, see the sections on basic alternative conceptions in Chapters 13, 14, and 15.

Applying What You Know

Identifying Experiences Students Have Had with Magnetism

Refer to your responses to the *Exploring Your Ideas* activity at the beginning of this chapter. Using the two experiences with magnetism you suggested young children might have prior to kindergarten, what new experience would you plan for them in kindergarten? Describe what component(s) it might add to their knowledge schema for magnetism.

(continued)

In the *Exploring Your Ideas* activity, you also described two additional experiences kindergarten children might have during the elementary school years. As their middle school teacher, what new experience would you plan for them? Describe what component(s) it might add to their knowledge schema for magnetism.

WHAT IS AN EFFECTIVE STRATEGY FOR CONCEPTUAL CHANGE?

To help students learn about science, teachers must go far beyond traditional teaching strategies. Students must be involved in science activities that foster conceptual change. Effective conceptual change requires:

* Motivating students to recall related prior knowledge.
* Connecting the new science idea to students' prior knowledge.
* Allowing students to compare (confront) prior knowledge with the new science idea.

Confrontation of prior knowledge involves providing opportunities for students to use the new idea successfully. It also involves helping students alter their ways of perceiving, and reconstructing their prior knowledge. Specific implications for teaching are to:

1. Build an awareness of, and use prior knowledge in, teaching science.
2. Motivate students to learn science.
3. Link new science ideas to prior knowledge.
4. Encourage growth of cognitive and metacognitive processes.

Figure 2–1 incorporates these implications for teaching in some detail. It identifies the "building blocks" for developing students' conceptions of the world. Each block is important. When just one is missing, the whole structure falls apart. The four major implications for teaching to promote conceptual change in students include these building blocks. Each of the implications is discussed below.

Implication #1: How Do Teachers Build an Awareness of, and Use Prior Knowledge in, Teaching Science?

Students are likely to have ideas about scientific concepts before they experience any formal teaching regarding them. These prior ideas enable them to explain and predict familiar phenomena to their own satisfaction. Their prior ideas tend to be stable over time and quite resistant to change. Sometimes they depend on the situation in which the prior knowledge was learned, or on the place and conditions under which they recall an idea.

Students' understandings of the world often conflict with the ideas they are expected to learn in school. When students are presented with more scientifically appropriate conceptions in science lessons, they may reject them or make them fit into their own ideas. The result may be a mix of "taught science" and "intuitive science." Teachers must realize students already have their own alternative conceptions for many science concepts in the curriculum. Therefore, teachers need to diagnose, or identify, these alternative conceptions before they begin teaching the scientifically appropriate idea.

Since conceptions of the world are part of students' prior knowledge, teachers facilitate learning through conceptual change more than they help students construct completely new concepts. Effective teaching aims at changing students' existing knowledge. It goes beyond merely linking new information to that knowledge, or having students become aware of the restricted situations in which their view is valid. Students frequently

Students are likely to have ideas about a scientific concept before they experience formal teaching.

experience conceptual conflict or a confrontation during a lesson when their prior knowledge about an idea does not coincide with the new knowledge. The reasons for this are:

- Students usually understand the world based on interpretations of their own everyday experiences.
- Students' experiences do not include organized observations and usually are severely limited in scope.
- Rather than being interested in a theory that explains a variety of world events, students tend to be interested in particular explanations for specific events.
- The use of specific language causes confusion in students when terms that have one meaning in the culture have another meaning in science. For example, students may think of "conservation" as "turning off the light when you leave the room and not wasting electricity." The teacher may be referring to the concept as "when energy is used, it doesn't disappear, it's just changed to a different form of energy." The students may be expecting the teacher to talk about conserving energy by not wasting it.

Approaches to teaching that are *unsuccessful* in helping students restructure prior knowledge include presenting information to students directly from textbooks, providing demonstrations and activities without helping students focus on the patterns that are similar in the activities, and providing a discovery-oriented lesson without specifically relating it to prior scientific knowledge (Driver et al. 1996; Smith & Anderson, 1984b). If the ideas held by students are taken into account, teaching is not "telling" or "giving" knowledge to students. It is helping each student construct scientifically accepted ideas for himself. The intuitive ideas students bring with them are where a lesson begins.

TABLE 2–1   *Learning conditions for conceptual change*

Learning Condition	Learning Example
1. Students must be aware of their prior knowledge.	A student makes predictions about what types of materials magnets will pick up. The student might predict, "Magnets will pick up all metals."
2. Students must be allowed to act on prior knowledge.	A student tries out her predictions about what types of materials magnets will pick up.
3. Students must confront, and become dissatisfied with, their existing idea.	When a student tests out a magnet with coins and finds out that the coins are not attracted to the magnet even though they are made of metal, the current understanding of magnetic attraction is confronted. The student might say, "These coins are made of metal. Why weren't they attracted to the magnet?"
4. Young students must interact with peers if conceptual change is to take place. Unguided and individual efforts to make sense of an experience usually result in poor understanding and an inability to apply knowledge.	When a student discusses his experiences with pieces of metal that are not picked up by a magnet with other members of his small group, he finds that they had the same experiences. Together, they decide that there may be only certain types of metal a magnet can pick up.
5. Students must comprehend the new idea. Students need time to resolve the conflict between their ideas, their observations, and the new idea.	A student tries to pick up different coins with a magnet several times. He also tries other pieces of metal such as aluminum and brass and finds that they, too, are not affected by the magnet.
6. Students must find the new, more appropriate idea to be as plausible and more useful than the prior, less appropriate idea.	After trying to pick up a variety of metal pieces with a magnet, a student comes to the conclusion that only some metals are attracted to magnets.
7. Students must extend the new idea and connect it to new situations.	A student is given additional kinds of metal pieces to try to pick up with a magnet.
8. Students must be encouraged to use and transfer the new idea to relevant experiences in their lives.	A student takes home a magnet and tries it on materials around the house.

In order to facilitate students' learning, teachers consider several different learning conditions needed to help students modify or discard old beliefs and construct new ideas (Driver et al., 1996; National Research Council, 1995; Osborne & Freyberg, 1985b). These are described in Table 2–1. Effective teaching creates learning conditions in which students are:

- aware
- able to act
- confronted and dissatisfied with their own ideas and skills
- able to interact with others
- using an explanation of the new idea
- able to make sense of the new idea
- able to make connections
- using and transferring the new idea

Facilitating conceptual change involves helping students become aware of inconsistencies in their way of viewing the world (Driver et al., 1996; Mayer, 1995; Nussbaum & Novick, 1982; Posner, Strike, Hewson, & Gertzog, 1982). The recognition of these inconsistencies is followed by a confrontation or discrepant observation that leads students to the conclusion that their original perceptions are not useful. Recognition of inconsistencies in their thinking can help students begin to make changes. This is not enough, however: a teacher must spend additional time guiding students in the construction of the new knowledge. Guidance might include:

1. Diagnosing the alternative science conceptions individuals, a small group, or the whole class have in relation to the new ideas being presented.
2. Responding to students' alternative science conceptions.
3. Presenting science content in a way that helps students make sense of the new concepts.
4. Leading students toward changing their alternative science conceptions to more scientific views. (Roth, Anderson, & Smith, 1986; Sexton, 1998)

These steps require an active teacher who is interested in understanding students' points of view. Such a teacher proposes new, alternative science concepts. The teacher creates conceptual conflict via discrepant events and leads students into constructing science ideas that logically fit together within a unit—for example, one on magnetism (Padilla & Pyle, 1996; Roth, Anderson, & Smith, 1986).

Implication #2: Motivating Students to Learn Science

Students do not learn science through repetition or simply by exposure to a situation; the student must want to learn. One way to help students want to learn is to give them opportunities to explore science and find satisfaction in doing so. A second way is to provide intrinsic reinforcements. While external rewards generally do not undermine interest in easy tasks, they tend to destroy motivation for difficult ones. This happens partly because students prefer to see themselves in control of their own actions rather than externally manipulated in ways determined by others. Also, external rewards are often misplaced so students see no personal significance in them and do not value the rewards. For example, students may be rewarded for simply getting a job done with no consideration as to whether they copied another's ideas or tried to think through an idea by themselves. Instead, teachers should encourage students to generate their own reinforcements and relate their personal experiences and prior knowledge to new science experiences. Students need to be challenged and have a goal and purpose in mind for their learning activities. What students learn is not so much determined by the science content presented in school, but by how significant the content is with regard to their own learning needs and expectations.

Implication #3: Linking New Science Ideas to Prior Knowledge

The linking of new science knowledge to prior knowledge begins before the formal teaching of that information. The teacher starts by helping students recall previous experiences, events, and remembrances related to the lesson topic. Then, students need to interact in some concrete fashion with the new science information to be presented in the lesson. This might include:

- Involving students in an open-ended activity where they can see cause-and-effect and link previous experiences with the new experience.
- Formulating and asking questions that elicit divergent responses from students, helping them link prior knowledge to new knowledge.
- Involving students in a focused activity accompanied by open and closed questions. The teacher tries to help students link their prior knowledge with the new experience.
- Focusing students' attention on key features of a specific learning situation.
- Helping students become more aware of how ideas are linked in their own minds.

What problem could be posed
using this photograph?

- Posing a problem and having students develop hypotheses or predictions based on prior experiences. These may not work; hopefully, students will see their prior knowledge was inadequate and try to change their conceptions.
- Demonstrating an event that is analogous to the concept being presented, using analogies, metaphors, and models.
- Linking old and new knowledge.

Implication #4: Encouraging Growth of Cognitive and Metacognitive Processes

Active and meaningful learning techniques stress the importance of having students think about their actions, engage in cognitive processes, and control their approach to learning. These techniques are known as "metacognition."

Science knowledge schema include thinking skills as well as concepts and generalizations. Strategies that help form new thinking skills are reflection, problem solving, decision making, and evaluating. Conceptual change occurs with thinking skills. A thinking skill, such as classifying, is also a concept. A young student in first grade is likely to think of classification as a way of putting a pile of objects into groups based on some characteristic they share. The student may sort the objects into groups based on their shape: those that are round go in one group, while those that are rectangular go in another group. A third group is composed of those that are neither obviously round nor rectangular (for example, a cone-shaped object). By the sixth grade, the same student is likely to have a different conception of classification. The student still understands grouping by a shared characteristic, but also groups in levels. The same set of objects used in the first-grade activity might still be grouped by shape, but then each shape group might be further recognized by size. The student has large and small round shapes, for example. Then, the student may group the large round shapes by texture: those that are rough and those that are smooth. The process can continue through many levels of grouping. The student's understanding of classification has changed to include levels of classification, or a hierarchy. Conceptual change forms thinking processes that resolve apparent contradictions in old thinking frameworks.

Awareness of one's own reasoning is important for conceptual change to lead to higher-level scientific thought processes. Teachers can help students learn *how to learn* in several ways. These methods include having students work with peers in safe, cooperative science learning settings and planning and setting science learning goals. When teachers actively select relevant science information, they facilitate student learning. Finally, monitoring what scientific concepts make sense to students is also helpful.

Students develop an understanding of how they learn when teachers model problem-solving situations for them. For example, the teacher can describe the thought processes she uses to solve a problem, then ask students to do the same, perhaps with prompting. Students should have opportunities to discuss their own metacognitive knowledge. This might involve planning the investigation of a problem, monitoring their thinking, and/or evaluating the actions taken. The focus should be on showing how these metacognitive strategies change depending upon goals and contexts.

A recent conversation between five elementary and middle school teachers centered on their views of teaching for meaningful learning. These teachers were trying to foster conceptual change in their students by encouraging them to use metacognition. For example:

- "I see students in a completely different way. For the first time, I am really challenging them, not just spoon-feeding them."
- "I have started thinking about how to best teach science."
- "The idea of prior knowledge has transformed my view of science teaching."
- "It is enlightening to see what ideas the students have and how they can think through ideas if given the opportunity."
- "Teaching science for meaningful learning has made me more confident in my teaching. I really enjoy teaching this way. I feel I have learned more about my own teaching. My science class is approached in a different way and I prefer this way. I don't think I could have walked out of my classroom looking happy after teaching science if I did not teach this way."

Lesson plans that represent the type of teaching these teachers are describing can be found at the ends of Chapters 13, 14, and 15.

SUMMARY

Science teaching must take into account students' prior knowledge if it is to be effective in helping them construct meaningful science knowledge. Before any formal science lesson on a concept (e.g., magnetism) begins, students are likely to have their own ideas about the concept. Their ideas may enable them to explain and predict phenomena to their satisfaction. Science learning depends on the classroom environment and on students' prior knowledge and motivation. When students are presented with ideas in science lessons, they have to modify and reconstruct their prior knowledge in order to understand those new ideas. This requires a willingness and an effort on the part of the learner. Learning involves the construction of knowledge schema through experience with the physical environment and through social interaction. Developing links with prior knowledge is an active process involving the generation, checking, and restructuring of ideas. Learning science is not simply a matter of adding to or extending existing concepts: it may involve reorganization of prior knowledge while taking the new knowledge into account. Learning is not passive; students set their own goals and control their own learning. Teachers help each student construct scientifically accepted ideas. The starting points for teaching are the ideas students bring with them.

chapter 3

The Learning Cycle

▼▲▼ EXPLORING YOUR IDEAS ▼▲▼▲▼▲▼▲▼▲▼

How do students begin to learn about their environment in a meaningful way? How can teachers help students learn important science content so that it is meaningful to them? What science teaching procedures are based on an understanding of how students learn? You can explore these questions by designing a brief science lesson to teach the concept of soil layers. *How would you begin the lesson? What would you do next? How would you end the lesson?* The lesson plan should demonstrate your answers to these questions. Remember that the four basic layers found as one digs in undisturbed soil are leaf litter, topsoil, subsoil, and bedrock. The thickness of the layers varies greatly. Also, write down, perhaps in the lesson plan outline margins, some of the principal ideas that emerge from your thoughts about such a plan. *Write the outline of the soils lesson before you read the next section.*

When asked to plan a science lesson, many novice teachers begin by explaining the concept to the students and asking them to verify the explanation in a hands-on activity. Students bring personal experiences, ideas, and skills related to the topics of the science lessons they are taught. Teachers need to take this prior knowledge into account when helping students reconstruct their existing ideas and learn new ones. Teaching science effectively involves more than telling students what you want them to know.

Look at your lesson plan again. *What could be done to begin the lesson by bringing out students' prior ideas?*

Effective follow-up activities for a science lesson involve interactive teacher-student explanations, practice, closure, application, and transfer activities.

For further information, see the Companion Website at *http://www.prenhall.com/sunal* for a link to Sunal & Sunal, 1994a.

Companion Website

Can you suggest other changes for the lesson you originally planned? Discuss your results from this activity with a peer.

For additional information on planning and evaluating an inquiry lesson for soil layers see Chapter 15, Earth and Space Science Starting Points, or Sunal & Sunal, 1994a.

Chapter Objectives

1. Describe a strategy that can be used to help identify, enhance, and create meaningful learning of science ideas and skills in classroom settings.
2. Describe the essential parts of each phase of the learning cycle and explain why each is used.
3. Describe the purpose of the initial, explanation, and application phases of a lesson designed to promote meaningful science learning.
4. Identify appropriate types of activities for each basic phase of instruction in a learning cycle and explain why each is used.
5. Plan for and describe a science lesson to enhance meaningful learning of science ideas and skills.

WHAT STRATEGY IS EFFECTIVE IN TEACHING SCIENCE MEANINGFULLY?

The previous questions provide the focus for this chapter on how to assist student science learning through constructing knowledge. The chapter uses and describes a process for planning and teaching science for students in classrooms using a strategy and learning sequence that helps identify, create, and enhance meaningful learning through conceptual change. First, the nature of an effective science learning sequence is explored. The chapter then focuses on making appropriate decisions regarding how to teach key science ideas. Finally, applications of the essential components of this strategy are provided in more depth through discussions, activities, and examples.

This chapter section is organized to help you actively explore the parts of an effective science lesson, which helps you understand the pedagogical sequence aimed at creating conceptual change. Activities have been constructed that require you to make observations and draw conclusions based on your past experiences. The problem in the following extended activity simulates the experience of an elementary teacher attempting to understand a new science idea and relate it to her students' previous experiences and prior knowledge. First, an introductory problem activity is presented. It involves an activity promoting conceptual change. *Perform the activity* and focus your attention on your own thinking during this part. Afterward, a discussion is presented, allowing you to compare your answers to those others have found.

In this first activity, you will investigate a problem concerning properties of everyday materials while receiving only tactile feedback. Few people can immediately make appropriate conclusions under these conditions. You may wish to work with a partner and discuss the problem. Question your thoughts. Try to become conscious of your own thinking while you are investigating the problem. In particular, observe the sequence of events you proceed through to arrive at an appropriate solution. After you have finished this problem, think over and exchange ideas with others about the steps you took in arriving at this conclusion.

Predict how warm or cool these objects would feel if touched.

A Conceptual Change Learning Sequence

Everyday Encounter with Materials: A Problem

Take a look around the room you are in and note the different types of material you find there (i.e., wood, glass, metal, plastic, concrete, and cloth). List several of the different types of material found in your surroundings in column 1 (Material Type) of Table 3–1, Everyday Materials Data Record Sheet, or make a similar table on a sheet of paper. You do not need to identify the kind of material, like rayon cloth. Do not choose objects near a heat outlet, an outside wall, or in the sunshine.

Next, imagine touching a sample of each type of material. In column 2 (Prediction), use the list of materials and write in your prediction of how warm or cool it would feel if you touched a representative sample of each type of material.

Finally, actually touch a sample of each type of material on your list. In column 3 (Observation), write an observation by indicating how warm or cool each object actually felt. For example, you might list wood from a chair leg, predict it would feel cool to the touch, and observe that it feels warm to the touch.

After completing the Everyday Materials Data Record Sheet, answer the following questions, completing each question before reading the next.

A. Which type of material felt the warmest? _____

B. Which type of material felt the coldest? _____

C. List, in rank order, the material types from warmest to coldest.

   Warmest

   _____

   _____

   _____

   _____

   _____

   _____

   Coldest

D. Why do you think the materials feel different?

   _____

   _____

   _____

TABLE 3–1   *Everyday materials data record sheet*

EVERYDAY MATERIALS DATA RECORD SHEET		
Material Type	**Prediction**	**Observation**
1.		
2.		
3.		
4.		
5.		
6.		

E. Melissa, a fourth-grade elementary teacher in Tuscaloosa, Alabama, when asked why the objects feel different, answered question D in the following way: "The different materials do not have different temperatures. Each of the materials is about as warm as all the others even though they feel different." Why do you think Melissa made this statement?

_____

_____

_____

F. What evidence would you need to come to the same conclusion as Melissa did?

_____

_____

G. Melissa tested her statement by measuring the temperature of each object with a thermometer. She held the thermometer on each object for about 60 seconds so that the reading would have time to respond to a temperature change. She found that all of the objects were within one degree of each other; for example, within one degree of 30 (29 to 31) degrees Celsius or 86 (85 to 87) degrees Fahrenheit. The differences measured did not correspond to the differences felt. She reasoned that this made sense since the air temperature all over the room was about the same. All materials in the room are about the same temperature if they have all been in the room for any period of time. What do you conclude now from these additional observations as to the cause of the differences felt in the materials?

_____

_____

H. Melissa concluded that, if the materials were all about the same temperature, the difference in the way they felt to her must be due to some other property of the materials. What property do you suspect might be involved?

_____

_____

I. Melissa used her prior knowledge to conclude that, since the various materials conduct heat at different rates, differences in the heat conduction of the materials was the cause of the differences noted in the materials. Thus, metal objects on a table feel cooler than the wood tabletop since metal conducts heat away from your hand faster, making your hand feel cooler. The wood tabletop feels warmer because little heat is conducted away from your hand by the wood. The rate at which various materials conduct heat away from your hand differs. Melissa next tried to predict the results of the following question posed by one of her students: "On a cold winter day, why do the handlebars of my bike feel colder than the handlebar grips?" How would you answer this student's question?

_____

_____

_____

If you responded that the handlebars (made of metal) conducted heat away from her hand faster and thus felt colder than the handlebar grips (made of plastic), you were probably following the same line of thinking as Melissa.

The following questions refer to items A through I on page 38. They are designed to help you reflect on the first set of activities. Discuss them with a peer partner, if possible.

1. Identify the different kinds of thinking processes used in attempting to solve the problem in items A through I. _____

   _____

   _____

   _____

2. What was the sequence, in time, of thinking steps you used to solve the problem?
   A. What was the first thought you had?_____
   B. What was the second? _____
   C. Third? _____
   D. _____
   E. _____
   F. _____
   G. _____
   H. _____

3. In what way did your understanding of the idea change while you tried to answer the problem? _____

   _____

   _____

4. What feedback from your actions was especially helpful? _____

   _____

   _____

When you have finished answering the four questions above, read the next section for a discussion and interpretation of your reactions.

Explanation of Everyday Encounter with Materials: A Problem

Compare your responses in the reflection activity above to patterns noted by many others when they attempted the same problem. The general thought sequence you used in working with the problem should have been similar to the sequence identified in Figure 3–1. When you started to solve the problem, you were using prior knowledge and past experience with heat and temperature. You interpreted the problem by accounting for different temperatures in terms of existing ideas already in your long-term memory. Your responses to the sensory information may have been awkward at first, making them inconsistent or inappropriate to the information supplied in each additional step.

These initial difficulties may have made you pause to reflect on your actions. You may have tried to take into account the sequence of each object touched or the object's location in the room. Perhaps you concentrated on how hard you pressed each object or on reference directions such as "heat flowing away from your body" or "heat moving toward your hand." In other words, you may have introduced elements that were not obvious parts of the situation. Discussing the problem with someone else or watching another person perform the same task may also have given you ideas on how to proceed. However,

First, assimilation of information and disequilibrium occurs:

The student, while reacting to the problem:

begins with prior knowledge of the science idea or skill.

observes and makes a mental list of observations, gaining information about the problem.

tries to interpret the new experience using prior knowledge but fails (may be repeated many times).

attempts to recall if the event was seen or experienced before.

tries to explain or solve the problem but finds the new solution is, again, not appropriate.

The student tries variations of it; some tests may work, while some may not or will not be appropriate.

shares reactions with other peers. The statements usually include a description of feelings and emotions such as frustration, confusion, or even disappointment felt throughout the original activities. This is an important event in a learning activity.

realizes there is a problem with the prior knowledge, is confronted by it, pauses, reflects, and *determines* something happened that was different and unexpected.

Next, building mental network connections, equilibrium begins:

The student:

tries different strategies not originally used in past experiences and gradually becomes aware of the new ideas or skills being used. The first trials may prove mostly inadequate or inappropriate. Gradually, partially correct responses are given.

observes others working on the same problem, or listens to another person describing a possible solution. The student tries these suggestions, then again attempts to restructure the knowledge schema using this new information.

finds more success. This may occur gradually. The newly modified strategy is tried out to check its usefulness. The student gradually feels better and is less confused. The student feels a need to share success with others.

finds solutions that appear to work in all cases. The student may initially feel uncomfortable using these different modified strategies.

begins to form a new science idea or skill as a mental schema by modifying old ones.

applies the new idea or skill to a variety of similar tasks and, by creative repetition, stabilizes the new schema.

transfers the new science idea or skill to other contexts and times. This may take several trials using the new science idea or skill. The student feels comfortable with it and has a feeling of success from reaching this solution to the problem.

FIGURE 3-1   *Sequence of responses from a typical student confronted with a problem leading to conceptual change*

information from others may have made little sense to you until you attempted to solve the problem first, by yourself, through your own actions. The attempts made it *your* problem—one needing to be solved. When a teacher tells a student about a solution to a problem, it may make little sense to her since it is not her problem and she has not related it to any previous experience. If a student was given a solution, she most likely would have accepted it and stored it in memory. This memory item probably would not be recalled at a later time since it is not connected to any other past experiences, other ideas she knew, or even feelings she had at the time. Any of these connections are helpful ways of accessing the memory.

In summary, when confronted with a new science idea a student generally responds in a learning sequence beginning with recalling prior knowledge of the science idea or skill, making a mental list of observations of the problem context, and then trying to solve the problem through repeated failure. Only after many trials will some attempts work, and the sharing of knowledge will then become useful. Later, after applying the new idea or skill to a variety of similar tasks and transferring it to other contexts and times, the student begins to feel comfortable with it and has a feeling of success from reaching this solution to the problem. This learning sequence is called "the learning cycle" and is more effective in planning science lessons for elementary and middle school children than traditional science lesson approaches.

WHAT ARE THE ESSENTIAL ELEMENTS OF EFFECTIVE SCIENCE LESSON PLANNING?

The state and national standards for teaching science encompass many of the changes now taking place in elementary and middle schools. These changes are seen in many aspects of a teacher's life. The greatest changes have been observed in classroom actions and interactions in teaching science. Encompassing the changes taking place, the National Science Education Standards (National Research Council, 1996) describe science teaching in classrooms with less teacher direction, student isolation, and coverage of science topics and with more active student inquiry and interactions (see Table 3–2). The guidelines for effective science teaching encompass the need for student learning through inquiry promoting conceptual change (see Figure 3–2). Inquiry incorporates diverse ways of investigating the natural world and proposing explanations based on evidence. Student inquiry involves such activities as making observations; considering alternative explanations; critical and creative thinking; planning investigations; using tools to collect, analyze, and interpret data; proposing and communicating explanations; and applying the explanations to other, more novel situations (National Research Council, 1996).

TABLE 3–2   *Changes in emphasis in teaching science in today's classrooms*

Less Emphasis on:	More Emphasis on:
Student acquisition of information	Student understanding and use of scientific knowledge, ideas, and inquiry processes
Presenting science content using lecture, textbook, and demonstration	Guiding students in active and extended inquiry
Rigidly following the textbook and its coverage of all topics	Selecting and adapting the textbook to change learning approaches and reduce coverage to fewer key ideas
Testing students for factual information at the end of the chapter	Continually assessing student understanding
Treating all students alike and responding to the group as a whole	Understanding and responding to an individual student's interests, experiences, and needs

Teaching Standard A: Teachers plan inquiry-based science program	Teaching Standard B: Teachers guide and facilitate science learning	Teaching Standard C: Teachers use ongoing assessment of science teaching and learning	Teaching Standard D: Design and manage science learning environment	Teaching Standard E: Develop communities of science learners
Select science content; adapt and design to meet students' needs	Focus and support inquiry while interacting with materials	Use student data and observations to guide teaching	Provide enough time for investigations	Respect diverse ideas and experiences
Select teaching strategy that supports student understanding	Plan for discourse among students	Guide students in self-assessment	Classroom setting should encourage and support student inquiry	Nurture collaboration among students
	Challenge students to accept responsibility for their own learning			Facilitate discussion in small and large groups
	Encourage and model scientific inquiry			Model skills and attitude of scientific inquiry

FIGURE 3–2   *National Science Education Standards related to effective classroom science teaching*

Source: Adapted with permission from National Research Council. Copyright 1996 by the National Academy of Sciences. Courtesy of the National Academy Press, Washington, D.C.

For further information, see the Companion Website at *http://www.prenhall.com/sunal* for links to the National Science Education Standards.

The teaching strategy that incorporates the changing emphases in teaching science must be a classroom inquiry process that is structured to help students and teachers become more involved in student-guided interactive learning. Robert Karplus (1979) named this approach to teaching science the **learning cycle** (see Figure 3–3). Beginning in the 1950s, the learning cycle has had a rich history of research, development, and examples as a classroom pedagogical strategy for teaching and learning science (Barman, 1989, 1992; Driver & Oldham, 1986; Hewson & Hewson, 1988; Lawson, Abraham, & Renner, 1989; Osbourne & Whittrock, 1983; Renner & Marek, 1990; Renner, Stafford,

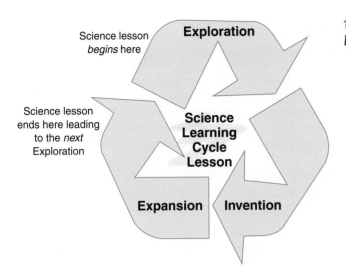

FIGURE 3-3 *The science learning cycle*

Lawson, McKinnon, Friot, & Kellog, 1976; Sunal & Sunal, 1991a, b, c, & e, 1994a; Weber & Renner, 1972).

The overall goal of the learning cycle is to help elementary and middle school students construct new scientific knowledge by creating conceptual change through interaction with the social and natural world. The inquiry teaching strategy takes into account students' developmental levels and helps them use their prior knowledge as they learn new thought processes, develop higher levels of thinking, and become aware of their own reasoning. This strategy is designed to adapt instruction to help students:

- *become aware* of their prior knowledge.
- *compare* new science ideas to their prior knowledge.
- *connect* new science ideas to what they already know.
- *construct* their own "new" scientific knowledge.
- *apply* the new scientific knowledge in novel situations.

The learning cycle has been effectively used with students at all levels because it helps them apply science knowledge gained in the classroom to new areas or to new situations (Renner & Abraham 1986; Renner et. al., 1976; Weber & Renner, 1972). Also, students who attend classrooms led by teachers more experienced in teaching science using the learning cycle have a deeper understanding of science ideas and less rote-memory surface knowledge (Hedgepeth, 1995). The learning cycle fosters learning in science because students:

- are more aware of their own reasoning.
- can recognize shortcomings of their prior knowledge as a result of being encouraged to try their existing ideas and skills out.
- can search more effectively for new patterns in their environment.
- are more likely to apply successful procedures for making decisions and solving environmentally related problems.
- can apply the science they learn more often in new settings.

Classroom science teaching must strengthen these areas in all students and discourage the unquestioned acceptance of poorly understood science principles and procedures.

Applying What You Know

Sequencing Teacher Actions during a Lesson

Teaching for meaningful learning in science requires thought and careful planning by teachers. The list of statements below represents a set of actions to be taken by a teacher planning a science lesson. Sequence these actions in the order of performance based on helping students construct an understanding of a scientific concept. Do this by placing a number in front of each statement. Use the number 1 to identify the *initial actions* to take place during the lesson, the number 2 to identify the *actions to be performed in the middle of the lesson,* and the number 3 to identify the *final appropriate actions in the science lesson.* The lesson should:

_____ provide clear examples of the new science idea or model the new skill.

_____ provide students with situations where they practice using the new science idea just explained.

_____ ask probing questions to diagnose students' prior knowledge about the scientific concept.

_____ provide a clear explanation of the new scientific concept.

_____ provide activities to help students transfer the new scientific knowledge to real world situations.

_____ focus students' attention on science experiences.

_____ provide additional practice to help students use terms, definitions, and explanations experienced in the lesson.

_____ ask students to clarify the new idea and justify their statements with evidence.

_____ provide application activities in new, relevant contexts while helping students recall their original alternative explanations.

_____ encourage students working cooperatively to recall and relate prior knowledge to the new science concept.

_____ elicit and make public students' prior knowledge.

_____ help students confront their prior knowledge.

_____ ask students to reflect on and explain related experiences, concepts, and terminology in their own words.

_____ summarize the important events in the science lesson.

_____ provide closure regarding the lesson's main ideas.

The order of teacher actions relates to the conditions needed to help students modify or discard prior knowledge (conceptual change). It also relates to helping them construct a new scientific knowledge schema for the focus ideas of the lesson. See Figure 3–4 for an appropriate time sequence of teacher actions.

The initial actions, labeled 1, to be taken in a lesson are found in the Exploration Phase of the lesson on Figure 3–6. The actions to be performed in the middle of the lesson, labeled 2, are found in the Invention Phase in Figure 3–7. The final actions to be taken in a science lesson, labeled 3, are found in the Expansion Phase in Figure 3–8.

This strategy for teaching is a "cycle." One set of actions leads to another. The last set of actions can be the lead-in for another lesson.

These questions are designed to help adapt science instruction to assist student learning in a science lesson. Based on the learning activities planned:

1. Exploration (Initial Actions)

- Did students *become aware* of their prior knowledge and reasoning about the new science idea?
- Were the students able to *compare* their prior knowledge to the new science idea and recognize shortcomings in their prior knowledge?

2. Invention (Next Actions)

- Did the students *connect* the new science idea to what they already knew?
- Were students able to *construct* their own "new" scientific knowledge based on the new idea and to search more effectively for new patterns and regularities in their environment?

3. Expansion (Concluding Actions)

- Did the students *apply* the new scientific knowledge in novel situations?
- Were the students able to develop successful procedures for making decisions and solving problems while *transferring* the new science idea to other settings?

FIGURE 3-4   *Brief outline of questions to evaluate the effectiveness of lesson planning decisions*

PREPARATION FOR PLANNING A LEARNING CYCLE

What Are the Important Components of an Effective Strategy for Teaching Science?

Teaching is a continuous process of decision making, involving planning, implementation, and evaluation. If teachers base their decisions on an understanding of how students learn science effectively, they can increase their ability to develop science lessons that work. The learning cycle sequence is not a blueprint for teaching science, but a set of decision points and criteria that all teachers must address in the process if they are to adequately help students learn science.

Phases of the Learning Cycle Lesson

Science teaching involves a complete planning sequence, the learning cycle, for effective science learning (Barman & Kotar, 1989). The learning cycle has three parts or phases, each requiring different student actions and interactions (Beisenherz, 1991). The lesson begins with students becoming actively involved in exploring a new science idea, **Exploration (Ex)**. This Exploration is followed by a more guided explanation and student invention of the idea, **Invention (I)**. The lesson culminates with the expansion of the idea through an application and transfer into new settings, **Expansion (Exp)**. Each learning cycle phase has a specific purpose related to the science learning needs of the student. All three phases need to be completed in a lesson before a single idea can be meaningfully learned (Renner, Abraham, & Birnie, 1988). If one phase of the learning cycle science lesson were dropped out, significant loss in the achievement of the new science idea would be expected. A significant loss in achievement of the new idea was also found when the sequence of the phases was changed; for example, putting Invention first (Abraham & Renner, 1986).

The learning cycle uses several pedagogical methods to accomplish its purpose, so that during each phase a teacher of science has a number of decisions to make. The choice of science pedagogical methods (e.g., student inquiry activities, reading a textbook passage, visiting a website to gather information, a hands-on approach, a film, lecture, cooperative learning, field trip to the school grounds, and so on) is determined by the:

- type of *science* idea(s) or skill(s) to be taught.
- prior knowledge and specific learning needs of the *student*.
- part of the learning cycle and *pedagogical methods* with which the student is involved.

The type of student learning activity the student is involved in is an important decision to consider during the learning cycle lesson. Pedagogical methods that involve students in active experimentation versus passive listening or guided hands-on activities with little student reflection create more long-term understanding of the new science idea presented (Renner, Abraham, & Birnie, 1985). Students participating in classrooms that focus on learning by reading science textbooks were poorly prepared for science achievement tests (Musheno & Lawson, 1999; Renner, & Marek, 1990). Students whose textbooks were modified to reflect the learning cycle performed significantly higher on science achievement tests. Students who participated in hands-on learning as part of a learning cycle had significantly higher science achievement and more positive attitudes toward learning than students in classrooms that focused on learning by reading science textbooks whether they were involved in hands-on learning or not (Allen, 1992; Kyle, 1986).

Effective science teaching requires making a match between the student, science content, and the science teaching approach (Figure 3–5). The criteria for making planning decisions in science lessons vary with each part of the learning process. A brief outline summary of the decisions and their sequence is provided in Figure 3–4. The criteria, in the form of questions, summarize the important points of student learning found in Karplus (1979), Driver (1986), Cavallo & Laubach (2001) and Glasson & Lalik (1993).

The learning cycle is best used as part of an instructional program that stresses creativity, development of self-worth, self-reliance, and respect for the opinions of others in a safe learning environment. This teaching approach is compatible with knowledge gained from developmental studies involving students, information processing studies

Figure 3–5 *Effective teaching requires a match*

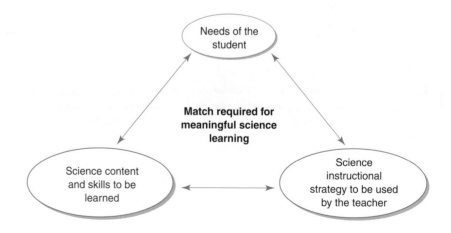

examining the functioning of the brain, and constructivist approaches to learning discussed in Chapter 2 (Clarke, 1990; Lawson, Abraham, & Renner, 1989; Tolman & Hardy, 1995).

Preparation for Planning a Learning Cycle

When a teacher begins to plan a science lesson, several decisions must be made. First, she selects a topic and develops a science objective that is relevant to the curriculum guidelines and to the students' past experiences in the area. The state science curriculum guidelines or national science standards are often sources that teachers first use. Sometimes, it is best to begin planning for a science objective by focusing on a science thinking skill students should be able to perform with the new science idea. With this skill in mind, it may be easier to develop a focus for the lesson objective. Often, however, teachers initially have a science activity in mind that involves students exploring the science objective. Most experienced teachers plan their lesson focus this way (Clark & Peterson, 1987; Shapiro, 1996). For example, a teacher may be planning a science lesson using the learning cycle for a textbook chapter discussing the topic of soil. He may be thinking about an activity in which students are asked to dig a small hole in a corner of the school grounds. Imagining the activity or trying it out will lead the teacher to focus on the properties of the soil, layers of soil, and how the goal is to be reached. The activity involves science skills that need to be developed along with the science content. The student thinking skills include observation and classification of various soil properties, making inferences about patterns found in the information, communicating inferences, and predicting and hypothesizing leading to generalizations about soils. Thus, the science lesson objectives on properties of soils include:

1. Observing and classifying properties of soil by (a) color, (b) particle size, (c) stickiness or clumping, (d) water-holding capacity, and (e) depth.
2. Communicating and identifying patterns in the information discovered about soils.
3. Predicting and inferring patterns at other "dig" sites or using indirect sources such as the textbook and library research materials.

The activity chosen for this initial exploration phase of the soils learning cycle lesson may be related to other new science ideas in later lessons. For example, the students may discover the layering of soils while digging a small hole in a part of the school grounds. In a later lesson, they are reminded of their discovery and describe the activity that led to it. The students can explore this idea further through building a simulated example of soil layering by filling a glass jar half full of water, adding several types of soil to it, shaking it, and examining it after the soil settles to the bottom. The first activity serves as part of the Exploration phase for this later lesson.

Planning the Exploration Phase of the Learning Cycle

After identifying the objectives of a lesson, the teacher decides how the initial part of the lesson, the Exploration, can best be planned to prepare students for meaningful learning of the lesson's key science ideas and skill(s). To make this decision, answers to questions about actions that will accomplish the following are needed:

What initial activities will confront students' existing knowledge of the new science idea?

What initial activities will help diagnose students' prior knowledge on the new science idea?

What initial activities will encourage students to recall and relate prior knowledge to the new science idea?

What initial activities will bring out and make public what the students now know about the new idea?

The Exploration part of a lesson involves students with a new science idea, makes their existing personal knowledge public, and relates old learning to new learning while the teacher diagnoses their existing ideas. The Exploration is a very important part of a science lesson that is not experienced by students in traditional classrooms. Research indicates that deleting this part of the lesson and beginning the lesson instead with an explanation of the new science idea seriously reduces student achievement (Abraham, 1989). Planning effective Exploration activities involves several important learning characteristics. First, several activities are usually designed to encourage learning through students' own inquiry and to focus their interests. Second, the activities include minimal teacher guidance or expectation. Third, the activities begin with a well-planned "key" question(s) from the teacher, or student questions developed from earlier activities. The questions are designed to encourage students' observation of the natural world and raise questions that confront students' old ways of thinking. Fourth, students typically work in cooperative learning groups during the Exploration phase. Exploration activities provide for student interaction with ideas and materials. Such interaction usually involves collecting and organizing data, selecting resources, participating in discussions, and debating. Students try out prior ideas, suspend judgment, predict, hypothesize, and test out their ideas. Fifth, students need adequate time to relate prior knowledge to the new idea. The activities help students become aware of the purpose and key science idea of the lesson. Finally, and most importantly, the Exploration process allows teachers to know students' present understanding of the key science idea.

Examples of Exploration activities include student observation and exploration of an event, a problem to be solved, a perplexing event (discrepant event), field trip, demonstration, decisions to make, or question-and-answer discussions in small groups. Planning the initial phase of the learning cycle involves four general steps.

Help students try out and confront existing knowledge with the new science idea.
The initial learning cycle activities provide a common background experience that allows students to learn through their own actions and reactions. It also helps them try out and confront their prior knowledge in a new setting. Teachers start with a "key" question involving students in a physical and mental activity that focuses their attention. For example, for the soils learning cycle lesson you may ask, "What does soil feel like, look like, smell like, and sound like?" or "What are the properties of soil?" or "Describe this soil sample to another student so that she can pick it out of a group of different soil samples."

Key questions are open or divergent questions for which there are many answers. This type of question allows all students to search their prior knowledge and respond with an answer. Many times these questions are centered on a **discrepant event**, an event that is confusing because it is not easily explained using prior knowledge.

For example, in a soils learning cycle lesson, while viewing soil layers in a hole dug on the school grounds, students are asked to describe how the soil got that way. To begin a different lesson cycle science lesson for the key idea of "temperature," the teacher asks students to touch different objects made of different materials and describe how warm they feel. In a cells learning cycle lesson, students are asked to draw and describe

Chapter 12, Starting Points in Teaching Science, describes the development and use of discrepant events in science lessons. Key questions can be asked in many ways.

what a thin piece of onion skin looks like through a microscope. In another learning cycle lesson, to introduce the "cause of sound," the teacher asks students to demonstrate how they would make a sound using common, everyday objects. In the Exploration phase the teacher may use a game, verbal statements of procedure, thinking aloud, a demonstration, or a problem situation to frame a question and focus students' attention.

As a lesson begins, students' minds are in different places. They may be thinking about what they are going to do during recess, what they will eat for lunch, or how they will do on a test later that day. The earlier students' attention is focused on the intended science idea, the greater the chance of learning. The first few minutes of any lesson are important. Sensory information, whether derived from the student's own actions or from a short teacher lecture, is held in the student's memory for less than one second before the mind decides what to hold on to and what to forget. Most sensory information is perceived by the student, but is disregarded. If the teacher does not help a student focus on the lesson's key science ideas and skills, the student may not obtain information relevant to the meaningful learning. This is necessary to help students connect the lesson's experiences to their prior knowledge.

The student's focus is drawn to the lesson's key science ideas and skills when he is involved in a problem or task that is puzzling and actively invites him to become involved in solving the puzzle. When a teacher asks students to touch different types of soil and describe how they feel, for example, the students may be surprised and puzzled to find little difference between them even though they have different colors and shades. Their attention is then focused on why there seems to be no difference between the soil types since they expected to feel a difference. By asking students to demonstrate how to make a sound using common, everyday objects, the teacher focuses their attention on sound, how to get sound from an object, and why different objects produce different sounds.

Diagnose students' prior knowledge of the new idea.   During the initial, or Exploration, phase of instruction, teachers need to determine students' current understanding of the ideas and/or skills being taught. Informal activities provide this information. Observation of students as they participate in discussion or an activity enables teachers to diagnose their level of understanding of content previously learned.

During the initial activity of the soil lesson example previously given, students observe several examples of different soils, then classify them by common properties. These properties may include grain size, color, shape, stickiness, and roughness. While students are actively participating in these experiences, an effective teacher observes how they interact with the materials, the content of their discussion, what type of meaning they begin to make of their explorations, and what properties they discover on their own. This information helps the teacher decide how relevant the new ideas are to the students in view of their prior knowledge. It also helps the teacher decide how much guidance the students need in the next part of the lesson.

Relate students' prior knowledge to new science ideas.   Meaningful science learning involves making connections between ideas and experiences and creating a knowledge schema. Open-ended questions and examples of materials that call attention to their past experiences help students remember what they have learned and transfer that knowledge to related ideas. This process helps students recall ideas from their long-term memory. Effective teachers help students retrieve as many related experiences, ideas, or skills from long-term memory as possible. The retrieval of relevant prior knowledge provides a knowledge schema into which new ideas can be placed or interconnected.

Chapters 8, Assessing and Evaluating Science Learning, and Chapter 12, Starting Points in Teaching Science, describe how to set up and perform informal and formal observations, interviews, and assessments of students.

Bring out prior knowledge related to the new idea and make it public.   The retrieval of prior knowledge allows students' ideas on the science topic to be made public. The student is made personally aware of his prior knowledge in a nonthreatening way, as are his peers and teacher, through small group interactions, through oral reports to the teacher and others in the class, and through shared written journals and drawings. This is important. The student checks how well his prior knowledge predicts real world events. This allows the student to determine the adequacy of his view, or to suggest a better one to replace it. Unless the student confronts her misconceptions about the real world, she will keep them intact. In this case, she is likely to use the new knowledge on the next test, but to forget it afterward since she is unable to transfer it to any new setting.

Recall from long-term memory alone is not a sufficient beginning for a lesson. Asking students, for example, to recall what happens when they drop different objects in water at home, or to discuss their experiences while swimming, won't relate previous learning about sinking and floating to new learning about these ideas. However, encouraging second graders to explore sinking and floating with a set of objects, to make predictions as to whether they will sink or float in a small bowl, and to record the results as the objects are placed in the water can result in an effective first activity introducing the concepts of sinking and floating. A discussion of their past water experiences after students have worked with a sinking and floating activity will tie the activity more completely into their prior knowledge. Often, one or two well-chosen activities for the Exploration can accomplish all the important purposes of the beginning of a science lesson: confrontation, diagnosis, relating old learning to new learning, and making personal knowledge public. Figure 3–6 provides a summary of criteria to evaluate the adequacy of a set of planned Exploration activities or the actions of a teacher in beginning a classroom science lesson using the learning cycle.

Planning the Invention Phase of the Learning Cycle

Invention builds on Exploration by using a more direct teaching format to guide students to experience and develop the new idea or skill more fully, or to a higher order. The purpose of Invention is to explain and provide examples of the key new idea or skill that leads students to mentally construct new patterns of reasoning. This part of the lesson is usually more teacher guided than are other parts of the lesson. The teacher brings this phase of the lesson to a close by clearly defining and describing the idea or skill.

When planning the Invention part of the science lesson, teachers make decisions on the following questions:

How can Exploration experiences be further developed to focus on the basic science idea or skill to be taught?

How is the key science idea best explained?

How should the science idea or skill be practiced, modeled, or demonstrated?

What strategies or techniques should be used to make sure all students understand the science idea?

Planning effective Invention activities requires the consideration of several important characteristics. First, Invention activities continue the development of the new science idea or skill through directed reflection and discussion, begun in the Exploration phase. Activities here communicate information about the new idea to help resolve confrontation or puzzlement. Second, these activities allow learning from "explanation" through an interesting variety of planned teaching actions, multimedia, and interactions of students. The explanation describes all important aspects, ranges, contexts, and uses of the new science idea or skill. Third, the planned activities introduce the new idea or skill in

---

EXPLORATION PHASE SUMMARY

The Exploration phase allows students to confront and make evident their own thinking/ knowledge schema of the science idea or skill to be learned.

Purposes

- Provide common background science experience allowing learning through students' own actions and reactions.
- Help students try out and confront their prior knowledge of the new science idea or skill.
- Bring out and make public students' prior knowledge on the new science idea or skill.

Evaluation Criteria: Exploration Activities Planned and Implemented

1. Encourage learning through students' own inquiry and focus their interest.
2. Involve minimal guidance or expectation on the teacher's part.
3. Often provide an experience that confronts students' old way of thinking.
4. Begin with a preplanned open or divergent question.
5. Involve students working in cooperative learning groups.
6. Encourage observation of the natural world and raise questions for the students.
7. Provide for student interaction with ideas and materials as well as the collection and organization of data.
8. Encourage students' reflection in selecting resources, discussion, and debate.
9. Encourage trying out prior ideas, suspending judgment, predicting, hypothesizing, and testing.
10. Provide students with adequate time to relate prior knowledge to the new idea or skill.
11. Allow students to know the purpose and objective of the science lesson.
12. Allow teacher to know students' present understanding of the idea or skill.

FIGURE 3-6   *Criteria for sequencing science instruction — the Exploration phase of the learning cycle*

a structured manner through additional student experiences using demonstrations, analogies, audio-visual materials, several sense modalities, textbook readings, or other media. Fourth, the activities encourage students to develop as much of the new idea as possible by providing more than one form of explanation, giving clear examples, modeling, and checking for understanding. For example, explaining the properties of soil using concrete examples, a field trip to the school grounds, a chart, and pictures may all be needed before the explanation of the idea becomes clear to students. Students need to have time to question, try out, and practice the new science idea. The Invention ends with a concise closure describing the main idea or skill introduced.

How students react to new ideas they encounter.   When presented with an idea, students can either assimilate or accommodate it into their own thinking. An idea presented to a student who is familiar with it in some way can be **assimilated** into that student's existing thoughts. We can say that the idea was assimilated into his knowledge schema. An idea presented to a student that is unfamiliar in some way may have to be **accommodated** into that student's existing knowledge structure. The knowledge schema is reorganized or a new one is built to accommodate the new idea.

What initial activities will confront these students' existing knowledge?

During the Exploration phase of the learning cycle, students are usually unable to assimilate the new ideas or skills presented. They were confronted and became confused or perplexed over the meaning of the experience they were involved in. When information cannot be assimilated, students may try to accommodate it. The students' minds accommodate by changing or adding to their knowledge schema (Piaget, 1977). The confrontation or puzzlement the students experienced in the Exploration activity upset their mental equilibrium, causing **disequilibrium.** Disequilibrium is an imbalance occurring when a person encounters an event or object that he is unable to assimilate due to the inadequacy of his cognitive structures (Ginsburg & Opper, 1988). In such a situation, there is a discrepancy or a conflict between the person's schema and the requirements of the experience. This is accompanied by feelings of unease. When faced with a disturbance, the person reacts with responses that attempt to restore her equilibrium.

During the Invention phase, teachers help students to accommodate their thinking to new science ideas or skills. The students are ready for the experiences of the Invention phase because they provide opportunities for students to accommodate the new ideas or skills, restoring their equilibrium (Martin, Sexton, Wagner, & Gerlovich, 1994). The Invention phase helps students modify the structures in their minds in reaction to their experiences.

In some situations, especially for young students, where the distance between the experience and prior knowledge is very great, the students do not perceive the difference as important. Such information does not confront or puzzle them, although it may be interesting enough to add to what they already know. Soil layering is an uninteresting observation for a three- or four-year-old (assimilation), but is highly interesting to a nine-year-old because he sees it as an observation that should make sense but does not with his present knowledge schema (accommodation). For example, students may enjoy listening to a singer with a deep bass voice. They may not have heard such deep singing before so they assimilate it into their schema for singing. Since they have heard singing voices that are deep, just not quite so deep, they are not confronted by this experience; rather, they assimilate it.

Provide explanations of the new science.   Explaining a new science idea that facilitates students' accommodation of it usually requires a variety of methods. These might include a student-teacher discussion of findings resulting from the exploration activities; students working with software; students working with materials in guided science activities; data collection and discussion of a problem in a cooperative learning group; a brief lecture; viewing a videotape; and reading short passages of a textbook, Internet website, or reference book. Since the student's short-term memory has a limited capacity, teachers must make certain that they provide important information as concretely as possible. When more concrete materials or visuals, such as hands-on materials, pictures, graphs, demonstrations, and modeling, accompany verbal explanations, more information can be stored efficiently. The use of concrete materials facilitates meaningful learning and long-term memory storage. To concretely demonstrate a new idea, teachers provide students with examples of all aspects of a concept, such as *absorption properties of soils*. These aspects include grain size, color, and shape differences between soils; rate of absorption; and upper limits of the amount of absorption. To accomplish this, students can repeatedly work with a generalization, such as some soils absorb and store more water than others, using concrete materials.

See Chapter 15, Earth and Space Science Starting Points, for additional examples of students investigating soils.

For further information, see the Companion Website at *http://www.prenhall.com/sunal* for a link to Sunal & Sunal, 1994a.

Companion Website

Also, note-taking guides, for information or data, often help make the structure of an idea or skill more concrete when provided to students at the beginning of the Invention phase. By working with concrete materials, which allow more efficient use of their short-term memory, students can process more meaningful knowledge than through reading text, viewing pictures, or listening to teacher lectures.

Provide examples of the new idea.   Students need to see clear examples of what the new science ideas or skills represent. At first, students' practice of an idea or skill is guided or modeled by the teacher. This enables the students to receive feedback. Without such guidance, students might practice errors, creating misconceptions that require a great amount of effort to unlearn. One or more examples demonstrating the idea or skill are presented at this point in the lesson. Sometimes this consists of demonstrating a science idea or skill through guided practice, analogies, or working models. It can also involve taking the students through a step-by-step process. The more ways in which an idea or skill is modeled for students, the more meaningful it will be to them (Clarke, 1990; Potari & Spiliotopoulou, 1996).

An Invention example in a learning cycle lesson with the key idea *properties of soils* should involve young students with experiences demonstrating that the range of soil types can be observed by differences in color, grain size, type of soil material, and other physical properties. Clay, sandy soil, and humus are examples students should touch, observe with a magnifying glass, and see in the classroom, on the school grounds, and elsewhere in the community in order to observe differences and investigate soil behavior in different situations. Dry, wet, warm, and cold soils should be observed using all senses except taste; records should be made; and discussions should be held on what was found. Terms should be provided during the follow-up discussion. To learn the property of *absorption*, which states some soils absorb and store more water than other soils, older students are asked to make predictions about the amount of water each soil sample can hold. Sand, clay soil, humus, and soil obtained from home and school can be used to make comparisons. Putting each soil type on the top of a paper towel in a large funnel, students can compare the amount of water held by each sample. Students will need to develop controls such as using equal amounts of water and measuring tools (i.e., marking a plastic soft drink bottle) to investigate the relationships involved. Communicating and discussing the results of predictions is best done in small groups, with summaries given in whole class meetings. Terms should again be provided during the follow-up discussion. A previous learning cycle lesson would explore the idea that soils are built up very slowly and vary with location because there are several processes that cause rocks to break down into small pieces to make soil. Also, depending on the type of rock and the type of climate, different types of soil will form.

Using a different science lesson, an analogy is used in the following example of a fourth-grade investigation of simple electric circuits. Students are first introduced to the concept of an electric circuit in a learning cycle lesson Exploration. This can be done by asking students to light a bulb using only a battery, a bulb, and a wire. Following students' lighting attempts and small group discussion, the teacher in the Invention part of the learning cycle uses a water pipe analogy when asking students to further investigate simple electric circuits: "When water flows into a pipe, its flow at the end will be determined by what happens to it inside the pipe." This analogy is demonstrated using student help, or by student investigation, with a piece of clear plastic aquarium tubing attached to a faucet or container of water. Pinching the tubing in the middle, increasing the water amount by opening the faucet handle, or using smaller diameter tubing changes the water flow. The Invention activities should describe all necessary aspects of the water circuit, including water source, water pipes, resistance of the tubing to water flow, and a water return drain where water can eventually return to the source. If water does not return to the source, the faucet will cease to function because the source will run dry. Then students are provided with many circuit example drawings on a worksheet in which students predict whether different circuit designs will light a bulb. Students are investigating the question: Will the current flow through the bulb? This is followed by students checking their predictions by observing the results of their trials with batteries and wires, which is followed by a discussion of the patterns discovered. In this learning cycle Invention, the analogy provides an organizational structure and a focus that helps students see patterns in the examples given. The worksheet provides them with clear examples of the main idea of the lesson, *open and closed circuits.*

Practice the new idea.   Students need to practice using the new idea or skill through concrete activities similar to the situations just experienced in the explanation activity. For example, students are shown a sample of soil and asked, "How does this new soil compare to the others in its ability to hold water?" In a different lesson, students are shown several additional drawings of a circuit worked with earlier and asked, "Will a bulb in each of these circuits light? Try it and see if your prediction works."

These activities let the teacher know how well the students understand the new science idea or skill. Observation of student performances helps the teacher to decide which students have sufficient experience with the science idea and are ready to move on to the Expansion activities, and which students need more practice or explanation. The teacher may circle back, explaining the idea further by involving students in new activities that help them invent the idea.

Closure for the new science idea.   Some students "discover" the new science idea during the Exploration phase. Others "invent" it during the Invention activities. Still other students may not yet be clear about the new science idea experienced. It is important to make certain that all students have a clear description of the idea or skill with which they have been working and will apply in the last part of the lesson. A closure can be completed with the teacher providing a brief, clear description, demonstration, or modeling of the main science idea or skill, orally and in writing, at the end of the Invention phase. The closure should state or show clearly and concisely the main objective of the lesson. Alternatively, students may state the main idea of the lesson orally, write the idea on the board, or demonstrate the skill. The teacher might ask in general, "What have you learned from the science experiences so far?" or in a soils lesson, "What is similar or different between soils found in our community?" or in an electric circuit lesson, "What is needed to have an electric bulb light?" Have several students respond to check their perception of the new idea. If they do not clearly state the main idea of the lesson, the teacher should state the main science idea or demonstrate the main science skill.

In a middle-grade lesson, a closure summarizing the key idea of the concept of *properties of soils* should include a statement that soils vary in their range of properties and that soil types can be observed to determine the range of color, grain size, type of material, and other physical properties. The different characteristics of soils, including the size and material of the particles that make them up, affect other properties, such as their ability to hold water.

Figure 3–7 provides a summary of criteria to evaluate the adequacy of a set of planned Invention activities or the actions of a teacher in the middle section of a classroom science lesson using the learning cycle.

INVENTION PHASE SUMMARY

Invention builds on Exploration by using a more direct teaching format to experience and develop the science idea or skill more fully, systematically, or to a higher order.

Purpose
- To explain the new science idea or skill, leading students to apply new patterns of reasoning to their experiences, encouraging accommodation.

Evaluation Criteria: Invention Activities Planned and Implemented

1. Continue development of the new idea or skill in students through more teacher-directed reflection and discussion of Exploration experience. Lead students through information and ideas that offer alternative ideas (solutions or explanations) for the confrontation experienced earlier.

2. Introduce the new idea or skill in a structured manner through additional student experiences using a variety of mediums including student senses, teacher explanation, technology interface, video, textbook readings, field trips, cooperative group discussions, Internet searches, guests to be interviewed, and others.

3. Allow learning of the "explanation of the new idea" through an interesting variety of teaching actions, multimedia, and students' hands-on, minds-on interactions describing aspects, ranges, contexts, and uses of the new science idea or skill.

4. Provide for the learning of explanations by additional practice where students use labels, definitions, personal explanations, and skills in new, but similar, situations. It is important to use personally relevant examples, not abstract, repetitive practice.

5. Offer students sufficient time to question and try out the explanation of the new idea.

6. Encourage students to develop as much of the new idea or skill as possible by providing more than one form of explanation, giving clear examples, modeling, and checking for understanding.

7. Provide a concise closure on the new idea or skill describing the main idea or skill introduced.

FIGURE 3-7   *Criteria for sequencing science instruction — the Invention phase of the learning cycle*

Planning the Expansion Phase of the Learning Cycle

Following the Invention, or explanation, phase of the lesson, it is necessary to help students apply and transfer the new science idea or skill to different situations. This is the purpose of the Expansion phase of the lesson. The expansion is a very important part of a science lesson that many times is not experienced by students in traditional classrooms. Research indicates that deleting this part of the lesson seriously reduces student achievement involving the new science idea (Renner, Abraham & Birnie, 1988). Practice and application helps students retrieve the science idea from their memory when they need to do so. Providing additional experiences that help students transfer the new idea to other settings and contexts is necessary for students to add this knowledge to their long-term memory. These experiences help students to restructure old thought forms and fully develop new thinking processes that integrate the new ideas/skills and resolve apparent contradictions discovered during the Exploration phase of the lesson. Expansion activities involve students in:

1. Analyzing problem situations.
2. Considering tentative solutions based on one's previous experience.
3. Trying out the tentative solutions.
4. Evaluating the effectiveness of the tentative solutions.
5. Using new solutions in different contexts.

Awareness of one's own reasoning is important for meaningful learning, especially as it leads to higher-level thinking processes. Specific aspects of Expansion to concentrate on during this phase of the learning cycle include broadening the range of application of a new idea, differentiating the new idea from other related ideas, asking students to describe not only the solution to the problem but what they did and how they came up with a solution, and relating previously held prior knowledge to the new idea or skill learned. Examples of Expansion student experiences include reflection on hands-on activities, field trips, problems to solve, decisions to make, interviewing or surveying other children or adults, making drawings of events, playing a part in a simulation, playing a game where the idea is involved in a successful conclusion, creating an analogy or model of the new idea and describing how it works, using the Internet to find applications of the new idea, paper-and-pencil exercises, and question-and-answer discussions in small groups.

Application and transfer of the new science idea.   In order for an idea or skill to be automatically retrieved from long-term memory, sufficient application and transfer of the new idea is needed. The experiences are spaced out over time and the idea or skill is used in situations similar to, but different from, those experienced in the lesson. For example, third-grade students in a soils learning cycle lesson are shown a sample of soil and asked, "Is this the type of soil to put plants into that need a constant source of water? What would you do to find out? How can you make the soil even better to carry out this task?" In an electric circuit learning cycle lesson, the teacher demonstrates a problem circuit and asks, "What is wrong with this circuit? Why doesn't it light? Make changes so that the bulb will light."

After students perform and apply the new science skill or idea in settings similar to those experienced in the lesson, they are ready to transfer it to different situations. Often, this step is omitted because students have given some evidence of learning the new idea or skill earlier in the lesson. This is thought to be sufficient. However, students need experience in using the science idea in a new context over a period of time before the new thought can be stabilized in the long-term memory (Baker & Piburn, 1997; Perkins & Salomon, 1991).

An example of transferring the new idea for the learning cycle lesson *soil properties* can be performed by asking students to design and construct a product that could be sold to people that would help clean up a water spill from a home plumbing problem.

In a different learning cycle lesson, transfer can occur by following up the electric circuit Invention activities with a question asking students to construct a circuit to perform a specific task, such as testing whether or not a material is a conductor. Transferring the new idea to another context can also involve asking students to make predictions and investigate the inside of a flashlight or other simple battery-powered toy device. Drawing, constructing, and using the new idea helps transfer the idea of the open or closed circuit or the soil properties concept to situations outside of the classroom and make connections with other aspects of students' lives. Reflection on their prior knowledge, discussion, and sharing of student ideas follows these application and transfer activities.

Give a lesson summary.   Following the application and transfer activities, a brief chronological summary of the lesson events is given. The summary is important to help students put the lesson's experiences together into a whole related event. This is especially important if the learning cycle takes place over more than one day. The summary includes the important ideas and events in each phase of the learning cycle lesson just completed. It is best to ask students to provide the summary. A student might begin by saying that ". . . when we were outside viewing soil layers in the hole we dug near the school fence, we first made predictions as to how soil layers got that way. . . ."

Figure 3–8 provides a summary of criteria to evaluate the adequacy of a set of planned Expansion activities in the final part of a classroom science lesson using the learning cycle.

EXPANSION PHASE SUMMARY

Expansion activities allow students to apply the idea or skill just taught in the Invention phase. They often include experiences that cause students to extend the range, modality, and context of the science idea or skill.

Purpose
- To apply the new idea or skill to additional examples fostering real understanding and long-term memory.

Evaluation Criteria: Expansion Activities Planned and Implemented

1. Provide additional time and experiences for students to ask questions, observe, record, use explanations, make decisions, and design experiments to apply the new idea or skill in new, but similar, situations. Additional time and experiences are needed for the science idea or skill to become part of the students' thought processes (conceptual change).

2. Encourage transfer of the new knowledge to various real world contexts and other times where the new idea or skill was explained. Relate student activities to personally relevant settings, thereby helping complete abstraction from classroom and textbook concrete examples.

3. Encourage retrieval from long-term memory by helping students form an abstraction from concrete examples.

4. End with a lesson summary that highlights and focuses attention on the experiences where the new knowledge was learned.

FIGURE 3–8   *Criteria for sequencing science instruction — the Expansion phase of the learning cycle*

Student Assessment at the End of Each Phase of the Learning Cycle

See Chapter 8, Assessing and Evaluating Science Learning, for a more complete description of assessment and evaluation of student learning.

Assessment of each student takes place throughout the science lesson. Three types of assessment related to the science new idea are necessary for effective science teaching. They are assessment of prior knowledge, monitoring of student learning actions, and checking for student understanding.

During the Exploration phase, assessment involves finding out students' prior knowledge and developmental levels with regards to the new science idea and monitoring student interactions with the planned activities. In the Invention phase, assessment usually consists of monitoring student participation and checking for levels of understanding in learning experiences that explain the new science idea. During the Expansion phase, assessment involves monitoring student participation in applying and transferring the new idea. Finally, following the Expansion phase, assessment involves determining the extent of change in students' ideas and checking for student understanding.

See Chapter 8, Assessing and Evaluating Science Learning, for sample checklists and "rubrics" to evaluate student learning.

Feedback responses from individual students and student groups are monitored in the Exploration and Invention Phase in several ways. Individual and small-group assessment is usually performed through informal student interviews and teacher observation of student responses, actions, and products during learning activities in each phase of the learning cycle. Assessment in small- and whole-group settings can be performed by having every student respond to teacher questions with a yes or no card they hold up. Another procedure is to ask the entire class a question and get responses from representative members of each cooperative learning group. Other response types are possible, such as asking students to quiz each other on the main idea of the lesson during the Invention closure. Checklists and lists of performance levels guide the recording of assessment information.

During the Expansion phase of the science lesson, observe students in their group discussions, as they work with activities, and as they share their answers. This includes asking the students in groups to apply the science idea in a new situation, providing a problem situation in which the individual student must apply the new science idea, and asking students to summarize the events of the lesson leading to the successful application of the main idea of the lesson. Following the Expansion phase, checking for understanding is best done through quizzes or assignments involving application-type assessment questions and performance activities. A general rule many teachers use is to plan more Expansion phase activities than needed for the lesson plan and to use the excess for quizzes following the lesson.

See Chapter 8, Assessing and Evaluating Science Learning, for a more detailed discussion of science assessment.

The information gained from these forms of assessment allows a teacher to decide whether to move on, stop and clarify, or recycle students through another set of activities. This is done, for instance, in a soil properties lesson if students do not use all of their senses, with the exception of taste, in describing a new soil sample during the Invention or Expansion phase. Reminding the student or small group of and/or modeling the appropriate investigative actions with new soil samples may be appropriate actions to take based on the feedback obtained from monitoring. Students having difficulty completing an application activity in an electric circuit lesson may be helped by providing students with a few circuits drawn on the board to classify, or by having students construct an example of an open and closed circuit to test it out. Providing explanations, giving examples and modeling, and checking for understanding of prerequisite ideas or the new idea may be repeated to improve comprehension. Additional practice and application learning activities are helpful if more than one prerequisite is poorly understood, or if the new science idea is abstract or contains several related pieces of information. See Figure 3–4 for an outline of criteria to consider in planning assessment for science lessons.

WORKING WITH THE LEARNING CYCLE

The best way to begin planning a science lesson to teach a key science concept is to visualize the student and teacher roles for a complete lesson. The lesson Exploration begins with the teacher raising questions about a familiar event and facilitating student exploration. The students play an active role of observing, asking questions, and testing out their prior knowledge. This leads to more teacher-guided activities that explain the concept and create interactions between students. The student role is to mentally construct, question differences in meaning, and practice the new concept. To finish the lesson, the Expansion phase is a time for the teacher to provide and encourage opportunities for application and transfer of the new science concept to other settings. Students concentrate on applying this new explanation and make connections to the real world. See Figure 3–9 for an overview of teacher and student roles in the learning cycle.

This sequence of learning and teaching activities is more likely to produce meaningful science learning than more traditional teaching using teacher explanations and science textbooks. In order for the sequence to be effective and for meaningful learning to result from a science activity, there are several prerequisites that need to be fulfilled. First, the attempted change in a science idea or skill should not be too large. Students should be challenged but not overwhelmed. Second, the new science idea or skill should be related to the background experiences of the students. This helps create a mental network to which the new idea or skill is tied. If students have no background or prior knowledge with the new science idea, then common experiences must be planned for before the

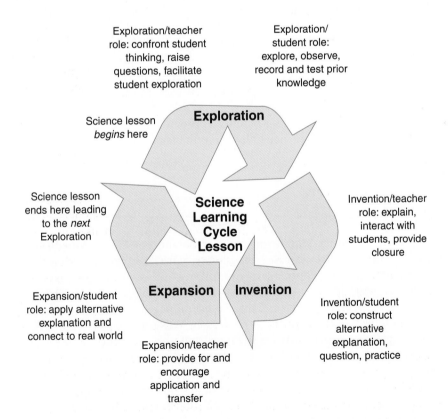

FIGURE 3-9   *Teacher and student roles in the learning cycle*

Using yarn, students are asked to create a tree cross-section like the one in the photograph.

lesson begins or during the lesson. Fifth-grade students, for example, may have little or no prior experience with soil layers or electric circuits. A field trip before the lesson begins, or Exploration phase experiences, will result in data and background experiences that the students can interpret throughout the science lesson. This is important if the new idea or skill is to be easily retrieved from long-term memory. Third, many concrete examples are used in interactive situations during a learning cycle. Fourth, students have opportunities to work through practice situations using real or simulated interactions with their environment. Fifth, students are given time to reflect, make mistakes, and interact with the new ideas or skills. Other prerequisites may exist in various situations, but these five are always essential.

The following activities are designed for practice to provide feedback on your level of understanding of the pedagogical sequence followed in the learning cycle.

Applying What You Know

Identifying and Sequencing Appropriate Lesson Activities

Below are two sets of activities, one for primary-grade and one for intermediate-grade students. These activities are used in a lesson with objectives relating to: (1) identifying different patterns of tree growth resulting from varying weather and other environmental conditions, and (2) observing and classifying skills. Begin with the primary-grade lesson activities. From the list on page 61, select an activity for the Exploration phase of the primary-grade lesson. Write down your choice in the space given. Then select an activity for the Invention phase, another for the Expansion phase, and write down these choices. Then, read the intermediate-grade lesson activities and choose activities appropriate for the Exploration, Invention, and Expansion phases of an intermediate-grade lesson having the above objectives. When you have made your choices for each lesson, reflect on or discuss your response with a partner, if available.

Primary-grade Lesson

Tree Growth and the Skills of Observing and Classifying

Possible Activities for Phases of the Learning Cycle:

1. Read a story about lumberjacks, foresters, trees, and so on. Choose one readily available in your room or school library. After reading the story, ask the students to recall differences observed in sizes, shapes, or other characteristics of trees. Discuss birthdays and how we are different from one birthday to the next. Use the above discussion to lead students to the conclusion that people, animals, and plants all show changes in growth over the years.

2. Ask students to create a tree cross-section by rolling yarn or clay in rings, alternating colors for each year's growth. Colored drawings may be substituted. After completing the tree cross-section, ask students to write or dictate a short narrative describing the life of their tree and how it was illustrated in their cross-section.

3. Ask the class to describe differences in the various trees they have seen around their homes, school, or local forest. They also may want to discuss differences between trees found in the same location.

4. Recalling what the students have previously observed about trees, discuss common tree cross-section characteristics leading to the idea that growth rings tell us about the growth history of a tree. Use a picture or transparency. Depending on the age of the students, discuss the size of rings, possible causes for their size differences, the number of rings for the age of the tree, and/or possible irregularities in rings that may indicate environmental influences during a tree's lifetime. Apply knowledge about growth rings to a discussion of the possible growth history of a tree. Ask the students what senses they use when they make their observations of trees. Make sure they discuss the importance of using all senses, except taste, to make observations.

5. Pass out examples of tree cross-sections so students can classify/observe and note similarities and differences among them. Ask students to classify the wooden pieces. Then, ask them to think of other ways to classify the wood pieces—most favorite, least favorite, similar color, size, scent, texture, buoyancy, sound-making qualities, and so on.

Primary-grade Lesson

Write down the number of the activity you chose for each phase of the learning cycle in the space below.

Exploration Phase　　＿＿＿＿

Invention Phase　　　＿＿＿＿

Expansion Phase　　　＿＿＿＿

Intermediate-grade Lesson

Tree Growth and the Skills of Observing and Classifying

Possible Activities for Phases of the Learning Cycle:

1. Have students identify and label tree parts and important characteristics of a tree cross-section drawing on a fact sheet (e.g., heartwood, sapwood, slowest growth, annual ring, most rapid growth, and environmental effects).

(continued)

2. Set up a laboratory activity with drawings or actual wood pieces of tree cross-sections, each illustrating a different environmental situation. Ask the students to measure the ring spaces to determine the average width of the light and dark rings found in the cross-sections. Ask them to describe some possible locations or environments where each tree may have grown.

3. Ask the students to describe differences they noted in the various trees seen around their homes, school, and local forests. Discuss differences between trees found in the same location.

4. On a transparency, label the parts and the growth events of a sample tree cross-section and point out evidence for each item discussed to help students develop the concept that "tree rings tell us about the growth history of a tree."

5. Ask students to observe and record characteristics of cross-sections of three to five tree samples. After they have made their observations, ask students to classify the samples using shape, texture, features, or another criterion of their choice. Have students compare their data with other students in their group. Ask them the following questions: What significant differences did you notice? How are the cross-sections alike? Could you identify common parts that all cross-sections show? What may have caused the differences you have found?

Intermediate-grade Lesson

Write down the number of the activity you chose for each phase in the space below.

Exploration Phase   _____
Invention Phase   _____
Expansion Phase   _____

Appropriate responses for both the primary-grade and intermediate-grade practice questions follow.

Exploration Phase. The approach best representing an Exploration activity upon which later conceptual understandings can be built is activity #5 for both the primary-grade and intermediate-grade lessons. It represents the Exploration phase of a learning cycle designed to encourage knowledge construction. In this activity, students have a chance to ask their own questions, try out their own ideas, and learn from their own mistakes. They gain background experience with the different wood samples they will use for the explanation that follows during the Invention phase.

Activity #3 for each lesson involves students in describing their own past experiences. However, identifying the relationship between the physical features of trees and differing patterns of tree growth due to environmental conditions using classifying and observing skills is not so obvious. Because this relationship requires a large mental jump, this is not a good beginning activity by itself. Choosing activities #5 and #3 together provides a more effective alternative exploration compared to #5 alone.

During Exploration, students learn through their own actions and reactions in a new situation. They confront the views they previously held. In this phase they explore new materials and ideas with minimal guidance or expectations for specific accomplishments. The new experience should raise questions they cannot answer with their existing ideas and skills. For many students, having made an effort that was not completely successful will help them to be ready for conceptual restructuring in the more guided explanation activity of the Invention phase that follows.

Invention Phase. The second phase of the learning cycle, Invention, formally introduces the new idea or skill that leads students to construct new knowledge from their experiences (as compared to the idea or skill with which the students started the lesson). The Invention phase first causes students to reflect on and discuss the Exploration activities. The new science idea may then be explained by the teacher, the textbook, a video, or another medium. This learning phase always follows the Exploration. Students are encouraged to construct as much of the new idea as possible for themselves in the exploration before it is explained to the class. However, expecting students to form all complex ideas themselves is not always realistic. *Invention activities naturally relate to the questions students were asking themselves at the conclusion of the Exploration.* The students' own questions are answered in an effective Invention. A combination of discussion, story, pictures, fact sheets, and transparencies found in activity #1 or activity #4, in each of the primary-grade and intermediate-grade lessons, is an effective Invention involving students in using their observing and classifying skills to explain the relationship between the physical features of trees and differing patterns of tree growth due to environmental conditions.

Expansion Phase. In the Expansion phase, the last part of any effective lesson designed to teach science ideas and skills meaningfully, students apply the new idea with which they are working in additional situations. The Expansion part of any lesson plan extends the range of applicability of the new idea or skill. Expansion provides additional time and experiences for the knowledge reconstruction process to stabilize the new idea or skill in the mind. Without a number and variety of applications, the idea's meaning will remain restricted to the examples used during its definition. Students may fail to abstract it from its concrete examples or generalize it to other situations. Asking students to construct their own models or measure other examples of the main lesson idea and interpret the meaning would be an effective Expansion activity with which to conclude the lesson. This is found in activity #2 in both the primary-age and intermediate-grade lessons. The Expansion activities help students evaluate their own understanding of the new science ideas. The students demonstrate and practice their own construction of the idea just explained. Using activities #3 and #2 together is an effective combination if time permits.

Expansion activities also help students whose knowledge construction takes place more slowly than average, or who did not adequately relate the teacher's original explanation to their own experiences. Talking to individual students with these difficulties helps identify problems and allows for prescriptive planning to resolve their problems.

The following practice activity is designed to look at the learning cycle as a complete learning sequence.

Applying What You Know

Identifying Major Lesson Characteristics

To guide your practice in planning science lessons, examine the third-grade learning cycle, Classifying Rocks: A Sample Learning Cycle Lesson, found in Figure 3–10. The objective of the lesson is enhancing the process skill of classifying. Quickly read through the lesson, looking at major headings and at the

(continued)

activities following each heading. What are the major characteristics of the lesson? Describe them.

———————

A description of the major characteristics includes the following points. The lesson does not begin by defining the science idea and skill involved in the lesson. The lesson activities first place students in a situation where they consider alternative ideas for patterns by which rocks can be classified based on their own experiences and expectations. These activities serve as the Exploration.

Next, the lesson activities involve students in concrete explanations of classification patterns supported by evidence and using the language of science. The science terminology is introduced only after students have experiences that enable them to understand the terms introduced. These activities are found in the Invention phase of the lesson.

The Expansion phase of the lesson allows students to practice the lesson's science skill in similar situations and also to apply and transfer the ideas to different contexts, including the real world.

CLASSIFYING ROCKS   **GRADE 3**

  I. Main Topic: Classifying and identifying rocks so that they fit into the same group.

 II. Objectives:
   A. The Students will observe and record observations of rocks and identify different observed rock properties (Exploration Phase).
   B. The students will describe the term "rock property" and provide two examples (Invention Phase).
   C. The students will regroup rocks based on their observed properties (Invention Phase).
   D. Students will apply additional rock properties and the newly invented classification system to unfamiliar rocks (Expansion Phase).

III. Exploration: Have students bring in five to ten rocks each from their neighborhood to mix in a box for a varied rock sample. Put the students in groups of three. Assign roles of materials manager, recorder, and reporter. All students will be active observers.
   A. Give each group a tray, a classification sheet divided into six boxes on which rocks are laid down [approximately ten rocks, a magnifying glass, a plastic knife (for scratch test), and a small piece of glass (for scratch test)]. Ask the key questions: Which rocks belong together? Why? Tell students to make and record observations for each of the rocks. Use all senses but taste.
   B. Ask students to handle their rocks, make observations about them, and share those observations with their partners. Observations will be made by all group members rotating around the group.
   C. Following each observation, have a group member put the rock in one of the six boxes. Not all boxes need to have a rock in them. When all rocks have been observed, ask the students to provide a label for each box to identify why they grouped them together.

FIGURE 3-10   *Classifying rocks: A sample learning cycle lesson*

IV. Invention:

    A. Have the student groups discuss and share their first findings with the class.

    B. Help students identify rock properties using their chosen labels. Examples include weight, size, texture, color, and size of crystals.

    C. Ask students to classify their rocks on the basis of rock properties invented by others that they did not use originally.

    D. Introduce, demonstrate, and discuss rock concepts: texture, color, size, fracture, crystal grain size, density, and so on.

    E. Assist and challenge students in other classification attempts.

    F. Provide closure describing various rock properties by demonstrating a variety of possible rock groupings.

V. Expansion:

    A. Give six additional rocks to each student group.

    B. Ask: "What are their properties and how would you put each rock into your classification system?"

    C. Have students write their responses, and ask another group to check their work.

    D. Give a homework assignment asking students to find a "different" rock around their house when they get home and bring it in to classify it the next day. Note: an alternative activity would be to take the students on a ten-minute field trip around the school building to find a rock. They should classify the rock using two rock properties when they return to the classroom.

VI. Evaluation as a Quiz or Part of a Unit Test:

At stations around the room, ask the students to classify three rocks using two rock properties experienced in the lesson.

FIGURE 3–10 *Continued*

As a summary, review the outline of questions to evaluate the effectiveness of lesson planning decisions given in Figure 3–4. A summary outline of the format of a complete lesson plan designed to facilitate students' construction of ideas and skills is given in Figure 3–11.

APPLICATION OF THE LEARNING CYCLE AS A SCIENCE LESSON PLANNING PROCESS

Each learning cycle phase must be experienced by the student in the order described (Exploration, Invention, Expansion). Deleting a phase or changing the order reduces meaningful science learning in students (Abraham, 1989; Tolman & Hardy, 1995). However, a teacher may return to an earlier phase of the lesson if the students need additional confrontation, explanation, or practice. Also, the Expansion of one lesson may lead into the Exploration of the next lesson. The learning cycle must be planned around a specific science idea or skill. Do not mix several important new skills, concepts, or generalizations in a single learning cycle lesson plan.

Perform the next application activity. Focus on the learning activities making up each phase of the lesson.

A complete learning cycle lesson plan contains the following sections:
Key idea
Goal (with connections to the state and national science standards)
Objectives for each learning cycle phase
Introduction to lesson
Lesson activities:

1. Exploration Phase
Materials
Student activities that:
Confront students' prior knowledge
Diagnose students' prior knowledge of the new science idea or skill
Relate previous learning to the new science idea or skill
Make "public" students' prior knowledge of the new science idea or skill

2. Invention Phase
Materials
Student activities that:
Reflect on and discuss the exploration activity
Provide explanations of the new science idea or skill
Provide clear science examples
Closure on the new science idea or skill

3. Expansion Phase
Materials
Student activities that:
Provide practice with the new science idea or skill
Provide applications of the new science idea or skill in different, relevant contexts
Transfer the new science knowledge to increasingly real world situations
Help students evaluate their own understanding
Lesson summary

FIGURE 3–11 *Learning cycle science lesson plan format*

Applying What You Know

Identifying Activities for Different Lesson Phases

List some possible appropriate learning and teaching activities for each phase of the learning cycle. Begin by identifying the activities used in the different phases of the lessons presented in this chapter. Examples are provided for a start.

1. *Exploration* Phase
   - introducing a problem to solve
   - structuring exploration (of an event)
   -

      •
      •
2. *Invention* Phase
      • watching and discussing a film
      • discussing Exploration activities and their results
      •
      •
      •

3. *Expansion* Phase
      • solving a related problem
      • taking a field trip to observe a natural process occurring
      •
      •
      •

Additional learning activities besides those listed above might include:

Exploration—demonstrating a discrepant event, developing evidence for an idea to support a prediction, unstructured exploring (of an event or skill), short field trip to school grounds to make observations, or reviewing similar and related past lesson activities.

Invention—giving a short lecture, using a variety of classroom "laboratory" activities such as a skill attainment lab in which students practice using an instrument or simple science process skill, giving a demonstration, reading a textbook passage, and participating in a computer tutorial or computer simulation.

Expansion—returning to the discrepant event in the Exploration, or using one or more of the following: an application problem, field trip, simulation, homework activity to further explore the new idea, game, art or social studies related activity illustrating the key science idea, or a creative or informational writing activity demonstrating the key idea.

For additional information on evaluating a learning cycle for physical science ideas, see Chapter 13, Physical Science Starting Points.

You have studied conceptual change and pedagogical sequencing using the learning cycle. Reflect on what has been discussed using the activity below. The activity involves a single learning cycle lesson. Discuss your results from this activity with a peer.

Applying What You Know

Planning a Learning Cycle

Plan a brief learning cycle lesson to teach the concept of position of objects, or for intermediate grades, the motions of objects (National Research Council, 1996).

For further information, see the Companion Website at *http://www.prenhall.com/sunal* for links to the National Science Education Standards.

Companion Website

Use the space provided to write down some of the principal ideas that emerge from your thoughts about such a plan. Remember that the position of an object can

(continued)

be described by locating it relative to another object or the background. Tracing and measuring its position, direction of motion, and speed can describe the motion of an object. The motion can be represented on a graph.

1. Design an *Exploration* activity that might be suitable for introducing the concept of position or motion in a science lesson.

_____

_____

2. Design an *Invention* activity to follow the Exploration above. _____

_____

_____

3. Describe an *Expansion* activity to follow the activity you gave for Inventing the idea of position or motion of an object. _____

_____

_____

For additional information on evaluating a unit using the learning cycle to teach electricity, see Chapter 15, Earth and Space Science Starting Points, or the National Science Education Standards (National Research Council, 1996, pages 134, 159, and 160).

As an additional application activity, outline a design for a science unit involving several lessons on a broad key earth science concept such as properties of earth materials, observation of objects in the sky, or changes in the earth and sky which will minimize learning difficulties your students might have. Discuss your results from this activity with a peer.

Companion Website

For further information, see the Companion Website at *http://www.prenhall.com/sunal* for a link to the National Science Education Standards.

Applying What You Know

Planning How to Teach a Science Concept

1. Locate a science concept for a unit in the state or national standards, or a chapter in a science textbook involving electricity for primary-age or intermediate-grade students. What science process skills are involved in the topic? What science ideas, concepts, or generalizations are students expected to already know? What ideas and/or skills are they expected to learn?
2. Describe areas in the unit where difficulties in learning might occur due to a difficult activity or the sequencing of the activities. These are both factors that hamper meaningful learning.
3. Briefly describe modifications in this unit that minimize the learning difficulties you have identified.
4. Organize subject matter ideas and skills so they follow a progression from concrete to more complex ideas and skills. List them in order. Use a learning cycle approach to instruction for each important idea. Star each important idea that requires a learning cycle.

SUMMARY

The purpose of this chapter is to introduce the teaching of science using the learning cycle. The learning cycle idea was introduced and then developed using activities for the reader. Looking back over the chapter, one can see that the chapter was organized using the learning cycle approach. The chapter was constructed keeping the three phases of the learning cycle in mind. First, an introductory activity with soils and an extended problem activity involving heat and temperature through an *Everyday Encounter with Materials* were presented. These activities included a consideration of the sequence of pedagogical events that naturally take place in conceptual change learning. This was the Exploration phase of the chapter. In addition to promoting conceptual change, the activities focused the readers' attention on their own thinking. It began the process of thinking about how science can be taught meaningfully to elementary and middle school students.

Afterward, a discussion of the learning cycle was presented, allowing readers to compare their activity outcomes to those others have found. It led to an explanation of effective lesson planning through the learning cycle using two key science concepts with soils and electric circuits. Additional practice activities in using the learning cycle were completed with key concepts found in tree growth and classifying rocks. This was the Invention phase of the chapter.

Finally, a series of application activities involved working with the essential components of the learning cycle. These included types of learning activities used with each phase of the learning cycle, the position and motion of objects, and earth and space science concepts. This was the Expansion phase of the chapter.

The following points summarize the learning cycle as it is used to facilitate students' meaningful learning of science.

1. The most worthwhile objectives of science units are major concepts, generalizations, and process skills. These require a strategy of instruction different from traditional teaching used to recall facts.
2. For these important science ideas and skills, students need a learning strategy, the learning cycle, to create meaningful understanding.
3. Identify the important key science ideas and skills to be taught in advance of using the learning cycle.
4. The learning cycle consists of a three-phase sequence of purposeful, interactive activities: the Exploration, Invention, and Expansion phases (EIE). These phases help students explore their prior knowledge, integrate new ideas into their thought patterns, and apply the new ideas and skills in diverse settings.
5. Use learning cycles to teach each key idea or skill. Each phase is experienced by the student in the order described (EIE). Teachers may return to an earlier phase if students have not experienced confrontation, need further explanation, or need more application of an idea or skill.
6. Begin using the learning cycle slowly through trial lessons. This helps you and your students become comfortable with the new learning strategy.
7. As a novice, you will meet with problems and have disappointments. Any complex professional skill takes time to develop.
8. Plan a learning cycle for a specific idea or skill. Do not mix several important concepts or generalizations in a single learning cycle.
9. Demonstrate a questioning and reflective attitude toward the content you teach. Generate a hypothesis, examine alternative explanations, and encourage students to do the same. Ask students: What do you know about . . . ? Why do you think . . . ? How do you explain . . . ? What evidence do you have? Reward appropriate responses from students.

chapter 4

Science as Inquiry

▼▲▼ Exploring Your Ideas ▼▲▼▲▼▲▼▲▼▲▼▲▼▲▼

Textbooks contain many statements. Read the sample sixth-grade science textbook passage below:

> (1) How does temperature affect your life? (2) Does temperature affect the way you dress and the things you do during the day? (3) Temperature is important to many people in their jobs. (4) A farmer is interested in knowing the temperature. (5) A few days of cold weather in the spring might kill a farmer's new crop. (6) Veterinarians take animals' temperatures to decide if they are sick. (7) Scientists record temperatures during some experiments. (8) Temperature is measured using a thermometer. (9) Temperature is measured in units called degrees. (10) Most people in the world measure temperature using a thermometer that has degrees Celsius (SEL-see-us). (11) The Celsius temperature scale is used by all scientists.

Respond to the following questions:

- Which science inquiry skills are fostered by reading the passage?
- Which statement(s) lead(s) to growth in inquiry skills? Identify these statements by number.
- Which statement(s) should be selected as a goal for a science lesson on inquiry skills?
- What activities should be used to encourage learning of the science inquiry skill(s)?

Discuss the passage and your responses with a peer if possible. We will return to this passage at the end of the chapter for additional reflection.

Chapter Objectives

1. Describe the basic science skill areas for developing meaningful learning in students.
2. Describe the difference in emphasis in planning for science inquiry skills at the primary-age and intermediate-grade levels.
3. Explain the attitudes and dispositions that promote meaningful science learning.
4. List the conditions necessary for effective teaching of science inquiry skills.
5. Describe the process of teaching science inquiry skills in classroom lessons.
6. Describe methods for assessing science inquiry skills planned as outcomes during a lesson or unit.
7. Explain the importance of planning for the development of science inquiry skills as one major outcome of the science curriculum.

HOW ARE INQUIRY SKILLS USED IN DEVELOPING STUDENTS' IDEAS IN SCIENCE?

Scientific inquiry relates to the diverse ways in which we study the natural world and propose explanations based on evidence. Inquiry also refers to the activities students engage in to develop their knowledge of scientific ideas and to investigate the natural world. Within their developmental capacities, scientifically literate students ask, find, and determine answers to questions derived from everyday experiences. Teaching involves helping students develop scientific inquiry skills (National Research Council, 1996). The general abilities needed to perform scientific inquiries are shown in Table 4–1.

Most elementary and middle school students are not developmentally ready for the abstractions of science knowledge without concrete inquiry experiences (Anderson, 1997; Renner & Marek, 1988). They are ready for experiences that give them concrete foundations for understanding abstract ideas. These foundations are the inquiry skills. Which inquiry skills can we usefully encourage our students to attempt, learn, and practice? For everyday classroom purposes, there are four categories of inquiry skills:

- early inquiry skills
- science process skills
- inquiry attitudes and dispositions
- critical response skills

We develop and use these skills on three different levels: the generic, the discipline or science topic, and the specific task. For example, we can work on a skill such as classification on a generic level. This means that classification is used in all areas of science. In that regard, we might classify leaves by their shapes or planets by their brightness. Classification is also generic because it is used in all subjects. For example, in social studies students will classify communities based on their population. Inquiry skills are also discipline- or topic-specific. For example, we use certain characteristics, such as hardness, to classify rocks but might not use those characteristics to classify leaves. Finally, we have to develop inquiry skills related to specific tasks. In a task, we need to decide whether a skill such as classification will help us solve the problem with which we are working. Perhaps

TABLE 4–1 *Abilities needed to do scientific inquiry identified in the National Science Education Standards*

ABILITIES NEEDED TO DO SCIENTIFIC INQUIRY	
Grades K–4	**Grades 5–8**
Ask a question about phenomena in the environment.	Identify questions that can be investigated.
Plan and perform simple investigations.	Plan and conduct scientific investigations.
Use simple equipment and tools to gather data.	Use tools and technology to gather, analyze, and interpret data.
Use data to develop descriptions and explanations.	Use a range of inquiry skills to develop generalizations and models using data.
Communicate descriptions of investigations and explanations.	Communicate scientific procedures for investigations and explanations.

Source: Adapted with permission from *National Science Education Standards.* Copyright 1996 by the National Academy of Sciences. Courtesy of the National Academy Press, Washington, D.C.

another skill, such as sequencing, would be more appropriate. Teachers help students develop inquiry skills at each level.

The effective use of scientific inquiry skills leads to the development of an "explanation" for what is observed or investigated. The explanation students develop is the science "idea" or "knowledge" to be learned in the lesson. Students at various age levels and with various types of experiences develop different explanations from their personal experiences depending on the inquiry skills used or available. The challenge for the teacher is to make common experiences meaningful to students through the use of inquiry skills so that they can create meaningful science knowledge.

WHAT ROLES DO INQUIRY SKILLS HAVE IN SCIENCE?

Knowledge begins through experiences with the world and other individuals. Students use their prior knowledge and information from their experiences to construct new science knowledge. The success of this learning process depends on the level and kind of science inquiry skills available to students.

Planned experiences in a science unit focus on helping students derive meaning from their experiences. When teachers encourage the development of students' science inquiry skills, they are helping them make meaning of their experiences. It is best to help students begin developing key inquiry skills through exploratory experiences. When students have developed the skills needed in a unit, the focus of science teaching can change from a skills emphasis to a skills *and content* emphasis.

A year-long science program incorporates the development, practice, and use of science inquiry skills in every unit. If the use of inquiry skills is left out of a unit, or is poorly developed, the ideas learned by the student are less meaningful, and rote memorization is likely to result (Howe, 1996; Paul, 1991).

The transfer of an inquiry skill from one context or science topic area to another is an important goal. It cannot be assumed that transfer occurs (Costa, 1991a). Transfer of an inquiry skill is likely to occur automatically only after a student has had many opportunities to practice the skill. For example, a unit on organisms involves students in identifying and classifying organisms in order to distinguish fungi from molds. A few weeks later, the class begins working with a unit on rocks. The classification skill students developed in the earlier unit on organisms will not automatically transfer when they try to classify types of sedimentary rocks such as limestone and sandstone. At a particular grade level (for example, second grade), skills such as ordering and classifying might be taught eight or more times (at least once with each science unit), because transfer of the skills to a new unit is not expected. The discussion below describes and examines science inquiry skills in an effective K–8 science program.

HOW ARE EARLY INQUIRY SKILLS DEVELOPED?

People use their five senses (sight, hearing, taste, touch, and smell) to investigate their environment. Very young children develop, refine, and apply their senses to develop numerous early inquiry skills as they play. Early inquiry skills include pushing, pulling, sliding, and rolling, which facilitate the investigation of the young child's world. When children play, the early inquiry skills they develop are diverse. One example is observation, a science process skill. Sand and garden dirt are the favorite play materials of many children; with the senses of touch and sight, these early skills may include packing, molding, pouring, pounding, pressing, shaping, and flattening.

TABLE 4-2   *Sample activities that develop early inquiry skills*

Activity	Sample Early Inquiry Skills
Water Play	Pouring, wetting, dropping, splashing, filling containers, emptying containers, spilling, spreading, stirring, mixing, smelling, listening
Motion Play	Pushing, pulling, sliding, rolling, jumping, skipping, running, hopping, lifting, carrying, throwing
Plant Play	Soaking, tearing, ripping, opening, digging, watering, supporting, mashing, squeezing, pressing, smelling, touching, listening
Sound Play	Striking objects with different intensities, striking different objects together, shaking objects, scratching objects, plucking objects, shouting, crying, giggling, whining, whispering, blowing, hiccuping

Applying What You Know

Inquiring about Dirt

What other early inquiry skills, besides observation, can a child gain through play- ing with sand or dirt? Think about the use of other senses besides touch and sight, or different combinations of senses.

Early inquiry skills are learned before any of the science content involved in the ex- periences through which children learn the skills. For example, young children pack, mold, and pour sand before they understand how sand is formed and what happens to sand in the formation of sedimentary rocks. These early skills are basic and are prerequi- sites for understanding science concepts related to rock formation. They are also prereq- uisites for later scientific inquiry skills. Early science experiences are important and fo- cus on building these early inquiry skills.

There are many other activities for which one or more early inquiry skills are devel- oped and used. Sound experiences, for example, are connected with skills related to mak- ing and listening to sounds. Striking objects with different intensities, striking different objects together, shaking objects, scratching objects, plucking objects, shouting, crying, giggling, whining, whispering, blowing, and hiccuping are all ways of making sounds. Some of these skills are learned, such as plucking objects and whistling, while others are part of our genetic inheritance, such as hiccuping and crying. All of these are early inquiry skills used to develop concepts about sound. Other activities for developing early inquiry skills are shown in Table 4–2.

HOW ARE SCIENCE PROCESS SKILLS DEVELOPED?

Early inquiry skills are combined to form scientific process skills and other more complex in- quiry skills needed to develop scientific literacy. Science process skills are basic and integrated thought processes, which are important in science because they are beginning skills that make exploration and investigation of natural phenomena possible. Most children and many adults, however, are not very good at using them (Glatthorn & Baron, 1991; Lawson, 1995). Examples of science process skills include observing, communicating, classifying, measuring and estimating, inferring, predicting, isolating and using variables, interpreting data, and formulating hypotheses. The later science process skills integrate the more basic process skills, so the basic science process skills are prerequisites for the more complex science skills. Examples of student behaviors related to each science process skill are given in Table 4–3.

TABLE 4-3 *Samples of student actions when performing science process skills*

Science Process Skill	Sample Grade K–8 Student Actions Involved When Using the Skill
Observing	1. *Identify* and *name* properties of an object or event by using at least four senses. Use of the sense of taste is restricted to specific teacher-designed situations. 2. *Be aware of the need* to make numerous observations of objects and events. 3. *Pose questions* focusing on observations of objects and events. 4. *Construct* statements of observations including quantitative terms. 5. *Construct* statements of observations describing observable changes in properties of an object. 6. *Distinguish* between statements based on observations and those based on inference.
Communicating	1. *Describe* the properties of an object in sufficient detail so that another person can identify it. 2. *Describe* changes in the properties of an object. 3. *Use pictures, tables, and graphs* to communicate results obtained from observations. 4. *Describe* relationships and trends in results orally, in writing, or in a picture, table, or graph.
Classifying	1. *Identify* and *name* observable properties of objects that could be used to classify the objects. 2. *Order* a group of objects based on a single property. 3. *Construct* a one-, two-, or multi-stage classification of a set of objects and name the observable characteristics on which the classification is based. 4. *Construct* two or more different classification schemes for the same set of objects—each scheme serving a different purpose. 5. *Construct* an operational definition of a single object or event based on a classification scheme.
Inferring	1. *Construct* one or more statements or explanations from a set of observations. 2. *Identify* observations supporting a given inference. 3. *Describe* alternative inferences for the same set of observations. 4. *Identify* inferences that should be accepted, modified, or rejected on the basis of additional observations.
Predicting	1. *Construct* a forecast of future events based on observed events. 2. *Order* a set of forecasts or predictions in terms of your confidence in them. 3. *Identify* predictions as (a) interpolating between observed events or (b) extrapolating beyond the range of observed events.
Measuring and estimating	1. *Demonstrate* the use of simple tools to describe length, mass, and time. 2. *Be aware of the need to consistently use* measurements to describe objects and events during investigations. 3. *Construct* estimates of simple measurements of quantities such as length, area, volume, and mass. 4. *Apply* rules for calculating derived quantities from two or more measurements such as rate distance divided by time. 5. *Distinguish* between accuracy and precision. 6. *Demonstrate* the use of technology hardware and software measuring tools.

(continued)

TABLE 4-3   *Continued*

Science Process Skill	Sample Grade K–8 Student Actions Involved When Using the Skill
Organizing, Interpreting, and Drawing Conclusions from Data (An integrated skill)	1. *Describe* the information provided by the shape of graphed data. 2. *Construct* tables and graphs representing results obtained from observations. 3. *Construct* one or more statements of inferences or hypotheses from the information given in a table of data, graph, or picture. 4. *Use and construct* graphs of various types to interpret data. 5. *Describe* data, using the mean, median, and range. 6. *Use* technology hardware and software to gather, analyze, and interpret data. 7. *Distinguish* between linear and nonlinear relations in data.
Isolating and Using Variables (An integrated skill)	1. *Identify* factors that may influence the behavior or properties of a system or event. 2. *Name* variables manipulated, responding, or held constant in an investigation or description of an experiment. 3. *Construct* a test to determine the effects of one variable (manipulated variable) on a second variable (the responding variable). 4. *Distinguish* between conditions that hold a given variable constant and conditions that do not hold a variable constant.
Formulating Hypotheses (An integrated skill)	1. *Distinguish* between statements of inference and hypotheses. 2. *Construct* a hypothesis relating potentially interacting variables. 3. *Construct* a hypothesis describing a test of a hypothesis. 4. *Distinguish* between observations that support a hypothesis and those that do not. 5. *Construct* a revision of a hypothesis on the basis of observations made to test the hypothesis.
Generating Hypotheses in Designing and Conducting an Experiment (An integrated skill)	1. *Acquire* background information. 2. *Establish* initial conditions for the investigation. 3. *Write* focus questions to guide inquiry. 4. *Collect and analyze* data while attempting to formulate tentative explanations. 5. *Re-examine and rewrite* explanations into hypotheses.

During play with sand, for example, students work with early inquiry skills such as pouring and flattening. These early skills lead to the development of more complex inquiry skills, such as observing, comparing, and contrasting different samples of sand and the capacities of different containers. Different samples of sand can be grouped and ordered by grain size, texture, or color. When observing, grouping, and ordering, science process skills are being used.

During sound play, students' early inquiry skills, such as striking and plucking, lead to science process skills such as inferring what is causing a sound and predicting what action will cause a higher-pitched sound. Other samples of activities with early inquiry skills leading to the use and development of science process skills are shown in Table 4–4.

Each science process skill has a number of subskills that need to be addressed. Basic behaviors that are required when elementary and middle school students use each science process skill appear in Table 4–3. For instance, as younger students learn the skill of observing, teachers will address the need for them to make many observations using all of their senses. Teachers also encourage students to examine quantitative as well as qualita-

TABLE 4-4   *Sample activities combining early inquiry skills and science process skills*

Activity	Combined Early Inquiry Skills and Science Process Skills
Water Play	Mixing—observing, communicating, classifying Filling containers—observing, comparing, ordering
Motion Play	Pushing—observing, inferring, ordering Throwing—observing, predicting, communicating
Plant Play	Watering—observing, inferring, interpreting data Squeezing—observing, comparing, contrasting, communicating

TABLE 4-5   *Functions served by science process skills*

Data Gathering	Data Organizing	Data Processing	Communicating
• observing	• classifying	• constructing tables	• reporting
• measuring and estimating skills	• ordering		• writing
• using library and reference skills	• isolating and using variables	• finding patterns	• graphing and drawing
• questioning	• using technology to organize data	• predicting	• formal discussing
• interviewing and surveying		• interpreting observations	• informal discussing
• reading books, charts, graphs, and maps		• finding relationships	• using technology to communicate data
• hypothesizing		• inferring	
• using technology to gather data		• evaluating hyphotheses	
		• using technology to process data	

tive characteristics. If an event involves change, students are encouraged to make observations of the event during the change process as well as before and after it. For example, throughout the entire dissolving process, a student continuously makes observations of a sugar cube put in water. The good observer describes the sugar cube using all his senses including taste, a qualitative aspect. The size and shape of the sugar cube are described by comparing it to the size of a unit of measurement, a quantitative aspect. Descriptions are given at regularly scheduled times before, during, and after the event. Good observation statements do not go beyond the observed data.

Four basic areas of science process skills are defined by the functions they serve: data gathering, data organizing, data processing, and communicating (Table 4–5). This order is used when planning an inquiry science lesson or unit. Early in the lesson, several data gathering science process skills are planned. Later, data organizing and data processing science process skills are encouraged. Student activities involving communication occur throughout the lesson, with a stronger focus near the end of the lesson. A well-planned science lesson or unit involves skills from each area.

HOW DO STUDENTS DEVELOP THE SKILLS OF MAKING OBSERVATIONS, INFERENCES, AND HYPOTHESES?

Everyone has been involved with science process skills in previous school experiences. Many people, however, have difficulty distinguishing between them or describing them. This is especially so with the skills of observing, inferring, and hypothesizing.

Applying What You Know

What Skills Are Being Used?

This activity asks you to use your present knowledge to determine the skill used to form each of the statements below.

Classroom Event

A container with a 2-inch layer of damp potting soil was placed on a table in a classroom. A piece of white bread was then placed on the soil. The container was covered with a lid and allowed to sit on the table for 9 days. During this time, students were asked to make statements about the container and its contents. Listed below are some of the statements students made during the week. Read their statements and identify which are statements of observation, inference, or hypothesis. Blacken the "O" corresponding to your choice.

Statements	Observation	Inference	Hypothesis
1. "The bread looks soggy," said one student (day one).	O	O	O
2. "The container is glass," one group reported (day one).	O	O	O
3. "All clear containers are made of glass," another group responded (day one).	O	O	O
4. "The top of the bread has three green spots about the size of a dime on it," said another student (day three).	O	O	O
5. One small group stated, "When uncovered, the bread has a musty smell" (day four).	O	O	O
6. "Laboratory analysis would reveal the spots to be patches of mold," said one group of students (day five).	O	O	O
7. "All types of bread will mold if put in the container," was a statement given by a small group of students who brought in several types of bread to try out in the container (day five).	O	O	O
8. "Mold is the stuff that grows in damp places," was a summary statement given by a small group of students (day five).	O	O	O

9. "The bread has seven quarter-sized patches of color on it," was reported by a small group of students (day eight).	O	O	O
10. "As the number of days increases there will be more patches of mold on the bread," another group stated (day eight).	O	O	O
11. "Someone must have poured something on the bread to make it mold," was a statement given by another student (day nine).	O	O	O
12. The following statement was given by a small group of students as a starting point for a project: "The higher the temperature in a moist environment, the more mold spores will increase in number on the bread on day nine."	O	O	O

How did you do? Check the possible responses below.

Statements 1, 4, 5, and 9 are observations.

Statements 2, 3, 6, 8, and 11 are inferences.

Statements 7, 10, and 12 are hypotheses.

What Are Observations?

Observations state characteristics of objects or events observed through the use of the senses. You should be able to identify the sense that is used to make an observation. For example, "the bar felt smooth with small, regularly spaced depressions," clearly involves the sense of touch. The bar *feels* smooth to this student. The student also feels depressions in the bar that are regularly spaced. Indirect observations are those made by another person: "Jack told me that the powder from the salt shaker tasted like sugar, not salt." Observations represent a single case or event. Observations may be valid but have no predictive value; they lead to statements of fact.

What Are Inferences?

Inferences are based on observations or factual statements, but extend beyond what has been observed with the senses. Inferences are not created to be tested. They are "best guess" statements such as, "It looks like it's raining outside," or "All the sugar disappears when I put it in water." They are only partially supported, or even unsupported, descriptions or explanations of what has been observed. Inferences usually summarize and go beyond a group of observations having common characteristics.

Classifying, predicting, and generalizing often result in inferences. Classification inferences define an object or event, and usually apply to all observed and unobserved cases. Statement 8 in the *Applying What You Know* feature above is a classification inference. Prediction inferences attempt to determine the state of an object or event for which insufficient data was gathered to make an observational statement. In making a prediction, one must go beyond the data gathered and extrapolate, or make judgments, about an event based on information pertaining to closely similar events. Statements 2, 6, and 11 in the *Applying What You Know* feature are prediction inferences. Generalizing inferences summarize and make conclusions about gathered information and may go beyond previous information about an object or event. A generalization is an example of this type of inference. Statement 3 in the *Applying What You Know* feature is a generalization inference. Inference statements can lead to the creation of concepts.

Applying What You Know

What Statements Might Students Make?

Based on the previous discussion, construct one statement that a student might make for each skill area using the bread mold test example in number 12 in the last *Applying What You Know*.

1. Observation:
2. Inference:

_____

Compare your answers to those below.

Observation—"The spots have a green color."

Prediction inference—"The spots on the bread will increase in the afternoon."

What Are Hypotheses and How Do Students Learn to Develop Them?

A **hypothesis** describes the relationship of two or more variables. The hypothesis is constructed so that it can be tested. Simple hypotheses usually contain only two variables: the manipulated variable (or cause) and the responding variable (or result). For example, "the colder the temperature, the smaller in volume a balloon filled with air becomes" is a hypothesis. Additional control variables may be added to make the relationship described by the hypothesis clearer and more possible to test. The hypothesis about shrinking balloons can be rewritten with more control variables: "All of the balloons will be the *same size, color,* and *material.* They will be put *in the freezer at the same time.*"

Based on personal observations and inferences, a scientist may make a generalized hypothesis for situations that have not been observed. Such a hypothesis states that whenever the same variables are combined, the same event will result. Hypotheses typically condense large amounts of data and are general statements that cover all cases, not only those that are actually observed.

Why Is a Hypothesis Only a Statement That Can Be Tested?

Once a hypothesis has been stated, it is then tested, since it must be possible to construct a test to investigate the relationship stated in the hypothesis. If no test can be designed or performed, the statement is not a hypothesis. The proposal made by Albert Einstein at the beginning of the 1900s, "Time slows down when an object approaches the speed of light," was not a hypothesis. It could not be tested until decades later. It became a hypothesis

What hypothesis might a student develop to investigate "sour milk"?

when particle accelerators were able to obtain speeds near the speed of light and data was obtained that supported the original statement as a hypothesis. It must be possible to set up an experiment, control variables, and collect data.

How Do We Test Hypotheses?

If the data pattern is consistent with the hypothesis, many people will say that the hypothesis is "proven." However, hypotheses can be proven only if *all* possible cases have been tested. Testing all cases is an impossible task. Therefore, hypotheses can never be proven; they can only be well supported so one feels quite confident about the relationship. Thus, each individual set of observations may support the hypothesis, but not prove it. However, the first set of data that is contrary to the hypothesis results in the hypothesis no longer being supported. An unsupported hypothesis must either be dropped or restated to account for the new findings.

Effective problem solvers design tests of hypotheses that require observations of the proposed relationship between the variables. Testing a hypothesis involves conducting a test that will *most likely* provide data supporting or not supporting the hypothesis. For example, a test of the hypothesis "all substances dissolve more quickly in hot water than in cold water" would involve mixing many substances, each with at least three different temperatures of water, and recording their dissolving times. However, this statement about the relationship between the variables is not as clear as it could be. A better hypothesis statement is, "The higher the temperature, the more quickly substances dissolve in water." The manipulated variable is temperature, and the responding variable is dissolving time.

Why Is it Important to Develop a Hypothesis That States a Clear Relationship between Variables?

Consider the hypothesis, "Some objects produce a higher pitch of sound than others when struck." This is a poor hypothesis. We cannot design a good test of it since we don't know what characteristic of objects has an effect on the pitch of the sound made. A good hypothesis statement clearly relates two variables in a general way. Without a clear relationship, a useful test cannot be designed. A useful test makes it possible to obtain data that *will not* support the hypothesis. A better hypothesis statement is, "The *longer* an object, the higher the *pitch* of sound it makes when struck." In this revised statement, the manipulated variable is length and the responding variable is pitch of sound. A test can be designed that involves testing the sound made by objects of various lengths. A plastic ruler held at different lengths over the side of a desk would provide a suitable first test. Try the test yourself. You will find that the sound made decreases in pitch as the amount of the ruler overhang gets longer. Therefore, the hypothesis is not supported.

How Do We Evaluate Our Hypotheses?

After data is collected, it is presented for consideration. Students must decide whether or not their hypothesis is supported. Four results are possible:

1. If the data are inadequate for making a decision, students decide they need additional data.
2. If the hypothesis is supported, the students invent a generalization.
3. If the hypothesis is not supported by the data, students reconstruct their hypothesis.
4. If the hypothesis is not supported by the data, students may reject the hypothesis and construct a new tentative hypothesis based on additional information.

In Chapters 5 and 6, the importance of differentiating statements of observation (facts), inferences (concepts), and hypotheses in planning science lessons is discussed in detail.

Whether a scientist discusses an event or is just thinking about it, it is important for her to decide whether the statement to be tested is an observation, inference, or hypothesis. Deciding which kind of statement she is working with is important because the instructional strategies differ depending on what type of content she is trying to help students develop.

How Are Hypothesis Statements Modified?

Students must have lots of practice with developing a modified hypothesis from a rejected hypothesis. It is not an easy task. For example, let's say that we tested the hypothesis considered earlier, "The higher the temperature, the more quickly substances dissolve in water." When we tested the hypothesis, we found some data that did not support it. We found that some substances did not dissolve in water at any of the temperatures we tried. Therefore, we must revise the hypothesis. A revised hypothesis might be, "The higher the temperature, the more quickly most substances dissolve in water." This revised hypothesis is not going to be a very useful statement when we try to design a test for it. "Most" does not tell us much because we don't know which substances it refers to. Our new revised hypothesis should concentrate on patterns we found in the exceptions that did not support the hypothesis we tested. A better revised hypothesis is, "The higher the temperature, the more quickly soluble substances dissolve in water." Here, the term "soluble" is a control variable. We are now ready to design a test and decide whether the data we collect support our revised hypothesis.

A **hypothesis:**

- describes the *relationship between variables* and is *general* since it covers observed and unobserved cases.

- includes a manipulated variable (cause), responding variable (result), and the control variables (variables kept constant).
- must be testable.
- may be disproved when one set of observations does not agree with what the hypothesis predicts.
- cannot be proven until *all* possible cases have been tested.

Applying What You Know

What Hypothesis Statement Might a Student Make?

Based on the above discussion, construct one statement a student might make while hypothesizing about the results from the bread mold test example in number 12 in the previous *Applying What You Know*. The test for the hypothesis on the bread mold indicated that increasing the temperature did not produce more mold spots. After a certain point, the number decreased. Write a modified or new hypothesis for mold growth.

Hypothesis:

_____

Compare your answer to the one below.

Modified hypothesis — "In a moist environment with a temperature range between 0 and 40 degrees Celsius, the higher the temperature, the more mold spots will increase in number on the bread."

How Do We Help Students Develop Testable Hypotheses?

Let's analyze a specific problem/question used to begin a science lesson for which hypothesizing is a lesson outcome: "What determines the rate at which the human heart beats?" In this question, the manipulated variable, or **cause**, being explored is why the rate at which the heart beats varies at different times in an individual or between individuals. The responding variable, or **result**, is the measured rate at which the heart is beating. The number of heartbeats depends on a variety of possible environmental and biological conditions. Students attempt to develop their own method of measuring heart rate in the *Exploration* phase of the learning cycle lesson.

Once students know what the problem or question is, and want to pursue it, they should be helped to systematically and creatively think about a solution. Hypothesis formation can be taught (Baker & Piburn, 1997; Quinn & George, 1975). The hypothesis is developed as a solution or answer to a specific question. This process occurs in the *Invention* phase of the learning cycle. Students are asked some questions to get them thinking about what is needed to decide whether their original question can be answered. Some questions the teacher might ask are:

"What do you need to know to answer your question?"

"What do you now know about this?"

"What do you need to try out?"

"How could this material or event help us come up with answers to our question?"

"What should be changed?"

"What should be kept the same?"

"What will happen as a result of the change?"

"How will I know if a result occurred?"

"Based on what we have discussed, what are some results you can expect to come up with?"

During the Invention phase of the learning cycle, the skill of measuring the heart rate is taught. The unit of measurement known as a "heartbeat" is discussed. Students learn that a heartbeat is measured over a specific period of time and is calculated as the number of beats per minute.

Cooperative learning groups offer an opportunity for the give-and-take of ideas, and are effective when trying to develop a hypothesis. The use of cooperative learning groups to form hypotheses is usually less stressful, more fun, and more productive than individual attempts (Eggen & Kauchak, 1988; National Research Council, 1996). When a hypothesis is developed in a small group, it is more likely that each student is involved. A variety of ideas, developed from each student's prior experience and knowledge, are usually more fully discussed.

If students have examined the collected data and decided the hypothesis they developed is supported, they expand its use during the *Expansion* phase of the learning cycle. They try out the generalization that resulted when the hypothesis was supported by the data. They use it in different situations to determine whether or not it continues to be supported. For example, their hypothesis may have related a strenuous level of activity, such as running, to an increased heart rate, and a low level of activity, such as sitting in a chair for ten minutes, to a lower heart rate. During the Expansion phase, they could record heart rate when trying out other strenuous activities, such as climbing stairs, and additional low level activities, such as lying on a cot for five minutes. If the data they collected did not support their hypothesis, the Expansion would involve them in modifying the hypothesis or in constructing a new hypothesis.

Applying What You Know

Identifying Better Hypotheses

Determine which statement of each pair below is a better hypothesis statement, and put a check mark before that statement. Consider the following criteria: describes the relationship between variables and is general; includes a manipulated variable, responding variable, and the control variables; and is testable. The following statements by elementary and middle school students were made as hypotheses to test in hands-on activities over the next week.

1. a._____ The later the hour in the day, the more likely it will rain.
   b._____ It rains more often on September 20 than on October 20.
2. a._____ A paper clip is a better conductor of electricity than a stick.
   b._____ The greater the metallic content of an object, the better it conducts electricity.
3. a._____ The colder the temperature, the slower fish will move.
   b._____ Temperature has an effect on fish.
4. a._____ The longer a magnet, the more small iron objects it can pick up.
   b._____ Placing a magnet in a box of small iron objects will give us an answer.

5. a._____ Students taller than 7 feet have higher heart rates than shorter students.
   b._____ The taller the student, the faster the heart rate.
6. a._____ The water boiled at 100 degrees Celsius.
   b._____ The clearer the liquid, the lower the temperature of its boiling point.
7. a._____ The higher the altitude of the sun, the higher the temperature of the surface of the ground.
   b._____ The more unstable the magnetic field of the sun, the higher the temperature of Earth.
8. a._____ Vinegar reacts faster with baking soda at a higher temperature.
   b._____ The higher the temperature, the faster the rate of a chemical reaction.
9. a._____ The more hours of light green plants receive, the larger the leaves will grow.
   b._____ The more light green plants receive, the better they will grow.
10. a._____ The higher the phosphate content of detergent (read from a detergent box label), the quicker it cleans soiled clothes.
    b._____ Sun detergent cleans solid clothes better than Bright detergent.

Answers and rationale.

1–a, 2–b, 8–b, 10–a — Hypotheses are generalized statements.

3–a, 9–a — Hypotheses show clear relationships of two or more variables (manipulated, responding, and control variables), and are more readily disproved.

4–a — Hypotheses attempt to describe relationships between variables.

5–b, 7–a — Hypotheses are testable; in this case, testable with materials available to students in a classroom.

6–b — Hypotheses are generalized statements that show a relationship between two or more variables (manipulated, responding, and control variables).

WHAT ATTITUDES AND DISPOSITIONS PROMOTE MEANINGFUL SCIENCE LEARNING?

Attitudes and dispositions are affective responses that reflect our feelings and personal likes and dislikes. The development of attitudes promoting meaningful learning is a fundamental goal of the science curriculum (Figure 4–1). Attitudes that can be planned for, modeled, and encouraged in a science lesson include curiosity, respect for evidence, flexibility, responsibility to others and the environment, and appreciation of nature. These attitudes are important not only for learning science, but also for being a scientifically literate citizen. With these attitudes, students begin to perceive science as a search for knowledge and understanding.

How Can Curiosity Be Fostered?

A curious student wants to know, try a new experience, explore, and find out about things around him. This is an attitude promoting all kinds of learning. Curiosity is often shown through questioning. Teachers foster curiosity by welcoming student questions about objects and events. Inviting students to pose questions is one way of valuing curiosity. Questioning brings satisfaction if it helps students share their pleasure and excitement with

1. Curiosity
   - questioning
   - wanting to know
2. Respect for evidence
   - open-mindedness
   - perseverance
   - willingness to consider conflicting evidence
3. Flexibility
   - willingness to reconsider ideas
   - recognition that ideas are tentative
   - willingness to consider other methods
4. Responsibility to people and the environment
5. Appreciation of nature

FIGURE 4-1   *Attitudes of value in learning science*

others. Satisfaction resulting from the expression of curiosity helps students sustain interest for longer periods and ask more thoughtful questions.

Curiosity is *wanting to know,* rather than a mere flow of questions. Wanting to know stimulates efforts to find out. A teacher encourages curiosity by asking students to explain a discrepant event related to a key idea. Young students learning classification, for example, can be asked to put a diverse set of objects into groups. Older students investigating aerodynamic lift can be asked to make paper airplanes with different wing shapes. One of the goals of the Exploration phase of the learning cycle is to create curiosity.

How Can Respect for Evidence Be Fostered?

To examine the physical world and construct meaning about it, evidence is gathered and used to develop and test ideas. An explanation or theory is not useful to a student until it fits the evidence and makes sense of what the student already knows.

How Can Open-Mindedness toward Evidence Be Fostered?

Students show they know that an unsupported statement is not necessarily true when they ask, "How do you know that's true?" or they say, "Prove it." Adults often expect students to accept scientific statements because of the authority scientific research is thought to have. This may reduce the students' desire to ask for evidence and be open-minded enough to consider evidence that does not support their hypothesis. If a teacher appears to accept statements from students without evidence, or offers no evidence for a statement she makes to students, the attitude that's transmitted is that evidence is *not* necessary. Asking for evidence and being open-minded enough to consider a range of evidence is essential in science teaching. It conveys the true nature of science as an effective process society invented to solve specific types of problems.

How Can Perseverance in Obtaining Evidence Be Fostered?

Obtaining convincing evidence takes perseverance. Sometimes the gathering of evidence to support their explanations seems impossible to students. Perseverance doesn't mean one should keep on trying if something is not working. It involves waiting for new evidence to be reported, being willing to try again, learning from earlier difficulties, and changing one's ideas as a result of what is learned. Teachers model perseverance and involve students in some assignments that require seeking out information rather than just accepting the most easily available evidence.

How Can Consideration of Conflicting Evidence Be Fostered?

It is not easy to believe evidence that may conflict with what you think you already know. Cultivating a respect for evidence involves a willingness to do so. Students are more likely to consider conflicting evidence if their teacher models this behavior, accepts mistakes, and rewards students' efforts. Teachers provide practice by involving students in drawing conclusions. Students can, for example, be provided with a data table or new account of common and relevant events. Students are then asked to draw conclusions and give evidence for each conclusion. In everyday science lessons, students are asked questions such as the following when they give explanations: "How do you know?" "What evidence did you use?" "What additional evidence do you need to make such a conclusion?"

How Can Flexibility Be Fostered?

Mental flexibility relates to the *products* of science activities, while respect for evidence relates to the *processes* occurring in science activities. The concepts and generalizations formed when trying to understand the physical world change as evidence which contradicts them is developed. Such changes are most rapid in students' early years since their limited experiences mean their conceptions are often quite inaccurate. Unless there is flexibility, each experience that conflicts with existing ideas causes resistance. It becomes a rival idea instead of a part of the process of modifying and developing an existing one.

The ability to be flexible, and the recognition that conclusions are tentative, are important qualities for students to cultivate. Elementary and middle school students may not be able to fully understand the tentativeness of ideas, but teachers need to promote attitudes that enable them to eventually develop this understanding. One way of doing this in the classroom is to preface conclusions with a statement like, "As far as we can tell . . . ." It helps to occasionally talk with students about how their ideas have changed and how they used to think. Asking students to write and read about what they have learned in a small group helps them develop flexibility. Having students construct portfolios of their science experiences and receive feedback also promotes flexibility.

How Can Responsibility to Others and to the Environment Be Fostered?

Students are encouraged to investigate and explore their environment in order to understand it and develop skills for further understanding. Growth in inquiry skills should be accompanied by the development of sensitivity and responsibility. This is expressed as an attitude of respect for, and willingness to care about, the physical and social environment.

A sense of responsibility toward someone or something is more likely to occur when a student has had experience with that person and thing or knows something about them. For example, students who have picked up litter from the school grounds understand the effort that goes into this task. These students are more likely to take care of their school or community than someone who has not been so involved. Knowledge and experience help, although they are not enough to create an attitude of responsibility. Many of the concepts relating to responsibility for, and sensitivity to, people and the environment are complex.

The interdependence of plants and animals in an ecosystem is not routinely considered when citizens make decisions in local communities. Concepts are often controversial, such as in the production of energy using nuclear power. It is still possible for teachers to help students develop respectful attitudes toward the physical and social environment through examples and rules of conduct. Rules that teachers and students form together help to establish a pattern of response, but only when students begin to act responsibly. These rules can be expressed by expecting students to feed the class hamster every day and care for others' property. The way to accomplish this is to gradually transfer the responsibility for making decisions about how to behave in the physical and social world to students.

Values and the Aesthetics of Nature

Values are decisions about the worth or importance of something based on a standard we have set. When we value something, we believe it is important or that it has worth. The standards used to make value decisions are **morals**. Elementary and middle school students are developing values as well as the moral standards used in determining what to value. As they learn to recognize others' values, they begin to notice how their own are similar to, or different from, these values. During the middle school years, many students begin to question specific values. With their increased cognitive skills, they begin to examine the moral standards people use to make value decisions. The examination and questioning in which they are involved can be used as a basis for understanding how people and societies can most effectively use science knowledge and its applications in technology.

Appreciation of the beauty of nature is a worthwhile goal in science (Sunal & Sunal, 1990, 1991d). It is only through the development of an appreciation of natural events and of the beauty in nature that one begins to value it. **Aesthetics** is the recognition of beauty and the assignment of value to it. People value that which they consider beautiful. Artists, through painting, sculpture, ceramics, and weaving, express the beauty they see in nature. Musicians and writers, through their works, also express the beauty they find in nature. Aesthetics encompasses all forms of expression, including music, literature, and art. Aesthetic activities allow students opportunities to search for beauty and examine values that people over the ages have assigned to the many designs and relationships found in nature.

Nature's creations are vulnerable. Massive mountains disintegrate, eroded by the elements of wind, cold, rain, and heat. At the same time, other landmasses are built up by processes involving the folding and faulting of Earth's materials. Vegetation and animal life persist, but are constantly modified by nature's various cycles of growth, life, decay, and death. When human technological advances are coupled with nature's own forces, the resulting changes in the design and balance of nature can be unpredictable and harmful to human well being.

Technological development frequently leads to significant consequences for woodlands. Humankind's potential for destruction is well documented throughout history. Consider the elimination of many animal species from our planet, the shrinking of productive natural land sites due to urban growth, and the increasing problem of contamination of Earth's natural resources, such as water. Many of these events are consequences of people's endeavors to advance society through technology. The Internet is a good source of recent information related to human effects on our planet.

Companion Website

To look at the Greenpeace site containing information about Earth's destruction, visit the links for Chapter 4 on the Companion Website at *http://www. prenhall.com/sunal*

Each generation must be educated to recognize and preserve the relationship between the natural environment and human development. There is a need to raise concern about, and awareness of, the disappearing woodlands, natural plains, and wetlands. There is a need to examine and institute ways that allow nature and people to coexist. Developing an appreciation for nature's beauty is a starting point for students to learn to live in, and value, the natural environment. Some objectives appropriate for a science lesson include the following:

- Demonstrating increasing knowledge of woodlands, forests, and other natural sites through drawing and writing.
- Observing and recording interrelationships between people and nature at natural sites.
- Developing one's own description of a natural site.
- Analyzing data/ideas in order to form personal interpretations about the importance of preserving natural resources and natural lands.
- Predicting possible outcomes of any change introduced to a natural site or area.
- Discussing and analyzing the positive and negative aspects of displacing a natural site through any change, such as urban or industrial development.
- Developing a "natural beauty impact statement" for a specific site.
- Modeling the concept of aesthetics as related to nature in classroom activities. (Sunal & Sunal, 1990, 1991d)

WHAT CRITICAL RESPONSE SKILLS PROMOTE MEANINGFUL SCIENCE LEARNING?

In everyday life, people use critical response skills to make decisions, evaluate them, and form judgments about the natural and physical world in which they live known as *critical response skills*. The critical response skills are *critical thinking, problem solving and decision making, experimenting,* and *creative thinking* (see Table 4–6). These critical response skills are more than tools. Determining the best color of clothing to wear in the winter, the best design for a model airplane intended to fly a long distance, or the proportion of sand and mulch that will hold the most water around a tree when there hasn't been much rain for weeks are all reasons to use critical response skills. The four skills described below are the most common ways of grouping critical response skills for specific purposes.

How Do We Foster Critical Thinking?

Critical thinking helps us develop good reasons for what we believe. **Critical thinking** involves careful, precise, persistent, and objective analysis of any scientific knowledge claim or belief in order to judge its validity and/or worth (Beyer, 1985; Ennis, 1991; Lawson, 1995; O'Reilly, 1991). Both before and after arriving at a conclusion, students need to be aware of, and willing to consider, the thought process they followed to reach a conclusion. Are their methods logical? Are they making unwarranted assumptions? Are they skipping a necessary step? Does the evidence support the conclusion? A willingness to consider the methods used helps students evaluate the process with which they worked, discover problem

TABLE 4–6   *Critical response skills in learning science*

Critical Response Skills	Sample Student Behaviors Involved When Using the Skill
Critical Thinking	Understanding new knowledge.
Problem Solving	Resolving a difficulty.
Experimenting	Testing an idea or explanation.
Creative Thinking	Creating novel ideas or products.

- Being open-minded.
- Asking questions.
- Focusing on a question.
- Distinguishing relevant and irrelevant knowledge statements, value statements, and reasoning.
- Willingness to analyze arguments and knowledge statements in terms of their strength.
- Desiring to use credible sources.
- Judging credibility of an argument or source.
- Tolerating ambiguity.
- Respecting evidence.
- Waiting for considerable evidence before judging.
- Being willing to search for more evidence.
- Being willing to revise in light of new evidence.

FIGURE 4-2   *Abilities, attitudes, and dispositions fostering critical thinking*

areas, and reflect on how they might do things differently. Wanting to improve on their ideas and on the processes they use to come to conclusions is an important goal. It is a creative process that helps students identify problems and seek alternatives. Figure 4–2 lists the abilities, attitudes, and dispositions fostering critical thinking.

Critical thinking involves a complex set of dispositions and abilities. These dispositions include seeking reasons, trying to be well informed, taking into account the total situation, and looking for alternatives (Ennis, 1991; National Research Council, 1996). In addition, critical thinking involves abilities such as focusing on a question, judging the credibility of a source, making and evaluating value judgments, defining terms, and deciding on an action.

Critical thinking doesn't come spontaneously to elementary and middle school students. It is encouraged by active use and by example. Because critical thinking is a complex set of dispositions and abilities, students cannot be expected to fully accomplish it in the middle school. However, they can begin to develop the dispositions and abilities that make up critical thinking during the elementary grades if they have appropriate assistance. Science teachers must plan lessons which include critical thinking, and work to develop its components in their students.

How Do We Foster Problem Solving and Decision Making?

Problem solving is a thinking strategy that attempts to resolve a difficulty. Students are natural problem solvers. They are novices, however, and instruction helps them become more capable problem solvers. The systematic approach used in science is especially useful to students as they learn to become better problem solvers. A good problem solver is familiar with, and capable of, using a variety of problem-solving strategies. Problem solving involves a complex sequence of thought processes beginning with problem finding and moving on to identifying, selecting, carrying out, and validating problem solutions. Figure 4–3 describes the processes involved in problem solving. Becoming a better problem solver requires that students be able to reflect on their thought processes in order to decide what a "good problem solver" does (Barell, 1991).

Since reflective problem solving incorporates science process skills and critical thinking as well as other thought processes, it is not well developed in elementary and middle

- Sensing a problem.
- Identifying important components of the problem: variables, relations between variables, and goals.
- Putting elements of the problem into your own words by representing the problem through imagination, writing, or graphs.
- Constructing or identifying a problem statement.
- Defining terms and conditions.
- Identifying alternative solution plans.
- Selecting a plan appropriate to the type of problem identified.
- Anticipating and planning for obstacles.
- Trying out the solution plan.
- Monitoring the solution plan process.
- Adapting procedures as obstacles are encountered.
- Describing the solution resulting from the procedure.
- Validating the findings in terms of the procedure and goal.
- Determining the efficiency and effectiveness of the overall process.

FIGURE 4-3   *Processes involved in problem solving*

school students. Teachers help students become reflective problem solvers by: (1) listening to students' ideas; (2) modeling thinking; (3) acting as an aid and guide for students; (4) designing science activities which involve learning as problem solving and experimentation; (5) planning, monitoring, and evaluating student progress; and (6) empowering students toward self-direction (Barell, 1991; Bereiter & Scardamalia, 1993). As an example, Ms. Wright asks her second graders in Ohio about the best type of clothes to wear in the winter after they have experienced a lesson on the effects of color and heat absorption. She encourages students to suggest aspects of the problem related to the situation posed. She also might describe the predicament she had as a youngster outside on a cold day. Next, Ms. Wright carries out a problem-solving activity where students are asked to go outside to the school playground and stand in the sunlight. While each student is standing, a partner wraps a piece of black cloth around one arm and a piece of pale yellow cloth around the other arm. After a while, additional colors of cloth are added to replace the black and yellow cloth pieces. The student reflects on the comfort he feels with different colors wrapped around his arm. Ms. Wright monitors the students' activities as they resolve the problem. She guides the students into making an informed decision about which color of clothing contributes most to keeping them warm on a cold day from among the alternative solutions. The students are encouraged to reflect on their thinking processes in order to decide what a good problem solver does:

1. Takes irrelevant information or events out of the problem.
2. Looks at the problem from different angles, and then develops and tries out sample solutions, weighing them against each other.
3. Makes an informed decision by choosing the best alternative based on information obtained from the samples.
4. Considers and supports ideas provided by others, adding on to someone else's thinking.
5. Represents the ideas concretely, perhaps by writing or drawing them on a piece of paper or with a computer application. (Barell, 1991)

- Identifying the variables.
- Identifying variables to be controlled.
- Writing operational definitions as needed.
- Constructing a question to be answered.
- Writing a testable hypothesis which answers the research question.
- Planning a test that will provide data to answer the question.
- Carrying out a test.
- Collecting and interpreting data related to the hypothesis.
- Writing a report of the experiment, including a statement about whether the data support the hypothesis.
- Developing and carrying out additional tests for other contexts or conditions to become confident about the hypothesis.

FIGURE 4-4   *Processes involved in experimenting*

How Do We Foster Experimenting?

When teaching the skill of experimenting, the teacher assists students in designing investigations that will help them pose a wide variety of "what if" questions throughout their lives. Human life involves continual experimentation, acting "in order to see what follows" (American Association for the Advancement of Science, 1993a; Schon, 1987). Most people are not very good at "experimentation" in either the laboratory or in daily life. Becoming proficient at experimenting is necessary if students are to develop an understanding of the nature of science.

Experimenting involves testing hypotheses or explanations (see Figure 4–4). The test, if successful, provides evidence to support the hypothesis. If not successful, the hypothesis is changed to incorporate new information or it is dropped from consideration.

How Important Is Data Collection and Organization during Experimenting?

Poorly organized data collection is likely to lead to false conclusions. The way in which data is presented also may lead to false conclusions. For example, students may test the hypothesis, "The higher the temperature, the more quickly materials will dissolve," in two trials using different temperatures. They do not find significant and systematic dissolving differences between the trials. Therefore, they conclude that no differences are found in the dissolving rate of a piece of candy at a higher temperature.

What Are Three Common Errors Students Make during Data Collection and Organization?

Small measuring errors are common and can influence data collection. There are three other common errors students make in data collection. Examples of these in relation to students experimenting with the hypothesis, "The higher the temperature, the more quickly materials will dissolve," follow.

1. Error I.   *Data Collection Error.* Collecting too few pieces of data can lead to the erroneous conclusion that dissolving time decreases with temperature.

Temperature of water in degrees Celsius	Dissolving time of piece of candy in minutes
1. 51	12
2. 48	11

2. Error II. *Data Organization Error.* Collecting more data points provides more information, but the data must be shown in an organized list. Otherwise, relationships between the pieces of data may not be obvious.

Temperature of water in degrees Celsius	Dissolving time of piece of candy in minutes
1. 51	12
2. 48	11
3. 38	13
4. 43	11
5. 46	12

3. Error III. *Data Collection Error.* Even when ordering the trials according to temperature, too small a range may result in data that isn't very helpful.

Temperature of water in degrees Celsius	Dissolving time of piece of candy in minutes
1. 51	12
2. 48	11
5. 46	12
4. 43	11
3. 38	13

While doing the experiment, students may decide that the information does not support the hypothesis and that a modified hypothesis, "The higher the temperature, the more slowly candy (materials) dissolve," should be used. What is needed to test this hypothesis are multiple observations (five or more) planned in advance and addressing a wider range of values for the manipulated variable or cause of the change. Take, for instance, the following test of the hypothesis, "The higher the temperature, the more quickly materials will dissolve." Even with measurement errors, the information supports the hypothesis.

Temperature of water in degrees Celsius	Dissolving time of piece of candy in minutes
1. 70	3
2. 60	7
3. 50	11
4. 40	13
5. 30	16
6. 20	18

What Is the Purpose of Sharing Information?

Teachers should encourage students to share their information with the class. Data collected by one group of students may lend or reduce support for one or more of several competing hypotheses. The sharing of information is likely to broaden students' understanding of a problem since they come into contact with a wider range of data. Student understanding can also be broadened when data is presented in varying formats by different groups.

During a learning cycle lesson involving the critical response skill of experimenting, students are encouraged to take different paths depending on whether the data they collected are inadequate, support the hypothesis, or do not support it. Figure 4–5 describes the paths of developing and reconstructing hypotheses. To some extent, this is a never-ending process because hypotheses cannot address all possibilities.

What Happens When No Decision Can Be Made Regarding Whether a Hypothesis Is Supported?

If the data collected are inadequate and no decision can be made regarding whether or not a hypothesis is supported, students should decide whether there is a way to collect more data and/or more appropriate data. If this can be done, they will plan how to do it and then collect the additional data. Students sometimes find that it is not possible to obtain adequate data, since the information may not exist in a form available to them. For example, they may be interested in how much oxygen still exists in a sealed jar af-

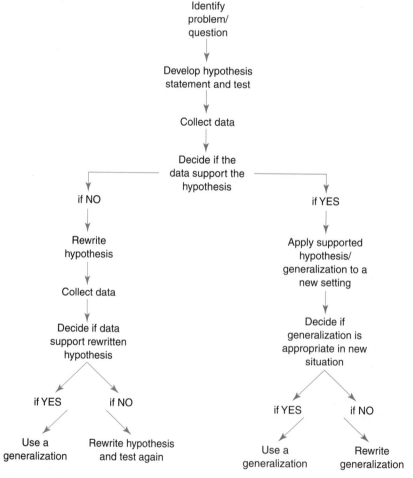

FIGURE 4–5   *The process of developing and revising generalizations*

ter a candle placed in it goes out. No methods may be available that give them the information they need. Students may, however, be able to make inferences based on information available on the Internet, in resource books, or in a film that shows mice leading an active life for an hour after a candle went out in the same jar. Under such circumstances, the students are asked to tell how confident or reliable they feel about their hypothesis. Or, they may wish to pursue a different but related problem for which more information is available.

How Do We Foster Creative Thinking?

Creative thinking uses the basic thought processes to develop constructive, novel, or aesthetic ideas or products. The emphasis is on the use of prior knowledge to generate other possibilities in the same context, similar possibilities in other contexts, or to extend ideas in new directions (see Figure 4–6). Creative thinking includes the intuitive as well as the rational.

Thus, teaching for creative thinking involves planning lessons that allow students to use and build on science attitudes and dispositions. Creative ability builds on and extends awareness, interest, and willingness to explore, create change, and generate novel thoughts, products, and solutions. In science lesson activities, students generate or select among different purposes for exploring and understanding basic concepts. Rather than being given narrow, convergent ideas in final form, students explore the range of meaning ideas have. Lessons on the water cycle, for example, include such divergent purposes as the effect of rainfall on the school grounds, how the water cycle affects our lives in our local area, and an understanding of the water cycle throughout history. Students select and revise a problem related to a key idea, choosing the methods to study the problem and defending ideas gained from their study.

Students are challenged to use what they already know at a higher level. They are challenged to perform in ways they never have. For example, students can participate in a water cycle play as actors, set designers, and script writers. Such a play enhances their creative thinking more than would reading and discussing a textbook passage (Sunal & Sunal, 1991d).

- Demonstrating an interest in exploring the novel and the unexpected.
- Willing to try to create innovative or original thoughts, patterns, products, and solutions.
- Willing to take risks in creating and exploring new ideas and different viewpoints.
- Aware of the potential of generating alternatives.
- Aware of the potential of applying ideas, analogies, and models in new contexts.
- Ready to change ideas or approaches as the situation evolves.
- Willing to work at the edge of one's competence and to accept confusion and uncertainty.
- Learning to view failure as normal, interesting, and challenging.
- Willing to set products or ideas aside and come back later to evaluate them from a distance.
- Feeling comfortable with, and being motivated by, intrinsic rather than extrinsic rewards.

FIGURE 4-6   *Processes involved in creative thinking*

These observations and reflections might lead to a question such as, "What do you think will happen if you do it this way?"

HOW DO WE CREATE CONDITIONS FOR STUDENT THINKING IN SCIENCE?

Teaching for thinking requires deliberate planning and classroom conditions that facilitate student interaction. Effective science teaching involves posing problems, dilemmas, and discrepancies, and raising questions involving students in a variety of inquiry activities related to the science content. Three strategies help create a proactive approach to teaching thinking: questioning, structuring, and modeling (Baker & Piburn, 1997; Costa, 1991c).

What Is the Role of Planned Questioning?

Planned questioning helps students connect prior knowledge, gather and process information into meaningful relationships, apply those relationships in new situations, and be aware of their own thinking during these processes. Teaching for thinking starts with students' prior knowledge of an idea and leads to current experiences with the idea. Teachers follow-up on student responses with questions such as: "What can you tell me about your past experience with events such as this?" "What is your evidence for that statement?" and "What can you now do to become more sure or comfortable with your answer?" Effective science teaching involves helping students ask more questions and providing them with fewer answers. To accomplish more effective questioning, teachers must be aware of, and plan for, higher-level thought questions that ask for evidence to support responses and require students to become aware of their own thinking. Teachers must plan for time in which students can ask questions.

Planning for questioning requires the use of wait time. Wait time is a research-supported technique that has been connected with increased student thinking about science ideas, longer responses from students, and more effective use of evidence in constructing responses (Rowe, 1987). The proper use of wait time involves waiting 3 to 5 seconds before asking students to respond to your higher-order question and before responding to their answers. Teachers of science need to be aware of the need for wait time and should practice using it.

What Is the Role of Structuring?

Structuring relates to planning for interaction between students and the environment. Structuring involves planning for adequate instructional time, interactive encounters, appropriate space, and sufficient resources to facilitate thinking. It is important that teachers maintain and extend student thinking in science goal areas for greater periods of time than is now common in classrooms. The classroom and outside-school environment are arranged so students have real objects and experiences with which to interact. Students talk about their thinking using an inquiry learning strategy. Students are also involved in some risk-taking in the learning process.

A safe environment is created so students can put their energy into exploration rather than self-consciousness and defensiveness. A safe feeling requires a positive and creative atmosphere, in which students listen to each others' ideas and work with each other in cooperative learning groups. Collaborative thinking is regularly encouraged to help students look at problems from multiple perspectives.

What Is the Role of Modeling?

The modeling of intellectual behaviors is planned in advance and frequently demonstrated until students regularly use them. Modeling is an effective strategy for helping students perform complex science behaviors. Modeling has two components: posing a problem, and thinking out loud while demonstrating a solution. Using materials to provide observable cues is effective. For example, a teacher demonstrates the proper use of measuring tools by acting out a complete procedure for their use, explaining each step.

Putting into action planned questioning, structuring, and modeling encourages students to integrate higher-order thought processes with science content.

HOW IS THE USE OF INQUIRY SKILLS ASSESSED?

Students of any age vary widely in their development. It is often difficult to determine whether all students in a group have mastered a particular skill. Yet, many teachers are not familiar with inquiry performance. Students' level of performance in using inquiry skills is poorly assessed by standardized and paper-and-pencil tests. Such tests are often concerned only with lower-level science content objectives. Assessing skills places a higher value on them and focuses learning toward higher-order inquiry skills. The difficulty in assessing skills usually relates to a lack of familiarity with keeping records of student activities and progress. Appropriate record keeping makes the assessment of skills "doable" within the demands of a busy teaching day. The type of record kept depends on whether it is intended for the parent, the teacher, or for another purpose, such as assessment by special education personnel.

The main question about the format of student record keeping seems to be, "Should it list task performance or skill development?" A record based on task performance uses the events that occur within a single science unit. For example, a student task record for use in a primary-grade unit investigating sound involves the completion of specific tasks such as making sounds using a variety of materials, creating sounds of different loudness and pitch, and constructing a musical instrument using ideas developed earlier in the unit (see Figure 4–7).

Student records based on skill development are related to the performance levels of various skills in the science unit. For a primary-grade sound unit, entries might include: (1) use of more than one sense while investigating the origin of sounds, (2) classification of a variety of sources of sound by the intensity of sound they produce, and (3) identification of the variable of force as the cause of the loudness of sounds (Figure 4–7). The skills related to these three assessment criteria are observing, identifying variables, and classifying.

SCIENCE PERFORMANCE RECORD

Topics	Students			
	Ann	Benjie	Makisha	Jose
Making sounds using a variety of materials.				
Creating sounds of different loudness and pitch.				
Constructing a musical instrument.				

SKILL DEVELOPMENT RECORD

Topics	Students			
	Ann	Benjie	Makisha	Jose
Observing				
Use of more than one sense while investigating the origin of sounds.				
Classifying				
Classification of a variety of sources of sound by the intensity of sound they produce.				
Identifying Variables				
Identification of the variable of force as the cause of loudness of sounds.				

FIGURE 4-7   *Records of student science performance and skill development*

Assessment of student thinking skills involves using different types of records for different purposes (see Sunal & Sunal, 1991b and 1991c for additional examples). The type of information recorded using these assessments ranges from a simple check mark to a numerical rating scale, rubric, or a narrative comment. A check mark indicates the student demonstrated or completed the task. Check marks may be useful as a progress check for the teacher, but they're usually not sufficient for evaluating student progress. The use of numerical, rubric, and narrative assessment ratings are informative to indicate the student's progress by diagnosing strengths, and weaknesses. Rubrics use criteria to assess and evaluate learning performance; see Figure 4–8 for a sample rubric assessment. Rubric and narrative assessment ratings are useful in prescribing future science instruction for students. When using skill development assessments, it is important to be aware of the stages in the student's progress toward more advanced skills (see Figure 4–9). The listing can be done on an individual or classroom chart. Comparing student progress to the overall development of the skill or to other students allows a teacher to provide a more supportive science program.

HYPOTHESIS QUALITY SCALE		
Level	**Criterion_____**	
0	No explanation; for example, a nonsense statement, a question, an observation, a single inference about a single concrete object.	
1	Nonscientific explanation; for example, ". . . because it's magic" or ". . . because the man pushed a button."	
2	Partial scientific explanation; for example, incomplete reference to variables, a negative explanation, or analogy.	
3	Scientific explanation relating at least two variables in general or nonspecific terms.	
4	Precise scientific explanation with qualification and/or quantification of the variables. A specific relationship between the variables is provided.	
5	In addition to a level 4 hypothesis statement, a test is given.	
	An explicit statement of a test of a hypothesis. An inference is made that the student who states a test also hypothesizes adequately and precisely.	

FIGURE 4-8   *Writing and evaluating hypotheses*

Source: Quinn, M. E. and George, K. D. (1975). *Teaching hypothesis formation.* Science Education, 59(3), p. 290. Reprinted by permission of Wiley-Liss, Inc., a subsidiary of John Wiley & Sons, Inc.

Applying What You Know

Rating the Quality of a Hypothesis

Part 1

Students have been found to write better hypotheses when they first write the hypothesis and then immediately test it (Quinn & George, 1975). A rubric for evaluating hypotheses helps students develop their hypotheses formation skills (see Figure 4–8).

Rate the following statements using the writing and evaluating hypothesis quality scale found in Figure 4–8. If the rating is not a 5, modify the statement to give it a higher rating.

1. Temperature affects the rate at which materials dissolve.
2. Plants need sunlight to grow.
3. Big rubber bands are stronger.

A discussion of possible answers to this activity is found on the Companion Website at *http://www.prenhall.com/sunal*

Companion Website

Part 2

The hypotheses stated below on the relationship of human variables and heart rate are rated as a 5 on the Hypothesis Quality Scale.

Problem: What determines the heart rate of students?

1. *Hypothesis:* The heavier the student, the faster his heart rate.
   Test: Have the students find their pulse and measure it. Then, weigh each person. Graph the heart rate (result) compared to weight (cause).
2. *Hypothesis:* The taller the student, the faster her heart rate.
   Test: As with (1), record the heart rate and the height and graph the results.

(continued)

3. *Hypothesis:* Girls' heart rates are slower than boys'.
   Test: Record the girls' heart rates and compare them to the boys'. Perhaps use the average rates for both.

Now, write one level 5 hypothesis for the following problem:

Problem: What determines how fast materials dissolve in a liquid?

   Hypothesis:
   Test:

A discussion of possible answers to this activity is found on the Companion Website at *http://www.prenhall.com/sunal*

CURIOSITY ASSESSMENT

Lesson or Activity _____

Rating Levels	Student			
	Ann	Benjie	Makisha	Jose
Level 1 Unaware of new things and shows few signs of interest even when these things are pointed out.				
Level 2 Often seems unaware of new things, showing little interest even when these things are pointed out.				
Level 3 Is attracted by new things but looks at them only superficially or for a short time. Asks questions, mostly about what things are and where they come from, rather than about how or why they work or relate to other things.				
Level 4 Usually shows interest in new or unusual things and notices details.				
Level 5 Shows interest in new or unusual things and notices details. Seeks, by questioning or action, to find out about, and explain, causes and relationships.				

FIGURE 4-9 *Sample development assessment for curiosity*

Although it is difficult for teachers to carefully evaluate students during their very busy days, evaluation is a critically important task. It is more than record keeping. It is necessary for planning effective science lessons, providing feedback to students to enhance their learning, and for interacting meaningfully with students during classroom teaching.

Chapter 8 provides an in-depth discussion of the use and techniques of science assessment.

WHAT IS THE HIERARCHY OF SCIENCE INQUIRY SKILLS?

The categories of inquiry skills previously described provide a way to scaffold the introduction of these skills in primary-age and intermediate-grade science lessons. The emphasis in kindergarten and early elementary grades is on using the early inquiry skills in as many science content areas as possible. Creative repetition and transfer across science content areas are necessary if the skills are to become automatic. During the early elementary grades, science lessons also focus on basic science process skills such as observation, classification, communication, and measurement. At the middle school level, science lessons focus on the development of higher-level inquiry skills (see Table 4–7). This emphasis should be evident in 40 percent or more of the science lessons at these grade levels.

Throughout all grade levels, a variety of science inquiry skills are attempted and used by students during science lessons. Modeling a variety of skill levels in science lessons where they are appropriate is important. The attitudes and dispositions relevant to the lesson's science content also should be a focus at all grade levels.

TABLE 4-7　*Developmental use of thinking skills in science lessons*

Thinking Skill	Components of Thinking Skills Used in Science Lessons		
	Kindergarten	Elementary School	Middle School
Observation	descriptive, all senses used, real experiences	quantitative, observe change, familiar situations	relate theory and observations, imagined situations
Classification	single variable	multiple attributes, use hierarchical system	create hierarchical system
Communication	description of direct sensing, begin recording data	inferences form experiences, begin graphical representation	mathematical description
Measuring and estimating	comparison	begin accuracy, begin estimation	abstract measures and relations
Inferring	use, but unaware	distinguish between observations	use in developing theory
Predicting	use, but unaware	descriptive, concrete	quantitative, abstract variables
Using variables	use single variable	identify, select and use multiple variables	control multiple variables
Hypothesizing	begin fair test	simple, concrete, identify hypotheses	identify, formulate, construct tests
	use of fair test	judge hypotheses, inductive	hypothetical-deductive
Experimenting	begin developing concept of fairness	hypothesis testing	hypothesis testing and generating

---

PHASE AND PLANNING REQUIRED

Exploration

Help students try out and confront their prior knowledge of the science inquiry skill(s).

Provide an opportunity for students to display the skill that is the focus of the lesson. Start students thinking with a "key" question involving them in an activity using the skill.

Relate previous experience to the lesson skill.

Invention

Discuss the results of the Exploration activity, providing connections to the skill that is the focus of the lesson.

Provide an explanation of the new skill, describing how to use it, when it is used, for what purpose it is used, and how to know when it is used appropriately.

Provide clear examples or model the new skill.

Provide closure for the new skill, describing the steps necessary to use it.

Expansion

Provide practice activities for the new skill. Use interesting examples, not repetitive practice.

Provide activities where the new skill is applied in new, relevant contexts.

Provide activities helping students transfer the new science inquiry skills to increasingly real world events.

Provide a summary of the skill's use, when it is used, and how to use it correctly.

FIGURE 4-10   *A learning cycle lesson plan focused on a science inquiry skill*

HOW IS THE LEARNING CYCLE USED TO TEACH SCIENCE INQUIRY SKILLS?

Inquiry skill learning requires relating the new skill to prerequisite skills, modeling the new skill, becoming aware of its components, and practicing and transferring it sufficiently so that it is performed automatically. The learning cycle accomplishes these necessary steps while building students' interest and proficiency (Figure 4–10).

Applying What You Know

Analyzing a Lesson

Answer the following questions using the classroom scene that follows:

1. What skill is the primary focus of this lesson?
2. What part of this narrative represents the Exploration phase of the learning cycle?
3. What part of this narrative represents the Invention phase of the learning cycle?
4. What part of this narrative represents the Expansion phase of the learning cycle?
5. What type of assessment record is appropriate for this lesson?

CLASSROOM SCENES

Second-grade students at Matthews Elementary School have just come in from outside recess and are getting ready for lunch. Mr. Ferrera is planning a lesson to help his students identify soil characteristics necessary for plant growth. As a beginning activity, Mr. Ferrera uses a naturally occurring classroom situation. While students are washing their hands in the classroom sink before lunch, he asks them questions informally and individually: "What is that you are washing off your hands?" "Where did it come from?" "Is it good for something?" The students' answers vary but, in general, they say that "dirt" is being washed off their hands, that dirt comes from the ground, and that dirt is not good for anything.

After lunch, Mr. Ferrera continues the daily science lesson. After the students are seated in the classroom in cooperative learning groups, he gives each group a potted tree seedling that he'd dug up from the side of the playground on the previous day. He asks the students to role-play how this plant grew to its current size. He asks, "Where must seeds be so they can grow?" and "How do seeds in the forest get into the ground?" The students' responses include role-playing seeds falling to the earth, the sun shining, rain wetting the seeds, the seeds laying on dirt, and the seed becoming a seedling. Then Mr. Ferrera takes the class on a short field trip outside in a small wooded area near the school parking lot and asks them to find examples of seeds and tree seedlings. After 5 minutes, he calls them back. The students report what they found, then he asks, "Why is dirt good for seeds?" and "What is it about dirt that makes it good for seed growth?"

The next day, Mr. Ferrera sets out four buckets of dirt containing sand, clay, rocky soil, and loamy soil. He gives each group of students four 2-liter plastic soft drink bottles that have their tops cut off. He directs each group to place a piece of cloth over the top of each bottle and put rubber bands around the top of each container to hold the cloth in place. Next, the groups collect one cup of soil from each of the buckets. They put the cup of soil on the cloth top of each bottle. Lastly, they slowly pour one cup of water on top of the soil on each bottle.

While the water drains through the soil, the teacher asks the groups to report what is happening in their bottles. He asks them to continue to watch how fast water drains through each type of soil and to notice the amount of water found at the bottom of each container. After a few more minutes, Mr. Ferrera provides each group with a sheet containing three questions. The first is, "Which container has the most water at the bottom?" After students answer this question, they are instructed to order the containers from the one with the most water to the one with the least water. The next question is, "What happened to the soils as the water was being poured?" The third question is, "Which soil best absorbs water?"

After a teacher-led discussion, the students conclude that the loamy soil absorbed the most water and allowed little water to pass through. The sandy soil absorbed the least water and allowed the most water to pass through.

Next, each group is asked to collect a plastic drinking cup full of soil from each bucket. They are given pipe cleaners and asked to push them through the soils as far down as possible. Mr. Ferrera asks them to report what they discover about the difficulty of pushing the pipe cleaners through the soils. The students wet the soils to see whether this makes any difference. The tree seedlings are again placed in each group's work area. The students are asked how the roots of a seedling are like the pipe cleaners in their ability to push through different types of soils. The students conclude that tree seedlings growing in loamy or sandy soils may have the easiest time.

To sum up, Mr. Ferrera asks each group to discuss the following questions: "What might happen if seeds were to fall on each of the four types of soil?" "How well would a seed be able to grow on each of the soils?" and "Why do you think so?" Following this discussion, Mr. Ferrera summarizes the students' discoveries about the type of soils seeds and plants need to grow: *Soil that is able to absorb and hold some moisture, soil loose enough that roots would be able to penetrate easily, well-drained soil so that the seed would not rot, and soil compact enough to allow the roots to keep the plant from falling over.*

The next day, Mr. Ferrera provides each student with a bean and a plastic cup. He then directs them to examine four buckets of soil. Each bucket contains a type of soil with which the students have not previously worked. Mr. Ferrera asks the students to use the soils in the buckets to create a potting soil they think would be the best for a bean plant. They are free to mix the soils if they choose. Each student is asked to justify his choice by describing the actions he took to the members of his group.

As a concluding activity, Mr. Ferrera takes the class outside to three different places on the school grounds and asks them to make observations of the soil by testing it with small shovels. He encourages them to comment on those characteristics of the soil that support plant growth. He asks for evidence if the students did not provide it in their statements.

Applying What You Know

Analyzing Inquiry Skills in a Lesson

Return to the *Exploring Your Ideas* feature on temperature at the beginning of the chapter. Reread the sample sixth-grade textbook passage and answer the questions below:

1. What statement(s) led to a growth in inquiry skills?
2. Which statement(s) should be selected as a goal for a science lesson in inquiry skills?
3. What activities should be used to encourage learning of the science inquiry skill(s)?

1. Statement 1 can lead to growth in inquiry skills if students are allowed to pursue this question.
2. Statements 1 and 2 should be selected as a goal for a science lesson in inquiry skills. Possible skills involve observing, measuring and estimating, predicting, formulating hypotheses, experimenting and/or attitudes developing such as curiosity and respect for evidence.
3. Inquiry activities should be planned that involve students in a learning cycle related to determining how temperatures affect behavior. These inquiry skills are important for students to understand and are part of the National Science Education Standards (National Research Council, 1996, pages 122, 145, and 148) for grades 5–8.

SUMMARY

Students' experiences with the world and other individuals are the beginning points of science knowledge and their ideas about how the natural environment works. Ideas are made up of information and the related inquiry skills necessary to use and interpret the information meaningfully. Students perceive and interpret information from their experiences and use their prior knowledge in order to construct new knowledge. Construction of new knowledge is totally dependent on the level and kind of science inquiry skills available to them. Beginning science experiences focus on helping students derive meaning from their everyday experiences by encouraging the development of their science inquiry skills. After students have specific science experiences in an area and have developed basic science inquiry skills, the focus of science teaching moves from a skills emphasis to a skills and content emphasis. A shift in emphasis of this kind is appropriate for middle elementary and beginning middle school students. Thinking about skill development requires purposeful unit and lesson planning and the use of teaching/learning methods that facilitate student interaction through a hands-on and minds-on approach. Assessment and evaluation of a wide range of science inquiry skills places a higher value on them and focuses instruction on meaningful learning in students.

chapter **5**

The Content of Science:
Conceptual Learning

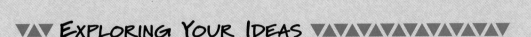

▼▲▼ EXPLORING YOUR IDEAS ▼▲▼▲▼▲▼▲▼▲▼▲▼

Textbooks are filled with statements. As a science teacher, you determine which ones are important enough for students to learn. Read the typical fourth-grade science textbook passage below. Identify the numbers of the statements you consider important science content for which you will plan lessons to create meaningful learning:

(1) Children often play with magnets. (2) Magnets are objects that pick up or stick to some things. (3) A magnet is made up of a metal called iron. (4) It can pick up a needle, a paper clip, or a pin. (5) A magnet cannot pick up paper, coins, wood, or plant leaves. (6) A magnet can pick up objects made of iron. (7) Steel is a metal made from iron. (8) Steel usually can be picked up by a magnet.

(9) The child in the picture is using a magnet. (10) It is sticking to the stove. (11) Why does it stick to the stove? (12) The stove is made of steel. (13) So, the magnet sticks to the stove.

(14) There are different sizes of magnets. (15) There are different shapes of magnets. (16) There are many ways to use magnets. (17) Have you ever used a magnet? (18) Maybe you used one but did not know it was a magnet. (19) Look at the pictures above. (20) How is each child using a magnet?

Discuss the passage and your responses with a peer, if possible. Share your ideas about the following questions: (1) What do you conclude about the science content in the passage? (2) Which concept statements should be selected as goals for a science lesson? and (3) What activities should be used to encourage learning of the science concept(s) selected for the lesson? We will return to this passage at the end of the chapter for additional reflection.

Chapter Objectives

1. Describe the rationale for science content that primarily consists of concepts and generalizations.
2. Distinguish concept statements from other types of statements such as facts, generalizations, and lesson procedures.
3. Identify and classify different types of concepts.
4. Identify and classify different levels of abstraction between concepts.
5. Classify science concepts on the basis of the complexity of reasoning patterns needed to understand them.
6. Describe the rationale for assessing and planning for alternative science conceptions.
7. Describe important elements of a teaching strategy that encourages and facilitates concept re-learning or replacement.

Applying What You Know

Identifying Facts

Indicate which of the following are facts:

_____ 1. The seed is red.

_____ 2. Seeds have a hard outer shell called the seed coat, an embryo, and soft inner material called the cotyledon.

_____ 3. The moon repeats the same shape every 28 days.

_____ 4. In 1609, Galileo reported that he observed four dim stars around Jupiter that appeared to move around the planet over many days.

_____ 5. The bone found in Northport, Alabama may have been from a mastodon.

_____

Of the five items above, numbers 1 and 4 are facts. Number 1 describes a specific observation. Number 4 identifies a specific event.

Number 2 is a concept statement defining a seed. Number 3 is a generalization since it describes a pattern relating shape and time. Both numbers 2 and 3 describe and summarize a set of similarities found between the facts from which they were formed. Number 5 is an inference, a statement that goes beyond the observations made.

Don't be concerned if you are finding it difficult to identify facts. It takes some practice before you can quickly and easily do this. The following discussion of concepts should help you better distinguish facts from concepts.

WHY SHOULD WE FOCUS ON TEACHING SCIENCE CONCEPTS AND GENERALIZATIONS?

Recent science education research gives us a better understanding of the difficulties students have in learning science. It is evident that meaningful learning in science only occurs if changes are made in traditional classroom teaching (Gil-Perez & Carrascosa, 1990; Manganus, Rottkamp, & Koch, 1999). Many teachers think about their courses in terms of topics, terminology, and concepts. However, this is *teacher-oriented* thinking in which the teacher mentally checks off content on a list. The goal of learning is coverage of a body of knowledge. Meaningful learning of content is *student oriented*: students must be actively involved in the process of reshaping and restructuring their own knowledge (Dreyfus, Jungwirth, & Eliovitch, 1990; Huntley, 1999). The science curriculum for elementary and middle school students must be seen as a program of experiences from which knowledge and skills are constructed (Driver & Oldham, 1986; Eckhaus & Wolfe, 1997).

Science or *scientific literacy* involves an awareness, appreciation, and understanding of the key scientific concepts and processes required for personal decision making, participation in civic and cultural affairs, and economic productivity (American Association for the Advancement of Science, 1993a; National Research Council, 1996). **Scientific learning** includes:

• Understanding factual information, concepts, and generalizations needed in everyday life.

- Developing proficiency in using and transferring the content of science into personal decision making.
- Acquiring attitudes and dispositions related to the appropriate use of science knowledge and the willingness and ability to make informed decisions about the risks and benefits of science and technology in everyday life.

More discussion of science literacy and scientific learning can be found at the websites of the NSES and Benchmarks standards. For further information, see links to these websites on the Companion Website at *http://www.prenhall.com/sunal*

Factual information or fact statements are based on observations about objects and events. Examples of facts are: "The temperature of the liquid is 35 degrees," "The helium atom has two protons in its nucleus," and "In 1644, Torricelli used a device, the barometer, to measure air pressure."

Concepts summarize a set of factual statements that have a common reference. These are generalized to all examples. A **concept** can be defined as the set of characteristics common to any and all instances of a given type, or the characteristics that make certain items examples of a type of thing and that distinguish any and all examples from non-examples. Some examples of concepts include type of rock, such as sedimentary or igneous; properties of a rock, such as its color and hardness; parts of a flower, such as the pistil or stamen; and the idea of force. Each involves a definable set of factual statements by which it is possible to identify the concept.

Generalizations are statements that relate concepts. They show how two or more concepts are connected to each other. Generalizations involve a range of statements, from simple unsupported ones to statements of theory, law, and principle that have extensive evidence supporting the relationships among concepts.

Facts are statements about observations of objects and events. They provide meaning for the concepts and generalizations formed from them. Without an adequate background of facts based on concrete experiences, a student's understanding of concepts such as *food chain, consumer,* or *producer* remains vague. Concepts, and the relationships among concepts found in generalizations, are the important aspects of science content.

The different kinds of content, facts, concepts, and generalizations require different types of instruction if meaningful science learning is to occur. The type of instruction is also dependent on students' developmental abilities. The focus of this chapter is on facilitating students' learning of science concepts. Since students usually come to class with preconceived ideas about the natural world, teachers of science must plan and implement activities that encourage conceptual change.

WHAT IS THE ROLE OF FACTUAL INFORMATION IN SCIENCE CONTENT?

Facts are single occurrences, taking place in the past or present, which result from observations. Facts do not allow us to predict an event or action (Eggen & Kauchak, 1988). Effective strategies for learning factual information differ greatly from those used in learning other kinds of science content. While science content is not acquired by learning factual information, factual information is recalled when constructing or interpreting concepts and generalizations. It is also used as a source of data in higher-order learning, such as critical and creative thinking (American Association for the Advancement of Science, 1993a).

Fact-learning strategies have often been mistakenly used to teach all science content. Elementary and middle school students can learn a lot of everyday science facts but be weak in higher-level science learning (National Research Council, 1996). A good portion of what we call traditional teaching of science has involved the use of fact-learning instructional strategies. Rarely should facts be the objective of a lesson and rarely should they be evaluated.

There is too much factual information to learn. The number of scientific facts available doubles every few years. However, facts have little power to create useful or meaningful knowledge by themselves. "Knowing" facts is related to a student's ability to recall from memory, a low-level thought process. The heavy use of fact-learning strategies treats important scientific concepts and generalizations as though they were facts and leaves little time to meaningfully teach science. Being able to name and label the parts of a plant, for example, can be a primary goal of instruction but should not be treated as something to be memorized. *Stem, leaf,* and *roots* are concepts and should be taught using concept-learning strategies.

When recall is needed, a rote memory learning strategy can facilitate the learning of scientific facts. Rote memory learning requires repetition, immediate feedback, breaking the content down into small pieces, associating new material to be memorized to information previously learned, mnemonics, and attention to the motivational needs of the student (Joyce & Weil, 1992). Games, rewards, mnemonics, and quick pacing of instructional events are all effective techniques for facilitating the memorization necessary for fact learning.

Again, science content is not acquired by memorizing facts. These rote techniques should make up only a small part of a science unit's instructional time, perhaps less than 10%. Terminology, symbols, and spelling are some of the factual information that might be included in a school science curriculum. Specific examples of some useful factual information are names of chemical elements and compounds; indexes of plants and animals in a range of biomes; constellations; stars; prehistoric plants and animals; and procedures for using basic science equipment such as the microscope and/or balance. The memorization of facts is planned in advance and is related to a useful goal. In a fourth-grade unit on the solar system, for example, the names of specific planets, such as Mercury, Mars, and Saturn, are facts that are considered a minor goal of the unit. Background experiences involving factual information are an important part of classroom science learning. They are the only common experiences a teacher knows the students have had. Direct experiences and the use of references for information provide important classroom data sources for developing concepts and generalizations.

WHAT IS A CONCEPT?

Concepts are formed by finding similarities between many facts and temporarily emphasizing those similarities. For example, *tree* is a concept we form by focusing on its structure of bark, leaves, and branches, as well as its usefulness for creating wood products and energy. We emphasize the similarities between the structure and functions of the concept we call *tree* and ignore tree differences, such as size, where we find them, and the fact that some have visible flowers or seeds.

How Are Concepts Formed?

Providing Examples and Non-Examples

As concepts are formed, a number of examples and non-examples of the concept must be examined and reorganized (Baker & Piburn, 1997; Eggen, Kauchak, & Harder, 1979). Concepts are best introduced through experiences with the concept during the Exploration phase of the learning cycle. The Exploration of a concept is followed by providing its name as well as examples and non-examples of the concept during the Invention phase of the learning cycle. **Examples** are any and all individual items or events that have the characteristics of a given concept (Seiger-Ehrenberg, 1991, p. 291). If a class was working with the concept of *planet*, for instance, a teacher might provide factual information and use examples such as Mars, Jupiter, and Earth. Students would look for planets in the sky and in pictures. They would use the naked eye, a telescope, and sky photographs. They would also look for them in pictures and multimedia taken from telescopes and spacecraft.

Non-examples are any and all individual items that may have some, but not all, the characteristics that make items examples of a given concept (Seiger-Ehrenberg, 1991, p. 291). As part of the process of constructing the concept of *planet*, students might examine non-examples such as stars, asteroids, and planetary satellites. While these have some characteristics similar to those of a planet, they are not similar enough to be considered a planet. Stars look like planets in the sky to the naked eye. Asteroids and satellites look like planets through a telescope. See Figure 5–1 for examples and non-examples that can be used in teaching the concept *planet*.

EXAMPLES AND NON-EXAMPLES ILLUSTRATING ASPECTS OF THE CONCEPT *PLANET* FOR A STUDENT

Object appearing as a star in the night sky

Example: Viewing Mars, Venus, and Jupiter with the naked eye shows a point of light only, no disk. These planets are indistinguishable from stars.

Non-example: Viewing Earth's moon shows a disk with light and dark features.

Object changing its position among other stars seen in the sky over weeks or months

Example: A planet seen in different positions at different times when compared to other stars in the area (check star calendars, newspapers, or the journal *Science and Children* to find the best viewing times or sky location).

Non-example: A stationary object or one appearing to move within a few seconds, minutes, or hours in the night sky when compared to other stars in the area.

Object which looks like a round disk through a telescope

Example: All planets in the solar system only appear as small circular objects in telescopes. Viewing or photographing Mars, Venus, and Jupiter through a telescope shows a disk, possibly with color and features such as bands and white and dark spots.

Non-example: Viewing or photographing a star does not show a disk. Color may be evident but surface features do not appear. To the naked eye and through telescopes, stars appear as points of light without physical size, except for the sun. Stars are too far away to show a small disk.

Unique size and motion in the solar system

Example: Planets are relatively large bodies in the solar system orbiting around the sun.

Non-example: Satellites, while they look like some of the planets, have orbits around another object in addition to their own orbit around the sun. Asteroids have orbits similar to the planets. However, asteroids and satellites are typically smaller than planets, being less than 2,000 miles in diameter. Most are less than 500 miles in diameter.

Source of light that makes planets visible

Example: Planets reflect light that strikes them from the sun. Planets do not give off their own visible light.

Non-example: A picture showing stars in a nebula. Stars give off their own light. The picture shows that hydrogen clouds in space are illuminated by stars and reflect that light to make them visible.

FIGURE 5–1   *Forming the concept of "planet"*

Identifying All Important Characteristics of Each Concept

For effective instruction, it is important to identify all the characteristics *essential* to the science concept. For example, in learning the concept *magnet,* young children may consider "attraction" an essential characteristic. With help, students experience the other characteristics associated with magnets and basic elements of each characteristic: (1) magnets attract and repel other objects; (2) only certain materials are attracted to, and repelled by, a magnet; (3) the attraction works at a distance; and (4) different strengths of attraction exist in different parts of the magnet. For older students, teachers add characteristics such as the existence of magnet poles, the attraction of objects most often made of iron, and the existence and structure of the magnetic field around a magnet, for example, by using iron filings. It is important to help students distinguish nonessential characteristics; for example, size and shape are useful in determining some differences in attraction along the length of the magnet, but are not essential in the overall concept. In other words, a horseshoe or bar shape is not an essential characteristic of a magnet.

The teacher plays an important role in helping students identify the essential characteristics of a science concept. The teacher might, for example, use a learning cycle with each essential characteristic of the magnet to produce conceptual change in younger students. For older students, a learning cycle could involve them in testing characteristics of magnets to determine which seem essential.

Exploration phase: ask students to make and discuss predictions and carry out tests in learning stations for several essential characteristics.

Invention phase: involve students in discussing the results of the tests of their predictions. As the discussion progresses, provide them with clear explanations of examples and non-examples. The examples make obvious the essential and nonessential characteristics of the concept.

Expansion phase: involve students in making further applications and in transferring the concept to situations outside the classroom context. A setting concerning an everyday use of a magnet and a setting associated with a person on the job are appropriate. For example, ask students, "How would you retrieve a quarter that has just fallen into a sewer grating and is still visible? (*Note:* coins are usually not made of iron so one could not use a magnet on a string.) A job situation might involve the question, "How would you solve a tool storage problem on a manned space station? You have a box full of small tools you use frequently, but when you open the box, screwdrivers and hammers made of iron float out of it."

How Do Concepts Differ from Facts?

Concepts differ from facts in two major ways. *First,* factual statements are isolated bits of information acquired directly through the senses: seeing, hearing, tasting, feeling, and smelling. Concepts go beyond this initial contact and involve more than simple observation. *Second,* concepts summarize and group observations into categories. Similarities are identified and generalized; for example, "A planet may or may not have an atmosphere, can have any surface condition, must be a primary object in orbit around a star, must be of substantial size, and does not give off its own visible light." Among the facts summarized into these characteristics are those that help students distinguish planets from asteroids, satellites of a planet, and two or more stars in orbit around each other (a multiple star system).

The summarizing capability of a concept is very important. The categories represented by concepts are chosen by a group of individuals or a society. Without concepts, it is difficult to remember or use all the facts we learn. For example, if students are involved with a unit on the concept of *magnetism,* a teacher might use magnets shaped as a long bar, horseshoe, round disk, rectangle, and many other shapes of various thicknesses. Some examples would not have a metallic luster but would be made of a dark material and might be flexible (such as magnets found on refrigerators at home). To remember each magnet with a separate name or all types (categories) with a unique name would take up a lot of mental capacity, so concepts are formed by grouping together similar objects with shared characteristics under the concept name *magnets.*

Applying What You Know

Analyzing Concepts in a Textbook Passage

Identify and list the concept(s) found in the sample science textbook passage below. Describe the characteristics provided in the passage for the concept(s). For each concept found, determine whether examples and non-examples are provided. If provided, describe them.

> Pond scum is a kind of algae (al-jee). Algae have chloroplasts like plants. But, algae do not have stems, leaves, or roots. Algae do not look like trees, bushes, or flowers.
>
> Many kinds of algae live in the waters of the world. Plankton and diatoms (dy-ah-toms) are kinds of algae found in oceans. Some algae are one-celled organisms. Some, like pond scum, live together in chains. Others live together in large groups and have root-like ends. These ends help them hold on to rocks or soil. Some of these algae become very large.
>
> Most algae are green. Green algae may grow on rocks. Other algae are brown, blue-green, or red.

The concept introduced in the sample textbook passage is: algae. The characteristics provided are: have chloroplasts; do not have stems, leaves, and roots; live on rocks, trees, and soil; one and many-celled organisms; and have many colors and sizes. Examples provided are: pond scum, plankton, diatoms, and green algae. The non-example is: do not look like trees, bushes, or flowers.

Operational Definitions of Concepts

Simply labeling something does not convey its meaning. It is important to provide hands-on experience, discussion, and time to reflect in order for meaning to be constructed. Meaningful science instruction focuses on helping students construct an operational definition for a concept.

Operational definitions describe a concept by providing a test for deciding whether an object or event is an example of the concept. The test is described in terms and experiences familiar to the student. The definition excludes all reasonable statements that do not represent the concept for elementary or middle school students. If the object or event does not meet the test, then it does not represent an example of the concept. An example of an operational definition is, "Oxygen is a gas that, when present, causes a glowing piece of wood placed in a container of the gas to burst into flame."

Frequently, operational definitions have two parts. The first is a description of the *conditions* (i.e., what is done in an event or to an object being defined, such as "when the wood is placed in a container of the gas"). The second part is a description of the *effect* (i.e., what is observed or what happens as a result of what is done, such as "Gas that causes a glowing piece of wood to burst into flame").

In different science areas or at different grade levels, more emphasis may be put on one of the parts of the description. In physical science, operational definitions usually emphasize the first part—"*what you do or what operation you perform.*" For static electricity, this includes "the attraction between materials and sometimes the light and sound effects obtained while rubbing two materials such as wool and rubber together." In biological science, descriptions of important aspects of an object or event are more common. These include descriptions of a part of a plant; for example, "The petiole is the thin, stem-like portion of some leaves that connects the leaf to the stem of the plant." If the object is a thin, stem-like portion of a leaf and it connects the leaf to the stem, it is a petiole.

Formal definition of the concept is very different from constructing an operational definition of it. A formal definition is like the definition found in a dictionary. Formal definitions use abstract terms. To understand the formal definition, the abstract terms used in it and the relationships between those terms must be understood. Students find it difficult to understand the meaning of formal definitions. An example of a formal concept definition is, "Air is the mixture of gases, mostly nitrogen and oxygen, in Earth's atmosphere." Understanding the concept of *air* as it is presented in this formal definition requires knowledge of what is meant by mixture, gas, nitrogen, oxygen, and atmosphere. Formal definitions of concepts are common in elementary and middle school textbooks.

Concept names are the labels or terms used to communicate the concept. *Magnet* is a concept name used to describe a class of objects. Some of the many concept names important in science are *push, magnet, air, force, pressure, electricity, energy, conservation of energy, strong nuclear force,* and *gluon* (an elementary particle in an atomic nucleus). Concept names communicate different meanings to individuals. Young students may focus only on the "attraction" aspect of the concept of *magnet.* Older students, when encountering the concept of *magnet,* may visualize an object that has attraction and repulsion forces associated with "poles" located within the object. Giving an event or object a concept name is a common textbook approach to science instruction. However, just giving the concept a name does not give it meaning. The experiences students have with the concept, and the opportunities they have to reflect on and discuss those experiences, are what gives the concept meaning. When a student uses a concept name, the teacher cannot be sure what meaning the student is giving the concept. Only an operational definition conveys the meaning the student has constructed for the concept.

Applying What You Know

Working with Operational Definitions

The following activity should help identify and develop the skill of *defining through the use of operational definitions.* For students, this skill is closely related to the skill of communicating. Making clear statements to peers and others about the world is an important student outcome. Also important is the idea that there is more than one satisfactory statement that can be used to define a concept. Operational definitions define concepts so that they can be used both inside and outside of classrooms in everyday situations.

Part I

Indicate whether each of the following statements represents an **operational description** of a concept, a **formal definition** of a concept, or a **concept name**.

_____ 1. Energy is the capacity for doing work.
_____ 2. A calorie is the amount of heat necessary to raise one liter of water one degree Celsius.
_____ 3. Density.
_____ 4. An object has a metallic luster if it is not transparent and reflects light that is white, yellow, or copper-colored. For example, copper, silver, and brass have a metallic sheen.
_____ 5. Metallic luster appears as a glaze or glistening surface, usually with metallic reflections.

Numbers 1 and 5 are examples of formal definitions. These definitions involve language and terms that require additional definition. Numbers 2 and 4 represent operational definitions. These definitions adequately describe a procedure, concept, object, or property of an object in the situation in which it is used. Number 3 is a concept name.

Part II

Two definitions are provided for each of the following concepts. Choose the more appropriate operational definition for a sixth-grade student.

Weight

1. The amount of Earth pull as measured by attaching an object to a spring and determining the length the spring has stretched, as in a spring balance.
2. Measuring the heaviness of an object.

Pressure

1. Pressure is the reading on a pressure gauge and is usually measured in pounds per square inch.
2. How hard one object presses on another object.

Air

1. Air is the mixture of gases that support life on Earth.
2. Although air is a transparent, odorless, and tasteless gas, it takes up space, can be compressed, and has weight.

Weight and pressure are more appropriately defined operationally using the first definition. The second choice is the more appropriate operational definition for air. More appropriate definitions allow the student to follow a procedure or carry out an operation whose result defines the concept. The less-operational statements refer to abstract procedures or terms and involve experiences that students are not likely to have had.

In the *Applying What You Know* activity above, it has not been difficult to identify the more appropriate definition—one that students should be working with and learning. Other operational definitions may be more difficult to use or construct. For example, in the definition of a weed, one might say that it is *a plant that is growing where it was not intentionally planted.* However, forests are usually not planted by people, yet the trees in forests are not considered weeds. Likewise, some flowers seed themselves and come up every year but are not considered weeds. Operational definitions may be more appropriate in some situations than in others. An additional description may be added to the definition if it fails to convey meaning. The definition of weed may be made more appropriate by including *a plant that is not valued* and *a plant that is not desired* in a specific location.

Applying What You Know

Developing Better Operational Definitions

Read the definitions that follow. Determine how appropriate each definition is in all classroom contexts, then add to the definition to make it more appropriate.

1. Bird—a bird is an animal that walks on two legs and flies.
2. Rain—rain consists of drops of water falling from a cloud in the sky.
3. Earthworm—an earthworm is an animal that lives underground, is soft and damp to the touch, pinkish in color, and pipe-like in shape.

Students are asked to define concepts as operational definitions on the basis of their own observations, thoughts, and experiences. These may not be the same as yours since your experience is much more extensive than theirs. A definition that seems adequate to students according to their own experiences and observations may be more appropriate than one based on the teacher's experiences. To require students to use only the teacher's definition, one that is not based on their own experience, defeats the important process of helping students construct their own meaning. As students learn more science, they progressively construct more complex definitions for concepts through revising past definitions. Therefore, an operational definition is a "doing" definition and one that is ever-changing. More important than the exact content of the definition is the ability of students to understand concepts based on their own experiences and their willingness to change old definitions when new ones become more adequate.

Interrelationships among Concepts

Concepts are interrelated. Two concepts often share some of the same facts, and most include other concepts as sub-concepts. For example, a key concept in elementary and middle school science is *ecosystem*. Ecosystem includes the sub-concept of "food web." *Food web,* in turn, involves the sub-concepts of "predator-prey," "decomposer," and "food chain," as well as other sub-concepts. *Predator-prey* and *decomposer,* in turn, include "camouflage" or "molds and fungi" in addition to other sub-concepts. Related concepts such as these form a hierarchy (see Figure 5–2). In a hierarchy, a key concept can incorporate many sub-concepts. In turn, a concept can be a sub-concept to another, more inclusive concept. As another example, *sound* is a concept that requires the learner to first understand such sub-concepts as "sources of sound come from vibration," "what makes things sound different," "pitch or frequency," "loudness or amplitude," "echoes and acoustics," "sound can be bounced off things, as in echoes," "sound can be bounced off things and absorbed," "hearing sounds," and "the speed sound travels." However, sound is a sub-concept in a unit on energy. Providing and having students make concept maps (see Figure 5–2) is an important tool the teacher can use to help students assess their own learning and to diagnose student learning problems.

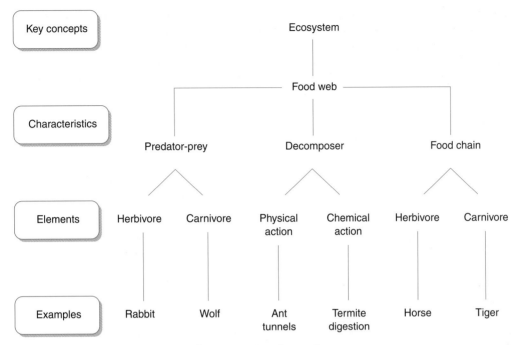

FIGURE 5-2   *A concept map showing interrelationships among concepts*

A **concept map** helps students develop interrelated knowledge and understanding. The concept map has been defined as a process that involves the identification of concepts in a set of materials being studied, and the organization of those concepts into a hierarchical arrangement from the most general, most inclusive concept to the least general, most specific concept (Novak, Gowin, & Johansen, 1983). A concept map can be thought of as a process rather than a product because it is always changing as we have different experiences and as we discuss our experiences with others. In other words, a concept map is a method of thinking through ideas and events by trying to figure out how they are related to each other. An example of a concept map that includes a hierarchy is shown in Figure 5–2, in which *ecosystem* is the most general, most inclusive concept in the hierarchy. Among the most specific concepts in the hierarchy are *rabbit, ant tunnels,* and *tiger.* Linking any two concepts in the hierarchy shows that the person developing the concept map thinks those two concepts are logically connected. In Figure 5–2, *predator-prey* is shown as logically connected to *herbivore* and *carnivore.* Teachers encourage students to link concepts in the concept map and to use words in the link such as "in" or "by." This describes the relationship between the ideas. In Figure 5–2, for example, the student might add the words "are part of " to describe the relationship between herbivores and predator-prey. The student might also add the words "are a," creating the relationship "*ant tunnels* are a *physical action.*"

A very simple concept map is:

throat—swallows—food

Such a concept map shows how two concepts are related, but does not describe a hierarchy. Teachers sometimes draw a concept map for students and leave some blank spaces in it. In this case, the students fill in just the blank spaces. Students may discuss the concepts that should be written in the blanks, or may carry out investigations and other activities to decide how to fill in the blanks. In Figure 5–2, for example, the teacher may leave a blank space where "wolf" is found. The students have many options for filling in the blank. In another case, such as with "herbivore," there may be just one acceptable option. Teachers may use a concept map throughout a unit, beginning with students' prior knowledge and adding to it and revising it as the unit progresses.

A **concept web** is very similar to the concept map. However, it is often a simpler hierarchy. In a concept web, the most general and inclusive idea is placed in the center. Sub-concepts is arranged around it and connected to it with a line. Another layer of sub-concepts are then arranged around the outside of a sub-concept and connected to the sub-concept with lines. A partial example of a concept web is shown in Figure 5–3. This concept web uses some of the same concepts that are found in Figure 5–2's concept map.

Most key concepts, such as *ecosystem* and *sound,* include several sub-concepts. To accurately construct a concept, students need to understand its sub-concepts. The facts summarized to form a key concept must be meaningful to students. For the concept *source of sound,* students must experience how all sounds they make or hear come from some matter that vibrates. Matter that has slow vibrations and fast vibrations should be experienced. These experiences enable students to acquire important facts that are needed to understand the sub-concept of "pitch." It is important that a unit on sound incorporate many opportunities to experience and interact with all sub-concepts and to compare and contrast the sets of characteristics that describe these concepts and the relationship among them. *Teachers must understand the hierarchy among concepts if they are to successfully teach concepts and diagnose the difficulties students are having in constructing these concepts.*

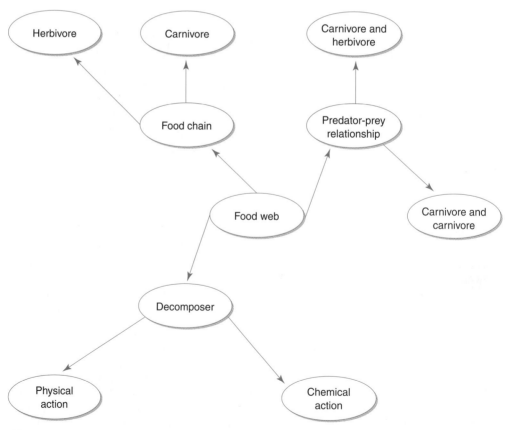

FIGURE 5-3   *Example of a concept web*

Applying What You Know

"Light" Is a Concept

Can you identify a concept that includes "light" as a sub-concept? _____

_____

Can you identify one or more sub-concepts of *light*? _____

_____

_____

A concept that includes light as a sub-concept is *energy*. Possible sub-concepts of *light* include "sources of light" and "light interacts with matter." A sample concept map for a sixth-grade unit on light is given in Figure 5–4.

Concepts are a major portion of the science content constructed by students. They take a large number of facts and process them into manageable pieces. Individuals must learn each concept and process the information it represents on their own. As a result, each of us has a somewhat different understanding of a concept. The strength of well-defined concepts is such that even though we each form our own mental construction of a concept, its essential characteristics are recognized by all of us.

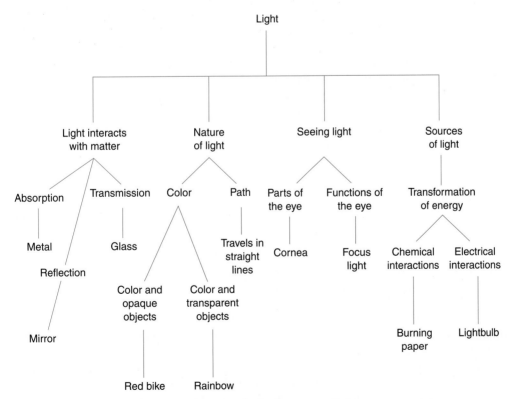

FIGURE 5-4   *A concept map for a sixth-grade unit on light*

Concepts Differ in Complexity and Abstractness

Concepts range widely in their *complexity* and *level of abstractness* (Klausmeier, Ghatala, & Frayer, 1974; Langley, Ronen, & Eylon, 1997). Because of this difference, the level of abstractness of concepts must match the students' developmental level of thinking. Consider the concepts listed earlier—*push, magnet, air, force, pressure, atmosphere, gas, electricity, conservation of energy, strong nuclear force,* and *gluon*. Of the concepts listed, *push* and *magnet* can be understood by very young children. Both are closely tied to everyday experiences in a child's world. A name and an operational definition can easily be associated with *push*. A *magnet* is an object that a child can handle and play with. It has the unique characteristic of "attraction" when brought close to certain kinds of materials. While each of these concepts is complex, each is also tied to a number of concrete experiences the child can have. As a result, children having these experiences typically form an appropriate partial concept before or during the early grades. Later experiences throughout the science program build a more complete understanding of each concept.

The concepts of *air, force, pressure, atmosphere, electricity, gas,* and *energy* are appropriately introduced to, and partially understood by, elementary students. The more directly observable aspects, or sub-concepts, of each key concept are the starting points. First- and second-grade students can experience properties of the sub-concepts of *air* through interactions with air blown by fans, bubbles in water, blown-up balloons, and large thin sheets in the wind. Fourth- and fifth-grade students should investigate sub-concepts of the *mass of air* using balloons attached to balanced metersticks. They can investigate "air density" and "buoyancy" by building hot air balloons from thin plastic bags. These and later experiences build an increasingly deeper understanding of the key concept of *air*. These understandings, in turn, become part of more inclusive concepts, such as *pressure, atmosphere,* and *gas*.

Among the most complex and abstract of the concepts listed above is *strong nuclear force*. It refers to the type of force between elementary particles found in the nucleus of the atom. It differs from gravitational and electrical forces that can be experienced. This is a concept typically learned in high school or later, although it is found in many middle school science textbooks. *Strong nuclear force* is complex, as is the concept of *magnet*. *Strong nuclear force,* however, has few if any concrete or directly observable characteristics that can be appropriately experienced by elementary and middle school students. Because its characteristics are complex and more abstract, students have great difficulty understanding it. How easily a concept can be learned depends on:

- The number of characteristics it has.
- How concrete these characteristics are.
- The reasoning skill level required to provide meaningful learning of all aspects of the concept. (Tennyson & Cocchiarella, 1986)

Robert Gagne (1965) described a teaching technique which focused on beginning with the simplest concepts, or simplest versions of a concept, and gradually moving to the more complex. He stressed the need to examine the entire learning sequence, then work in small steps from the simple to the complex.

Jean Piaget defined and categorized the levels of mental development based on the thought processes typically available to students (Piaget, 1963, 1970c). The developmental levels of concern to us here are preoperational, concrete operational, and formal operational. Piaget found that most students enter school capable of performing preoperational thinking, develop concrete operational thinking during the early elementary grades, and begin to use formal thought processes during their middle school years.

Thought processes typically associated with each of the developmental levels described by Piaget are listed in Figure 5–5.

Jerome Bruner (1961) applied the developmental principles in discovery learning. He focused on the child's involvement with the learning process. The teacher served as a guide and advisor to the child during the investigations. Concrete materials were to be used to begin learning. Bruner identified three stages of the mental representation of information. The first is enactive representation and is similar to Piaget's first stage, sensorimotor learning. At this time, the child develops motor skills, self-awareness, and an awareness of the surrounding environment. Bruner's second stage, the ikonic, occurs when the child's mental representations are strongly affected by her perceptions and these perceptions are unstable and egocentric. Therefore, the child is inconsistent in her observations and perceptions of the world. The last stage is symbolic representation: language develops extensively and the world is represented by words and ideas. At this stage, the child moves toward, and into, the stage Piaget labels as formal operational.

The preoperational reasoning patterns most frequently required for the understanding of general science concepts are:

P1 *Symbolic behavior* develops the idea that symbols and words stand for objects and classes of objects.

P2 *Deferred imitation* imitates or models another's behavior, providing an additional means of learning.

P3 *Centration* focuses on one aspect of the environment while neglecting others.

P4 *Being perception bound* distinguishes by appearance, rather than reality; fails to distinguish fantasy from reality; sees and draws what is known, not what is seen.

P5 *Giving animistic and artificialistic explanations* gives phenomena and objects living attributes and considers all objects and events as being made by humans.

P6 *Being egocentric* views everything from one viewpoint.

The concrete reasoning patterns most frequently required for the understanding of general science concepts are:

C1 *Making simple classification* and successfully relating systems to subsystems, and classes to subclasses.

C2 *Applying conservation* reasoning to objects.

C3 *Establishing one-to-one correspondences* and arranging data in an increasing or decreasing sequence.

C4 *Understanding concepts* defined in terms of familiar actions and examples that can be directly observed.

The formal reasoning patterns most frequently required for the understanding of general science concepts are:

F1 *Understanding concepts* defined in terms of other concepts, theories, idealized models, or abstract relationships such as ratios or mathematical limits.

F2 *Imagining all possible combinations* of conditions even though not all may be realized in nature.

F3 Recognizing and applying functional relationships, such as direct and inverse proportion.

F4 *Separating the effects of several variables* by varying only one at a time.

F5 Understanding the nature of probability and recognizing its implications for experimental design and data analysis.

FIGURE 5-5   *Thought processes typically associated with preoperational, concrete-operational, and formal-operational developmental levels*

A large portion of science content requires the use of diverse and higher-order reasoning. Yet, most students' abilities to do abstract thinking is very limited. It is important to plan the learning of science concepts according to the reasoning patterns needed to understand the content communicated in the lesson. Although not limited to these specific stages, concepts may be called "preoperational," "concrete," or "formal," depending on the type of thought processes required to begin constructing meaning for the concept. These labels indicate differences in the thinking required to understand a concept. Effective teachers begin with "preoperational" or "concrete" concepts and gradually progress to higher-level concepts. The differences between these categories of concepts might be summarized as follows. Preoperational concepts develop from students' use of early inquiry skills in physical activities. Concrete concepts develop as students begin to use a full range of inquiry skills, especially when introduced through real objects and experiences. A concept can usually be considered "concrete" if one can grasp its meaning through direct experience. If a concept derives its meaning from the proficient use of inquiry skills, involving a concept's position within a theoretical system, it is classified as "formal." Using the above classification, *push* and *magnet* are classified as "preoperational." *Air, force, pressure, atmosphere, electricity,* and *gas* are classified as "concrete" concepts. *Conservation of energy, strong nuclear force,* and *gluon* are classified as "formal" concepts.

Applying What You Know

How Do You Plan Lessons That Develop Concepts?

Some concepts introduced in elementary or middle school science classrooms are *atom, rough* (as in texture), *genotype, dissolve, round, density,* and *cell.* In planning a unit, it is important to decide whether students could develop an initial understanding of these concepts through: (1) *the senses by direct interaction and play* with the physical aspects of the concepts over an extended period of time, (2) *direct experience and the use of more concrete reasoning patterns* (such as classification, conservation, and one-to-one correspondence), or (3) *inferences* abstracted from experience and *the use of more formal reasoning patterns* (reasoning with theories, models, and other concepts). The planned lesson activity matches students' prior knowledge and their proficiency levels in using the thinking skills required to understand the concept. In deciding how to classify the concepts, it is helpful to describe to yourself some activities you would use to help your students understand each concept. Then, analyze the knowledge and thought processes required of students when they are involved in these activities. Use Figure 5-5 to assist you in your classification.

Classify the concepts *atom, rough, genotype, dissolve, round, density,* and *cell* as either (1), (2), or (3), and describe the knowledge and thought processes required of students when they are involved in learning each concept.

Rough and *round* can be developed through the direct use of the senses. Students directly interact during play with the physical aspects of the concepts over a period of time. Modeling of the concepts is possible. The student first repeats the gross outward aspects of the concept, later incorporating its more subtle distinctions. Such aspects of these concepts can be derived meaningfully using preoperational reasoning patterns. Reasoning patterns of deferred imitation (P2) and centration (P3) can be used to develop meaning.

Dissolve and *cell* can be understood in terms of familiar actions: observations using tasting and smelling, observations of color, observations through a magnifying glass or microscope, and classification of many examples, drawings, and models of each of the concepts. In other words, important aspects of these concepts can be derived from direct experience by using more concrete reasoning patterns. Classification (C1), one-to-one correspondence (C3), and use of familiar examples (C4) can be used to develop meaning.

The concepts of *atom, genotype,* and *density* must be understood in terms of other concepts (patterns in the properties of matter, gene, inherited trait, mass, and volume), functional relationships (ratio), inferences, assumptions, and/or idealized models. These understandings are not the result of direct experiences and require the application of formal reasoning patterns. Use of concepts defined in terms of other concepts (F1) or functional relationships (F3) can be used to develop meaning.

Preoperational Concepts

Preoperational concepts are concepts whose meaning is developed through the basic senses. Direct interaction through playing with the physical aspects of the concepts over an extended period of time is required. The use of imitation, mimicking, and modeling is

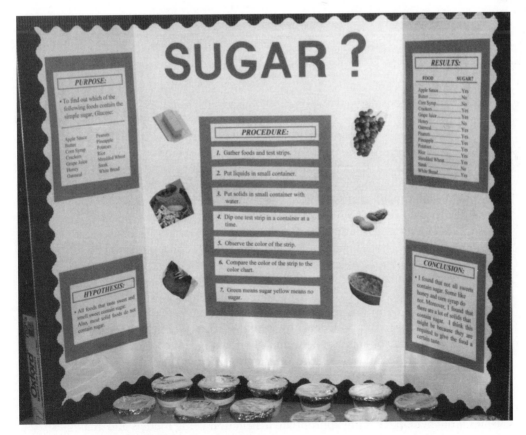

What properties make up the concept "sugar"?

necessary. Verbal descriptions, diagrams, or models are not effective with students who use preoperational thought processes. *Push* and *round* in the previous practice activity are examples of preoperational concepts.

Meaningful concepts can be developed before a concept name is given to the experiences. In learning the concept *ball,* and later the form *spherical,* very young children will use all their senses with each ball encountered. They see, touch, smell, and perhaps lick or bite each ball. They also lay on it, kick it, throw it, put it under and into other things, and so on. These investigations are repeated with each ball they encounter until they are able to group all of these characteristics into the concept *ball.* Then, when a ball is encountered, not only will the young student label it as a ball, but she'll understand it as a meaningful concept. The same events occur with many other concepts, such as *cat, dog,* or *tree.*

One instructional method that can be used in helping young students understand the concept of *lever* as a preoperational concept is to have them play on the school playground on a seesaw over two weeks. During recess each day, the students will experience different variables on the seesaw; they may sit near the end or have a heavier student sit on one end. At the end of the two-week period, a discussion with a small group of students can bring out the differences encountered. It should be possible to ask a student whether he can balance the seesaw. The student will have developed categories of the effects of weight on the ends of the seesaw, but may not be able to identify the important variable of distance of the weights from the fulcrum.

Concrete Concepts

Concrete concepts are concepts whose meanings can be derived from first-hand experiences with objects or events. Some concrete concepts are intuitive. This occurs when the entire meaning of the concept can be gotten through the senses. The color *green* is an example. Concrete concepts can be developed through science process skills. Important aspects of meaning can be derived for common objects such as *flower* or *leaf.* Learning a musical scale by playing it makes a concept concrete. Temperature, when read as a numeral or as a color range on a thermometer, can be related to the students' feelings of comfort in the room. Temperature is a concrete concept when the operational definition of a thermometer reading is used. Concrete concepts can be developed using higher-order inquiry skills. In these and all examples of instruction with concrete concepts, first-hand experiences and the manipulation of the objects must occur, or the experiences must be common to the students involved. *Dissolve* and *cell* in the previous *Applying What You Know* feature are examples of concrete concepts for which higher-level inquiry skills are needed.

Drawings, maps, globes, and models establish many concepts as concrete concepts. However, learners must be able to develop meaning from direct experience with a concept in order for it to become concrete. If the concrete materials themselves represent abstract models whose origins are divorced from the experience of the students, the materials will not fit the definition of a concrete concept. A molecular model is an example of concrete materials used in classrooms. In second-grade textbooks, pictures of molecules containing sticks and spheres can be found. Students have no concrete experience with the origin of this representation or with its outcome in everyday life. It is a concept that, when presented, can only be memorized and not meaningfully understood. It may also result in students forming a misconception. Diagrams and models demonstrating the phases of the moon or the use of water for electricity may lead to student misconceptions. Chapter 9 offers help for more appropriate instruction using models and analogies.

An instructional method that helps students understand the concept of *lever* as a concrete concept is to have the students answer the question, "What affects the balance of a see-saw?" Student groups freely experiment with a model balance using a ruler on their desk and objects in a junk box. The inferences students have drawn from the exploration are then discussed. Next, the teacher provides a set of materials and an experimental procedure for all student groups to follow for an investigation of the problem. Groups investigate the effect of the important variables of weight, length, and placement of the fulcrum on the balance of a lever. The groups' data is shown on a chalkboard and discussed. At this point, the teacher helps students focus on the idea that the significant variables are the weight and distance of the weight from the fulcrum. This is followed up by having students construct levers using different materials, weights, and fulcrum placements and having them report on what they have found. These levers can be related to different uses, such as a nail-puller or catapult. This learning cycle lesson follows a *teacher-guided approach* to concept learning.

A *student-oriented approach* at this level has a different focus. For example, students are given string, weights, rulers, and a junk box full of various objects. A large clock with the seconds indicated on it is available in the room. Before the students begin, the teacher holds a whole group discussion, encouraging them to describe the procedure they will use in answering the questions, predicting what some important variables might be, and predicting some possible difficulties in finding the answer. Following the students' work, a discussion is held with each group in which the members describe their results and the evidence used to support these results. Groups are asked to verify the final results and apply them in solving a real world problem. Both the teacher-guided and student-oriented instructional procedures follow a learning cycle strategy.

Formal Concepts

Formal concepts derive their meaning from an established relationship with an assumption, model, or some other hypothetical–deductive system. Meaning is not given to these concepts by information from the senses, but through imagination or through developing logical relationships within the system. The concept's meaning is developed from the properties or relations given to it by the set of assumptions within which it is a member. *Atom, genotype,* and *density* in the prior Applying What You Know activity are examples of formal concepts.

The concept of the *atomic nucleus* is formal because it represents a hypothetical–deductive system based on observations; we have not been able to "see" an atomic nucleus. When temperature is described as the result of the motion of atoms and molecules, it is a formal concept. *Genotype, neutron star,* and *graviton* all represent formal concepts, because they are all based upon postulates, and they cannot be seen, heard, felt, smelled, or tasted. While musical scales represent a concrete concept, any relationship between two or more musical notes—*harmony*—represents a formal concept. When concepts can be modeled using concrete objects, events, or symbols (for example, using the model of the solar system), the concepts can be described by individuals using concrete reasoning patterns. They may have an initial understanding of the concept by memorizing aspects of the actual model, but they are denied useful or complete comprehension of the concept until more formal thinking operations occur. When this occurs, they are able to construct the hypothetical–deductive system within which the concept derives its full meaning.

In assessing the comprehension of formal concepts, it is important to avoid an evaluation based solely on the examination of parts of the concrete models. This type of evaluation does not test meaningful learning of a concept's implications and its transfer to other contexts. Can the student predict that planets like Mercury and Venus are only seen close to the sun? They will not be seen far from the sun at sunset or sunrise. Don't be misled by concrete learners' ability to use labels or rules to work with formal concepts. Learners can identify planet names or use rules to name the order of planets in the solar system, but once the activity is over the rule will probably be forgotten. In other words, the model of the solar system they understand will not help them organize or predict what they see in the night sky. Such difficulty occurs because concrete thinking does not allow the students to comprehend the concept upon which the rule is based.

A sample instructional strategy used to help older students understand the concept of *lever* is to have them derive the concept from experimental data and an analysis of the mathematical relationships of the variables. The students should be able to conclude that the weights on one side multiplied by the distance to the fulcrum equal the weights multiplied by the distance on the other side of the fulcrum. To be successful, students must have had earlier direct, related experiences with levers and familiarity with the meaning of each variable, the symbols used, and the rules of arithmetic relating the variables in this mathematical statement. Many of these experiences should have begun in the elementary and middle school years.

Applying What You Know

Matching Concepts with Appropriate Activities

Being able to select important concepts and activities that help students develop the meaning of those concepts is an important skill for science teachers. The activities work through the appropriate matching of concepts to students. Determine whether the concepts below can be taught meaningfully, not through rote memory, to students of various grade levels. Some of the concepts can be taught at several levels. The levels are as follows:

"P"   refers to preoperational concepts with students in preschool.
"C"   refers to early concrete operational concepts with students in elementary school.
"F"   refers to formal concepts with students in middle school and later grades.

Sample responses for the first two items are given. For each concept below, indicate the levels at which meaningful instruction could take place. Provide a reason for your selection by describing the type of activities which relate to the thinking level.

Concept	P, C, F	Reasons and Example Activity
A. Closed Electric Circuit	C	Directly observable effects occur when a bulb is attached to a battery by wires.
	F	A closed path along which an electric current might flow, even though a bulb or other part of the circuit might not be operating because the current is too small.
B. Pressure	C	A barometer reading.
	C	Pressure differences can be found using a manometer, a "U"-shaped tube with water at the bottom of the "U". The height of the water can be measured in centimeters. Pressures can be compared.
	F	Force per unit area (includes force concept and proportions). Pressure can be used to calculate gas volumes or forces exerted on container surfaces.

Provide your descriptions of the concepts below, patterning them after the examples given above. Give at least one example for each concept.

C. Seasons
D. Gas
E. Hard versus Soft (as in texture)
F. Neutron

The student who primarily uses concrete reasoning patterns does not reason beyond concrete objects, events, or experiences; has little power of reflection; and does not construct theoretical systems. Hearing a lecture or reading about density, particle models, genotypes, or other formal concepts will not provide such a student with the necessary experiential background to understand these concepts. Instead, instruction should begin with exploratory experiences and "concrete" concepts.

The fact that science concepts can be interpreted either as "preoperational," "concrete," or "formal" helps in planning a teaching activity leading students to construct their own meaning. Learning that begins with a concrete version of a concept is likely to make a more secure connection with the students' previous understandings and preconceptions.

The learning cycle is a way to help students achieve meaningful understanding of a concept. Most students are likely to have an understanding of *temperature, pressure, digestion,* and *animal* as concrete concepts. Through Exploration activities, they can apply their understanding and also discover the limitations of their concrete concepts. For instance, they can discover the difficulty of making quantitative predictions from pressure defined completely in terms of a barometer reading.

There are some differences among students. Some develop complex inquiry skills much earlier than others. For this reason, you should make allowances in the amount of time available for investigation by different students.

Instructional Requirements for Meaningful Learning of Science Concepts

Students of all ages describe science concepts differently from those accepted as accurate in scientific literature. In the past, these alternative conceptions have been called "critical barriers to learning," and "misconceptions." Techniques to identify alternative conceptions among students are discussed in Chapter 9.

Students may have the alternative concept that *magnets are attracted to all metals.* They may have formed the concept on the basis of the limited facts available. Students may only have various iron items available, so they generalize the magnetic attraction to all metals. The very young student may not recognize that there are different kinds of metals. Since iron is so common and has magnetic attraction, he concludes that all metals are attracted to a magnet. Another student may decide that magnets are attracted to all silver-colored metals and not to other-colored metals. Common examples of unpainted metals that students have available to them usually include silvery iron objects and yellowish objects made of copper or brass. It is only later, with more experience, that the student realizes the metal objects may have been painted or coated. The color of metals is not a good indicator of attraction.

Another student may decide that *magnets are attracted to all metals except soft or pure metals such as copper or gold.* The student may have tested only iron objects, which are hard metals, and a few copper or silver objects, which are soft metals. Although the concept is inaccurate, it represents an effort by the student to abstract similarities. As more facts are acquired, or when the student reviews the inventory of facts, the concept may be changed and become more accurate. Teachers have an important role. They provide opportunities for students to have experiences that will add to their inventory of facts. Teachers also provide opportunities for students to discuss the facts they have acquired and relate them to the concepts formed. Students may have hundreds of alternative conceptions about each area of science. A few possible alternative conceptions are given in Table 5–1.

In order to learn a new concept, students must be mentally involved in conceptual change, a process of reshaping and restructuring their prior knowledge. The starting point in the process of conceptual change is students' prior knowledge, or commonsense knowledge. It has proven successful for the student in the past but is different from the intended knowledge to be gained as an outcome of the science lesson (Champagne, Gunstone, & Klopfer, 1983; Sanger & Greenbowe, 1997).

During the early part of a science lesson, the Exploration, each student identifies her own existing concept. A problematic science experience and discussion related to the concept encourages students to think about their views. Thinking about their views leads to a confrontation between their alternative conception and the conception intended by the science lesson. Dissatisfaction with existing conceptions is critical to the process of conceptual change. Only at this time do students realize they must reorganize or replace their prior knowledge because their existing concepts are inadequate to understand the new experiences. To be useful, retained, and transferred to a new setting, the new conception must be clear, understandable, plausible, and successful for the student (Berliner & Casanova, 1987; Posner, Strike, Hewson, & Gertzog, 1982; Suares, Pias, Membiela & Dapia, 1998).

This process of *awareness, reconstruction,* and *application* makes up the sequence of events in the learning cycle. Using learning cycles to teach concepts is an effective strategy that results in meaningful learning; it is teaching for understanding. Using the instructional strategy for teaching facts only creates the memorization of words or vocabulary definitions associated with the concept. It does not result in understanding of the concept.

Teachers may influence students' thinking and conceptions in the ways that are intended, in unanticipated ways, or not at all (Baker & Piburn, 1997; Duit, 1987). When might teaching have little effect on students' concepts? There are four types of instances that may result in small effects:

1. *Students have already formed concepts on their own, sometimes by giving the idea a lot of thought* (Feldsine, 1987; Rye & Rubba, 1998). Many concepts develop as students try to make sense of their physical environment. These concepts are likely to be firmly held. In school, students are sometimes involved in situations using concepts that the teacher defines differently than the students. One or two instructional experiences in school may not be enough to convince students to reconstruct their own concept.

2. *Teachers are often unaware of students' inaccurate or incomplete concepts.* Through setting up an open-ended exploration activity, teachers observe, listen, and work with students, noting their current understanding of a concept.

3. *Teachers often make unfounded assumptions about the teaching and learning process.* Sometimes teachers assume students have not formed prior concepts. At other times, teachers assume that if students have developed concepts prior to teaching, these are easily replaced by the new concepts they're taught. Both assumptions are often false. Much

TABLE 5-1   *A sample of alternative conceptions students bring to science lessons*

Science Area	Sample Alternative Conceptions That Can Create a Learning Barrier in Science Lessons
Physical Science	
Light	Magnifying glasses make light bigger.
Electricity	Electricity is used up when it passes through a lightbulb.
Magnetism	A compass needle points in the direction you are going.
Heat	Heat and cold are two substances.
Temperature	Temperature relates to an object's size.
Force	Force, pressure, and energy are the same thing.
Motion	Constant motion requires a constant force.
Matter	Molecules expand when matter is heated.
Conservation	Sugar disappears when dissolved.
Earth Science	
Earth	Thrown objects may fall off Earth when dropped in the southern hemisphere.
Prehistoric life	Dinosaurs and "cavemen" lived at the same time.
Rocks	Rocks must be heavy.
Soil	Soil must always have been in its present form.
Rain	Empty clouds are refilled by the ocean, or the sun boils the ocean to create water vapor.
Oceans	Oceans are so large that they never change, or they can be changed by humans.
Seasons	Seasons are caused by Earth's distance from the sun.
Night	Day and night are caused by the sun going around Earth or Earth's revolution around the sun.
Moon	Different countries see different phases of the moon on the same day.
Solar system	The solar system includes everything in the universe.
Planets	Planets cannot be seen with the naked eye, or they appear to the naked eye as small disks.
Stars	Stars are all at the same distance.
Zodiac	Astrology (location of the planets among the stars) predicts the future.
Sun	The sun is directly overhead at noon.
Biological Science	
Fruits	A tomato is a fruit.
Plants	Plants need fertilizer for food.
Animals	Acquired characteristics can be inherited.
Osmosis	Fluids move freely in and out of cells no matter what type or kind of material is involved.
Amino acids	Amino acids come from the cytoplasm of a cell.
Chlorophyll	When part of a leaf loses its green color, that part of the plant is dead.

of the time, students have prior concepts which they do not easily reconstruct since conceptual change is a difficult and demanding process.

4. *Teachers and students often don't communicate with each other.* Teachers try to convey meaning using words, diagrams, or symbols. When focusing on these, the student has to find meaning in them. The constructed meaning may not be the meaning intended by the teacher. This is particularly likely if the language used by the teacher, textbook, or worksheet is not familiar to the student. In this case:

- The student may ignore what the teacher is saying.
- The teacher may ignore what the student is saying.
- The teacher may insist that students use the *correct* words. Students may sound like they understand the concept but, actually, they don't.
- The teacher rephrases student responses, making them accurate without addressing the students' misunderstandings. (Harlen, 1985a)

How can teachers influence students' science concepts? There are five important actions that must take place. These actions are summarized in the learning cycle sequence in Table 5–2.

TABLE 5–2   *A learning cycle lesson plan format focused on a science concept*

THE LEARNING CYCLE: TEACHING A CONCEPT	
Phase	**Planning Required**
Exploration	
	Help students try out and confront their prior knowledge of the science concept.
	Ask probing questions to diagnose students' prior knowledge of the science concept.
	Focus students' attention on science experiences.
	Encourage students working cooperatively in groups to relate prior knowledge to make students' prior knowledge of the concept public.
Invention	
	Ask students to reflect on and explain Exploration experiences, concepts, and terminology in their own words to provide connections to the concept that is the focus of the lesson.
	Provide definitions, terminology, clear explanations, all characteristics, and elements of the new science concept as concretely as possible.
	Involve students in clear examples and non-examples of the new science concept.
	Ask students to clarify the new idea and justify statements with evidence.
	Provide for student practice using the new science concept.
	Provide concise, brief closure for the new science concept.
Expansion	
	Provide additional practice to help students use terms, definitions, and explanations of the concept experienced in the lesson.
	Provide application activities for the science concept in new, relevant contexts while at the same time helping students recall their original alternative explanations.
	Provide activities to help students transfer the new science concept to increasingly real world events.
	Provide a summary of the important events in the science lesson leading to the new science concept.

1. Teachers need to provide students with an opportunity to become familiar with the context in which the concept to be discussed belongs. Whenever possible, this involves students trying out their ideas in first-hand experiences by explaining objects or a science event for themselves. The Exploration phase of a learning cycle is an appropriate time to accomplish these activities.

2. To successfully influence students' concepts, teachers are aware of, and help students become aware of, ideas they bring to the lesson. Bringing out prior knowledge begins during the Exploration phase of the learning cycle. This part of the science lesson focuses attention on encouraging students to describe, write, draw, and act out their understanding or meaning of the data related to the concept goal of the lesson. Questions are asked to find out what the students think about the object or event. What words do they use to describe or explain it? What evidence are they using to describe or explain the phenomenon? Activities that help include sorting activities, student-only group discussion, small and large group discussions with the teacher, and one-to-one informal discussions with the teacher during class activities. Students' ideas, presented on paper or computer, are just as important. Annotated drawings and diagrams, sequenced drawings, structured writing, and personal logs are encouraged. A more complete description of ways to bring out students' prior knowledge is found in Chapter 9.

3. Communication is important, particularly during the Invention phase of a learning cycle when students are guided to construct a new concept or reconstruct an existing one. Students present their ideas to others and learn to appreciate the ideas of other students and the teacher. Often, small group discussion challenges students to find evidence for their ideas. Large group discussions bring a number of ideas together for consideration.

4. During the activity and discussion process of the Invention phase of the learning cycle, students experience many examples and non-examples of the concept and are encouraged to explore for themselves all the characteristics and aspects of each concept. Don't present ready-made concepts and expect students to understand them without some time in which to construct their own meaning.

5. The value of the concept presented by the teacher is made evident through expansion, the last phase of the learning cycle. Students use the new concepts to make sense of a variety of new experiences. Through reflection, the consideration of observations and communication, students realize the usefulness of the new concepts in interpreting the world around them.

TEACHING CONCEPTS USING THE LEARNING CYCLE

Concept learning requires students to relate new knowledge to prior knowledge, apply the new knowledge, become aware of all of its important characteristics through many examples and non-examples, and have sufficient application practice so that it is used appropriately and automatically. The learning cycle accomplishes these necessary steps, motivating students to learn the new concept so it is well understood.

Applying What You Know

Analyzing a Learning Cycle Focused on Concept Development

Read the *Classroom Scenes* feature that follows and answer the following questions related to teaching science concepts:

1. What key concept and sub-concepts are the primary focus of this lesson?

(continued)

2. Describe the concept and sub-concepts in terms of level and appropriateness of match for these students.
3. List examples and non-examples provided in the lesson.
4. List at least two important characteristics of each concept given in the lesson.
5. What part of this anecdote represents the Exploration phase of the learning cycle?
6. What part of this anecdote represents the Invention phase of the learning cycle?
7. What part of this anecdote represents the Expansion phase of the learning cycle?
8. What type of assessment record is appropriate for this lesson? (Refer to Chapter 4.)
9. How would you assess the progress of Makisha's and Benjie's groups? (Refer to Chapter 4.)

CLASSROOM SCENES

Characteristics of Natural Watersheds

On Tuesday, students in Mrs. Washington's fourth-grade classroom at Crestmont Elementary School brought in empty half-gallon cardboard milk cartons and gallon plastic milk containers. At the beginning of the science lesson, Mrs. Washington asked the students to get into their usual science groups and assign each other roles as follows: reporter, checker, spokesperson, materials person, and observer. She asked the materials person from each group to come to the tables in the front of the room and pick up three cardboard milk containers, three plastic milk containers, three funnels, two measuring cups, and a felt marking pen.

To get them started, Mrs. Washington asked the key question: "What determines how fast and how much water gets into our rivers after a heavy rainstorm?" Then she told the students, "Knowing this might help us predict when and where flooding conditions will happen." Following small group discussions, several students made reports. Jose said, "Flooding will happen when there is lots of heavy rain." Raising her hand excitedly, Makisha said flooding usually happens "in streets near the river." Ann lives on a hill in an area surrounded by trees and said, "Even when it rains really hard, I don't see water around on the ground." Benjie, remembering a previous lesson where students investigated soils and the amount of water they can hold, said, "People living where the dirt is dark probably won't get flooded because it soaks up more water than other kinds of dirt." Mrs. Washington summarized the students' comments by writing their reasons on the board.

She then asked the students to focus on two ideas: "Does the number of plants or amount of vegetation covering a soil affect how much water runs off of it and how fast it runs off?" "Does the steepness of a hill affect how much and how fast water runs off a hill?" She asked three of the six groups to investigate the first problem and the other groups to investigate the second problem. The students were told to:

> Use the materials you collected earlier to find an answer for your group's problem. I have brought pieces of soil that are the same size and have different amounts of vegetation. They are in boxes in the back of the room. Each one has a label: *thick grass, little grass,* or *no grass.*

Then Mrs. Washington pointed out that each of the cardboard milk cartons had a hole cut out in one side and one side completely cut out so that they could put in different soil pieces. The students were told to use the plastic milk containers to collect the water for their investigation. Mrs. Washington asked whether there were any questions before they began their investigation.

The student groups began discussing their problem and finding ways to test out their predictions of the effects of vegetation or slope on running water. For example, Makisha's group was investigating vegetation and decided that, if they put one of each type of soil in their three cardboard milk containers, they could determine how much water came through the soils. Benjie's group investigated slope. They put different soils in each of the three milk containers and put a different number of books under one end of the cartons to make different sloping hills. All the student groups designed experiments to test out a solution to their problem. They recorded their actions, the amounts of water they added, and the amount of water that drained out.

Mrs. Washington asked the three groups investigating each problem to get together, share what they did, and talk about what happened. In their groups, students noted that when water was sprinkled over the container it flowed from various areas and collected at fewer spots until it reached the drain point. Mrs. Washington provided them with the label "watershed" to describe areas that contribute to where water collects in an area (as in a stream or lake). She then asked the materials person to return the materials. Each group cleaned up its workplace.

The group working with each problem talked about the conclusions they reached. The spokesperson from Makisha's group reported that the amount of plants in the soil made a difference in how much water came through the soil. Therefore, the amount of plants makes a difference in a watershed. Benjie's group reported the higher slopes had more water draining through the soil.

Mrs. Washington asked the spokesperson in each group to go to the board and write down their group's results with regard to water runoff. She then asked the other students whether they had questions they wanted to ask Makisha's and Benjie's groups about what they did and what they found out. Mrs. Washington provided closure by stating that places called watersheds are different depending on the amount and kind of plants that grow on the soil and the hilliness of the soil. The more plants or vegetation an area has, the smaller the rate of water runoff following a rainstorm. This keeps more water in the soil for the plants to use and allows time for more water to evaporate into the air, providing some protection against flooding in heavy rainstorms. There are watersheds with lots of vegetation and some with little vegetation. Also, when rain falls on steep hills, more water goes into the rivers below. People building homes at the bottom of large hills near creeks or rivers need to be watchful in heavy rainstorms. There are hilly watersheds and flatter watersheds.

Mrs. Washington asked the groups to discuss the questions, "What would happen if all of the water that fell on the ground in a rainstorm went into the river?" "Does this ever happen?" Following the students' group discussions and a general class discussion of the question, Mrs. Washington asked each group to draw two watersheds: one drawing to show a watershed where it would be dangerous to build a home, and a second drawing to show a watershed where someone would rarely have a problem with flooding, with a descriptive explanation written to describe the drawings. The materials collector from each group collected the drawings, narratives, and art materials at the end of the lesson.

The next day, Mrs. Washington took the students out on the school grounds for a fifteen-minute field trip. They visited three different locations, discussing whether they saw evidence of water in the drainage area and relating what they saw to the lesson they had learned the previous day.

Source: D. Sunal (1992). Natural watersheds. Natural Resources Education Series. Parsons, W. V.: U.S. Department of Agriculture, U.S. Forest Service.

What concept might be emphasized using these materials with a young child? With an older student?

THE HIERARCHY OF CONCEPTS THROUGH DIFFERENT GRADE LEVELS

Concepts provide structure for science content in elementary and middle school lessons. The science program in kindergarten and primary grade classrooms begins with preoperational concepts and early inquiry skills in many science areas. Creative repetition and transfer across all science content areas are necessary for the skills and knowledge to become automatic. See Figure 5-6 for examples of energy concepts addressed at different concept levels.

During later elementary grades and middle school, science lessons emphasize concrete concepts in conjunction with the inquiry skills necessary to develop meaningful learning of the concepts. Lessons begin with concrete concepts and move toward the introduction of experiences relating to the attainment of formal concepts.

Applying What You Know

Reflecting on Your Earlier Ideas

Return to the *Exploring Your Ideas* activity on magnets at the beginning of the chapter. Reread the sample fourth-grade textbook passage and answer the questions below.

1. Identify which statements are facts.
2. Identify which statements are concepts.
3. Identify statements that are procedures or other information about the science content.

4. Identify the statements you consider part of the science content every student should understand and for which lessons are planned to create meaningful learning.

---

1. Statements 1, 9, and 10 are factual statements and should not be memorized by students. They provide facts to build the concept *magnet*.
2. Statements 2, 3, 4, 5, 6, 7, 8, 14, 15, and 16 are concepts or descriptions of properties of a concept. Only two concepts are introduced in the passage: *magnets* and *steel*.
3. Statements 11, 12, 13, 17, 18, 19, and 20 are procedures or other information about the science content.
4. Students should understand the concept *magnet* and the properties of the concepts that distinguish it from others. These statements are 2, 3, 4, 5, 6, 14, 15, and 16. This concept is important for students to understand and is included as part of what the National Science Education Standards (1996, page 127) identify as science standards for grades K-4.

Preoperational concepts relating to *sound, light, heat,* and *mechanical energy*.

1. Observe the presence or absence of different types of energy.
   Observe on and off (lights, water, machines).
   Observe pushes and pulls.
   Observe hot and cold.
   Observe sound and no sound.

2. Classify energy types according to the sense used to observe its characteristics.
   Observe effects of current and static electricity.
   Observe the different forms of light.
   Observe the effects of mechanical energy.
   Observe the effects of heat.
   Observe the effects of sound.

3. Observe sources and non-sources of energy.
   Observe sources of mechanical energy (cars, trucks, toys, simple machines).
   Observe sources of electricity (lightning, outlets, batteries, static).
   Observe sources of sound.
   Observe sources of heat.
   Observe sources of light (lamp, sun, fire, lightbulb).

4. Classify into two groups, within energy type, observed characteristics (relative).
   Classify by fast and slow.
   Observe shadows.
   Classify by light and dark, bright and dim.
   Classify by hot and cold.
   Classify by loud and soft (auditorily, tactually, visually).

FIGURE 5-6 *Hierarchy of energy concepts through different grade levels*

5. Observe the proper use of energy forms.

Observe safety procedures in relation to all forms of energy.

Observe conservation measures in relation to all forms of energy.

Transition to concrete concepts relating to *sound, light, heat, mechanical, electrical,* **and** *chemical energy.*

1. Classify objects in everyday living by the type of energy used.

Identify sources of heat (stove, sun, fire, friction).

Identify objects that make sound.

Observe chemical reactions (vinegar, baking soda, chemical garden).

Identify sources of electricity (outlets, batteries, rubbing, hand generator).

Identify gross sounds in the environment (trucks).

Identify objects that use mechanical energy (toys, simple machines, and so on).

Identify more sources of light (flashlight, moon, star, and so on).

2. Classify according to energy receivers and producers.

Identify objects, appliances, and equipment that use different types of energy.

Identify objects, appliances, and equipment that produce energy.

3. Demonstrate a simple system which produces each type of energy.

Experience the use of different forms of energy.

4. Classify, in a variety of ways, the characteristics of energy types.

Observe the behavior of instruments that measure energy (thermometers, meters).

Classify high and low sounds (auditorily, tactually, visually).

Classify temperature (hot, warm, cold).

Classify hues and shades of colors (light, bright, dark, dull, shiny, tan, gray, and so on).

Classify the effects of electricity.

5. Measure the relative degree of energy present in a system.

Classify substances by temperature (hot, cold, warm, cool).

6. Observe different characteristics of energy transmission.

Observe conductors and insulators of electricity.

Classify various opaque, translucent, and transparent materials.

Observe conductors and insulators of heat.

Observe objects that reflect light and images (metal, mirror).

7. Demonstrate the proper use of energy forms.

Demonstrate safety procedures.

Demonstrate conservation procedures.

Concrete concepts relating to *sound, light, heat, mechanical, electrical, chemical,* **and** *nuclear energy.*

1. Classify characteristics of energy transmission for each form of energy.

Classify good and poor conductors and insulators of heat.

Classify good and poor conductors and insulators of electricity.

Observe sound traveling through solids, liquids, and gases.

2. Observe energy transformation between different types of energy.

Investigate the transformation of energy (heat to light, sound to mechanical, mechanical to electrical, fuel to heat, chemical to heat).

Identify the transformation of energy in objects in everyday living.

FIGURE 5-6 *Continued*

3. Measure degrees of energy present, using the metric system (construct instruments).

   Measure the freezing and boiling temperatures of water.

   Observe the use and function of an audiometer and an audiogram.

   Measure sound in decibels.

4. Observe and order characteristics within each energy type.

   Observe the colors of light broken down by a prism.

   Investigate that sound travels in waves.

   Investigate vibration and its relation to sound.

   Classify differences between static, current, and potential energies.

5. Construct and observe energy systems and their components.

   Discriminate between simple open and closed circuits.

   Construct systems that produce shadows.

   Construct and investigate three simple machines (lever, wheel, inclined plane).

   Classify objects in everyday living according to their functions within an energy system.

   Construct an electromagnet.

   Construct simple electrical systems.

   Construct simple sound systems.

   Construct simple heat systems.

   Construct light systems using lenses and mirrors.

6. Predict the outcome of an arrangement of components in an energy system.

   Predict how the placement of the light source affects the shadow produced.

   Investigate objects that reflect light and images (metals, mirrors).

7. Identify the improper use of energy forms.

   Demonstrate the improper use of environmental materials.

   Demonstrate improper safety procedures.

Transition to formal concepts relating to *sound, light, heat, mechanical, electrical, chemical,* and *nuclear energy.*

1. Construct combinations of simple energy systems (transmission, transformation).

   Predict the outcomes of different types of circuitry (series, parallel).

   Plan and investigate characteristics of light (heat producing, travels in a straight line, can be reflected or refracted, absorption, black as the absence of light, white as the presence of all light).

   Plan and investigate the nature of transformation of energy within systems.

   Construct and investigate electrical systems with multiple components (telegraph, electromagnet).

   Plan and investigate lenses (concave, convex) and mirrors (plane, curved).

   Plan and investigate the nature of energy systems in terms of conduction and insulation.

   Plan and investigate how sound travels (waves; rarefaction; compression; molecules; reverberation; through solids, liquids, gases).

2. Observe and analyze simple energy systems in everyday life, including their components, transformation, and generation (flashlights, toys, firecrackers, telegraph).

   Investigate vocal production in terms of intensity and pitch (talking, singing, yelling).

   Investigate the properties of electricity (static, AC, DC, batteries).

3. Classify simple energy systems by measuring degrees of energy present.

   Measure the properties of electricity (static, AC, DC, volts, amperes, ohms).

FIGURE 5-6   *Continued*

137

Measure quantities of heat in systems.

Measure the properties of light (spectrum, X-ray, ultraviolet, gamma, cosmic, laser, candle power).

Measure expansion and constriction of substances.

Measure freezing and boiling temperatures of various substances.

4. Predict the quantitative effect of arrangement of components in everyday energy systems.

Investigate sources of heat.

Investigate sources of sound (traffic, music, body sounds).

Investigate sources of light (electric bulbs, flames, fluorescent materials).

Investigate sources of electricity (different size batteries, different types of batteries—e.g., wet cell with lower and dissimilar metal pieces).

5. Evaluate and make judgments about the proper and improper use of energy systems.

Formulate safety measures for the use of energy.

Formulate conservation measures for the use of environmental materials.

FIGURE 5-6   *Continued*

SUMMARY

Concepts are a basic component of science content taught in classrooms. Although factual information is necessary for forming concepts, science content is not acquired by memorizing facts. Teachers planning science lessons identify and distinguish between the concepts they teach. Different instructional methods are used to teach different concepts to students. Most concepts have more than one level of meaning and may be "preoperational," "concrete," and "formal," depending on the methods used in classroom instruction. Thus, temperature as read on a thermometer is a "concrete" concept, while temperature as a measure of the average molecular kinetic energy is a "formal" concept. Before being classified, a concept must be clearly defined. All concepts are abstract because they are abstracted from many specific instances and examples.

Teachers use what they know about their students' ideas, and encourage students to talk about their ideas. When students have expressed their own ideas, learning activities help test them out. Four conditions need to exist to help students discard old beliefs and accept a new idea based on real world facts:

1. A student must be dissatisfied with his existing idea.
2. Any new concept must be comprehensible to the student through the introduction of all important characteristics essential to the understanding of the concept.
3. A new concept must appear as plausible as the student's own alternative conception.
4. A new concept or explanation has to be more useful for making sense of the environment than the previously held belief.

The learning cycle helps students become aware of their prior knowledge; fosters cooperative learning and a safe, positive, learning environment; compares new alternatives to prior knowledge; connects new ideas to what students already know; and helps students construct their own "new" knowledge and apply it in ways that are different from the situation in which it was learned.

The Content of Science:
Constructing Generalizations

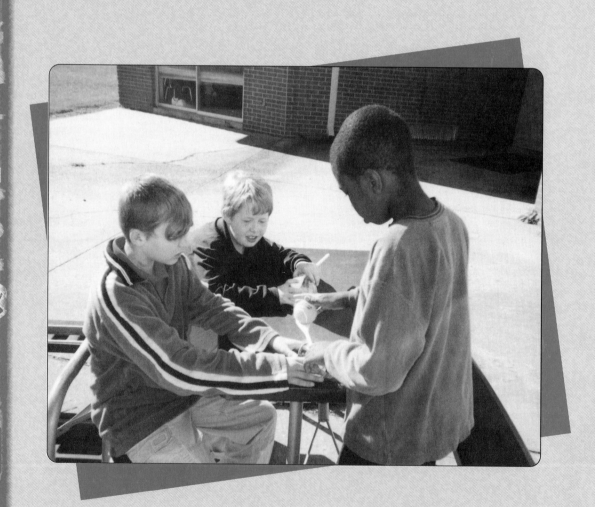

▼▲▼ EXPLORING YOUR IDEAS ▼▲▼▲▼▲▼▲▼▲▼▲▼

In addition to concepts, textbooks contain other important science content statements called generalizations. Can you identify these statements? How are they useful for building scientific literacy? What determines the type of activities that encourage knowledge growth through generalizations? Read the sample third-grade science textbook passage below on the properties of matter. Use the numerals next to the statements to identify generalizations for which science lessons should be planned:

> (1) Have you ever made sugar water? (2) How did you make it? (3) First, you got some water. (4) Then, you mixed the sugar into the water with a spoon. (5) Did the sugar stay on top of the water? (6) Did it sink to the bottom? (7) It sunk to the bottom. (8) You had to mix it into the water with a spoon. (9) After you mixed it up you couldn't tell the water from the sugar. (10) The sugar dissolved in the water. (11) When something mixes with a liquid so that you cannot tell the two things apart, something has dissolved. (12) You add sugar to water to make it sweet. (13) Would it be easier to dissolve the sugar in warm water? (14) The tiny pieces of sugar mix more easily with warm water. (15) They don't mix as easily with cold water. (16) A solution is a mixture formed by dissolving a solid or a liquid in another liquid. (17) Sugar water is a solution. (18) Ocean water is also a solution. (19) It has a lot of salt dissolved in it.

Discuss the passage and your responses to the following questions with a peer:

- What did you conclude about science content in the passage?
- Which statement(s) is a science generalization in the passage?
- Which generalization statement(s) should be selected as a goal for a science lesson?
- What activities should be used to encourage learning of the science generalization(s) you identified?

We will return to this passage at the end of the chapter for additional reflection.

Chapter Objectives

1. Describe the role of generalizations in science content.
2. Suggest appropriate activities for an inquiry lesson that teaches a generalization.
3. Describe the teacher's role in an inquiry lesson developing a generalization.
4. Describe how the process of developing and revising generalizations is continuous.
5. Describe the thought processes used to construct generalizations to solve everyday problems.

THE EXPLORATION PHASE OF THIS LEARNING CYCLE: HELPING YOU CONSTRUCT YOUR IDEAS ABOUT TEACHING GENERALIZATIONS

Scientists involved in scientific inquiry search for patterns of change and relationships in nature, thereby forming generalizations that become the content of scientific knowledge (Martin, Sexton, Wagner, & Gerlovich, 1997; Schwab, 1974). The most useful and powerful ideas in science content are generalizations. They enable us to explain the processes and events we experience. Generalizations are often explanations of cause and effect that allow the prediction of future events. Generalizations develop from inferences about many observations. They also arise from results gained from testing hypotheses. A generalization provides more information than a concept statement because statements of generalizations describe two or more concepts and the relationship among them. It is necessary to actively help students construct meaningful generalizations.

This chapter involves the reader in activities that enhance the understanding of scientific content. In order to accomplish this goal, it is organized as a learning cycle. You will be working through the learning cycle as you read the chapter and perform the activities.

Before formal schooling starts, students construct alternative or inaccurate generalizations from their limited experience with the physical world (Driver, Leach, Millar, & Scott, 1996). For example, a student might construct the generalization, "Heat and cold are things that enter substances and flow from place to place." This generalization leads to statements such as, in the winter, "Cold is coming through the crack under the door," and in the summer, "Close the door, you are letting the cold out." Often, early reasoning patterns allow students to form alternative generalizations from single experiences; for example, "The metal of a bike's handlebar is colder than the plastic grip." Other alternative generalizations are formed from analogies made from seemingly related events, from statements of adults, or from information gathered from the mass media (Thagard, 1992). Many students, for example, think that a thermostat regulating the furnace is similar to a faucet. Students note that, "The more one turns the handle of a faucet, the greater the amount of water that comes out." Therefore, the students inappropriately apply this generalization to heat and a thermostat and decide that "turning a thermostat to 10 or 15 degrees above the desired temperature will make the house heat faster than simply setting it to the desired temperature." Science experiences in school provide students with a great number of opportunities to help them investigate relationships in the physical world, construct generalizations through experiencing the interaction between concepts, and develop the knowledge and skills needed in reconstructing existing generalizations they brought into the classroom.

Let's begin our consideration of how to help students construct generalizations by completing the exploration activity presented below in the *Applying What You Know* feature below.

Applying What You Know

Exploring Your Ideas about a Generalization

Patterns in Paper Planes

Answer the following questions:

Why can planes fly? _____

What helps planes fly better? _____

One possible generalization is, "The lighter its weight, the better an airplane will fly." The activities below are designed to help you investigate and understand the predictive quality of this generalization with paper airplanes.

For this activity, use a sheet of paper, 8 1/2 by 11 inches, and three to six paper clips. Construct a paper airplane by folding the sheet of paper in half. Then lay the folded piece down, pick up one corner away from the first fold, and fold this corner so that one side of the paper lays on the first folded edge. Repeat this operation a second time with the same corner. Repeat this corner folding on the other side of the paper.

When you have completed your paper airplane, gently throw it part of the way across the room with a small force, enough to allow the plane to sail only several feet. Mark the distance the plane flew with a small piece of paper labeled "Trial 1." Now, attach a paper clip to the "nose" of the paper airplane. Gently throw the airplane across the room again with the same force. Mark the distance the plane flew with a small piece of paper labeled "Trial 2." Attach a second paper clip to the airplane. Gently throw the airplane across the room again, with the same force used in Trial 1. Mark the distance the plane flew with a small piece of paper labeled "Trial 3." Now, try putting one or two paper clips on the paper airplane in different locations. You might try one wing, both wings, the tail, or one on front and one in back.

Record your data:

How far did the paper airplane fly with no added weight? _____ .

Collect some additional information:

- How far did the paper airplane fly with one added paper clip on the
  a. front? _____ .
  b. side? _____ .
  c. back? _____ .
- How far did the paper airplane fly with two added paper clips on
  a. the front and back (one on each)? _____ .
  b. one of the sides? _____ .
  c. the back? _____ .
- How far did the paper airplane fly with two added paper clips, one on
  a. the front? _____ .
  b. either side? _____ .
  c. the back with one on the side? _____ .

You may wish to try more than one trial for each above design. Also, you might try other experiments using three or more paper clips. Record the results of these new trials.

When you have completed all of your additional trials, describe the patterns you find among the variations in weight and the distance the paper airplane flew.

1. Does it help, in general, to add more weight? _____
   Why, what happens? _____
2. Is more weight always better? _____
3. Does adding weight to one part of the paper airplane always result in a greater distance flown? _____

(continued)

4. What combination of weights produced the greatest distance? _____

_____

5. Make a new generalization about weight and paper airplanes. _____

_____

6. Think about other paper airplanes, model airplanes that are unpowered gliders, and real, full-sized gliders people use to sail in the sky. Do you think weight
   and weight distribution are important in obtaining long-distance flights in
   these examples? _____

7. What could you say to people using these other non-paper gliders as the result
   of your activity above? _____

_____

8. State a generalization about the effects of the amount or location of weight on
   the flight performance of gliders. _____

_____

_____

In the activity above, you tried various combinations of weights on a paper airplane.
Then you tried to identify whether the amount of the weight or the location of the
weight made a difference in the distance the plane flew. You were then asked to combine both the weight and location and determine what combination produced the
greatest flight distance in the airplane. You were then asked to suggest possible combinations of weight or location of weight useful for non-paper airplane gliders. To
do this, you probably used some of the information you collected in your activity
with paper airplanes. Finally, an answer to a problem was attempted when you were
asked to "explain the effects of the amount and location of weight on the flight performance of gliders." Actually, two generalizations could be developed to explain
the events, one with weight and flight performance and the other with weight, location, and flight performance.

In a lesson constructing a generalization, a *problem* or *question* is presented or
asked. Questions are raised in the learner's mind by having students interact with
data related to the topic during the Exploration phase. Teachers help students identify questions by using several strategies. Teachers can put students in a discrepant
event situation where information they acquire sets up some conflict or raises a
question. First-hand observations of objects or events also provide an intrinsic motivation that can lead to a sense of conflict and raise questions. This is different from
the extrinsic motivation provided to learners when they are asked to memorize generalizations. Student involvement in hands-on activities requires them to recall information they already have. They often find their prior knowledge isn't sufficient
to resolve the conflict they are experiencing or to answer their questions. The activity encourages students to organize the information they have in a more systematic way to determine whether it is sufficient.

In this Exploration, you collected the data by investigating paper airplane flight.
At the end of the Exploration, a tentative answer to a problem on flight performance
was attempted. It was a problem arising naturally from the activity with which you
were involved.

What happens to the length of the flight when more weight is added?

THE INVENTION PHASE OF THIS LEARNING CYCLE: HELPING YOU CONSTRUCT YOUR IDEAS ABOUT TEACHING GENERALIZATIONS

Generalizations

Generalizations describe a relationship between two or more concepts. They are reconstructed as students gain more experience with concepts. The form of instruction designed to help students construct meaning and learn generalizations is typically called "inquiry learning." Distinguishing generalization statements from other statements is critical in determining the appropriate instructional strategy. Science experiences with generalizations as outcomes begin with primary-age students. Exploration and investigation are possible in most science areas. However, generalization-constructing inquiry lessons make up a *major* part of the science program with older students since they have the mental capacity, skills, and concepts necessary to work effectively with generalizations.

It is important to select and teach appropriate ideas that help students construct meaningful generalizations (Bianchini, 1998; Songer & Linn, 1991). These are concrete rather than abstract, and macroscopic rather than microscopic. Generalizations are "big" ideas that are quantitative as well as qualitative. Generalizations are general statements that:

- are different from facts and concepts.
- identify relationships between two or more concepts.
- give explanations of cause and effect.
- predict a future occurrence of the relationship stated in the generalization. (Driver et al., 1996; Eggen & Kauchak, 1988, p. 58; Greenwood, 1996)

In the discussion below, a third-grade student named Jennifer uses both concepts and a generalization to describe an experience:

> My dog knows where to find his food in the morning. He meets me at the door when I come home from school. He comes when you call his name. He goes far down the street sometimes,

but always finds his way back home. He barks when someone comes to the door and plays with me without hurting me. Dogs know a lot. They must be pretty smart.

Jennifer uses several concepts, including *dog, food, morning, meet, door,* and *street,* as well as others. These concepts summarize Jennifer's experiences with each of these events and items. Jennifer also makes a generalization that goes further than the concepts with which she is working. She relates her pet's actions and skills in many areas to the intelligence of the animal.

Distinguishing Generalizations from Facts and Concepts

Since goals for science lessons can be facts, concepts, or generalizations, teachers make distinctions between them. The choice of instructional strategy in a science lesson is matched to the type of statement selected as the learning goal. Sometimes people mistake generalizations for facts. For example, "The sun rises in the east" is a generalization for two reasons:

1. The statement wasn't formed from one observation alone. We may have seen the sun coming up in the morning. We may have noted the direction. However, we have not seen the sun rise every day, on cloudy days, or from many different locations on Earth. The statement is a summarization, not a report of a single event.
2. The statement involves two concepts and a relationship. Predictions of future occurrences can be made from the statement. These characteristics distinguish it from a concept statement. (Eggen & Kauchak, 1988; Seiger-Ehrenberg, 1991)

We make inferences from experiences we have had and generalize them to include all possible examples. If tested through predictions (or better still, by using hypotheses to gather data), the resulting conclusion is a generalization.

Observations made after adding weight to a paper airplane might lead you to state and test the hypothesis, "The greater the weight added, the straighter the plane will fly." Because you have not seen all possible cases, you generalized from what you did see to make a statement. For that reason, your statement is a generalization from what was observed. You agree with the statement because you have not observed a contradictory case. If a contradictory case eventually is observed, the generalization can be changed. For instance, putting weight on only one wing might cause the paper airplane to fly in a circular path. You would have to reconstruct the generalization to become more confident in making predictions about the flight path of the paper airplane.

Which of the following do you think is a generalization? "The water is cold." "Freezing means to change from a liquid to a solid." "Cooling causes liquids to become solids." The first statement is a fact. The second is a concept statement. The third statement is a generalization since it is not formed from observation alone. It attempts to explain the effect and predicts a possible future occurrence.

How Are Generalizations Used to Predict?

Generalizations are used to organize facts and concepts as they summarize them and describe the relationships among them. Once the organization occurs and a generalization is formed, it can be used to make predictions of actions and events. Using the generalization about "the sun rises in the east," we can predict the location of the sunrise.

Generalizations can be a starting point that leads to the creation of a hypothesis and a test. If we live in a house facing east and have houses directly across the street, we should be able to predict the month when the sun will be seen between two of the houses. We may observe many sunrises and find that the sun does not rise exactly in the east on most days. For example, each day from October to December, the sun rises farther and farther to the south of due east. The sun rises the farthest south of due east on December 21st of each year. Only around March 21st and September 21st does the sun rise directly in the east. The results of our data collection may lead us to change our original hypothesis and create a new generalization.

Using the new generalization, "The sun rises south of due east every day from September 21st to March 21st," what prediction can be made about the location of the sun in the early morning sky next December? In late November 2 years from now? On a date in February 25 years from now? Using this generalization, you could more confidently predict that the sun will be in the southeast sky in the early morning at each of these times.

The predictive ability of generalizations is important because being able to predict events and actions gives us some control over our lives. Science education helps students learn to predict, understand, and control events in their lives. Their chances of survival in a difficult environment, whether it is an urban or rural one, are increased. Success in understanding or minimizing everyday problems leads to less anxiety, greater satisfaction in daily routines, and the potential ability to help others. Teachers help students form generalizations about their everyday environment and use them to make predictions that will affect their daily lives. They also help students discover inaccuracies in the generalizations they have formed and reconstruct them so that they have better predictive value.

Types of Generalizations

Generalizations have different levels of acceptance by people. For example, they can describe a simple relationship among a few concepts with only limited explanatory and/or predictive power. The statement, "The greater the weight added to a paper airplane, the straighter the plane will fly," is a generalization for which we can find exceptions. This generalization is not accepted as accurate without common exceptions. Generalizations exist at different levels of accuracy. Some are best called simple generalizations. Other generalizations are highly complex and relate many concepts, show complex relationships, and/or make predictions with a higher degree of certainty or accuracy, and a greater degree of confidence. These are laws, principles, and theories. For example, "The sun can be seen in the western sky in the early evening, local time," is a generalization that can be accepted as accurate and with confidence for people living in temperate and equatorial latitudes.

The difference between a law, principle, and theory is its generalizability and predictability. Laws, principles, and theories are types of generalizations. A **law** is a generalization that applies to all members of a broad class of phenomena. A **principle** is highly general, or fundamental, and laws are derived from it. A **theory** is an explanation of events based on laws, principles, and known consequences of other phenomena. Examples of generalizations, laws, principles, and theories are:

"The time it takes for a pendulum to swing back and forth is related to its length."
  (generalization)
"Friction results in heat." (generalization)
"Different kinds of cells do different kinds of work." (generalization)

"The farther from the center, or fulcrum, one pushes down on a lever, the greater the weight that can be lifted on the other side of the lever." (generalization)

"A magnet is strongest at its poles." (generalization)

"Heating most liquids will cause them to boil." (generalization)

"The colder a liquid, the less evaporation will occur from its surface." (generalization)

"Like poles repel, unlike poles attract." (law of magnetism)

"An object will continue in straight-line motion at the same velocity unless a force acts on it." (law of motion)

"An object floating in a fluid displaces its own weight in fluid." (law of flotation)

"If a number of independent influences act on an object or system, the total influence is the sum of the individual influences acting alone." (principle of superposition)

"Global motion of continental crust plates results in continent formation and mountain building." (theory of plate tectonics)

"Explanation of the behavior of matter is based on the assumption that it is composed of large numbers of particles in constant motion." (kinetic theory)

Applying What You Know

Analyzing a Generalization

Students often memorize and use generalizations, laws, principles, and theories without knowledge of their origin, use, or areas of appropriate application. If students are to apply a generalization at the appropriate times, teachers must help them understand the concepts and relationships found in the generalization. Memorization of a generalization with little understanding of the concepts it includes is a limited type of learning. Students will not be able to use it or even judge when to apply it. Consider the generalization, "The rate of two touching wheels turning in is inversely proportional to the circumference of the two wheels."

1. Describe its meaning in your own words. A sketch may help.

2. What concepts do you think students have to know to understand it? _____

3. What skill(s) might they have to understand? _____

_____

1. A way to describe the generalization is: the larger the circumference of one wheel as compared to a second touching wheel, the greater the difference in the rate of turning of the two wheels. See Figure 6–1 for a sketch of the wheels. Using this sketch, another description could be given: Gear A turns two times every time Gear B turns once.
2. Concepts you might have identified include: rate, turning, inversely, proportional, circumference, and wheel.
3. A student needs skill in measuring and visualization to understand this generalization. Students: (1) have to understand how to measure circumference,

(2) need the spatial ability to imagine two wheels (or imaginary circles) rolling on each other, (3) have to visualize 360 degree rotation in the wheels, and (4) have to concretely perform the wheel action with real wheels at their desks. In middle school, students demonstrate the appropriate use of a ratio operation (Circumference #1 $\times$ Circumference #2 = Turning Rate of Wheel #1 $\times$ Turning Rate of Wheel #2).

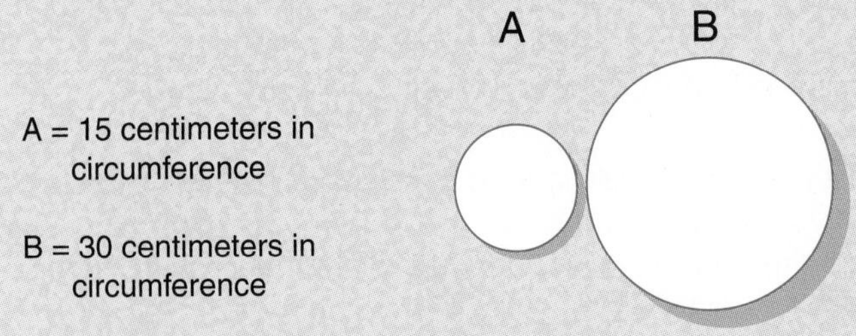

A = 15 centimeters in circumference

B = 30 centimeters in circumference

FIGURE 6-1   *Touching wheels with different circumferences*

The Learning Cycle: How Do We Teach Generalizations Meaningfully?

Generalizations are the most powerful form of science content for understanding and having some control over our physical environment. However, generalizations are the most difficult form of science content to learn. To meaningfully understand a generalization, a student must not only first develop an understanding of the concepts used in the generalization, but must repeatedly experience the relationship among these concepts, both physically and mentally. Repeated "playing" with the generalization is effective and necessary. Students need to find that changing one concept (variable) creates a change in the other concept. In the previous gear example, turning one gear that is touching a second gear and noticing their differing rotation rates needs to be related to gears of varying sizes before meaningful learning is accomplished. This is a time for checking poorly made predictions developed from prior knowledge against reality and modifying those predictions until the student comes up with a more adequate generalization.

A lesson focusing on a generalization begins with an Exploration activity in which a problem or question is identified directly or developed through student action. This is the first phase of the lesson. The complete learning cycle used in teaching a generalization consists of the student actions in the sequence described in Table 6–1.

To illustrate the use of the learning cycle with a generalization as the outcome, consider the following fourth- or fifth-grade sequence. The generalization involved was, "Heat causes liquids to evaporate." This example highlights National Science Education Standards A and B (National Research Council, 1996). For further information, visit the NSES website.

TABLE 6-1   *A learning cycle lesson plan format focused on a science generalization*

THE LEARNING CYCLE: TEACHING GENERALIZATIONS	
Phase	**Planning Required**
Exploration—	Help students try out, and confront, their prior knowledge of the science generalization. Provide an opportunity for students to identify a problem or question that is the focus of the lesson. Start students thinking with a "key" question that involves them in an activity. Encourage students working cooperatively in groups to relate prior knowledge to the problem or question. Bring out, and make public, students' prior knowledge of the problem or question.
Invention—	Ask students to investigate a science generalization as a response to the problem/question in the Exploration activities. Allow students to gather data (information) to provide evidence for a solution to their problem while exploring the generalization. Ask students to analyze the data and formulate a conclusion to their problem, comparing it to the generalization introduced earlier. Provide closure on important aspects of the new generalization.
Expansion—	Provide application activities for the science generalization in new, relevant contexts while at the same time helping students recall their original alternative explanations. Provide activities to help students transfer the new science generalization to increasingly real world events. Provide a summary of the important events in the science lesson leading to the new science generalization.

For further information, see the link to the NSES website on the Companion Website at
http://www.prenhall.com/sunal

CLASSROOM SCENES

Exploration

The teacher presents the students with a story related to the generalization:

> On a warm Saturday at 3:00 p.m., you and two friends were out at the park several miles from home. Your father planned to take you to the movie theater at 4:00 p.m. However, a surprise shower caught all of you out in the open. Your clothes got wet. If your dad picks you up soaking wet, he will take you home to get dry clothes. The movie showing starts at 4:10 p.m. There will not be enough time to go home to change your clothes and get to the theater in time to see the movie.

The teacher asks the class to discuss this story and come up with the *problem* facing these students. Group roles are assigned, and group reports are made.

Invention

The students are asked to plan, then write out, an investigation to determine whether their problem could be solved. To focus the problem, the teacher asks the students to consider ways they could get their clothes to dry quickly. Old clothing is available in the room for each group. After the student groups plan their investigation, they are encouraged to carry out the plan by gathering data. The students record the results of wetting various clothing items, such as socks, shirts, jeans, and shoes. They use various methods for drying. Some choose moving the items through the air. Others use a fan. Some use a space heater. Others use combinations of all three methods.

After collecting data, students analyze their records, comparing them with their original plan. They write a conclusion based on the evidence gathered, indicating whether the three students in the park could go to the movie.

The groups report their investigation and results to the class. Following the reports, the teacher leads a discussion as a closure to the invention of the generalization, "Heat causes water (liquids) to evaporate," which is that movement of air past a liquid increases evaporation by increasing the amount of energy available to the water and removing water vapor from the clothing's surface.

Expansion

The next day, the student groups are asked to work at learning stations throughout the room. Each station presents them with a problem to solve. The stations involve applying the generalization formed the day before about the relationship of heat and the evaporation rate. A different liquid is tested on cloth samples at each station: rubbing alcohol, cooking oil, and various solutions with water, gelatin, soy sauce, and milk.

The groups present their results and discuss them, applying the generalization. A take-home assignment is provided in writing, asking each student to involve a family member in an activity. Students and family members observe and identify processes that increase the evaporation rate, which takes place at home that evening.

The next day, students are asked to report the results of their home assignment to their group. Next, each group is asked to use these results, along with research in the library and on the Internet, to develop a report on how processes that increase the evaporation rate help us in our daily lives. Reports include processes occurring with clothes dryers, evaporative cooling for homes, cooking, baking, and ceiling fans. Each process is described in relation to the lesson generalization.

Asking Questions and Posing Problems

The question or problem developed in the Exploration phase is the starting point of a lesson whose outcome is a generalization. The question can be posed by the teacher or, more meaningfully, by the student or student group. Good questions stimulate students, making them take a closer look at something in their environment as in the above example (Spargo & Enderstein, 1997). Good questions lead to action with objects, events, or ideas. The question or problem focuses the student on a cause and its result, or on an explanation. Good questions often start out as general "what" questions, followed by more specific ones. General questions might include: "What happens?" "What do I see, hear, or feel?" "What does it do?" "What do you think?" "What happens if _____?" "How many?" "What group _____?" "Can you make _____?"

Poor first questions ask students about their knowledge of words or what the text or teacher said earlier. They make science the recall of information. Good first questions ask students to focus their observation on an event, pose problems, start actively collecting data, cause measuring or counting, lead to comparisons, and facilitate additional thinking.

In a discussion related to evaporating water, a later specific question may arise: "What sensations do you feel when you are wet?" This can be a problem leading to the construction of a generalization, particularly if it is developed further into a question such as, "Why do you feel cool when you are wet?" There are two important parts to this question: (1) the sensations one observes or feels, and (2) the reason for the sensations. Students describe the sensation they feel as coolness. Evaporation is the *cause* of the sensation of coolness. Coolness is a *result* of the evaporation. Thus:

$$\text{Evaporation} \rightarrow \text{Coolness}$$

$$\text{Cause} \rightarrow \text{Result}$$

When students feel the coolness, they search for the cause resulting in the coolness. This cause is called a variable. The variable can be changed. If your arm is wet and you feel a coolness as the wetness evaporates, you can put a thick towel around the wet arm, which will reduce the rate of evaporation, and the arm will not feel so cool.

A generalization relates concepts, such as *evaporation rate, coolness felt,* or *temperature,* in some way. In order to understand the relationship, the teacher helps students to separate out the concepts involved in the generalization and decide how they are related (cause and result). The relationship between the two concepts in this example is a direct one: the more of one (evaporation), the greater the other (coolness or change in temperature).

At this point, when students have investigated reducing the evaporation rate and the sensation of coolness on their arm, they can develop the generalization, "Evaporation of water causes cooling."

If the student cannot: (1) clearly identify the concepts, (2) determine which is the cause and which is the result, (3) identify the relationship in a generalization, and (4) actively engage in experiences and data involving the relationship, it is unlikely that the student will understand the generalization (Driver et al., 1996; Eggen, Kauchak, & Harder, 1979; Sutman, 1995). The teacher must be aware of the limitations hindering students' abilities to work through an inquiry and construct a generalization. These limitations include:

1. Poorly developed prior knowledge containing alternative conceptions and misconceptions of concepts.
2. The limited number of ideas they can hold in their short-term memory at one time.
3. Their need for help in addressing a question systematically.
4. Their need for concrete materials and experiences to try out *while* they are "thinking" through the process.

Before beginning the lesson, teachers think about these limitations in terms of the concepts involved in the problem or question, possible generalizations that could resolve the problem, and what kind of information students will need to collect to determine if their generalizations are supported by evidence.

Data Gathering

The Invention phase continues as students gather data, or information, on their problem/question. Teachers provide guidance by asking questions such as:

• What are some possible sources of information to be gathered?

What are some ways these students might record the information gathered?

- What methods will help us gather the most useful information (for example: direct observation, carrying out experiments, library and Internet research, surveys, interviews with individuals, or a combination of a few methods)?
- What materials and equipment will we need to carry out our planned investigation?
- Will the method we picked provide us with enough data (information) to check our problem or will we need to combine it with another method to gather some different data?
- How will we record and store the information obtained?
- How will we communicate the information obtained to others?
- How will we analyze the information we gathered?

Once students have decided how they will gather data or information, they are given enough time to do this. Some data gathering may be done out of school. Some in-school time is necessary, however, because students often need to discuss a next step in data gathering with their cooperative learning groups or they need advice on how to find and use a data source not considered earlier. As an example of data gathering, let's return to the question about the "sensation you feel when you are wet" and the generalization that "evaporation of water causes cooling." Students should be able to wet paper towels and pieces of cloth with water. They should let the water evaporate under three or more conditions: still air, blowing air gently with a hand fan, and using an electric fan to blow air. They will be able to determine, using thermometers, the conditions and relationships experienced in the generalization about evaporation and cooling.

As students gather data, they decide how to organize, classify, and categorize it. Data is presented in a way that allows it to be easily and clearly shared with others. Students might use tables, charts, graphs, bulletin boards, drawings, oral reports, written reports, dramatic skits, panel discussion, models, or demonstrations. Well-organized data enables students to more successfully use it to decide the level of confidence they have in a generalization. Poorly organized data collection or presentation is likely to be of little use. It may not display identifiable patterns, thereby encouraging false conclusions about the generalization.

THE EXPANSION PHASE OF THIS LEARNING CYCLE: HELPING YOU CONSTRUCT YOUR IDEAS ABOUT TEACHING GENERALIZATIONS

Teachers help students construct a usable generalization. They also help students understand that once they have a usable generalization, they need to apply it and transfer it to a variety of settings. It can be reconstructed later if they find it no longer addresses the data they have. For example, if students determined that a piece of candy dissolves more quickly in water at higher temperatures, they could test another sugar product or other soluble material such as salt. When they do this, they will be deciding whether their generalization is appropriate in another context. If it is not appropriate, they reconstruct their interpretation of the generalization based on the collected data.

Next, students consider the question, "Is our generalization always a good predictor?" Students decide how widely the generalization can be applied; for example, "Does all soluble matter dissolve more quickly at higher temperatures?" At this point, students can be asked to check how soluble gases stay dissolved in liquids. The test can involve taking three bottles of a soft drink beverage at three different temperatures: one cold, one room temperature, and one warmed in warm water. Put a transparent plastic bag around the bottle and your arm and unscrew the top while the bag is tightly closed around your arm with your hand inside the bag. Your observations will provide some limitations to the generalization about dissolving materials, "Gases dissolve less readily in liquids at higher temperatures." The students may decide that they can confidently say, "All soluble *solids* dissolve more quickly in liquids at higher temperatures." They may also decide that, although there is some evidence encouraging them to apply their generalization to still other situations, they need to collect more data before they can generalize beyond the materials they used. When students begin to apply a generalization, it is always necessary to encourage them to think about the limits present by asking the questions, "When is this generalization useful?" and "Does the generalization always make good predictions?"

Applying What You Know

Reflecting on Your Earlier Ideas

Return to the *Exploring Your Ideas* feature at the beginning of this chapter on properties of matter. Reread the sample third-grade textbook passage and respond to the following.

1. Which statement(s) is a generalization?
2. Which statement(s) is a concept?
3. Identify statements that are procedures or other information about the science content.
4. What activities should be used to encourage learning of the science generalization(s) identified?

1. Statements 14 and 15, taken together, form a generalization relating the temperature of water, mixing, and the solubility of solids forming a solution.
2. Statements 9, 10, and 11 identify, provide an example, and define the concept *dissolved*. Statements 16, 17, 18, and 19 identify, provide examples of, and define the concept *solution*. The concept statements are not complete. Only two concepts are introduced.
3. Statements 1 to 8 and 12 are procedures or other information about the science content.
4. Inquiry activities should be planned that involve students in a generalization learning cycle related to the solubility of solids and water at differing temperatures. Statement 13 attempts to involve students in such an activity. The problem must be identified by the students, an investigation must be planned and carried out, and results must be applied in several different settings. This generalization is important and is identified in the National Science Education Standards for grades K-4 (1996, page 12).

Evaluating the Inquiry Process

Students should be assisted in reviewing their investigative activities to determine which were productive and which could have been done differently. For example, some data sources may be very helpful while others are limited. Some ways of organizing data may be more effective than others. Evaluating their activities enables students to make better decisions, better direct their own learning, become more aware of their own thinking and planning, and become more dependent on internal rather than external reinforcement. This is important to teaching meaningful science and developing citizens who are independent judges and decision makers capable of performing the jobs of the 21st century.

Applying What You Know

Planning an Inquiry Lesson

Briefly describe an inquiry lesson focusing on a generalization that involves students in investigating a problem in their immediate environment. This may be some event that intrigues you in the topics of light or sound or some phenomenon in the biological or Earth science areas.

Lesson Objective: _____

Possible Student Alternative Conception: _____

Exploration Activity: _____

_____

_____

Problem or Question That Might Be Generated by the Exploration Activity: ___

_____

(continued)

Invention Activity: _____

_____

_____

Two Possible Sources or Activities from Which Data Might Be Gathered:

1. _____

2. _____

Closure: _____

Expansion Activity:

Application:_____

_____

Transfer:_____

_____

Lesson Summary: _____

_____

SUMMARY

The development of generalizations is a primary goal in elementary and middle school science teaching. It is the most powerful type of science content a student learns. Facts and concepts do not allow personal prediction. Only knowledge of generalizations provides meaningful predictions or control of events in our daily lives. In order to create meaningful learning, students must be able to interact with the concepts and relationships involved in a generalization in a relevant way. Generalizations are meaningfully understood only through active involvement. Such involvement is both physical and mental. It enables students to work with the data used to construct the generalization and to predict the outcome of a generalization. It is checked each time it is used.

In teaching generalizations, the three phases of the learning cycle help students identify a problem/question related to the generalization (Exploration), collect data with which to check the validity of the generalization and predict the results of the generalization (Invention), and either apply or transfer the use of the generalization to different contexts (Expansion). One important part of planning a generalization learning cycle is the inclusion of the significant step of checking the application of the generalization in a new situation during the Expansion phase. Students need to use generalizations they learn in a variety of situations if they are to stabilize them as a usable piece of knowledge. They also need to discover that a generalization they construct may not satisfactorily explain a different situation, their investigation did not use appropriate procedures or resources, or it needed additional or diverse information. Since the modern world involves students in complex situations and changing technologies, it is important that they use generalizations in a variety of situations and learn when they are appropriate and when they need to be reconstructed. If they are not able to do this, they will be less able to participate fully as scientifically literate citizens of the 21st century.

chapter 7

Teaching Science Meaningfully

▼▲▼ EXPLORING YOUR IDEAS ▼▲▼▲▼▲▼▲▼▲▼▲▼▲▼

Obtain a school's science textbook and review one chapter. Identify the science text-book and grade level. Pay particular attention to the "teaching" approach the textbook uses to develop a key science idea. Would you describe the approach as "hands-on" or not? Why? Discuss the results with others so that the teaching approaches of several science textbooks can be compared. What do you conclude about the science text-books' approaches to learning science?

Chapter Objectives

1. Describe the knowledge dimensions of effective science teaching.
2. Describe effective pedagogical strategies in helping students construct meaningful science learning outcomes.
3. Describe and evaluate the effective use of cooperative group learning in a science lesson.
4. Describe and evaluate the teacher's role in science lessons focusing on fact acquisition, concept attainment, understanding generalizations, and developing inquiry skills.
5. Describe the potential effects of varying the amount of teacher control over a lesson's activities on science learning outcomes.
6. Describe important areas to be addressed in an effective classroom management plan for teaching science content or inquiry skills.
7. Describe and evaluate science safety for a classroom lesson in a specific science area (e.g., electricity, plants, or animals).

WHAT PEDAGOGICAL KNOWLEDGE IS IMPORTANT FOR EFFECTIVE SCIENCE TEACHING?

There are three dimensions of effective teaching in science. Each is important in planning for science teaching with elementary and middle school students. First, there are a number of general characteristics appropriate for effective teaching in any setting and subject. An example is using wait-time when asking and answering students' questions. This dimension is termed *pedagogical knowledge.*

See Chapter 13 for a discussion of how to teach the concept of heat.

In addition to these characteristics, an effective science teacher uses strategies that work well with science content and inquiry skills. For example, most students confuse the concepts of *temperature* and *heat.* If this problem is not addressed in a science lesson on heat, students will complete the lesson unable to understand and cope with everyday life and laboratory-related problems, which range from efficient use of air conditioning and heating controls in homes to the appropriate selection of insulation for homes, clothing, and appliances.

Such teaching requires knowledge of specific methods that go beyond general classroom teaching. This second dimension is called *science pedagogical knowledge.*

A third dimension of knowledge for which a foundation is needed is *science content knowledge.* For example, knowing that "energy" is not a physical substance but rather a means of accounting for the way changes take place in objects and events allows for science teaching that creates less confusion and misconceptions about the physical world. This chapter focuses on pedagogical and science pedagogical knowledge, which are both important for the effective teaching of science.

In general, the effective teacher is one whose students end up possessing at least the knowledge, skills, and attitudes judged to be appropriate for those students. Effective classrooms require teachers who foster learning to the extent that most of their students learn most of what they are supposed to learn (Berliner, 1987b; Roth, 1996, 1997). Educational research has identified a number of factors associated with good teaching in an effective classroom. These factors include *clarity, variety, task orientation, student engagement, questioning,* and *cooperative learning.* Each factor is important for all phases of the learning cycle.

What Is Clarity?

Clarity, or clear instruction, has many components (Jacobowitz, 1997). Effective teachers provide directions that students can understand and follow. It is especially important to provide a focus before and during students' hands-on activities. The experiences in which students are involved are relevant and relate to their prior knowledge. Students know about the general learning procedure and outcomes of the lesson, so they are more self-directed in their learning. The lesson begins by relating new knowledge to students' prior knowledge. Its organization allows students to develop more control over their own learning by providing regular opportunities for interaction, feedback, and self-evaluation. The lesson revisits science content several times in different formats.

What Is Variety?

Effective lessons are planned and taught with experiences that gain students' attention (Jacobowitz, 1997). Teachers who display enthusiasm, use a variety of question types, and incorporate student ideas are especially effective in holding students' attention. Effective lessons involve as many learning modalities as possible. Reading about a topic alone is not sufficient. Using a hands-on activity alone is not generally effective either. The combination of hands-on activities, student discussion, reading, teacher questioning, school grounds field trips, inquiry activities, group problem solving, and writing journals brings the whole lesson together so that meaningful learning of an important idea or skill occurs.

What Is Task Orientation?

Lesson planning and teacher actions carried out in the classroom influence the task orientation of students. Educational research has shown that classrooms vary greatly in the amount of time and emphasis devoted to specific educational goals (Berliner, 1987a; Perie, 1997). Weekly averages ranging from 5 to 60 minutes per day for science in the same school are not uncommon. Scientific literacy for all students requires involvement for a significant amount of time each day at every grade level. Effective teachers manage and reduce interruptions, plan for transitions between topics, organize materials distribution and return, and are aware of efficient techniques for managing student traffic flow. Science lessons involve cycles of active learning and feedback, build on one another, and lead to the unit focus. They accomplish local curriculum goals and address national science education standards.

What Is Student Engagement?

Effective classrooms create and sustain a learning environment where students focus on lesson activities with few interruptions or disruptions. Classrooms vary greatly in the rate of student engagement and the use of manipulatives (Shaw & Hatfield, 1996). If the school allocates 40 minutes for science and the students are engaged in learning only half of the time, scientific literacy will be lowered for all students.

Effective teachers continuously involve students in activities related to the lesson's goal. Behaviors that do not fit with those activities are kept to a minimum. The more consistently and completely students are engaged with the lesson activities, the higher the student achievement. Effective engagement requires an instructional setting that is not threatening to students. If they are comfortable in the physical and social environment of the classroom, students are better able to truly engage in learning activities.

Effective teachers continuously monitor students' engagement with the lesson's activities. To effectively monitor, the teacher works with students individually and in small groups rather than with the whole class. The use of global monitoring skills at intervals of a few minutes helps provide the information needed to decide if the current learning activity should be stopped and students should move on to the next one, whether certain students should be refocused back to the activity, or whether the activity needs to be modified to increase student learning.

What Is Questioning?

Teacher questions are an integral part of teaching science. The type of questions used guides the learning outcomes and student engagement in the lesson (King & Rosenshine, 1993; Penick, 1996). The amount of time a teacher waits between asking a question and calling on students significantly changes the students' responses (Rowe, 1996). Similar results occur when wait-time is used after a student responds to a question and before a teacher acknowledges that response. Classroom research has found the average teacher waits less than a second before calling on a student or responding to a student's comment. Waiting three or more seconds before calling on a student or acknowledging a response can increase the length of student responses, the number of appropriate responses, and the cognitive level of the responses. It is also related to increased performance on standardized science tests (Berliner, 1987a).

The types of questions asked during a science lesson are planned in advance and relate to the lesson's activities (Magnusson & Palinscar, 1995). Learning cycle lessons begin with questions that all students have a chance to answer. Questions such as the following may be used in a learning cycle related to the concept of *habitat,* "Where do you find frogs?" "What kind of home do you think frogs need?" "How do places where frogs live differ from the homes of other animals?" "What is needed for an animal to live well?" These types of questions are **open questions**. There are many answers, all of which are accepted by the teacher. This engages all students since everyone is able to provide an answer.

Asking several open questions during the Exploration phase of the lesson is a technique that encourages students to recall and share prior experiences. A central **key question** is planned for the Exploration phase of every learning cycle. In the lesson focusing on the concept of *habitat,* a key question can be, "What do you think is needed for an animal to live well?" It is an open question that involves each student in thinking about the main idea of the lesson.

During the Invention phase of the lesson, questions are used to focus student inquiry on the main ideas of the lesson. After watching a film of several animals taking care of their daily needs in the natural environment, the teacher might ask, "Where does the frog get its food?" "What type of food does it need?" These are **closed questions** because they have a narrow focus. Usually, these questions either have one or a few appropriate answers. The Invention may involve an open question, but closed questions are mostly used during its activities.

During the Expansion phase of the lesson, questions help students apply the concept in a new context. There is a greater emphasis on open questions in this phase than during the Invention phase. Usually, there is a mix of open and closed questions to engage the students in activities. For example, an open question used during an Expansion might be, "If you are going to design a habitat for frogs, what needs to be in it?" After the students have presented their ideas, the teacher might ask the closed question, "What is missing from our design for the frogs' habitat?"

What Is Cooperative Learning?

Cooperative learning is an approach and a set of strategies specifically designed to encourage student cooperation while learning. In a review of research on the use of cooperative learning, Slavin (1989) reports that students learn as well, or better, when using cooperative learning than with competitive and individual learning strategies. Johnson and Johnson (1986) point out that the use of cooperative learning results in a wide range of positive mental health benefits including a positive self-image and an improved attitude toward, and acceptance of, classmates.

Traditional classroom grouping has problems that can limit and create barriers in learning (Johnson, Johnson, & Holubec, 1990a). Some of these barriers include leadership dominated by one person and work performed by a few in the group. Figure 7–1 lists some problems associated with traditional grouping in classrooms. Some problems with classroom groups are the result of misconceptions held by teachers, such as the need for competition between students to simulate the real world. Many misconceptions also exist about the effects of cooperative learning groups (see Figure 7–2). However, students in cooperative groups show higher academic achievement and increased motivation.

Students experience:

- a free ride.
- doing all the work.
- leadership falling to high-ability students.
- having to do all of the explaining/learning if they are high-ability students.
- a dysfunctional division of labor.
- dependence on authority.
- ganging up on others.
- pressures to suppress individual ability.
- competition with others.

These experiences can be avoided when group work is structured cooperatively.

FIGURE 7-1   *Traditional learning groups*

Source: Johnson, D., Johnson, R., and Holubec, E. (1990). *Circles of learning: Cooperation in the classroom.* Edina, MN: Interaction Book Company, 8.

1. Schools should emphasize competition because it is a dog-eat-dog world.
2. High-achieving students are penalized by working in heterogeneous cooperative learning groups.
3. Every member of a cooperative learning group has to do the same work and proceed at the same rate.
4. A single group grade shared by group members is not fair.
5. Using cooperative learning is simple.
6. The schools can change overnight.

FIGURE 7-2   *Alternative conceptions about cooperative learning*

Source: Johnson, D., Johnson, R., and Holubec, E. (1990). *Circles of learning: Cooperation in the classroom.* Edina, MN: Interaction Book Company, 129–136.

Small cooperative groups increase the opportunities for positive reinforcement and reduce the risks of negative reactions and ridicule for giving a wrong answer. To be successful, group interpersonal skills are carefully planned for, taught, and reinforced by the teacher (Johnson, Johnson, & Holubec, 1990b; Simsek & Simon, 1992).

Cooperative learning fosters four important goals for students (Johnson & Johnson, 1991). The first is positive interdependence among students through the division of workload, responsibility, and joint rewards. Groups establish positive interdependence when they learn to work together to earn recognition, grades, rewards, and other indicators of group success (Slavin, 1989). Students know they are relying on each other for a successful outcome to each experience. They learn to work together for the common good. Discussions, explanations, questioning, and other verbal exchanges play an important role in sharing, exploring, discovering, applying, reviewing, and rehearsing the content. Traditional group work often fails because one student takes over and makes decisions that only affect his own learning (Slavin, 1989). In cooperative groups, students are linked to group mates so no one member can succeed unless all members do. Techniques used in lesson plans include creating mutual group goals, joint rewards, divided resources, and complementary roles.

The second goal, positive student interaction and accountability, holds students individually accountable for their own learning and also for the learning of others in the group. Assignments are frequently divided, with each student mastering a part and then instructing the other students. Lesson planning includes peer-to-peer teaching, accountability, verbal and nonverbal interaction, and commitment to the task.

Individual accountability, in which the work of each individual contributes to the success of the group, is an important part of the success of the cooperative learning group. Each student knows the others are depending on her. If one student chooses to do poor work or make trouble, the other members of the group are sure to be affected and use peer pressure to change the student's behavior. Recognition, including grading, is done with an eye to the success of the group as well as of the individual. Grades are often partially assigned by combining individual scores and the group's mean scores. Teachers and students also evaluate and grade the working process of the group as well as the final product or presentation.

The third goal involves having adequate interpersonal skills and small group skills. Student interpersonal skills are not taken for granted. Students are taught skills such as effective communication, the willingness to accept and support each other, the ability to resolve conflicts, and acquiring knowledge about each other.

When the implementation of cooperative learning programs fails, it is often because the teacher either does not understand the theory behind cooperative learning or has not planned sufficiently for lessons to be effective (Martens, 1990). Cooperative learning is complex, often requiring years to become an expert. Deepening knowledge and consistent practice are needed for a teacher's expertise to develop.

Students also need practice and time to develop effective learning groups. Instruction in cooperative learning begins with short lessons or with carefully structured activities presented by the teacher. For example, the teacher may ask students to classify a set of pictures in a cooperative group activity. As students become more familiar with the group processes, activities may be longer and involve the students in selecting topics and assigning membership responsibilities.

A fourth goal is awareness of the need for group processing. This involves students in face-to-face encounters with each other on the topic being studied. They are encouraged to discuss the group process, how well the group accomplished its goals, and how to evaluate individual roles in the group. Some discussion topics include sequence of the tasks, procedures to carry out the task, and student responsibility for the tasks.

Students and the teacher monitor how well the group functions. The teacher instructs students in effective group processes, creates and facilitates a nonthreatening work environment, and intervenes when members encounter difficulty with group processes. Group processes include group formation skills, group achievement skills, and group interaction skills.

A detailed list of these skills is found in Chapter 8.

Teachers plan heterogenous and small cooperative groups (Scharman, Hampton, & Orth, 1995). The method used in grouping students for cooperative learning experiences is an important factor in the success of these groups. A typical group includes four students: one high achiever, two average achievers, and a low achiever. With this type of grouping, less chance exists that a student will be isolated. If two students enter into a discussion, then the remaining two students can talk to each other. The *Classroom Scenes: Characteristics of Natural Watersheds* in Chapter 5 is an example of the use of cooperative learning groups in a science lesson. Other examples are found in the literature, such as activities involving the human body (Brennon, 1997), projects in science (Marx, Blumenfeld, Krajcik, & Soloway, 1997), designing experiments (Stein, 1997), and investigating the planet Mars (Canizo, 1997).

Leadership responsibilities for both the lesson's content and the group's success are given to all group members. For example, one student may be the group's *recorder,* writing down what decisions are made and keeping notes; another might be *in charge of materials,* collecting those needed and organizing them; another may be the group's *spokesperson;* and another may be the group's *organizer,* making sure everyone has a chance to contribute to the discussion and that each person has a clear task to do. These roles usually alternate among members of the group if they work together over a period of time on different topics.

When students are ready to work cooperatively with larger amounts of material, they divide up a topic. Each member may work with students in other groups who have the same task or question. The result is then shared with the students' original group. This procedure is called a *jigsaw* and is best used when there is so much material available on a topic that it has to be broken down into subtopics. Another approach is to have each group member develop a response by herself, then share it with her group. For example, one teacher used the jigsaw method in a month-long unit on weather. Each group in a fourth-grade class gathered data by setting up its own weather station. One student in every group was assigned to one of the following tasks: determining wind direction, wind speed, temperature, or humidity. Students assigned to wind direction met in a temporary subgroup to research, design, and build their instruments. When they completed their wind direction instruments, they returned to their cooperative group. They instructed the others on the origins, functions, and meaning of the information obtained from the instrument. Other students in the group taught their peers about the measurement of wind speed, temperature, and humidity. The whole group was now able to go about its task of setting up a weather station, relating the combined data from all the instruments. They kept daily and weekly records, inferring patterns, asking questions, making predictions, and relating their data to regional weather information. Finally, they discussed how human activity is influenced by weather data. Cooperative learning enables students to work with both large and small amounts of material. Each student's strengths are used as each makes a recognizable contribution.

Elementary and middle school science is the perfect subject for cooperative learning, since the learning cycle is designed for use with small groups of students. Cooperative groups work with hands-on materials, make observations, and develop inferences and hypotheses. Discussion with other members of the group is essential. Working in groups gives students time to talk to one another and share their thoughts as they construct knowledge (Hannigan, 1990). In this way, science concepts and skills become reflective and more meaningful.

In science classrooms using cooperative learning, teachers tend to have less difficulty with classroom management. Students, rather than teachers, assume the responsibility for materials. They help each other by answering questions and assisting in the completion of assignments (Hannigan, 1990). This gives the teacher more time to work with others needing help in the class.

Many students may feel apprehensive about the science content they are learning. They may feel intimidated when making inferences or predictions in front of the entire class. When these same students get involved in small group work, however, they are often more eager to make contributions to the group's effort. Because students realize they have valid contributions to make, they become even more willing to participate in small group work (Hannigan, 1990). Using this instructional strategy allows students as a group to use their creativity to solve more difficult and complex science problems (Foster & Penick, 1985).

The collaborative nature of science is demonstrated in a cooperative group activity.

Real world science involves the work of many people. Although one person may be credited with a theory or discovery, the work of many people helped him reach that point. Teaching science through collaborative learning exemplifies the collaborative nature of science (National Research Council, 1996).

WHAT IS SCIENCE PEDAGOGICAL KNOWLEDGE FOR EFFECTIVE SCIENCE TEACHING?

Teachers' Views of Effective Science Teaching

Teachers have alternative conceptions of the way science teaching and learning take place within the classroom. One popular conception sees science teaching mostly as *fact acquisition*. The content to be learned is a listing of facts and definitions of terms. Students receive and remember the information presented. Repetition is the key learning process. Students are evaluated by repeating the facts and definitions provided by the teacher and textbook. The teacher's role is to plan and expose students to facts, provide drill and recitation sessions, and encourage motivation in students through a variety of media and external rewards. Today, many teachers still see science simply as fact acquisition.

A second conception of science teaching and learning in the classroom involves *idea attainment*. Attainment requires students to figure out the attributes and attribute values of a concept by comparing and contrasting examples and non-examples of the concept. For example, the concept *apple* has several characteristics distinguishing it from *orange*. Size, color, and taste are important characteristics of the concept *apple*. Each of the characteristics has a range of values. For instance, the color of apples ranges from green to red.

Idea attainment views concepts as already created by others in the biological, physical, and Earth sciences. Learning occurs when students search for and identify these same patterns and relationships in examples and non-examples to develop their own understanding of the concepts. The teacher's role is to present and explain these concepts in a coherent and interesting way through involving students in using examples, demonstrations, and laboratory activities to illustrate the ideas. Today, many teachers are beginning to use student interaction and involvement as their primary focus of teaching.

See Chapter 5 on conceptual learning.

A third conception of science teaching and learning in the classroom actively engages students in developing important science ideas on their own and in identifying and using them in the real world. The emphasis in *idea formation* is on student activities involving them with interpreting and constructing representations of what they read, observe, and try out. Students decide what to investigate and what methods to use. Students are encouraged, in a safe setting, to challenge their previously learned ideas with new ideas. The students then integrate this information with their prior knowledge, making changes or replacing old ideas as they are appropriate and make sense to the student. The teacher's role involves guiding student learning and monitoring students' behaviors, ideas, and interpretations. Today, many teachers are becoming more of a guide by presenting alternatives and leading students to be dissatisfied with their old ideas. New alternative ideas are attempted by applying them and by providing new evidence and situations which allow the student to choose the appropriate new idea (National Science Teachers Association, 1993).

See Chapters 2 and 6 for a discussion on conceptual change and constructing generalizations.

Effective science teaching through idea attainment or through idea formation changes traditional roles of the teacher and student. No longer is the teacher's primary role to give information, nor is it pushing students to memorize the concepts as understood by the teacher or text. The teacher's ideas and those in the text were developed from a set of experiences and a knowledge base that are different from those of the students. In lessons aimed at idea attainment and formation, students actively participate in the learning process using exploration, testing of their prior knowledge, and application of ideas in a variety of situations. Teachers take on the role of a guide in helping students learn, and reduce their role as the knowledge authority.

Effective science teaching contributes to meaningful learning among students in at least three ways:

1. Observations and investigations provide students with a more extensive experience of the physical world.
2. The "safe" student classroom grouped for cooperative learning gives students a positive and supportive social setting.
3. The use of appropriate instructional methods in a learning cycle format leads students to reorganize their own reasoning by allowing them to experience its inadequacies, by suggesting more fruitful approaches, and by permitting them to use and apply the new ideas.

How Do Teachers Match Science Instructional Methods to Science Learning Outcomes?

One aim of education is to help students be self-directing (National Research Council, 1996, pp. 22–23). The amount of student control during the learning process is a key factor that varies with the different instructional activities used in classrooms. Instructional activities may involve lecturing, reading a book, observing a video, or using computer-assisted tutorials. Contrast these activities with creating a journal or language experience story, completing a science fair project, and asking a question and being allowed to follow-up the answer through one's own investigations. Significant differences occur when the more-active approaches are used in the Exploration, Invention, or Expansion phases of a learning cycle lesson.

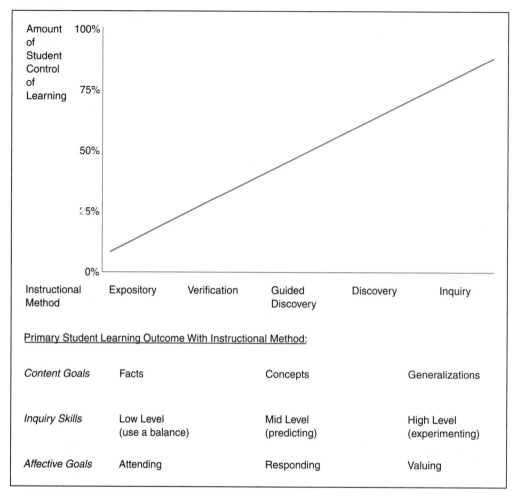

FIGURE 7-3   *Matching learning outcomes to instructional methods*

The amount of control students have over their science learning activities is an important factor to consider in selecting an instructional method to help students create meaningful learning (Simsek, 1993). Instructional activities for teaching science can be grouped into five categories of instructional methods based on the amount of student control. Sequenced from least to greatest student control, the categories are expository, verification, guided discovery, discovery, and inquiry (see Figure 7–3). The categories are described in detail below to demonstrate the range of science instruction methods (see Table 7–1). An appropriate instructional method is chosen to match the science content objectives students are to accomplish in the lesson as well as their developmental needs. Each instructional method is particularly effective and appropriate in helping elementary and middle school students accomplish a particular level or type of learning objective (Figure 7–3). If used exclusively, one instructional method is less effective than a combination of methods for accomplishing all learning outcomes.

It is important to understand how and when each category of methods is used. No science instructional method is bad or good by itself. However, the use of expository and rote memorization methods for a large proportion of any science unit is inappropriate (Collins, 1997). They are also inappropriate methods for teaching science generalizations

TABLE 7-1 *Range of science instructional methods based on roles of the student and teacher*

Activity	Role of Student	Role of Teacher
Expository	Attends to what the teacher is doing and saying	Provides problem, carries out activity/investigation, determines appropriateness of results (e.g., short lecture with demonstration)
Verification	Performs activity	Provides problem, procedure, materials, expected results, and determines appropriateness of student results
Guided Discovery	Investigates and determines answers	Provides problem, procedure, and materials to carry out an investigation and determines appropriateness of results
Discovery	Determines procedure and materials needed and performs investigation	Provides problem, determines appropriateness of results, and facilitates student decisions
Inquiry	Determines problem, procedure, materials, performs investigation, and determines appropriateness of results	Facilitates student decisions

or higher-order thinking skills. See Figure 7–3 for an overview of the instructional methods and their outcomes for elementary and middle school students.

Applying What You Know

Comparing Instructional Methods

Compare the following two instructional methods by describing the:

1. amount of student control over the lesson activities and direction.
2. potential student learning outcomes for a first-grade or a sixth-grade student.

Method 1: A 30-minute teacher lecture describing the characteristics of plants with a particular emphasis on the different structures that serve different functions.

Method 2: A 20-minute school yard field trip where students are asked to find different plant parts, tape them on a sheet of paper, and discuss what each part does for the plant. This is followed by a whole group discussion.

What difference would be expected in student learning outcomes?

What Are Expository Instructional Methods?

Expository instructional methods provide students with little control over the direction or extent of the learning process. Lesson activities using expository methods include the following characteristics. The teacher controls the situation and must provide adequate directions and motivation. If it is skills practice, the teacher provides ample opportunities to practice the skill in a wide variety of situations. The teacher supplies immediate and continuous feedback. Verbal communication emphasizes teacher monologues and closed questions. The teacher or instructional device controls the situation but must provide extensive and adequate directions for the student.

When expository instructional activities focus on practice, such as using a thermometer, a wide variety of examples and situations are needed to motivate the student to practice. Immediate feedback must be supplied with each example. External motivation and careful classroom management are required for success. For young students, expository methods only produce the lower levels of learning: recall and memorization. For example, the usual result of lecturing to a first grader is factual knowledge by rote memory. The same result is obtained from viewing a video or through computer-tutorial instruction. These methods may produce some growth in lower-level skill areas such as using simple observation tools and carrying out observation procedures. They facilitate the lower-level affective areas of attending and willingness to receive information. Expository methods are occasionally useful in the Invention phase of the learning cycle where the teacher explains the key idea of the lesson, and the lesson focus involves the need for recall. While the category of expository methods represents low control over the student's own learning, other categories of methods allow for increasing amounts of student control.

What Are Verification Instructional Methods?

Verification instructional methods are used to demonstrate to the student the fact or concept just explained by the teacher or textbook. The teacher creates a problem to investigate, determines the procedures and materials needed, specifies how students are to collect and analyze data, and evaluates the students' results as they relate to the original problem. The student knows what the results should be when verification is the instructional method. The teacher, in a cookbook fashion, carefully guides the use of materials, procedures, or data collection. Verbal communication by the teacher involves closed questions and reactions to students by accepting or clarifying their responses.

A teacher uses a verification method when she explains that *only some metals are attracted to magnets,* and demonstrates that, out of a set of metals—iron washers, pieces of brass keys, aluminum foil, or silver coins—only iron is attracted to a magnet. In these activities, students know what the results should be. The teacher either demonstrates or carefully guides the students in a step-by-step fashion. The materials, procedures, data collection, and results are all provided for the student to observe. Sometimes the student or group's data are pooled and trends in that data are noted. This method is used when the teacher: (1) does a demonstration with hazardous materials, or (2) when important observations need to be made and pointed out by the teacher after the students have completed the activity on their own. As with the previous category, the chief outcomes expected for young students using these methods are rote memory and lower-level skills and attitudes. Verification methods are useful in the Invention phase of the learning cycle when the teacher explains the key idea or skill and students practice using the key idea or skill.

What Are Guided Discovery Instructional Methods?

With guided discovery instructional methods, students are involved in activities related to a concept and form an understanding of them before the teacher explains them or they read about them in a textbook (Stefanich, 1992). The teacher creates a problem to investigate and determines the procedures and materials needed. However, students collect and analyze data and evaluate the results as they relate to the original problem. Students are provided with the time and opportunity to study relationships in data and to form the new idea. Only one concept, generalization, or skill is the focus of each activity. There are multiple (2 to 5) activities illustrating the concept, generalization, or skill. Students pool, discuss, and display class data obtained through the activities. The students' main role is to investigate and discover the answers to the questions posed. Students do not know the answer beforehand. The role of the teacher is to provide directions and ask questions that help students begin their activities. The teacher also provides the materials and describes the procedures needed to complete the activity.

An example of a guided discovery instructional method is an activity that helps students develop the concept of *flower* by dissecting several different types of flowers, looking for patterns, and then discussing what they found. Only one key concept is the focus of the activities. A number of discovery activities involving the concept may be needed during the lesson. Students learn mid-level inquiry skills such as the science process skills of inferring, predicting, measuring, estimating, organizing, interpreting, and drawing conclusions from data. Use of the learning cycle in teaching concepts requires a sequence of guided discovery instructional methods with a medium amount of student control (Magnusson & Palinscar, 1995).

What Are Discovery Instructional Methods?

Discovery instructional methods provide students with a problem centered on a key science concept, generalization, or skill. Students are encouraged to decide how and when to collect data, analyze the results, and evaluate the results as they relate to the original problem. The teacher decides what content and process skills students should learn. The teacher presents the problem to the class. Prerequisite practice with skills such as measuring, identifying, and controlling variables is provided as needed. Students investigate and report the results of their investigation. The teacher's main role is to stimulate students to begin investigations through appropriate questions and act as a facilitator and resource person for materials and ideas during the rest of the experience.

An example of an open discovery activity is asking students to investigate ways of keeping cold objects, such as ice cubes, cold for a long period. Before instruction begins, the teacher decides what content and inquiry skills students are to learn. The teacher then designs the question and environment to guide the students' investigation. Students investigate questions such as: "What can be done to keep ice cubes from melting?" "What materials should be used to keep ice from melting?" "Do the same procedures and materials keep hot objects from cooling?" The students meet in cooperative learning groups and plan an investigation leading to a presentation of results and further discussion.

Students involved in discovery methods can meaningfully learn science concepts, generalizations, and mid- and upper-level science process skills, attitudes, and critical response skills. Discovery methods take more time than the previous categories of methods. Using the discovery method reduces the amount of material that can be covered if this method is used to the exclusion of others. Meaningful learning of most science concepts, generalizations, and inquiry skills are the expected outcomes. Compare these outcomes to the rote memorization and lower-level skills that are expected for the previous categories. Use of the learning cycle in teaching generalizations requires a sequence of teaching methods with high student control. The discovery method is appropriate for these lessons.

What Are Inquiry Instructional Methods?

The fifth science instruction method, inquiry, involves significant student control over the direction the lesson takes (Fitzsimmons & Goldhaber, 1997). Instructional activities in this category require the student to create a problem to investigate, determine the procedures and materials needed, collect and analyze data, and evaluate the results as they relate to the original problem. Students must be competent in basic science process skills and create problem areas to investigate. Students generally work in groups and orally report the results of their investigations. The teacher guides students in narrowing down the problems to be investigated and is well-prepared to act as a resource person. The teacher is a facilitator and resource person who ensures that the classroom environment is safe and supportive (Marx, 1997).

Inquiry method activities are intrinsically motivating because students are directing their own learning. A first grader involved in these instructional activities is likely to use higher thought processes. A young student's science project, for example, could involve making a clay model of an insect that lives in bushes and successfully hides from most predators. In this project, the student is asking questions, communicating information, making inferences, and building predictions. In writing stories about the science experience, facts may form the basic content of the narrative, but students also often make inferences and construct generalizations. For example, a first grader may ask, "Why don't all bugs get eaten by birds?" The teacher may encourage the student to find insects in bushes in the school yard and describe what they look like, to see if that helps provide an answer. The student is developing attitudes about insects and about the value of investigative experiences, as well as many inquiry skills.

Students involved in inquiry method activities have a lot of practice with the full range of inquiry skills as well as science generalizations. These methods take more time than do the previous categories of instructional methods. Using inquiry methods requires careful selection of the key science ideas and skills covered in inquiry activities. Inquiry methods reduce the amount of material covered to an even greater extent than in the previous categories. Meaningful learning of generalizations and higher-order inquiry skills, as well as improved long-term memory and transfer of learning, are the expected outcomes. Compare these outcomes to those expected for the previous categories. Use of the learning cycle for teaching generalizations requires a sequence for learning that involves instructional activities with high student control. Inquiry method activities are appropriate for these lessons.

Science lessons focusing on low-level inquiry skills and knowledge require expository or verification instructional activities with less student control. Science lessons focusing on mid-level inquiry skills and concepts require a set of guided discovery instructional activities that consistently provide for some student control sequenced in a learning cycle. Science lessons focusing on generalizations and higher-level inquiry skills require discovery or inquiry instructional activities with high student control sequenced in a learning cycle.

How Are Instructional Activities Matched to Each Phase of the Learning Cycle?

The effective teacher of science selects instructional activities to match the science learning outcome desired. The teacher also determines which activities fit the sequence required for each phase of the learning cycle. The learning cycle is a strategy for decision making, thereby providing a guide for sequencing instructional activities in a science lesson. Teachers first choose a set of science activities that belong to either guided discovery, discovery, or inquiry methods, depending on the planned lesson outcomes. Specific instructional activities that fit the chosen method are selected for the Exploration phase of the learning cycle. If the guided discovery method was selected to teach the concept of *habitat* for a first-grade class, for example, a structured Exploration activity of several animal habitats might be chosen for the Exploration phase of the lesson (see *Structured Exploration* in the next section of this chapter). The Invention activities help students search for regularities in observations and provide explanations of the key idea or skill. Since the guided discovery method was selected to teach the concept of *habitat,* a teacher-guided discussion and field trip observation of an animal habitat might be chosen for the Invention phase of the lesson (see *Outdoor Instructional Activities* in a later section of this chapter). During Expansion, students apply what they learned in new contexts. Using the guided discovery method for teaching the concept of *habitat,* an activity having cooperative groups of students draw and role-play an animal habitat might be chosen for the Expansion phase of the lesson (see *Games, Simulations,* and *Role-Playing* in the next section of this chapter). A repertoire of appropriate teaching activities for each phase of the learning cycle is helpful in planning science lessons. The types of activities listed below have been suggested by classroom teachers for use in the context of the learning cycle, although others are also possible.

What Instructional Activities Are Useful during the Exploration Phase?

Exploration activities are used to gain students' attention and relate the ideas and skills to be learned to past experiences. Chapter 3 supplied a listing of characteristics for an effective exploration. This listing provides a set of criteria for judging the appropriateness of a particular instructional activity. During Exploration, the students learn through their own actions and reactions. They explore new materials and new ideas with minimal guidance or without the expectation of specific accomplishments. The activity raises questions they cannot answer with their usual patterns of reasoning. Having made an effort that was not completely successful, the students are ready for the Invention phase of the learning cycle. Successful sample teaching methods for the Exploration phase of a lesson are described below. These are sequenced from low student control to high student control.

Review.   Review related concepts and generalizations studied in previous lessons and relate them to the new idea that will be invented in the current lesson. For example, following a guided discovery lesson on the concept of the complete electric circuit, a review of the concept might be effective for the Exploration phase of a next lesson on the parts of an electric circuit: (1) energy source—battery; (2) energy user—bulb; and (3) energy transmitter—wire.

Structured exploration.   Allow students to explore a structured environment leading to a concept or generalization to be invented in the next part of the learning cycle. Begin with an open key question to help organize experiences. For example, "What might happen in an electric circuit when extra electric bulbs are added?" Next, give students a series of activities on 3 by 5 inch cards to perform. Ask, "What happens when a second electric bulb is added?" Tell them to "predict what you think will happen and then try it." Next, have the students predict what will happen when a third electric bulb is added and have them try it. Ask them to describe what is happening in each activity using a question such as, "What patterns do you see?"

Cooperative group challenge.   Describe what you are going to do and ask students to predict what will happen. For example, hold a mystery object over a jar of water and ask, "What will happen when I put this in the water?" Divide the students into cooperative groups based on their answers. You may have a group that predicted the object would sink, another that predicted it would float, and another that predicted it would stay in the middle. Ask each group to provide evidence for its answer. Then, provide each group with objects of different materials and sizes, along with a jar of water, and ask them to make, and test, their predictions.

Discrepant event.   Discrepant events confront students' conceptions of the way the world works, thereby challenging their prior knowledge. For example, show students two pictures, each showing a potato cooking in a pot of boiling water on a stove. One pot is cooking over a low flame while the other one is cooking over a high flame. Ask, "Which will cook the potato faster?" The discrepancy is that boiling water stays at a temperature of 100 degrees Celsius and will not rise in the pot until the water boils out. Both potatoes will cook in the same amount of time. The characteristics of a discrepant event activity include the following:

1. The discrepancy relates to past experiences of the student. If it does not, the event is most likely of little interest.
2. Familiar materials are used in the activity.
3. An inconsistency is introduced in one of several ways: through a silent presentation, having the event operating as students enter the room, cueing the students verbally, or using films or pictures.
4. Materials are ready for the students to have something to manipulate.
5. Inquiry into all discrepancies, even those not expected, is encouraged.
6. Only requested information, and only information that cannot be obtained through the student's own inquiry process, is provided.

Discrepancies are sometimes difficult to devise and students might expect "magic" all the time. Therefore, discrepancies are not used in each learning cycle.

Problem exploration.   Present students with an open-ended problem and have them attempt to find a solution. For example, have students investigate the problem of pouring water. Ask questions such as: "When pouring water out of a pitcher, why does the stream of water not fall straight down?" "Why does it appear to fall toward the pitcher?" Provide buckets, water, pitchers, and instant cameras for groups requesting them.

Open exploration.   Allow students to explore an unstructured environment leading to the formation of a concept in the next phase of the learning cycle. Begin with an open key question. For example, on a field trip to a wooded area next to the school, ask students to observe the growth of small plants as they walk under a large tree. Ask them to describe what they see and why this happens.

What Are Instructional Activities for the Invention Phase?

The second step in the learning cycle, Invention, explains a new concept or skill, leading the students to practice new patterns of reasoning about their experiences. Verbalization of the new idea and terminology are introduced in this phase.

Chapter 3 lists the characteristics of an effective invention. They provide the criteria for selecting a particular instructional activity. The concept may be introduced in a discussion of the results found in the Exploration phase activities, a teacher-guided activity, the textbook, a film, or another information medium. This phase follows the Exploration and relates to the Exploration activities. Some instructional methods that have been successfully used during the Invention phase are described below.

Expository instructional activities.   Expository methods develop fact acquisition such as the names of the planets. They are also used to develop lower-level skills such as counting events, telling time, and measuring using a thermometer or double-pan balance. Some examples include practicing of a simple skill, such as using a thermometer, lecturing, reading a textbook, or viewing a film.

Verification instructional activities.   Verification activities provide evidence in support of a concept or skill described in a textbook or lecture. Students practice them by repeating activities or labs described or demonstrated for them. Some examples of verification methods are step-by-step student laboratory exercises or "cookbook labs," the film of an event followed by a lecture explaining it, student demonstration of a procedure under teacher direction, or a student field trip to the school grounds to find an example of a braided streambed or cold-blooded animal following an explanation in the classroom.

Guided discovery activities.   Guided discovery activities are teacher-structured events centered on a concept or skill. The teacher provides the question, materials, and suggested procedure; the students do not know the expected result. Examples of guided discovery activities involve students in hands-on activities with the concept of predator-prey, or the inquiry skill of making predictions.

See Chapters 4 and 5 for additional guidelines in developing skills and concepts.

Discovery instructional activities.   Student discovery of a concept, generalization, or skill occurs through a situation partially structured by the teacher. A problem is presented, then the students decide how and when to collect data. Generally, students work in groups, write in journals, write reports, and present the results of their activities. The teacher only provides the question to be answered and the materials to be used. Examples of discovery activities include students investigating the generalization of interaction-at-a-distance with magnetic and electric fields or students reserving judgment until a sufficient amount of evidence is gathered.

See Chapter 6 for additional guidelines in developing generalizations.

Inquiry instructional activities.   Student investigation of a generalization or skill through an inquiry situation is structured by the student. The student formulates the main question and directs the data-gathering and analysis activities. The teacher only acts as a facilitator. A group of students investigating a question they thought up during a science lesson, student-developed science collections, and project work related to a science unit or a science fair project for which students create their own questions to investigate are examples of inquiry method activities.

See Chapter 6 for additional guidelines in developing generalizations.

This outdoor measuring activity involved solving everyday problems.

Outdoor instructional activities.   Outdoor activities of a short or long duration should be a common unit, if not a weekly event. These activities include everything from a trip to the school playground to find out whether the moon can be seen in the daytime sky to a trip to a planetarium. Most field trips do not need to be costly or require a bus. However, field trips do require more advance planning than classroom activities. Be sure to visit the site prior to the activity to determine the potential for learning and problem situations that might arise.

The school, school grounds, and local neighborhood are surveyed to determine the potential for the variety of topics covered throughout the year. Soil erosion on parts of the ball field, the types of streams in soil near the parking lot, examples of cold- and warm-blooded animals in the litter and bushes around the school, the efficient use of energy in the school building, and evaluation of the nutritional value of the school lunch are some examples of 10- to 20-minute local field trips.

Field trips have objectives similar to those for classroom-based activities. For example, one might conduct a field trip to develop his observation or measuring skills. Field trips with varying amounts of student control are matched to the type of objective to be learned. Practice or skill attainment is involved when the objective is fact acquisition or lower-level skills such as measuring long distances, measuring the speed of sound, and use of a variety of sampling techniques for plants and animals. Concept verification or expository learning is involved when the objective is verification of a concept or skill read about in a textbook through replicating it in an activity. Guided discovery is involved when the objective involves attaining a concept or skill through a hands-on activity the teacher structures. Discovery is involved when the objective is attaining or developing a concept, generalization, or skill through a problem activity the teacher partially structures. Free inquiry is involved when the objective is student discovery of a concept, generalization, or skill through a problem investigation the student structures.

Demonstration.   A demonstration is the use of real objects, physical analogies, or models to illustrate a concept, generalization, skill, or attitude. Students look for a particular event, or one student performs the activity for others. A short film clip may be appropriate for demonstrating certain skills, although it is sometimes necessary to decide between a classroom activity and a demonstration. The following criteria are important in making the decision to use a demonstration:

1. Lack of availability of equipment.
2. Safety problems.
3. Phenomena requiring long-term observation.
4. Difficult or complex task.
5. Mixed developmental level of the students.

There are a variety of types of demonstrations. The type with the highest amount of student involvement possible is best. The following order is considered:

1. Student demonstrates; if not appropriate, then use number 2.
2. Student demonstrates under teacher direction; if not appropriate, then use number 3.
3. Student directs teacher; if all else is not appropriate, then use number 4.
4. Teacher demonstrates.

Games, simulations, and role-playing.   Games, simulations, and role-playing involve students in acting out concepts, generalizations, and inquiry skills. Games have a win-or-lose aspect while simulations do not need an ending event to be effective. Many games found at toy stores can be adapted for educational purposes. Simulations are found in educational journals, software, and in teacher stores. Role-playing can be as simple as creating a panel of experts (students) discussing an event they researched in the library. The teacher directs student actions. Students must understand their roles and the rules. These activities are useful for studying controversial issues.

Discovery invitation.   This method helps focus students' attention on the higher-level inquiry skills such as selecting variables, data interpretation, data analysis, and determining the meaning of a set of data or an event. This is done by presenting data for a given problem or situation. The students do not gather or collect data, which is a time-consuming process. This method provides students with experience in the later parts of the inquiry process where they tend to be weakest. Examples include bringing in a newspaper article about a particular event (Mount St. Helen's eruption); providing a table of data (sunspot numbers for the last 100 years); or showing a picture or diagram of an event (tracks of a dinosaur in sandstone). Most invitations are begun with open questions such as, "What does this mean to you?" or "What happened here?" The method is less time-consuming than going through the entire inquiry process; students need less equipment and fewer data-collecting skills. This method is appropriate for all levels. A "correct" answer does not have to be given or even arrived at. Weekly invitations every Friday can be a motivational activity. Cooperative learning groups provide an effective approach for structuring the classroom for this type of activity.

Closure statement.   A closure statement describes in clear, simple terms what the students should understand as a result of the lesson activities to this point. For example, "When placed in a light of high intensity, the dark-colored object will absorb more heat than lighter-colored objects."

General considerations for invention instructional activities.   Some general considerations in using these Invention phase activities include allowing students the time and opportunities for repeated experiences with the new concept or generalization. The amount of material covered in the textbook may have to decrease. Some teachers report that the pace quickens later because more students have a much better foundation in the science inquiry skills.

When introducing a new terminology, concrete concepts defined operationally through demonstration, examples, and actions are used. Only later are more formal definitions of the concepts presented. Diverse activities help students construct relationships between concepts. Students often need to work with a relationship in a variety of ways before they are able to accomplish conceptual change. Students are asked to justify their conclusions, predictions, and inferences regardless of whether these are correct or incorrect using questions such as: "Why are you sure of that?" "What is the evidence?" and "What are some other ways of thinking about solving the problem?" Teachers also ask students to explain their ideas.

Students are encouraged to interact with one another during discussions and problem-solving activities. By learning about the viewpoints of others, they become more aware of their own reasoning. Students using advanced reasoning patterns serve as role models for those using less-developed reasoning patterns. The latter, because of their more limited understanding, challenge their advanced classmates' reasoning, making them rethink their ideas. Conceptual difficulties that might never have been revealed can be dealt with by peers.

When students are allowed more control over the lesson, they become aware and critical of their own reasoning. Many are accustomed to teaching that delivers information without challenging their thinking. Discovery activities and open-ended questions are, at first, likely to be uncomfortable for some students because they must take some responsibility rather than having their teacher decide what is right or wrong.

An effective strategy is modeling thinking to be facilitated in the students. The teacher thinks out loud when presenting an explanation or answering a student's question. Using this method, students know the teacher considers alternative possibilities and is, at times, unsure of how to proceed. The class is invited to join the teacher in this activity by commenting on the teacher's ideas, proposing others, and evaluating suggestions. Some questions are left unanswered, because they may be too difficult or the answer may be completely unknown.

The effective science teacher is receptive to ideas or hypotheses that are different. These are encouraged by drawing attention to their good points and to unusual points of view. To help students re-examine an inadequate reasoning pattern or alternative conception, the teacher might suggest a lab activity, further reading, or discussion. Attention is called to the reasoning behind a right or wrong answer rather than merely mentioning the answer itself. The following behaviors are avoided because they tend to encourage thinking only at a superficial level:

- Allowing so little time for responses to a question that few students have time to think about their answers.
- Evaluating the first answer and then taking control of the discussion without waiting for comments from other students.
- Suggesting all or part of an answer to the teacher's own questions rather than inviting students to propose even partial solutions.
- Requiring students to primarily recall pieces of information as opposed to relating or evaluating information.

What Are Instructional Activities for the Expansion Phase?

In the third step in the learning cycle, Expansion, students apply the new concept, generalization, and/or skill to additional examples. This step is necessary to extend the range of applicability of the new idea. Without many widely varied applications, the idea's meaning remains restricted to the examples used during its introduction in the Invention phase. Many students fail to abstract the idea from its concrete examples or generalize it to other situations. Two or more Expansion activities using more than one type of activity are recommended. The instructional activities found here are similar to others previously suggested and have been ordered by the amount of student control in a typical activity. Select the method(s) that appropriately applies the new idea. Others are also possible.

- Practice using the lesson idea in new situations or with technology. For example, ask students to find five objects at home. Predict, and try out, whether they sink or float.
- Discovery invitation involving an application of the idea.
- Field trip involving an application of the idea. At a local boat marina, for example, students can observe boat design, relating it to what they have learned about sinking and floating, and can measure the effect putting several students in a boat has on the height of the boat floating above the water.
- Games and role-playing involving an application of the idea.
- Art activities illustrating or using the new idea.
- Social studies activities integrating the new idea.
- Mathematics activities integrating the new idea.
- Discrepant event. Return to the event that students attempted but did not completely answer during the Exploration, or provide a new discrepant event using a different context. For example, if students were challenged with determining whether a small mystery object would sink or float in the Exploration, they could be challenged with

another in the Expansion. A counter-intuitive example is also used in the Expansion phase. Therefore, if a small object that sinks was used in the Exploration, a large object that floats will be used in the Expansion.

- Problem involving an application of the idea. For sinking or floating, ask students to make pieces of clay float.

Lesson Conclusion

Summarization of the lesson is accomplished by one or more of the following methods:

- The teacher initiates a sample problem for student discussion that relates the objectives of the lesson.
- The students or teacher provide(s) a review of the lesson events.
- The teacher provides a question and answer review.
- Students are led into a discussion of the lesson's events. The teacher could begin with, "What have we found out about. . .?"

Student assessment occurs throughout the lesson. Monitoring and checking for understanding are continuous, ongoing assessment tasks. At the end of the lesson, summative assessment is performed.

Summative assessment test items ask students to justify their answers so that their reasoning patterns, as well as their knowledge, are assessed.

A summary of the instructional management procedures promoting meaningful learning that are not usually found in traditional classrooms includes the following:

See Chapter 8 for development of a plan for assessing and evaluating science learning.

1. Group students heterogeneously and encourage peer interactions throughout the science lesson.
2. Call attention to discrepant events or create them, if necessary, for each science lesson.
3. Ask students to explain or justify their conclusions, predictions, and inferences, rather than accepting a simple answer, whether accurate or not.
4. Propose discrepant observations, unsatisfactory hypotheses, or incorrect conclusions and challenge students to evaluate these. For example, ask students to respond to the statement, "All small objects float and all large objects sink."
5. Always introduce a new term by using several concrete examples, a demonstration, or an activity. Use the Invention phase of the lesson to introduce new terminology. Without an experience to which the term relates, it will be forgotten.

Applying What You Know

Planning for Instruction during the Invention

Describe an appropriate instructional method for the Invention phase of the learning cycle for: (1) learning a concrete concept, (2) learning a generalization, and (3) learning the skill of measuring volume accurately with a graduated cylinder. Discuss your responses with others, comparing your choices and rationales for selection.

Classroom Management with Hands-On Science

Teachers using a traditional approach to classroom management have difficulty learning to use the more hands-on approach of current science curricula. Since the role of the student in the learning process has changed, the teacher's classroom management must also change (French, 1995). Students use more materials and are involved in a greater number of student-to-student interactions. There is more movement about the room, more questions, and more student control of their own learning. General classroom management guidelines designed for a hands-on, minds-on science program include advance planning, giving directions, distributing materials, creating an organized beginning, grouping students, using classroom rules, lesson smoothness, and being a facilitator. These lead to more effective learning in a stimulating and safe classroom.

Advance Planning

Preplanning lessons is critical to effective classroom management and high student achievement. Teachers try out the activities and experiments students perform in the classroom *before* they are used. Activities described in textbooks and other sources have a tendency not to work as advertised, or they may contain problem points that stop student activities. Problem points can be evaluated and modifications made by the teacher in procedures or materials if try-outs occur in advance. Special materials required for a lesson have to be prepared ahead of time. Much of this advance preparation is simple and not very time consuming if started at an early date. For instance, growing small plants from seeds or from shoots takes little time or can be accomplished by volunteer students if started two or more weeks in advance. Preparation eliminates delays that can cause teacher frustration.

Giving Directions

Before students receive materials, they are given directions on how the materials will be used. If not, students may use the materials in ways that the teacher had not planned. Students are creative and, unless guided, they will set their own agenda. The directions do not have to be specific or step-by-step. They can include a statement such as, "You will be receiving a box of materials. When you get your box, make observations of each object in the box and group them. Write your observations on the sheet provided." This approach does not provide the students with answers, but introduces a focus for the next student-directed activity. Providing instructions while students are involved in activities with materials is usually not effective because the students are too busy to listen. Having students set materials aside following an activity rather than collecting them is often more effective because students can demonstrate what they did by using the materials during discussions.

Distributing Materials

The distribution of materials to students can be the most difficult part of a science lesson. For hands-on science, it is important to set up stations and locate materials to be used where they are easily accessible. This eliminates confusion and reduces the time students need to obtain materials. Having preplanned how the students will receive and return the materials with which they work creates smoother lessons with fewer transition problems. Appointing science helpers is an effective technique which involves rotating two or more students per week so that every student has a chance. Lessons with large amounts of materials often have additional helpers appointed.

Distribution methods based on those used at restaurants and home at mealtime provide a good analogy for planning science materials distribution in classrooms (Table 7–2). For example, science materials can be distributed family style. Designate a table or row of students as a group. A student distributes a set of materials to each group. Students in the

T_ABLE_ 7-2   *Approaches to the distribution of classroom science materials*

Distribution Style	Teacher and Student Involvement
Family Style	One student distributes a set of materials to each group. Students in the group redistribute the materials among themselves.
Waiter/Waitress Style	One student from each group picks up all of the materials on a tray and delivers items to each individual member of the group.
Boxed Lunch Style	All materials needed for each person are put in a box. One student picks up the boxes and distributes the boxes to each member in the group.
Cafeteria Style	All students from each team proceed through a line where items to be used by the individual are picked up in sequence. Or, one student from each team proceeds through a line where items to be used by the team are picked up in sequence.
Food Court Style	Students go to different locations or stations in the room to pick up their needed materials.
Home Style	Using student helpers to distribute materials to student group locations before the science lesson begins.

group redistribute the materials among themselves, much like passing around a bowl of mashed potatoes at the dinner table.

A second distribution method, using a waiter/waitress style, involves identifying a student from each group to come up and collect a set of materials to be used by the whole group. The student delivers items to each individual member of the group, or brings the whole tray to the group as a single set. Modifications to this method include a boxed lunch style, where all materials needed for each student are in a box to be picked up and brought to the group.

A third strategy uses a cafeteria-style approach. One student from each team proceeds through a line where items to be used by the team are picked up. A second version of this strategy involves all students from each team proceeding through a line where items to be used by the individual are picked up in sequence.

A fourth method, the food court style, involves students going to different locations in the room to pick up their needed materials, avoiding crowding of students in one area of the room.

A fifth method, home style, involves distributing materials to student group locations before the science lesson begins. This can be done by students earlier in the day or by assigned science helpers at lunch or break time. Variations of all these methods may also occur.

When making a decision about a materials distribution method, it is important to consider the following factors. *Time* is the most important factor, so reducing the amount of time needed is the primary concern. The second most important factor is the *amount of student involvement*. A distribution method that increases student involvement is preferable. This provides additional time for those students involved to become aware of the materials and to understand how to use them, resulting in an increase in science learning. A third factor to consider is the *amount of teacher time*. The method that most reduces the involvement of the teacher is often best. This time is better used working with individual groups or monitoring the classroom. A fourth factor to consider is *efficiency and smoothness*. The distribution method that gets materials to students quickly, without causing disruption, should be used most often. The application of these factors depends on the classroom context. This context includes the age of the student, the number of materials to be distributed, the type of materials (breakable or not), safety concerns, and the amount of potential mess that could be caused during the distribution process. While no one distribution method works in all lessons, there are probably one or two methods that work best in a specific classroom, with occasional variations.

Organized Beginning

The beginning of the lesson is an important classroom management point in hands-on, minds-on science. When all materials are ready to be distributed and students are ready for the science lesson to begin, it is important to provide an introduction or overview to the lesson. Many times, this introduction provides students with an expectation of what is to come next, giving them a focus for relating the events of the activity. Most introductions do not involve telling students the expected outcomes of the activities, or even the specific objectives of the lesson if they take the excitement of discovery learning away from the student.

Grouping Students

Before beginning science lesson activities, it is important to group students for cooperative learning. This usually involves dividing the students into small groups of two to four students. Cooperative learning groups provide for effective learning and are useful in organizing the classroom for the distribution and return of science materials. These groups can be given names or numbers to facilitate materials distribution.

Using Classroom Rules

Effective classroom management in hands-on, minds-on science requires teaching and modeling all classroom rules. This process can be fun and interesting to the student. One technique is to post daily and weekly classroom schedules and student-helper lists. Students have a right to know when they will be involved in activities and what their roles will involve.

During the beginning of the lesson, teachers monitor and redirect the behavior of students who are not on task. Nonverbal communication is best where possible, including hand signals or facial expressions. If necessary, ask misdirected students to describe their task and their present responsibility. If further redirection is required, use a quiet discussion including the effects of the present behavior if continued and the positive effects of the requested behavior on fellow classmates if completed.

Lesson Smoothness

Students keep on task when teachers provide smooth, evenly paced, relevant lessons. Science teachers are aware of the various ways the flow of learning can be disrupted or enhanced. Lesson confusion is handled by appropriate *lesson planning* before the lesson begins. For example, lessons involving discrepant events are particularly effective in motivating learning in students and creating more manageable and on-task student behaviors (Kounin, 1970). Clearly knowing the sequence of activities, having all materials ready, and anticipating management problems creates a smoother lesson. Specific classroom management practices used during the teacher-led part of the lesson increase the smoothness and pacing of a hands-on, minds-on science lesson. These include:

- Completing instruction on the original idea before switching to instruction on a new idea.
- Staying with an instructional activity and avoiding repeated switching and returning to the original activity.
- Announcing only ideas or information relevant to the activity at hand.
- Avoiding disrupting the whole-group student activity by over-attention to minor student misbehavior. (Kounin, 1970)

Being a Facilitator

Effective classroom management during student activities involves teachers helping students who are having difficulty and monitoring the progress of individuals and groups (Jacobowitz, 1997). The teacher moves around the class from group to group asking questions to help focus or redirect student learning. These questions are usually open ended. Rather than focusing directly on a teacher-perceived answer, teacher questions create more thought on the part of the student. The questions help focus the students' attention on what they are doing. Examples are: "What evidence do you have for making that statement?" "Why did you say that?" and "Why have you been doing that?" In small groups, students usually feel freer to ask questions or to provide explanations that may not be well thought out. It is important that the teacher creates an atmosphere where students are willing to try out new ideas and explanations without fear of embarrassment. The teacher's role during the student activity part of the lesson is one of a facilitator and helper in fostering student learning (Ross, 1997).

The guidelines for classroom management just provided do not cover all situations. These are suggested only as a sample of the kinds of classroom management teachers use when they involve students in effective hands-on, minds-on learning. See Figure 7–4 for a brief outline of the major methods discussed. It takes practice to develop a teaching style that is effective in providing meaningful science learning activities to students.

No longer is the teacher's role one of giving information and facts. The roles of the teacher and students have changed. Some recommended practices and ideas for classroom management are:

- Locate materials where they are to be used.
- Prepare your plan and materials ahead of time.
- Provide an overview before beginning.
- Give directions first.
- Plan your distribution.
- Assign students to work in small groups.
- Direct students' energy toward lesson objectives.
- Conduct smooth lessons.
- Post schedules.
- Reduce confusion.
- Serve as a guide.
- Ask thinking-type questions.

FIGURE 7-4 *Classroom management for hands-on elementary science teaching*

*Even young students can learn
science safety.*

Applying What You Know

Analyzing Classroom Management

Evaluate one of your previous science lesson plans, or an observation of a science lesson, for the appropriateness of the classroom management methods preplanned or implemented. Use Figure 7–4 as a checklist of areas to be addressed in an effective classroom management plan. Discuss your responses with others, comparing potential problems and your rationale.

SAFETY IN SCIENCE LESSONS

When planning lessons, the teacher should be aware of safety problem areas and suggested safe practices (National Research Council, 1996, p. 44). Safety rules and guidelines have been established by national organizations such as the Occupational Safety and Health Administration (OSHA) as well as by local and state education agencies. It is strongly suggested that copies be obtained of science safety precautions for science topics you will be teaching and have had little experience with. These can be obtained from the Internet, science safety guides for teachers from your state department of education, or professional science teachers organizations.

Specific information for science teaching is found in publications by the National Science Teachers Association, The Eisenhower National Clearinghouse for Mathematics and Science, and The American Chemical Society. Links to these organizations can be found on the Companion Website at *http://www.prenhall.com/sunal*

When planning a lesson, check the science topic to be planned with an outline of general safety guidelines for that area. This will be a first check on possible safety precautions. An outline of a planning reference guide for science safety is found in Figure 7–5. The figure lists general ideas and suggested practices to be aware of when planning classroom science lessons. In particular, review areas that are unfamiliar. The topics include reference guidelines for safety glasses, first aid, open flames, field trips, animals, plants, chemicals, electricity, high-risk materials, and rockets (Feldkamp-Price, 1994; McBride & Chiapetta, 1992; Rossman, 1993). Also, read through related topics as a reminder while planning your classroom management for the science lesson. Obtain additional, in-depth guidelines from other sources, such as those suggested above, on the Internet or publications from your state department of education or local school system.

Safety Glasses
1. Demonstration areas should be protected by a plexiglass shield.
2. Students must wear safety glasses if there is the possibility of flying objects, splashing, or spattering. Eye protection devices must be sanitized after each use.

First Aid
1. If an accident occurs, contact the principal's office and the parents or guardian immediately after checking for severe bleeding and breathing failure.
2. Wash cuts with soap and water. Do not apply antiseptic.
3. Do not apply greases or oils to burns.
4. Do not touch an electrical shock victim while he is in contact with the current.
5. Do not give an unconscious person liquids.
6. If bitten by a warm-blooded animal, try to confine the animal for future examination.
7. If an allergic reaction occurs from an insect sting, rush the victim to the hospital immediately.
8. The phone number of the Poison Control Center is _____.

Open Flames
1. Candles should always be placed on a tray or protective mat.
2. Avoid using alcohol burners.
3. When using Bunsen burners, never turn on the gas before lighting the match.
4. Propane or portable burners should never be used by the student.
5. Never place a warm or burning material in the wastebasket.
6. Never reach over an open flame.

FIGURE 7-5   *Some general safety guidelines for hands-on, activity-oriented science teaching*

7. Hair and articles of clothing should be tied back during activities using open flames.

8. Check fire regulations in your school before you plan a lesson using open flames. Electrical hot plates are a possible substitute.

9. Know the proper procedures in case of a fire.

10. Flammable liquids should be properly labeled and kept in a locked cabinet.

11. Flammable liquids should not be handled by the students.

Field Trips

1. Even the most experienced teacher must be alert to potential dangers while on a field trip.

2. Proper student conduct is extremely important in the out-of-doors.

3. Proper clothing is necessary for a comfortable trip.

4. Students should be able to identify poison ivy, poison oak, and poison sumac before taking a field trip.

5. Glass containers should never be taken on a field trip.

6. If exposed to very cold weather, never rub a numb area. It may result in tissue damage.

Animals in the Classroom

1. No experiment should be performed which will cause pain, suffering, or discomfort to an animal.

2. Animals must be housed, fed, and cared for to maintain normal growth.

3. Wild animals should never be brought into the classroom.

4. Handle animals only when necessary.

5. Animal bites and scratches should be washed and reported immediately.

6. Animal wastes and bedding should be disposed of in a safe and sanitary manner.

7. An unusual odor from the cage could indicate illness.

8. Wash hands after handling snakes, turtles, fish, frogs, toads, and so on.

9. After observation, all cold-blooded animals should be returned to their natural environment.

10. Poisonous snakes should never enter the classroom.

11. Treat all bacteria as if they were pathogens (disease-producing).

12. Aquariums should be emptied with a siphon.

Plants and Molds in the Classroom

1. Don't place any plants or plant parts in the mouth.

2. Apple seeds, mistletoe berries, and other common seeds are toxic.

3. Seeds may be coated with toxic insecticides.

4. Petri dishes should be sealed and disposed of after use.

5. Fungicides, pesticides, and fertilizers must be stored in a locked cabinet.

6. If a toxic plant or chemical is consumed, contact the Poison Control Center immediately for advice.

Materials (Chemicals) and Equipment in the Classroom

1. Protective clothing and glasses should be worn if there is a possibility of the splashing or spilling of chemicals.

2. An ABC-type extinguisher should be readily available when using flammable chemicals.

3. Students should never carry apparatus in congested areas.

4. Students should never taste, smell, or touch an unknown chemical.

5. All chemicals should be labeled. Unmarked chemicals must be discarded.

6. Proper disposal of chemicals is mandatory.

7. Some acid vapor is toxic.

8. Do not directly look at magnesium ribbon if it is burning.

FIGURE 7-5   *Continued*

186

9. Dry ice produces carbon dioxide, a gas. Do not put it in a closed container.
10. Never use an 110-volt source or incandescent light in an electricity experiment.
11. The smoke and dust resulting from burning ammonium dichromate (used in volcano demonstrations) is toxic.
12. Mixing baking soda and vinegar may cause an explosion if put in a closed container.
13. Formaldehyde may cause an allergic reaction.
14. Asbestos is carcinogenic (cancer-producing).
15. Mercury thermometers (or the mercury metal) are not recommended for use in the classroom.
16. When using knives of any type, the student must cut away from herself.
17. Plastic, rather than glass, apparatus is recommended when heat is not involved.
18. Cracked or broken equipment should be discarded.
19. Use a lubricant and safe procedures when inserting corks or stoppers with tubes. Do not allow students to do this.
20. The floor should be clean and dry where machines and tools are being used.
21. Pumps and belt-driven machines must be fastened securely and have a belt guard.

Electricity in the Classroom
1. During experiments, students should use dry cells rather than wet cells or 110-volt A/C outlet current.
2. Never leave an 110-volt socket open and accessible to students.
3. Appliances and cords should be checked regularly.
4. When inserting or removing an electric plug, always hold it by the plug, not the cord.
5. All electrical devices should be properly grounded.
6. Secure loose clothing, jewelry, and hair when using machines with moving parts.
7. A short-circuited dry cell can produce a high temperature.
8. Use only carbon dioxide fire extinguishers on electrical fires.
9. If skin is exposed to battery acid, thoroughly flush the area with plenty of water.

Model Rockets and Other Propelled Objects
1. Propellants or fuel for model cars and planes should be stored in a cool, locked cabinet.
2. Do not launch planes near a crowded area, trees, power lines, or buildings.
3. Model rockets should never be made of metal.
4. The launching site should be roped off when using model rockets.
5. A countdown system should be used when launching model rockets. Follow published guidelines.
6. Never attempt to retrieve a rocket or kite from a power line.

FIGURE 7-5   *Continued*

Applying What You Know

Identifying Science Safety Considerations

Locate a section in an elementary or middle school science textbook involving electricity.

1. Describe important science safety considerations to be included in a science lesson plan involving hands-on electricity activities for this textbook section. Use Figure 7–5 as a guide.

(continued)

2. Find an additional source on the Internet or elsewhere to add to the possible guidelines to consider.
3. Discuss your responses with others, comparing potential problems and your rationale for concern.
4. Identify areas in electrical safety on which you need more information.

SUMMARY

Teachers with a basic foundation in each of the three science teaching dimensions—pedagogy, science pedagogy, and science content—have the knowledge and skills to create meaningful science learning. While it has been found that teachers who have little or no science content knowledge are not effective, teaching success relates to knowing general procedures in effective teaching and learning, effectively using a repertoire of science-content-related teaching and learning methods, having adequate science content knowledge organized in a meaningful way, and knowing where and how science information can be obtained if additional information is needed.

chapter 8

Assessing and Evaluating Science Learning

▼▲▼ EXPLORING YOUR IDEAS ▼▲▼▲▼▲▼▲▼▲▼▲▼▲▼

Evaluate the appropriateness of the planned assessment in one of your previously written science lesson plans or a set of pages in a teacher's and a student's edition of a science textbook. If possible, work with a partner on this activity. Answer the questions below:

1. Where in the lesson did assessment occur? Where in the lesson plan did evaluation occur?
2. Evaluate the effectiveness of the assessment and evaluation in the lesson plan using Figure 8–1. Provide evidence supporting your evaluation.

Chapter Objectives

1. Differentiate between testing, assessment, and evaluation in science teaching.
2. Describe the broad evaluative functions of assessment information.
3. Describe the purpose of assessment and evaluation in science.
4. Differentiate traditional assessment from alternative assessment for meaningful learning.
5. Describe the uses of assessment in a unit and lesson evaluation.
6. Identify and describe the types of assessment.
7. Discuss and develop alternative assessment measures of science learning outcomes.

Formative Evaluation
1. Finding out what students' ideas and skills are prior to instruction in science.
2. Monitoring student science learning.
Summative Evaluation
3. Determining the extent of change in students' ideas and skills.

FIGURE 8-1   *Evaluative functions of assessment information*

WHAT IS ASSESSING AND EVALUATING SCIENCE LEARNING?

Assessment and evaluation occur daily in our lives. For example, one might ask, "How do I know if I am an adequate cook or an adequate gardener?" She answers this question by first assessing her work. If she constantly burns vegetables, giving them an unnatural taste, or if her kitchen is cluttered with boxes and dirty cookware, she can evaluate her performance as a cook as "weak." Or, if she has an organized and efficient work area for her tools, and healthy plants, she can evaluate her performance as a gardener as "strong." The characteristics of her abilities and the products she cooks or grows have been used as an assessment. The information provides the basis for an evaluation of her performance as a cook or gardener. Assessment and evaluation involve a purpose, criteria, methods and tools, evidence, people, and consequences (Rowe, 1991).

Assessment and evaluation of students involves teachers in consideration of their abilities and products, and in recognition of students' developmental needs. Assessment and evaluation examine the abilities and products that are important in the lives of students. They consider students' abilities and products in the situation in which they are learning, and in situations in which they use what they have learned.

Assessment and evaluation are a major part of a classroom teacher's role. Effective teaching and continued self-improvement as a teacher are possible only with good skills in student assessment and evaluation (Harlen, 1991; Rowe, 1991). Students own self-improvement is more likely to occur when the teacher effectively assesses and evaluates them. Improvement is more likely because teachers skilled in assessment help students obtain the feedback they need to decide where to make changes in their thinking and in how they perform learning activities.

This chapter describes the classroom assessment process in teaching science and the types of assessment that can be used. Having skills in using a wide range of tools and methods that address different purposes for assessment is important. Assessment, and the evaluation of that information, recognizes students' developmental needs. It also recognizes that science learning involves working with inquiry processes and content. When evaluation recognizes both of these, it helps teachers plan lessons that promote meaningful learning and measure progress for a wide range of human development.

Recent reforms have called for science instruction incorporating physical and mental student involvement, higher-order thinking skills, cooperative group work, and interdisciplinary learning. Forms of assessment must change as curricula and instruction change to reflect these diversified goals (Lehman, 1994, p. 48). Traditional testing provides information focusing on whether the student recognizes or recalls what is learned in an artificial setting. Meaningful learning is best assessed through finding out whether a student can use an idea or skill to solve a real problem.

Assessment, testing, and evaluation are different processes. **Assessment** is a part of instruction, helping teachers gather information for specific purposes. **Testing** is a tool or instrument teachers use at widely spaced intervals to measure what a student knows at that time; it's only a part of the assessment process. Assessment is much more than testing; it's a continual and integrated part of instruction, not just something that follows a lesson (Foster & Heiting, 1994). It involves student knowledge and skills, as well as actions and products. Students learn through assessment experiences as well as in regular instructional activities.

Assessment in science involves gathering information with three evaluative functions:

1. Finding out what ideas and skills students have prior to their instruction in science (prior knowledge).
2. Monitoring student learning (monitoring).
3. Determining the extent of change in students' ideas and skills (summative evaluation).

The first two evaluative functions represent formative evaluation, or making decisions during the instructional process. The last evaluative function provides summative evaluation, or making decisions about the result of the instructional process or summing up (see Figure 8-1). Assessment involves documenting observations, student verbal exchanges, and student products. It considers what students do and how they do it. When the information gathered from assessment is interpreted and used to make judgments and decisions, **evaluation** is occurring.

The purpose of a given assessment has implications for the *type* of information gathered, *how* the information is gathered, and *what kind of evaluation* results from the assessment. There are many evaluation purposes for assessing students' science learning that fit under the three evaluative functions. For example:

1. A teacher may want to determine the prior knowledge of students in a specific area of science, such as energy.
2. To monitor students' learning, a teacher may want to:
   * provide feedback to students about their own hands-on performance and collaborative learning during or following a science activity.
   * provide feedback to students about their collaborative efforts as the science activity is underway.
   * provide feedback about students' use of inquiry skills during and following a science activity.
3. To sum up, the teacher may want to:
   * determine the students' depth of understanding in science learning outcomes.
   * determine student development toward the goals of the science unit.
   * determine student development toward the goals identified by state or national science standards.

WHY DOES TEACHING FOR MEANINGFUL LEARNING INVOLVE MULTIPLE USES AND FORMS OF ASSESSMENT?

If assessment is narrowly defined as factual recall by a teacher, students will believe that the only important learning outcomes are the facts that were recalled to answer the majority of the questions on the last quiz. Students are likely to believe that once you have taken and passed a quiz, you can forget those facts. The problem with the assessment of areas beyond the memorization or recall level is that most students and teachers have little experience with such assessment. Since traditional assessment often tests for memory or recall of facts, it is difficult to think of a more appropriate way of assessing learning. Teaching and assessing for meaningful learning involves assessing higher-level outcomes with much less emphasis on recall or comprehension. **Science assessment** involves gathering information on

TABLE 8–1   *Changing the emphasis of assessment in science learning*

Traditional Science Testing More Often:	Alternative Science Assessment More Often:
• Determines student grades and ranks students.	• Is used as feedback for teachers to plan and carry out lessons and provide student learning.
• Uses paper-and-pencil, quick-answer objective tests (e.g., true/false, fill-in-the-blank, multiple-choice).	• Uses paper-and-pencil, essay, interviews, observation,and performance testing.
• Focuses on science facts.	• Focuses on student understanding and the use of scientific concepts, generalizations, and inquiry skills.
• Uses mean test scores to compare students.	• Uses criteria (rubrics) to judge students' performance as well as to set student goals.
• Tests students weekly and at the end of the unit.	• Continuously assesses students' skills and products of learning.
• Has students working alone on tests.	• Combines assessment from individuals and work with other students.
• Focuses on student recall of information.	• Focuses on what students are able to do.
• Focuses on science information.	• Focuses on critical and creative thinking.

capacities and products we think are essential in the context where they were learned and are to be used. During assessment, teachers consider what skills and content students bring to the lesson, what students are doing during the learning activities, what information best describes the skills and content students are expected to gain from the lesson, and what information best describes students' development. In science, teachers do not view assessment as involving tests only and as an after-the-fact way of finding out what students have learned. Instead, teachers view assessment as a part of instruction: clarifying, providing feedback, and setting goals toward which student activity is directed (Jones, 1994). See Table 8–1 for a comparison of traditional testing and the alternative science assessment required in today's classrooms.

Do we judge our students to be deficient in writing, speaking, and listening to science? In analyzing scientific data and ideas? In doing scientific research? In creatively approaching science ideas? In forming scientific attitudes through thoughtful analysis, problem posing, and problem solving? If students are deficient, then teachers actively involve them in doing, thinking, and communicating these science outcomes. As part of this process, teachers assess students by allowing them to write, speak, and listen interactively in science, analyze science-related situations, pose and solve science problems, do scientific research, create science, and express themselves in diverse ways. Alternative science assessment tasks gather information about students' performance in the science lesson activity, simulation, project, experiment, game, play, debate, or recital. They also gather information on how students use science knowledge and inquiry skills in solving everyday problems they encounter.

Effective ways of observing and recording require skills not usually required in traditional classroom teaching. Turning a goal into purposeful assessment does not require more work; it requires a different kind of work (Foster & Heiting, 1994; Jones, 1994). A second-grade plant unit where students are expected to understand the concept of *plant* can serve as an example. The concept of *plant* involves understanding the essential parts of the plant, the functions of each part, and the diversity among plant parts and functions. Traditional instruction and assessment involve students in spelling and writing the name of the parts of the plant (root, stem, leaf, and flower), reading a simple description of these parts, and copying a large diagram with the plant parts labeled. These lesson objectives reflect low-level knowledge as the desired outcomes. Following instruction, the teacher continues by testing students' knowledge. Students are asked to spell each word, and label the parts on a plant diagram. Students who have spelled and labeled a majority of the plant parts correctly are evaluated as having successfully completed the lesson. Those who have misspelled or mislabeled two or more terms are judged as unsuccessful.

This process does not represent useful assessment, nor does it represent good instruction. To test the validity of the traditional assessment process, teachers show a live common plant to these students or take them into the school yard and point out a common plant. Try a grass plant, a "common weed," or a maple tree. Ask them whether they think it is a plant and request evidence for their answer. If, for example, they have been asked to identify grass or a "common weed" plant, they may have trouble answering the question, "Where is the stem?" or, in most cases, "Where is the flower?" In the case of a maple tree, they may be able to quickly identify a stem, but they may have trouble finding a flower.

The students are likely to have trouble with an assessment such as the one just described because the lesson did not involve them in meaningful, hands-on, minds-on activities. Students must investigate essential aspects of the concept of *plant,* such as its size, shape, color, texture, and growth patterns. Nor did the lesson involve them in understanding the functions of a plant. Students did not have minds-on experiences that involved them in transferring the lesson's activities to the real world outside the classroom.

The same problems exist in the lesson assessment. Because of the poor instruction, it is difficult for the lesson to be aligned with more meaningful science assessment. The lesson is focused only on low-level knowledge. However, in addition to a test, the teacher could observe student performance during hands-on activities (Jones, 1994). The teacher could consider how appropriately students were using the basic science skills of observing and communicating. In order to assess and evaluate meaningful learning, the teacher considers both the *content learned* and the *skills used* to learn the content.

See Chapters 4 and 5 for an outline of the components of meaningful instruction.

WHAT ARE THE PURPOSES OF ASSESSMENT IN SCIENCE LESSONS AND UNITS?

Because assessment is a necessary part of effective instruction, a teacher needs to determine the purposes of the assessment and the uses of the information being gathered. Assessment helps the teacher make judgments that evaluate the learning process. Important questions assessment can help answer are: "What do students need to know to be effective learners?" "What do teachers need to know about students and their own teaching to be effective teachers?" and "What do families and schools need to know about student performance in order to determine the developmental progress their children are making?"

Evaluation of today's standards-based, hands-on science lessons uses a range of information. To be effective evaluators, teachers consider students' prior knowledge, hands-on performance, collaborative efforts, use of the range of inquiry skills, depth of understanding, and developmental level. Each of these is considered in terms of the knowledge and skills identified as outcomes in the goals of a unit (see Figure 8–2). Each of these has specific types of assessment tools and procedures useful in evaluation.

The teacher begins the process of assessment when determining the **goal** of a unit or lesson based on a national, state, or local science standard. Students are assessed to determine whether they meet the goal. Clear goals are crucial to effective assessment. A goal can be assessed in relation to each of the uses of information identified above. Several, or all, of these uses of information are involved in every unit evaluation.

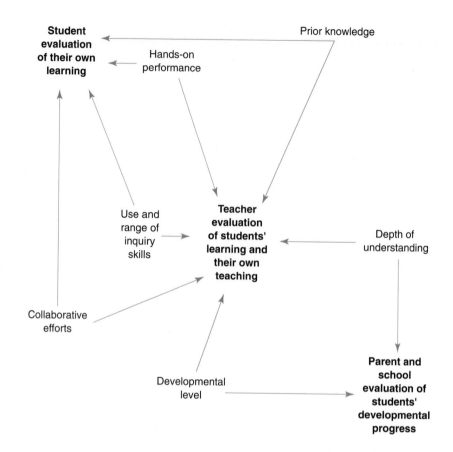

FIGURE 8-2 *Primary uses of assessment information for making judgments in evaluating the learning process*

To be most effective, assessment must be a real part of instructional planning and of the teaching process in every science unit. Assessment is a natural activity connected to the flow of each lesson. It ends each day with a reflection on changes in students' ideas and inquiry skills (see Figure 8–3). Goals developed from science standards form the basis for a general unit assessment plan. The lessons use learning cycles that include assessment for information needed by students, teachers, and schools to implement meaningful science learning. Assessment helps teachers create change in students' ideas and inquiry skills.

Different parts of the learning cycle require different assessment information. For example, information on prior knowledge is needed during the Exploration phase by both students and the teacher. Depth of understanding and developmental level are important assessment information when the lesson and unit learning experiences are concluded. Table 8–2 provides a guide for gathering information during different parts of the learning cycle.

Prior Knowledge

Chapters 2 and 5 have discussed prior knowledge and its effects on learning.

Assessment at the beginning of a unit and lesson occurs during the Exploration phase of the learning cycle. It focuses on what students bring to the lesson from a developmental perspective (Driver, 1990). Their past beliefs and experiences are related to the unit's topic to make up their prior knowledge.

Listening to what students say and observing what they do takes place during individual and group activities, one-to-one discussions, small group discussions, and class discussions.

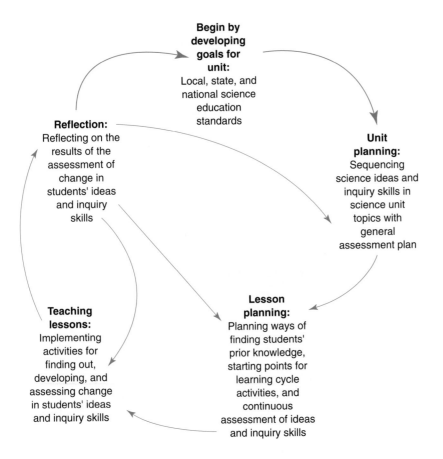

FIGURE 8-3 *How does the assessment fit the approach taken in instructional planning and teaching?*

TABLE 8-2 *Assessment forms during each phase of the learning cycle*

Part of Lesson (Evaluation Priority)	Primary Assessment	Secondary Assessment
Exploration phase and before the lesson begins (Finding out students' ideas and skills)	Prior knowledge Developmental level	Hands-on performance Collaborative efforts Use and range of inquiry skills Depth of understanding
Invention phase (Monitoring student learning)	Hands-on performance Collaborative efforts Use and range of inquiry skills	Prior knowledge Depth of understanding Developmental level
Expansion phase (Monitoring student learning)	Collaborative efforts Use and range of inquiry skills	Prior knowledge Hands-on performance Depth of understanding Developmental level
At the end or after the lesson (Determining the extent of change in students' ideas and skills)	Use and range of inquiry skills Depth of understanding Developmental level	Prior knowledge Hands-on performance Collaborative efforts

FIGURE 8-4 *Annotated drawing of the digestive system*

Draw and tell what you think happens to food inside your body.

My body has three stomacks inside. I have a candy stomack. It gets very full allot. I have a water stomack. It gets thirrsty alot. I have a food stomack. I love my food stomack.

The types of assessment often used to provide information about students' prior knowledge include student observation, interviews, annotated drawings/diagrams, sequenced drawings, structured writing, journals, and problem-solving tasks involving counter-intuitive or discrepant events related to the topic of the unit. See Figures 8–4 and 8–5 for examples of annotated drawings and diagrams to assess prior knowledge. This

Draw what you think happens in an egg.

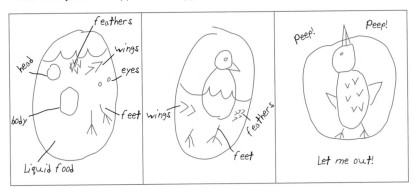

FIGURE 8-5 *Sequenced drawing of the development of a chick in an egg*

process is usually integrated with the lesson's Exploration activity. The assessment then becomes part of the instruction.

See Chapters 12 through 14 for examples of using discrepant events to help students become aware of their prior knowledge.

Hands-On, Minds-On Performance

Hands-on performance is a phrase that has been widely used to identify physical actions students perform with manipulatives during a lesson. In assessment, hands-on performance includes student actions relating to how the students met the goal of the lesson. There are critical experiences that students must have during the lesson if their learning is to have personal meaning (Kulm & Stuessy, 1991; Reichel, 1994). Throughout a science lesson's planned activities, hands-on involvement must engage students' minds in all phases of the learning cycle.

Assessment takes place throughout the lesson to determine whether students are engaged in hands-on performance. This includes being physically involved with their hands and bodies and having their minds engaged through writing, reporting, informal discussing, or cooperatively working with a group of students. Assessment includes students' actions, comments, and products. Their products include what they write, draw, make, or set up. The types of assessment useful in evaluation of hands-on performance include observation, interviews, work samples, portfolios, journals, and group discussion.

Collaborative Efforts of Students

The interaction of students with others is an observable event, yet it has rarely been used as a part of assessment in traditional classrooms. These interactive experiences require intense, minds-on involvement of students. When a teacher builds purposeful, diverse, and extensive interactions between and among students into a lesson, learning becomes more meaningful to those students. They must report, explain, justify, and evaluate from multiple perspectives to work successfully in a group. The teacher, in turn, has an opportunity to obtain meaningful assessment information about the learning process (Reichel, 1994). Assessment of cooperative efforts takes place in all phases of the learning cycle. The types of assessment useful with cooperative learning include observation, interviews, group work samples, group tests, portfolios, journals, and group discussions (Johnson & Johnson, 1991).

Use of the Range of Inquiry Skills

In traditional classrooms, problem solving often focuses on memory use and lower-order thought processes. Effective science assessment puts a greater emphasis on higher-order thinking and is accomplished by providing students with challenging learning activities. Events, challenges, and problems are presented which include new and different contexts so students begin the process of transferring learning from the classroom to the real world. The assessment of science inquiry skills appropriate to the new idea is most useful during the Invention and Expansion phases of the learning cycle.

Teachers have become much more aware of the importance of students' feelings about how and what they learn. Students' feelings are a critical factor in their depth of understanding and ability to transfer knowledge to the real world. If a student's belief about an idea is challenged in a setting that causes anxiety or dislike, the student is not likely to change the idea. A misconception, a naive understanding, or an inaccurate view of an aspect of the natural world will remain with the student when the lesson is over. When required to use this knowledge in everyday situations, the student uses this original belief as a basis for action. It is important for teachers to be aware of students' attitudes and dispositions in a science topic area. This information is used to guide the instructional process and to assess the whole student.

Attitudes and dispositions are assessed in the Exploration and Expansion phases of the learning cycle. In a unit, it is useful to begin assessment of student attitudes and dispositions in the Exploration phase. Later assessments are best made in lessons during the middle and later parts of a unit. This approach allows the teacher to compare student progress in an attitude or disposition over a period of time and across different units.

The types of assessment effective here include written formats, such as multiple-choice tests, short essays, and papers, and using observation, interviews, group discussion, portfolios, and performance testing.

A discussion and examples of attitudes and dispositions that are important in elementary and middle school science learning are found in Chapter 4.

See Chapter 4 for a listing of inquiry skills.

Depth of Understanding and Developmental Level

Assessing depth of understanding in traditional assessment usually involves having the students give correct answers that repeat the teacher's or text's definition of a term or concept. However, teachers need to move beyond this narrow perspective. Effective science assessment includes having students construct narratives that describe their understanding of the experiences they have and how they use their understanding in solving problems. Effective science assessment does not ask the student to mimic the idea taught. A more valid measure of the depth of understanding of an idea assesses the capacity of a student to create products in diverse contexts built on the idea. The student should be able to transfer what was learned to the real world in a meaningful way.

Assessment of the depth of understanding is best performed following the Expansion phase of the learning cycle through tests, field trips, and projects. The types of assessment effective in assessing depth of understanding include activities similar to those used in the Expansion phase of the lesson, written formats such as multiple-choice tests, short essays and papers, drawings and diagrams, and observational formats such as interviews, group discussions, portfolios, and performance testing.

Part of the knowledge students learn in school science includes recall of facts such as the names of objects, events, and procedures for carrying out various tasks. For example, students are asked to memorize the identity of common tree species, constellations, and elements. They also might memorize events such as the dates and number of years between the appearances of Halley's Comet. Memorized procedures often include the steps in mounting a specimen on a microscope slide and accurately determining the mass of an object on a double-pan balance. Assessment of memory occurs best after the Expansion phase of the learning cycle. The types of assessment used include multiple-choice, matching, true/false, fill-in-the-blank, and short essay tests, labeling drawings, role-play, performance testing, and demonstrating the skill.

Students' progress is not limited to one facet of development (Driver, 1990). Assessment of different types of progress is needed, including inquiry skills, the formation of more abstract and more widely acceptable scientific ideas, and the social skills supporting investigations by student groups. Being alert to students' progress allows teachers to encourage their development (Driver, 1990). Assessment can begin with a comparison of students' progress toward local, state, or national science standards. Student development includes the ability to do scientific inquiry, physical science, life science, Earth and space science, science and technology, science in personal and social perspectives, and the history and nature of science (National Research Council, 1996).

A comparison of students' abilities to do scientific inquiry usually involves developing a **rubric assessment**. This is an ordered sequence of performance levels that students in a class are expected to have at that time. Rubrics include a list of actions by individuals or groups of students to be observed during the lesson. For instance, a third-grade teacher considers whether his students can ask questions about objects or events without prompting, whether they seek information from observations to answer their own questions, and whether they identify those questions that can be answered by simple investigation. These and other behaviors are part of a developmental sequence used to compare students' progress toward a science standard. Table 8–3 contains a sample rubric sequence for the development of scientific questioning and planning, and for conducting investigations (National Research Council, 1996). The items in the sequence can be grouped into fewer levels or be refined to create more levels (Price & Hein, 1994). The types of assessment useful in determining developmental level include observation, interviews, short essays, drawings with narration, portfolios, and performance testing.

TABLE 8–3 *Sequence of developmental levels based on two science standards*

STUDENT ABILITIES NEEDED TO PERFORM SCIENTIFIC INQUIRY		
Developmental Level	Scientific Questions	Planning and Conducting Investigations
1	Asks questions about an object or event.	Able to make systematic observations with all senses.
2	Answers own questions about an object or event by seeking information from observations and investigations.	Able to conduct simple experiments suggested to answer questions.
3	Identifies questions of others that can be answered through observation and investigation.	Able to design and conduct simple experiments.
4	Refines and refocuses broad and ill-defined questions about objects or events.	Able to identify and use a fair test in an investigation.
5	Identifies own question with a specific scientific concept, formulates a plan, gathers accurate data, interprets and uses evidence to propose explanations to a question.	Able to design and conduct a scientific investigation.

Applying What You Know

Reflecting on Your Earlier Ideas

Return to the *Exploring Your Ideas* activity with which this chapter started. Answer the questions below, preferably while working with a partner.

1. What is the purpose of each assessment planned in the lesson? For example, you may note that hands-on performance will be assessed. You may decide that the purpose of this assessment is to determine whether students are engaged by the task or are ready for the next level of the exercise. Therefore, you decide that the teacher is monitoring students' science learning. Now, identify the assessment (if it exists) and its purpose in the lesson plan you are examining for each of the following phases:
   a. Exploration
   b. Invention
   c. Expansion
2. Evaluate the quality of the assessment in the lesson plan.
   a. Is information gathered for each evaluative function?
   b. Is information gathered for a variety of purposes?
Provide evidence supporting your conclusions.

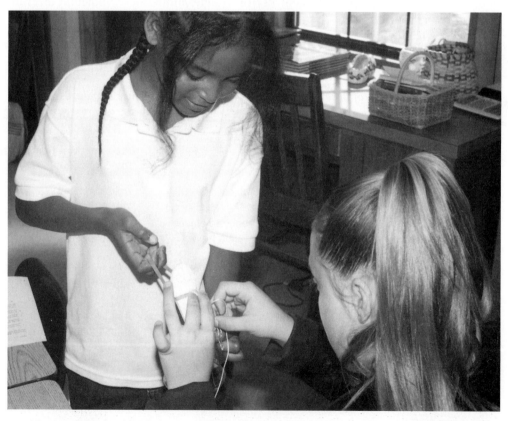

Could a simple knowledge test evaluate the learning taking place in this activity?

HOW DO YOU EVALUATE SCIENCE LEARNING?

The choice of assessment type sometimes influences and limits the use of hands-on learning by students. It is relatively easy to test students' knowledge when they have been asked to memorize lists of data. It is much harder to assess science learning from direct observations of experience.

Assessment involves more than giving a test for the purpose of a grade. Effective science assessment involves a variety of tools and methods. There are three evaluative functions (see Table 8–4) into which the various types of assessment tools and methods fit. The first evaluative function is finding out what students' ideas and skills are. This is known as *assessing for prior knowledge* for instructional decision making. It is necessary to determine the knowledge and experience students bring to the lesson in order to know where to start and to identify those experiences on which to focus.

The second function involves *monitoring student science learning* during the instructional process. Monitoring assessment provides immediate feedback to the teacher and students about the learning process taking place. It gives information regarding hands-on performance, collaborative efforts of students, and the use and range of inquiry skills.

The third function involves *summative assessment.* This assessment provides information about student actions and products resulting from a learning activity, lesson, or unit. The types of tools used determine whether students have meaningfully

TABLE 8–4　*Types of assessment useful in evaluating science learning*

Type of Assessment	EVALUATIVE FUNCTION OF INFORMATION		
	Prior	Monitoring	Summative
Observation			
Anecdotal record	X	X	
Checklist	X	X	X
Interview	X	X	X
Annotated drawing	X	X	X
Portfolio	X	X	X
Discussion	X	X	X
Journal	X	X	
Peer rating	X	X	
Self-rating	X	X	
Presentation	X	X	X
Group evaluation		X	X
Performance testing	X	X	X
Multiple-choice	X		X
Matching	X		X
True/false			X
Fill-in-the-blank			X
Short answer	X		
Essay	X	X	X
Project		X	X
Webbing/Concept Map	X	X	X

Note: The X indicates the categories evaluated using each form of assessment.

learned the key ideas or skills of the lesson, whether they are ready to proceed to the next idea, and the effectiveness of the teacher's approach in the lesson. Summative assessments give information about students' depth of understanding and their development of the ideas and skills with which they have worked. Types of assessment used in this area are many, including observation, teacher-made and standardized tests, and portfolios. Technology can be used to obtain or record the information in an assessment for all three functions of evaluation. Software programs frequently have evaluative functions written into them.

Testing is the most common form of science learning assessment. Alternative evaluation formats usually involve collecting information in a learning environment without direct testing. There are several types of alternative evaluation formats, including observation, interviews, portfolios, discussions, group evaluations, and performance testing.

Observation

Teachers continuously make observations of their students, watching them work, plan, discuss ideas, express frustration, and so on (Airasian, 1994). These observations are usually informal and quick, often taking less than a minute. Teachers use their observations to adjust the pace and content of a lesson. Informal notes can be taken during observations and recorded for later use. At other times, teachers make more structured observations, particularly when they want to find out how a student or a group of students is progressing. Such observations are more systematic. The teacher makes an observation at a certain time or at a particular point in a lesson. Notes of the observations are generally recorded. For example, the teacher may observe the interactions occurring in a cooperative learning group every 5 minutes to develop an estimate of how well the students are working together. A teacher may also observe an individual during the beginning of lessons over several days to decide whether the student is able to adjust quickly to a new activity.

To carry out more systematic observation of an individual or a group of students, teachers develop instruments that provide them with specific types of information about student actions and products. These are usually integrated into the science lesson and unit. Checklists are useful for identifying science ideas and how well students work with them during inquiries. Observations assess specific behaviors or student products. It is not possible to make observations of everything. Therefore, deciding which behaviors contribute to meaningful science learning and making observations of those behaviors are important.

Underlying the assessment of specific behaviors is the students' need for feedback. If they are going to be able to solve problems, make decisions, and reflect on their thinking, students continuously need specific feedback. For example, they need feedback on how well they performed during the decision-making process, whether they had adequate information to make a good decision, and whether evidence supported their decision after it was made. Such specific feedback gives students information to compare their progress against appropriate models of decision-making behavior. Students need to receive credit for making progress toward an appropriate model rather than being marked down for not succeeding. Teachers give students feedback that helps them develop higher-order thinking skills by making systematic observations of the behaviors that contribute to those skills.

Anecdotal Records

Two ways of making and recording systematic observations are through anecdotal records and checklists. The anecdotal record lists the student's name, the date, the time of day a behavior occurred, and a description of the behavior observed. In describing the observed behavior, the teacher tries to be objective and does not draw conclusions. For example, the teacher might use an anecdotal record to determine whether a student is having difficulty organizing the equipment needed for a laboratory activity.

Useful anecdotal records report observations of the same behavior over a period of time. The teacher may observe the student at the beginning of every laboratory activity for a week. Some teachers carry around post-it notes or blank adhesive labels and make notes on them while observing. They then stick the notes in the student's file. In the example above, the teacher may note that the student has more difficulty on Thursday and Friday than earlier in the week. These observations may lead the teacher to make another set of anecdotal records that observe a behavior that might be responsible for the student's difficulties on Thursday and Friday. The teacher may also construct a checklist that allows for the observation of all the students to determine whether they have more difficulty organizing their equipment for laboratory activities on specific days of the week. Anecdotal records can provide information about behaviors that teachers use later to develop assessment checklists. Anecdotal records are often best used with students about whom the teacher has concerns. They enable the teacher to get a picture of the behavior of a single student or of a few students when several systematic observations of behaviors are made.

Checklists

Checklists are lists of student behaviors of interest to the teacher. They may be sequential, as in rubrics, or a list of separate actions to observe. They guide the observation because they enable the teacher to collect specific pieces of information for individuals or groups of students observed during the lesson. The teacher can observe many students when a checklist is used because the observation is shorter and less intensive than with an anecdotal record. However, checklists do not always follow up on information gathered first through anecdotal records. A teacher may begin systematic observation by using a checklist. Checklists do not have to be sequential, as in a rubric, but can be a list of items to observe. An example of a rubric for a science idea checklist appears in Table 8–5.

In a typical class of 20 or more students, it is difficult for a teacher to systematically use checklists and anecdotal records. When a teacher is actively involved with students,

TABLE 8–5   *A checklist rubric assessing a middle-grade student's progress in using the concepts of location and position of objects*

LOCATION AND MOTION OF OBJECTS	
Circle the appropriate level.	
Level of Skill	**Observed Student Actions**
1	Describes an object in ambiguous terms (e.g., close or far, fast or slow).
2	Describes an object by locating it relative to another object, and indicating its position at different times.
3	Describes an object by estimating or measuring its distance from at least two other objects and at two points in time.
4	Describes an object by quantitatively indicating its location and speed.
5	Describes an object by quantitatively and graphically indicating its position, direction of motion, and speed.

it is not always possible to stop and make careful observations. With planning, a teacher can identify times and specific students to observe systematically. For example, during small group work time, individual study, or practice sessions, a teacher can move freely among students. Such observations are designed to require little time. A checklist is helpful in this observation. If recorded immediately following work with an individual or group, checklists are accurate and rapidly completed.

Validity and reliability issues are considered in selecting the type of observation procedure to be used. To increase its validity, a checklist should match the purpose of the observation. To increase their reliability, observation procedures should be simple, since complex formats may introduce error into the assessment. Preplanned, specifically defined assessment observations are performed more easily with fewer errors than unplanned, global observations. One example of a global behavior observation is a "poor experiment report." If the checklist combines a number of important skills together, the teacher is unable to identify the cause of poor performance. A checklist is used several times to provide a more complete and accurate view of a student's ability, thus increasing its reliability. The observation time may be too short if a checklist is used just once to record key student actions that are only occasionally displayed.

The process of creating appropriate and useful observations begins with determining the *purpose* of the assessment. Next, it involves setting an *objective* on which all students will be evaluated. Then, the *behavior* that is related to the accomplishment of the objective is determined. Next, the variety of *levels* at which students will be performing the behavior is decided. Finally, to make record keeping easier, it involves the creation of a *checklist* rubric on which student performance will be recorded. When developed in this way, the phrase "assessment rubric" is generally used to describe the checklist. For instance, to measure a student's ability to make observations of the characteristics of plants, the teacher might include the following levels of observational behavior in an assessment rubric:

- A *low level of behavior* is identified when a student makes an observation of plant parts only when they are pointed out. For example, the student notices the plant parts named stem, stamen, and pistil only after they are pointed out to her.
- An *intermediate level of behavior* is identified when a student makes qualitative observations that do not involve analysis and measurements, such as whether each plant seems tall or short.
- A *higher level of behavior* is identified when qualitative and quantitative measures are used appropriately, such as height in centimeters, and involve utilizing several senses to make observations with reasonable accuracy. These provide only a limited amount of detail, and are missing one or more key elements (see Tables 8–6 and 8–7 for example rubrics showing levels of performance).

The checklist provides the teacher with an easy-to-use assessment. It includes clearly described specific observable behaviors so that there is little misunderstanding about the level on which the students are performing. If used over the course of many lessons, a unit, or throughout the year, a student's progress in a particularly important area is documented. When this information is provided to students, they are better able to assess themselves. This feedback provides students with a target level of behavior and builds their self-confidence and willingness to take charge of their own learning. The information might be used by fellow members of a cooperative learning group to assess each other. At the end of a grading period, this record displays the degree of student progress in an area and can be translated into numerical grades on a fixed scale, if necessary. For example, if the skill of classification is being evaluated (see Table 8–7), administering the

TABLE 8-6   *A checklist rubric assessing observation skills in a unit on plants*

OBSERVATION SKILL	
Circle the appropriate level.	
Level of Skill	**Observed Student Actions**
0	Does not make plant part observations, even when they are pointed out.
1	Only rarely makes plant part observations, even when they are pointed out.
2	Makes qualitative observations that do not involve analysis or measurement. Makes very limited use of senses, noticing only some things visually. Mixes statements of observations and inferences indiscriminately.
3	Uses quantitative measures when making observations (i.e., nine leaves). Uses several senses with reasonable accuracy. Orders observations consistently, and does not repeat those already made. Provides only a limited amount of detail. Sometimes mixes statements of observations and inferences indiscriminately.
4	Makes detailed, wide-ranging, accurate observations using all the senses. Selects those relevant to the particular inquiry. Provides an adequate amount of observed detail for each plant part. Asks for more samples to make additional observations.

TABLE 8-7   *Checklist rubric assessing classification skill*

CLASSIFICATION SKILLS	
Circle the appropriate level.	
Level of Skill	**Observed Student Actions**
0	Does not notice patterns in observations.
1	Looks for classification patterns but often suggests ones which are not justified by the evidence.
2	Consistently classifies according to one criterion and provides evidence for the classification pattern.
3	Classifies according to more than one criterion when it is pointed out.
4	Consistently classifies using several criteria. Makes reasonable inferences that fit the evidence, and attempts to explain the patterns found in instances outside the lesson examples (i.e., generalizes).

checklist rubric on four different occasions could result in a score of 16. A teacher may choose to give a grade of "A" for 16 to 14 points, a "B" for 13 to 11 points, and so on.

In addition to science content, checklists are helpful in assessing hard-to-measure areas such as science inquiry skills. These are found in lesson activities involving hands-on learning and cooperative learning. Students are usually asked to perform a wide range of actions in science lessons, such as classifying, formulating a question relating to cause and

TABLE 8-8   *Checklist rubric assessing problem-solving skills for elementary students*

PROBLEM-SOLVING SKILLS FOR A SPECIFIC CLASS OF PROBLEMS	
Circle the appropriate level.	
Level of Skill	**Observed Student Actions**
0	Unable to approach a problem without help.
1	Needs help to view the nature of the problem and then tries one or more ways of tackling it without much forethought as to what is likely to be relevant.
2	Sees nature of problem, begins to attempt steps toward its solution, but does not move systematically and/or has difficulty in carrying out each step in attempting to find an answer.
3	Investigates a simple problem systematically and sees the need for "fair testing," but rarely suggests possible explanations.
4	Investigates problems systematically, sees the need for "fair testing," and is beginning to make and test hypotheses.

See the discussion of operational definitions in Chapter 4.

effect relationships, identifying a variable, problem solving, performing an experiment, posing a research question in the form of a hypothesis, drawing conclusions based on data, or applying learning. An example of a checklist rubric for assessing problem solving is shown in Table 8–8.

To develop a checklist for any of these skills, it is important to decide on the highest level of skill expected of students. Writing the statement as an operational definition is a good first step in developing this highest level.

This characteristic is given the highest number. The teacher might use a "3," or a greater point scale such as level 4 found on Table 8–8. The next step in developing a checklist is to determine the lowest level of performance to be expected from students. This level is given a "0" or "1." See level 0 on Table 8–8 for an example. To complete the checklist, the teacher decides on steps of performance that partially fulfill the highest level. See levels 2 to 3 on Table 8–8. These intermediate steps clearly describe the expected behavior. Depending on the need for detail, there may be only one or two intermediate levels. At times, it is more efficient to develop the checklist while students are learning the skill during a unit. The observed behaviors are the basis for writing the intermediate levels.

Applying What You Know

Constructing a Rubric

Construct a checklist rubric for one of your science lesson plans. If possible, work with a partner on this activity. Choose an inquiry skill or science concept described as an objective for the science lesson. Answer the questions below:

1. What is the inquiry skill or science concept to be assessed?
2. What is the highest level of progress students are expected to reach with this skill or concept? State the skill or concept using an operational definition. What

do you want the students to be able to do, or make, if they have reached the highest level? Label this statement as "level 3."

3. Write down the lowest level of the skill or concept you expect to find among your students at the beginning of the lesson. Label this statement "level 1."

4. Write down one additional level below the highest level you expect students to reach. Label this statement "level 2."

5. Write the three levels from 2, 3, and 4 above in a new list that is appropriate as an observational checklist rubric to be used for assessing students during the lesson.

Interviews

Interviews provide an opportunity to explore students' ideas, discuss their planning, and talk about how they evaluate their own work (Meng & Doran, 1993). A highly-structured interview involves the interviewer asking a set of questions in a specific order. In a less-structured interview, the interviewer has a few leading questions but allows the discussion to follow the students' perspective or directions. The interviewer develops additional questions based on the responses given by the interviewee.

Interviews commonly involve students' alternative conceptions about a science idea or skill topic during the Exploration phase, and the assessment of learning outcomes near the end and after the lesson. The intended learning outcomes assessed in an interview are science content and inquiry skills. Memorized information and specific answers are not emphasized; how students arrive at an answer is more important.

The interview is used with a variety of other assessments during the unit so that students with different learning styles have the opportunity to demonstrate what each has learned. Within an interview, multiple learning outcomes are considered. An interview uses different techniques to assess students' accomplishment of various learning outcomes. For example, students are asked to generate their own questions about a concept or a skill. The interview follows up by asking for the thinking behind the students' questions. A student might, for instance, ask a question regarding circular motion, relating satellites' motion to that of a string with a weight on the end, "Why, when the weight is being spun around, when you let go of the string, doesn't the weight move straight out (perpendicularly outward) from you?" The interviewer reflects on the thinking that was involved in forming the question. Evidently the student may believe that the string acts as a rubber band. When it is cut, the student thinks the weight, or satellite, will move directly out away from the planet rather than in the line of motion in which it is traveling. The interviewer follows up the student's question by asking the student to explain, and provide evidence for, the ideas expressed in the question. This may confirm that the student has an alternative conception to the scientifically accepted view. The information allows the teacher to provide experiences that help the student confront this naive idea. If this interview occurs near the end of a lesson, the questioning may also help the student correct the naive belief by reflecting on the lesson's experiences. This student might, for example, demonstrate circular motion by releasing the weight while comparing what he believes and what he is experiencing.

The most common interview usually involves one student talking with one adult. However, it is possible for an interviewer to work with a cooperative learning group or some other small grouping of students. The interviewer has a list of prepared questions or topics to guide the interview. The information is recorded during or immediately after the interview. The interviewer does not comment or offer information unless it is necessary

---

PARTS OF A PLANT INTERVIEW GUIDE

For this interview, the students are presented with a flowering plant and questions on the parts of the plant, functions of those parts, and relationships among the parts.

1. Identify the parts of this plant.
2. Describe the part of the plant you think is most important for the plant to survive.
3. How is this part related to the functions of the other parts of the plant? *(Make sure the student relates the functions of all parts of the plant to each other.)*
4. In what ways are the parts of the plant related to where we find it, (i.e., its habitat)?
5. Ask one question that you have about the parts of the plant and their functions.

FIGURE 8-6   *Interview guide on the parts of a plant*

to restate or otherwise clarify a question. The interviewer's primary role is that of listener and prober. Watch that you don't give an answer through nonverbal positive or negative responses. Be neutral in your responses. Figure 8–6 gives an example of an interview guide. An interview allows the teacher to obtain information of greater depth than that gleaned from written tasks or group activities. The teacher is prepared to ask additional questions as the need arises to confirm inferences regarding the student's abilities.

Student responses are often recorded in writing, on a tape recording, or on a checklist. Interviews often provide a lot of information, so it is easy to forget some of it if it isn't recorded quickly. A tape-recorded interview can be played back to the student a couple of times during the interview to help the student reflect on her own ideas. Because interviews often provide lots of information, the interviewer reviews notes, organizing and summarizing them soon after they are completed (Sunal & Haas, 1993).

Portfolios

A portfolio contains a variety of work demonstrating a student's range of knowledge and skills (National Education Association, 1993). It is a grouping of materials and products created over a period of time showing the level of a student's engagement and quality in learning. Portfolios are a way of organizing an evaluation of assessment information or an assessment process. Students are asked to put a specific list of items they produce over a period of time into an organized portfolio.

As an assessment process, the portfolio involves a small number of student-selected productions along with other teacher-administered performance tasks and tests. These items form the basis upon which the evaluation is made. In this case, the portfolio is a way of organizing qualitative and narrative types of assessment items that are otherwise hard to handle and score. Examples of such items are student journals, reflections on their work, annotated drawings, group evaluations of their own performance, and videotapes of student performances. The implementation of portfolios is best done in a planned and evolving process. Begin with a unit and add units over time to create a year-long portfolio process.

There are three roles to consider in using portfolio assessment. How we identify each role affects how a portfolio is used. The roles to be identified are: (1) the person who is responsible for *setting up* the portfolio, (2) the person *constructing* the portfolio, and (3) the person *evaluating* the portfolio. Each of these roles can vary. Three questions need to be asked:

POSSIBLE PORTFOLIO CONTENTS

Annotated drawings

Charts

Journals of things learned each day during the science unit

Writing samples

Questions that need answers

Written reports of investigations

Audiotape recordings of reports

Videotapes of demonstrations or presentations

Computer disks of word-processed reports

Lists of references used in developing a report

Student-created poems or stories related to the science topic or unit

News stories and pictures of events related to the science topic or unit

Peer assessment sheets

Self-assessment checklists

Personal goal statements

Descriptions of main themes of lessons

Parent comments on portfolios

FIGURE 8-7   *Sample portfolio contents*

1. What does the portfolio contain? (see Figure 8–7)
2. What will count as evidence?
3. How should the evidence be weighed and the final evaluation made?

The three roles and three questions need to be considered together to design an effective plan for using portfolios in science teaching.

The person(s) responsible for setting up the portfolio can be the teacher, the student, a student group, or a school. The curriculum guide in a school system or state may require portfolios and specify what they contain and how they are organized.

The basic design of the portfolio determines its purpose, which may be the assessment of hands-on performance, depth of understanding, or any of the other purposes of using information for evaluation described earlier. For instance, a school may have set a priority on facilitating the development of its students' thinking skills. The teacher asks students to present materials providing evidence that they developed science inquiry skills during a particular unit. It might be suggested that they submit six pieces of evidence. These could be observations made during a science activity or an experiment designed and carried out by the student. Alternatively, the teacher could ask students to submit only materials in support of a specific set of skills such as observing, classifying, or creative thinking. All students in the class can be assessed on the same set of skills. An individualized approach may also be taken so that specific groups or individual students address different skills and submit different types of evidence.

Assessing Prior Knowledge Using Portfolios

The types of evidence making up a portfolio can reflect each of the evaluative functions of assessment: prior knowledge, monitoring, and summative assessment. Each category determines a particular approach to selecting materials for the portfolio. For example, if the teacher wants to find out what ideas students bring to class before the lesson begins, examining specific work samples from previous science units and initial activities in a unit provides valuable information about students' background experiences, alternative conceptions, and inquiry-skill levels.

Typically, students are more reflective about their work when they are asked to select samples of what they believe to be their best work. Teachers of younger students provide children with opportunities to select and talk about products from some of their science work that will be included in the portfolio. Older students are asked to write an explanation about what this work represents and why it is special.

Portfolio items include a variety of products including drawings, language experience stories, poems, paragraphs, practice work, laboratory reports, and summary reports. Very young students often do not want the teacher to keep their work because they want to take it home. When this happens, the teacher may want to make photocopies, or a teacher might ask students to place their science work samples in a student-decorated special folder given to parents periodically. It is helpful to focus other adults' examination of the portfolio by listing specific items of interest.

Monitoring Using Portfolios

A second evaluative function of a portfolio is monitoring. In this case, students select samples of science work throughout a time interval such as a unit. Science work samples are collections of student work for a specific purpose. They are discrete and do not represent a final or end product or the student's highest level of science achievement. Work samples provide a structured view of student performance across a wide variety of objectives.

The first evidence of work in an early unit activity, followed by evidence in later activities, provides information regarding consistency, growth, and level of attainment. In traditional assessment, this type of evidence of student learning is usually lost and rarely considered when monitoring the growth of a student. Examples include first drafts of lab reports, annotated drawings, data collected before it is put on a formal table, or a tape of conversations in a cooperative group at the beginning of an investigation.

Summative Evaluation Using Portfolios

Summative evaluation primarily involves evidence demonstrating that the goals of the lesson or unit are being met by the individual student. Examples include observation checklists, multiple-choice and matching paper-and-pencil quizzes and tests, library reports, laboratory worksheets, and laboratory reports.

A second area of evidence includes documents produced by others in the setting. Such evidence includes community service related to the science unit topics, letters and newspaper reports of student involvement in the community, and notes in the portfolio involving effective participation in the student's cooperative learning group.

A third area of evidence asks students to reflect on how the portfolio illustrates what they have learned in science. The information is gathered through interviews with young students or short essays by older students. Students explain why this portfolio contains evidence of their growth. Notes attached to the front of specific documents or to the collection of documents explain the portfolio contents and how the pieces and the whole relate to students' own science learning.

The nature of the evaluator is an important consideration in determining the organization and format of the summative science portfolio since it can be evaluated by a diverse group of evaluators for a variety of purposes. The portfolio is used by the teacher for prescribing learning activities, grading, and planning future work. It is used by the student for self-reflection and feedback. Parents examine a portfolio to gain information regarding the progress of their child and about current science work. Portfolios can be used as a culminating activity, providing information on science experiences used as a transition to, or for graduation from, elementary to middle school, middle school to high school, one grade level to another, or one school to another. A science portfolio is also used during parent-visiting evenings, public displays, and science fairs. In each case, the organization and amount of effort put into the format of the overall portfolio differs. The teacher usually needs no more than a simple format. Portfolios for parent nights, public displays, and transfers to other schools involve more elaborate and creative approaches.

No matter the evaluative purpose of portfolios, it is important that students be personally involved and have a sense of ownership in the work they are presenting. To increase their sense of ownership, the students should have some control over the portfolio process. The teacher may determine the format and the content of the portfolio, allowing students some choice as to which experiment or journal item they might include. Alternatively, the teacher might gradually give students more control by allowing them to determine the number of documents in a category, the number of categories, or the entire format of the portfolio. The teacher specifies the purpose but allows students to make important decisions regarding what information provides the best evidence demonstrating their experience and growth in science.

Students can determine what kind of evidence and how much evidence needs to be supplied for a fair evaluation to take place. They are encouraged to think about whether each document provides evidence of a type of growth that otherwise would not be known to the evaluator. This helps students understand the problem of redundancy and trivial materials. The process also helps students develop higher-level thinking skills, especially with regard to planning, monitoring, and reflecting on their own behavior.

An additional approach is to allow small groups to make cooperative decisions regarding the evidence needed to demonstrate the group's learning. This can involve peer evaluation of documents or of evidence submitted by others in the class as one part of the evaluation process. Students in a cooperative group can rank each member's contribution toward the completion of a specific role or task (see Table 8–9). Simplified evaluation keys help students in this process (Collins, 1991; Hein, 1991; Meng & Doran, 1990; Wolf, 1989).

One other important aspect of the use of portfolios is the need for regular student maintenance of the portfolio. Students review their portfolio and organize its contents every one to two weeks. The teacher might help students at the beginning of the year with

TABLE 8-9 *Cooperative group self-ranking scheme for four group tasks*

Student Names/ Scores	Jeff	Melanie	Pablo	Yusuf	Total
Role or Task	Rank Order of Contributions Made toward Task Completion				
Contributing ideas	3	1	4	2	10
Collecting data	1	4	2	3	10
Organizing data	2	1	4	3	10
Reporting data	1	3	2	4	10
Total	7	9	12	12	40

TABLE 8-10   *Partial yearly schedule for science portfolios*

Due Date	Science Portfolio
Sept. 12	Summer science experiences portfolio (for teacher use)
Sept. 25	Light unit portfolio (for teacher and student use)
Oct. 10	Electricity unit portfolio (for teacher and student use)
Oct. 20	First-term science experiences portfolio (summative evaluation for parents)

this process, but later simply provides instructions for them. All items entered into the portfolio are dated and indicate the student's name and group. Each item indicates whether it was completed by the individual, with a peer, or with a group. A regular schedule for evaluation of the science portfolio is given to the students to indicate when peers, the teacher, or parents will be reviewing the materials (see Table 8–10).

Discussions, Journals, and Presentations

Classroom science, characterized by hands-on, minds-on activities, engages students in two different ways. First, students are engaged through active investigation of physical and natural events including natural creatures as well as batteries and electric bulbs. It involves using diverse tools for investigation, such as rulers, video cameras, computer interface temperature probes, and microscopes. Just as important are the social dimensions of science and of students' interactions, such as interviews, conversations, formal discussions, group tasks, and parent and family events (Piaget, 1950; Vygotsky, 1962). Ideas, as well as materials brought into the classroom, are shared, examined, and reconsidered in various ways.

Discussions and social interactions can be formal or informal and spontaneous. Informal discussion is evaluated by listening to, or videotaping, students' conversations and focusing on the key words being used. These words provide the teacher with clues about student thinking. Specific ideas or questions that persistently come to the surface allow the teacher to evaluate students' prior knowledge, growth, and understanding of a concept. Teachers consider questions such as: "Are the terms 'heat' and 'temperature' used indiscriminately?" and "Do students confuse observations with inferences?" Teachers note whether all group members contribute to an informal discussion.

Formal discussions occur in more structured or whole-class sessions. During these discussions, students present their experiences and observations related to science activities. Planning for discussions for assessment involves the teacher or a small group in a conversation sustained by student-initiated questions and ideas. This allows students to control the direction of the discussion. Teachers' open-ended questions and their role as a guide bring out evidence for assessing students in a variety of objective areas. Guidelines for holding group discussions are:

1. Begin with open-ended questions such as: "What can you tell me about the life cycle of butterflies?" or "Where do you experience electricity in your daily lives?"
2. Welcome students' comments when they are made without correcting or modifying them.
3. Involve the students in the discussion.
4. Keep records of students' comments using a coding scheme.

Evaluating students' comments for the purpose of assessing prior knowledge gives insight into planning and deciding upon the appropriate points to emphasize during a unit. A coding scheme can be used with informal or formal discussions to determine the nature of students' prior knowledge (Chittenden, 1990; Price & Hein, 1994). Five categories of statements can be found across all discussions. These are: (1) *announcements*—statements of a fact or bits of information such as, "Mammals have fur," (2) *reported observations*— personal or second-hand observations made by the students such as, "When you dig into the soil you see different colors," (3) *explanations*—statements relating events and objects together in order to deal with cause and effect such as, "The more leaf litter found in sand, the more it will hold water," (4) *questions*—statements inquiring into problems facing students such as, "Why do some materials stick to magnets and others don't?" and (5) *references*—statements identifying the sources of information such as books, Internet sites, television, "I tried it at home," or "My father told me." Some statements may be classified under more than one of these categories. Taking note of the level of student statements in each of these categories makes it possible to develop better inferences about the nature of students' prior knowledge.

As an assessment strategy, discussions are "staged" observations involving a part of classroom life that ordinarily remains undocumented. Especially with primary students, teachers may get the feeling that conversation is "just talk" since no evidence of learning— such as drawings or graphs—is produced (Chittenden, 1990). However, there is a need to assess students' conversations. This assessment validates the idea of cooperative and interactive learning of science in classrooms. Methods of assessment should tap the information gathered during hands-on, minds-on science.

Journals are a way in which students record their ideas and social interactions in science. Many students have kept journals, particularly if they have been in whole language

---

Name: _____ Date: _____

SCIENCE JOURNAL

What was the main idea of the lesson?

_____

_____

What questions do you have about the lesson now?

_____

What else would you like to know about the main idea of the lesson?

_____

_____

What else would you like to say?

_____

_____

_____

FIGURE 8-8   *Structured science journal*

classrooms. Journals are used so that students write about science through leading questions such as:

What was the main idea in the science lesson today (or this week)?
What questions do you have about the science you learned today?
What did you do in science today?
What did you like best in science today?
What did you like least in science today?
What do you think was the most important thing you learned?
What confused you or bored you?
What else do you want to mention?

Students write in their journals daily, weekly, or at other intervals. They are encouraged, but not required, to respond to all the questions. Science-related responses that do not directly answer the questions are encouraged. The length of response is not important.

A shorter, more structured version of a journal is a *log,* a form that students fill out (see Figure 8–8 for an example). A log is an effective way for students to sum up what they liked or did not like about a lesson or unit, and the key idea they learned in the lesson (Sunal & Haas, 1993).

Asking students to use, modify, and construct webs and concept maps supplements and extends the information provided in a log. For example, asking students to complete entries in a concept web provides feedback about students' connections between concepts (see Figure 8–9).

See Chapter 10 for additional information on concept webs and Chapter 2 for concept maps.

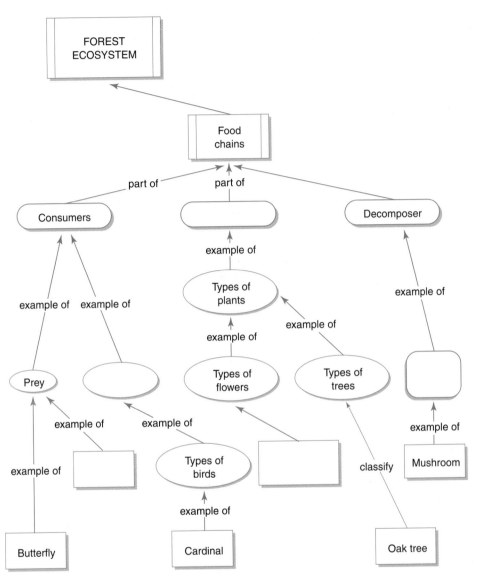

FIGURE 8-9   *Concept map completion item*

Groups can use journals to keep track of their work. They help group members evaluate how well their planning process went, how well their plans worked out, and what they will do next. Journals serve as the basis for discussion when students use them as notes for evaluating their own work and the science program.

Students often use journals to express very private feelings. When encouraging students to use journals to evaluate work in a group or in other ways through which the content of the writing becomes public, it is important to use caution since students should not be put in a position where they feel their privacy is violated. If the journal is going to be read by the teacher, or shared in any other way, students must be aware of this before they are encouraged to write.

Presentations are an attractive means of evaluation for both students and teachers. Presentations can be informal and daily events. A cooperative group member, for example, can report the plans decided on by the group to begin an investigation, or a group can plan a creative drama to act out their interpretation of a physical event in nature (Reichel, 1994). Formal presentations provide information about the results of an extended science investigation or science fair project. This type of assessment is concrete because it allows students to see the results of the work that led up to the presentation. Peers are provided with a means to evaluate other students' work. It creates social interaction at a high level of thought. The teacher sees growth in students if presentations are used several times during the year.

Group Evaluation

Having students work in cooperative groups to solve problems is a natural way for them to study science. It is also a natural way for teachers to assess students or for students to assess themselves (Johnson & Johnson, 1991). Group assessment is a necessary part of cooperative group learning. Students become more active members of a group when they are involved in interdependent tasks and are provided feedback through the assessment of group experiences. Providing feedback for students in cooperative settings increases the value they place on working in such settings.

Teachers make sure students are always involved in some part of the process. Self-evaluation is an important experience enabling students to develop an awareness of their own performance and behavior. It is a necessary element for the successful functioning of cooperative learning groups (see Chapter 7). Students' self-evaluation can involve assessing their planning, monitoring their own behavior, and evaluating the results of their actions. Students can use a checklist and group discussion to evaluate work periods, group cooperation, data sources, study skills, and information-gathering activities as well as the progress of their plan.

Peer evaluation can be one part of a student's grade on cooperative tasks. Peer evaluation examines the ideas contributed, the information or data collected, the organization of the data, and the reporting of the results. The *ideas contributed* are assessed by the number of comments made and by the relevance of the ideas to the problem at hand. The *data collected* are assessed by examining each student's involvement in setting up the materials needed, the number of measurements made, the drawings made, the models constructed, and the number of pieces of information recorded. The *organization of the data* collected is assessed through the construction of a table of the information, rewriting the data in a more usable form, the number of points plotted on graphs, and the suggestions made about patterns discovered in the information. *Reporting of results* is assessed by the number of sentences written by the secretary, the number of sentences suggested for the secretary to write down, offering a plan for completing the report, word processing the report, making graphs and artwork that are part of the report, and the level of participation in the presentation of the report. Students rate each other on the extent of their participation in each of these basic areas.

An average score for each student in the group is computed from the individual ratings. The groups can be asked to evaluate each other on just one of these four areas during a particular task, or they can assess each student's contribution to all of the tasks. This is done by having each student independently rate the other students' contribution in the specific role or task area (see Table 8–9). Over time, each student's contribution is a record of the amount of effort expended. This assessment data is reported as part of a group discussion on how well the group is performing. It can also be used as a part of individual student grades or a cooperative group grade. A discussion about individual participation may help group members realize that it is not necessary for everyone to do all tasks equally well. Some members may contribute more to one phase of a project or activity than to others. It points out to them that different science tasks may require different types of skills. All members do not have to contribute equally in each area.

Learning in cooperative groups requires students to develop and use the same social skills that are necessary in everyday life. Social skills are essential in an effective cooperative learning group (Johnson & Johnson, 1991). Interpersonal and group social skills are taught, and as discussed in Chapter 7, face-to-face positive interaction and accountability are fostered. With appropriate information and feedback, students self-correct their social behaviors.

What social skills are assessed? How are student social skills assessed in the context of cooperative learning? Social skills can be divided into three areas.

1. Those skills enabling students to form successful groups; for example, how to move into the group setting quickly, take on assigned roles, and, with little transition time, begin academic tasks.
2. Those skills helping a group achieve academic goals or successfully carry out academic tasks. These skills help a group manage the steps for completing a task. They facilitate learning and understanding of the science content or inquiry skills involved in the lesson.
3. Those skills facilitating positive interaction between group members (they like each other during and after a task). These skills help group members feel better about themselves and each other, and lead to group stability (Figure 8–10).

Social skills are assessed within the context of cooperative learning. Focus on one social skill at a time. You can determine the focus skill by observing the groups and noting the behaviors hindering group action. When beginning the next cooperative group task, explain, model, and describe examples of the appropriate behavior for the focus skill. This establishes an acceptable level of behavior in the area. Tell students you will be watching their performance and will provide information on how well they did during the lesson. Assessment of the skill is accomplished in two different ways. To provide feedback for older students, develop a scale with a score of "5" indicating that every time the group was observed, their target social skills were appropriate. A "4" indicates that, at least one time, the target social skill was not appropriately displayed during the lesson. Additional inappropriate displays produce lower ratings of "3", "2", or "1". It is important to set a lower limit whereby some action from outside the group will occur. This may be at a rating of "2" or "1". For very young students, this process is made more concrete by placing a chip on a group's table when they are monitored and found to be demonstrating appropriate behavior. A maximum of five chips and five observations might be set. A certain level of chips at the end of the science lesson week can determine a reward, such as free-reading time in the classroom or school library.

One strategy for involving the students in group evaluation is to provide the class with a series of questions that are generalizations related to the unit. For example, in a middle school unit on *Experimenting With Matter,* the teacher asks: "Does all matter expand when heated?" "Do liquids, solids, and gases expand?" "Do all solids melt when heated?" "Do all liquids evaporate?" and so on (Small & Petrek, 1992). Each group of five students in a classroom decided on a question the group would investigate. They developed a hypothesis and a test to answer the question. Next, a written report and an oral presentation of the project were developed and finalized by all group members. The guidelines each of the groups used in carrying out the activities and assessing the written and oral reports were used to assess all students in the group. Guidelines for the hands-on activities included skillful use of laboratory equipment, the condition of the laboratory

Group Formation Skills

Move into the group location quickly.

Stay with the group while it is working.

Speak in quiet voices.

Let each person have a chance to share ideas.

Listen with interest.

Keep your hands and feet to yourself.

Share materials.

Group Achievement Skills

Review what to do before starting.

Offer ideas about the best way to get the task done.

Make a plan for what you are going to do.

If you don't understand what someone says, ask him to explain it.

Ask questions.

Ask for help.

Offer help and explain ideas or what to do.

Pay attention to how much time you have to carry out your plan.

Say what you think someone else has said to find out if you have got it right.

When you are trying to solve a problem, say out loud what you are thinking.

Say why you think this is the best idea and give your evidence for it.

Ask for, or give, other answers to the problem or task.

Check your group's conclusion to decide whether you carried out your plan and did what you were supposed to do.

When you are done, make a summary of what you have learned and say it out loud.

Group Interaction Skills

When two other students don't agree, compare and contrast what they are saying.

When two other students don't agree, try to put together parts of their ideas to come up with a compromise idea.

Make sure everyone is part of the plan and gets a chance to do their part.

Make sure everyone has a chance to say what they think before someone gets a second chance.

At least once, give each person in your group a compliment about something she is doing or saying.

Give your compliment aloud or in a silent way (like with a smile).

Show everyone in your group that you like them and are friendly to them.

Don't say things to others in your group that you wouldn't want them to say to you (don't be mean).

Tell the others whether you do or do not like something, but do it in a nice way.

Talk about each person's idea and why it might not work, but don't criticize the person.

Show that you are interested in what you are doing so others will stay interested.

When things get tough, joke a little so that everyone relaxes.

Listen to everybody's idea before you decide together on the group's conclusion.

FIGURE 8-10 *Assessing cooperative group skills*

station and equipment, attention to safety rules, honesty in reporting gathered data, and use of project time. Points were given for each section of the written project report: introduction, hypothesis, procedure, results, conclusions, and further questions. Each section was given equal weight. The sections were assessed on completeness of information, organization, clarity of language, clear representation of the data, and accuracy. The oral presentation was assessed using eight criteria: (1) appropriate length of the report, (2) interest generated in the audience, (3) creativity, (4) quality of visual aids and props, (5) completeness, (6) honesty in reporting the data, (7) use of voice and body expression, and (8) participation by all group members. Each group member received a grade for carrying out the activities, the written report, and the oral report. Each of these assessments could carry different weights. For instance, the written report might be worth 50 percent of the project grade, while the activity guidelines could be worth 20 percent and the oral presentation worth 30 percent.

Teachers can provide sets of questions similar to those found in Figure 8–10 to guide a group in evaluating itself or to guide the individual student as he evaluates his own, and the group's, work. The teacher encourages students to summarize, and, as appropriate, review planned strategies and the timeline for carrying out work. As students identify things they have done well and the problems they come up against, they are encouraged to suggest and record ways of correcting their problems with the teacher. These recommendations are listed and saved, so that the next time the class works on a similar project, the teacher can review these points to remind the students of the desired behaviors they need to use to continue being successful or to improve upon their skills.

Performance Testing

In using the phrase "hands-on, minds-on" approach, classroom science teaching has finally recognized that learning best takes place when the learner is actively involved (Brown & Shavelson, 1996). In today's classrooms, science learning and teaching are activity-based, oriented toward problem solving, and involve interactions with many students (Kleinheider, 1996). When students engage in hands-on, minds-on science activities, they apply both intellectual and practical skills in order to use and develop a body of knowledge. This teaching enables students to develop and use their understanding across a range of content and a variety of everyday tasks. Because of this, teachers have concluded that paper-and-pencil tests do not assess the full range of knowledge and skills gained in today's classrooms. Performance assessment is a critical component in evaluating the effectiveness of today's science learning (Hein & Price, 1994; Reichel, 1994). In performance assessment, students are asked to perform a skill they have learned or to apply a concept in a new situation. In a unit on simple machines, for instance, a performance test occurs when a student is asked to set up a lever to lift a heavy weight with the least amount of force.

Student performance assessment utilizes written assessments, creation of a product, creative drama, stations, individual practical work at desks, or practical work in cooperative groups in a variety of formats. There are at least six formats for performance assessment:

1. The use of graphic and symbolic representation, such as reading or presenting information from graphs, tables, or charts.
2. The use of apparatus and measuring instruments involving estimating, measuring, following instructions, and solving problems.

3. The categories of observation involving making, interpreting, and using observations to solve problems.

4. Interpretation and application involving data already gathered and applying that information in various science contexts.

5. Planning investigations with a focus on sequencing elements and planning the entire investigation.

6. Performing investigations where students implement combinations of the preceding categories.

The assessment of student problem solving uses a variety of practical actions. These are assessed individually or in combination with each other. They include problem perception, problem reformulation, planning and carrying out, recording and interpreting, and evaluation by the student.

Developing performance assessment items for written tests and tasks for practical work is done easily if a few guidelines are followed. Keep performance items direct and simple so they are easily performed by the whole class. Do not make any one assessment too long; keep it to 10 minutes of practical work time. Provide diagrams and clear instructions students can follow with little guidance. Use materials that are familiar to the students. Involve students in evaluating their own work. Written items assess skills and content areas developed in the lesson or unit. One strategy is to construct tasks similar to the activities found in the Expansion phase of the lesson learning cycles just completed. Once a task is determined, develop scoring criteria for the range of acceptable answers. Performance, not content, is the focus of the task and is reflected in the scoring. Tables 8–7 and 8–8 provide examples of scoring using observational checklists that are appropriate for performance assessment.

Among the types of tasks and projects used for performance assessment are group assessment, role-playing, creative drama writing assignments, portfolio assessment, simulations, displays, projects, and models. Both process and product are measured when students are given a set of questions asking them to describe the skills and steps used in completing the project.

Assessment with Tests and Quizzes

Multiple-choice, matching, true/false, fill-in-the-blank, idea webs, concept maps, short-answer questions, and essays are assessment formats used in tests and quizzes. With very young students, a version of a short essay test is given by asking students to dictate stories related to science activities with which they have been involved. Primary-grade students can often write and illustrate short-answer questions related to science content. Paper-and-pencil items can be used to measure higher-order learning outcomes (O'Sullivan, Reese, & Mazzeo, 1997).

Effective items include short-answer or multiple-choice responses following a problem or a description of an event (see Figure 8–11). Other item formats involve interpreting a data table or graph describing the results in a multiple-choice format, a multiple-choice question for which a written justification is requested, or printed text from mass media for which multiple-choice questions are written. Asking elementary and middle school students to explain, modify, or construct and discuss idea webs and concept maps related to the key lesson idea effectively assesses higher-level thinking. All types of paper-and-pencil items are carefully adapted for use with young students.

All test items are written to determine whether students met the objectives of the units and lessons. The match between the objective and the test item is critically important. Test items used to assess factual knowledge relate to those objectives that specify a factual-knowledge learning outcome. Questions for knowledge objectives are the easiest

Some fourth-grade students were doing a project for their science class. They were trying to find the answer to the question, "Do beetles choose to live in bright light or in the shade?" The picture shows one way that a student set up an experiment to find out if beetles choose to live in bright light or in the shade.

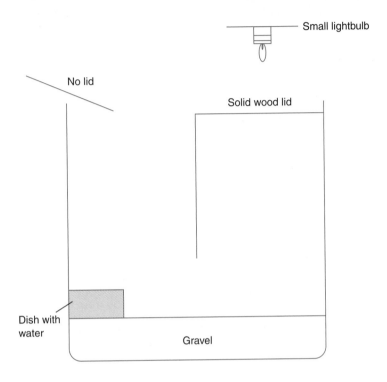

Is this a good way to set up this experiment? Tell why or why not.

> yes cause of the wall
> that blocks the light. But I
> would put a water dish in the shad
> to so the water can be on which
> ever side he choces.

FIGURE 8-11   *Sample short-answer paper-and-pencil item using a problem event*
Source: O'Sullivan, C. Y., Reese, C. M., Mazzeo, J. (1997). *NAEP 1996 science report card for the nation and the states.* Washington, D.C.: National Center for Education Statistics, U.S. Department of Education.

to construct. Testing higher-level science content and inquiry skill objectives requires that new data be provided for the student to use in answering the question.

The text of the NAEP 1996 *Science Report Card for the Nation and the States* is available at *http://www.ed.gov/NCES/naep*

Before writing test items, the teacher considers the objectives of the lesson or unit by deciding which objectives have a priority in assessment. Those most heavily stressed objectives in the unit are assessed. The teacher then decides what type or combination of types of questions to use in the test and writes the test items. Guidelines for writing appropriate science essay and objective test items follow:

- Decide what science concepts, generalizations, or inquiry skills you want students to use before you write any questions.
- Write essay questions with clear tasks (for example, are students to describe steps in completing an activity?).
- Write essay questions that require more than the repetition of information.
- Use only a few questions, and make sure they require answers that are not lengthy.
- Make sure the questions vary in difficulty.
- Give clear directions (students should know whether an answer should be in outline form or paragraphs, its point value, and what criteria will be used to evaluate answers). (Good & Brophy, 1986; Sunal & Haas, 1993)

Objective Test Questions

Science objective test questions in the formats of multiple-choice, true/false, fill-in-the-blank, and short-answer items ask students to respond to important content. Guidelines for such objective questions are:

- Present a problem, event, graph, or data in the question.
- Make the question as short as possible.
- Give short-answer choices.
- Use the negative infrequently and make it noticeable by underlining the *not* when it is used.
- Give only one correct or clearly best answer.
- Make all answer choices plausible.
- Keep all responses similar in length since a different length suggests a particular response is the answer. (Good & Brophy, 1986; Sunal & Haas, 1993)

In assessing concept mastery, parts of the full concepts are provided and requested. Full concept descriptions include the concept name, relevant attributes, irrelevant attributes, examples, non-examples, related concepts, and the meaning of a concept as expressed in a formal or operational definition. Concept mastery questions ask the student to identify a missing aspect of the concept description. For example, the name of the concept is given and students are asked to select an example or relevant attributes. Or, examples of the concept are given and students are asked for the relevant attributes and name of the concept (see Figure 8–11) (Meng & Doran, 1993).

HOW IS MULTIPLE ASSESSMENT USED IN TEACHING AND LEARNING SCIENCE?

Whenever student learning is assessed in a topic area, teachers include essential abilities and products in the types of situations where they were learned and are used. Teachers ask themselves: "What performances should our students do well?" and "What are the challenges our students should be able to meet?" This type of assessment is a global approach for assessing science learning. In a global approach, **multiple assessment** is used. Teachers do not view assessment as tests or as an after-the-event way of finding out what students have learned. Instead, they view assessment as an instructional process. It is a way of determining students' prior knowledge, monitoring student learning, and determining summative learning outcomes. Multiple assessment, used with standards-based curriculum and instruction, is a way of clarifying, providing feedback, and setting goals that direct a meaningful student science learning activity.

Applying What You Know

Evaluating Assessments

Select a science textbook for a particular grade level. Obtain both the student's and teacher's editions. Choose one chapter and review the suggested assessment in both. If possible, work with a partner on this activity. Respond to the items below.

1. Textbook publisher and author:
2. Chapter title:
3. Chapter goal(s):
4. Complete the following chart:

Assessment Suggestions

Page Number	Type of Assessment (e.g., True/False test)	Evaluative Use of This Information (i.e., prior knowledge, monitoring, or summative)

5. Write a general description of the assessment suggested in the chapter. What areas are covered? What is missing? Evaluate the adequacy of the assessment suggested for a standards-based, hands-on, minds-on science program. What must be added to create effective assessment?

The following classroom scenario gives an example of the use of multiple assessment practices in a third-grade lesson on adaptation in nature.

CLASSROOM SCENES

The goal of the lesson is to explore the relationship between animal parts and the habitat in which the animal is found. Skills involved include observation, classification, communication through discussion, reporting, and making inferences. The lesson begins by having the students sit around the teacher in a circle on the floor. The teacher quickly pairs off the students and asks the pairs to discuss the following key question: "Pick a particular kind of bird. What does it look like?" When each pair has completed their discussion, the teacher asks a small number of pairs to name and describe their bird. Next, the teacher asks each pair to discuss the following statement: "Describe differences between birds." After discussion, some pairs are asked to report their discussion to the group. The process continues with each statement that follows: "Discuss what your bird eats." "Describe how your bird gets its food." "Describe what your bird uses to eat with." and "Do you think all birds eat the same things?" While the students are working, the teacher moves from pair to pair while making observations of the general classroom activity. During this process, the teacher becomes aware of the students' prior knowledge and the presence of some alternative conceptions about animals.

Next, the teacher asks the students to return to their seats. Each pair of students is provided with a set of materials and instructions on an index card. They begin following the instructions. Students are instructed not to put any of the items used in the lesson in their mouths but only to bring the item close to their lips without letting it touch their lips. Some of the pairs are given gummy worms on plates and straws. Their instructions require them to try to get a gummy worm near their mouths using the straws. Other pairs are given paper cups with the bottom cut out, pieces of uncooked pasta, and some paper plates. These pairs are instructed to get the pasta near their mouths using only the cups. Other pairs are given thin slices of pears and bananas. These students are asked to put the fruit near to their mouths but are not given any tools with which to do it. These students cannot use their hands or anything else but their mouth to pick up the fruit. Each pair will describe their experiences with this activity to the whole class.

Each pair is then asked to draw a mouth or mouthparts that would be useful for an animal like a bird to have. The drawing should be of a mouth or mouthparts that would make it as easy as possible to eat the food they were given. The teacher asks the students to write below the drawing those types of tools that could more easily pick up the food they were trying to get into their mouths.

The teacher next puts pairs of students together into groups of four. Each pair places the drawing it has just completed into a group portfolio. Each small group is provided with a set of pictures of birds. They are asked to classify the pictures based on the bird's mouthparts (beaks). When finished, each group is asked to draw and name the type of beak found in each category on a chart they construct. Some examples developed by the students are a shovel beak, a chopstick beak, a short beak, and a long and thin beak. For each category, the teacher asks the groups to respond to the question, "What kind of foods would be most easily picked up by this kind of beak?" After the discussion, the charts are placed in the group's portfolio.

Next, the teacher shows pictures of three different types of habitats: a swamp with small insects floating on its surface, a lakeshore with small fish swimming in shallow water, and a rotting tree with insects under the bark. The teacher asks the students to determine which of the beaks just described would be best at getting food in each of these places. During a discussion of the students' ideas, the teacher draws the different types of beaks that were discovered by the students on the chalkboard. The groups include predator birds, seed-eating birds, birds that find food in water, insect-eating birds, and birds that have other food sources. The teacher provides closure to this part of the lesson by stating that the shape of an animal's parts are related to living successfully in a particular habitat. The small groups are then asked to role-play birds whose beaks are useful in one of these categories.

The next day, during the morning break, the teacher asks several students to help set up six learning stations. Some examples of materials at the stations are dry cereal such as Kix® floating in water to represent small, aquatic animals floating in a pond, popcorn flicked off of a shelf to represent airborne insects, gummy worms in loose oatmeal to represent small animals in the soil, water in a tall, thin vase to represent nectar in a flower, and an apple tied to a string hanging from the ceiling to represent fruit on a tree or insects under bark. Pairs of students from each small group are given a kit of tools and are asked to determine the best tool to get the food at each station to their mouth. They are asked to keep a journal of their activities and to conclude, for each station, what type of beak this tool represents. The kits contain a straw, two wooden skewers, pliers, tweezers, two spoons, spoon with slots, and some other materials. When finished, their journals are placed into the small group portfolio.

On a front table, the teacher has placed a number of pictures of birds. These pictures include birds such as a hawk, sparrow, duck, pelican, swallow, snipe, hummingbird, toucan, and warbler. Each pair of students is asked to match each station with a type of bird found in one of the pictures. For one of their answers, the teacher asks each pair to discuss their results with the class indicating why they chose that particular bird. The teacher summarizes the lesson by describing the activities of the past two days. After the discussion, the students write a brief summary paragraph of the lesson's main idea, which is placed in the small group portfolio.

Applying What You Know

Identifying Assessment Practices

Multiple assessment during a lesson or a unit is a way of determining students' prior knowledge, monitoring student learning, and determining summative or learning outcomes. It is an ongoing part of instruction. In the previous scenario, identify the various assessment practices in the lesson and group them into the three basic assessment categories.

1. Determining students' prior knowledge—
2. Monitoring students' learning—
3. Determining summative learning outcomes—

SUMMARY

Assessment is much more than testing. It involves gathering information for three basic evaluative functions: determining prior knowledge, monitoring student learning, and summing up or summative assessment. Science assessment requires considering many student abilities and products. It examines those abilities and products important in the lives of students. It considers their abilities and products in the situations in which they are learning, and in situations in which they use what they have learned.

Assessment is a natural and integrated part of instruction, not just something that follows a lesson. It is not separate from instruction. Students learn through experiences in the assessment as well as in regular instructional activities. Assessment and the evaluation of that information are a major part of a teacher's role. Performed with planning and reflective thought, student assessment and evaluation are keys to providing information to teachers about whether their teaching is effective. Such information is necessary for a teacher's continued self-improvement.

chapter 9

Planning Science Units

▼▲▼ Exploring Your Ideas ▼▲▼▲▼▲▼▲▼▲▼▲▼

Select a topic useful for planning a science unit from a science textbook. Identify the grade level(s) for the unit, and construct a brief outline describing the focus of the unit and the types of activities that might be incorporated within it; for example, experiments or use of related trade books.

Chapter Objectives

1. Describe conceptual organizers which are useful as evaluation criteria in the development of science units.
2. Describe the differences between description-, inquiry skills-, and conceptual and inquiry skills-based units built around a similar science area.
3. Describe the potential impact of interdisciplinary and multidisciplinary approaches to key science ideas in designing science units.
4. Describe the differences between theme-, issue-, project-, and case study-based units built around a similar science area.
5. Describe a rationale and criteria for determining appropriate topics for an integrated science unit.
6. Describe the general techniques for planning an integrated science unit.
7. Write rationales and goal statements demonstrating the differences between theme-, issue-, projects-, and case study-focused units built around the same science topic area.

HOW DO WE PLAN THE APPROPRIATE FOCUS FOR A SCIENCE UNIT?

Effective teaching organized around key science concepts, generalizations, and inquiry skills is unit based. The science unit can be subject oriented or focused on a cross-cutting theme integrating other subjects. The **unit** is a set of interconnected, related lesson plans that explore, fully invent, and expand a topic. There are basic developmental steps which are helpful in planning science units. The unit-planning process is a critical professional skill because key ideas are interrelated with each other and with the students' prior experiences to make them useful.

Some of the most meaningful science units interrelate multiple school subjects studied at the same time as the science unit (Martin-Kniep, Feige, & Soodak, 1995). An **integrated unit approach** involves using a focus to interconnect significant and relevant knowledge from various disciplines in a coherent manner (Richmond, 1994). Developing integrated units increases the complexity of planning because the topic of the unit is dealt with from a number of viewpoints.

Integrated science comes under a variety of names, including interdisciplinary teaching, thematic teaching, and multidisciplinary teaching. At the local and national level, much is being written and tried as teachers make interconnections between school subjects. National and state science standards promote an interdisciplinary and integrated development of knowledge (American Association for the Advancement of Science, 1993a; National Research Council, 1995). The American Association for the Advancement of Science (AAAS) describes science literacy as knowledge organized around themes that interconnect the natural sciences, social sciences, mathematics, and technology. The AAAS gives the following rationale for an integrated approach: "To ensure the scientific literacy of all students, curricula must be changed to reduce the sheer amount of material covered; to weaken or eliminate rigid subject-matter boundaries; to pay more attention to the connections among science, mathematics, and technology. . ." (American Association for the Advancement of Science, 1993b, p. 104). Language arts specialists encourage elementary teachers to involve their students in writing and reading activities that are integrated with their subject matter studies. In the mathematics standards, mathematics is viewed as a process involved with themes in all subject areas (National Council of Teachers of Mathematics, 1989).

Integration is an important goal for education. Real-life experiences form the basis of an effective science program. Good science programs are active, involving lots of hands-on activities beginning in the earliest school years. Reading, writing, social studies, and mathematics play a vital role in a hands-on, minds-on emphasis in learning science and facilitating growth in these same basic skill areas (American Association for the Advancement of Science 1993a; Butler, 1991; Glynn & Muth, 1994; National Research Council, 1995; Texley, 1996). If science is to be taught in ways that foster meaningful learning by students, several questions must be answered. Among these are: "What steps are needed for planning a science unit that helps students develop meaningful learning about the natural world?" "What does it mean for an elementary or middle school teacher to integrate science with other subject areas?" "Why is integration important in planning meaningful learning for students?" "What kinds of integrated teaching develop meaningful learning in students?" "What is the place of science in an integrated science unit?" and "What conceptual organizers and organizational patterns are useful as evaluation criteria in the development of science units?"

Purposeful organization is needed to plan science units focusing on the key ideas, addressing students' needs, and incorporating appropriate instructional strategies. There are three conceptual organizers which are useful as evaluation criteria during the construction of science units. The first is *significance*. The content taught is important to the discipline and to students' needs for scientific literacy. The unit teaches the nature of scientific knowledge, not the products of science. Interdisciplinary and multidisciplinary connections are used to tie the unit's ideas into students' prior knowledge and to facilitate their transfer to a wider set of experiences (American Association for the Advancement of Science, 1993a). Less is more in the unit. Fewer concepts are taught, but the ones that are represent the most critical concepts related to a topic and are therefore taught in depth (National Research Council, 1995).

The second conceptual organizer for a unit is *coherence*. Science unit content is related to the integrity of the discipline. Therefore, unit activities are consistent with the nature of scientific inquiry, reflecting scientific values, and giving students direct experience with the kinds of thought and action that are typical of work in the scientific disciplines. Since science is characterized by intellectual discovery, memorization is only one of many thinking processes utilized during the unit. To ensure coherence, a science unit's emphasis is on science inquiry skills. Inquiry skills are used to promote the conceptual understanding, application, and transfer of scientific knowledge to the student's own world.

The third conceptual organizer for a unit is *relevance*. The science unit content and skills impact a student's thinking, personal interactions, social interactions, and career decisions. Science content, activities, and breadth of experiences concern and reflect the students' current life in addition to their future goals and aspirations. Science content and skills in science units include the daily life and decisions of students. The teacher always considers the question, "What science does an 8- or 11-year-old student need to know to be an intelligent consumer, make informed decisions, or have a better quality of life?" This includes being able to effectively use, read, select, or purchase consumer items students *regularly use in their daily lives*. What science does a student need to know to be able to effectively use toys and body care products, read appropriate-level magazines and books, view television advertisements and movies, or read labels and instructions on items of clothing and technology devices such as personal radios? Science units in school classrooms portray science as impacting human decisions and the quality of life.

The planning of units can involve a single teacher, a teacher pair, a group, teachers from various subject areas, a whole school, or several schools through the use of e-mail and the Internet. Selecting a focus for a unit involves determining the guiding goals of the unit. The emphasis can vary in science content, science inquiry skills, and the amount of integration with other subjects. Different approaches to planning a science unit include description with a focus on content, an inquiry skills focus, a conceptual and inquiry skills focus, a theme focus, or an issues focus. Each focus has its own organization (see Figure 9–1).

Description-Focused Units

Traditionally, the most common science units have a **descriptive** approach. Sample topics focus on content such as matter and energy, light, plants, and weather. In these units, content plays the major role. Skills, when covered, are typically integrated into the content-focused lessons. Usually there is little emphasis on skill development or on student assessment, since skills play an incidental role (see Figure 9–2).

The sources of such units are most often textbooks. The content topics frequently spiral through the curriculum. Topics are introduced in the early grades and are repeated at various points in higher grade levels. Each time they are repeated, new, more complex and abstract information is introduced. Generally, the breadth as well as the depth of the topic

1. Descriptive focus
    example: a unit on sound, electricity, or mammals
    (inquiry skills play a lesser role)
2. Inquiry Skills focus
    example: a unit on observation, classifying, or experimenting
    (content plays a lesser role)
3. Conceptual and Inquiry Skills focus
    example: a unit including sinking and floating, observation, classifying, selecting
    relevant variables, mass, volume, experimenting, or buoyancy
    (in a single unit, inquiry skills and content play equal roles)
4. Theme focus
    examples: units on interaction, interdependence, or patterns
    (in a single unit, inquiry skills and content play equal roles)
5. Issues focus
    examples: units on pollution, endangered species, or flood control
    (in a single unit, inquiry skills and content play equal roles)

FIGURE 9-1   *Focus and organization of the science unit*

FIGURE 9-2   *Sequence of descriptive- and concept-focused science units*

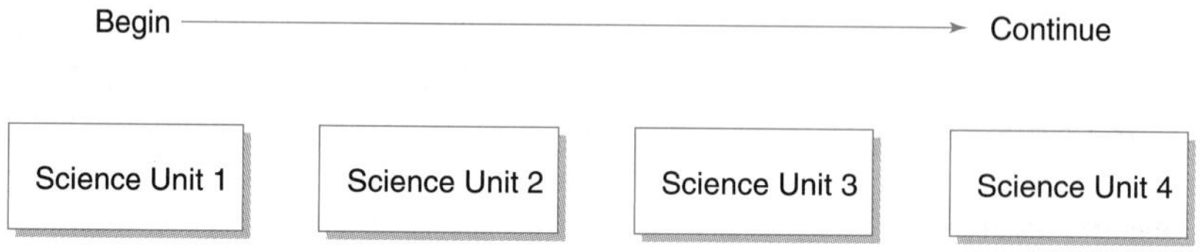

Begin ──────────────────────────────→ Continue

| Science Unit 1 | Science Unit 2 | Science Unit 3 | Science Unit 4 |

is expanded. When these topics are taught thoroughly, they build on the foundation students bring from earlier grades. The topic's development is matched closely to students' own intellectual development, gradually building an in-depth understanding of the topic.

There are difficulties and problems in using this approach to science unit organization. Sometimes, earlier teachers may not have taught the topic, or they may have taught it with a factual emphasis, neglecting to change to a strategy of science instruction that focuses on conceptual development.

See Chapter 5 for an effective strategy.

As a result, students are unprepared for the more advanced exploration of the topic they find at a higher grade level.

Because skill development is mostly incidental in this type of unit, students don't have many opportunities to develop the thinking abilities that help them understand the topic at a higher and more complex level. Even when teachers cover the topic appropriately, students may focus on fact learning and on memorization because they haven't developed the thinking strategies needed to explore and understand the more complex ideas presented.

With an emphasis on content, description-focused units may provide a clear and discrete view of a topic such as weather. However, connections with other topics, science disciplines, or knowledge are not made clear to students. There is little application and transfer of content learning with this approach.

Description-focused units are taught sparingly during the year and are supplemented with greater emphasis on science inquiry skills. The best approach is to greatly modify descriptive text materials through centering on the key science concepts and inquiry skills suggested for the topic area in state and national standards.

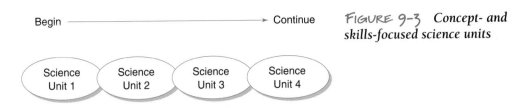

FIGURE 9-3 *Concept- and skills-focused science units*

Inquiry Skills-Focused Units

In an **inquiry skills-focused unit**, the specific content learned is less important than the skills to be developed. An inquiry skill such as classification can be taught with almost any content. Students can classify rocks and minerals, clouds in the sky, plant leaves, or the colors of stars. The teacher recognizes that the students learn content, but is focused on the development of the skill. Hence, the unit is organized around a significant critical or creative science thinking skill. This skill is developed and practiced within a set of content.

See Chapter 4 on the development of inquiry skills.

A strength of an inquiry skills-focused unit is that it allows the teacher to provide remedial help for students who have difficulty in science. Students are more focused on *how* they are learning. Such a focus facilitates the transfer of learning. These units emphasize hands-on/minds-on learning. It is the lack of developed thinking skills that often creates learning problems in science. Inquiry skills-focused teaching enables students to develop new skills or further develop a skill so they may work with ideas in greater depth. It also helps them work with more abstract ideas. The full range of inquiry skills is considered in planning these science units. Teachers order and select science inquiry skills, problem-solving skills, and other skills based on the students' developmental needs.

See Chapter 4 for a discussion of inquiry skills teaching.

The weakness of focusing solely on an inquiry skills-focused unit is that scientific ideas may not be covered systematically. The day-to-day activities may jump between concepts without full development of any one concept. Higher-level concepts may not be learned because the sub-concepts providing a foundation for them were not adequately or systematically addressed. General connections between science and other subjects are usually not developed in inquiry skills-focused units.

Skills-focused units must be taught from a systematic curriculum plan. They can be interspersed with other types of science units throughout the year and from grade to grade. These units ensure that students develop an inquiry skill needed in upcoming units. For example, at the first-grade level, three or four units throughout the year focusing on observing, classifying, measuring, and communicating results using diagrams and drawings provide a foundation of important skills that are necessary in order to understand important science concepts (see Figure 9–3).

Conceptual and Inquiry Skills-Focused Units

Units can combine science concepts and inquiry skills with equal emphasis. This **conceptual and inquiry skills-focused** type of unit works best with an inquiry or investigative instructional strategy. The students work with a coherent set of content. At the same time, they develop the skills necessary to systematically study and construct an understanding of the concepts. For example, students can investigate why objects such as little boats made of pieces of clay sink or float. Their investigation involves students in making predictions about which objects will sink or float, testing these predictions, classifying objects based on their sinking or floating properties, selecting those relevant properties (variables) of the objects that appear to be related, and investigating whether those properties are related. The concepts involved with sinking and floating include

FIGURE 9-4   *Theme-focused science units*

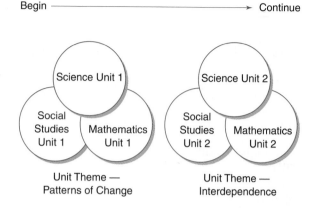

Begin ──────────────────────→ Continue

Unit Theme —
Patterns of Change

Unit Theme —
Interdependence

mass and volume. These experiences also help students build the concept of buoyancy as applied to real world events. Mass, volume, and buoyancy are the conceptual goals of the unit.

The strength of this type of unit is that students develop skills enabling them to use the content they are learning in meaningful ways. A criterion for selecting appropriate topics for this type of unit is that key ideas lend themselves to investigation by the students using concrete materials. This type of teaching requires significantly more time than does the traditional approach. Fewer concepts are taught during the school year. Therefore, it is important to select key ideas fundamental to scientific literacy (see Figure 9–4). These are found in state and national science standards.

Applying What You Know

Reflecting on Differences between Types of Units

Select an appropriate science topic for a unit from a science textbook. Identify the topic of the unit selected and the grade level(s). Describe the differences between description-, inquiry skills-, and conceptual and inquiry skills-based units built around the same science topic.

Theme-Focused Units

Themes which cut across traditional science topics focus on powerful ideas used often by people, which provide tools for thinking about the world and solving problems (American Association for the Advancement of Science, 1993a; National Research Council, 1996). Some examples include systems, patterns of change, interaction, models, time, distance, interdependence, and scale. Other less-broad but useful themes are concepts such as *forces, energy, evolution, the living cell, the dynamic Earth, aeronautics,* or *space exploration* (Mayer, 1995; National Aeronautics and Space Administration, 1992). **Themes** address broad ideas such as the interactions between materials, rather than simply a study of magnets. An "interaction" unit examines the changes brought about through interactions of materials in direct contact with each other, such as the absorption of water by cloth, the completion of an electric circuit when wires touch each other,

TABLE 9–1   *Using interconnections between disciplines to plan integrated science units*

Interconnections between Disciplines	Sample Interconnections
Constancy	Speed of light, conservation of mass
Patterns of change	Positions and motions of objects
Interdependence	Predator-and-prey, ecosystem, solar system
Evolution	River systems, organisms in a changing environment
Equilibrium	Stationary objects, water in a hot water tank, and a floating object
Direct interactions	Scissors cutting paper, paper soaking up water
Interaction-at-a-distance	Magnetic and electrical forces
Systems	Organisms, machines, solar system, dynamic Earth
Subsystems	Reproduction, power source, Jupiter and satellites, weather
Organization	Periodic table, classification of organisms
Form	Shape, structure, or organization of parts in a whole
Function	Cutting, holding weights, or facilitating motion
Measurement	Length, time, mass, and productivity
Conceptual models	Physical objects, mental constructs, conceptual maps, mathematical relations or computer simulations of a living cell, operation of an electric circuit, or the water cycle

the effects of adding vinegar to baking soda, and the separation of materials using a knife or scissors. It also can deal with interaction between objects at a distance. This involves magnets drawing in nails from a distance or creating a pattern among iron filings, a balloon attracted to a wall after being rubbed on someone's hair, and an object falling to Earth from a student's hand. See Table 9–1 for additional examples of broad interconnecting themes.

Development of **theme-focused units** begins with planning a time of the year when meaningful integration of the selected subjects around an important theme can occur. After comparing the yearly topics of each of the major subjects, select a theme that fits the curriculum and arrange for appropriate topics in each of the subject areas to be developed in a set of lessons or a thematic unit. For example, the theme "patterns of change" could be investigated during the primary-age years in a unit that integrates the topics of:

- Observation and classification of day and night and seasonal events (science).
- Examination of how people change their dress and everyday activities during daily and seasonal change (social studies).
- Investigation of number sets and problems related to changes in seasons through activities, such as counting the number of hours of daylight in winter and the number of days in each season using a yearly calendar (mathematics).

A strength of this type of unit is its ability to make connections to subjects other than science. These same themes are important ideas in social studies, music, mathematics,

What does the attire of these people tell you about the weather?

or any other content area. Interactions between cultures and societies, for example, also create change. Students are more easily motivated because these units can be highly relevant.

A weakness of this type of unit is the difficulty of focusing on significant aspects of the theme in each subject area. In the early grades, "interactions" should refer to physical events (American Association for the Advancement of Science, 1993a). It may be difficult to relate meaningfully to physical events in all subjects. In planning an early-grades unit on the theme of interactions, teachers need to consider whether strong examples of interactions have been selected as the social studies, music, and mathematics components, or if the examples stretch to fit the topic? Are they trivial? Are they tangential, barely addressing the topic? For young students, interactions between societies is a difficult idea. It may not be possible to involve students in developmentally meaningful experiences that will help them create this idea. In a departmentalized setting, theme teaching across subjects requires lots of collaboration and flexibility between teachers.

Issues-Focused Units

An **issues-focused unit** can be considered as an attempt to answer a question that is relevant to somebody—an individual, a group of individuals, or society as a whole. An issue does not always have an answer. Many issues are complex and not easily resolved. Students can explore such issues, identify possible solutions, examine the arguments

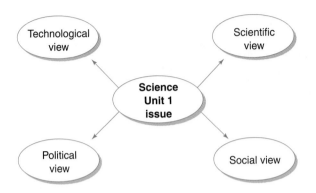

FIGURE 9-5 *Issues-focused science unit*

for and against each solution, predict which solution(s) might be best implemented, and try out a possible solution. The strength of an issues-focused unit is that students are highly motivated to investigate the issue because they perceive it as relevant. This type of unit allows a combination of content and skills development. All students are involved in the investigation at some level. Another strength is that the unit requires an understanding of the problem or issue from a variety of viewpoints. In addition to a scientific context, an issue generally has social, political, economic, and technological contexts.

The selection of appropriate key ideas for this type of unit begins with identifying an issue relevant to students. The topic of endangered species, for example, cannot be meaningfully investigated by first graders because of the abstractness of the issue.

Choosing a yearly curriculum based on issues can create a haphazard approach to learning science skills and content. This type of unit is best interspersed with other units in a well-sequenced curriculum based on a course of study. The issues-focused unit might follow-up a previous unit, enabling students to investigate in some depth an issue discovered in the earlier unit.

Finally, an issues-focused unit is not easily managed. The students are often pursuing different aspects of an investigation at the same time. The teacher makes sure there is an underlying organization, that all information is sequenced and communicated to all participants, and that information is analyzed and shared in relevant and clearly understood formats. Graphs, maps, charts, computer databases, and other means of organizing and communicating information are used. A reliance on library research papers, which are then read to the class, often produces boredom among the students and does not allow them to recognize which information is relevant (see Figure 9–5).

Incorporating Projects and Case Studies into Units

All of the types of units can include **projects** and **case studies**. See Figure 9–6 for examples. Projects involve students in investigating a problem, theme, or issue in small groups. These groups identify the problem, determine methods for investigating the problem, and carry out an investigation leading to a group conclusion. Examples of investigative projects include studying the effect of planting bushes and flowers on the diversity of wildlife around a school; determining water quality of a stream, lake, or tap water; finding out what is needed for safe housing construction in earthquake-prone areas; and determining the impact of mining, deforestation, or housing construction on people living downstream from them.

Project Method

examples: units on analysis of the impact of mining operations in the area, water quality in streams, or strategies for earthquake survival (in a single unit, skills and content play equal roles)

Case Study Method

examples: units on management of household insects in the city, urban forests or air quality, or noise pollution around the school (in a single unit, skills and content play equal roles)

FIGURE 9-6   *Problem-solving methods in science units*

An example of an issues-focused unit best approached as a project at the fourth- or fifth-grade level is one involving students in studying the Endangered Species Act in the United States and its implications on the environment, people's jobs, and landowners. This is approached as a project. Upon investigation, students usually find that an endangered species is part of an ecosystem that is endangered. The particular species no longer lives in an ecosystem that can support it. People are faced not just with the loss of a single species, but with the loss of an ecosystem. Protecting the species means protecting the ecosystem in which it lives, which means that some people may lose their jobs or that landowners may not be able to do what they wish with their land. However, it also means that future generations will have access to that ecosystem. This is a complex issue with no easy solution.

Case studies involve students in developing an explanation or conclusion for a specific small set of individuals, objects, or events related to the problem, theme, or issue. First graders might explore the issue of, "Why don't we have more kinds of birds around our school?" This is best approached as a case study. One solution to the issue is to focus on the needs of a single bird or a few species. This might involve putting up a birdhouse or bird feeder meeting the needs of a single species outside the classroom window. Bushes might also be planted around the school to provide nesting and sleeping areas for several species of birds. The students record the different species visiting the bird feeder, bushes, and wildflowers, and compare their findings with their records of birds around the school before the bird feeder and plantings were put in place. As part of their unit, the students might use e-mail to find out what birds first graders at other schools find around their school. They might visit a store and a plant nursery to see what types of wild bird food are found and to find out what kinds of birds are attracted to different types of food.

Applying What You Know

Considering Differences between Types of Units

Select a science topic useful for planning a science unit from a science textbook. Identify the topic of unit selected, and the grade level(s). Describe the differences between theme-, issues-, projects-, and case study-based units built around the same science topic.

Classify these farm animals by their physical characteristics.

WHAT TOPICS ARE APPROPRIATE FOR INTEGRATED SCIENCE?

Perhaps the best way to start to think about the types of decisions required and the problems in planning integrated science is to consider an example of a first-grade theme-focused unit that was recently planned in an elementary school. The unit's topic was farm animals. Science, social studies, mathematics, and language arts were to be connected in the theme-focused unit. The teacher began planning the unit by considering inquiry skills objectives appropriate for a primary-age grade level. These included mapping, observing, identifying and describing, inferring, and classifying. The teacher then wrote the goals of the unit to include outcomes where students will be able to:

1. Describe the location of animals and farm implements on a farm, using a three-dimensional model farm laid out on a large table in the classroom.
2. Observe, describe, and identify farm animals and their family members.
3. Classify animals by their physical characteristics.
4. Name and infer foods people get from farm animals.
5. Classify animal coverings.
6. Order and classify the life cycles of animals.
7. Compare animal life cycles to human life cycles.

The unit began with students being shown print pictures and a videotape of various farms: dairy farms, egg and poultry farms, cattle farms and ranches, grain farms, catfish farms, fruit farms, flower farms, vegetable farms, and farms where multiple uses were evident. The students were asked to identify common features of a farm and to map the location of plants and animals on a farm.

The students were then given pictures and asked to group and identify the various products of a farm. They observed and participated in the processing of milk into butter using a butter churn. They classified farm animals according to their coverings such as fur, skin, scales, or feathers. They then identified the life cycles of the animals whose coverings they had classified. The unit concluded with a visit to a working farm in the local area.

Social studies, mathematics, and language arts were connected in the daily activities of the theme-focused unit. These activities included using print pictures, CD-ROM pictures on a computer screen, plastic replicas, and animal crackers. The students used interactive CD-ROM and bulletin board activities involving travel around the farm, as well as a learning center including crafts, computer programs, pictures of farm animals, and books related to farm life.

Mathematical processes during these activities included counting animals, adding groups of animals to come up with a total number, and subtracting animals when groups were split. Social studies processes included listing the chores done every day by the farmer to ensure the animals were well cared for, and making a map of the location of barns and feeding areas of a three-dimensional model farm in the classroom. After a visit to a farm, students identified the products produced from each type of farm animal they studied.

Language arts connections in the unit activities were made when stories were read to students, when a class book on farm animals was written and constructed, when students wrote thank-you notes after the farm visit, and when students wrote poems about farm animals. Woven into the unit were considerations of the acquisition of new farm-related vocabulary, examinations of the literary elements in trade books read, development of reading strategies and comprehension in materials read, and development of listening and speaking skills.

The teacher started planning the unit with some specific concerns about thematic units (Crawley, Barufaldi, & Salyer, 1994). She thought there was something important missing from the typical thematic approach. Analyzing her outline and organization, she concluded that an emphasis on student science thinking skills was a good organizational theme. However, she felt uneasy about the content of the unit.

This teacher appropriately felt that thinking skills are an important part of a primary-age thematic unit. Inquiry skills are recommended as an organizing focus for any grade level, but especially in the primary-age years. In the later elementary and middle school years, both inquiry skills- and content-focused description units are needed. Examples suggested by the American Association for the Advancement of Science include interdisciplinary themes such as patterns of change, interaction, systems, and models (1993a).

Even if inquiry skills are the major focus of the primary-age unit, the unit cannot be content free; an underlying content theme is needed. To address the uneasiness the teacher felt about the farm animals unit, an alternative approach might have been to work with an underlying content-organizing theme such as "interdependence." If the theme of "interdependence" is chosen, farm animals and farms serve as a catalyst for studies of interdependence. The focus can be "Farm animals need us and we need them." This is supported by an integrated set of concepts such as:

> Farm animals have life cycles. Farm animals depend on us for their food. Farm animals provide us with our food in terms of milk, cheese, and meat. Farmers and their farm animals provide people who don't live on farms with their food. Farm animals also provide us with products that are not food, such as leather and wool. The food production process has many steps. Farm animals are part of a food chain, as are humans. Technology helps make food production more efficient. We pay the farmers money so they can buy the things they don't grow or make for themselves and their farm animals. We can classify animals by their outer coverings.

The long-term goal for this theme-focused unit is the development of the key concept of interdependence of all living things in an ecosystem. This concept is dealt with time and again in higher-grade units.

Other problems with this integrated unit develop from the fact that the overall theme of farm animals does not suggest a sequence and organization for the development of inquiry skills or basic concepts and generalizations in support of the theme. For instance, why is it important to classify animal coverings? How does it fit with the theme of farm animals? When in the unit should this take place? The same can be said for many of the activities suggested earlier for the farm animals unit. What is the place of questions and ideas centered around describing and classifying animals in a variety of ways? The biological concept of animal? The concept and events taking place in a biological food chain or local version of a food web (leading in the future to the concept of ecosystem)? The nature of asking questions and gathering evidence involved in an investigation? The nature of a scientific way of thinking?

This idea of a sequence without an appropriate content theme can lead to inappropriate planning and trivial learning. A unit designed around "turkeys" traditionally has been used in elementary classrooms around the Thanksgiving Day holiday. The students are given name tags in the shape of a turkey, they read stories about turkeys, make turkey drawings after tracing their hands, write stories about turkeys, make observations of a turkey egg and turkey feather, and visit a turkey farm. Thoughtful decisions about appropriate knowledge, interconnections between concepts and generalizations, and the use and practice of inquiry skills are supplanted by one theme and how well the activities fit this particular theme. A curriculum that moves from one thematic unit to the next with themes such as "turkeys" produces trivialized knowledge and learning that is not meaningful to the students' present needs or future success (Martin-Kniep, Feige, & Soodak, 1995).

How to Choose Appropriate Themes for Integrated Units

In selecting a theme, the questions asked include what will be the:

- Important *key concepts* central to each of the subject areas integrated?
- *Guiding questions* that lead students into inquiry?
- *Activities* that will engage the students in reflective inquiry?
- Natural and significant *connections* between key concepts?

An appropriate theme involves teachers and students in making choices that do not compromise the quality of student learning outcomes or lower the teacher's own feeling of the worthwhileness of the science unit (Yager & Lutz, 1994). While most themes interconnect subjects, *many* will not provide meaningful learning for students. Some examples of themes that are difficult to appropriately address in a thematic unit are rabbits, zoo animals, farm animals, dinosaurs, the Constitutional Convention, written communication, Thanksgiving, and Mesopotamia. Thematic units are best when used occasionally; they should not be the organizing factor for the yearly curriculum.

Mesopotamia, for example, is better understood when its habitat is studied; when irrigation is understood in relation to the types of food plants its inhabitants depended upon; and when the effects poor farming practices had on erosion of soils, and ultimately on the decline of the culture, are considered. Science can inform this social studies topic immensely. However, students' understanding of plants is better served when they directly study them, investigating photosynthesis, soil conditions, the water cycle, and so on.

A second, more extended example is the concept of the birth of a nation, such as the United States' history from 1750 to 1820. This is an important concept in school social studies curricula that is better understood when studied along with the other events in the social and natural world of that time. The successful integration of science with this topic should be well planned in advance. A focus on electricity, natural resources, and Earth processes that were being discovered at the time can be connecting ideas for science and provide several possible direct study topics with many connections to other subjects.

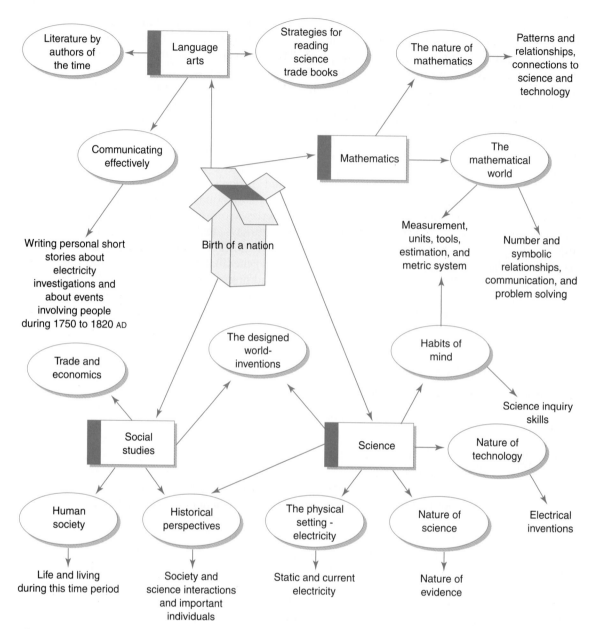

Literature by authors of the time

Language arts

Strategies for reading science trade books

The nature of mathematics

Patterns and relationships, connections to science and technology

Communicating effectively

Mathematics

The mathematical world

Writing personal short stories about electricity investigations and about events involving people during 1750 to 1820 AD

Birth of a nation

Measurement, units, tools, estimation, and metric system

Number and symbolic relationships, communication, and problem solving

The designed world- inventions

Habits of mind

Trade and economics

Science inquiry skills

Social studies

Science

Nature of technology

Human society

Historical perspectives

The physical setting - electricity

Nature of science

Electrical inventions

Life and living during this time period

Society and science interactions and important individuals

Static and current electricity

Nature of evidence

FIGURE 9-7   *Web diagram for planning an integrated science unit across four subject areas*

Choosing electricity provides many appropriate and practical learning activities that can be successfully tied together in a meaningful science unit. The example uses the *Bench- marks for Scientific Literacy* outline for including key idea areas (American Association for the Advancement of Science, 1993a). See Figure 9–7 and the additional connections in *Benchmarks for Science Literacy* (American Association for the Advancement of Science, 1993a, "The Physical Setting," pp. 93–95; "The Designed World," pp. 193, 194, & 198; "Habits of Mind," p. 293). For example, science outcomes are planned in "The Physical Setting" through activities focused on electricity, static and current activity, interaction at a distance, forces exerted by charged objects, batteries, lightning, circuits, types and conditions of charged objects, and planning and carrying out investigations with electricity. Science outcomes in "The Designed World" involve the development of electrical devices that (1) build up and store charge (capacitors), (2) increase voltage (van de Graff generators), (3) those that plate metals (electroplating), and (4) leak electrical charge (pointed metal rods used as lightning rods). Mathematics outcomes in "The Mathematical World" include the measurement of forces, distances, and electrical charges through experiences with charged balloons, pieces of charged paper, and lightbulb intensity in an electrical circuit. Other mathematics outcomes involve appropriate units and tools (metric system), estimation, communication, problem solving, and developing formulas for expressing predictions. Social studies outcomes involve historically concurrent political (the Revolutionary War) and economic (trade and monetary system) events in the lives of the people of the times, important individuals and groups influencing events, the importance of rules and laws affecting personal safety (electrical safety), and geographic locations of events. Language arts involves strategies for reading science trade books, reading poems and short stories by authors of the time, strategies for writing stories and reports about electrical investigations, and writing a review of a film about the time and of interactive CD-ROMs about events affecting the United States between 1750 to 1820 AD.

As another example, "dinosaur" is a topic that does not lend itself well to integration with social studies. The social world is the focus of social studies. People and their societies were not found during the Mesozoic period. Students could explore the lives and work of the scientists who have been important in the study of dinosaurs. They could also talk about laws preserving important dinosaur sites and controlling access to specimens. Each of these social studies-related considerations would inform students in the study of dinosaurs. However, social studies concepts might be better served by an in-depth study of the process of developing and passing a law and of the pressure groups that influence the passage of a law.

In the case of topics such as "dinosaurs" and "laws," mathematics content is a forced choice. Mathematics is involved in each case. For example, it is involved in understanding the relative sizes of various dinosaurs or how a majority vote in the passage of a law is calculated. Mathematics is found everywhere. However, if mathematics is always viewed in terms of integrated units, basic mathematical concepts may not be learned by children. If thematic units are always used, basic understandings of concepts such as *photosynthesis* and *laws* may be lost.

The study of a less-effective theme leads to students' understanding of the ideas related to the theme at a very low level. They may be able to describe objects related to the ideas on a factual basis, but cannot explain the interactions between those objects. Knowing the names of the animals on a farm and describing their coverings (fur, feathers, and so on) is meaningless unless one can explain the interactions among the different kinds of farm animals and the importance of diversity in a food web or local ecosystem. Studying animals on a farm without an accompanying study of the plants on the farm is also a weak approach. Animals depend on particular plants. Where do these come from? Does the farmer grow them? Does the farmer have to buy them? What happens when there is a shortage and the farmer can't get the plants his animals need to eat? What is the difference between a farm and a natural ecosystem? In the farm unit described earlier in this chapter, it is difficult to find a powerful science idea that the students learned. It is not important for them to know the names of all the different animals. It is more important for students to develop a way of thinking that involves problem solving, the gathering of evidence, and developing conclusions from that evidence.

Less-effective themes usually lead to a unit that teaches one subject well at the expense of others. When selecting a theme, one must ask, "If students followed through on the activities, what important science, social studies, and mathematics ideas will they have learned?" These ideas must be part of the year-long curriculum design for the classroom. Thematic units are taught because they more fully inform students. However, they do not completely replace science units because thematic units do not teach all the key ideas that need to be addressed if students are to meet the state and national guidelines for scientific literacy.

Planning Integrated Units

There are two major planning techniques for integrated teaching. The first involves choosing a single key idea that interconnects the disciplines. This type of planning is more limited in scope and focuses on a significant interconnection during a science unit. The American Association for the Advancement of Science (AAAS) developed a framework for integrating key ideas in order to foster scientific literacy (1993a). Interconnections are made between the key idea and 12 areas of knowledge. See Figure 9–8 for a listing of the 12 areas of possible interconnected knowledge centered on the key idea in a science unit. Figure 9–9 provides a description of each area of possible connected knowledge. When planning a unit, lessons involving the key unit ideas are interconnected with several of

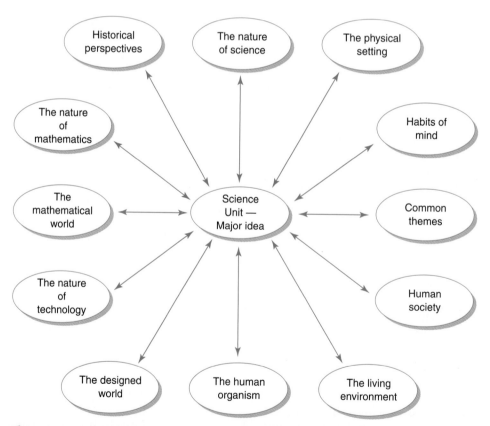

FIGURE 9-8   *Possible interconnections between knowledge areas in a science unit as described in Benchmarks for Science Literacy (AAAS, 1993)*
From *Benchmarks for Science Literacy* by American Association for the Advancement of Science, copyright 1993 by the American Association for the Advancement of Science. Used by permission of Oxford University Press, Inc.

Historical perspectives—displacing Earth from the center of the universe; Earth's place in the universe; relating matter, energy, space, and time; extending time; motion of the continents; understanding fire; explaining the diversity of life; discovering germs; and harnessing power.

The nature of science—the scientific worldview, scientific inquiry, and the scientific enterprise.

The physical setting—the universe, Earth, shaping Earth, the structure of matter, energy transformations, motion, and forces of nature.

Habits of mind—Science inquiry skills.

Common themes—Systems, patterns of change, interaction, models, time, distance, interdependence, and scale.

Human society—cultural effects of behavior, social change, political and economic systems, social conflict, and global interdependence.

The living environment—Diversity of life, heredity, cells, interdependence of life, flow of matter and energy, and evolution of life.

The human organism—Human identity, human development, basic biological functions, learning, and health.

The designed world—agriculture, materials and manufacturing, energy sources and use, communication, information processing, and health technology.

The nature of technology—technology and science, design, and systems and issues in technology.

The mathematical world—numbers, symbolic relationships, shapes, uncertainty, and mathematical reasoning.

The nature of mathematics—patterns and relationships, mathematics, science and technology, and mathematical inquiry.

FIGURE 9-9   *Possible interconnections between knowledge areas in a science unit*

the areas to develop application and transfer. The more natural the interconnections and the greater the number of interconnections made, the higher the quality of scientific understanding of the unit's key ideas. See Figure 9–10 for a listing of possible interconnections with the key idea of "forces" among intermediate-grade students in the AAAS's 12 areas of knowledge. *Benchmarks for Scientific Literacy* is a rich resource for planning integrated science units (American Association for the Advancement of Science, 1993a). This source can be accessed on the Internet at *http://www.aas.org/benchmarks.*

For further information on *Benchmarks for Scientific Literacy,* see the accompanying Companion Website at *http://www.prenhall.com/sunal*

Companion Website

Applying What You Know

Making Connections between Science Areas

Select a key idea from a science textbook useful for planning a science lesson. Create an outline making connections to other science-related areas involving a single science concept. Include at least four of the areas listed below. Use Figure 9–10 as a model. Identify the concept used and the grade level in which it will be taught.

(continued)

	Key Concept—	Grade Level—
Historical perspectives—		
The nature of science—		
The physical setting—		
Habits of mind—		
Common themes—		
Human society—		
The living environment—		
The human organism—		
The designed world—		
The nature of technology—		
The mathematical world—		
The nature of mathematics—		

The second major planning technique for integrated teaching involves planning the yearly curriculum concurrently in several subjects. Teachers look at curriculum goals throughout the year. The goals for science are matched to those for social studies, mathematics, and so on across several units. If the Constitutional Convention and the history of the Revolutionary War period is a major goal in social studies, and electricity is important in science, they should be taught at the same time. Interconnections occur when the students study the following:

• Benjamin Franklin can be studied as a participant in the Constitutional Convention and a major personality during the Revolutionary War, and also can be investigated for his experiments with static electricity.

Historical perspectives—Issac Newton.
The nature of science—everybody can reason scientifically.
The physical setting—changes in speed and direction are caused by forces.
Habits of mind—estimation skills.
Common themes—sketches and diagrams showing interactions and interconnections of objects and events.
Human society—forces can be used to help or hurt human beings.
The living environment—substances may change or move but never appear or disappear out of nothing.
The human organism—senses can be used for observation.
The designed world—new materials and techniques have been developed to withstand natural forces.
The nature of technology—tools are used to do things better and more easily.
The mathematical world—sometimes changing one thing changes something else.
The nature of mathematics—things move, or can be made to move, along straight, curved, circular, and jagged paths.

FIGURE 9-10   *Possible interconnections between knowledge areas in a science unit focusing on the main idea of "forces in the natural world"*

- A study of Benjamin Franklin can lead to a consideration of inventions and discoveries of that time period. These include the link between nerve action and electricity by Galvani (1771), liquid batteries by Volta (1800), electromagnetism by Oerstead (1819), electric generators by Faraday (1821), and laws of electrical interactions by Ampere (1822). Other inventions, such as electroplating, development of batteries, and the concept of basic circuits, could be connected with events in history during and following this period.
- The invention of the metric system occurred during this time period; therefore, the metric system can be connected to historical events. A study of metric units of measurement can also occur.
- Other interconnections within science are found in the measurement of forces between magnets, the distance between objects, and the effects of adding batteries and bulbs to circuits.

WHAT IS THE GENERAL PROCESS OF PLANNING SCIENCE UNITS WITH AN APPROPRIATE FOCUS?

Teaching science through well-planned units helps students become scientifically literate and can be focused to make interconnections with many relevant areas of students' lives. Effective science unit planning requires thoughtful consideration of basic planning steps, purposeful organization, and reflective evaluation. Using any of the unit-planning approaches described earlier in the chapter requires a similar sequence of planning steps. These planning steps are summarized in Figure 9–11 and described with the examples below.

1. Generate topic selection.
2. Select a title.
3. Research the topic, beginning with state and national standards.
4. Identify special needs among the students.
5. Identify focus questions.
6. List intended learning outcomes.
7. Categorize intended learning outcomes.
8. Create a web.
9. Develop a rationale.
10. Begin the KWL. (What do I *know* about this topic? What do I *want* to learn about this topic? What did I *learn* about this topic?)
11. Write learning objectives.
12. Develop lesson plans.
13. Make accommodations for technology and safety.
14. Develop an assessment plan.
15. Implement the unit.
16. Complete the KWL.
17. Reflect on the unit.

FIGURE 9–11   *Steps in planning the science unit*

Step 1: Generating Ideas for the Topic of a Unit

Once a theme is chosen, terms, words, and phrases related to the unit are generated. Generating ideas creates an initial list of possible objectives and activity topics. It will be revised and changed as the unit development process continues. The ideas should flow when integration with other subjects is the goal. Some examples of initial topic generation for an integrated unit on electricity at the fifth-grade level follow:

energy; communications; distance; machines; observation; problem solving; sources of electricity; uses of electricity; how electricity is transmitted; calculating electric bills; comparing the costs of electricity by graphing; the role technology plays in the production, distribution, and use of electricity; identifying who discovered electricity; mapping routes of electric transmission; Benjamin Franklin; Alessandro Volta; critical thinking; change in lifestyle with electricity; ways people in the past lived without electricity; stories about people and electricity; data gathering; hypothesizing; and experimenting.

Step 2: Naming the Unit

Units need focus, and naming them is a way to arrive at a focus. The name can capture the importance or value of the unit, as well as its content. The name a unit is given is a way of making sure that the initial ideas are logically connected to each other. The following are the names of some science units that have been developed:

Atoms, Molecules, and You; Australia Is a Unique Habitat; Physical and Chemical Reactions with Food; Electricity and Models; Living Things and How They Adapt; Rules—For People and in Nature; Transportation Is How We Move People and Things; Properties of Matter; Conserving Our Environment; Sounds of Music; and Using the Skies.

An alternative way of naming a unit is to use a question. The unit then serves to answer the question. For example:

What Is Electricity? What Are the Properties of Matter? How Do We Measure the Solar System? What Steps Can Be Taken to Conserve our Environment? How Do People and Things Move from Place to Place in Our Country? Why Should We Consider Space Travel? What Have Been the Critical Events in Space Travel? How Do We See Colors?

Step 3: Researching the Topic

Researching the topic to be taught is critically important. It enables teachers to assess their prior knowledge, add to this knowledge base, identify alternative conceptions that may be held, and modify those alternative conceptions. Journals, encyclopedias, science texts, and trade books have traditionally been used in planning units. However, structured ideas already linked to diverse concepts for planning science units can be found by creating a concept search on the Internet. They are also available in *Science for All Americans* (American Association for the Advancement of Science, 1993b) and *Benchmarks for Science Literacy* (American Association for the Advancement of Science, 1993a), by accessing other national and state courses of study, and by sending e-mail queries to other teachers and scientists on the Internet.

Step 4: Identifying Special Needs among Students and Making Accommodations

A list of the special needs found among the students in the class is created if it does not already exist. The list indicates those needs identified through the special education program.

It also indicates any recognized needs that do not fall within the purview of the special education program. The list includes students: (1) who are having difficulties academically, (2) whose native language is not English and who are not yet fluent in English, (3) who have physical and emotional difficulties, and (4) who are experiencing severe stress in their families such as divorce, death, a move from another state, or a major illness. All of these students require adaptation of the lesson plans if they are to be taught effectively.

Greater discussion of addressing students' special needs is found in Chapter 11.

Step 5: Developing Focus Questions

Too often, teachers don't consider what the main points or questions for a unit are, especially when the ideas have been planned for us, as in a textbook chapter. Textbook chapters typically contain more information than students need to know. Their focus is often on breadth rather than depth. Without a focus or central questions, it is difficult to help students see the main point of a chapter or a unit. **Focus questions** help students make a link with their prior knowledge as well as establish a rationale for studying the unit. Some examples of focus questions are:

How can knowledge about the elements and compounds affect my choice of foods?

How should people interact with the environment?

What can families do to prepare themselves for natural disasters such as tornadoes, floods, hurricanes, and earthquakes?

What are the major forces involved in designing efficient transportation vehicles?

How has science helped change transportation in this century?

For a single unit, several questions are appropriate. A focus question guides the development of a single lesson or of several lessons. For example, a middle school unit on "Electricity and Models" could have a question set including the following:

What is electricity?

Who discovered electricity?

Why and how is electricity used in my house?

Where does electricity come from?

What are some devices that use electricity?

How do you measure electricity?

How did people in the past live without electricity?

Once an initial list of focus questions is developed, teachers ask: "Which of the focus questions really get at the heart of the unit?" "What kinds of questions are being asked?" "Are they mostly 'where' or 'when' questions?" "Are there any 'how' or 'why' questions?" "Do the questions represent a variety of science inquiry skills and thinking levels from recall and comprehension to application, analysis, and evaluation?" and "To what extent do the questions relate to the students' interests and needs?"

Evaluating the list of focus questions generated for the "Electricity and Models" unit can lead the teacher to modify the questions. Modifications are made to include a variety of science inquiry skills and students' interests and needs. As an example, one of the questions above can be modified and three new questions added. The question, "What are some devices that use electricity?" is modified to, "How do devices that use electricity work?" The new focus questions are: "How can I tell the difference between static and current electricity?" "Who in our community works with the production and distribution of electricity and electrical devices?" and "How will our use of electricity change in the future?"

How does a lightbulb work?

Step 6: Creating Intended Learning Outcomes

The initial list of ideas and the teacher's reflection on the focus questions in steps 1 to 5 helps create a list of intended learning outcomes that are usually written as learning objectives. Intended **learning outcomes** (objectives) are statements of what the teacher wants the students to learn. These statements can include inquiry skills, concepts, and generalizations. The process of identifying learning outcomes begins with a consideration of the initial list of topics generated in step 1. Learning outcomes are not activities or things the students will do. If the teacher has a favorite activity or field trip, she considers what the students will learn from the experience to derive an intended learning outcome. The following is an initial list of ideas for a middle school unit on "habitats." Those with an "X" best represent the potential, intended learning outcomes. Those with an "O" are activities not intended as learning outcomes:

1. X Predator-and-prey relationship.
2. X Food chains.
3. X Animals and plants are sensitive to changes in their habitat.
4. O Write a letter or use the Internet to ask a soil conservationist about obtaining information resources for an investigation.
5. X A habitat is a complex system of interrelationships between plants, animals, climate, and soils.
6. X Maintaining a habitat has economic costs and benefits.
7. O Use of a learning center.
8. X Planning and community action is necessary to foster the conservation of threatened habitats.
9. O How to determine the ratio of predators to prey.
10. O Damage caused by natural disasters.

11. O Measuring the area covered by a habitat.
12. O Using specialized measuring equipment such as that used by foresters to measure the height of trees.
13. O Field trip to a habitat.
14. X Food web.
15. X Using the computer to measure temperature changes in a habitat.
16. X Finding patterns in the location of types of plants in a habitat.

Step 7: Categorizing Intended Learning Outcomes

The next step is grouping the intended learning outcomes into categories. Identify each idea as a generalization, concept, or inquiry skill. Inquiry skills can be grouped into several levels. Check to see that outcomes are expected in each of these categories. The statements in step 6 can be grouped as follows: concepts: 2 and 14; generalizations: 1, 3, 5, 6, and 8; inquiry skills: 15 and 16, and other statements: 4, 7, and 9 to 13.

Step 8: Creating an Idea Web

Now that possible goals and intended learning outcomes have been explored, the technique of webbing is used to evaluate and complete the important ideas and skills students will learn in the science unit. To develop a **web**, the information and ideas from the previous steps are used. Other ideas or skills needed to support the topic are added to help create bridges between similar concepts. Ideas and skills can also be added as ladders between lower-level concepts and a more abstract concept. Ladders help students understand and integrate skills, concepts, and generalizations. Two types of webs are generally used: a hierarchical web and a schematic components web. The teacher chooses the one that best fits the topic.

To construct a hierarchical web (see example in Figure 9–12), the teacher:

1. Selects the key idea(s) or skill(s).
2. Lists ideas and skills related to the key ideas considered as important learning outcomes.
3. Ranks the ideas and/or skills from the most general to the most specific.
4. Groups the ideas and/or skills into clusters, adding more specific ideas and/or skills if necessary.
5. Arranges the ideas and skills in a two-dimensional array on a computer webbing program, spreadsheet, or drawing program. If using paper or index cards, the teacher writes or arranges the ideas and skills as they appear in the two-dimensional array.
6. Links the ideas and skills, and labels each link.

The following list includes sample responses for the development of a hierarchical web in the sequence above (see Figure 9–12).

1. ECOSYSTEM and FOREST.
2. Food webs, Beetle, Types of plants, Types of flowers, Picking seeds out of a dried flower, Types of trees, Predators, Prey, Food chains, Producers, Types of birds.
3. ECOSYSTEM, FOREST, Food webs, Food chains, Producers, Consumers, Predators, Prey, Types of plants, Types of birds, Types of flowers, Types of trees, Beetle, Butterfly, Picking seeds out of a dried flower.
4. (a) ECOSYSTEM and FOREST; (b) Food webs; (c) Food chains, Producers, Consumers, Decomposers, Predators, Prey; (d) Types of plants, Types of birds, Types of flowers, Types of trees; (e) Beetle, Butterfly, Woodpecker, Cardinal; (f) Picking seeds

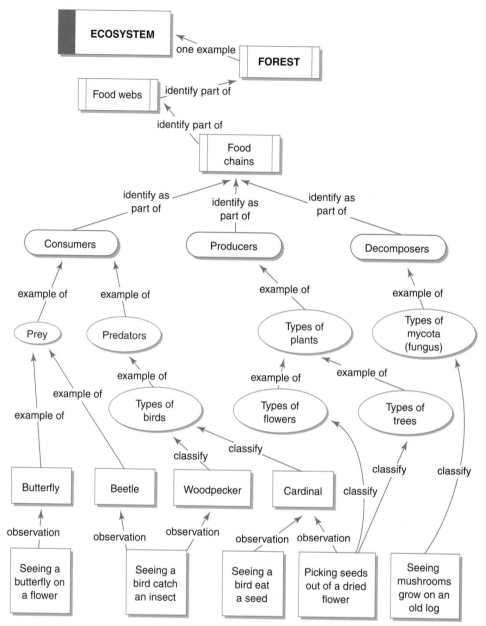

FIGURE 9-12   *Partial example of a hierarchical web used for planning a science unit on a forest ecosystem*

out of a dried flower, Seeing a bird catch an insect, Seeing a butterfly on a flower, Seeing a bird eat a seed, Seeing mushrooms grow on an old log.

5. See Figure 9–12.
6. See Figure 9–12.

Many of the procedures listed above for the hierarchical web are followed in creating a schematic-components web. In the schematic-components web in Figure 9–13, the unit topic is located in the center of the web. Both web types connect the main ideas and skills with interlinking and inquiry skills terms such as "students will observe," "identify," and

F<small>IGURE</small> 9-13 *Partial example of a schematic-components web*

"find an example." These terms define the inquiry processes used in learning this content—inferring, measuring, and so on.

Using a webbing technique helps to analyze the nature of the unit at this stage. Does the web show meaningful ideas and skills? Are there too many abstract ideas? What concrete ideas, bridges, and ladders can be added to help the students understand other concepts or more abstract ideas? Are there any values or attitudes included?

If a textbook serves as the source for a unit, the teacher lists the important ideas and skills from the book. The list is then used to create the web. Using the process outlined in steps 6 and 7, as well as national and state standards, the teacher will find it necessary to modify the web by changing or adding the concrete ideas or inquiry skills missing from the textbook's approach to the topic. Typically, science textbooks contain a large amount of content. The teacher de-emphasizes and eliminates textbook ideas and facts that are not compatible with the standards to plan a unit based on appropriate key ideas for science literacy. For example, a second-grade textbook chapter on "materials" may be modified by deleting the discussions and diagrams on atoms. It may be further modified by adding activities where students investigate the properties of a variety of materials through experiences such as melting, evaporating, odors, and colors.

Applying What You Know

Webbing Different Types of Units

From a science textbook, select a topic chapter useful for planning a science unit. Create three webs for the science unit showing the differences between description-, inquiry skills-, and conceptual and inquiry skills-focused units built around the same science topic. Identify the textbook and section selected, the grade level(s), and a unit title that distinguishes the specific focus of the science unit.

Step 9: Development of a Rationale and Goals

Now that some time has been spent in thinking about the initial ideas of the unit, categorizing them as ideas and skills, and analyzing them by making a web, it is important to think about why the unit will be taught and how the **unit rationale** will be communicated to students. A statement describing the rationale for the unit answers these questions: "How does the unit affect the future of the *students,* as well as their current individual needs and interests?" "How does the unit contribute to *societal* issues and help students deal responsibly with them?" "How is the unit *developmentally appropriate* for the students?" and "How does the unit reflect the spirit and character of inquiry and the nature of science as a *self-learning enterprise* as compared to the view of science as knowledge created by authorities?"

A rationale statement is determined by the values influencing the teacher's perception of students, students' relationship to society, and students' interaction with science as a discipline. Unit rationales can also be influenced by current trends and directions in science teaching and education in general. For example, since the 1970s, there has been a shift toward a more student-centered (hands-on) science approach for the learner. In the 1990s, the necessity for more reflective inquiry for all students added to the previous trend to create a hands-on, minds-on approach to teaching science.

The rationale also includes a statement of goals. These are broad statements of intent reflecting the integration of ideas concerning students, society, and the nature of science. For example, a rationale for a unit on "life on Earth" might contain a goal statement such as, "This unit is designed to give sixth-grade students insight into, and an appreciation of, life as it existed in the past, ideas concerning how life changed, and the diversity of life that now exists on Earth."

A complete rationale contains a goal statement, as well as an explanation of how the unit attends to conceptions of the student, society, and the nature of science. Added to the goal statement above, a rationale for the unit "life on Earth" could end with the following:

The unit begins with evidence on past life as found in local area rocks and through samples from nearby regions. The unit continues with searches on the Internet and library resources for other examples, for general patterns of change found in fossils, and for the ways change is investigated through ideas such as extinctions, change in form and complexity, and changes brought about by environmental conditions. The unit concludes by investigating modern-day local and global descriptions of life's diversity and the loss of diversity due to extinctions. Environmental change due to natural causes and the role of society is addressed to provide students with an appreciation of their actions as having consequences and the role of stewardship for life in their community and planet.

Applying What You Know

More Practice in Planning Units

Select a science chapter topic useful for planning a science unit from a textbook. Create three webs for a science unit showing the differences between theme-, issue-, projects-, and case study-focused units built around the same science topic area. Write a brief statement for each one, giving a rationale and goal statement. These rationale and goal statements should reflect the differences between each of the unit focuses. Identify the textbook and section selected and the grade level(s). Give a title for the unit that distinguishes the specific focus of the unit.

Step 10: Beginning the KWL

The **KWL** is a three-step procedure that gives the teacher some indication of students' prior knowledge and of what they would like to learn about the science unit topic. First, at the beginning of a new unit, a teacher asks students, "What do you *know* about _____?" Second, the teacher asks students, "What *would* you like to learn about this topic?" Third, after the unit has been taught, the teacher asks students, "What did you *learn* about this topic?" Students' comments are recorded on a chart with three columns: K (know), W (would like to learn), and L (what was learned).

Step 11: Development of Learning Objectives

In this step, the initial learning outcomes are revised, written as objectives, and categorized into practical categories for teaching. There are many ways to write learning objectives. All **objectives**, whatever their specific format, focus on what the student will learn and how success can be achieved.

Objectives identify many types of potential learning. Ideas include concepts and generalizations. Inquiry skills are another area in which objectives are written. A third area deals with attitudes and values. With many topics, basic inquiry skills are taught, particularly in measurement, science laboratory experiences, handling materials safely, and recording events. Examples of objectives that require students to construct *ideas* are:

Students will give examples of how temperature influences how much gases and solids dissolve in liquids.

Given a list of famous scientists and their accomplishments, students will make a list of the personal characteristics that have contributed to making people famous.

Students will give examples of pollution that they have personally read about or observed.

Examples of objectives that require students to use and develop *inquiry skills* are:

Students will gather data by conducting a survey.

Students will organize data into bar charts comparing two variables.

Students will list their criteria and decision options in chart form when making a decision relating to the environment.

Objectives that indicate *attitudes or values* with which students will work are:

Students will share their knowledge about an endangered local ecosystem with other people in their community.

Students will demonstrate respect for the plantings around the school.

Step 12: Development of Lesson Plans

Potential activities emerge from the list of learning outcomes. One way to look at the activities is to consider the resources available and possible related activities with these resources. Then the appropriateness of the resources and activities for the special and developmental needs of the students is considered. Examples of resources include textbooks, field trips, games, guest speakers, the Internet, computer software, laboratory equipment, commercial videos, TV cameras and homemade videotapes, manipulatives from common materials, case studies, debates, and simulations. Each of these resources can serve as a focal point for a type of experience designed to facilitate the accomplishment of an objective. In a science unit on scarcity, for example, one objective might be that students will give examples of natural resources that do not exist in their local area. Possible resources and resource strategies for this objective could be:

A field trip to a mine or a gravel pit.

Use of the Internet to search for natural resources.

A video clip of a field geologist at work.

Newspaper articles on resources imported into the local area.

Pages in the science textbook.

Each of these resources and resource activities has an integrity of its own. Each can be used to achieve one or more different outcomes.

The lesson plans are drafted using the list of resources and resource activities for the intended learning outcomes. They are also based on the rationale and learning objectives that have been designed. Search for examples of a web-based unit on the Internet. As the science lesson plans are written, the teacher considers how the lesson can be adapted to the special needs identified among the students using step 4 results as a starting point.

Step 13: Development of Accommodations for Technology and Safety

Additional accommodations are made for all students. Ask yourself questions about how learning can be enhanced or what activities require special attention for safety. How can technology enhance learning in this setting? If concrete materials are available for the concepts and skills involved, can technology help facilitate meaningful learning? If concrete materials are not available, can technology provide the bridge to help students learn the concepts meaningfully?

Are there objects, chemicals, or events in the lesson where special care is needed? Remember "Murphy's law": if something can go wrong, it usually will. Students must learn how to deal with these problems. Do not address a problem simply by telling students that there is a problem; they must be taught how to handle each situation. Find out what students already know about the problem. What attitudes do the students have about the personal harm that can result? Decide on an action and develop instructional activities to train students in this setting to deal effectively with the problem. If the science activity is too dangerous for students to do at their desks, will you provide a demonstration or use electronic media in an interactive way to foster student learning of the concept involved? Can technology provide additional practice or transfer experiences that are not safe in the real life situation?

Step 14: Development of an Assessment Plan

Two purposes of assessment are important at this stage in planning a unit. Assessment provides: (1) feedback with regard to student learning of a key idea, and (2) data regarding the effectiveness of the lesson plans on student learning outcomes.

The most common or traditional approach to this step is to prepare a post-assessment instrument, a quiz or test, that is administered when the students complete the unit or a component of the unit. Assessment is also used to provide feedback to students on their learning and provide feedback to teachers about the effectiveness of the unit.

Other forms of assessment are used in addition to, or instead of, a quiz or test. Among these might be a student writing project, graphs and charts, cooperative group work, artwork, a design for an experiment, an interview, or a group/individual project. The observation of student actions and recording of data on more than one or two students often cannot be successfully carried out in a short amount of time. Techniques for group and individual assessment are planned at the beginning of the unit.

Assessment also includes other methods and approaches. Informal and semiformal methods, as well as having students develop portfolios of their work, can be incorporated into a more effective assessment plan. The assessment is designed to evaluate each type of learning outcome included in the unit. This requires several types of assessment methods. Measures are developed to evaluate ideas, inquiry skills, and effects.

See Chapter 8 for examples and procedures in effective science assessment.

As part of a complete assessment plan, students are asked for feedback on how they reacted to the unit. A student feedback form can be used (see Figure 9–14).

Step 15: Implementation

After planning, the unit is taught. Adjustments and fine-tuning are necessary if a science unit is to meet the needs of the students and the context of the learning experience. Remember, key science ideas and skills are incorporated within the context of the learning experience. A pleasant, safe setting where students do not feel threatened is reflected in the attitude and value outcomes planned for the unit.

Step 16: Complete the KWL

The students are asked, "What did you learn?" Their comments are written under the "L" column on the KWL chart begun prior to writing the unit's lesson plans. The students are asked to compare the comments in each column and determine if the lessons changed what they knew and addressed what they wanted to know.

Step 17: Reflection

Unit development and instructional planning are part of a large cycle. One of the most important parts of the cycle is a period of time devoted to gathering feedback on the unit and reflecting on its effectiveness. Some questions to consider are the following:

1. What evidence of motivation to learn about the science topic was found?
2. What evidence of learning about the science topic did you see?
3. To what extent did students attain the learning objectives?

1. During the unit, how satisfied were you as a learner?

   _____ very satisfied   _____ satisfied
   _____ unsatisfied   _____ very unsatisfied

2. What could your teacher have done to increase your satisfaction?

3. What were your favorite activities? Why?

4. What were your least favorite activities? Why?

FIGURE 9-14   *Sample student feedback form*

4. Did the ideas in the lessons flow together well?
5. What did the students remember and not remember from day to day?
6. Which lesson was the best? Why? Would you have predicted this?
7. Would you use this unit again in its present form? If not, how would you change it? What specific modifications would you make?

Applying What You Know

Outlining a Unit

Outline a science unit following the first 14 steps described above. Select one of the webs and one of the seven types of units completed earlier in the chapter to develop a full unit outline. Identify the textbook and section selected, as well as the grade level(s). Give the unit a title that distinguishes its specific focus.

SUMMARY

The unit-planning process is a critical professional skill because key ideas must be interrelated with each other and with students' prior experiences to make them useful. Units can be developed with an emphasis on key ideas from a science discipline or on integrated ideas from several disciplines.

There are three conceptual organizers that are useful as evaluation criteria during the construction of science units: significance, coherence, and relevance. Selecting an appropriate focus for a unit involves determining the rationale and goals of the unit. Emphasis can vary in science content, science inquiry skills, and the amount of integration with other subjects. Different approaches to planning a science unit include description with a focus on content, an inquiry skills focus, a conceptual and inquiry skills focus, a theme focus, or an issues focus. Each focus can incorporate a project or a case study. Each focus has its strengths and weaknesses.

In planning an integrated science unit, an appropriate integrating theme involves teachers and students in making choices that do not compromise the quality of student learning outcomes or lower the teacher's own feelings about the worth of the unit. In selecting a theme, the questions asked are: "What are the important key concepts central to each of the subject areas integrated?" "What are the guiding questions that lead students into inquiry?" "What activities will engage students in reflective inquiry?" and "What are the natural and significant connections between key concepts?" There are two major planning techniques for integrated teaching. The first involves choosing a single key idea that interconnects the disciplines. This type of planning is more limited in scope and focuses on a significant interconnection during a science unit. The second planning technique involves planning the yearly curriculum concurrently in several subjects. The goals for science can be matched to those for social studies, mathematics, physical education, fine arts, or language arts across several units.

Effective science unit planning of any appropriate focus requires thoughtful consideration of the basic planning steps, purposeful organization, and reflective evaluation. Using any of the unit-planning approaches described in the chapter requires a similar sequence of planning steps.

chapter 10

Science for All Students

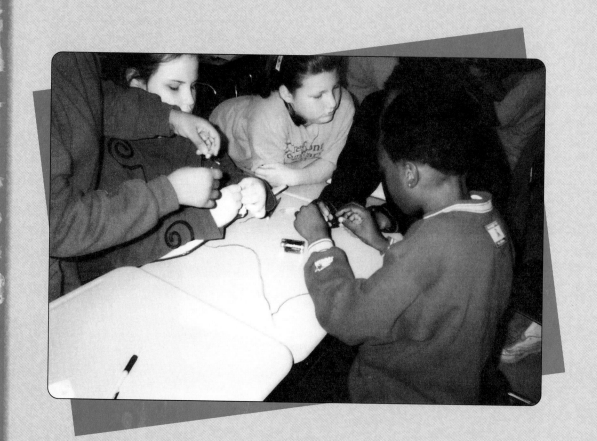

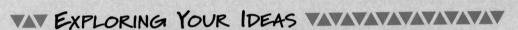

▼▲▼ EXPLORING YOUR IDEAS ▼▲▼▲▼▲▼▲▼▲▼▲▼▲▼▲▼

Evaluate a classroom lesson you have taught or observed recently that included one or more special needs students. Answer the questions below:

1. Describe the science lesson taught in the classroom. What types and number of interactions occurred between the students and the teacher, and between the students? What role in the learning process did the teacher play? What role did the students play?
2. What strategies did you observe that involved all students in the science lesson?
3. What learning outcomes do you infer for all students from the observed lesson? What difficulties did the students have in accomplishing the lesson outcome(s)? Provide evidence supporting your evaluation.

Chapter Objectives

1. Describe the purpose and rationale of science for all students.
2. Describe the factors that need to be considered when adapting science instruction for children with special needs.
3. Identify and describe accommodations that need to be made when adapting a science concept for several specific special needs.
4. Define multicultural science teaching.
5. Describe the general science pedagogical strategies needed to teach meaningful science to students of both genders and diverse cultural heritages.
6. Describe the strategies needed to assess science learning in diverse student populations.

WHAT IS SCIENCE FOR ALL STUDENTS?

Students are very curious about the world in which they live. Their curiosity often results in a natural interest in learning more about the environment. When teachers share this enthusiasm and have basic skills and teaching resources, the stage is set for effective learning in science for all students.

"Science for all" means that every student has an equal opportunity to learn science regardless of culture, gender, or disability. In recent years, the inclusion of students with special needs in regular classrooms has increased. The majority of all students in the United States now attend regular classes (U.S. Department of Education, 1989). One-third or more of our students are from diverse cultural backgrounds. However, 75% of African-American and 83% of Hispanic students are below the expected level of scientific literacy (Children's Defense Fund, 1991). We must step away from the traditional whole class approach to teaching science and encourage students to use, interact with, and respect not only their own heritage but also those of their peers. *Science for All Americans,* a document setting forth national science standards for all students, says that students respond to their own expectations of what they can and cannot learn. If they believe they are able to learn something, such as solving equations or riding a bicycle, they usually make headway (American Association for the Advancement of Science, 1990).

This chapter describes the process for planning, developing, and carrying out science lessons involving diverse students. It focuses on "science for all." The types of accommodations made in a lesson in order to involve all students will be not be large or difficult if they're included in a basic hands-on, minds-on approach to science.

Americans from all cultures, who use science to solve everyday problems and whose votes affect major technological decisions, continue to consult tarot cards and astrologers, believe tabloid stories about aliens, use all types of "unapproved and unverified" drugs advertised in magazines, and speculate whether Earth revolves around the sun. Science literacy allows a person to observe events perceptively, reflect on them thoughtfully, and understand the explanations offered to them. These internal perceptions and reflections provide a basis for making decisions and taking action (American Association for the Advancement of Science, 1993a, p. 322). It is the right of all citizens to be scientifically literate, since literacy affects the quality of life of every person. Therefore, the goal of every school and classroom is to provide for the attainment of science literacy for all students.

People who are literate in science are not necessarily able to perform science in a professional sense, any more than a musically literate person can compose music or play an instrument. As another example, a professional engineer can design a part for a car's engine while a mechanically literate person can change the spark plugs in the car. Scientifically literate people are able to use thought processes and the scientific knowledge they have acquired to think about and make sense of many ideas, claims, and events they encounter in everyday life (American Association for the Advancement of Science, 1993a).

Science, in the past, has been depicted as an expendable class subject. This is particularly true for special learners and diverse students. In a study conducted by Patton, Polloway, and Cronin (1986), a significant number of students in special education programs were found not to be receiving any science instruction at all. Science instruction is valuable to "special" students for many of the same reasons that it is valuable to all other students. Ditchfield (1987) provides a strong case for teaching science to all students: "As a means of studying the world around us, and making sense of it, science has much to offer as a way of practical everyday living. It begins by asking questions . . . and develops into posing (tentative explanations) hypotheses, testing out such hypotheses by experiment and interpreting the outcomes" (p. 37). A few other reasons for teaching science to all students are:

1. Science activities can broaden and enrich the experience base of students.
2. Special learners can benefit from guided or selected activities based on reality that have predictable outcomes.
3. The manipulation of concrete objects can facilitate conceptual learning.
4. Science activities can involve the learning of cause-and-effect relationships.
5. Science provides many opportunities to develop and refine thinking and problem-solving skills.

Applying What You Know

Science in Daily Work Activities

Interview a person in the local community who uses science in his or her daily work activities. If possible, this person should be a member of a minority group and/or a woman. Some examples of possible interviewees are a local paint contractor, a hair stylist, a mechanic who repairs automobile engines, a catfish pond farmer, a dental hygienist, a librarian, a pharmacist, a meat cutter, a baker in a supermarket, or a manager of a fast-food restaurant. If you are in a classroom setting, you can ask your students to conduct the interviews with someone at home, with a relative, or with someone in their neighborhood or in local businesses. The interview should include the following questions: (1) "What is your job?" (2) "What preparation is needed for a person to do your job?" (3) "What activities in your job relate to science?" (4) "What science is related to your work?" (5) "What science is needed to be good at your job?" (6) "Did you know someone who had a job like this?" and (7) "Was this person a role model for you?"

The following is an example of the results of an interview with a hog farmer guided by the questions above. Mr. G. said that raising hogs consisted of a lot of trial and error. He said he uses science in a practical manner. He constantly observes his animals to determine their production and consumption. He classifies the animals by how well they produce offspring and how fast the offspring grow and mature. Mr. G.'s observations are placed in a computer. Each pig is analyzed and projections are made about its productivity and earnings. He said that by doing this, he makes inferences about each animal. He is constantly interpreting the data about these animals, and this data helps him determine whether or not to keep a sow.

He is constantly measuring and recording the information because he runs a moneymaking operation. He is constantly experimenting with his pigs to determine ways to make them more productive with the least amount of input and expense. Variables are controlled by maintaining a constant temperature in the hog barns, eliminating disease, and providing a constant, healthy food supply.

Mr. G. has a high school diploma. He studied science classes in high school, has taken some classes at the local community college, and goes to workshops offered by the Farmer's Federation and the state Agricultural Bureau. These classes have dealt with anatomy, animal disease, animal nutrition, computer literacy, business accounting, and applied chemistry. He keeps trying to learn more because that is the only way he can keep his hogs healthy and profitable. His family has been farming for generations, but he is the first one to specialize in hogs.

WHAT IS SCIENCE EDUCATION FOR STUDENTS WITH DISABILITIES?

The U. S. Department of Education has interpreted the Individuals with Disabilities Education Act (IDEA) to mean that "the regular classroom in the neighborhood school should be the first placement option considered for students with disabilities" (Riley, 1999). IDEA requires that, to the maximum extent appropriate, children with disabilities are educated with children who are not disabled, and that special classes, separate schooling, or other removal of children with disabilities from the regular environment only occurs when the nature and severity of the disability is such that education in regular classes with the use of supplementary aids and services cannot be attained satisfactorily (IDEA Sec. 612 (5) (B)).

Researchers have found that students with disabilities who are placed in the regular classroom must have appropriate supports and services to succeed. These students need supplementary aids and services and instructional strategies adapted to their needs. Some supplementary aids and services that educators have used successfully include modifications to the regular curriculum, the assistance of an itinerant teacher with special education training, special education training for the regular teacher, the use of computer-assisted devices, the provision of note takers, and the use of a resource room. In these classrooms, students are viewed not as separate groups (disabled and nondisabled), but as students with shared characteristics who vary regarding a wide range of attributes.

A review of the literature on appropriate classroom science strategies for special needs students gives the following suggestions:

- Make your science instruction activity-oriented.
- Attempt to relate science topics to students' everyday experiences.
- Choose science activities that are interesting to students and to you.
- Consider the linguistic and conceptual demands of the science curriculum, as some students may have great difficulty with these areas.
- Establish an efficient system of managing the classroom, paying particular attention to establishing ground rules and procedures for science activities.
- Focus on process skills throughout science activities.
- Examine textbooks for the impact they may have on your students.

Textbooks continue to play a crucial role in science education for many students. Four areas that should be examined to help students comprehend science texts are vocabulary level, content in terms of conceptual complexity (concrete versus formal ideas), writing style and organization, and special features such as illustrations and graphs.

A primary reason for including students with special needs in the regular classroom is to increase their contact with a broader range of students. Excellent opportunities exist during science activities to promote such contact. Students of differing abilities and backgrounds benefit both academically and socially from cooperative learning (Putnam, 1993). Most science curricula hold the potential for a wealth of activity-centered small-group experiences appropriate for a wide range of students. When students work together to achieve a science objective, the potential for positive interactions within the group is enhanced. Constructive interactions in the context of a group experience reinforce the interaction skills of all students and develop an appreciation of differences among peers. Conversely, an instructional strategy that encourages competition or purely individualistic learning does little to promote the integration of all students, fostering continued isolation of students even though learning may occur. The identification of conditions needing accommodation may require the modification of the learning experience in order to most fully benefit the student. Student abilities and characteristics, combined with the specifications of the Individualized Education Plan (IEP), determine the degree of modification of instructional strategies, curriculum, and evaluation procedures necessary to best serve the student.

What Are Some General Instructional Strategies for Inclusive Classrooms?

1. *Hands-on science activities* during each phase of the learning cycle provide positive experiences for all students since motivation is enhanced through working with science materials. The multi-sensory nature of these activities is especially suitable for students with special needs. Meaningful science activities occur throughout the learning cycle in an integrated manner, enabling students to construct their understanding of science content. All students benefit when they construct a science concept in stages rather than when the fully-formed concept is presented to them in a lecture or through a reading assignment. Fully-formed concepts don't convey the process involved in developing them or the evidence used in that developmental process. Fully-formed concepts are separated from any context and are hard to tie together. They can't be applied to the real world by students because they seem to exist fully developed with no connections to anything else. For example, if a parent were presented with a fully grown 18-year-old, instead of a baby, the parent would not understand that individual's personality, motivations, dreams, or worries. There would be little context in which to understand who this person really was. Open-ended, exploratory learning approaches are seen in the literature as being effective with students who have learning disabilities and related mild disabilities that affect learning (Wang & Zollers, 1990).

2. *Cooperative group activities* can provide needed science help for students and aid in their social integration. Cooperative learning involves grouping students of varying abilities into productive work teams in order to learn new material, prepare for tests, and carry out projects. Each student within the group has a role with a specific assignment. For example, a student might record responses, encourage contributions, or manage materials. Research on cooperative learning involving special needs and regular students indicates that cooperative learning experiences, compared to competitive and individualistic ones, promote more positive attitudes toward peers who have disabilities (Johnson & Johnson, 1978). Student progress can be measured both individually and within the group.

Chapter 7 discusses cooperative learning in greater depth.

See Chapter 8 for more discussion.

Ideas for classwide peer tutoring have been described by Charles R. Greenwood (Vandercook, York, & Forest,1989).

3. *Classwide peer tutoring* involves assigning science tutoring activities to all students in a classroom. Students work with an idea, a demonstration, or a procedure, then teach it to other students, perhaps through a group activity such as a jigsaw. When they have mastered the science idea, demonstration, or procedure, they return to their home cooperative group and teach it to the members of that group. Having opportunities to teach peers can reinforce students' own learning and motivation.

4. The *peer buddy system* involves students serving as friends, guides, or counselors to fellow students who are experiencing problems. A variation pairs a student with disabilities, such as one with a severe visual impairment, with another student whose vision is normal. Another variation is to occasionally pair two students who are experiencing similar problems so that they can give each other moral support. This might occur between two students who have orthopedic problems; for example, they might both use wheelchairs. The opportunity to talk with someone else about how she has approached problem situations can lead to a sharing of advice, greater motivation, and better learning.

The peer buddy system enables students to help each other solve problems.

5. *Reciprocal teaching* involves students in learning strategies to improve their comprehension of textual science material by questioning, summarizing, clarifying, and predicting what is in the text. Textual material can appear in science textbooks, trade books, children's magazines, Internet sites, software programs, and in instructions for carrying out an activity. Students take turns leading discussions in a cooperative group that focuses on each of the strategies; a student may lead a discussion about:

- Questions the text raises.
- How to best summarize the ideas in the text.
- How to explain or clarify the ideas in the text.
- The predictions they can make based on the ideas in the text.

It is important to teach students these four strategies before they utilize them.

6. *Reading alone* may present difficulties for all students, yet it is an integral part of most science activities and curricula. While materials are chosen to reflect the reading levels of most students, wide variations in individual reading levels within the classroom are still likely. Reading *follows* students' experiences with the events discussed in the reading materials. Reading is most effective when it is part of the Invention phase of a learning cycle. It should occur after students have explored the lesson's idea and formed the idea in their minds through hands-on experiences.

7. A *lecture-based* presentation should primarily be used to give instructions, describe procedures, and provide short explanations of events. Lectures present problems when students in the class have very short attention spans. They can result in both inappropriate behavior and students simply "tuning out." When lectures are used, they must be brief. Important concepts and vocabulary are learned best through a variety of hands-on, minds-on activities involving a range of modalities. If repetition is necessary, short lectures may be easily tape-recorded so the student can hear them again.

Some teachers stress the importance of *over-learning* by students with disabilities. Over-learning is useful, but these students sometimes work with material long after they have mastered it. This can cause them to become bored with the material if they have constructed a meaningful and useful understanding of it.

8. *Media presentations* and the use of all types of *technology* can be a positive aspect of the curriculum for all students. Students with low reading abilities benefit from a multi-sensory approach. Media content may require reinforcement before and after its presentation. Repeated opportunities to work with the media presentation may be of value to any student in the class. Materials are selected with the students' ability levels in mind.

Additional strategies for improving student achievement can be found in many sources including Schrag & Burnett (1993), Kysilko (1995), Roach, Ascroft, and Stamp (1995), Vandercook, York, and Forest (1989), and Sunal and Sunal (1983).

General Curriculum Adaptation for Inclusive Classrooms

A variety of activity-based science curriculum materials currently available requires little or no modification for appropriate use with many students with disabilities. Many teachers have successfully adapted science curriculum materials to meet their individual needs (Klumb, 1992). General steps in adapting science materials for students with disabilities include:

1. Identifying the learning needs and characteristics of the students.
2. Identifying the goals for instruction.
3. Comparing the learning needs and goals to the teaching materials to determine whether the content, instructional techniques, or setting require modification.
4. Determining specific modifications to the teaching materials.
5. Modifying the materials.
6. Conducting ongoing evaluation as the materials are used.

Successful adaptations include using organizational aides such as pre-organizers, overviews, or highlighting; chapter or section summaries; and changing the medium through which the information is conveyed.

What Factors Are Considered in Adapting Science Curricula and Science Instruction?

Time is the variable which, more than any other, frequently distinguishes the learning behavior of students with disabilities. Students with visual impairments, for example, often have no lead time and no opportunity to size up an event before they are in the midst of it. These students should be given the opportunity to explore while materials are being set out for other students to eventually pick up. Students with hearing impairments usually get less experience at abstracting information and gathering it into convenient bundles for mental manipulation because they may have fewer opportunities to discuss their experiences with others. Their response time may be longer than that of other students in a specific situation. Emotionally conflicted students often cannot suppress competing responses or ignore one stimulus in order to pay attention to another. As a result, they have less time in which to anticipate the course of some event and adjust accordingly. Students with mental retardation often cannot integrate events, assign meaning to them, and pick out an appropriate response. For all these students, making predictions over a short interval of time may be difficult, but the reasons for this difficulty are different and depend on the kind of disability.

Different modalities take in information at distinctive rates. An individual's eyes, for example, can display a whole spatial array at one time. Take, for example, falling objects of several sizes and masses. When either the observer or the objects in the array start moving in relation to each other, the eyes keep track of that information as a whole set. By contrast, information coming in over auditory tracts is strung out in time and must be sequenced and patterned by the listener before it becomes intelligible.

The wide range and depth of distance over which the eyes pick up information permit people to "see ahead in time." Before an event reaches its conclusion, or even before it takes place, people who can see may anticipate it and adjust their responses accordingly. Because vision permits interaction at a distance, it provides a little lead time in which to adjust one's response before an event happens.

Students with visual impairments ordinarily do not have that kind of lead time. To experience events, they usually must arrive in the midst of them. They may use sound and other perceptive cues, but since these appear over a much shorter distance and range than vision, the lead-time variable must necessarily be shorter. The visual cues, which tell an inquirer into a physical or biological system what to look for and when to collect data, must be supplanted for visually impaired students with other devices. Since students with hearing impairments have so little information before arriving on the scene compared to sighted children, they require more time to collect the comparable cues.

Students with hearing impairments often don't get sufficient early practice at representing experience in some kind of language context. The task of abstracting information from the environment and then accumulating it into language bundles that are logically manipulated depends on the availability of language models or appropriate communication substitutes for sound. Schools frequently spend an exorbitant amount of time teaching language per se rather than language in the context of some concrete event. As a result, students with hearing impairments are often denied the chance that normal students get of trying to map experience into language through science.

Whereas students with visual impairments may suffer from a kind of "time binding" at the point in inquiry where the physical or biological systems to be investigated must be observed, students with hearing impairments may become bound in the present at the point of converting experience into abstractions. Since categorizing experience into abstractions frees students from the necessity of manipulating factors mentally, students with hearing impairments need to engage in science activities where they can observe the history of systems or events. Students with visual impairments usually come to use verbal information very efficiently. They usually can hold longer chains of directions and verbal information in their memory than can sighted students.

Doing Science with Students with Visual or Hearing Impairments

Probably the first major conception that students with visual impairments must acquire has to do with *exploring spatial relations and dimensionality.* Space and time, which may be taken for granted by the sighted and must eventually be dimensionalized for them, must also be dimensionalized for students with visual impairments. A possible sequence of activities that can help develop a strategy for exploring spatial relations in a system might progress through the following steps:

1. *Use of the body*—begin with large objects where the children's bodies serve as the center of the coordinate system.
2. *Serial ordering*—have students order objects by size.
3. *Surfaces*—have students explore and describe the surface of the objects.

4. *Measurements*—have students use string to measure the size of the objects and then compare the lengths of the strings resulting from the measurement of the objects.

Students with hearing impairments mainly have problems at two points: talking over what happened in an experiment and getting directions. Students with hearing impairments must rely heavily on visual cues. It is suggested that students with visual impairments be encouraged to assemble all the apparatus they use, or all that is practical for them to assemble; the same is true for students with hearing impairments. This helps establish some continuity between what one does to a system or event. Continuity helps students understand the changes a system or event goes through during an experiment or activity.

Students with hearing impairments require early and frequent exposure to physical and biological systems whose histories they can observe and change. Language in use is not simply a labeling process. It is more like a mapping process in which the words and the logical connectives work together to reveal the thought. Deprivation of oral language experience, whether through real or functional deafness, may be remedied to some degree by frequent and somewhat prolonged exposure to directed experiments designed to focus attention on patterns of interaction in physical and biological systems.

Much of what is done in modern science programs can be adapted for use by students with visual and hearing impairments for whom early science instruction is even more important than for other students. The following steps have been successfully used to adapt science materials for students with visual and hearing impairments (Sunal, C. & Sunal, D., 1983; Sunal, D. & Sunal, C., 1982):

1. Identify the variables in an event.
2. Identify the kinds of evidence that could be associated with the variables.
3. Identify all the modalities or combinations of modalities that could be used to supply evidence that is equivalent to what would normally be collected.
4. Adapt the apparatus where necessary.
5. Devise a technique for recording data.

Doing Science with Mentally Retarded or Emotionally Conflicted Students

Emotionally conflicted students and mentally retarded students often have a common problem: their attention spans are short. Almost without exception, however, teachers who involve these students in science activities report that their attention to science activities persists much longer than their attention to more passive tasks. These students return voluntarily to science tasks. They often make the system go through the same interactions many times. It is as though they carry on a kind of silent dialogue with it. Perhaps this is one of the times when they can structure their own thoughts, since other parts of the day may be devoted to the necessary business of trying to respond to conventional modes imposed on them.

WHAT IS SCIENCE EDUCATION IN A CULTURALLY DIVERSE SOCIETY?

All societies are culturally diverse to some extent. However, the United States is more culturally diverse than most countries. This diversity has led to an important question in science education: "How can all students participate in, and meaningfully learn, science?" (Hodson, 1994).

Classrooms are becoming more diverse. Some students are recent arrivals from other countries and are learning English as a second language. Many children are raised in urban settings that differ greatly from the national mainstream experience. Some students have moved from an urban area to a small town.

In the United States, three significant minority student groups, African-American, Hispanics from numerous Latin American countries, and Native Americans, are underrepresented underachievers in science. Asian-American immigrants generally have limited English proficiency yet are more successful in science in the United States than are members of some other minority groups who are native English speakers (Tobin & McRobbie, 1996). The needs of various groups within the culture differ, as does their current participation and success in science education.

Teachers need to think and learn about what makes a multicultural science program successful. In what ways is it different from a traditional program? The classroom has a content and a context, and both must respond to the needs of all students. To be responsive, programs must provide science experiences that are rich in promoting learning. They need to address connected and relevant strands of content and context so that students can be successful in learning from their experiences. Just providing a science program with a variety of experiences and an environment where students are free to explore is no longer adequate. The science program must consistently invite all students to participate in scientific inquiry. Adapting and designing experiences that meet the particular interests, knowledge, and backgrounds of students helps teachers recognize and work with student diversity. This includes fostering the different forms of communication: spoken, written, graphic, and mathematical. It also includes allowing students who cannot communicate effectively in English to demonstrate what they have learned.

There are many definitions of multicultural education. One of the most comprehensive definitions describes multicultural education as at least three things: an idea or concept, an educational reform movement, and a process. Multicultural education incorporates the idea that all students—regardless of their gender, social class, and ethnic or cultural characteristics—should have an equal opportunity to learn in school (Atwater, 1993). There are three basic premises in multicultural science education. First, all students can learn science. Second, every student can participate effectively in the science program. Third, cultural diversity is appreciated in the science program because it enhances rather than detracts from the richness and effectiveness of science learning (Atwater, 1993).

Five goals have been identified in order for teachers to meet the needs of culturally diverse student populations. These are fulfilled through a multicultural approach to science education:

1. Acquire the knowledge and skills needed to study children's learning (the constructivist approach to conceptualizing learning).
2. Present appropriate lessons for particular students and use indirect, but powerful, teaching strategies such as role-playing and cooperation to increase instructional effectiveness with diverse groups of students in the classroom.
3. Eliminate school and teacher stereotypes and expectations that can narrow student opportunities for learning and displaying competence.
4. Create and sustain a communal setting respectful of individual differences and group membership, where learning is valued, engagement is nurtured, and interests are encouraged (Holmes Group, 1986).

5. Assess students in the context of science activities, assess student understanding of the nature of science, and also assess students' unique culturally based science understandings (Tippins & Dana, 1993).

Strategies for Multicultural Science

Historical Approach

In classrooms where all students learn science, three major strategies have been successfully used. The *first strategy* is to use *historical science* and the lives of scientists as illustrations relating to the concepts being taught. Well-chosen examples of science from other cultures involving scientists of both genders demonstrate that science is a specific way of thinking about the world. In teaching astronomy, for example, use the example of Maria Mitchell. She was a scientist who studied comets, satellites, and sunspots in the 19th century. As another example, when teaching the human circulatory system, use Charles R. Drew, the physician and surgeon famous for developing the blood bank system. The Persian philosopher and physician, Avicenna, who wrote a medical text used for 500 years, is another possible example. In addition, examples from the history of Western science can be used to illustrate how the purposes and methodologies of Western science have changed and are part of larger cultural changes (Stanley & Brickhouse, 1994). In so doing, students learn that the form of contemporary Western science is not universal, inevitable, or unchangeable. This kind of understanding is needed to encourage critical thinking about the purposes of science.

For further information see the Companion Website for links to sites that identify scientists of both genders and different cultural groups at *http://www.prenhall.com/sunal*. Some sites include photographs of the scientists.

Current Science and Scientists

The *second strategy* is to *provide examples and references from present-day science activity and the scientists who are involved with it*. Some examples include Tania Ruiz, astronomer; Stephen Hawking, physicist; Penny Okamoto, researcher on DNA sequences; Jewel Plummer Cobb, cancer researcher; and Jerome Kagan, brain researcher. This strategy also includes providing information on how to prepare for science-related careers and helping students understand that early preparation in mathematics and science is critical.

Using Student Culture

The *third strategy involves using examples and applications of science that fit a student's culture and ethnic background.* Experiences students have at home, in school, and in the community are rich opportunities for the development of science-relevant concepts. If experiences used in science lessons relate to students' personal experiences, they have greater ownership of the learning outcomes. It is important that science activities, problems, experiments, and variables used in lesson plans relate to students' daily lives.

In planning culturally relevant science units, teachers ask themselves the following questions: "Does the science unit promote respect for the skills, experiences, and abilities of all student cultures represented?" "Are all students active participants and engaged learners in all phases of the lesson?" (Lopez-Freeman, 1995). If the answer to these questions is "yes," then we are moving toward a culture of science for all students.

Applying What You Know

Using Student Surveys

In a classroom to which you have access, survey the children about their life experiences. Ask questions such as: "What pets do you have?" "What type of games do you like to play outdoors and indoors?" "What are your favorite television programs?" "What trips or vacations have you made away from home?" "Who is your favorite relative?" "What job does he or she do?" "What are your favorite foods?" "Who cooks them?" (Several additional questions could be added.)

Using the information gained from the survey, develop a culturally relevant activity for a specific phase of the learning cycle designed to teach a science concept. Indicate the learning cycle phase, the science concept, and describe the activity.

The information gained from such student surveys is used in developing problems, examples, and experiences for science lesson plans. For instance, in a unit on light and color that builds on the heritage of Appalachian students, the quilts made in the area could be a focus for the lesson's activities. As an Exploration occurring over several days, students could make vegetable dyes to dye pieces of cloth that are later made into a quilt. As they are making the dyes, they may note the concentrations of vegetable matter needed to produce a lighter or darker dye, investigate how difficult it is to remove spots produced by various vegetable dyes, and determine the effect of exposure to the sun on pieces of cloth dyed with various vegetable dyes. As an Expansion, many of these activities can then be carried out with commercial dyes and their results compared to the results obtained with vegetable dyes. As another example, students could examine the patterning found in Appalachian quilts during the Exploration of a lesson on symmetry. All these activities tie into the heritage of students from Appalachia.

As an extension, surveying students' families or other members of the community may suggest additional activities for culturally relevant science. Questions asking for information about local customs, hobbies, celebrations, and interesting local sites and people to visit can generate information for use in developing science activities that utilize the local community and the cultural backgrounds found among its people.

Positive Role Models and Relevancy

A career in science or engineering is seen as unachievable by many people. Science and mathematics courses are viewed as boring and unnecessary. Some have considered this problem to be particularly acute in the African-American community (South Central Bell, 1994). The factors that have produced this problem are complex. Among them are the lack of positive role models, relevancy, and career information.

Positive Role Models

African-American scientists and engineers have made outstanding contributions in their fields. Still, African-American youth are often not aware of these historical and contemporary scientists. Also, many African-American youth do not realize the need for a strong, early education in mathematics and science, or understand how to prepare for a scientific

Parents are role models when they work with children.

career. The same situation often exists with youth from other groups such as Hispanic Americans and Native Americans.

The investigation of the lives of scientists and engineers, both historical and contemporary, is important if all students are to have opportunities to succeed in science. Such an investigation moves beyond the individuals typically studied; for example, George Washington Carver, a botanist and agricultural researcher, and Benjamin Banneker, a self-taught mathematician and astronomer who helped determine the outline for the city of Washington, D.C., in 1790 to 1791. These individuals are worthy of study, but sometimes few others are investigated; therefore, students hear about the same few people over and over again. Among the others who could be studied are Harvey Pickrum, a microbiologist who has worked to discover the causes of toxic shock syndrome and diaper rash; Patricia Cowings, who works with NASA training astronauts to deal with motion sickness; and Walter Massey, a theoretical physicist who has worked on superconducting materials. Most important of all is the chance to talk with local scientists, engineers, and science teachers who are members of the community. These people may never be as famous as Benjamin Banneker or George Washington Carver, but they are real and meaningful to students. When they come from the local region, they demonstrate to students what can reasonably be achieved with some effort and guidance.

Relevant Science

One way of addressing the needs of all students is to utilize science activities that contextualize science concepts through the use of everyday objects and experiences. For example, when you stumble into your shower in the morning and turn on the water, the shower curtain seems to come at you and attack you. You push it away but it comes right back. Instinctively, you shut off the water and the shower curtain calms down. You turn the water back on and the shower curtain moves toward you again. This is a common experience which serves as a real-world instance of Bernoulli's principle: the pressure in a moving stream of fluid is less than the pressure in the surrounding fluid. Using such an example contextualizes science concepts. The example makes use of an experience that many students have had.

Career Information

Appropriate science teaching for students from minority groups has many of the same characteristics as appropriate teaching for students in the mainstream culture. Using examples such as the one above helps all students in the classroom. It is good teaching for everyone.

CULTURE AND GENDER DIFFERENCES IN STUDENT–TEACHER INTERACTIONS

Many teachers interact differently with various students. Male students are often given extended teacher help when answering questions. Females who give wrong answers are usually not asked to elaborate on their answers. Females are often rewarded for the neatness, but not the correctness, of their work. African-American males are often ignored in science class until they misbehave. Few African-American females are praised for their science learning. Native Americans are often introduced to science concepts in a manner that is not meaningful to them (Atwater, 1993; Bellamy, 1994). Teachers need to pay attention to their own teaching behaviors as they occur during the flow of a lesson. This can be difficult since they are so involved in the lesson. However, it is important to determine how each student is approached and whether the teachers have any patterns of behavior that should be changed if all students are to be meaningfully involved in science.

Although it is a time-consuming complex, teachers must read about the cultures represented by their students and interact closely with students and their families in order to learn about those cultures. Over time, teachers will develop an understanding of the cultural backgrounds of the students with whom they work. Teachers can address gender concerns by paying attention to how they interact with boys and girls, how they respond to both passive and active behaviors from boys and girls, how their expectations for behaviors from boys and girls differ, and how they work to include both male and female scientists in the curriculum.

For further information, links can be found on the Companion Website to sites that contain ideas and activities for working with families. See *http://www.prenhall.com/sunal*

In addition to general science pedagogical strategies, specific teaching strategies are needed to provide meaningful science for students of both genders and of all cultural heritages. Strategies shown to be effective in the research literature (Hampton & Gallegos, 1994) include:

1. *Having high science expectations for all students.* Girls and students from all cultural heritages are told that they are expected to succeed and that careers in science are a real option for them.

2. *Varying science learning activities.* Students learn more through interesting, relevant, interactive, problem-solving situations. Small group work is an effective strategy for such situations. Small groups give students opportunities to develop mutual respect and understanding. Teachers need to modify groups at times so that all students feel comfortable and not isolated.

3. *Addressing the affective dimension.* If students come from backgrounds with low academic success, the teacher makes additional efforts to assure that they are accepted and appreciated. The teacher models respect for the various cultures represented in the classroom. Students are helped to look for the diverse talents and viewpoints of their classmates. Guests from cultures represented by the students in the classroom are regular visitors to the classroom in order to participate in interviews, demonstrate special skills, and assist students in after-school or weekend study programs.

4. *Overcoming language barriers.* The teacher shows students that science is more of a process than a language. Students find that scientists who do not speak English make great contributions to the world. Science ideas are the same in any language. For example, the concept of the water cycle remains the same no matter which language is used to describe and discuss it. Students whose first language is not English can be helped by working in groups, perhaps with peer interpreters. Visuals and objects labeled with key terms and concepts are useful. Students whose first language is not English are asked to share their native language's terms for the concepts introduced in class.

5. *Respecting different cultural mores and traditions.* Teachers investigate students' cultural heritages and traditions. The information gained can ensure respect for cultural mores and traditions. Sometimes, traditional stories present alternative scientific concepts. Religious beliefs may conflict with scientific teaching. Religious beliefs are respected, but students learn that religion and science often approach the same events in different ways.

6. *Discussing gender and cultural inequities.* Students learn that all groups are not fully represented in scientific and technical careers. There are differences, based on opportunity, in how well individuals from different ethnic groups succeed in science. Yet, there is a growing need for scientists and engineers. The scientific and mathematical potential of a person should not be wasted because of his gender or ethnic group.

7. *Analyzing classroom management for equity.* Some students, particularly girls, may allow others to dominate their learning. Teachers find themselves focusing attention on students who demand attention, particularly if the students demonstrate ability and achievement. Teachers must provide at least equal experiences and opportunities for girls and minority students in science. Students are encouraged to respect each other and participate equally in class.

8. *Providing role models who are women and/or represent a range of cultural heritages.* Teachers use professional organizations and institutions of higher education to locate scientists and engineers who are role models for girls and students of different cultural heritages. These individuals are invited to visit the classroom. They can communicate with students via e-mail, letters, or telephone. They might also arrange a field trip to their workplace.

9. *Acknowledging and using the culture and home environment as a vehicle for learning.* Using the students' home and culture in science activities helps them apply science to their daily lives. Family members are asked to work with the teacher to provide ideas that can be tried out at home or that bring the culture into the classroom. For example, students might investigate the properties that make the peppers used in Thai or Mexican food so hot. They might also investigate traditional farming practices in Africa where multicropping (the planting of a mixture of crops together in the same field) occurs. In instances where the culture and/or home environment does not view girls as having the potential for success in science, activities involving the home enable girls to demonstrate accomplishment of science outcomes to family members.

ASSESSMENT OF SCIENCE LEARNING FOR ALL STUDENTS

See also Chapter 7 for detailed information on cooperative learning.

Test scores alone are poor measures of student potential (Quality of Education for Minorities Report, 1990). Tests fail to consider interpersonal skills, language abilities, and talents that students need in the real world. Culturally relevant alternative assessment is necessary to improve educational options for students from diverse backgrounds.

Group assessment through cooperative learning is one means of assessing students from diverse backgrounds.

Students engage in discussion to construct and negotiate a shared meaning of their science experiences. Group members benefit by helping one another. In the process, students begin to understand and appreciate cultural differences. Research on cooperative learning involving different ethnic groups and male and female middle school students indicates that cooperative learning experiences, compared to competitive and individualistic ones, promote more positive attitudes toward members of a different ethnic group or sex (Johnson & Johnson, 1978).

Graphic organizers, including student and teacher use of concept maps, semantic webs, and Venn diagrams, become tools for negotiating meanings between students when a culturally diverse group of students must share, discuss, and agree upon meanings.

Oral interviews encourage self-confidence when teachers pose questions that allow students to describe science learning experiences without imposing requirements for the use of specific vocabulary. Students have opportunities to share science experiences through personal narratives. This enables them to demonstrate their individual questions, perspectives, and understandings.

Portfolios provide a developmental record of growth in science documented by a range of assessments. Examples include experiment and project reports, creative writing examples, diagrams and graphs that have been constructed, concept maps, journals, oral interviews, and cooperative group assessments. Use of the portfolio provides multiple sources profiling student growth and helps ensure equitable treatment of culturally diverse students.

Journal writing encourages students to connect science to personal experiences. It helps students make connections between their experiences and concepts. It is more culturally relevant when it becomes a personal process in which grammar and punctuation are unimportant. Journaling can be as simple as asking students to write an entry describing what they know about a scientific concept or the main theme of a lesson just taught. These continuous entries throughout the unit provide evidence of learning in the context of the student's life experiences.

Asking students to *share their journal comments* in pairs or in their cooperative group enables them to communicate with each other about their learning. They can write responses to each other's thoughts. A continuous sharing of ideas back and forth helps students accept each other's ideas and the evaluation of their own ideas by others. Another type of journaling involves students in creating a class journal. In this journal, each student shares her ideas about a shared science experience. As the journal is passed around the class, the breadth of ideas and perspectives on the shared experience becomes evident.

Applying What You Know

Reflecting on Your Planning for a Culturally Diverse Classroom

Evaluate one of your previously written science lesson plans. Consider how appropriately the lesson involves culturally diverse students in your classroom. If possible, work with a partner on this activity. Answer the questions on the following page.

1. What strategies would involve all students in the science lesson?
2. What additional strategy could be added to increase the effectiveness of the science lesson for students from all cultural backgrounds?

SUMMARY

Science for all students is a planned and deliberate effort to help students regardless of special needs, cultural heritage, or gender. It is an effort to maximize their potential for success in science. This effort focuses on student learning and on the teaching methodologies that make science relevant and meaningful to each student. It includes the idea that all students can learn science and that science is worthwhile for them. Science opens doors for all students, enabling them to see themselves in careers that utilize scientific knowledge and processes of thinking. The goal of science for all students is scientific literacy among all citizens.

chapter 11

Developing an Effective Classroom Science Program

▼▲▼ EXPLORING YOUR IDEAS ▼▲▼▲▼▲▼▲▼▲▼▲▼▲▼

It is July and you have just been assigned to teach fourth grade after three years of teaching first grade. You will spend most of the next several weeks planning your overall teaching program. You decide to begin with the science program. What are some basic questions you intend to think about before you construct a plan for the yearlong science program?

Chapter Objectives

1. Describe the basic preplanning questions that need to be explored before designing a yearlong science program.
2. Identify the criteria useful in designing a yearlong plan for science.
3. Describe an effective strategy for designing a yearlong plan for science.
4. Describe the purpose of technology during the different phases of a science lesson.
5. Evaluate software, multimedia programs, or interactive laser disk materials for effective use in a science lesson.
6. Identify the basic classroom facilities that should be available to support a yearlong science program of active student science learning.
7. Identify the basic science materials that should be available in classrooms to support a yearlong science program.

FIGURE 11–1 *Key elements of an effective classroom science program*

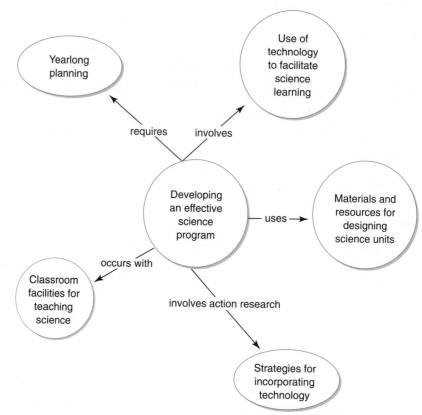

WHAT FACTORS RESULT IN AN EFFECTIVE SCIENCE PROGRAM?

Students must actively integrate new information using science facilities, resources, and technology effectively in a setting that facilitates learning if they are to create meaningful science knowledge. Active and thoughtful teaching requires expert teacher planning and ongoing evaluation. An effective science program requires teachers with general pedagogical knowledge and specific science pedagogical knowledge.

What students learn is influenced by how they are taught, the quality of the individual and social processes occurring in their classrooms, and the perceptions and understanding of science as an enterprise and as a subject to be taught and learned (National Research Council, 1996, p. 28). To implement these assumptions in teaching, the National Research Council identifies science teaching standards that describe the basic design of an effective science program (see Figure 11–1). This chapter describes the process of planning, developing, and carrying out science lessons in a learning community that includes inquiry, teacher facilitation, and ongoing assessment. These actions are supported by appropriate and adequate technology, classroom facilities, and resources.

YEARLONG PLANNING

Basic Preplanning Questions

Designing the yearlong science program is as important in creating meaningful student outcomes as is the daily planning of lessons. Before designing the yearlong science program, several questions need to be answered:

- What is a good science program for these students?
- How do I incorporate an inquiry and student reflection mode as an integral part of the science program?
- What ties together this year's science program with the program students had in previous, and will have in future, years?
- Is the yearlong program aligned with the teaching strategies to be used and the assessment to be performed?
- Will the program promote a community of science learning within the school and community?

What Is a Good Science Program for These Students?

Local, state, and national science standards define an effective program as one designed around key science knowledge, skills, and attitudes (see Figure 11–2). This knowledge is

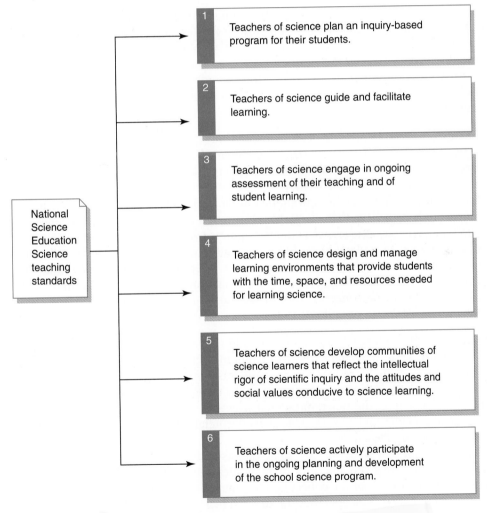

1 Teachers of science plan an inquiry-based program for their students.

2 Teachers of science guide and facilitate learning.

3 Teachers of science engage in ongoing assessment of their teaching and of student learning.

4 Teachers of science design and manage learning environments that provide students with the time, space, and resources needed for learning science.

5 Teachers of science develop communities of science learners that reflect the intellectual rigor of scientific inquiry and the attitudes and social values conducive to science learning.

6 Teachers of science actively participate in the ongoing planning and development of the school science program.

National Science Education Science teaching standards

FIGURE 11-2   *Science teaching standards section of the* National Science **Education Standards**
Source: Adapted with permission from National Research Council. Copyright 1996 by the National Academy of Sciences. Courtesy of the National Academy Press, Washington, D.C.

embedded in a yearlong inquiry-centered curriculum that is developmentally appropriate, interesting, and relevant (National Research Council, 1996, p. 3). The science program is an integral part of the daily lives of the students. It is also integral to the activities students have in other subjects and at other times during the school day. Science is experienced as a necessary and important component in every student's life.

Consider the following from the National Science Education Standards (NSES) (National Research Council, 1996).

> *Primary-Age Grades*: The children cannot understand a complex concept such as energy. Nonetheless, they have intuitive notions of energy (National Research Council, 1996, p. 126).
>
> *Middle School*: Energy is a property of many substances and is associated with heat, light, and electricity . . . energy is transferred in many ways (National Research Council, 1996, p. 155).

These statements from the NSES standards document indicate that energy is an abstract concept important in a wide variety of scientific understandings. Most people think of energy as a concrete substance with properties similar to matter. This idea begins early in life and disagrees with even the simplest energy concepts taught in school science. Students' early ideas about energy are created from a wide array of personal experiences. In research studies describing alternative conceptions about energy, four categories continue to recur in students' interviews:

1. Energy relates to living things and moving things. Students think that, without energy, things get less active or fatigued (Solomon, 1985; Stead, 1980).
2. Energy makes things work. Students relate energy to stationary objects only when energy storage is evident, such as in batteries, power stations, oil, or coal (Watts, 1983).
3. Energy changes from one form to another in a material way, like the way water changes to ice. Students believe that energy travels through electronic devices, machines, and wires, changing its appearance at different points (Watts & Gilbert, 1983).
4. Energy is a vague concept related to events in the world. Students do not differentiate energy from other learned or experienced concepts. Energy, force, power, acceleration, muscle strength, fatigue, and other physical and biological terms cannot be distinguished as unique concepts (Bliss & Osbourne, 1985; Clement, 1978; Duit, 1984; Viennot, 1979; Watts & Gilbert, 1983).

Although valuable for teachers as a starting point in developing a science lesson, students' ideas and words describing energy have different meanings than are found in the science curriculum. As seen in the research above, students' ideas of work, power, force, and energy have little to do with the scientific use of the term. When a student encounters the science idea in school, the newly presented concepts are incorporated and mixed into these prior alternative conceptions. This new interpretation at the end of the lesson is not the one intended by the teacher.

It is important that students have some understanding of the concepts that make up energy before they are given labels for them. Students should be allowed time to discuss and reflect on their ideas of the concepts. They must be provided with extensive experiences related to energy concepts they are to learn before those concepts are formally introduced. Appropriate experiences involve numerous everyday situations with different conditions, types, forms, and strengths of energy. Students should experience different results and products with energy.

How Do I Incorporate an Inquiry and Student Reflection Mode as an Integral Part of the Science Program?

Interactive learning where students use and experience an inquiry approach to understand the world around them is the main ingredient that should bind science together throughout the year. Students need regular opportunities to engage in, and reflect on, natural phenomena. Students should learn how to question, explore, find answers, and solve problems in science that are relevant to their personal lives. Science units can reflect different focuses: conceptual inquiry, inquiry skills development, or integrated—theme, issue, project, and case study.

For example, considering the NSES standards energy statements previously cited, students should experience science in a way that engages them in active construction of ideas and explanations and enhances their abilities of doing science (National Research Council, 1996, p. 121). Inquiry assumes the existence of learners' preconceptions and the need for active use of them, as a beginning point, in making sense of new situations. Only through inquiry can students restructure their own energy concepts and reach a higher level of understanding, known as science literacy. Teachers must be concerned action researchers who are informally investigating students' ideas. Teachers can use the learning cycle to incorporate student viewpoints in a setting with interactive student learning and dialogue. The lessons and activities selected should help students clearly differentiate key energy concepts such as *speed and acceleration, heat and temperature,* and *kinetic and potential energy.*

What Ties Together This Year's Science Program with the Program Students Had in Previous, and Will Have in Future, Years?

The science program must build on the prior knowledge the students bring with them. It should recognize, address, and reconstruct students' prior knowledge. Students need to build an attitude and a repertoire of investigative skills to continue to be successful in future science inquiries. Every year's science program should emphasize real-world applications and societal implications (American Association for the Advancement of Science, 1993a, p. 152).

For example, in response to the specific energy standard, energy should be connected to four basic energy-related concepts:

1. Energy transport (transfer of energy from one place to another).
2. Energy transformation (changing energy from one form to another).
3. Energy conservation (if energy is reduced in one place, it must be increased in another).
4. Energy degradation (during energy transformation, some energy is spread around to other places, usually in the form of heat).

Science unit experiences should begin with the first two energy-related concepts in the early elementary grades. In the middle elementary grades, unit experiences continue the first two and begin the last two energy-related concepts. The later elementary and middle school units continue the development of these four energy-related concepts in all science areas: life, physical, and Earth science.

Is the Yearlong Program Aligned with the Teaching Strategies to Be Used and the Assessment to Be Performed?

Successful change requires a systematic approach using the curriculum goals of state and national standards. District, school, and classroom policies, professional development practices, and teacher resources must be aligned. This, in turn, requires some changes in classroom teaching and assessment, which are integrated with the science curriculum it-self. A curriculum focusing on higher-level understanding of key concepts uses nontra-ditional teaching strategies and assessment that allow students to demonstrate their un-derstanding of science.

Use of the learning cycle facilitates meaningful learning of the concept of *energy* fol-lowing the guidelines in the NSES standards document. An inquiry process is used in the learning cycle. Students use their current experiences and reflect on energy ideas to re-construct their prior knowledge. Planning a unit using the learning cycle creates a set of decision points that all teachers continuously address in order to adequately help students learn important ideas through inquiry. Recognizing these decision points helps teachers decide what actions to take to foster meaningful learning by students. When planning a classroom lesson using the learning cycle for an energy concept or thought process, the following decisions are made:

During Exploration

1. Confront the existing energy knowledge of students.
2. Focus students' attention on experiences related to the new energy concept.
3. Encourage students to recall and relate their previous knowledge.
4. Bring out and make public what the students now know (i.e., their prior knowledge).
5. Provide an opportunity for students to try out their prior knowledge in the new setting.
6. Assess students' prior knowledge and monitor students' progress in bringing out and confronting their alternative conceptions.

During Invention

1. Ask students to reflect on, and discuss, the results of the Exploration activity to pro-vide connections that focus on the idea of the lesson.
2. Provide a clear explanation using multimedia and interactions with students to de-scribe aspects, analogies, contexts, and uses.
3. Provide clear examples or model the new skill.
4. Provide student practice using the new knowledge.
5. Provide a concise brief closure.
6. Use assessments of students' prior knowledge in implementing Invention activities and monitor students' progress toward developing a more scientific understanding of the energy concept.

During Expansion

1. Provide additional personally relevant student practice activities as needed.
2. Provide student application and transfer activities in new contexts relevant to stu-dents' personal needs.
3. Provide a summary that highlights and focuses attention on the experiences in which the new knowledge was learned.
4. Use assessments of students' prior knowledge in implementing Expansion activities while monitoring and assessing the progress of the students' explanation of the en-ergy concept.

WILL THE PROGRAM PROMOTE A COMMUNITY OF SCIENCE LEARNING WITHIN THE SCHOOL AND SOCIAL COMMUNITY?

Student learning of a concept is not an individualized task. Meaningful understanding requires the cooperation of a community of learners. This community can involve a student's cooperative learning group, a teacher's grade-level planning team, school staff and administrators, input from parents in a variety of roles, and the experiences of concerned and interested citizens in the local area. In studying the concept of *energy*, for example, students ask questions about objects, events, and processes relating to energy which they can answer through investigation. They might ask: "Do different properties of objects affect how much light is absorbed?" and "What does energy have to do with sound?" Students cooperatively plan and conduct simple energy investigations. For example, a cooperative group may plan a procedure for determining whether color affects the amount of light absorbed by a material. As a member of a cooperative group, students construct explanations and communicate them along with the supporting evidence. They consider questions such as, "How do the group's results compare to the results of other groups?"

Applying What You know

Using the Basic Preplanning Questions

Respond to the basic preplanning questions below. Consider the following specific life science content goal for grades 5–8 from the National Science Education Standards:

> Cells carry on many functions needed to sustain life. This requires that cells take in nutrients that they use to provide energy for the work that cells do and to make the materials that a cellular organism needs. (National Research Council, 1996, p. 156)

Resources to assist you as you develop a response for this activity can be found in the *National Science Education Standards* (National Research Council, 1996: "Inquiry," pages 121–123; "Life science," pages 155–157; "Technology," pages 161–166; "Social perspectives," pages 166–179; and "Nature of science," pages 170–171). Another excellent source to use is *Benchmarks for Science Literacy* (American Association for the Advancement of Science, 1993a: "Cells," pages 110–112; "Nature of science," pages 15–18; "Health," pages 143–145; "Health technology," pages 204–206; and "Historical perspectives," pages 256–259).

See the Companion Website that accompanies this text at *http://www.prenhall.com/sunal* for links to the *National Science Education Standards* and *Benchmarks for Science Literacy.*

Companion Website

Basic Preplanning Questions:

Respond to each specific question considering the life science content standard quoted above:

1. *What is a good science program for these students?* This basic question can be developed into a specific question, "How does this concept fit into a good science program for grades 5–8 students?"
2. *How do I incorporate an inquiry and student reflection mode as an integral part of the science program?* This basic question can be developed into a specific question, "How can I incorporate an inquiry and reflective mode in teaching this concept?"
3. *What ties together this year's science program with the program students had in previous, and will have in future, years?* This basic question can be developed into several specific questions: "What would you do differently each year if you

(continued)

were developing this concept with students over several years?" "What are the prerequisite ideas?" Sequence a set of ideas over several years to develop the standard above as a final understanding.

4. *Is the yearlong program aligned with the teaching strategies to be used and the assessment to be performed?* This basic question can be developed into a specific question, "What is a teaching and assessment strategy that matches this curriculum goal for a specific student activity?"

5. *Will the program promote a community of science learning within the school and community?* This basic question can be developed into a specific question, "How can a community of science learners be structured for this curriculum goal?"

Becoming an Effective Planner and Teacher of Classroom Science

It takes time and effort to become an effective planner for science teaching. Teachers carry out their own research and direct their personal development as a professional as they become effective planners. A supportive school environment helps teachers more fully develop their planning skills.

Teachers carry out research in their classrooms all the time. They work on situations in which a student is having difficulty reading and recording the cooling of water in a jar, or is having difficulty in applying a science concept in a new experience. Most teachers benefit from further developing their skills at carrying out practitioner research. Practitioner research is purposeful and practical. It involves methods and skills teachers use to solve their own problems in their classroom. It begins with a focus question or problem that narrows down their attention to one key factor. This leads to an informal investigation by asking: "What information is needed to answer the question?" "How can I get the information needed and what observations must be made?" See Figure 11–3 for an overview

FIGURE 11–3 *Steps in performing action research*

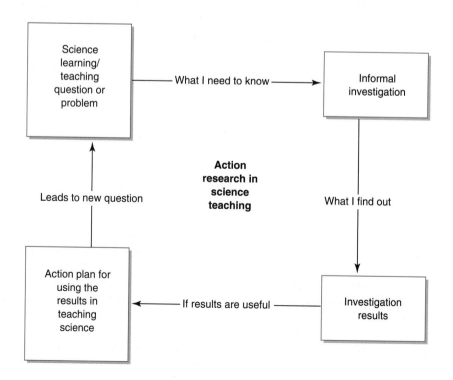

of the process. If the results of the problem's investigation are evaluated as significant, the practitioner researcher develops a plan to implement those results. The implementation is further evaluated to check whether the results provide a solution to the question or problem originally asked. Questions such as: "How big a group should work at one computer while using the Internet?" and "When students use sensor probe technology, do they understand the science principles better than when using textbook lessons?" are best answered by a teacher carrying out informal practitioner research in the classroom.

Practitioner research creates a deeper understanding of the ideas questioned as well as more effective science learning outcomes in students. A teacher asks questions about everyday science teaching assumptions believed to be true, but which have not have been checked out in the classroom. Teachers who purposely use practitioner research generate more questions. They use more effective strategies for systematically observing classrooms, testing out their questions, and solving science teaching/learning problems. They are more likely to value their results and formulate effective plans of action based on what they have learned. Further information and help in carrying out practitioner research in daily classroom routines can be found by searching the Internet for terms such as "practitioner research" and "action research."

Some useful sites appear on the Companion Website at *http://www.prenhall.com/sunal*

What Criteria Are Used in Planning the Yearlong Program?

After considering the basic preplanning questions, the yearlong program is planned. Criteria based on research results and the National Science Education Standards that are considered in planning the yearlong program include:

- Continuously spaced science experiences.
- Concepts integrated with other classroom subjects.
- Science activities that are parallel and interactive with other classrooms in and out of the school.
- Provision of equal learning opportunities for all students.
- Science units matched with future scheduled local and national science events. (American Association for the Advancement of Science, 1993a; Lowery, 1997; National Research Council, 1996)

Additional criteria may be added using state and local school system guidelines. For example, most states specify the science content area to emphasize at each grade level, whereas the national standards specify only the developmental sequence of each science content area over several years.

Continuously Spaced Science Experiences

The effective science program includes daily lessons every week throughout the school year. The National Science Teachers Association recommends a minimum of 150 minutes per week of science instruction in grades 1–3, 225 minutes in grades 4–6, and 250 minutes in grades 7–8 with at least 60 percent of the science instructional time devoted to hands-on experiences in the field or laboratory (Lowery, 1997, p. 138). Local and state guidelines may slightly differ.

A critical element in long-term planning is that the spacing of learning over time produces markedly higher learning achievement than massed learning over short time periods (Dempster, 1988). This element has two parts: the "spacing effect" and the "massed-versus-distributed practice effect." In the "spacing effect," learning in lessons taking place over a short time period produces lower achievement than occurs when several lessons are spaced out over a longer period. The difference in achievement between the extremes increases as the frequency of lessons increases. Science taught during one time of the year and deleted at another time of the year produces below-expected-grade-level science learning outcomes. For example, science taught in the fall and not in the spring, or science taught for several weeks and not again until a month or two later, is not an effective science plan. Consecutive, continuous science experiences throughout the year produce greater science knowledge.

In the "massed-versus-distributed practice effect," learning taking place in a few longer, closely spaced sessions produces lower achievement than several shorter sessions spaced out over the same time period. Science that is taught once a week to fourth graders for one 225-minute period is not as effective as science taught every day for 45 minutes per day. Science that is taught as an unplanned incidental subject coming in irregular spurts of time produces below-grade-level science learning outcomes. Planning for an effective year-long science program involves daily lessons throughout the year at all grade levels.

Concepts Integrated with Other Classroom Subjects

Identification of science curriculum goals starts with the state or local science course of study and the national science standards. A developmental sequence of goals is considered. The goals are then compared with the curriculum goals in mathematics, social studies, and literacy. Commonalities in skills and content between the subject goal areas are identified. Students make sense of the world in a very concrete way, and literature and storytelling involved in other school subjects, unaccompanied by scientific experiences and explanations, can lead to misconceptions (Miller, Steiner, & Larson, 1996). Sequencing these science commonalities can result in a systematic plan involving not only science but all subjects in a classroom for the school year. For example, when the National Science Education Standard stated in the last *Applying What You Know* is examined across the curriculum's subjects, many common elements are found. These common elements can be scheduled so they are considered in each of the subjects at the same time during the year. For instance, goals in science related to cells and nutrition can be correlated in social studies, mathematics, literacy, and drama (see Table 11–1).

Development of a community for science learning can be enhanced when teachers in the same grade and across grade levels align their curricula. At several points during the school year, science units can be matched across classrooms at the same grade level, for example, having all first graders investigating the same idea. Investigating the unifying concept of *constancy and change* in a local community environment, for example, stimulates informal student discussion during lunchtime and makes possible cross-classroom group presentations. A school play for all third graders demonstrating the effect of soap

TABLE 11–1   *Cell and nutrition science activities that are parallel with other subjects in the classroom*

Science	Social Studies	Mathematics	Literacy	Drama
Cells (plant and animal) require nutrients and minerals.	Government guidelines for nutrition.	Measurement or calculation of specific and daily food units and calories for different individuals.	Informational reading and writing.	Role-playing nutrient actions in a cell.

molecules in water (MacKinnon, 1998) can involve students from several classrooms. A mini-science fair and investigations of a local community environment with roles shared between classrooms at the same grade level are other examples. Creating learning communities between classrooms at the same grade level fosters teacher creativity as ideas for activities are shared and teachers are motivated by working with other teachers.

Effective interactive activities have been documented in many schools across grade levels and schools (e.g., Daisey & Shroyer, 1995; Gondree & Doran, 1998; McLaughlin, 1997). Cross-age tutoring between small groups of students in the first and fifth grades are possible on topics such as "characteristics of organisms." Cross-age tutoring can take the form of a younger student asking questions to a small group of older students whose answers provide background on the diversity or range of organisms in a specific habitat. Students in the first and fifth grades can work together in small groups investigating a problem or relationship out-of-doors on the school grounds in a key aspect of a science unit. Family members can participate in science school carnivals, field trips, science career days, and community environmental surveys as a part of the science unit (Gardner, 1996; Nichols, 1996; Scribner-Maclean, 1996).

Provision of Equal Learning Opportunities

The yearlong science program facilitates equity for every student regardless of gender, background, learning style, or ability. An equal opportunity to learn, however, may require an unequal distribution of time. Students for whom English is not a native language, for example, may need additional time or teacher aid in order to participate in science experiences. At-risk students may need help in focusing their attention. Minority students may need role models that are not available in the materials provided by the school (National Research Council, 1995, pp. 221–222). Teachers' expectations are the key to planning for equity in science for all students. It is not enough to say you know that "equity is important." Teachers must actively change what they do and the activities in which students are involved before measurable change occurs in providing for student equity. Planning for equity occurs at this time in the yearlong planning phase and is carried out during the implementation of the units.

See Chapter 10 for specific changes that can be made for teaching science to all students.

Science Units Matched with Future Scheduled Local and National Science Events

As yearlong planning is occurring, it is important to look ahead. When is Earth Day? Is there a space shuttle launch scheduled that has relevance to one of the year's science topics? What astronomical events, such as a bright comet, are predicted? What seasonal constellations are visible?

Relate important scientific dates to appropriate science units. During a unit on the atmosphere, celebrate the anniversary of Jeannette Piccard, the only woman to reach the stratosphere at a height of 17,543 meters (57,559 feet), which occurred on January 5, 1935. Other examples include September 12, 1992, the anniversary of Mae Jamison's flight into space. She was the first African-American woman to do so. Marie Curie's birthday, November 7, 1867, commemorates the first woman to receive a science doctoral degree and a pioneer physicist who studied radioactivity. Angeles Alvarino's birthday on October 3, 1916, commemorates the discoverer of 22 new ocean species. A useful resource in coordinating dates and events is *Every Day Science: An Enrichment Calendar,* available from the National Science Teachers Association (NSTA).

Has a conference on global warming been scheduled or an earthquake been predicted? Searching the Internet is one means of identifying such anniversaries and events. For example, the NSTA at *http://www.nsta.org* or AAAS at *http://www.aaas.org* are sites where such information can be found.

For further information, see links to NSTA and AAAS on the Companion Website at *http://www.prenhall.com/sunal*

Encyclopedias and calendars also contain information about historical and current science events and people. Some useful resources include *African and African American Women of Science* (Bernstein, Winkler, & Zierdt-Warshaw, 1998a), *Multicultural Women of Science* (Bernstein, Winkler, & Zierdt-Warshaw, 1998b), and *Science for All Cultures* (National Science Teachers Association, 1993). Useful trade books are also available, such as *Marie Curie* (Lepscky, 1992).

A Strategy for Designing a Yearlong Program

Planning a meaningful course of study in science requires clustering outcomes, seeking appropriate connections, and then sequencing the results into coherent units of science instruction. There are several components to be addressed in the design of a yearlong science program. These are:

- Goals and rationale.
- Alignment with local, state, and national science standards.
- Overall science learning outcomes.
- Science units of study.
- Repertoire of instructional strategies appropriate to science.
- Science assessment and portfolio construction.

These components are shared and discussed with students as a regular part of instruction during the year to help set expectations. Information from exploratory work done in answering the earlier preplanning questions is used here to begin development of the yearlong program. The following sections provide a description of the components of the design of a yearlong science program.

Goals and Rationale

The goals and rationale for the science program were considered as part of preplanning. These initial ideas are now expanded into a complete rationale. The following questions guide this expansion of the preplanning questions. First, "What are the broad goals in science for your students during the school year?" Identify these and list or describe them. Second, "What is your rationale for choosing these goals?" Sketch out the rationale. Third, "How do the goals fit the students' developmental levels? Cultural backgrounds? Interests?" Include your description of the "fit" in the rationale. Fourth, "What are the key science knowledge, skills, and attitudes your students should learn?" Use these to further refine the goals and the rationale.

General yearlong science program goals recommended by the National Research Council (1996) for a K–8 science program are the following (see Figure 11–4):

- Science is an investigative and problem-solving set of unified activities.
- Science activities are centered on basic, crosscutting themes including: (1) systems, order, and organization, (2) evidence, model, and explanation, (3) constancy, change, and measurement, (4) evolution and equilibrium, and (5) form and function.
- Science activities and themes are developed through a study of key ideas in the physical, life, Earth, and space sciences.
- Connections and applications are sought in technology, personal and social perspectives, and the history and nature of science.

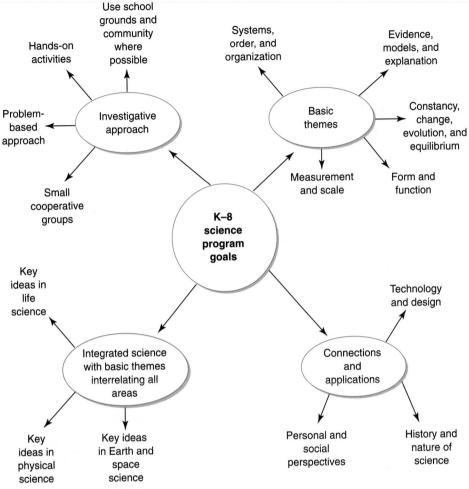

FIGURE 11-4   *Components of an effective yearlong science program*

Goals for a fourth-grade classroom may include the following:

Goals That Are Part of an Investigative Approach:

1. Collecting and sharing data from a variety of sources.
2. Using simple equipment and tools to gather data.
3. Working collaboratively in collecting and interpreting data.
4. Communicating ideas about what is found in a variety of ways.
5. Describing changes in objects and events.
6. Making predictions.
7. Designing simple, comparative tests.
8. Gathering information to answer their own questions.
9. Identifying patterns of change.
10. Drawing inferences from data.

Goals That Are Basic Themes:

11. Investigating many parts in a system that influence each other.

12. Exploring a simple model that suggests how either a part of, or the whole, system works in the natural world.

13. Finding that changes in objects and events can be steady or irregular.

14. Observing and sequencing the many forms of an organism due to growth and development.

15. Representing an object by a larger or smaller version—a plant cell or the solar system.

Goals That Are Included as Integrated Science:

16. Life cycle of organisms.

17. Position and motion of objects.

18. Changes in the Earth and sky.

Goals That Are Connections and Applications:

19. Changes in environments and their effects on humans.

20. Science as a human endeavor.

21. Technology design skills such as designing materials to solve a problem.

An example of a yearlong science program rationale for fourth grade is the following:

> Science involves meaningful experiences for all students in their daily lives. Science is best learned through inquiry. Students should be encouraged to question, investigate, and evaluate results of experiences to answer their own questions. Therefore, science concept and skill outcomes should be relevant to students' interests and developmental levels. Throughout the science unit students should readily apply what they learn in their home setting and to the local community. This application is necessary for students to be able to transfer their science understandings to future life experiences.

Alignment with Local, State, and National Science Standards

At this point, local and national standards, which will be addressed during the school year, are identified. School system, state, and national science standards documents identify specific themes and sets of concepts to focus the yearlong science program. Develop an initial list, then evaluate your choices. Developing a planning web is a useful tool for many teachers. See Figure 11–5 for a fourth-grade example. Decide whether the goals are relevant to students' interests, backgrounds, and developmental levels. Make regular connections to other subjects taught during the year. The planning sequence of social studies and mathematics, also based on local and national standards, can be coordinated to regularly intersect with science throughout the school year. Narrow down the list to a set of standards that best fits these considerations. Planning adequate time for in-depth investigation of fewer science concept areas is more important than coverage of a large number of science topics during the school year.

Overall Learning Outcomes

What do you want your students to know and be able to do at the end of the school year? The answer to this question represents the learning outcomes your students will be able to demonstrate. As an example, you may have identified the theme of "systems, order, and organization." Specifically, students will be exploring the idea that "a simple model may suggest how either a part of, or the whole, system works in the natural world." At this point in your planning you consider the question, "What will students know or be able to do as an outcome of their study of this theme?" An answer might be the following:

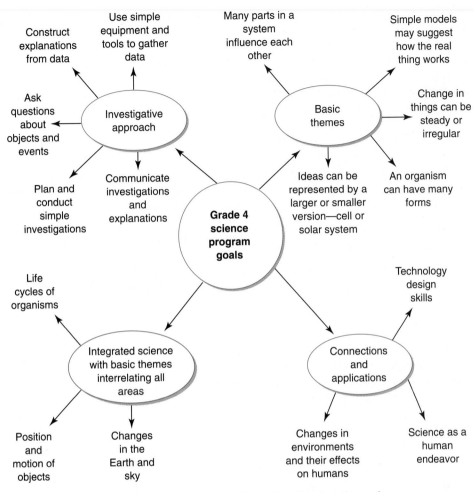

FIGURE 11-5   *Designing a sample yearlong plan for fourth grade*

As an outcome of their study of the theme of systems, order, and organization, students will demonstrate a meaningful understanding that:

> The natural and designed world is too large and complicated to investigate and comprehend all at once. We can be more successful in understanding the world by defining small portions of it to investigate. The idea under investigation can be referred to as a "system." Systems can consist of organisms, stars, growth and development, numbers, or objects.

This unifying concept will be taught and retaught through each of the units relating to life, physical, Earth, and space sciences.

Units of Study

Identify and list the key units to be studied during the year. Build on the decisions you already made identifying the rationale, goals, alignment, and overall learning outcomes for the yearlong plan. Your yearlong plan should be flexible so it can take advantage of student questions and current and historical science events that occur during the year. For example, students may become interested in a related science topic (e.g., evidence for living organisms on Mars), or the community may become involved in a science-related contro-versy (e.g., recurrent flooding in an area of the local community). The science topic or con-troversy should be integrated with the planned science curriculum in such a way that the students understand the basic concepts and principles underlying these current events.

An example of a yearlong plan for a fourth-grade sequence of units that complies with state standards, in this instance the *Alabama Course of Study—Science,* is: "The Universe," "The Earth in Space," "The Dynamic Earth," "Matter," "Energy," "Force and Motion," "Di-versity," "Heredity," "Cells," and "Interdependence" (Teague, 1995). This sequence of units integrates the sciences since the units include the three strands of Earth and space science, physical science, and life science.

The content of a science unit addresses *science knowledge,* concepts, and generaliza-tions, as well as *science inquiry skills.* For example, checking the Alabama state science standards in the example above, some of the science inquiry skills these units address in-clude utilizing techniques and habits essential to scientific investigations; communicat-ing scientific content effectively; constructing mental, verbal, and physical representa-tions and models of events and objects; recognizing the effects of manipulated and controlled factors on the outcome of events; using appropriate instruments and proce-dures when learning new information; and applying mathematical knowledge and skills to scientific investigations.

A third area of importance is the *application of science skills and knowledge.* In the pre-vious example sequence of units, this involves recognizing that uniformity, quantity, qual-ity, and cost effectiveness of manufactured products improve with the use of technology; recognizing relationships among science, technology, and society; becoming aware of ways to deal with discarded products that create waste disposal problems; relating goods and services to the technologies that make them available; applying scientific knowledge and processes from one domain of science to other fields of study; recognizing the importance of science to many careers; and serving the community through a science-related project.

Repertoire of Instructional Strategies

Describe the range of instructional strategies to be used in each of the units for this year-long plan. Later, it will be necessary to determine the specific instructional strategies that fit a particular science unit. At this point, list those that appear to be workable in at least some of the units. An inquiry framework involving use of the learning cycle, for instance, can include the following instructional strategies: discrepant events, cooperative learning, laboratory activities, field trips, problem-solving activities, discussion, role-playing, case studies, live demonstrations, simulations, virtual field trips using videotapes and the In-ternet, guest speakers, and cross-age tutoring.

Assessment and Portfolio Construction

Describe the assessment and evaluation plan to be implemented during the year. How will you know whether the students have accomplished the learning outcomes previously identified? Since the students will be involved in a variety of learning activities, the as-sessment should reflect this range and be appropriate to the diversity represented by the students. An example for the fourth grade follows:

- Each student will maintain a portfolio of his work, with some components identified by the student and some identified by the teacher.
- Each student will work in a cooperative team and will be evaluated for her individ-ual and team effort.

- An investigative project will be carried out by each cooperative group twice during the year, once in late fall and once in early spring. Presentation of the project results will be made to all of the school's fourth graders at a grade-level assembly.
- Performance activities involving the understanding of concepts and science skills will be used in each unit.
- Students will keep journals describing their weekly experiences in science. These will be written each week on Friday.
- Quizzes, with part of the questions submitted by students, will be given for each unit.

Applying What You Know

Describing Components of a Yearlong Science Program

Obtain a yearlong plan of study for a science program at a specific grade level, such as a local or state course of study or a classroom teacher's plan. Identify and describe the following components in the design of the yearlong program or plan:

Goals and rationale.

Alignment with local, state, and national science standards.

Overall learning outcomes.

Units of study.

Repertoire of instructional strategies.

Assessment and portfolio construction.

Discuss the adequacy of this program in meeting the planning criteria above.

HOW CAN TECHNOLOGY BE USED TO FACILITATE SCIENCE LEARNING?

Planning and development of the yearlong science program involves coordination of the program goals with the National Science Education Standards. The technology used to support the teaching of science should reflect the goals and learning outcomes established in the yearlong plan. State and national guidelines for the teaching of science may recommend or imply general and specific components. The National Science Education Standards state that ". . . teachers of science design and manage learning environments that provide students with the time, space and resources needed for learning science" (National Research Council, 1996, p. 43). The design and management involves ". . . making available science tools, materials, media, and technological resources accessible to students and engaging students in designing the learning environment"(National Research Council, 1996, p. 43).

Technology provides a means for communicating and interacting with others. It is also a means for exploration that helps students construct new knowledge and reconstruct existing ideas. In order to develop technology as a tool that facilitates exploration, gathering of data, understanding, and science literacy, it is useful to envision technology as: (1) an information resource, (2) a learning tool, (3) a storage device, (4) a facilitator of communication, and (5) an integrator of information (Perkins, 1992). The need for student-centered instructional environments accompanies the growing comprehension and acceptance of learning as explained by the new national science standards (American Association for the

Advancement of Science, 1993a; National Research Council, 1996). When students are in student-directed, collaborative classrooms supported by teachers who start with the students' prior knowledge, provide meaningful tasks, and emphasize connections between ideas, they learn more (Nicaise & Barnes, 1996). How can technology assist students in learning science that is meaningful to them? What learning conditions are optimal for the use of technology? How and when does technology facilitate the basic elements of instruction? What technology applications are useful in science learning?

Rationale

Traditional classrooms involve students in direct instruction with textbooks. Hands-on materials and computer programs are used to reinforce the ideas presented in the textbook. Lecture and discussion, in addition to individual activities and homework, round out the traditional strategy of classroom science teaching. Assessment involves participation in class discussion, presentations, and tests. Technology generally plays a small role in traditional science teaching. It is often used to reinforce the strategy of teaching as telling, or simply providing information to be memorized. Students in this setting have great difficulty in remembering material over time or transferring learning or skills to other school settings or to the real world. This type of instruction and classroom environment does not support or nurture meaningful learning. Overall, in many schools the use of technology has resulted in very little change in the way teachers teach science in K–8 classrooms. Instead, the use of technology mirrors traditional instructional practices.

Using technology to expand students' control over their own learning and to increase the quality and extent of experience is vital to creating an interactive and information-rich classroom. Students are active seekers and constructors of knowledge. They not only bring to the classroom their everyday interests and curiosities, but increasingly bring a view of technology as a personal tool used in the home for communication and exploration. Meaningful science learning starts with the student and involves the discovery and transformation of information about the natural world into meaningful knowledge (Brooks & Brooks, 1993; Fosnot, 1993). It also involves real-life situations and social activities that help students shape their own understanding. Cognitive development depends on a student's social interaction with others where language plays a central role (Vygotsky, 1978). Traditional classrooms do not provide students with the essential contextual features for science learning, thus forcing them to rely on superficial surface-level features of concepts and events without the ability to apply or use the knowledge (Chi, Feltovich, & Glaser, 1981). Meaningful science learning should occur within the world students experience so that when they deal with problems and situations simulating and representing reality and relevance, they learn more (Bednar, Cunningham, Duffy, & Perry, 1992).

Optimal Learning Conditions

Technology has been used to support traditional reinforcement and simple transmission of knowledge in a classroom setting. However, technology has a much greater potential to facilitate and enhance learning activities to create meaningful science learning (Vockell & Schwartz, 1992). Some of these areas include:

1. Science concepts that are difficult to teach using lecture, textbook, or video media; for example, the impact of the changing environment on animal life and the importance of environmental monitoring can be facilitated with student engagement in the

simulation *SimAnt* by Maxis (see Figure 11–6 for the addresses of software and multimedia companies). Tom Snyder Productions and MECC, offer many simulations appropriate for elementary and middle school students (see Figure 11–6).

2. Science concepts that are logistically difficult to teach; for example, the interplay of latitude and local environmental conditions in the dates of the first signs of spring in the United States. The movement of first sightings of robins or forsythia blooms can be coordinated with partner classrooms in locations north and south of your location. Such sightings are communicated among the participating classrooms by posting them on Internet sites. The Journey North website offers such a service.

See link to The Journey North website on the Companion Website that accompanies this text at
http://www.prenhall.com/sunal

3. Motivating students to actively take part in a learning activity; for example, the impact of making decisions where the changing natural environment leads to a change in the

---

ADDRESSES OF SOFTWARE AND MULTIMEDIA PRODUCERS

Davidson Corporation
19840 Pioneer Ave.
Torrance, CA 90503
800-545-7677
http://www.education.com/products/ lead products

Decision Development
2680 Bishop Drive Suite 122
San Ramon, CA 94583
510-830-8896
http://www.ddc2000.com/

Inspiration Software, Inc.
7412 SW Beaverson Hillsdale Hwy.
Suite 102
Portland OR 97225
800-877-4292
http://www.inspiration.com

Maxis
2 Theatre Square, Suite 230
Orinda, CA 94563
800-336-2947
http://www.maxis.com/index.html

MECC
6160 Summit Dr. North
Minneapolis, MN 55430
800-685-6322
http://www.mecc.com

Scholastic
730 Broadway
New York, NY 10003
800-541-5513
http://www.scholastic.com

Sunburst
101 Castelton St.
Pleasantville, NY 10570
800-321-7511
http://www.nysunburst.com

Tom Snyder Productions
80 Coolidge Hill Road
Watertown, MA 02172
800-342-0236
http://www.teachsp.com

Vernier Software and Technology
13979 SW Millikan Way
Beaverton, OR 97005-2886
http://www.vernier.com

Videodiscovery
1700 Westlake Avenue N. Suite 600
Seattle, WA 98100
800-548-3472
http://www.videodiscovery.com/vdyweb

FIGURE 11–6 *Addresses of software and multimedia companies*
Note: website addresses are subject to change. Use a search engine if a new address is needed.

quality of life, and the importance of environmental monitoring can be facilitated with student engagement in the simulation *SimEarth* by Maxis (see Figure 11–6).

4. Providing individualized student practice with generalizations in science through software demonstrating relationships between variables such as using a teacher-constructed database to provide data for the temperature and depth of ocean water, or its temperature and altitude. Sunburst offers many programs appropriate for elementary and middle school students (see Figure 11–6).

5. Implementing instruction that is not safe to carry out; for example, field trips to dangerous sites or equipment too dangerous to use can be performed through the use of the Internet or other instructional software. Videodiscovery offers many video programs appropriate for elementary and middle school students (see Figure 11–6).

6. Incorporating instruction in the science program that is too costly; for example, field trips to sites not in the local area or equipment too expensive to use. Davidson Corporation or Scholastic offer media and programs appropriate for elementary and middle school students (see Figure 11–6).

How Does Technology Facilitate the Basic Elements of Science Instruction?

Technology facilitates science learning in five basic elements of instruction: (1) authentic science learning activities, (2) collaborative groups, (3) information-rich classrooms, (4) teacher bridging, and (5) authentic evaluation tasks. Computers and access to the Internet assist instruction in becoming more efficient and effective if used for appropriate learner needs. Teachers are the major element of instruction in science lessons. Technology should be regarded as a tool teachers use to enhance student learning. The effects can improve the general science learning environment for students and free the teacher from less-productive and more time-consuming instructional tasks.

Authentic Science Learning Activities

Meaningful learning in science implies activities in which students guide their direction and pace and have some control over the learning outcomes. Authentic science activities involve the creation of science learning environments containing multiple sources of starting points, perspectives, and sources of information. Teaching strategies that appropriately utilize technology encourage the development of meaningful learning (Jonassen, 1995).

In planning to use technology to structure authentic learning activities, teachers are aware of students' developmental levels, interests, and prior knowledge. Units and lessons aimed at helping students construct meaningful science learning have several important elements. First, they motivate students to become involved, activate their prior knowledge, and challenge students' existing science knowledge. Technology can provide the curiosity and challenge needed. For example, students may examine pictures of the moon downloaded from the Internet and be surprised to find many scars, blemishes, and cracks in addition to the mountains and plains. A stereotype of a smooth moon or one that is a jumble of rock piles may be challenged by this information.

Next, using magnetic or optical media, the teacher guides students through explanations and examples of the new ideas. The teacher might have students use library reference materials, CD-ROMs, and the Internet to get information on the moon's history, as well as recent observations and exploratory visits to it. These references have a great deal of information that enables students to obtain a realistic view of the rocks, surface features, and processes of change present on the moon.

Finally, students expand their new knowledge as they apply it to a range of different contexts. Students might undertake a project in which they view and compare observations of the moon with another class in a different part of the country. They might also explore other satellites of planets, using the vast amount of observations on CD-ROMs and the Internet to determine whether the moon is typical of other planets' satellites in the solar system. The integration of magnetic and optical media, the Internet, and broadcast media into the science curriculum gives power to students and teachers, enabling them to construct meaning from current information in an ever-increasing body of knowledge.

Students should work on problems and situations that simulate and represent the real world through using educational games and tool software (Bransford, Sherwood, Kinzer, Hasselbring, & Williams, 1990). Many examples of electronic and optical media enable students to experiment in self-contained worlds through simulations. Students assume various community roles such as soil investigator and data recorder. They solve problems in an interdisciplinary approach using biological, chemical, geological, medical, economic, and political perspectives. Four units each provide middle school students with about 10 hours of self-guided instruction.

Collaborative Groups

Students must have extended opportunities to collaborate (Slavin, 1995). Small-group learning and technology can play an integral role in encouraging student exploration and interaction. While students work on authentic tasks in collaborative groups, the teacher's role is that of facilitator, problem presenter, resource demonstrator, and question-poser.

Technology can assist teachers in developing a collaborative classroom. Available CD-ROMs, software, laser disks, or the Internet offer multiple possibilities for enhancing collaboration. One example is *Science Court* by Tom Snyder Publications, a CD-ROM and print materials series that utilizes courtroom drama, group collaboration, hands-on activities, and humor to teach science concepts and investigative skills. It is designed for students in grades 4–6. Students analyze, discuss, and perform experiments to gather information. They collaboratively come to a prediction of a science event. Sample conceptual areas involve the water cycle, machines, and sound. A television broadcast version is also available.

Information-Rich Classrooms

A rich array of science resources must be available for student exploration if science knowledge is to have a personally constructed meaning. The teacher's role needs to gradually change from information provider to facilitator and coach of learning. To be successful in real-world tasks, the classroom must be information rich and provide for more student-controlled learning. There are diverse magnetic and optical media and Internet sites that provide students with opportunities for relevant information. Some examples are electronic libraries found in videodisks (such as visual and text encyclopedias), student-constructed databases, microcomputer-based laboratory sensors, calculators and graphing calculators, and asynchronous communications as in "ask-a-scientist" formats with e-mail and the Internet. For example, information on birds can be found at the websites of "Birds of America" and "Ask-an-Expert" (for agricultural questions).

See the link to Birds of America and Ask-an-Expert on the Companion Website that accompanies this text at *http://www.prenhall.com/sunal*

Live broadcasts and taped-delay showings of science programs such as *Bill Nye the Science Guy or Newton's Apple* on the Public Broadcasting Service offer a rich diversity in science teaching resources.

Announcements of science programs are found in the local newspaper, *TV Guide*®, and in professional publications such as *Science and Children, Science Scope,* and *NSTA Reports.* The Internet provides access to worldwide resources. *The Great Solar System Rescue* and *The Great Ocean Rescue,* available either in videodisk or CD-ROM multimedia kits by Tom Snyder Publications, offer cooperative learning, group discussion, and team problem-solving experiences with interdisciplinary science puzzles for the whole class.

Connecting Prior Knowledge to the New Science Idea

Helping students reach the lesson's goal from the beginning of the lesson requires direct experience in science as well as an experience that will help transfer the goal to a new setting. If possible, this transfer should extend far beyond the time and space limitations of the classroom. Technology assists students in gaining first-hand experience in many ways through:

- Manipulating, organizing, and analyzing science information.
- Using science cyber-manipulatives (interactive objects on computer screens).
- Utilizing science cyber-equipment (interactive science equipment on computer screens).
- Discussing questions and posing problems to scientists and people who use science understandings on their jobs or who are directly involved in science events.
- Accessing current science news reports and documents.
- Obtaining photographs and short movies.
- Performing art renditions of events and experiences.
- Designing charts, tables, and maps.

Technology can provide the interactive activities required for connecting prior knowledge to the development of new science concepts by using simulations, interactive discussion, graphing software, and microcomputer-based laboratories. One example is *Rainforest Researchers* by Tom Snyder Publications, which provides materials to help students explore the nature, issues, and science concepts associated with rainforests. Interactive multimedia programs can provide meaningful learning and transfer for basic science concepts such as plant and animal adaptations, life cycles, and ecosystem relationships.

Alternative Assessment Tasks

In authentic evaluation, students carry out a variety of performances that show their understanding of an idea (Perkins & Blythe, 1994). Students express what they are learning by using word processing, desktop publishing, graphics, and multimedia display programs. Using *Power Point*™ to display or present ideas gained in an educational activity can be a useful learning outcome and assessment format. The results of a project can understandably be communicated through a graphics program or as part of a multimedia program. In these packages, students describe experiences and investigate a variety of science problems.

Useful Technology Applications in Science

Technology alone does not have the power to help students create, analyze, compare, examine, and ultimately understand the world. Teachers need to take an active role in order to maximize the computer's capabilities in fostering science learning. Technology applications that help teachers create meaningful science learning in students involve several broad categories, including productivity and resource software, problem-solving software and multimedia, cyber-materials kits, simulated environments, computer telecommunications and video conferencing (Dyrli & Kinnaman, 1995), the Internet, and microcomputer- and calculator-based science laboratories.

Productivity and Resource Software

Productivity and resource software include word processors, laser disks, digital images (from digital cameras and video cameras), scanned images, databases, spreadsheets, drawings and art work, graphic organizers, and multimedia programs that manage and display data. These applications allow data and text to be entered or collected, manipulated piecemeal or as a whole, and displayed in a variety of forms and colors. This software facilitates information processing and communication. Some are provided on any basic computer's hard drive. Examples of productivity and resource software are *Inspiration* from Inspiration Software, Inc., a graphical organizer for concept mapping, or *Timeliner* from Tom Snyder Publications for creating time lines. One resource example is *Telling Our Stories: Women in Science* by Tom Snyder Publications.

Problem-Solving Software and Multimedia

Problem-solving software and multimedia usually contain scenarios generated by a computer in addition to print resources, including teacher-planning and student-activity materials. These materials provide students with opportunities to use their inquiry skills in technology-based science investigations. Examples include *Science Sleuths* by Videodiscovery, *The Great Solar System Race* by Tom Snyder Publications, *Zookeeper* by Davidson, and *Puzzle Tanks* by Sunburst.

Cyber-Materials Kits

Cyber-materials kits allow students to move and put together a variety of computer-controlled objects. Examples include arranging a series of boxes having separate functions; each arrangement of boxes produces a different outcome. Another is *The Factory Deluxe* by Sunburst, which offers five environments which fourth through eighth graders can manipulate to build machine assembly lines in order to produce specific results with an industrial theme. Visual thinking and problem solving are emphasized.

Simulated Environments

Simulated environments create microworlds that simulate nature in simple and complex ways to help students learn science concepts and generalizations without burdening them with great amounts of facts. In *Odell Down Under* by MECC, students live in the ocean near Australia's Great Barrier Reef. Their goal is to survive and successfully move up the food chain. *Operation Frog* by Scholastic allows students to probe body organs and remove them for examination. *Science Court* and *Science Court Explorations* by Tom Snyder Productions and Delta Education ask student groups of second through sixth graders to solve science problems in an animated story context. For second to fourth graders, these multimedia programs use a CD-ROM, hands-on experiments, and cooperative teams in solving problems involving rockets, pendulums, friction, heat, flight, and magnets. *Science Explorers* by Decision Development allows students to explore many science topics through simulated experiments.

Computer Telecommunications and Video Conferencing

Computer telecommunication and video conferencing allow students to investigate and interact with the world outside their classroom. This includes e-mail communications with a school across town, or a free Internet website which can be created to allow students in many classrooms to post data and leave messages for specific students or for all of the classrooms involved. There is no need to coordinate class schedules with the day of the week, time of day, or time zones since the communication is asynchronous (always available). The messages are left on a message board to be read when the receiver is ready to read it. One example is *sites ALIVE!* by Tom Snyder Productions, where students interact with other students by carrying out science investigations at sites around the world. Video conferencing by the Internet gives students an opportunity to carry on a live visual discussion with another class, with researchers, or with government representatives. The computer cameras and software used for video conferencing are inexpensive.

Internet

The Internet has great potential for use in teaching and learning science. It provides a wide choice of resource materials ranging from holdings in the Smithsonian Institution to *OceanEXPO*, which follows a fleet of boats as they circle the globe.

Companion
Website

For further information on *sites ALIVE!* and *OceanEXPO*, see the Companion Website at *http://www.prenhall.com/sunal* for links to these two websites.

The Internet also offers opportunities for students to pursue their own research, communicate with other students and resource people around the globe, and participate in data collection on projects involving students at a variety of sites. However, simply having access to the kaleidoscope of information on the Internet does not guarantee that the information will be used by students to construct meaningful learning (Morrison & Collins, 1995). Students must be trained in the use of the Internet, practice using it, and be encouraged to integrate new information and possibilities from the Internet into their science learning activities if the Internet is to be a useful tool. This requires an active approach to science learning in which students use the Internet for reading, writing, observing, collecting data, utilizing data, and problem solving. Such an approach moves away from traditional roles for students and teachers and toward learning centered on students in real-world contexts. The elements of meaningful learning occur when students are actively involved in learning and encounter ways to integrate new understandings into a background of existing knowledge. Teaching strategies that utilize technology, such as the Internet, can encourage the development of rich cognitive structures emphasizing the qualities of meaningful learning (Harter & Gerhke, 1989; Jonassen, 1995).

Microcomputer- and Calculator-Based Science Laboratories

Microcomputer- and calculator-based science laboratories enable students to collect information about their environment and process it into tables and graphs. This technology extends students' senses so that data can be collected in unusual places, (e.g., under the ground) and at different times (e.g., every half hour for a 24-hour period). Although this technology is not common in today's elementary and middle schools, it is found in every home, automobile, and workplace in the United States. This technology soon will be an important tool helping K–8 students learn meaningful science. Student groups in a fourth-grade class designed and built models of a solar-heated house. They used a thermometer sensor to record the inside temperature in different parts of the house during morning and early afternoon time periods to see temperature changes as the sun varied its position in the sky. Sensors are available for young students and include temperature, sound, motion, and light probes, among others. For middle-grade students, Vernier Software and Technology also sells sensors for magnetic fields, electricity, forces, humidity, distance, acceleration, and many other phenomena. These devices are connected to a microcomputer creating a microcomputer-based laboratory (MBL) or to a graphing calculator using a calculator-based laboratory (CBL) unit. Graphing calculators and CBL-type units are available from Texas Instruments and Casio Corporations, among others.

Applying What You Know

Using a Software Evaluation Checklist

Choose three pieces of software, multimedia programs, or interactive laser disk materials. These are available from your school or library or as a demonstration copy from the software publisher. Software and multimedia are also available on the Internet, either in their entirety or as demonstration copies. Visit the publisher's websites for more information on the availability and additional information on the product. Evaluate each selection using the software evaluation checklist found in Figure 11–7. Use the software, program, or laser disk for enough time to understand possible problems students might have, options available, and possible ways to assess learning outcomes. Do a complete evaluation of each item.

Responses will be different for various items. Some media look interesting for possible use in the classroom, but prove to be difficult to use or have trivial content or skills. Without experiencing the program yourself, it is difficult to adequately judge its educational worth.

WHAT STRATEGIES ARE USEFUL FOR INCORPORATING TECHNOLOGY INTO THE CURRICULUM?

A technology-rich curriculum can facilitate meaningful learning by students in the day-to-day activities of the classroom. However, using technology as a resource and an instructional tool for teaching science poses a challenge to teachers. The greatest barriers to effective change in the use of technology for teaching science are teacher beliefs about the technology and/or a lack of knowledge of the technology. Teachers who believe technology can enhance the process of teaching and learning are more likely to include technology as an integral part of their science instruction. Teachers who have had professional development training in technology recognize that realistic expectations are needed (Mitchell-Powell, 1995). Technology cannot replace many types of activities in the classroom. Knowledgeable teachers recognize technology's limitations, and are more likely to implement change than are teachers who attempt poorly informed change and quit without having gained the necessary long-term experience needed for success. As with any

TEACHING SCIENCE USING A TECHNOLOGY MEDIA EVALUATION FORM

Media Title: _____

Publisher: _____

Subject area(s): _____

Type of media (floppy disk, CD-ROM, laser disk and so on): _____

1. Technical and program description: Use the program as a student until you understand the possibilities of student interaction.

    a. What type of software is this? (e.g., computer-assisted instruction, simulation application, game, skill practice or problem solving)

    b. Hardware and classroom requirements.

    c. What happens when a student begins, during the activity, and when it ends?

    d. Describe the program sequence and structure.

    e. Briefly describe the intended purpose (goal) of the program.

    f. Briefly describe the intended audience of the program.

    g. Briefly describe the intended use of the program.

2. Complete the checklist below:

Inquiry Skills Checklist

	Emphasis	
	Major	**Incidental**
1. Process Skills		
A. *Observing*—the program requires students to:		
1. Observe carefully	_____	_____
2. Recall/remember things, ideas, and events	_____	_____
B. *Classifying*—the program requires students to:		
1. Compare/contrast	_____	_____
2. Group/label—assign a descriptive label or phrase to a set of objects/ideas after grouping them according to a common attribute	_____	_____
3. Categorize/classify—group ideas or objects according to given criteria (labels are provided)	_____	_____
C. *Analyzing*—the program requires students to:		
1. Question (formulate relevant information)	_____	_____
2. Discriminate fact from opinion	_____	_____
3. Discriminate relevant from irrelevant information	_____	_____
4. Discriminate reliable from unreliable sources of information	_____	_____
5. Recognize part-to-whole relationships	_____	_____
D. *Inferring*—the program requires students to:		
1. Understand the meaning of statements	_____	_____
2. Identify probable causes and effects	_____	_____
3. Use generalizations to solve problems or justify decisions	_____	_____
4. Make predictions	_____	_____
5. Identify one's own assumptions or those of others	_____	_____

FIGURE 11-7   *Evaluation checklist for software*

2. Operations:

   A. *Logical reasoning*—the program requires students to:

      1. Use inductive reasoning—combine an assumption or hypothesis with provided information to draw a tentative generalization   _____   _____

      2. Use deductive reasoning—draw a conclusion that can be proved or disproved by using only the information provided   _____   _____

   B. *Creative thinking*—the program requires students to:

      1. Demonstrate fluency—produce a variety of responses   _____   _____

      2. Demonstrate flexibility—try several different approaches or apply a concept, idea, or rule to a variety of situations   _____   _____

      3. Demonstrate originality—produce novel, unexpected, but related responses   _____   _____

      4. Elaborate—extend or expand on a concept or idea   _____   _____

      5. Spontaneously create new ideas or rules to fit the available information (the "aha!" experience)   _____   _____

   C. *Problem solving*—the program requires students to:

      1. Make decisions/judgments—draw conclusions and/or determine what to do after discerning and comparing relevant facts   _____   _____

      2. Define/describe the problem   _____   _____

      3. Determine the desired outcome   _____   _____

      4. Search for possible solutions   _____   _____

      5. Select and apply a trial solution   _____   _____

      6. Evaluate the outcome   _____   _____

      7. Revise and repeat the above steps (except "a") if the desired outcome is not attained   _____   _____

3. Support materials: (Check one)

   Instructions only _____ Brief manual _____ Extensive manual _____
   Comments:

4. Learning Outcomes: Content

   a. How is reality simplified?

   b. What science misconceptions will the program create in students?

   c. What is the main science theme of the program?

   d. What are the primary concepts and generalizations in the program?

   e. Make mistakes with the program and see what the program does. Describe the result.

5. Learning Outcomes: Primary skills (Complete and summarize *Inquiry Skills Checklist* here)

   a. List the major skills emphasized in the program.

   b. List the incidental skills in the program (no more than three).

   c. List the prerequisite skills needed before starting the program. Note the special skills students must have to work through the program.

   d. Describe any attempt to transfer skills or concepts to other contexts or subjects other than science.

6. Summary of software evaluation:

   a. For what age/grade levels is this useful?(circle levels)? K 1 2 3 4 5 6 7 8 8+

   b. Describe the major weaknesses of the software. Provide examples.

Fɪɢᴜʀᴇ 11-7 **Continued**   *(continued)*

c. Describe the major strengths of the software. Provide examples. Also, what motivates the student to stay with the program?

d. Is the program confusing or hard to use academically or technically? Why?

7. To recommend the program for classroom use, the answers to question 6 a–g should all be "Yes." Circle the appropriate answer:

a. Does the program emphasize higher-order thinking skills?	Yes	No
b. Is the computer a good medium for presenting this material?	Yes	No
c. Does the program deserve a "good" to "excellent" rating in educational quality and program structure?	Yes	No
d. Is the program likely to maintain high student motivation?	Yes	No
e. Can the program be used by several students in a reasonable amount of time?	Yes	No
f. Is the program accurate in content, grammar, and spelling?	Yes	No
g. Is the program free from errors which inhibit student interaction?	Yes	No

8. Overall summary comment: Would you use this software with students?

9. Other comments:

10. In what science lessons or units would this program be useful?

a. Describe a specific teaching lesson and grade level where this software would fit.

b. In what part of the learning cycle lesson would this software be useful?

c. How should the software be used in the classroom (classroom management)?

11. Join with one other person who evaluated software. Compare and discuss her software program. Give your partner's name and software title. What were the main considerations that led to your partner's summary evaluation?

These evaluations can either be shared by posting them on an Internet website or printed off and put on reserve in a school library.

FIGURE 11–7   *Continued*

major ingredient in good teaching, skilled use of technology requires several years of informed practice through practitioner research by the teacher along with purposeful student support and training.

Use of the Internet in Teaching Science

The teacher's use of technology and technology software in classrooms parallels the use of the Internet in teaching science. There are five levels of Internet use by a classroom teacher (see Figure 11–8) (Sunal, Sunal, Smith, & Britt, 1996). These five levels provide a scale with which a teacher can evaluate the present level of Internet use. The scale also indicates the next higher level of usage to work toward. Teacher teams may want to use the levels in planning practitioner research to determine how the level of usage relates to student involvement in learning science. This scale is appropriate for evaluating classroom use with technology hardware or software in addition to the Internet.

Level 1 occurs when Internet resources are used to provide science content information for the teacher. This level involves teachers in using the Internet to find science and science-teaching information for planning lessons and units. Once some experience with

LEVELS OF INTERNET USAGE

Level 1
Internet resources are used to provide content information for the teacher.

Level 2
Internet resources are shared with students to provide content information.

Level 3
The teacher incorporates Internet information directly into a lesson.

Level 4
The teacher acts as a learning facilitator in a student-directed project using a variety of Internet materials.

Level 5
Students directly plan and implement their use of the Internet.

FIGURE 11-8   *Five levels of Internet usage by teachers*

navigating the Internet and visiting sample sites has occurred, level 1 is easily attained by most teachers.

Level 2 occurs when Internet resources are shared with students to provide science content information. The Internet is an extra resource for content information in addition to the normally used lesson materials. This level is best used in lessons where students are engaged in guided discovery activities. Learning outcomes best served with this level of technology use involve science concepts and low-to-mid-level science inquiry skills and affective outcomes.

See Chapter 7 for assistance in matching science instructional methods to science learning outcomes.

An example of such usage occurred when a sixth-grade teacher implementing a unit on the weather provided students with a set of reference materials in the library corner of the classroom. These included 50 pages of current U.S. weather maps, information on worldwide weather systems including the temperature at cloud tops from satellite observations, and color charts on ocean temperature in the Pacific Ocean related to the La Niña/El Niño effect. The materials had been printed from three Internet sites and served as current resources that students could use during the unit.

Level 3 occurs when the teacher incorporates Internet information directly into a science lesson. This level is best used in lessons and units where students are engaged in guided discovery activities. Learning outcomes best served with this level of technology use involve science concepts and mid-level science inquiry skills and affective outcomes. For example, a fifth-grade teacher printed off hourly weather reports from the *Weather Channel*'s website.

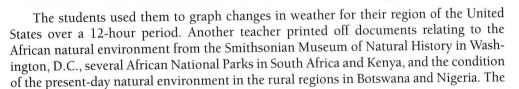

For further information on the Weather Channel, see the Companion Website at *http://www.prenhall.com/sunal* for this link.

Companion Website

The students used them to graph changes in weather for their region of the United States over a 12-hour period. Another teacher printed off documents relating to the African natural environment from the Smithsonian Museum of Natural History in Washington, D.C., several African National Parks in South Africa and Kenya, and the condition of the present-day natural environment in the rural regions in Botswana and Nigeria. The students read and analyzed these documents for their unit on differences in ecosystems. The sparse material available to them in their textbook and school library was extended through access to the Internet. It offered these students opportunities to compare several perspectives on an issue they were studying.

Level 4 occurs when the teacher acts as a learning facilitator in a student-directed science project using a variety of Internet materials. This level is best used in lessons and units where students are engaged in discovery science activities. Outcomes best served with this level of technology use involve science concepts and generalizations and mid-level science inquiry skills and affective outcomes. At this level, the fourth-grade teacher acts as a learning facilitator in a student-directed project using a variety of Internet materials. As part of a study of the world's rainforests, one group of students found several Internet sites dealing with rainforest-related information.

For further information, see the Companion Website at *http://www.prenhall.com/sunal* for links to rainforest-related websites.

The teacher often acted as a facilitator when students had difficulty locating a site dealing with the topics of interest. At one point, students found a website reporting a project by elementary school students in Ecuador in which they earned money and used it to buy a piece of the Ecuadoran rainforest that would then be held in its natural state. The students used e-mail to communicate with these Ecuadoran students, and the teacher used e-mail to work with Ecuadoran teachers to set up a process by which the students could contribute to the project of the Ecuadoran students.

Level 5 occurs when students directly plan and implement their own use of the Internet. This level is best used in lessons and units where students are engaged in inquiry activities. Learning outcomes best served with this level of technology use involve science generalizations and higher order science inquiry skills and affective outcomes. One group of four sixth-grade Alabama students studying energy resources and careers in energy-related fields decided they might get useful information by searching the Internet for scientific addresses set up by major governmental, commercial, and energy-research organizations within their state. Each student chose a different field of the energy enterprise. They considered different types of energy: electrical, petroleum, renewable energy, and fusion energy, and searched the Internet for a site that might relate to each. Their investigation included researching for resources, means of production, environmental and health issues, and conservation of resources. They found a fusion energy research site at Auburn University and a petroleum research source at the University of Alabama. Two of the students could not find a site for the type of energy in their selected fields, so they searched the Internet for e-mail addresses of university science and engineering departments in that state and requested information about their selected field for each type of energy. One student still did not find an e-mail address for the type of energy in the field selected. She used an Internet yellow pages search to locate the telephone numbers and addresses of two agencies in the state. She then contacted them via letter. The teacher encouraged the students to work through the problems they encountered and made some suggestions. However, the different searches were organized by the students and the content for which they searched was determined by each student.

The Internet is a vast and potentially frustrating source of materials and opportunities for meaningful science learning by students. Teachers can quickly use it at levels 1 to 3; however, moving beyond level 3 requires some initial experience with the Internet. The teacher should then consider carrying out one unit that involves students in level 4 usage. Once such involvement has occurred, it is important to use the experience to build the opportunities for level 4 usage into other units. The first experience with level 4 usage might be challenging, frustrating, and/or disappointing. Both students and the teacher will need to develop management, scheduling, and cooperative strategies that facilitate level 4 usage. Even a disappointing experience is useful because it demonstrates what strategies need to be revised. It also may indicate which topics are suited to level 4 experience and which are not.

Once students and the teacher have built a foundation of level 4 experiences, usage at level 5 can be tried. Again, initial level 5 experiences probably will not be smooth. The teacher and students will have to work to build usage strategies and to select the most appropriate activities and topics for level 5 activities. Usage at levels 4 and 5 requires experimentation, which should occur over an extended period of time. It may be that a teacher will work with level 4 usage for a year or two before trying level 5 usage. The time span is not important. Reflection on the experience at a particular level and building strategies for the best utilization of activities at a level are important. The gradual development of expertise among both the teacher and students is the goal. It is the exploration, reflection, and building of expertise that make the use of the Internet a meaningful part of the school science program.

Teaching science using the Internet requires practical and timely access to the Internet (Sunal, Sunal, Smith, & Britt, 1998). The best option is to have Internet access within the classroom, preferably at several computers. However, such access is not always available. Most schools first offer Internet access at one or more computers located in the school's library or computer laboratory. This is likely to result in the lower levels of Internet usage: levels 1, 2, and perhaps 3.

Management and scheduling problems arise when usage at levels 4 and 5 is attempted. At both of these levels, the students are the primary users of the Internet. Enabling each student, or even small groups of students, to have access to the Internet must be planned ahead of time when the computer used to access the Internet is not in the classroom. Work out a schedule for its use among interested teachers. Open-access time each day should be included in the schedule. Open-access times should vary, occurring in the morning on some days and in the afternoon on others. This gives flexibility and enables teachers and students to utilize the Internet as various subjects are taught or problems and interests arise. Whether the Internet is accessed in a classroom or outside, a two-hour block of time is a useful beginning point for a class of students. This allows usage by several students, or repeated usage by one or more students. It allows for time taken up by movement between the classroom and the computer's location. It also allows for some time spent in finding one's way through the Internet to the sources that are useful for the activity or project underway. Several two-hour slots during the week are preferable.

Finally, teachers must consider usage policies. Marker (1996) has an excellent discussion of developing a school policy to ensure the fair, appropriate, and ethical use of the Internet by students. Teachers should consider developing a form students can use to request permission to print off materials from the Internet. A permission form limits students' usual desire to print off all sorts of interesting Internet material (see Figure 11–9). The permission form asks students to give the address of the site from which they are printing, briefly explain why they need to print from the site, describe how they will be using the printed materials, and indicate how many pages will be printed. Also, be sure to remember to check web addresses before you ask students to visit them. All assigned websites should be inspected for appropriate materials and verified that the address has not been changed or dropped.

SAMPLE STUDENT INTERNET PRINTING REQUEST FORM

Name: _____

Date: _____

Address of the site: _____

Brief explanation describing how you will use the materials printed from this site:

_____

_____

Number of pages to be printed: _____

_____

FIGURE 11-9   *Sample Internet printing request form*

Modeling is important. Teachers should seek out opportunities to work through sample lessons or projects that utilize the Internet. They should demonstrate procedures so students can see the processes involved. Teachers and students should take an opportunity to read about and visit other classrooms in which students are actively using the Internet.

Applying What You Know

Planning a Science Lesson Incorporating Technology

Plan a science lesson using one of the technology choices listed below. Select a key science concept or generalization from the *National Science Education Standards*. For instance, one standard for grades K–4 is, "All organisms cause changes in the environment where they live. Some of these changes are detrimental to the organisms or other organisms whereas others are beneficial" (National Research Council, 1996, p. 129). Outline a learning cycle teaching the key concept or generalization. Include the grade level and objectives.

Choose one or more of the following to be included in this lesson: digital or video images, laser science computer software instructional programs, database or spreadsheet, *Power Point* presentation program software, or the Internet. Be sure to describe the specific equipment and materials necessary for use of the technology. For example, give the Internet address used or the name of the computer software.

WHAT CLASSROOM FACILITIES AND TEACHING RESOURCES FACILITATE SCIENCE LEARNING?

Designing the Physical Environment to Support the Yearlong Science Program

Planning and development of the yearlong science program involves coordination of the program goals with the *National Science Education Standards*. Classroom facilities and resources used in teaching science should reflect the goals and learning outcomes

What classroom resources facilitate science learning?

established in the yearlong plan. State and national guidelines for the teaching of science may recommend or imply general and specific components. Adequate facilities and teaching resources are needed for developmentally appropriate science investigations and instruction. Appropriate and sufficient facilities and resources are basic to providing an adequate and safe science education environment. No curriculum, system of discipline, or instructional strategy fully overcomes the limitations of inadequate facilities or materials (Lowery, 1997, p. 138). The *National Science Education Standards* cite time, space, and materials as critical components for promoting sustained inquiry. Excerpts from the national standards relating to the use of technology are shown in Figure 11–10.

While teachers generally have little control over the shape or size of the classroom, it is possible to arrange any classroom to more effectively teach science. Effective science teachers have a good room arrangement that reduces potential distractions for students and decreases the opportunities for inappropriate behavior (Emmert, Evertson, & Anderson, 1980). The National Science Teachers Association recommends facilities that allow students to inquire about science phenomena, provide space that facilitates active engagement in collecting, sorting, observing, graphing, and experimenting, allow students to work together to solve problems and inquire using a team approach, and provide for teacher-student and student-student interaction (Lowery, 1997, pp. 138–144; Rakow, 1998). These recommendations have implications for decisions about what facilities are available and how the classroom is arranged.

<div>
<p style="text-align:center"><strong>National Science Education Program Standards (Excerpts)</strong></p>

<p>All students in the K–12 science program must have equitable access to opportunities to achieve the National Science Education Standards.</p>

<p>All elements of the K–12 science program must be consistent with the other National Science Education Standards and with one another and developed within and across grade levels to meet a clearly stated set of goals.</p>

<p>The program of study in science for all students should be developmentally appropriate, interesting, and relevant to students' lives; emphasize student understanding through inquiry; and be connected with other school subjects.</p>

<p>The K–12 science program must give students access to appropriate and sufficient resources, including quality teachers, time, materials, and equipment; adequate and safe space; and the community.</p>

<p>Schools must work as communities that encourage, support, and sustain teachers as they implement an effective science program.</p>
</div>

FIGURE 11-10   *National Science Education Standards excerpts relating to classroom facilities for teaching science*

Source: Adapted with permission from National Research Council. Copyright 1996 by the National Academy of Sciences. Courtesy of the National Academy Press, Washington, D.C.

Criteria used in designing a classroom facility in which to effectively teach hands-on, minds-on science are:

- Permits easy monitoring of students during science activities.
- Provides for whole class and cooperative group activities or projects.
- Facilitates easy flowing traffic patterns for distributing, obtaining, or returning science materials.
- Provides adequate open and flexible areas, such as floor space, table space, and other work areas in and out of the classroom.
- Facilitates science community goals and needs of the students so that the teacher and student(s) can move and interact freely.
- Has appropriate adaptations for students with disabilities, meeting Americans with Disabilities Act requirements to be fully involved in science activities.
- Allows flexible furniture arrangement for a variety of science activities.
- Has a variation of furniture for student and teacher work space including flat-top surfaces.
- Has space for permanent and temporary storage of student and teacher science displays, collections, materials, and projects.
- Has adequate working space, appropriate fire and safety signs, and equipment for the safe conduct of science activities.
- Has display areas with manipulative science materials accessible to students.
- Has a lockable storage cabinet or closet in the classroom or elsewhere in the school for hazardous chemicals, as well as delicate or expensive equipment.
- Has adequate electrical outlets with ground fault interruption protection (so that several hot plates could be used at the same time).
- Has adequate lighting and window shades to allow light to be controlled for science activities.

TABLE 11–2   *Sample yearlong instructional strategies and matched special physical requirements*

Instructional Strategies and General Student Learning Activities	Special Physical Requirements to Be Met in the Classroom
Students will be collecting and sorting a great variety of materials.	Temporary storage space will be needed for these materials before and after sorting.
Students will use the computer to collect data.	Computers are accessible for use by a small group.
Students will be investigating marine organisms.	Space will be needed for aquariums and a wet area in which to study marine organisms.
Students will observe and investigate events in a natural setting.	A natural area on the school grounds is accessible for use by a small group.

- Has one or more computers with provisions for access for e-mail and the Internet.
- Has a wet area, a sink, and an adequate water supply for science activities.
- Has ready access to a natural study area out-of-doors on the school grounds for a variety of science activities. (Biehle, Motz, & West, 1999)

There are several steps in designing a classroom for effective yearlong science teaching. First, brainstorm possible instructional strategies and general student learning activities to be included in the yearlong plan. Refer to the facilities design criteria previously discussed. Develop a web diagram linking the general components.

Second, list the instructional strategies that will be part of the yearlong plan in a column. Next to each activity, note whether it poses any special physical requirements. These might include an electrical outlet, a wet area with a sink, or a workspace large enough so that safety will not be a problem. For example, if you are teaching first grade and know that students will be collecting and sorting a great variety of materials, temporary storage space will be needed for these materials before and after sorting. Pizza boxes take a small amount of space when stacked up and are good sorting trays. These can be bought or donated from a local pizza place or requested from parents. A sixth-grade teacher may want students to use the computer to collect data. Student groups can present data they have collected via a database or graphing program. Provisions must be made for computers to be accessible for use by a small group and visible for viewing by a larger group (see Table 11–2 for other examples).

Third, draw a basic floor plan of your classroom, including items that cannot be moved. These include electrical outlets, windows, built-in cupboards, and a sink, as well as other items. Make several photocopies of this basic plan, then draw different floor plans that consider the special requirements and arrangements needed to carry out the activities you listed in the first step. Involve the students in the planning. Show them your designs and ask them to suggest revisions or develop their own plans. Select one that seems to be a workable starting point. You may need to change this plan for different units or parts of units. As you try out the planned room arrangement and evaluate how it facilitates your goals for science learning, you probably will want to revise it. Use the facilities design criteria above as a means of evaluating the effectiveness of your plan.

Fourth, consider and plan for special problems that occur in managing science materials. Adequate space is required for a well-functioning inquiry-based science program. Many materials are required and must be stored. Shelves and cabinets will be needed. A cabinet with a lock is needed to store costly equipment and potentially hazardous materials.

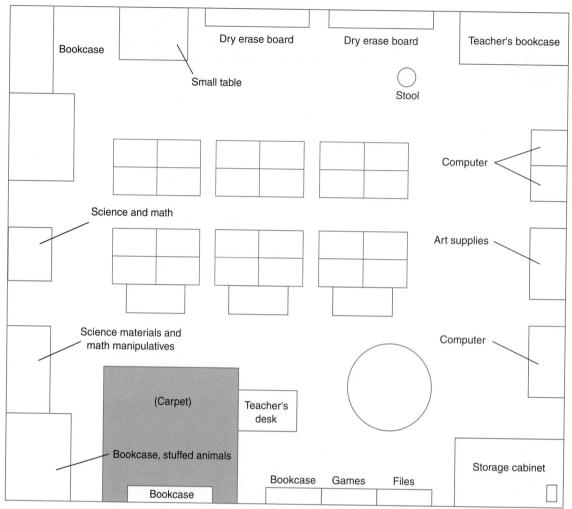

FIGURE 11-11   *Design for a fourth-grade classroom*

These materials can include glassware, dissection knives and pins, digital cameras, ammonia, and bleach.

Develop an organized plan for storing materials that will help students know where they belong when they are returned. It should help you make a quick, spot-check inventory to be sure that all the materials have been returned after a science activity. For example, storage areas can be labeled with the name of the equipment or material stored. These labels can be written or can be in the form of a drawing on the back wall of the shelf. Masking tape can be used to divide shelves into storage sections. The number of items in the section can be listed on a sticker attached to the section or on an index card taped to it.

Another consideration in managing materials is mismatched storage of different types of items. Separate storage areas are necessary for different types of materials. For instance, magnetic media such as computer disks and videotape should never be stored near magnets or equipment containing strong magnets. The magnetic structure of the computer disks and videotape will be disrupted by the magnets and the materials will become useless. Electronic equipment should not be stored near chemicals. The fumes from vinegar, ammonia, and bleach quickly corrode electric contacts. Glassware and other breakable materials should be stored on low shelves to prevent accidents caused by reaching too high and being unable to safely grasp such breakable items. Large plastic trays and containers should be available for the storage of items and for carrying items to various locations in the classroom.

Applying What You Know

Evaluating Classroom Design

This section of the chapter has attempted to provide you with ways to think about how your science goals influence the design of the classroom environment. Now, let's take a closer look at a sample fourth-grade classroom.

Study the arrangement of the classroom in Figure 11–11 using the criteria stated above and your local, state, and national science standards. What advantages and disadvantages do you see in this classroom design for teaching hands-on, minds-on science?

Applying What You Know

Using Criteria for Effective Science Classroom Design

This activity is designed to involve you in thinking about how the facilities enhance science teaching in a particular classroom. Visit a classroom in a local elementary or middle school. Conduct an interview with a teacher to find out how conducive the facilities are to teaching science. This activity can be done in groups of two to four. Evaluate each of the following items using a scale of 1 (low) to 5 (high) based on your observations and discussion with the teacher.

Criteria Useful in Designing a Classroom to Effectively Teach Science

Assessment Ranking Criterion

(1, 2, 3, 4, or 5)

_____ 1. The classroom design enables students and teachers to move and interact freely.

_____ 2. The classroom design provides for whole class and cooperative group science activities or projects.

_____ 3. The classroom design permits easy monitoring of students during science activities.

_____ 4. The classroom design allows a flexible furniture arrangement adaptable to a variety of science activities.

_____ 5. The classroom design has adaptations for students with disabilities so they can be fully involved in science activities.

_____ 6. The classroom design facilitates easy flowing traffic patterns for distributing, obtaining, or returning science materials.

_____ 7. The classroom design avoids congested areas such as at laboratory stations, demonstration tables, and work areas.

(continued)

_____ 8. The classroom design has space for permanent and temporary storage of student and teacher science collections, materials, and projects.

_____ 9. The classroom design has adequate working space for the safe conduct of science activities.

_____ 10. The classroom design has display areas with manipulative science materials accessible to students.

_____ 11. The classroom design has a lockable storage cabinet or closet in the classroom or elsewhere in the school for hazardous chemicals and for delicate or expensive equipment.

_____ 12. The classroom design has electrical outlets with ground fault interruption protection.

_____ 13. The classroom design has one or more computers with provisions for electronic communications.

_____ 14. The classroom design has a wet area and sink adaptable to a variety of science activities.

_____ 15. The classroom has ready access to a natural study area out-of-doors on the school grounds adaptable to a variety of science activities.

_____

After completing the ranking, you will be asked to report and describe the results of your assessment. Create a modified design of the classroom that remediates problem areas discovered in the assessment. In creating your modified design, make sure you consider the various types of instruction that will occur in the room during the day. Draw your design on a computer or a large piece of paper. Be able to defend your redesign of the room based on the principles of effective classroom facilities developed in this chapter as well as on local, state, and national science standards.

Teaching Resources That Support the Yearlong Science Program

The physical environment influences the direction and quality of student science learning. Science teaching resources and materials are essential for implementing and sustaining inquiry-based learning. Appropriate and adequate resources are critical for equity among students of various abilities and backgrounds.

Materials for Learning and Teaching Science

Science materials in a classroom naturally motivate as well as engage students, in addition to providing the means to accomplish hands-on, minds-on inquiry teaching. Science materials for an effective science program are diverse, falling under many categories including the following:

The classroom vivarium.   A vivarium is a collection of live plants and animals, perhaps on a large cart or bookcase, with which students can interact. These can include a terrarium, an aquarium, a mealworm or pill-bug habitat, potted plants, an earthworm habitat, a bird in a cage, and a hamster in its habitat cage.

Natural settings.   The effective science program provides students with access to natural settings where basic science concepts are studied. These include native plants on the school grounds, a garden, a greenhouse with a water source, a storage shed for garden tools, nature trails, natural outdoor areas with a variety of environments, and educational kiosks (Lowery, 1997).

Science kits. Science teaching materials can be purchased either as individual items or as kits designed around topics of study such as weather, magnetism, or ecology. Kits contain hands-on materials that are used to conduct activities that fit the yearlong science plan. Most kits are supplemented with a teacher's guide and multimedia support materials.

Magnetic, optical, Internet, and broadcast media. For many schools, this media format is now a primary source of educational support. Although film and overhead transparencies are still in use, the vast majority of new materials are recorded on magnetic tape, on optical disks, or are available electronically. This media includes VCR tape, audiotape, CD-ROM disks, microcomputer diskettes, the Internet, TV broadcasts, and laser disks.

Electronic and optical hardware. The hardware includes computers, television, video camera, digital camera, videodisk player, calculators and graphing calculators, and electronic sensors for microcomputer-based laboratories. These materials should be stored centrally in the library or the school science storeroom.

Everyday materials. To make science meaningful to students, the materials used must be familiar to them. When possible, use common household and community items rather than specialized scientific equipment. A plastic drinking cup does just as well as a beaker when salt is stirred into cool water. Family members and local commercial businesses are prime sources of everyday items. Eliciting their help is a way to stretch tight school budgets. When asked by letter, phone call, or classroom newsletter announcement, many family members and businesses will contribute what they can. Examples of everyday materials useful in science are small jars, plastic cups, straws, empty cans, string, shoeboxes and pizza boxes, baking soda, food dyes, nails, screws, wire, batteries, various-sized containers, food items, batteries, and plastic bags.

Science equipment. Not everything can be taught with everyday materials. Some concepts and skills can only be learned through the use of specialized equipment. For example, Pyrex™ glass containers such as beakers are needed if liquids are going to be heated. Ordinary glass containers will crack when heated. Some necessary specialized science equipment are a Pyrex test tube, balance, thermometer, electric hot plates, centimeter rulers and measuring tapes, safety scissors, prism, microscope, telescope, a stand and a clamp to hold an object being heated, litmus paper for testing acids and bases, and magnets.

Student-made equipment and materials. Many teachers have students carry out projects, some of which consist of making specialized equipment. As part of the learning experience and as a motivational factor, students are asked to either donate the equipment they construct or to make additional copies to be used for future science learning in the classroom. Some of this equipment might include string telephones, instruments for a weather station, a seismograph, model airplanes, a model of Earth's layers, photographs of unusual science events, rock samples, and tapes of interviews with people who use science in their jobs.

Charts, posters, and graphs. These materials offer a needed dimension to teaching science. They demonstrate how to communicate complex ideas to a large number of people. They integrate mathematics, language arts, and even social studies with science. There are many examples that are free for educational use. Attending a state or regional science education conference is an excellent way to obtain charts, posters, and graphs for use in the classroom. These materials can be used during a lesson, as part of the instructional media, as a reference, or as a learning center. Examples of some sources for these materials are given in the National Science Teachers Association quarterly newsletter, *NSTA Reports*.

Government agencies are another good source for information and can be accessed through the Internet or by letter. The U.S. Department of Energy, U.S. Geological Survey, and NASA Teachers' Centers are all sources of these materials.

Student magazines.   There are several children's magazines that can be used for science instruction. Among these are *Chickadee, Connect, Discover, Dolphin Log, Kid City, Kids Discover, National Geographic World, National Wildlife, Odyssey, Owl, Ranger Rick, Science Land, Science Weekly, SuperScience Blue, SuperScience Red, 3-2-1 Contact, WonderScience, Your Big Backyard,* and *Zoobooks.*

Resources for Science Teaching

Obtaining Science Supplies

Individual science supplies, science kits, computer software and hardware, as well as books providing ideas for inquiry activities are available from a variety of sources. Locally, family members, the community's environment, and the school grounds all provide excellent sources for science supplies. These local sources are also effective in creating a community of learners because the people involved are concerned about the program and interested in fostering it. Another local source is the commercial teacher supply stores and discount department stores that typically have a small selection of science materials. Science and/or museum stores in shopping malls are other local resources. Science print materials, computer software, and CD-ROMs are available in computer stores and many bookstores. Government agencies, including local offices of state and national agencies, are a source of print materials, CD-ROMs, maps, and charts. These agencies include the local extension agent's office, an office of the U.S. Soil Conservation Service, the office of the ranger in charge of a nearby national forest, a local or state National Aeronautics and Space Administration (NASA) teacher resource center, and an office of the state fisheries service.

Many other stores and businesses are local sources of science materials. For example, dry ice is often available from a dairy or food processing plant. Toys illustrating science concepts are found in discount stores. Simple scientific equipment such as microscopes, thermometers, and magnets are found in large discount stores and in toy stores. Many biological materials can be obtained from the local community environment. They can also be found in the supermarket. Samples of vegetables, fruits, grains, and animal parts (for example, a chicken wing to demonstrate muscle functions or bones to demonstrate the skeletal structure of the chicken wing). A local television and radio station is often willing to provide clips of weather broadcasts or a weather forecaster who will come to the classroom as a guest speaker. Teachers may make copies of many science programs broadcast for use in their classroom (see the information later in this chapter on permitted copying).

There are many sources that are nationally or internationally based. The Internet provides access to sources for science materials that are not local. A useful starting point on the Internet is *http://www.nsta.org.* This is the site for the National Science Teachers Association (NSTA). This professional group has a science store with print and magnetic materials. Each year in its January issues of *Science and Children* and *Science Scope,* NSTA publishes an annual companion resource guide of science-teaching materials. This is the most comprehensive guide to science materials sources available. Check the school library or a university library for this resource.

For further information, see the Companion Website at *http://www.prenhall.com/sunal* for links to the National Science Teachers Association, *Science and Children,* and *Science Scope* websites.

Professional organizations serve as sources for science teaching. Membership in a science-related professional organization opens up lots of opportunities for identifying and obtaining science materials as well as ideas for teaching and professional relationships with other effective teachers of science. The National Science Teachers Association and the School Science and Mathematics Association are two leading professional organizations that provide assistance in teaching all areas of science. The National Science Teachers Association may be contacted at 1840 Wilson Blvd., Arlington, VA 22201. The School Science and Mathematics Association may be contacted at Bloomsburg University, Bloomsburg, PA 17815.

Science textbook supply companies provide extensive materials for teaching science at the K–8 level. Some of the programs available that enhance an inquiry-based program are (see Figure 11–12): *Chemicals, Health, Environment and Me* (CHEM) from Lawrence

---

Chemicals, Health, Environment and Me (CHEM)
   Lawrence Hall of Science
   University of California at Berkeley
   Berkeley, CA 94720
   510-642-8718
   http://lhsinfo@uclink.berkeley.edu

Foundations and Challenges to Encourage Technology-based Science (FACETS)
   American Chemical Society
   Education Division
   1155 Sixteenth Street, NW
   Washington, D.C. 20036
   202-872-4076

Full Option Science System (FOSS)
   Delta Education, Inc.
   5 Hudson Park Drive
   Hudson, NH 03051
   800-258-1302
            or
   80 Northwest Blvd.
   P. O. Box 3000
   Nashua, NH 03061-3000
   800-442-5444

Great Explorations in Math and Science (GEMS)
   Lawrence Hall of Science
   University of California at Berkeley
   Berkeley, CA 94720
   510-642-7771
   http://lhsinfo@uclink.berkeley.edu

Life Lab and Physical Science Program
   Videodiscovery
   1700 Westlake Avenue N. Suite 600
   Seattle, WA 98109
   800-548-3472
   http://lifelab@eworld.com

Science and Technology for Children (STC)
   Smithsonian Institution
   Carolina Biological Supply Company
   2700 York Road
   Burlington, NC 27215
   800-334-5551

Science Curriculum Improvement Study 3 (SCIS3)
   Delta Education
   12 Simon Street
   P. O. Box 300
   Nashua, NH 03061
   800-258-1302
   http://www.delta-ed.com

Science for Life and Living (BSCS)
   Biological Science Curriculum Study
   Pikes Peak Research Park
   5415 Mark Dabling Blvd.
   Colorado Springs, CO 80918
   800-542-6657
   http://cmonson@cc.colorado.edu

Links to companies with website addresses can be found on the Companion Website that accompanies this text at *http://www.prenhall.com/sunal*

Companion Website

FIGURE 11-12   *Sample of publishers of K–8 science programs that focus on inquiry science learning*

**BROADCAST MEDIA AND COMPUTER COPYRIGHT LAW:
WHAT YOU CAN AND CANNOT DO**

Broadcast Media

What can you do?

1. You can make a videotape or audiotape copy of a broadcast for educational uses.
2. The taped copy can be kept for 45 calendar days and must be erased at the end of this period.
3. You can ask your media center or school system media coordinator to record a program for you.
4. The taped program can be used once in your classroom during the first 10 school days of the 45 calendar day period. It can be shown in its entirety or in part according to the instructional objectives.
5. The taped program can be used for student review as a second use during the 45 calendar day period.
6. School staff may view or listen to the program several times during the 45 calendar day period.
7. Several additional copies can be made of the program for educational purposes. These copies must be erased when the original taped copy is erased.
8. If you want to keep the copy longer than the 45 calendar day period, permission must be obtained from the copyright holder.

What you cannot do.

1. You cannot change the original content of the program.
2. When the program is used, you cannot skip the copyright notice in the program.
3. You cannot videotape premium broadcast channels without prior permission.

Computer Programs

What can you do?

1. You can make one backup copy of a computer program.
2. You can adapt a computer program to another language if such an adaptation does not already exist.
3. You can add changes to the program so that it better fits your instructional needs.

What you cannot do.

You cannot make additional copies other than the single backup copy of the computer program.

FIGURE 11–13   *Copyright law for broadcast media and computer programs*

Hall of Science; *Foundations and Challenges to Encourage Technology-based Science* (FACETS) from the American Chemical Society; *Full Option Science System* (FOSS) from Lawrence Hall of Science and Delta Education; *Great Explorations in Math and Science* (GEMS) from Lawrence Hall of Science; *Life Lab and Physical Science Program* from Videodiscovery; *Science and Technology for Children* (STC) from the Smithsonian Institution; *Science Curriculum Improvement Study 3* (SCIS3) from Delta Education; and *Science for Life and Living* (BSCS) from Biological Science Curriculum Study.

The science supply companies offer an enormous range of materials and equipment for science teaching. Three major supply companies are: (1) Carolina Biological Supply Company at 2700 York Rd., Burlington, NC 27215, (2) Delta Education at 80 Northwest Blvd. P. O. Box 3000, Nashua, NH 03061-3000, 800-442-5444 and (3) Flinn Scientific, Inc. at 131 Flinn St., P. O. Box 219, Batavia, IL 60510.

For further information, see links to the Carolina Biological Supply Company, Delta Education and Flinn Scientific websites on the Companion Website at *http://www.prenhall.com/sunal*

Copyrighted broadcast radio and television programs can be used in an educational setting. However, there are some limitations placed on such use. Figure 11–13 describes what you can and cannot do. Computer programs also have some restrictions on their use (see Figure 11–13). Purchased educational videotapes and computer programs can be used as many times as a teacher wishes in an instructional setting for educational purposes. Many CD-ROMs and other multimedia software packages developed for use in schools usually include permission and a license to use them in an instructional setting. Also, they usually permit modification of the contents for instructional purposes. Teachers should check the copyright notice on the material to make sure such permission is granted before using any CD-ROM.

Applying What You Know

Legal Use of Software

Access an educational CD-ROM or other multimedia software package. Determine your legal rights in using this material for a classroom science lesson. Report:

  the name of the material
  publisher
  a brief description of the material
  its legal uses in the classroom

SUMMARY

An effective science program requires good planning and management of facilities, technology, and science resources. Although state and national guidelines aid in planning a yearlong science program, the classroom teacher has the responsibility of creating the program. The teacher must consider many factors in this process. Having a basic set of criteria facilitates the decision-making process. Science materials are a critical component of the yearlong science program plan. They range from a bottle of vinegar to a laser disk player. Newer technologies such as digital cameras have a great potential for use in a meaningful science program. Planning is vitally important. If a teacher does not plan for using a digital camera, or even a simple item such as vinegar, as a key component in a unit, then the time may never be found to use these items as part of the science experience. During the school year, teachers are often too busy and have too many pressing demands to sit back and plan carefully. Advance yearlong planning saves time during the school year and produces a better coordinated, fuller, and more meaningful science program.

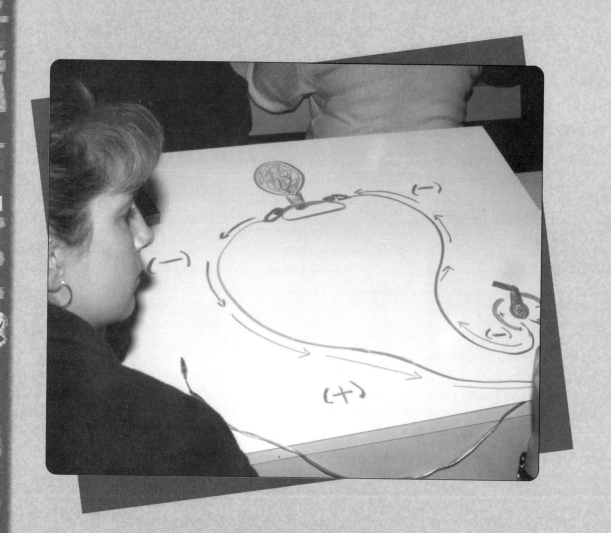

chapter

12

Starting Points in Teaching Science

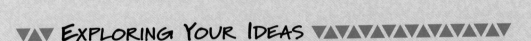

▼▲▼ EXPLORING YOUR IDEAS ▼▲▼▲▼▲▼▲▼▲▼▲▼▲▼

Evaluate the beginning or Exploration phase of one of your previously written lesson plans, or use one found in Chapters 13, 14, or 15. Consider the appropriateness of the questions in the lesson plan. If possible, work with a partner on this activity. You may wish to do two lesson plans, yours and your partner's. Answer the questions below:

1. Where in the lesson plan did teacher questions occur? What questions are suggested or inferred in the beginning of the lesson?
2. Do the questions in question 1 above enable students to elicit their prior knowledge? While some recall questions may be useful, they should not be the main focus of a well written Exploration phase. Provide evidence supporting your evaluation.

Chapter Objectives

1. Describe the characteristics of students' alternative conceptions.
2. Describe the means by which students' alternative conceptions can be identified.
3. Identify and describe decision points encountered by a teacher when planning lessons and units aimed at helping students reconstruct alternative conceptions so that they more accurately represent scientific ideas.
4. Describe the purpose and the characteristics of a discrepant event activity.
5. Describe the instructional and curricular implications of effectively using students' prior knowledge in teaching science.

WHAT ARE ALTERNATIVE CONCEPTIONS?

Before students experience any classroom teaching in science, they have created their own ideas to explain and predict everyday phenomena to their satisfaction. When students are presented with ideas in science lessons, they make them fit into their own preconceived ideas. The result may be a mix of taught science and intuitive science. In order to facilitate meaningful learning during classroom science lessons, many existing ideas must be changed. New ideas must be connected to existing knowledge, which requires a willingness and an effort on the part of students. Teaching involves helping students construct meaning for those ideas for which there is scientific evidence.

The starting point of a teaching sequence is the ideas students bring with them. When the lesson begins with the identification of student ideas, the teacher becomes a diagnostician, prescriber, facilitator, and monitor of appropriate science learning activities for the student rather than a dispenser of information. The learning cycle helps students complete this restructuring process.

The ideas elementary and middle school students construct from their everyday experiences have several major characteristics that make science teaching a complex process requiring careful planning. Each student constructs ideas of the world based on her personal experiences. The result is a "commonsense" science knowledge base, some of which is incompatible or in direct disagreement with knowledge held in the scientific community.

Commonsense ideas are generally unquestioned and untested. They differ from ideas based on a rational gathering and interpretation of evidence. Other names for these ideas are preconceptions, misconceptions, barriers to learning, or alternative conceptions. From a young child's viewpoint, the world has certain causes and effects. An appropriate phrase to describe these ideas is **alternative conception**. These are not misconceptions in the child's sense of knowing, since the child's knowledge comes from personal experience. However, the ideas are not compatible with scientific evidence. It's not that the child can't construct similar ideas, but rather that the child is still a novice who is developing his learning expertise. Students' alternative conceptions have common characteristics:

1. Students' alternative conceptions are inconsistent with the conceptions held by experts.
2. Similar alternative conceptions are usually held by many students.
3. Students' alternative conceptions are highly resistant to change by traditional science teaching methods.
4. Alternative conceptions appear natural or coherent to the student and are made up of a number of ideas linked in a network.
5. Some students' alternative conceptions coincide with similar beliefs in historical times. Science may have provided more successful ideas, but the alternative idea still forms in young students because it seems "logical" to a novice. Before 1789 A.D., heat and cold were thought to be substances. Before 1600 A.D., Earth was thought to revolve around the sun. Today, many of our students still bring these ideas to the classroom.

Why aren't these alternative conceptions obvious to teachers? There are several reasons. Students have learned various ways to keep their alternative conceptions from being challenged. Teachers only occasionally probe the depths of students' knowledge of a concept or generalization. Rarely are students asked to apply or transfer the idea to a different situation. The traditional use of textbooks, and having students spell their terms and recall their definitions, facilitates students' surface knowledge of concepts, but not meaningful understanding.

1. Language and word meanings.
2. Personal experiences with the real world.
3. Family, neighbors, and peers.
4. Mass media—books, newspapers, TV, and magazines.
5. Schools and museums.
6. Developmentally related views.
7. Personal theories.
8. Prior attitudes and values.

FIGURE 12–1 *Sources of students' alternative conceptions*

What Are the Origins of Alternative Conceptions?

Experiences are the primary source of student ideas (Figure 12–1). These experiences come from students' interactions with the natural world. They also come from the language used at home, on television, and at school. Analogies that make use of everyday objects or events are a source of students' ideas. Students' interpretations of their experiences reflect their level of cognitive and social development.

The words in our languages themselves cause students to attend to features that may be similes and metaphors of scientific knowledge. Students construct models and analogies from inappropriate inferences (Hesse, 1989; Sutton, 1992). For example, students' metaphors for the phrase "blanket of clouds" in a lesson on weather may involve meanings such as fluffy wool, suffocating, or warming. Some of these meanings may be barriers to constructing the scientific meaning.

Sometimes classrooms reinforce students' naive ideas. For example, "The cause of seasons is due to how close or how far Earth is from the sun" is an idea often learned in elementary school because textbooks show exaggerated oval views of Earth's orbit. Some teachers also have this alternative conception and reinforce it with their students. See Figure 12–1 for other sources of alternative conceptions.

Past student experiences are often narrow, limited, and have no regular pattern. As a result, students develop ideas about the world without much evidence for them. "Mutations in living things produce monsters" is an alternative conception widely broadcast in the mass media and accepted by students in elementary school. Scientific evidence indicates that while most mutations produce cells that do not function, others can result in welcome hybrids such as new fungus- or drought-resistant wheat.

An alternative conception can also result from inferences made from observations of a single event. "The battery has run out of electricity. The bulb doesn't have light any more" is an analogy developed by comparing the battery and bulb to a bucket with water or a box of cereal. No more comes out, so it must be empty. It makes sense based on what students have experienced or have been told. Students do not realize they have experienced only a small part of the event. The battery has just as much electricity now as when it was new. What's different is that the chemical reactions developing highly energetic electrons have ceased.

Students develop one set of concepts for school and another set for home. For example, at home they may use the concept that heavy objects fall faster than light objects. However, in a quiz at school, they tell the teacher that all objects fall at the same rate. Once formed, alternative conceptions are applied across different problems and situations. Even though "commonsense" knowledge was developed in one situation, students apply their idea to other settings that seem related to the first. Therefore, it is common to find a student using ideas about motion and inertia developed while watching a television cartoon. This may include, "Objects and people can have instantaneous motion or stopping" as though inertia did not exist. The student applies an idea she developed after watching a running cartoon character come to an instant stop. Learning a new science idea based on evidence in a specific situation may address a simple alternative conception. Dealing with alternative conceptions that span many experiences and situations, resulting in an alternative framework, requires more time. An effective teacher has to help the student transfer the more scientific idea throughout a scientific framework, not just modify an alternative conception in a specific situation (Burruss, 1999; Clough & Driver, 1986).

Young students often construct alternative conceptions of the real world because they lack some thought processes that are usually developed later. As students develop more mature thought processes, some alternative conceptions begin to disappear. These developmentally related conceptions of the world result from the reasoning ability of the student at a particular time (Piaget, 1976). Developmental literature describes many examples of this transformation (Piaget, 1970, 1978). One involves "drawing trees and a telephone pole perpendicular to the ground level, even up hills," rather than in the vertical direction resulting from gravity. Another involves deciding that "a large flat bowl of water or a pancake made of clay contains more matter than does a glass of water or ball of clay of the same volume shown at the same time." Many developmentally related conceptions result from the lack of ability to reason using conservation of number, amount of substance, area, volume, and volume displacement. Other thought processes whose lack of development lead to alternative conceptions include anthropomorphism, animism, artificialism, early forms of classification, and reversibility (Stepans & Kuehn, 1985). See Figure 12–2 for some sources of developmentally related alternative conceptions.

Alternative conceptions are often constructed when students are asked to describe or explain evidence gathered in their current experiences. The personal explanation constructed may be entirely new to the student or closely related to several previously constructed ideas. Students interpret the same event differently depending on the characteristics of the situation in which it occurs. These interpretations are an individual's own beliefs or theories. Because these interpretations are mentally connected to many other experiences and ideas, they quickly become stable. Some of these personal theories are strong and may last for decades. One example of a new alternative conception based on previous ones is when students are asked to predict the direction of a marble rolling through a curved hollow tube and out onto the floor when it reaches the end of the tube. Most students have not considered this event before and construct an answer to fit the situation, such as "the marble will leave the tube traveling in a curved path on the floor." Observing the event, students will find the marble, in actuality, does not continue to travel in a straight line on the floor. A second example involves showing a student an image produced from a lens. The image appears to be upside down. Seeing this image causes many students to report that the lens acts like water flowing down a drain and turning right in a swirling tornado fashion, "Stating the light comes out of the lens in a different way. It just depends on how much it turned going through."

Additional sources of alternative conceptions are prior attitudes and values. Every science-related issue has its nonscientific components, including ideological, political, emotional, religious, and moral concerns. Some strongly held science alternative conceptions come from a concern for justice and fair play. The concepts of predator and prey in nature are the basis for how a food chain functions and an ecosystem works. These concepts are based on scientifically derived evidence, not justice and fair play. The necessity of the roles of predator, prey, consumer, and producer among plants and animals in nature cannot be

Animism—the belief that nonliving things, such as the sun and the moon, are alive in the same sense that people are alive. A child may say, for example, that the moon knows it is alive.

Anthropomorphism—the belief that nonliving things have human characteristics, such as human form or personality. A talking rock in a children's story is an example of anthropomorphism.

Artificialism—the belief that natural things result from the actions of an outside agent. The natural object was not formed by a natural process. The outside agent could be God or a person. For example, a child may say the moon was formed by the intervention of God, not by a natural process.

Early forms of classification—grouping objects by one or more characteristics, but being unable to understand one or more of the following: (1) how the parts are related to the whole, (2) how the whole is related to the parts, or (3) how the parts are related to the parts. A child may, for example, take a set of pictures and group all the yellow daisies together and the white daisies together. However, the child does not understand that both yellow and white daisies are flowers. The child may say, "If you take out the white daisies, the flowers are left."

Lack of reversibility—the inability to mentally come to a conclusion, and then do the reverse mentally and go back to the original starting point. For example, a child may observe orange juice being poured into a glass, filling it to the top. The child may then observe the orange juice being poured from the glass into a short wide glass bowl. The child may decide the glass held more juice because the top of the column of juice in the glass was higher than is the top of the juice in the bowl. The child is unable to think back through the process. Therefore, the child's thinking is overwhelmed by the shorter appearance of the juice in the wide bowl.

FIGURE 12-2   *Sources of developmentally related alternative conceptions*

interpreted or changed using socially derived attitudes. In nature, it is not unfair for one animal to eat another animal; it just happens.

There are some attitudes that are critically important in giving meaning to science; these include questioning all things, longing to know, searching for data and meaning, demanding verification, respecting logic, and considering premises and consequences (Martin, Sexton, Wagner, & Gerlovich, 1997; Thelen, 1983). Without these attitudes, students form alternative conceptions that become barriers to learning science.

How Are Students' Alternative Conceptions Identified?

Since students bring alternative conceptions to a lesson before it begins, teachers need to assess them in order to effectively plan their lessons and instruction. The results of the assessment are used in each phase of the learning cycle. Being able to probe students' prior knowledge requires an assessment strategy. When you ask students questions, you usually get an unexpected answer if you probe deeply enough. One teacher asked fifth graders who had just finished a five-week unit on Earth science to give a written explanation of, "Where does the energy that warms Earth come from?" The answers received were interesting, if not surprising. Of the 28 students, three gave summaries of a scientifically appropriate answer. They were able to "explain in their own words" that the sun is made up of gaseous material increasing in density the deeper one goes into the sun. This material reacts at the nuclear level deep in the sun to produce enormous amounts of energy and new substances. The energy from these reactions gradually makes its way to the sun's surface. At the sun's surface, the energy is radiated away in the form of strong energy rays and particles that travel out in all directions. Some of them travel to Earth. When this energy strikes Earth, some of it is reflected back off and some is absorbed and remains as heat. The magnetic field of Earth and a layer in the atmosphere called the ozone layer keep much of the "strong" radiation from reaching Earth's surface.

Eleven students had an incomplete grasp of the idea. These students stated that the sun was made of hot gases and that light rays travel from the sun to Earth. It is these rays that warm Earth. However, in their discussion, this group expressed some well-known alternative conceptions about the sun. These were the same ones they had before the unit started. Some were: "The sun is a ball of fire" "The sun is a glowing iron ball" and "A star and a sun are two different things."

Twelve students knew little, if any, appropriate aspects of the idea. Some stated that: "The sun was hot because of air or winds flowing around the sun" and "When the air or wind reaches a certain temperature or speed, the air/wind will blow on Earth, warming it." Two students had no idea and could not answer the question. After having been taught a unit on Earth science, only 10 percent of the students appropriately explained where the energy that heats Earth comes from. Forty-five percent of the students had a partial grasp of the concept, and another 45 percent had inappropriate beliefs or no comment on the concept.

What do these findings mean for the teacher? The most important things students bring to the classroom are their own concepts and beliefs about the world (Martin, 1997; Wandersee, 1985). But what does the teacher do if most of the class has alternative conceptions about the concept or only parts of the concept? Researchers and classroom teachers have found that before a new concept can be learned, students must be aware of their prior knowledge and these ideas must be realistically tested or confronted (Philips, 1991). This identification process is usually the first activity of an effectively planned science lesson. To survey their ideas, one teacher asked students to write, in their own words, where they thought energy that warms Earth comes from. Along with their written explanations, the students drew pictures to help explain their ideas. Having students write down their ideas about the concept not only gives the teacher a clear idea of what the students think about it, but it brings the idea to a conscious level so students can reflect upon it in a concrete form (Eaton, et al., Anderson, & Smith, 1983; National Research Council, 1996).

Another technique used to find students' alternative conceptions is to interview a sample of students (Eaton, et al., 1983; Martin, 1997) and to encourage them to explain and clarify the concept to be taught in their own words instead of restating memorized facts (Baker & Piburn, 1997; Berliner & Casanova, 1987). Before beginning a unit on stars and the universe, one teacher interviewed students by asking them probing questions. She found that her fifth graders thought "there is only one sun in the universe, our sun. Stars are small objects that can't support life nearby." Outside of the context of a lesson, elementary students usually answer science questions "based on common sense." The source of their ideas is experience with the everyday world, instead of school-based knowledge (Stepans, et al., Beiswenger, & Dyche, 1986). Teachers must beware of elaborate memorized responses that can seem very accurate until the teacher probes further.

A useful and revealing way to discover alternative conceptions is through class discussion, especially in small cooperative learning groups. Students will use others' ideas and words and make comparisons with their own concepts (Eaton, et al., Anderson, & Smith, 1983). The discussion should be in a free and unrestricted atmosphere. Students should not be penalized or afraid to express their alternative conceptions or theories. En-

Students' artwork can help teachers diagnose their alternative conceptions.

couraging students to state their beliefs in a positive and safe context helps each student feel more comfortable about asking for clarification in the future.

After gathering data, teachers look for patterns in the alternative conceptions. Research finds that many alternative conceptions tend to be prevalent among the entire class (Baker & Piburn, 1997; Wandersee, 1985). Other alternative conceptions may be held by only a few students. Teachers concentrate on the most generally held alternative conceptions. There may be one to four of these. By knowing the most common alternative conceptions, such as "the sun is a ball of fire," teachers decide what to stress, allowing the students to test out the alternative conception and discussing it with students during the lesson (Eaton, et al., Anderson, & Smith, 1984; Howe; 1996). Teachers help students work carefully through these alternative conceptions, beginning in the Exploration phase of the lesson. Asking students "Why do astronauts wear space suits?" and "What are the things that a fire needs to continue burning?" may be a beginning. However, time and student interaction with the idea are needed for meaningful learning to occur. Activities in the Invention and Expansion phases provide for this. Alternative conceptions are resistant to change and are rarely altered by more traditional instructional methods in which teachers dispense information and students copy it down (Brody, et al., Chipman, & Marion, 1989; Osbourne, 1996).

Eliciting Alternative Conceptions

Helping students become aware of their prior knowledge is an important task accomplished during the Exploration phase of the learning cycle. Students' prior knowledge is explored in many ways. The age of the students, the time available, and the type of science objective at which the lesson aims are criteria used by teachers to decide how to explore students' prior knowledge. Some techniques are observational, such as noting student responses in informal settings, while working on a challenging task, during student-only group discussions, and in whole class discussions. Others are more direct, including questioning students individually or in small groups, asking students to make annotated drawings and diagrams illustrating their ideas or solving a problem, and asking students to write about their view of an event in journals or short stories.

An important part of the strategy for identifying students' alternative conceptions is asking appropriate questions in a context that creates a reflective response. The following classroom scene considers the question, "What can be done to get more useful student responses?"

CLASSROOM SCENES

During classroom activities when students were discussing a paragraph in their textbook on light, a student began reflecting sunlight off the reflective metal surface of her pen onto the ceiling. When the teacher, Mrs. Holt, saw this, she came over to the third-grade student and asked, "Why does the metal surface of your pen reflect sunlight?" The student did not respond. Not wanting to make the student feel bad, Mrs. Holt said, "All surfaces reflect light. Some reflect a lot and we can see them on the wall, while others do not." She then moved on to the next group of students.

Mrs. Holt asked a closed question. **Closed questions** focus student thinking toward a recall of information or thinking leading to a single, correct answer. They may involve many types of inquiry-thinking skills. However, closed questions do not allow students to freely express their prior knowledge surrounding a topic, as in this classroom scene. Student responses to closed questions tend to be short and lead to no additional response. A lack of response is common because students do not have the single correct answer or cannot think of how to find out the answer. Had Mrs. Holt, instead, asked the question, "What other materials or surfaces reflect light?" the student probably would have responded by describing a number of objects like mirrors, coins, and jewelry. After investigating other surfaces, like paper and cement, reflection by all surfaces might well be suggested by the student.

Let's consider another classroom scene.

CLASSROOM SCENES

In a third-grade classroom, Ms. Allen provided the students with inexpensive materials made of glass, clear plastic, and various other clear and opaque objects she had bought with PTA money at a recent garage sale. These included small glasses with a raised pattern on them, a couple of old glass candle holders, and geometric shapes made of clear plastic. Ms. Allen instructed the students to hold the materials up to the light. She asked, "What do you see? Draw and describe it." The students examined the pieces in the bright sunlight coming through the classroom windows. Ms. Allen asked a series of questions as students investigated the materials. They included: "Can you describe the light patterns?" "Where have you noticed these light patterns before?" and "With what types of objects have you seen these light patterns?" She then asked students to form groups with these objects based on how light passes through them. Each of these questions caused extensive discussion within each of the cooperative learning groups.

Ms. Allen asked open questions. **Open questions** move student thinking away from a specific, single answer, and instead involve divergent thinking (Spargo & Enderstein, 1997). Open questions may involve many types of inquiry-thinking skills. They allow students to freely express their prior knowledge surrounding a topic, as in this classroom scene. Student responses to open questions tend to be longer and lead to responses to every question asked. Every student can answer the question correctly. An open question leads to investigations where prior knowledge is tested in a safe environment. Student alternative conceptions are challenged without penalizing the student.

In general, it is best to ask open questions during the beginning of the lesson when each student can respond with an answer from his prior knowledge and make public his beliefs about the science idea. Some other examples of open questions are: "What do you think is happening inside the egg?" or "What do you think happens to food when you swallow it?" These can be followed with, "Can you tell me a bit more about that?"

Had Ms. Allen asked the closed question, "What causes light to come out of these things in a variety of colors?" or if she had asked the students to explain why sunlight turns into colors, they would have had little experience or language with which to construct a correct response.

Applying What You Know

Reflecting on Your Ideas about Questions

Return to the *Exploring Your Ideas* activity with which this chapter began. Reflect on your response, considering the following:

1. Did you find at least one open question in the lesson plan? There should be at least one open question if it is to be effective.
2. Were the questions asked of students before they began their activity?

Evidence supporting the appropriateness of each question should satisfy the following criteria:

1. Key questions in the Exploration are open questions.
2. Questions stimulate students' hands-on or minds-on reflection and investigation.
3. Questions are sequential in nature so that answering one leads to further work and to the next question.
4. Questions provide students with a common background of experience and recall of prior experience.
5. Questions do not introduce vocabulary but stimulate students' experiences relating to the vocabulary. Vocabulary is best introduced in the Invention phase of the lesson.
6. Questions focus on stimulating students' use of observation and information processing skills. Questions do not lead to conclusions.

How Do We Use Students' Alternative Conceptions in Teaching Science?

To create meaningful learning through conceptual change, students' prior knowledge is addressed in the science lesson (Berliner & Casanova, 1987; Loving, 1998; Posner, Strike, Hewson, & Gertzog, 1982). The lesson builds on students' experiences and modifies their alternative conceptions. After identifying the alternative conceptions, a search is made by the teacher for common themes running through them. These common themes provide information for a series of decisions made by the teacher during the learning cycle. The decisions are made in the process of constructing a cognitive bridge for students where they are able to develop a more adequate and useful understanding of a new idea.

The types of activities selected and questions asked in the lesson are the result of several teacher decisions. *Decision point one* occurs during the Exploration phase of the lesson. The teacher decides to use an activity that helps students become aware of their alternative conceptions.

Decision point two also occurs during the Exploration phase of the lesson. The teacher decides to use an activity designed to make students dissatisfied with their existing concepts. The science activity enables students to test their own ideas. Students use inquiry skills to investigate whether the evidence fits their predictions. If the students, for example, believe that wind from the sun warms Earth, they are challenged to explain cold winds on a sunny winter day. Using a discrepant event is an effective strategy (Hesse, 1989; Miller, Steiner, & Larson, 1996). **Discrepant events** may be concrete experiences with objects or events, or mental or computer (virtual) problems that pose a discrepant challenge. Such a challenge occurs when an activity brings out different interpretations of data by members of a small group.

Decision point three, making the new concept comprehensible to the student, occurs during the Invention phase of the lesson. Linking prior knowledge and lesson observations to the new idea occurs with several approaches. First, discussion involves the words students use to describe their ideas. Students are helped to recognize that words have different meanings in different contexts. When discussing the source of heat in the sun, most, if not all, fifth graders are able to understand that interactions and new combinations between particles of matter take place at very high pressures within the sun to create heat. They also may relate this to the creation of new materials during this process. However, they are not able to understand the concept of fusion in a thermonuclear reaction.

Another approach carefully differentiates the new idea from others. Many ideas in students' minds are confused. The difference between mass and weight, for example, is missed because too few experiences are provided with each concept. Relating students' prior knowledge to the new idea facilitates learning because it connects present observations of the new idea to past student experiences, thus broadening, linking, and creating a larger experience network.

Decision point four also occurs during the Invention phase of the lesson. Activities are planned to help the new concept or explanation appear as plausible as the student's own alternative conception. Students are given an ample opportunity to communicate their own ideas, think through them, and interact with others' ideas. If the student believes that "winds are responsible for warming Earth," for example, the teacher needs to challenge the students in a positive way to give an explanation of where these winds come from. When the students cannot give a response or agree on an explanation, they are more willing to think about an explanation based on evidence the teacher provides.

Decision point five occurs during the Expansion phase of the lesson. Activities are planned that show that the new concept is more useful than the previously held idea (Berliner & Casanova, 1987; Hynd, Alvermann, & Qian, 1997). Students are encouraged to generalize from one context to another to explain different, but related, events. They are helped to extend the range of evidence available by seeking further evidence, especially for events that are hard to observe directly. This can be made evident by a strategy as simple as discussing how this information helped scientists predict the effects of cloud cover on the daytime temperature of a region of Earth. The weather reports on television use this idea daily. The students could be asked to measure the air and ground temperature with a thermometer on two consecutive days, a clear day and a cloudy day, or on a partly cloudy day when at times the sun is blocked by clouds and other times it shines through.

How Can Discrepant Event Activities Be Used to Elicit Alternative Conceptions?

One successful strategy for helping students restructure their ideas involves creating a safe cognitive confrontation during the Exploration phase using activities built around a discrepant event. The students' alternative conception makes sense based on the experiences they have had. They apply it everywhere and really believe in it; therefore, they won't change their common sense idea based on the teacher or textbook telling them the "right" idea out of context with their experience. Students also won't change in response to classroom experiences that explain the scientific idea but do not connect the new idea with their own existing ideas or provide plausible evidence supporting the new idea. If the ideas students bring to the lesson are taken into account, teaching isn't "telling" or "adding to" the knowledge of students. Teachers purposely involve students in a series of experiences, confronting their original ideas with evidence for a different, more scientifically appropriate idea. Teachers help students as they begin to reconstruct their old ideas. This is the conceptual change process.

In order to do this, the teacher helps students test their ideas out in the real world. For most important ideas, an instructional activity that acts as a confrontation to students' thinking is planned. Teachers plan for things not to go the way students think they should go (Leyden, 1991). Students see a discrepancy between what they thought would happen and what actually did happen. Discrepant events help students focus on the inadequacy of their original idea while at the same time allowing them the opportunity to construct a new version that works better in the real world. They usually involve students in activities with concrete objects, demonstrations, and/or discussions relating to the variety of alternative conceptions held. The discrepant events expose the inadequacies of students' ideas. For example, many young students think "only shiny materials reflect light." Challenging students to light up a dark corner of the room using only poorly reflecting materials such as paper or cloth mats should prove to be a discrepant idea.

Chapters 13, 14, and 15 provide examples of discrepant events for specific concepts in Earth science, biological science, and physical science.

Helping students resolve problems in their thinking about the world, and developing a more appropriate understanding of the way the real world works, involves modifying existing ideas. Students tend to become self-motivated during discrepant event activities, while recognizing the need to modify their ideas or to accept another idea. During discrepant activities, teachers are supportive in small-group and whole-group discussions where students openly and freely give their own descriptions of how they think the world works.

Conceptual change learning can have several effects on students who bring in alternative conceptions. Various levels of mental conflict will occur with the science conceptions presented in the discrepant events. Effective teachers expect some frustration or "mental tension" among their students and plan activities that allow them to safely express their frustration while they struggle with reconstructing their own ideas. Only after working through the appropriate activities of a complete learning cycle are students' reconstructions of their ideas stabilized. At this point, students are able to apply the new idea in other settings.

Applying What You Know

Addressing Students' Alternative Conceptions

Evaluate the instructional activities in one of the lesson plans you have written or one of those in Chapters 13, 14, or 15 to address student alternative conceptions. If possible, work with a partner on this activity. Answer the questions below:

1. Describe the key idea in the lesson—concept, generalization, or skill.

(continued)

2. Identify the instructional activities planned in the Exploration phase of the lesson to address the alternative conceptions students may bring to class or possibly construct during the lesson.
3. Using the information in question 2 above, evaluate the instructional activities' appropriateness in helping students confront and test the ideas they bring to the lesson. Provide evidence and an evaluation statement of appropriateness.
4. Modify the activity or construct a new one to more adequately confront students' alternative conceptions.
5. Discuss and compare your responses with a peer.

CURRICULUM CONSIDERATIONS RELATED TO STUDENTS' ALTERNATIVE CONCEPTIONS

A few, but important, science ideas in the National Science Education Standards form the basis of the elementary and middle school science curriculum (National Research Council, 1996). The prior knowledge of students becomes more complete and more complex with age only if appropriate experiences are sequenced to address students' alternative conceptions in a conceptual area. Important ideas must be addressed repeatedly over the years in a **spiral curriculum**. Meaningful understanding of the science concept becomes broader and deeper with time, and science concepts are repeatedly revisited throughout the curriculum. For example, the concept *properties of matter* is first taught through exploring, observing, and classifying diverse materials in primary-age grades. It continues to be taught in middle school through the investigation of materials using conceptual tools such as the mineral hardness scale, Mohs, or the periodic table. Science experiences help students reconstruct their personal everyday ideas so they become more consistent with scientific evidence on each level of the spiral curriculum.

The process of reconstructing alternative conceptions has several implications for curriculum development. Traditionally, science is seen as a difficult subject because it may address abstract ideas and explanations for which the student has little experience or any direct contact. Students can't transfer information from memorized explanations of how things work to personal experiences in the real world. For example, students might memorize the theory describing the cause of air pressure. They might also study diagrams and memorize how this theory is applied to using a siphon, and how the siphon works. However, students may be unable to meaningfully understand the theory because it has only been taught through diagrams, models, or analogies. As another example, teachers use moon–Earth diagrams to help explain the phases of the moon and explain the atom by comparing it to the solar system. Students generally do not understand the first model in the comparison (the moon–Earth diagram explaining moon phases). Also, students usually have little prior experience with events linking the model to the real world. Therefore, the model becomes one more abstract idea to memorize. Then, if students don't have a meaningful understanding of the moon–Earth model, they probably don't really understand the solar system model they are introduced to. Finally, when the solar system model they don't meaningfully understand is used to teach them about the atom, they can't use it to understand the atom. In this case, one model that is not well understood is being used to teach yet another model. Students react by memorizing everything, or they just ignore it all and pay little attention to the lesson. Observations and experiences with the real world are lacking in many science curricula.

How does the moon change over a week's period?

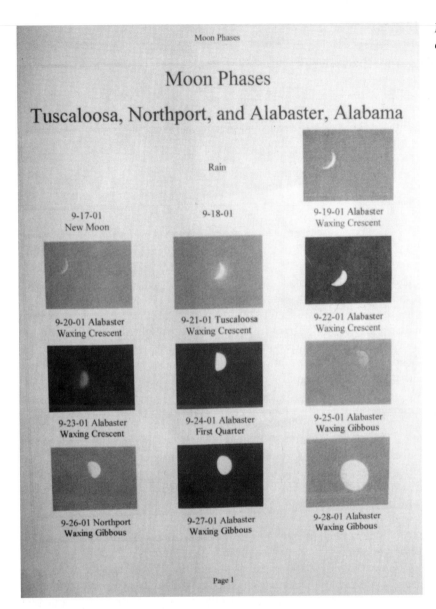

Moon Phases

Moon Phases
Tuscaloosa, Northport, and Alabaster, Alabama

Rain

9-17-01
New Moon

9-18-01

9-19-01 Alabaster
Waxing Crescent

9-20-01 Alabaster
Waxing Crescent

9-21-01 Tuscaloosa
Waxing Crescent

9-22-01 Alabaster
Waxing Crescent

9-23-01 Alabaster
Waxing Crescent

9-24-01 Alabaster
First Quarter

9-25-01 Alabaster
Waxing Gibbous

9-26-01 Northport
Waxing Gibbous

9-27-01 Alabaster
Waxing Gibbous

9-28-01 Alabaster
Waxing Gibbous

Page 1

Conceptual bridges are aspects of a lesson that facilitate students' conceptual change by helping create meaningful links between their experiences and an explanation of those experiences. All types of instructional activities, as discussed in Chapter 7, including discussion, videotaped events, simulations, and games, are conceptual bridges. Students create meaningful learning when they have lots of science experiences involving reflective observation, conceptual bridges, and explanations (see Figure 12–3).

Observations and Real-World Experiences

Relevant personal experiences are needed *before* conceptual bridges or explanations are introduced. Personal experiences include direct observation, play, exploring, discussing, writing about experiences, investigating, and reading about others' experiences. Experiences involving reflective observation provide an experiential bridge to the important new

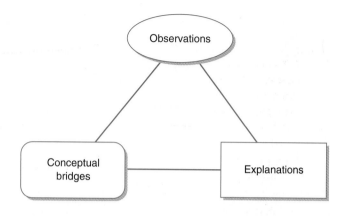

FIGURE 12-3 *Different types of student experiences are needed in science lessons and units*

idea of the lesson. Many personal experiences relating to the new idea are needed before an appropriate mental representation is possible and meaningful learning begins (Aldridge, 1992). Thoughtful representations help link student experiences with science ideas. "Observations of the shape and location of the moon in the sky over several weeks" or "experiences with the variety of characteristics of matter" are necessary to be able to meaningfully explain the moon's motion or the molecular nature of matter, but they must also be *linked* in a one-to-one correspondence as much as possible when explanations and models are introduced. Real-world observations must be related to the conceptual bridges used in the lesson and to the lesson's goal.

Conceptual Bridges

Bringing in a different model or creating a new model related to the idea of the lesson can facilitate conceptual change. Similes, metaphors, analogies, models, and stories are frequently used to create conceptual bridges in teaching science (Dagher, 1994). However, in practice, their distinctions are not always clear (Dagher, 1995b). Together, they refer to parts of a teacher's explanation in which a familiar situation is used to explain an unfamiliar, new phenomenon.

A curriculum sequence is needed in which experiences help students make sense of the similes, metaphors, analogies, models, and stories presented in a lesson. These conceptual bridge tools are not useful when presented as scientific facts; they were never even designed for this use. Examples of when conceptual bridges are taught as facts include presenting second-grade students with the idea of a molecule by using colored circles attached together; presenting third-grade students with a solar system model in which Earth, the sun, and the moon are represented by Styrofoam balls attached to each other; or presenting fifth-grade students with a Styrofoam ball with toothpicks stuck in, each ending with a small clay ball to represent the atom as electrons circling a nucleus. Besides the fact that conceptual bridge tools always break down when used as an explanation of the real world, two major difficulties result when they are used early in the lesson without considering the students' need for constructing meaning. One problem is that students don't have the real-world experiences needed to understand the conceptual bridge. The second problem is the great number of alternative conceptions that can result from the use of conceptual bridge tools. Physical models can be misleading (Harrison & Treagust, 1994).

Using Models

Mathematical expressions and graphs of events are two examples of models. Others are diagrams and physical models, such as charts or a plastic model of a human ear. The model is taught by making connections for students between real-world observations and the model. For example, when using a chart showing the solar system, the distance, location, and the size of the planets are always misrepresented. Students must understand that the distance and relative size of the planets are not being represented accurately in the model. Telling them is not enough. As a partial remedy for this problem, give students a roll of toilet paper and a table of each planet's distance from the sun and have the students mark each planet on the roll at appropriated distances for the solar system. As another example, the spacing between molecules in molecular models and drawings should be explored by students before the models or diagrams are introduced. There is much more empty space than matter in reality. Molecular spacing can be experienced through adding water to alcohol and finding out that the volume of the mixture is less than the original materials put in. In this case, the students measure how much water and how much alcohol have been put into a container. They then measure the water–alcohol mixture in the container, finding it is less than the total of the volumes of water and alcohol. Compressing a gas by pushing the plunger into a large plastic syringe is another example.

The connections linking models and observations are a reversible process. The model is linked to the real-world observations students make, which in turn are linked to the model. For example, students demonstrate the location of the third-quarter moon in an orange Styrofoam ball model, then test it by looking at the moon in the morning sky, or looking at a gibbous moon in the sky is followed by creating an orange Styrofoam ball model. Moving from experience to the model and then from the model back to experience a number of times allows students to become comfortable with the ideas and develop stable mental representations of them. To avoid confusion, the scale and any other primary element in the science idea is represented as accurately as possible. An expert teacher takes the time to do it. When using an Earth globe and a moon sphere one-fourth the diameter of the Earth, the teacher places the moon 30 times Earth's diameter away. As another example, the nucleus of an atom can be represented by the head of a pin 28 feet away from an electron that is represented by a cotton ball.

Using Similes, Metaphors, and Stories

As with models, teachers constantly use similes, metaphors, and stories because they are believed to help explain an idea and are easy to remember. **Similes** are figures of speech that compare two unlike things. **Metaphors** are words or phrases, or figures of thought, where one idea is used in place of another to suggest a likeness between them. Stories in books also attempt to represent or model real-world events. It is assumed that the characteristics of one well-known idea are immediately transferred to the lesser known idea, which is the new idea of the lesson (Stahl, 1992). A model is more elaborate and explicit than a metaphor. Some examples of similes and metaphors include the following:

Similes

- A rock can have stripes that look like layers.
- The solar system is like a merry-go-round.
- Talc is as smooth as a rose petal.

Metaphors

- An onion is made up of little boxes or blocks called cells.
- If a cell were a boat, the nucleus would be its captain.
- Little pieces of living matter float inside the cytoplasm.
- A cell is filled with a jelly-like liquid.

Consider the pictures students might form in their minds when the metaphors above are used and what inaccurate ideas might result! Students may take the metaphor literally. Much research has found that such figures of speech and thought are a great source of students' alternative conceptions in science (Dagher, 1995b). Students must discuss their interpretation of the meaning of figures of speech so that teachers know what they are thinking.

Applying What You Know

Barriers to Scientific Meaning

What meanings of words used in science lessons will students attend to? For the phrases listed below, describe at least two possible associations that could form part of the meaning. The first two are done for you.

1. "We live at the bottom of an ocean of air." (suffocating, heavy)
2. "Tree of life" (branching pattern through generations, living tree)
3. "Petrified"
4. "Noble gases"
5. "White noise"
6. "Hole in the ozone layer"
7. "Computer virus"
8. State another science term that might lead to multiple meanings with students.

Underline those associations that could create barriers to the scientific meaning intended in the lesson. For example, in example 1, *suffocating* may be underlined, and in example 2, *living tree* may be underlined.

Using Analogies

Curricula do not always successfully link similarities and differences between the analogies used and the new science idea. This creates another source of alternative conceptions (Harrison & Treagust, 1994). An **analogy** is more elaborate and explicit than a simile. An example of an analogy is the idea that, if one object or event agrees with another in two or more ways, they will probably agree in others. "The heart is a pump" relates to similar functions between a heart and a pump. However, they have different structures and origins. When analogies are used to teach science ideas, the new idea is first introduced during the Exploration phase of the learning cycle. The students gain experience with the idea at this time.

The second step during the Invention phase of the lesson is to review, explain, and identify the important characteristics of the known idea used in the analogy. This is followed by an explanation of the new idea. Its key characteristics are highlighted by comparing them to the better known idea used in the analogy. This link or bridge between the analogy and the explanation of the new idea includes identifying limitations where the analogy breaks down. Therefore, students need to talk about how the analogy, "The heart is a pump," has limitations. They might discuss the different structure of each, or the different materials out of which each is made. They can talk about the source of energy for each and the job each does. The Expansion phase of the learning cycle involves students in using the analogy and relating it to the new idea in new contexts to better understand the linkage and the new idea. This is the time to explore how often the linkage breaks down.

For example, if it is important that students understand an analogy found in a third-grade textbook such as, "An onion is made up of little boxes or blocks called cells," the analogy must be taught. Begin the Exploration phase by having students observe thin slices of an onion under a low-power microscope (this should be done after students have had some experience using the microscope). While observing the onion, the students are given other living and nonliving materials to observe. They draw what they see and group the set of materials based on how they look through a microscope. The student groups then provide oral reports on what they saw.

To begin the Invention, show students examples of different kinds of blocks, comparing them to the pictures they have drawn. Give each group sample blocks and ask them, "Which shape do the cells most look like?" It is not obvious through a microscope that the rectangular-like boxes in a two-dimensional field are really three-dimensional, rectangular-shaped solids. They should turn the blocks and look at them from different angles, including the top and back. They should examine the flatness of the sides, the angles in the corners, and compare the lengths of the sides. The teacher helps the students focus in on the living materials, especially the onion tissue and plant materials that come out of an aquarium. Each of these more readily show plant cell structures. The students are made aware that the total surface area of the blocks equals all six sides.

During the Expansion phase of the lesson, students are provided with onion cells stained using an iodine solution. They use blocks to construct the image they are seeing in the microscope. Ask them if they see any structure inside the cells. Provide some information about the internal structure of plant cells, and help students understand that the idea of the analogy of blocks or little boxes does not explain many things about cells. Cells have things inside them, including a nucleus, that are visible in the stained onion. Cells are less regular than blocks or little boxes. Their shapes vary in size and do not only have right angles. Some appear squeezed or distorted in shape.

Explanation

Explanations should be student generated from evidence as much as possible. The teacher helps facilitate student action and explains through teacher-guided activities where clarity and plausibility are needed. Explanations can be as simple as a generalization relating the shape of the moon to its position in the sky compared to the sun, or more complex ideas can be used such as, "The speed of a planet in its orbit is related to its distance from the sun." Links are made between experiences and conceptual bridges. Later, conceptual bridges and explanations are fully developed in the science lessons. For example, observations are made of the waning moon at the same time each morning, perhaps 9:00 A.M., over a period of a week to 10 days. This is done from a classroom window facing south or outside the school door after the moon is at full phase. Students begin to observe the gibbous moon every clear morning for a week, making drawings each day of the shape and location of the moon, sun, and the trees and buildings on the horizon. Comparing drawings made over time provides students with the evidence needed to develop a model and an explanation. Students are asked to look for patterns in their drawings. They discuss and orally report what they see, then sequence the drawings by date and by the size of the moon. Each sequence of drawings will be the same. The drawings show the changing shape and decreasing size of the moon over the time period. They also show the changing position of the moon each day, as it moves west about 12 1/2 degrees per day. The shape of the moon is related to its position in the sky compared to the sun.

Linking Observations, Conceptual Bridges, and Explanations

Observations, conceptual bridges, and explanations cannot be taught in isolation. Only with emphasis on the three different types of instructional activities, and the repeated use of the linkages between them, will the student be able to appropriately construct meaning (Aldridge, 1992). Figure 12–4 shows the sequence and relationship of different types of student experiences in a science lesson. Observations are the primary experiences through which models are constructed to help students learn explanations of the natural world.

All links between theory, conceptual bridges, and real-world observations should be revisited. It is also possible to develop reversible connections. Using the explanation just introduced, students practice making predictions, representing the predictions in the model, and observing predictions of the event. For example, students make a prediction from the explanation of the shape of the moon based on its revolution around Earth, and then show the prediction in a diagram or model. This links the explanation to the model and provides a check on the theory. The idea that the moon not only changes shape but also changes location can be shown on a diagram or model. This prediction is verified by the student through observing and drawing the moon in the sky at sunset every day over a period of a week. Comparing and discussing the drawings as evidence for the prediction reverses the connection, going from explanation to observation.

There are limitations to this curriculum structure. For some students, the ideas represented in the experiences and models are at least partially understood before the lesson begins. Teachers may want to use a more deductive approach, beginning with theory and leading directly to models and experiences. Even for these students, however, observations and experience with the idea are a necessary part of the lesson to help them validate the related theoretical ideas. Leaving out any one of the components or not providing repeated reversible linkages threatens meaningful learning in science.

FIGURE 12–4
*Relationship of different types
of student experiences in
science lessons and units*

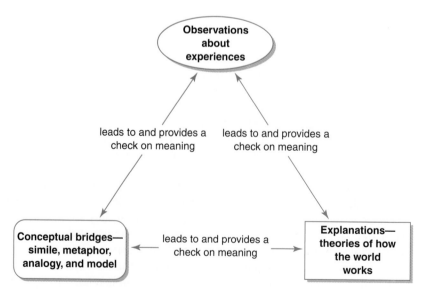

Applying What You Know

Finding Links

Respond to the following tasks, which are designed to help you look for links between theory, conceptual bridges, and real-world observations in a lesson plan or textbook chapter:

1. What is the grade level and title of the lesson plan or chapter you have selected?
2. What are the key ideas in the lesson or chapter?
3. Select a single key idea, then identify and describe the following from the lesson plan or chapter: the real-world observations available for the student, the conceptual bridges used during the instruction, and the explanation provided.
4. What links are made between each of these elements: theory, conceptual bridges, and real-world observations? Are the links appropriate and repeated so that students can construct meaningful science knowledge?

HOW ARE TEXTBOOKS ADAPTED FOR USE IN CONCEPTUAL CHANGE TEACHING?

Problems with Textbooks

Textbooks and traditional curriculum materials are dominant in many schools. A majority of teachers focus students' science learning on the textbook. These materials highlight science terms and statements of explanation. Although textbooks are gradually being changed to solve this problem, at present most rarely provide the evidence or the experience students need to construct their own meanings. The best science instructional materials today are full curriculum packages that de-emphasize the role of the textbook and provide primary learning through hands-on materials, multimedia resources, and group work.

Students incorrectly use common scientific terms and definitions because of limited or no relevant experiences, not because they failed to memorize the words. They mix and confuse scientific terms and definitions presented in textbooks. For example, students improperly use the terms "force" and "pressure," "force" and "energy," "weight" and "mass," and "density" and "weight" interchangeably. They also associate a term with the very specific situation in which the word was encountered and do not realize that the term has a broader or different meaning in other settings. The words "consumer," "producer," "food," and "work" are but a few examples. Students also link a scientific word to another word that may sound similar but has a different meaning. For example, students confuse the scientific definition of "work" as "force multiplied by distance" with their everyday use of the term "work" as "physical exertion." Pushing against a wall and not moving it is physically exhausting, but no work has been done in the scientific sense. When a definition is stated in a book or by a teacher, students may attach a different meaning because of these associations. Curriculum materials must involve students in experiences involving reflection that demonstrates the conditions and limitations of these associations.

Books may also use terminology, metaphors, idioms, or figurative language with which students are not familiar (some examples were described earlier in the chapter). Typically, too many ideas are presented in each chapter. Concepts are often shown as boldfaced words in textbooks; examples include *property, mineral, constellation, fuel, freezing point,* and *dissolve.* There are 200 to 800 concepts presented in many elementary science textbooks, and many more concepts exist in middle school science textbooks. If they are important, each must be taught meaningfully using a learning cycle approach. However, there are too many in most textbooks to do this in a school year (Connor, 1991). Important concepts require one or more complete lessons to be learned meaningfully. To do this, the number of concepts is reduced at each grade level (National Research Council, 1996). Merely teaching the correct spelling and reciting the textbook definition of the term allows a teacher to "cover" the textbook but produces only rote learning.

Diagrams, graphs, and pictures summarize many ideas. Some are clear, but many are confusing and lead to alternative conceptions based on the students' individual beliefs. Past research reports that many textbook graphs are not understood by students (Brasell, 1990). Students must be allowed to question and comment on graphs. Teachers must make sure the students can explain a graph's meaning. Pictures often have different meanings to students than the authors intended (Blystone & Detting, 1990), and may not provide the evidence necessary for students to construct meaningful knowledge.

A heavy reliance on books, whether they are a standard science curriculum series or nonfiction trade books, inadequately helps students change their alternative conceptions of a concept (Rowe & Holland, 1992). Books should be available as a resource for evidence. They should not dictate the curriculum or the instructional process. Students' meaningful knowledge of the natural world is constructed only through a curriculum that is both hands-on and minds-on (Rowe & Holland, 1992).

Although teachers' editions of science textbooks contain prepared lesson outlines and teaching suggestions, most teachers find it necessary to revise the sequence and content of chapters and of single lessons. While science textbooks differ in the quantity and quality of information provided to teachers and students, many offer sufficient structure and detail to make adaptation a better choice than starting from scratch. Experienced teachers prefer designing their own units, but teachers who lack either time or experience find adapting a textbook unit a workable compromise.

Selecting Science Content

Once the overall goal has been determined, the chapter materials are analyzed to identify the range of key concepts, generalizations, or skills to be taught. This listing is compared with national, state, and local curriculum guides. Several sources are available to help in this comparison. The most important are local and state science curriculum guides, the *National Science Education Standards* (National Research Council, 1996), and *Benchmarks for Scientific Literacy* (American Association for the Advancement of Science, 1993). The National Science Teachers Association has published two helpful books on how to use the National Science Education Standards: *NSTA Pathways to the Science Standards—Elementary School Edition* (Lowery, 1997a) and *NSTA Pathways to the Science Standards—Secondary School Edition* (Lowery, 1997b).

For each of the key ideas selected, a learning cycle is planned and taught. Using a learning cycle for each key concept takes additional time, but produces meaningful learning. Research shows students in this type of curriculum score as well, or higher, on standardized tests than do students in more traditional classrooms (Haury, 1993; Schafer, 1994). The research also shows that students using the learning cycle perform significantly higher than do more traditionally taught students in the areas of higher order thinking, attitudes, and dispositions. The professional literature and national standards propose that "less is more." Teaching only the important key ideas presented in a textbook results in higher science achievement. This requires a thoughtful approach to developing hands-on, minds-on lessons aimed at meaningful science learning.

What are the key concepts and generalizations that, if meaningfully learned, provide the foundation for students to understand other ideas in the topic area? What thinking skills and science inquiry skills do these key concepts and generalizations require if meaningful learning is to take place? For example, understanding the concepts of *solids, liquids,* and *gases* in a chapter on matter is important. Equally important is understanding the change of matter from one form to another (National Research Council, 1996). This includes examination of the concepts of *melting and freezing,* as well as *evaporating and condensing.* Various everyday examples of these concepts must be examined, such as boiling, simmering, clouds, dew, frost, snow, sleet, hail, ice, fog, rain, and steam. Examination involves observing, classifying, inferring, and measuring temperature and volume. There may be many other bolded words in the chapter, but as an introductory unit on matter, elementary science lessons focus on the ideas and skills just described. The textbook may not contain all of these selected key ideas. Some of the textbook ideas are dropped because they are not useful or not related to national, state, or local curriculum guides.

There may be some key ideas the teacher identifies through her own knowledge and research. Teachers examine their own background knowledge, carry out Internet or library research, interview resource people, and explore the topic to be taught in other ways in order to develop a broader and deeper knowledge of it. The National Science Teachers Association home page is a good start for a web search. Many excellent reviews of research on student alternative conceptions are available in science education journals and through ERIC, the Education Resource Instructional Clearinghouse online.

For further information on the National Science Teachers Association and ERIC, see the Companion Website at *http://www.prenhall.com/sunal*

Developing a concept web or using concept mapping in a hierarchical arrangement may be very helpful at this point. The teacher's professional decisions in matching student needs to the science content to be taught are important. All ideas, concepts, and generalizations require student thinking if meaningful learning is to take place. Concepts that require abstract thinking skills may be inappropriate for younger children. The textbook chapter, curriculum guide, student needs, and the results of the teacher's exploration of the topic and available resources provide a complete picture of the topic area from which the unit will be developed. This complete picture will be much broader than the final unit that is taught.

Planning Instructional Activities

The next step in adapting textbooks is to plan the instructional activities and their sequence. The sources previously cited are used for gathering activities that allow students to have hands-on, minds-on experiences with the objectives of the unit. Additional Internet sources can be accessed through a search using key words from the selected concepts and may include accessing the home page of organizations such as the National Aeronautics and Space Administration (NASA).

For further information on NASA, see the Companion Website at *http://www.prenhall.com/sunal*

A learning cycle is developed for each key science concept, generalization, and skill in the unit. Other less important but related concepts, generalizations, or skills can be covered in more traditional ways, such as by having students read and ask questions about the textbook, view a video, or listen to a short lecture. This coverage may occur during the Invention phase of a planned learning cycle or in a more traditional lesson near the end of the unit when broad coverage is viewed as important. In many cases, teachers find the textbook provides a portion of the Invention phase of a learning cycle for a concept or a generalization. In such instances, the teacher adds activities not found in the textbook for the Exploration and Expansion phases of each learning cycle. Sometimes activities suggested in the textbook are rearranged to create an effective Expansion activity.

This adaptation process demonstrates that the textbook is a useful tool in a lesson, but it is not the lesson. The textbook is best used as a resource. Usually, it can be used as one part of the Invention phase. The weakest point of textbooks in developing meaningful science learning is their lack of Exploration activities relating prior knowledge to the key idea of the lesson. Textbooks are also weak in providing Expansion phase application activities that help students transfer the ideas learned to other situations and everyday experiences.

Planning the Assessment

Following the selection and sequencing of instructional activities, science teachers review the textbook and curriculum guides for appropriate assessments of the objectives of the lesson or unit. Many of these assessments address only the knowledge or recall level, in which case a major adaptation effort is required. Based on the objectives for each learning cycle, assessments are constructed using diverse formats appropriate for meaningful learning.

These include prior knowledge, monitoring, and summative assessments. Having students develop a portfolio of their work is always a component of the unit assessment. Incorporating performance assessments is also a part of each lesson. The information from the assessment provides a teacher with a means to evaluate the level of meaningful learning that occurs.

See Chapter 8 for an in-depth discussion of assessment for meaningful learning.

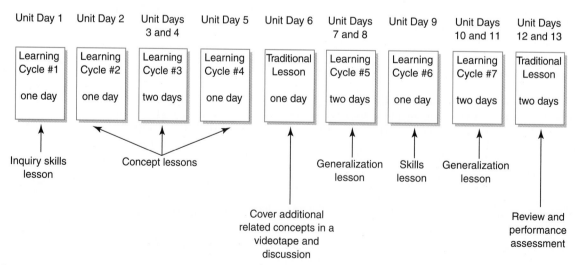

Sample Lessons in a Unit Sequence

FIGURE 12-5   *General unit sequence using the learning cycle*

A general sequence of lessons using an adapted science textbook chapter is shown in Figure 12–5. The unit begins with a skills-based learning cycle to introduce foundation experiences and connect them to the unit and chapter's main theme. If the chapter relates to static electricity, for example, the first lesson has students observe, classify, communicate, and develop inferences about static electricity in their daily lives. Balloons, combs, small pieces of paper, string, cloth, rubber, and glass rods, along with other objects, are investigated. This lesson might be followed by additional learning cycle lessons on key concepts such as the idea that there are two types of electric charge, as evidenced by attraction and repulsion. One or more lessons address generalizations formed from the concepts introduced in the first lessons. For example, the force of electrically charged objects varies with distance. The unit sequence can repeat itself for other concepts of static electricity (e.g., the effect of different materials, the amount or intensity of rubbing on the charge produced, and the effect of humidity on the electrically charged objects). If other topics are to be introduced for coverage purposes, traditional lessons might be scattered occasionally between the learning cycles.

Modification of textbooks requires developing an appropriate purpose and goal for the unit, constructing a broad outline of the elements of the topic to be taught, selecting key ideas and skills that will form the foundation of knowledge that students should understand about the topic, identifying and sequencing the unit's activities in a learning cycle format, and assessing student outcomes. The extent to which modifications of a textbook chapter are needed in any of these areas varies with each textbook level and textbook series. A checklist for developing single lessons in the learning cycle format is found in Chapter 3.

Applying What You Know

Adapting Material from a Textbook

Perform a partial textbook adaptation by completing the following tasks:

1. Select a chapter from a science textbook. Give the textbook title, publisher, grade level, and chapter title.
2. Examine the key ideas in the chapter. Identify the chapter's goal and objectives—key concepts, generalizations, and skills. Construct a concept web for these outcomes.
3. Examine the appropriate use of metaphors, idioms, or figurative language in the chapter. Look for scientific terms and definitions with which students may not be familiar because of their limited experience. Examine the appropriate use of diagrams, graphs, and pictures in the chapter. What potential problems exist?
4. Compare the goals and objectives you identified in task 2 above to the National Science Education Standards (National Research Council, 1996). Do the textbook's goals contain the basic outcomes described in the national standards as expected for each student at this grade level? What is missing, if anything?
5. Determine whether the chapter's sequence of topics and activities appropriately build students' knowledge interconnections. To do this, choose a single key concept and follow its development in the chapter. Describe the sequence of how this concept is introduced and taught. Does the sequence follow a learning cycle approach?
6. What types of assessments are utilized in the chapter and what learning outcomes are evaluated?
7. What adaptations would you recommend that a teacher make if this textbook is to be used to plan a science unit?

SUMMARY

Science teaching makes use of students' common ideas about science concepts. Effective teachers encourage students to talk about their ideas in small groups and as a whole class. Students become aware of their own ideas as they talk about them. When students talk through their ideas, they often can see the conditions, limitations, and problems involved. Students discover that various people think differently about the same events.

The process of teaching to help students reconstruct their alternative conceptions has important instructional implications. The teacher becomes a motivator, diagnostician, guide, innovator, and action researcher. Teachers experiment and try out a wide range of strategies as they identify students' alternative conceptions and help them reconstruct their personal ideas. The professional ability of the teacher to make decisions about the needs of students, the difficulty or level of science content, and the teaching sequence and strategy to be used is of greater value in the teaching and learning process than are the textbook or other written curriculum materials provided.

In order to plan and implement a sequence of meaningful learning activities, teachers must understand students' alternative conceptions. Teachers of science select concepts that are appropriate based on national, state, or local curriculum guides. These science concepts relate to the key ideas of the unit being taught. They then diagnose the alternative conceptions of the key ideas held by their students. When students have expressed their own ideas, teachers plan learning activities to help them test out a variety of ideas and theories. Finally, a series of instructional activities is planned to help students reconstruct their ideas. The activities clearly communicate the evidence for the specific idea to be constructed.

Changing students' ideas is a slow process. Teachers think in terms of long-range change rather than immediate change. Students are constructing new mental representations that explain events. This is not a process that can be hurried. It is a process that is frustrating and uncomfortable for students. It is much easier to be content with one's existing ideas. However, students enjoy the challenge, since science is interesting, motivational, and a highlight of the day for both students and teachers. Teachers provide a conceptual bridge for the student in moving from an initial conceptualization of an idea to a higher, more complex understanding based on wider evidence from the natural world.

chapter 13

Physical Science Starting Points

348

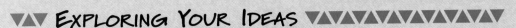

▼▲▼ EXPLORING YOUR IDEAS ▼▲▼▲▼▲▼▲▼▲▼▲▼▲▼

Describe your definition of the physical sciences. *Heat* is a physical science concept; *temperature* is another physical science concept. Give your definition of each of these concepts. While both concepts are used frequently and often experienced in our everyday lives, you may have found it difficult to write out a definition for these two concepts. This is not unusual; in fact, it happens with several major physical science concepts.

Chapter Objectives

1. Define the physical sciences.
2. Give several examples of students' alternative conceptions in one area of physical science.
3. Describe a procedure for interviewing students regarding their prior knowledge concerning ideas in the physical sciences.
4. Describe a discrepant event activity that confronts students' alternative conception of an idea in physical science.
5. Develop one or two key questions a teacher could use to create a "confrontation" and/or possible student investigation in the Exploration phase of a physical science lesson.

WHAT ARE THE PHYSICAL SCIENCES?

The physical sciences are concerned with the materials, events, and processes that make up the physical universe; they study various aspects of nature including the properties, composition, and structure of matter. They also study changes in matter and accompanying energy changes, describing them in terms of principles and laws. Whenever students directly or indirectly experience the environment, their prior knowledge determines what they observe and the meaning they give to their observations. Since the physical world is part of students' experiences from their day of birth, they have ideas about all areas of the physical sciences. In order to carry out their roles effectively, teachers must consider the following questions: "How do students learn physical science in a meaningful way?" "How can I assist students in learning important physical science content so that it is meaningful to them?" and "What teaching procedures are based on an understanding of how students learn physical science?"

This chapter discusses the starting points for teaching physical science. These starting points are students' prior knowledge about it and the alternative conceptions embodied within it. Alternative conceptions create a barrier to learning in most areas of physical science. Commonly held alternative conceptions in physical science have been identified in research studies.

As a general model and example for the physical sciences, this chapter begins with an overview of the basic concepts needed by all students, and later focuses on heat energy as an example, with commonly held alternative conceptions about heat energy presented. Specific needs that students have when learning about heat energy are discussed in order to demonstrate the learning cycle strategy useful when teaching all physical science concepts. Later, alternative conceptions in the areas of matter, energy, force, motion, light, and electricity are described. Following the discussion of students' alternative conceptions, examples of discrepant event activities and learning cycle lesson plans are given. These examples provide a foundation for lesson planning by teachers who wish to effectively address students' alternative conceptions in physical science and assist them as they reconstruct their ideas.

The physical sciences are concerned with a vast scale of complex events and continuously changing processes. Yet, scientists have created models to predict events and processes in such a way that only a relatively few key ideas are needed to make sense of the physical world. These key ideas are summarized in five general areas: matter, energy, interactions of energy and matter, forces, and motion. Selected key ideas in each of these general areas of physical science are found in Table 13-1.

WHAT SCIENCE KNOWLEDGE IS NEEDED IN THE AREA OF HEAT?

In the general area of "energy," *heat* is a topic often covered in a science unit or covered indirectly with other ideas at all grade levels in elementary and middle school. Basic concepts covered in heat units in textbooks, state curricula, national standards, and teacher-made lessons include the following:

Primary-age students (grades K–2) should have had experience with, and understand, the following:

1. Materials can be described by physical properties related to heat. These properties include:
   - How hot an object is to the touch.
   - How long it stays hot.
   - How long it stays cold.

TABLE 13-1   *Examples of key ideas in the general areas of physical science*

Nature and Structure of Matter	Energy	Interactions of Energy and Matter	Force	Motion
Early Childhood: Grades K–2				
Objects have many observable properties.	Light can be reflected (by a mirror), refracted (by a lens), or absorbed (by an object).	Materials can exist in different states—solid, liquid, and gas.	Pushing and pulling can change the position and motion of objects.	The position of an object can be described by locating it relative to another object.
Middle Childhood: Grades 3–8				
A substance has characteristic properties such as melting point, boiling point, density, and solubility.	Light interacts with substances during transmission (as in refraction), absorption (as in color change), and scattering (as in a mirror).	Substances react chemically in characteristic ways with other substances to form new substances with different properties.	A moving object that has no forces on it continues to move at a constant speed in a straight line.	The motion of an object can be described by its position, direction, and speed.

2. Heating and cooling cause changes in materials. The point at which materials change states has a name. These changes include:
   - Solids to liquids (*melting*)
   - Liquids to solids (*freezing*)
   - Gases to liquids (*condensation*)
   - Liquids to gases (*evaporation*)

   Each transformation is a fully reversible process that is repeatable. It never wears out if energy is available from, or to, the environment.
3. At the same temperature, different materials are in different states. At room temperature, only some materials are in a liquid state (e.g., water and oil). At a temperature lower than room temperature, fewer materials are in a liquid state (e.g., frozen water).
4. The senses can be used to observe the "temperature" of materials. The sense of touch can be used with a variety of temperatures, materials, and situations. The other senses should also be used: hearing (e.g., ice cracking when melting), sight (e.g., boiling water and rising steam), smell (e.g., perfume turning from a liquid to an invisible gas), and taste (e.g., dissolved materials in liquids and fruit juice popsicles still taste sweet even though they are frozen).
5. Heat energy can be transferred to or from an object by conduction, convection, or radiation. Students need to have many experiences with a wide variety of materials undergoing heat transformation. When cooler things are put with warmer things, both change. The warm ones lose heat energy and the cool ones gain heat energy.
6. Heat energy is produced during a variety of events through mechanical action (transforming motion energy into heat energy). Rubbing blocks of wood together or rubbing wood on cement are instances when mechanical action can be used to turn motion energy into heat energy. Other events producing heat energy are burning paper or a candle, mixing vinegar and baking soda, and turning on an electric light using a simple electric circuit with a battery, bulb, and wire.

TABLE 13-2   *Examples of changes in materials caused by heating and cooling*

Transfer	Effect	Example	Transformation Name
Heat into material	Solid changing to liquid.	Wax becoming a liquid.	Melt
Heat out of material	Liquid changing to solid.	Water changing into ice.	Freeze
Heat into material	Liquid changing to gas.	Water disappearing on a glass (water bubbling on a stove burner).	Evaporate
Heat out of material	Gas changing to liquid.	Water appearing on the outside of a cold glass.	Condense
Heat into material	Solid changing directly to gas.	Ice on a windshield disappearing without a trace of water (dry ice, frozen carbon dioxide, disappearing on a table).	Sublime
Heat out of material	Gas changing directly to a solid.	Frost appearing on a cold window without first appearing as water.	Sublime (frost creation)

Elementary and middle school students (grades 3–8) should have had experience with, and understand, the following:

1. Objects can be described qualitatively and quantitatively in terms of their heat properties:
   • Temperature.
   • Heat capacity.
   • State of matter.
   Heating and cooling cause changes in materials. Each transformation has a name. These changes are investigated by describing, measuring, recording, and graphing. The changes include the relationships between the transfer of heat into or out of a material, and changes produced by that transfer (see Table 13-2).
   Energy is given off to the environment during phase changes from gas to liquid to solid. Extra energy is needed from the environment for phase changes from a solid to a liquid to a gas.
2. Matter is made of small particles that are too small to be seen without magnification.
3. Matter is made of small particles that are held together by electrical forces.
4. The smallest particles of matter (atoms and molecules) are constantly moving.
5. **Temperature** is a measure of the average rate of motion, or speed, of the smallest particles of matter (atoms and molecules). Temperature is measured with a thermometer that indicates the amount of motion or speed energy each particle has. An increase in speed causes the average distance between particles to increase. This is seen in everyday life as the expansion of matter upon heating. Thus, liquids will rise as seen in an enclosed thermometer column.
6. Faster-moving small particles of matter have more energy of motion than slower-moving particles.
7. The **total internal energy** of an object is the sum of the energy of motion contained in all its particles. It is the total energy of an object that can be transferred out of the object.

8. **Heat** is internal energy in the process of transfer. **Heat energy** can be measured by its effect on the amount of ice it can melt. Heat is a measure of how much energy all the particles in an object have lost or gained. It indicates the total amount of internal energy transferred to or from a specific amount of a substance. Heat can be transferred to or from an object by contact, or from a distance. The three ways to transfer heat are:
   1. Conduction from particle to particle of matter.
   2. Convection or movement of a group of particles (in fluids) that have a specific amount of internal energy.
   3. Radiation of energy by conversion to light, infrared waves, or other types of radiative energy (energy emitted in the form of electromagnetic waves). Light often accompanies large gains or losses of heat.

9. Heat, as with all energy, cannot be created or destroyed, but *only transferred from one form to another.* Heat can be produced by changing:
   • Mechanical energy (moving particles or objects) into heat energy.
   • Chemical energy (changing the arrangements of the smallest particles) into heat energy.
   • Electrical energy (attraction and repulsion between the smallest particles) into heat energy.

10. The amount of internal energy an object has determines the state the matter is in:
    • Solid (least energy; smallest particles stay in one position and only vibrate).
    • Liquid (more energy; smallest particles stray and move past one another).
    • Gas (most energy; smallest particles are free from, or collide with, one another).

11. Different materials require different levels of internal energy to be in the same state because the forces between particles are different. At room temperature, only some materials are in a liquid state. In a freezer, fewer materials are in a liquid state.

12. Reversible processes in materials involving (caused by) transfers of heat are:
    • Melting and freezing.
    • Evaporation (or boiling) and condensation.
    • Formation of ice and sublimation (changing between a gas and a solid).

13. All change in the universe, whether biological or physical, involves energy being transferred from one form to another.

ALTERNATIVE CONCEPTIONS OF HEAT

Reviewing a specific area of science in more detail provides examples of how student experiences are used to plan discrepant events that confront their prior knowledge. Lesson plans that create meaningful learning consider the prior experiences and ideas of students.

Hot and *cold* are concepts all humans are aware of from the day they are born. Everyone is an expert on what causes heat and cold, where each comes from, how each affects us, and the times and places that they make us feel good or bad. When a third-grade teacher plans for a unit in a textbook chapter entitled "Heat" and reads the teacher's guide, she finds concepts such as *degrees, temperature, thermometer, freezing point,* and *heat* are mentioned. Students probably have already developed alternative conceptions related to each of those terms based on eight years of experience and thought. Research indicates that conceptual development of heat is influenced by familial and cultural experiences such as local climate, household experiences, and religious beliefs (Jones, Carter, & Rua, 2000). Phenomena competing with the heat concept, such as confusion with evaporation of liquids and dissolving of solids, also have an effect on new conceptual understandings related to heat.

An effective way to begin any lesson in a science unit on heat is to provide students with hands-on experiences relating to the concept. If these experiences are structured as an Exploration in a learning cycle format, the teacher confronts the students with an activity that elicits what they know and believe about the concept. Listening to student responses, directing students to listen to peer responses, and asking students to discuss each others' responses gives students and teacher the beginning points for an effective physical science lesson. These beginning points are students' current conceptions. These conceptions determine their understanding about the concept as they have already experienced it in the real world. These prior conceptions may act as a barrier to understanding new ideas investigated in science lessons. They also shape the nature of new ideas about heat. While some of these conceptions are appropriate for a third grader, many are considered alternative conceptions. If alternative conceptions are not addressed, they will continue to determine the meaning of future experiences students have in the lesson.

Applying What You Know

Identifying Heat Concepts and Generalizations

Respond to the following:

1. List some of the facts, concepts, and generalizations in a unit on heat that are appropriate for primary-age students.
2. What alternative conceptions do you think a primary-age student has about heat?
3. List some of the facts, concepts, and generalizations in a heat unit that are appropriate for an intermediate-grade student.
4. What alternative conceptions do you think an older intermediate-grade student has about heat?
5. Label the statements in questions 1 and 3 above with "C" for concept or "G" for generalizations. Do you have any facts listed? If so, put an "F" in front of the statement. Remember that when planning a lesson, the same instructional strategy cannot be used effectively for every type of content.
6. Now, look at the answers suggested below and compare your responses to them. The suggested answers do not summarize all possible ideas, but these concepts and generalizations are included when planning curriculum units on heat. Comment on the comparison of the answers below with your responses.

For questions 1 and 3, possible heat concepts and generalizations are listed in the preceding section. Others are found below in the discussion on students' alternative conceptions about heat or in state and national science education standards (for example, the *National Science Education Standards* published by the National Science Teachers Association in 1995). Compare your responses to those suggested.

For questions 2 and 4, examples of alternative conceptions are found later in this chapter.

For question 5, see Chapters 4 and 5 if you are in doubt about whether you have written a fact, concept, or generalization.

An incomplete understanding of heat makes it difficult for students to distinguish between heat, temperature, and the internal energy of objects. In addition, alternative ways of using the word "heat" are common both at home and at school. Student's ideas are re-inforced constantly in the media and by adults as they interact with children. One alternative conception is that some materials are naturally warmer than others. Teachers need to make a long-term effort to help students modify these commonly held beliefs. Examples of students' conceptions of heat include the following italicized ideas. The scientific explanation follows (Stahly, Krockover, & Shepardson, 1999; Brook & Wells, 1988; de Vos & Verdonk, 1996; Driver, Guesne, & Tiberghien, 1985; Erickson, 1985; Kesidou, 1990; Kesidou & Duit, 1993; Nakhleh & Samarapungavan, 1999; Osborne & Freyberg, 1985b; Solomon, 1985; Tiberghien, 1983; Wiser, 1986).

1. Students' Alternative Conception: *Heat and temperature are the same thing. More heat means higher temperature, and/or more cold means colder temperature. Larger objects have a higher temperature. Temperature is a measure of heat.* These ideas lead to a learning barrier when students are taught heat concepts or they are asked to solve problems related to heat. Heat is a measure of the amount of internal energy that an object receives or gives off. Temperature is a measurement of the expansion of materials given different amounts of heat. For example, in a thermometer, colored alcohol is confined in a thin tube. When the thermometer is put into warm water, the alcohol gains energy and increases its volume. Therefore, the level of the alcohol rises in the tube since it has no other place to go.

2. Students' Alternative Conception: *Heat and cold are opposites. They are two substances. When an object gains more of one of them, its temperature changes.* Only heat energy exists. There is either heat or less heat. Because all objects give off heat when they are in a cooler environment, their temperature decreases. When the environment, or a single heat source, has more heat energy than an object, the object in that environment absorbs more heat energy and its temperature rises.

3. Students' Alternative Conception: *Heat and cold are like liquids. They have the qualities of liquids. Hotness (as on a hot day) is explained as excess heat coming into the body from outside. Coldness is due to cold coming into the body from outside.* Heat energy flows into and out of objects. This is a reversible process. Younger students are often still struggling with the concept of reversibility. Therefore, they may not understand that while an object absorbs heat from the outside and becomes warmer, at the same time it transfers heat to the environment. This reversible process may cause the object to slowly increase in heat, remain stable, or cool down, depending on the amounts of heat being transferred.

4. Students' Alternative Conception: *Some substances, depending on what they are made of or where they are found, are naturally colder than others. Objects made of different materials are at different temperatures in the same room. Objects cool down or heat up at random.* Students often do not understand that substances that are in contact with each other are at the same temperature. Thus, a warm chair put in a cold room will become cold because of the cold air touching the surface of the chair. Heat is transferred to the air by conduction. The chair also loses heat energy in other ways, such as through the radiation of heat energy. A hot iron, for example, loses a great deal of its heat energy through radiation. Students often say that some materials, such as metal and concrete, have colder "natural" temperatures than do other materials, such as plastic and cotton. All objects in the same room will eventually have the same temperature as they either cool down or warm up to the overall room temperature.

5. Students' Alternative Conception: *All substances transfer or conduct heat at the same rate. Conduction depends on a material's strength or hardness. Some substances cannot heat up (for example, flour, salt, or air).* Objects feel warmer or colder to human touch because they vary in the amount of heat they can conduct to or away from the person's hand. A bicycle handle on a cold day will feel much colder than the plastic of the handlebar grip. A car sitting in the sun in the middle of summer will feel very hot to the touch as compared to a wool blanket that has been laying on the ground exposed to the same sunlight. When students become aware of conductivity, they may not understand that there are many degrees of conductivity in materials.

Students must be helped to change their belief that an object either conducts heat well or does not conduct heat at all to the idea that all objects conduct some heat and no object conducts heat perfectly. Most objects conduct heat somewhere in between these extremes. Another idea many students have attributes the ability of a material to pass along heat to unrelated properties of the object. Students may think that a harder, shinier, heavier, or stronger material conducts heat faster. These characteristics are not related to the rate of heat conduction. However, the color of an object does affect the rate of heat energy absorbed or radiated. Darker-colored objects absorb and radiate more heat than lighter-colored objects. As an example, try touching a dark shirt and a light shirt on a sunny day.

6. Students' Alternative Conception: *Some materials draw in heat so that they stay warm for a long time compared to other objects in the same location. Metals get hot quickly because they attract heat. Heat's ability to penetrate depends on its strength.* Substances vary in the amount of internal heat energy they possess, even at the same temperature. For instance, water has more heat energy than most other substances. Water will have a substantially greater amount of heat than an equal volume of iron at the same temperature. If we take two items with the same volume, such as a gallon of water and a concrete block, allow them to be warmed by the noontime sun, and then let them sit outside into the evening, we will find that the temperature of the water will be warmer than that of the cement block.

Water has a greater capacity for heat than most other materials. Therefore, more heat energy is needed to raise water to a specific temperature than is needed with most substances. Because it has more internal heat, water will also cool down more slowly. Sometimes students confuse the ability of the color of substances to absorb heat with the heat capacity of the material itself. While darker colors absorb more radiated heat, this color property does not relate to the heat capacity of the material itself.

7. Students' Alternative Conception: *A material sitting on a table or stove melts or boils at a variety of temperatures.* This alternative idea is related to students' common household experiences with melting and boiling. For example, when a pot is placed on a stove, the student first sees small bubbles coming up from the bottom. Later, as the pot of water is continuously heated, the student sees many bubbles violently coming up to the surface. The student interprets this as, "Water starts boiling at lower temperatures and boils more as the temperature increases." If the student placed a thermometer near the bottom of the pot when the first bubbles are seen, a boiling temperature of about 100° Celsius will be measured. At the same time, the thermometer may read slightly less than 100° near the top of the pot. As the pot is heated, the student will find more and more of the water reaching the temperature of 100°. However, additional heat is needed to change water to a gas, even though it has reached 100° Celsius.

Similar events occur with melting ice in a glass. A glass of ice water sitting in a warm room will remain at 0° Celsius until all of the ice has changed to water. It will rise above 0° only after all the ice has changed to water. In this case, heat gained by the water causes the ice to change its phase but doesn't cause the temperature of the water to rise. Everyday experiences are confusing because it takes some time for all of a substance to reach a boiling or melting point, and extra energy is gained or released for boiling or melting to occur. Observations are made on one part of the event and often generalized to the whole event. Students need to make and record systematic observations and measurements to gain the evidence needed to understand these basic ideas.

8. Students' Alternative Conception: *Particles (molecules) of substances get larger when heated and smaller when cooled. Particles of substances individually melt or boil as temperatures increase.* Most students perceive the action of molecules and atoms as similar to everyday objects, while some see matter as continuous, and others have a partially scientific (Newtonian) view. In each case, students provide explanations of the properties and processes of matter that were consistent with those beliefs. Students' prior conceptions differ in each grade level, and there is a gradual shift toward a more scientific view during development and hands-on, minds-on learning.

Students find it difficult to imagine things they can't experience or see, so they relate the expansion and contraction or melting and boiling effects of matter to the behavior of the individual molecules in a substance. Students with this alternative conception of matter may draw round molecules turning into oddly shaped blobs in order to illustrate melting on a microscopic level. This leads them to describe what they don't know in terms of what they do know about. The individual molecules of melting ice are imagined to fall apart into a liquid. Students apply the explanations of events between objects with which they are familiar (macroscopic events) to explain events between atomic-size particles that have different forces acting on them (microscopic events). The forces and actions of objects/particles on each level are very different. A scientifically accurate description involves the individual molecules moving farther apart as their speed increases and the forces of attraction between them decrease.

Discrepant Event Activities in Heat

After determining what ideas students bring to the classroom, the teacher designs instructional activities using students' prior knowledge and alternative conceptions as a starting point. In a unit on heat, it is best to help students gain background experiences involving the concept of *energy* first, delaying other aspects of the unit such as "measurement of temperature" and "phases of matter" to a later time. Where possible, use several activities for each of the basic concepts in the heat unit. For example, students should observe and inquire about the cooling and heating properties of many different substances. In later grades, focus on the observation that temperature does not vary during the changing states of matter. Several activities are needed to provide the necessary experience and measurements with each phase change. Just one activity in any area does not give students the time and experience needed to reconstruct their old ideas.

The following are examples of discrepant events appropriate for the Exploration phase of a complete learning cycle lesson. The activities below work with one or more alternative conceptions. The activities are designed to help students make their prior knowledge public and to create a confrontation in which they question their own ideas. A discrepant activity does not change students' understanding of these concepts. Understanding is developed over time through a series of learning cycle lessons. The numbers of the alternative conceptions addressed are indicated below and match those given in the previous list.

1. **Students' Alternative Conception:** *Heat and temperature are the same thing.*

   Discrepant Activity: The following activity can be done in small groups under teacher direction or at a learning station using an activity study guide sheet. Each student makes a prediction of an outcome before doing the activity.

   Fill containers such as Styrofoam cups with water at different temperatures, (e.g., 0° and 40° Celsius or 10° and 30° Celsius). The cups should have different amounts of water: one-fourth, one-half, or three-fourths full. Mark the cups so students can determine the volume of water in each cup. The water in the cups can be added together or added to a third, larger container. Younger students (for example, second graders) can study the differences between temperature and heat by feeling the water with their fingers before mixing. They then make a prediction, mix the water from two different cups, and feel the change in temperature. This experience enables students to observe the differences between temperature and heat. Older middle school students are taught to use a thermometer to do the same activities in addition to using the sense of touch. A series of activities to perform is written on a sheet of paper or on 3 × 5 inch cards. Specific activities include the following:

A. Ask students to fill two cups one-half full: one with ice water at 0° Celsius and one with hot water at about 30° Celsius. The cold water can be obtained from a large container with water and ice cubes. The hot water can be obtained from the tap in a sink or it can be warmed on a hot plate. It should not be so hot as to cause discomfort to the students. Students should feel the water in both cups and make predictions before measuring the results (see Figure 13-1). Mixing equal quantities of water at different temperatures produces a temperature midway between the two. Equal quantities of one-half cup of water at 0° Celsius and 30° Celsius produce one cup of water at 15° Celsius.

B. Next, ask students to mix a very small quantity (one-tenth of a cup) of hot water at 45° Celsius with a nearly full cup of cold water at 0° Celsius. Mixing these two together produces little change in the temperature of the cold water.

C. Other combinations to try include one-fourth cup of hot water with three-fourths cup of cold water, three-fourths cup of hot water with one-fourth cup of cold water, and a small amount of cold water with nearly a cup of hot water.

Student predictions about everyday events will not be accurate if they do not distinguish between heat and temperature. Typically, students believe hot water is more powerful and that it will greatly change the substance to which it is added to, no matter the volume of each. In the learning cycle lesson that follows, this Exploration activity involves students in discussing the results, guiding them to the conclusion that

Activity Step	Describe How the Water Feels	Measured Temperature	Prediction of Temperature When A and B Are Added Together
1. Cup A			X
2. Cup B			X
3. Prediction of temperature when cup A and B are added together	X	X	
4. Cup A and B are mixed together			X
5. Compare your prediction and measured results in steps 3 and 4			

FIGURE 13-1   *Student worksheet for heat and temperature activity*

temperature is not a measure of the amount of heat present, only of how hot a substance is. To determine the amount of heat present, it is necessary to know the amount of the substance, and the type of substance, in addition to the temperature.

2. **Students' Alternative Conception:** *Heat and cold are opposites. They are two substances. When an object gains more of one of them, its temperature changes.*

   Discrepant Activity: In small groups, have students discuss the following everyday events. Third-grade and older students should draw pictures of the first event that happens, the next event, and the final event. Demonstrate the event for students when they are grouped around a table following a discussion of their predictions.

   A. Ask students: "What happens to an object or substance, for example, butter or water, when you put it in a pan on a hot plate or in the sunlight?" and "What is the order of events?" Use a heat-resistant beaker or glass saucepan for this activity.

   The students observe that the hot plate is giving off heat. The object is heating up. Some of the heat from the hot plate does not heat the classroom.

   B. Next, ask students: "What happens to an object when you take it from the room and put it into a picnic ice chest?" "What is the order of events?" "What happens to the ice in the chest?" Use a small ice chest, ice, and a 2-liter bottle of hot water.

   A second example could involve liquid butter put into the chest. The students observe that a warm object put in an ice chest causes a lot of the ice to melt as the object cools down. Ask: "What is happening when ice melts?" and "Where does the heat come from to melt the ice in the chest?"

   In the following learning cycle lesson, the Invention phase illustrates how energy is being transferred from one substance to another. In the instance of heating objects on the hot plate or in the sunlight, the students may say that there is heat going from the hot plate or sun to the object. In cooling objects in the freezer or on a cold day, students may say that there is cold going from the freezer or cold air to the object. The students, after answering the questions about items in an ice chest, should become aware of the reasoning that "cold cannot be moving from the ice chest into the object in the ice chest since the ice is being warmed and melting. Instead, heat from the object is flowing into the ice, causing it to melt and form water."

3. **Students' Alternative Conception:** *Heat and cold are like liquids. They have the qualities of liquids. Hotness (as on a hot day) is explained as excess heat coming into the body from outside. Coldness is due to cold coming into the body from outside.*

   Discrepant Activity A: Fill a paper cup with water that is hot to the touch. Ask students to touch the water every 5 minutes and record their results. After the first time they have touched the water, ask the students to predict what will happen to the water over the next 15 minutes. Ask them why they believe their prediction is going to happen. Young students in first and second grade can rip off a thin strip of paper whose length is related to the temperature they have felt. They should tape it to a large sheet of paper after each observation. This produces a bar graph of the water's temperature over time. Older students in the third grade and above can use a thermometer and make a bar graph or a line graph with two axes, (temperature versus time). Later, they should be asked to predict the cooling of an object by drawing a line on a graph. Repeat this discrepant activity with very cold water while allowing it to warm up.

   Discrepant Activity B: Fill two large containers, big enough to hold common classroom objects, with very cold and very warm water. Ask the students to put various objects in the container. Predict how the objects will feel when they test them every minute over a 5-minute period and record these predictions (see Figure 13-2). Then, tell them to try out the activity to check their predictions. Use a variety of objects, such as silverware, pieces of metal, glass, wood, and coins, brought from a freezer in the cafeteria and from a hot water bath. The students should feel the cooling and warming effects of the solid objects. They should also note, or measure, the temperature of the water with a thermometer. Students probably will predict that "heat will go out of the hot water" and "cold will go out of the cold water." This explanation confronts the students with a problem when they methodically experience the events of objects cooling down or heating up. Very hot and cold objects hardly affect the temperature of water. These activities are followed by learning cycle lessons helping students develop the idea that hot and cold are the two ends of a continuum of the concept of *heat*.

4. **Students' Alternative Conception:** *Some substances, depending on what they are made of or where they are found, are naturally colder than others. Objects made of different materials are at different temperatures in the same room. Objects cool down or heat up at random.*

   Discrepant Activity: Students who have been taught the skill of measuring using thermometers can perform this activity. Ask students to touch five different kinds of objects made of different materials in their classroom. Ask them to describe and record what they observe when they feel the objects, especially how hot or cold they feel. Have older students construct a bar or line graph of the five objects, based on how hot or cold they feel, in order from the highest to lowest temperature. They can cut and label strips of paper to represent their prediction (see Figure 13-3). Following this activity, ask the student groups to discuss and record why the objects feel different. Each group should present its explanation to the whole class. Students usually describe differences in objects such as metal, paper, and cloth as due to the idea that

Temperature of Water (hot or cold)	Object	Prediction	Describe Temperature of Object by Touch	Measure the Temperature of the Water
Hot	Metal fork			
Hot	Metal fork			
Cold	Wood rod			
Cold	Wood rod			

FIGURE 13-2   *Student worksheet for cooling and warming curves*

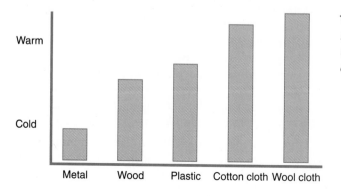

FIGURE 13-3   *Sample student prediction sheet for the temperature of classroom objects*

Group these items by how warm or cold they feel.

different materials are naturally at different temperatures in the same room. Then, allow the students to measure the temperature of each of the objects with a thermometer to the nearest whole degree. Ask students to put the bulb of the thermometer against the object. Again, ask them to use a bar or line graph to show the results in the same order as was done earlier.

The students are confronted with information from the thermometer measurements indicating that all of the objects are at about the same temperature. This result is an Exploration that is followed, in the Invention phase of the learning cycle, by a series of questions regarding why this result differs from what they expected.

5. **Students' Alternative Conception:** *All substances transfer or conduct heat at the same rate. Conduction depends on a material's strength or hardness. Some substances cannot heat up (for example, flour, salt, or air).*

   Discrepant Activity: Provide each group of four second-grade or older students with four different kinds of materials of the same length, such as a wooden rod, a metal spoon, a plastic ruler, a comb, or a length of bare aluminum, iron, or copper wire. Each group should have a container of hot water and a small piece of candle wax or margarine. The water should be hot (not scalding) to the touch and held in large bowls or containers. Tell the students they are going to have a race. They are going to try to find out which of the materials will most quickly pass heat from a bowl of hot water through the length of material. After they have made their predictions, have them rank the materials in order from slowest to fastest.

Instruct the students to take small pieces of the wax or margarine and stick them to the underside of each object at three different points: one-fourth of the way from the end, one-half of the way from the end, and three-fourths of the way from the end. The instructions can vary depending on the age level of the students. Have students put a small part of one end of each object into the hot water bath and observe what happens to each of the pieces of wax. Put all materials in at the same time to avoid difficulty in timing results. Have students hold two materials in the water. One student should make observations and one should record the observations. Ask the students to record the order in which the materials lose or drop their piece of wax. Which one loses its wax first? Which second, and so on? Ask them to compare their results with their predictions.

6. **Students' Alternative Conception:** *Some materials draw in heat so that they stay warm for a long time compared to other objects in the same location. Metals get hot quickly because they attract heat. Heat's ability to penetrate depends on its strength.*

Discrepant Activity: Provide each group of four third-grade or older students with four different kinds of materials of approximately equal volume, such as a quarter, a marble, a small plastic die, an equal volume of water, a small rock, a piece of wood, or a metal bolt. Have students fill five Styrofoam cups one-third full with enough hot water (about 45° or 50° Celsius) to cover the largest object. Put a thermometer into each cup and measure the starting temperature of the water.

Ask students to infer the current temperature of each of the objects. They should infer that they are equal. Ask them to predict the final temperature of the water after an object has been sitting in each cup for awhile. Have the students place one of the objects gently into each cup. Have them measure and record the temperature of the water every 30 seconds for 10 minutes. Ask the students to predict the final temperature of each of the objects and infer how each would feel. They should be the same as the final water temperature in each cup. Have the students compare the results of their predictions of the final temperatures with the results they obtained from their measurements. They should find that the final temperature of the water in the cups is different. An equal volume of water produces the greatest temperature change. Water takes the greatest amount of heat energy to warm up when compared to any common object of the same volume and temperature change. It also gives off the greatest amount of heat energy to cool down. A small rock and a marble require the next greatest amount of heat among the objects previously listed in this activity. Metals, plastic, and wood require the least amount of heat among the listed objects. Remember, answers should not be given to the students at this time. Explanations are given later in the learning cycle.

7. **Students' Alternative Conception:** *A material sitting on a table or store melts or boils at a variety of temperatures.*

Discrepant Activity: For this activity, students need to have had previous experience in reading a thermometer and in record keeping. Organize small groups of four students: a materials manager and container holder, a thermometer reader, a timer, and a recorder. Provide each group with a heat source, either a 2-quart bowl of very warm water or a hot plate. Provide students with a common food item that melts at a low temperature. The substance should have a melting point below the temperature of hot water, such as margarine, cheese, butter, or ice cream. Ask students to measure the temperature of the item (for example, cold margarine) in a small tin can such as a small tomato paste can. The margarine should cover 2 inches of the can's bottom. Provide the students with a cloth potholder with which to hold the can containing the cold margarine. Have them measure and record the temperature of the margarine. Ask each group of students to predict how the temperature of the margarine will change over a 15-minute period, or until completely melted, when the tomato can is put into a bowl of hot water. Ask them to predict how the appearance of the margarine will change over the predicted temperature range. Next, ask them to put the can, with the thermometer inserted in the margarine, into a bowl of hot water using a hot pad to protect their hands. The can should be put one-half of the way in the water. Ask students to read and record the temperature of the margarine and what it looks like every 30 seconds. As soon as melting begins, have students slowly stir the margarine with the thermometer. Ask them to construct a line graph with two axes labelled "time" and "temperature." Then, have students compare their results with their predictions. Ask student groups to report their results to the whole class. Students can repeat the activity to determine if the margarine solidifies and melts at the same temperature every time.

The students should find that the graph of the margarine's temperature will not be a straight line (see Figure 13-4). The temperature should steadily increase until the margarine begins to melt. At that point, the graph should flatten out as the temperature remains constant. If the heat source is hot enough to raise the margarine's temperature above its melting point, the now-liquid margarine should again show a steady increase.

8. **Students' Alternative Conception:** *Particles (molecules) of substances get larger when heated and smaller when cooled. Particles of substances individually melt or boil as temperatures increase.*

   Discrepant Activity A: Perform the following as a demonstration for the whole class, or by providing one equipment set-up for each group of third-grade or older students. Fill a plastic 2-quart soft drink container with room-temperature water colored with food dye. There should be no air in the bottle. Insert a clear straw about one-fourth of the way down into the water. Use clay to hold the straw in place and seal the top of the bottle. A one-hole rubber stopper is preferable, if available. When the straw is inserted into the bottle, make sure the water is partially up the straw. Ask the students to predict what will happen when the bottle is put in a hot water bath. Then, put the bottle into a plastic water bucket or other large container of hot water. Ask the

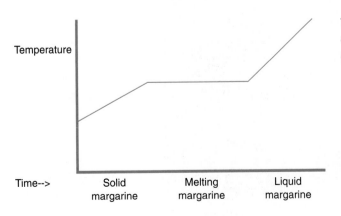

FIGURE 13-4 *Student plot of temperature while heating a substance*

students to make observations. Have older students measure the height (in centimeters) of the water's movement up the straw. The water will move up the straw because the water in the bottle is expanding as it warms; since the bottle does not expand, the water must move up the straw. Ask the students to discuss, describe, and draw what is happening as the water goes up the straw. The bottle could, at this point, be brought out of the hot water bath and be allowed to cool or be put in cold water.

The students will observe that the water in the straw goes down as it contracts. This can be repeated indefinitely, since the process is reversible and never stops. Renew the hot and cold water.

Discrepant Activity B: As a continuing activity for older students, ask them to draw an ice cube as it would be seen through a microscope that could see particles as small as a molecule. Have the students draw two other pictures of the ice cube: one when it is melting, and another when it is completely turned to water. Each drawing should show what the molecules look like and what they are doing. Have the students make additional drawings to show water that is at room temperature, at the boiling point, and as a gas (water vapor) in the air. Ask the students to discuss their drawings. At a later time, following the Exploration and during the Invention phase of the lesson, make drawings on the chalkboard of molecules at the various temperatures. The size and shape of the molecules will not change. The molecules should be close together and nearly stationary, but rocking slightly back and forth in solid ice (see Figure 13-5). Show the speed of particles with long or short arrows. In water, the molecules should be close together and move slowly in random directions, but will speed up as the temperature increases. As a gas, water vapor molecules should move quickly in random directions and be much farther apart.

Discrepant Activity C: Tell the students they are going to put on a play in which they simulate water molecules in a container. Ask for eight to ten volunteers to come to the front of the room. Use masking tape to make a large bottle shape on the floor. Place a piece of tape about halfway up the bottle to indicate the liquid level. Provide the following rules: (1) as molecules, students must stay inside the container (bottle) so they cannot cross the tape, (2) they will always be moving in random directions,

FIGURE 13-5 *A melting ice cube seen through an imaginary microscope*

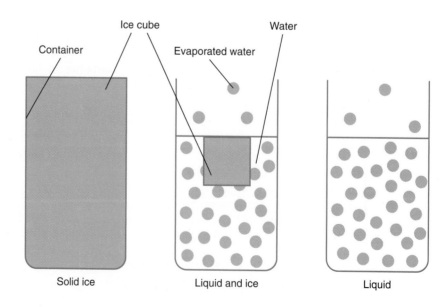

and (3) the speed of their motion will depend on the temperature of the water. You will provide them with instructions as to how fast they should move to simulate a variety of temperatures.

To begin, tell the ten students they are cool water filling the bottom half of the bottle. Ask them to place themselves in the bottle and move with tiny baby steps around the inside bottom of the bottle, sometimes bumping gently into each other, but staying inside the tape barrier. The other students should be watching and recording the events through drawings. Then, provide two additional temperatures at which the water in the bottle will be observed. One should be at a higher temperature with slow, normal steps, and another at a higher temperature with quick normal-sized steps. Care should be taken that all bumps are gentle.

The classroom observers should note and report that, as the students take faster and faster steps, their distance apart increases, the bumps are a little bit harder, and they will find it harder to stay in the bottom half of the bottle. The water will rise by a small amount as in a column of liquid in a thermometer. After a whole-group discussion of this simulation, small groups of the students should compare these results with their drawings and descriptions of the straw and ice cube they observed earlier.

The "water" expands as the temperature increases by the greater distance between the molecules. During the Invention phase of the learning cycle lesson, help students come to the conclusion that molecules do not get larger or smaller when heated or cooled. Also, molecules do not melt when ice changes from a solid to a liquid. The molecules speed up and move farther apart due to collisions. The change that occurs is in the speed of the molecules and in their distance apart.

IMPLICATIONS FOR CLASSROOM TEACHING OF A UNIT ON HEAT

What experiences may be helpful in developing students' ideas regarding a specific topic such as heat? In order to move toward a view of heat based on scientific evidence, students need to differentiate between their own sensory experiences and a scientific interpretation of these observations. This is fostered by: (1) experiences establishing that different objects in the same environment or in contact with one another are at the same temperature, despite the difference in how they feel, (2) experiences helping students make the conceptual distinction between temperature and heat, (3) opportunities to explain the sensations of hot and cold that they feel and measure, and (4) spending more time considering what they see happening when a range of substances are heated and changes of state occur.

It is a good use of time to study processes in reverse: heating and cooling, evaporation and condensation, and conduction of heat toward the body and away from it. What may appear to be a simple reversal for us may not be obvious to students.

Teachers need to plan to help students relate the observations they make from their sensory experiences to the scientific interpretation of these observations. For instance, the different temperature sensations experienced when touching metal and wood can be interpreted using ideas about heat transfer and the conductivities of different materials. Students, however, tend to fit their own ideas to their observations. Some students may reason that if the metal feels colder, it is colder. Allowing students to test their alternative ideas about their experiences may help them make the connection between theory and observations.

Students need to understand that scientists explain phenomena by describing a general situation, not one specific case. They also have to recognize which assumptions are appropriate in a specific situation. Relating the actual situation to the scientific model (general situation) used to interpret it may not be easy.

See Chapter 12 for a further discussion.

It is often valuable to give students time to understand a situation at a qualitative level, such as how hot something feels, before any quantitative ideas such as measurement are introduced.

Applying What You Know

Assessing Prior Knowledge about Heat

Assess and discuss the prior knowledge of a student in one of the eight heat areas described above. In advance, set up a schedule with a classroom teacher that will not interfere with normal class activities. Take notes during and following the interview. Complete a reflective journal entry for the student. Discuss the results with the teacher and observe the student in his daily classroom activities to see if his thinking fits your conclusions. Follow these steps in completing the activity:

Step 1. Select a discrepant event, phenomenon, or confrontational situation related to a heat concept or generalization. Use one of the heat alternative conceptions and activities above as an example of the content and format to be used, or construct one using a similar format. Consider the probable prior knowledge of this student in planning this activity. Gather the demonstration materials or draw the phenomenon or situation.

Step 2. Write a script of one or more key questions and possible follow-up responses you will make. Consider general open-ended questions, problem-solving tasks, garden-path tasks (walk student through the idea), or comprehension tasks. Ask the student to describe his understanding of the event. A good question is one to which you do not know the answer. Use questions such as: "Why do you think the water went up?" or "What is your evidence?"

Step 3. To start the interview, set the student at ease. Talk to the student about something that will be of interest to him. Begin the interview, starting with your key question.

Step 4. Find out what ideas the student already has about the phenomenon or situation. What does the student think is happening? For what reasons? What words does the student use to explain or describe it? You are not interested in the right answer; you are only interested in what the student's answer is and the reasoning that led to the answer.

Step 5. Take the student seriously. Give him the opportunity to discuss or try out his ideas by himself.

Step 6. Challenge the student to describe or find evidence for his own ideas. Probe to get at the deeper understanding of the ideas expressed and follow his line of reasoning.

Step 7. Thank the student for allowing you to listen to his view of the event. After the interview, write up the events as they occurred from steps 1 to 7 in a reflective journal format. Make sure to include your thoughts about each student statement or action taken.

Consider the following questions: "What does the student believe (prior knowledge) about the concept or event?" "Why does he believe this?" "Where did this belief originate?" "How does this belief relate to the scientific view?" To complete this activity, include a title page and label the parts of the assignment as indicated on the following page, organize them, and place them in a folder.

1. A description of the concept and the demonstration materials, or a drawing of the phenomenon or situation.
2. A script of the key question and possible follow-up responses you will make to your students.
3. A write-up of the notes of the interview and student statements as they occurred in a reflective journal form. Identify the student only by first name or use a pseudonym.
4. Your conclusion for the student, written in a short one-page paper format. As a teacher, what have you learned about this student?

A Learning Cycle Example Involving Students' Alternative Conceptions Related to Heat

In order to demonstrate the complete instructional process of: (1) identifying students' alternative conceptions, (2) developing a lesson plan, and (3) developing assessment of a specific concept in heat, an example of a complete lesson and assessment follows.

Alternative Conception Addressed by the Lesson Plan: *Heat and temperature are the same thing (alternative conception number 1 above).*

Lesson Goal: To allow students to investigate, develop inferences, and differentiate between the concepts of heat and temperature.

Grade Level: Grades 3–4.

Prerequisites: Can measure temperature to the nearest 2 degrees with a thermometer.

Exploration

Objective: The students will investigate mixing hot and cold water by making predictions of the resulting mixture accompanied with observations of the results.

Materials: For each group: two Styrofoam cups; a source of hot water (from a tap or hot plate at about 50° Celsius or 122° Fahrenheit); cold water with floating ice cubes in it (with a temperature of 0° Celsius or 32° Fahrenheit); one thermometer; paper towels; paper to make a bar graph and for recording results; one kitchen measuring cup with metric or English measures.

Procedure:

A. Place the students in groups of four and assign roles: a materials manager, readers/observers (two students), and a recorder.
B. State the key questions or problems: "What happens when we mix together two water samples that have different temperatures?" "Guess, or predict, what the temperature of the water will be when you mix together two equal-volume water samples that have different temperatures, one that is warm with one that is cold." Make a prediction, measure the water temperatures, mix them together, measure the result, and record all observations.
C. Describe the materials and instructions needed for student groups to carry out the activity of mixing various temperatures and quantities of water.
D. Let's start with a thought problem. Discuss it in your groups. Decide on an answer and write it down. Then, begin your group activity. Here is the problem: "If you mix

one-fourth cup of very hot water with three-fourths cup of very cold water, what will be the temperature of the mixed water?" Write down your prediction.

E. Ask the groups to do the activity explained above in number 1 of the "Discrepant Event Activities in Heat" section and write down what they find. The data could be recorded in a bar graph or data table.

F. Ask each group to discuss the results of Procedure E and the questions from Procedure C above.

Evaluation: Check to see if each group made predictions. Monitor their participation as a group by observing whether groups stay together while working and if each person has a chance to share her ideas.

Invention

Objective: The students will investigate heat in materials and determine that the heat energy possessed by an object is related to both the quantity of matter present and its temperature.

Materials: For each group: nine clear plastic drinking cups; a source of hot water from a tap or hot plate; crushed ice (do not use ice cubes); paper towels; paper to make a graph and for recording results; one kitchen measuring cup with metric or English measures; teaspoon.

Procedure:

A. Place the students in groups of four as was done in the Exploration.

B. Ask student groups to report the results of their Exploration activities to the whole class. Help students communicate the results of their activities using tables and/or bar graphs to justify their conclusions. Ask questions that help students compare the results of one group with another.

C. Write the following questions on the board and ask each group to discuss them and make a brief report to the class: "What can you conclude about mixing two equal samples of water that have different temperatures?" "What can you conclude about mixing a very small amount of water at one temperature with a lot of water at another temperature?" "What variables are important in predicting the temperature of materials in these activities?" "What is more important, the temperature of the water with which you started or the amount of water with which you started?"

While the students are reporting their results, at appropriate points discuss an alternative way of looking at heat as a means of describing matter. The students can be expected to have some difficulties at this point because their preconceptions create a barrier to understanding that both properties, the original temperature and the volume of the water involved, are important and real. The amount of water at a specific temperature is related to the amount of internal heat energy present. Temperature relates only to how fast the molecules of water move (the energy of a single molecule), which causes the thermometer column to expand and rise. It may be that single molecules have a large amount of heat energy, but if there are not a lot of molecules, there will not be a lot of heat in the entire sample.

D. Provide each group with a set of instructions on paper or 3 × 5 inch index cards. This activity relates the concept of *heat* to the amount of internal energy that various quantities of water possess by asking students to put together different amounts of hot water with the same amount of crushed ice.

To begin the activity, have students place one-fourth cup of crushed ice in each of five clear plastic drinking cups. Then, have them measure out the four different amounts of hot water (three-fourths cup, one-half cup, one-fourth cup, and one tea-spoon) into other cups. Finally, have them quickly pour the hot water out of one cup into a cup with crushed ice. They should repeat the process as quickly as possible with all the other cups of hot water. Ask the groups to make observations of all five of the cups in which crushed ice was initially placed for 5 minutes. At the end of 5 minutes, ask them to note how much crushed ice is left in each of the five cups. Finally, have them relate the amount of crushed ice left in a cup to the amount of hot water (heat) added to the cup. Older students can perform a second activity by adding the same amount of water (three-fourths cup) at different temperatures to the crushed ice. Similar results will be observed.

E. Ask students to record the results of their activity. At the end of each group report, ask each group why different amounts of ice were found in the five cups at the end of the 5-minute observation period. Also, ask each group to state the evidence from which they made their inference. At this point, the students may report that the amount of ice left is related to the amount of water added to the cup. Explain that the added water was all at the same temperature. The temperature did not vary; only the amount of water varied. Everything else was the same. If more hot water was added to the ice, it was the same as adding more heat to the ice, which caused the ice to melt faster. Help students focus on the smallest amount, (a teaspoonful) of water added to the ice. Even though that water had a high temperature, it did not melt much ice. So, very little heat was added to the ice.

F. As closure, explain to students that heat and temperature are two different properties of materials. *Temperature* is measured with a thermometer. It indicates the quickness of motion or speed energy each particle of water has. An increase in speed causes the average distance between particles to increase, and thus everyday objects (matter) expand. For example, liquids upon heating will rise in an enclosed thermometer column. *Heat energy* can be measured by its effect on the amount of ice it can melt. This is a practical way of measuring heat energy. Heat is a measure of how much energy all the particles in an object have lost or gained. It indicates the total amount of internal energy transferred to or from a specific amount of water.

Evaluation: When asked during the Invention to make an inference about the ice and water, the group reports the evidence upon which the inference was made. The evidence relates in a logical way to the inference. Group participation will be assessed by noting whether all members were part of the plan and had a chance to do their part.

Expansion

Objective: The students will solve everyday problems involving the heat and temperature in materials.

Materials: For each group: ten clear plastic drinking cups; crushed ice; paper towels; paper for recording results; one kitchen measuring cup with metric or English measures; a source of hot water from a tap or hot plate at about 120° Celsius; cold water with floating ice cubes in it with a temperature of about 0° Celsius or 32° Fahrenheit; thermometers; tablespoons.

Procedure:

A. Place the students in groups of four and assign roles: a materials manager, readers/ observers (two students), and a recorder.

B. At stations set up around the room, ask the groups to solve a variety of problems:

Station 1. Ask students to get one-half cup samples of very cold water and hot water from buckets located in the room. Ask them to predict the final temperature when the hot water is added to the cold water.

Next, ask them to follow these directions: Get one-half cup samples of hot and cold water. Measure the temperature of each cup of water. Then, pour the hot water into the cold water cup. After 30 seconds, take a measurement of the temperature of the mixed cup of water and compare it to their prediction. (The students should find a temperature midway between the temperatures of the starting cups of water.)

Station 2. Present the following problem:

> Mom is having a cup of coffee after dinner. She pours herself an almost-full cup of coffee. The temperature of the coffee is about 50° Celsius (122° Fahrenheit). She adds one tablespoonful of cold milk to the coffee. What temperature is her coffee now? Write your prediction on a sheet of paper. Describe the reasoning behind your answer.

Next, ask them to follow these directions: Get one cup almost full of hot water, a second cup one-fourth full of cold water, and one tablespoon. Measure and record the temperature of the hot water and of the cold water. Pour one tablespoon of cold water into the hot water cup. Measure and record the temperature of the mixed cup of water and compare it to their prediction. (The students should find a temperature that is still hot, perhaps 45° Celsius or 113° Fahrenheit.)

Station 3. Present the following problem:

> You are having hot chicken soup for dinner. Mom always serves it too hot for you to eat; it's about 50° C (122° Fahrenheit). You are really hungry so you do not want to wait for it to cool down. Therefore, you are going to add some cold water to it. There is about 60 milliliters (one cup) of soup in your bowl. How much cold water should you add to your soup so that its temperature will be about 40° Celsius (104° Fahrenheit)? Write your prediction on a sheet of paper. Describe the reasoning behind your answer.

Next, ask students to follow these directions: "Try out your guess using the hot water, cups, and thermometer at this station. If your guess didn't work, measure out more or less water until you get it to about 40° Celsius. Record all your work." (The students will need to measure out about 20 milliliters—one-third of a cup—of cold water.)

Teacher's Note: The following three stations may be discussed without performing the task. If time is available, the teacher may wish to have the students carry out the activity at the station, or one group of students could demonstrate the station's activity to the whole class.

Station 4. Present the following problem:

> Which will have a higher temperature after 1 minute on a burner: a small pot with one cup of water in it or a small pot with one-fourth cup of water in it? Write your prediction on a sheet of paper. Describe the reasoning behind your answer.

(For every degree of temperature increase, the larger amount of water requires more heat than does the smaller volume of water. Since the burner is giving off the same amount of heat during every 1-minute period, the smaller amount of water will rise to a higher temperature when compared to the larger amount of water.)

Station 5. Present the following problem:

> Which will cool to the lower temperature in 10 minutes: a plastic glass containing one cup of very hot water or a plastic glass containing one-fourth cup of very hot water?

(The larger amount of water has more heat, and therefore takes longer to cool down.)

Station 6. Present the following problem:

> Which has a higher temperature: a cup of boiling hot water or a swimming pool of water at air temperature? Which has more heat: a cup of boiling hot water or a swimming pool at air temperature?

(The cup of water has the higher temperature. The swimming pool has more heat. If the students are having difficulty with this question, ask them: "Which can melt more ice: a cup of boiling hot water or a swimming pool of water at air temperature?" "Which had more heat?")

C. Discuss the results of their station activities in a whole group. The teacher can summarize student ideas on the board.

D. Summarize the lesson by stating that when we started the activities, the students may not have been able to tell the difference between the words "heat" and "temperature." By mixing different amounts of water and by melting ice with different amounts of water, they should be able to apply the terms "heat" and "temperature" to their everyday lives. Whether they are talking about soup or coffee, they should be able to use the idea of heat to guess how long it will take things to heat or cool. They should also be able to guess how much cold water they need to mix into hotter water to make it the temperature they would like.

Evaluation: Tell the following story to the students:

> Juan had a carton of cold milk sitting on his lunch tray. Jill came by and said that she did not like the soup that came with lunch. It was steaming and looked like it was too hot to eat. She took a tablespoonful of her hot soup and poured it into Juan's milk. After yelling at Jill to "Stop it!" Juan decided to drink his milk even though there was some soup in it. He was surprised to find out that his milk was still cold.

Write down your ideas about whether or not Juan should have been surprised that his milk was still cold.

EXAMPLES OF ALTERNATIVE CONCEPTIONS IN ADDITIONAL PHYSICAL SCIENCE AREAS

Students' prior knowledge determines what they observe and the meaning they give to those observations. Since the physical world is part of students' experiences from the day of birth, they have ideas about all the basic physical science areas. As part of this prior knowledge, the alternative conceptions brought by students into the classroom can be numerous. Students' prior knowledge changes from year to year with the development of new thought processes and knowledge gained at home and in school. Therefore, it is difficult to list all the possible alternative conceptions students might have. A brief sample of the basic alternative conceptions commonly found in physical science follows. The list illustrates the depth and breadth of alternative ideas students bring to class and the awareness teachers must develop to plan effective science lessons. This outline includes the following areas: the nature and structure of matter, energy, force, and motion (Brown & Clement, 1992; Driver, 1995; Eckstein & Shemesh, 1993; Kesidou & Duit, 1993; Lee, Eichinger, Anderson, Berkheimer, & Blakeslee, 1993; Lehrer & Schauble, 1998; Sunal & Sunal, 1998). This brief sample is intended to introduce the range of alternative conceptions found among elementary- and intermediate-grade students in the broader areas of physical science.

Sample Alternative Conceptions about the Nature and Structure of Matter Students Bring to Class

1. Mass and weight of a substance are the same thing.
2. Matter is continuous, and is not made up of discrete particles.
3. There is no space between gas molecules.
4. Everything that is sensed is matter—including heat and light (very young students).
5. Matter does not include gases or things you cannot see (older students).
6. Matter you cannot see (air) is weightless.
7. Matter you cannot see doesn't exist (air is nothing).
8. If particles exist in matter, there is something in the space between the particles.
9. When substances change, as in a physical or chemical action, the quantity of matter does not remain the same. For example, sugar added to water does not make the water heavier. Sugar disappears when dissolved.
10. Mass and volume are the same thing.
11. An object, when cut into pieces, will have less mass than a whole object. For example, a powdered form of a solid weighs less than the solid weighs.
12. All molecules are motionless.
13. Molecules of matter have macroscopic properties similar to those of common objects. All molecules of substances get larger when they are heated.
14. The volume and quantity of substances are the same thing.
15. Gases can't be heated.
16. Gases exert force in only one direction.
17. Suction is a force.
18. Pressure and density are the same thing.
19. Weight is added during a chemical change. (Chemical changes tend to be viewed by the obvious features of the change. For example, when wood is burned in a closed container, the smoke that is produced leads students to suggest that weight is added).
20. Matter disappears when gases are given off or absorbed. When wood is burned, for example, the ashes weigh much less than the wood weighed.
21. Air, or oxygen, is not involved in burning.
22. Physical and chemical change are the same thing.
23. Molecules of matter do not attract each other.
24. Melting and dissolving are the same.

Sample Alternative Conceptions about Energy Students Bring to Class

1. Energy is associated only with humans or movement (very young students).
2. Energy is associated only with living things, growing, and food (older students).
3. Energy is associated with a substance like food or fuel that is used up.
4. Energy is not measurable.
5. Energy transformations involve only one form of energy at a time and only if they have perceivable effects. For example, transformation of motion energy to heat energy (air friction) is usually not obvious because there is no observable temperature increase.
6. Some forms of energy cannot make things happen, such as sound, light, or chemical energy.

7. Energy transformation means that energy is stored up in an object and then released back in its original form rather than changing from one form to another.

Sample Alternative Conceptions about Light Energy Students Bring to Class

1. Light is in the flashlight bulb or other light source (light is identified with its source).
2. Light is something, a substance, that travels from place to place.
3. The eye sees without anything coming to or from the object.
4. Light comes from the observer's eye.
5. Images seen with the eye require no mechanism to produce them (for example, the lens in the eye).
6. Light from a source moves out in only one direction (rather than radiating out in all directions).
7. Light fills space (for example, a room is full of light).
8. Light bends around corners, so it doesn't move in a straight line.
9. Only mirrors and shiny objects reflect light.
10. Magnifying glasses make light (pieces) bigger.
11. Light and color are not related.
12. Shadows are reflections.
13. Light, if unseen, is lost or destroyed (not conserved).

Sample Alternative Conceptions about Electricity and Magnetism Students Bring to Class

1. Electricity does not have describable properties.
2. Electricity leaving a battery or other electrical source is used up when it passes through an electric bulb.
3. Electricity coming out of a battery remains the same without variation.
4. Objects connected to an electrical source, such as a battery, can be connected in any way to make a lightbulb light. For instance, a wire coming from a battery to any point on a bulb will cause it to light.
5. All materials pass on electricity (very young students).
6. Only metals allow electricity to pass through. All other materials do not conduct electricity (older students).
7. Electric current and electric energy are the same thing.
8. Electricity and magnetism are unrelated.
9. Magnets attract all metals.
10. Magnetism can't pass through other materials.
11. Some magnets have poles while others do not.
12. A compass needle points in the direction in which you are going.

Sample Alternative Conceptions about Force and Motion Students Bring to Class

1. Force, energy, power, and pressure are the same thing.
2. Force is something that makes things happen or creates change.
3. Force is a property of an object. It exists within objects rather than as a relationship between objects.

4. Force exists only during observable actions. Passive forces, such as with an object sitting on a table, do not exist.
5. The amount water rises when an object is put into it is related to the object's weight. Therefore, the heavier an object is, the more the water will rise.
6. An object has weight if you can feel it; otherwise, it has no weight.
7. Weight, mass, and density are the same thing.
8. Constant speed requires a constant force.
9. The amount of speed is proportional to the amount of force. If an object is not moving there is no force acting on it.
10. If an object is moving, there is a force acting on it in the direction of motion.
11. It is difficult to move large objects quickly because of friction. Inertia is not an important factor of motion or an important property of objects.
12. The harder you push, regardless of its size, the more an object will increase in speed to the same amount.
13. Leaning against a wall requires no force pushing outward by the wall. If an object isn't moving, there are no forces on it.
14. An object with more of some observable property (for example, size) will exert the greater force.
15. Gravity is not a force. All objects naturally fall.
16. Air makes objects fall.
17. The heavier the object, the faster the force of gravity will cause it to fall downward.
18. Gravity increases with height above Earth.
19. An object thrown into the air has no forces on it.
20. An object in orbit around Earth has only one force on it, that of gravity.
21. There is no air or air pressure in space or on the moon, so there is no gravity.

Applying What You Know

Identifying Alternative Physical Science Conceptions

Evaluate one of your physical science lesson plans or a science textbook chapter to determine possible alternative conceptions students bring to the lesson. If possible, work with a partner on this activity. Answer the questions below:

1. What are the stated or implied physical science concepts and generalizations in the lesson plan or chapter?
2. What are possible alternative conceptions students might bring to the lesson plan? Check the concepts and generalizations against the sample lists provided above. List the alternative conceptions.

ACTIVITIES THAT HELP STUDENTS CHANGE THEIR ALTERNATIVE CONCEPTIONS IN PHYSICAL SCIENCE

Discrepant events can provide students with the confrontation they need to test out their prior knowledge about an idea. The discrepant events below demonstrate examples from several physical science areas. A sample alternative conception is followed by an appropriate discrepant event useful during the Exploration phase of a learning cycle lesson.

Discrepant Events with the Nature and Structure of Matter

Students' Alternative Conception:

   2. *Matter is continuous, and is not made up of discrete particles.*
   5. *Matter does not include gases or things you cannot see (older students).*
   6. *Matter you cannot see (air) is weightless.*
   7. *Matter you cannot see doesn't exist (air is nothing).*
12. *All molecules are motionless.*

Discrepant Activity: Give groups of students a magnifying glass, scissors, and a small piece of Styrofoam and ask them to divide the Styrofoam in half. Do this over and over until the students cannot divide it further. Ask, "Is there still Styrofoam left?" Ask students to do the same with some sugar crystals by crushing them. When the students cannot divide the sugar crystal into any smaller pieces, ask them "Is any sugar left?" Ask one of the students in each group to taste the smallest sugar crystal and describe its taste.

Provide each group of students with a half-cup of clean water. Ask them to put a pinch of sugar into the water. Have the taster in each group taste it after about 1 minute. Since the students will be able to taste the sugar in the water, ask them, "Are there sugar particles in the water even if you cannot see them?"

Teacher's Note: This activity provides evidence students can use to begin to understand the idea that matter exists even though it cannot be seen and that matter can be broken up into very small particles and still retain the same properties that larger-sized pieces have. Even though sugar was put in one part of the water, all parts will eventually taste sweet. Thus, molecules must move. Additional activities can be performed with flower-scented room spray and other materials that have a strong odor. "Invisible" perfume molecules travel across the room in a short time.

Discrepant Events with Light Energy

Students' Alternative Conception:

   2. *Light is something, a substance, that travels from place to place.*
   3. *The eye sees without anything coming to or from the object.*
   4. *Light comes from the observer's eye.*
   7. *Light fills space (for example, a room is full of light).*
   8. *Light bends around corners, so it doesn't move in a straight line.*

Discrepant Activity: Some preparation is needed to complete this discrepant event. Ask the students to bring in one flashlight for each of their cooperative groups. Ahead of time, cut out a circle of black construction paper to fit over the end of each flashlight. Cut a thin, 2-centimeter slit in the circle with a razor blade so that light comes out of the flashlight in a line.

Each group begins the activity with the following materials: a flashlight that produces a single thin line of light, two small mirrors, a manila folder, and lumps of clay to hold up the mirrors. Write the following problems on the board or on 3 × 5 inch index cards and ask the groups to work through each problem in order. Carry out these activities in a darkened room.

Problem 1: Draw and describe how you can see a pencil on your desk.

Problem 2: Lay the flashlight down on the floor so that the thin line on the end of the flashlight is vertical. Then, set the manila folder on its edge 1 meter from the flashlight. Stand the manila folder up in such a way that, when light from the flashlight is

Describe how the light gets from the flashlight to the card.

turned on, it shines on the folder. After you have placed the flashlight and folder, turn on the flashlight and find out whether your set-up works. If not, shut off your flashlight and make changes, then try out your changed set-up. Do not make changes with the flashlight turned on. Draw and describe how the light gets from the flashlight to the folder and then to your eye.

Problem 3: Lay the flashlight down on the floor. Set the manila folder 1 meter from the flashlight. Next, set a mirror in such a way that the mirror reflects the light from the flashlight onto the manila folder when the light from the flashlight is turned on. After your group has placed the items, find out whether your set-up works. If it doesn't, turn off the flashlight, make changes, and try again. Do not make adjustments with the flashlight turned on. Draw and describe how the light gets from the flashlight to the folder and then to your eye.

Problem 4: Set the flashlight down on the floor. Then, set a manila folder 1 meter from the flashlight. Next, set two mirrors in such a way that one mirror reflects the light from the flashlight to the second mirror. The second mirror should reflect that light onto the manila folder. After your group has set this up, find out whether your set-up works. If it doesn't, turn off the flashlight, make changes, and try again. Do not make adjustments with the flashlight turned on. Draw and describe how the light gets from the flashlight to the folder to your eye.

Each student group should report the results from the problems. Following the reports, the teacher should ask each group to answer the following questions in a short essay: "How do we see things in our world?" and "What is the rule about reflected light that tells us how to set-up the mirrors in the problems we just worked?"

Discrepant Events with Electricity and Magnetism

Students' Alternative Conception:
1. *Electricity does not have describable properties.*
2. *Electricity leaving a battery or other electrical source is used up when it passes through an electric bulb.*
3. *Electricity coming out of a battery remains the same without variation.*
5. *All materials pass on electricity (very young students).*
6. *Only metals allow electricity to pass through. All other materials do not conduct electricity (older students).*

Discrepant Activity: Provide each group of students with two batteries of different voltages (a 1 1/2-volt "D" cell, and a 9-volt battery); two wires with their ends exposed and with about 1 centimeter of insulation removed; a lightbulb or a bulb in a socket; and a bag of common objects such as pennies, seeds, twigs, a plastic spoon, a metal spoon, a foil gum wrapper, a paper-covered metal twist tie, a paper clip, a pencil, and a 6-meter piece of aluminum or copper wire without insulation.

This lesson follows lessons where students have developed an understanding of open, closed, and short circuits. The students should be able to connect the battery, bulb, and wire to make the lightbulb light. Instruct students to use what they have learned about electric circuits to test different materials to find out whether they would make good wires. Ask, "Do all materials conduct (pass through) electricity?" If so, "Do they allow electricity to pass through equally?"

Give students an instruction sheet with the following directions:

Answer these questions by constructing an electric circuit to test the objects in the bag. If the object is made up of more than one material, you must test all its parts. If an object is very long, you must test it at different lengths. For the long length of wire only, test the difference in its conduction of electricity using two types of batteries.

When the students have completed the tests, ask each group to report its results. Summarize their results on a chart on the board.

Discrepant Events with Force and Motion

Students' Alternative Conception:
6. *An object has weight if you can feel it; otherwise, it has no weight.*

Discrepant Activity: Provide groups of students with a magnifying glass and a bag of common items. Some of the items that can be included in the bag are marbles, pennies, grains of salt and sugar in small plastic bags, feathers or small Styrofoam or foam rubber pieces, a small amount of flour in a small plastic bag, peppercorns, dried seeds (such as corn, lima bean, or radish), a small amount of water in a small plastic bag, and a small amount of vegetable oil in a small plastic bag. Ask the students to group the items by weight. Ask them to do the grouping by considering single pieces of the substance only, rather than the collection of pieces in cases such as the total sample of salt. Give each group a grid sheet with at least ten boxes.

Ask the students to order the items by weight. Ask: "Which item weighs the most?" "Which item weighs the least?" and "Which has no weight?" Tell the students to place one piece or part of that item in the first box on a grid sheet and label it as the "heaviest." Repeat the process until all of the substances are ordered and labeled. They are to identify each box with a label that is appropriate to the item.

Have each student group report its results and reasons for grouping. Following the reports, compare the weight of the samples of the items against each other. For example, students might label a single piece of salt, sugar, flour, or water as having no weight.

Put ten pennies on the right side of a double-pan balance. Put a plastic bag of flour heavier than the ten pennies on the left side of the double-pan balance. Take flour out of the bag until it balances. Using the balance, make comparisons between the ten pennies and other materials such as salt, water, seeds, or a marble. The students should note the volume of the materials needed to balance the ten pennies. Ask the students to review their grouping of the items and their ordering of the groups by weight. They should be allowed to reorder the materials.

Applying What You Know

Assessing a Students' Prior Physical Science Knowledge

Assess and discuss the prior knowledge of a student in a specific physical science area, or assess and discuss the prior knowledge of a student in relation to a physical science unit currently being taught by a teacher in a local school. In advance, set up a schedule with a teacher that will not interfere with normal class activities. Interview the student, and complete a reflective journal entry. Discuss the results with the teacher and observe the student in her daily activities to see if the student's thinking fits your conclusions.

Step 1. Select a discrepant event, phenomenon, or confrontational situation related to a physical science concept or generalization. Use the physical science alternative conceptions and above activities as an example of the format to be used. Consider the background of this student when planning this activity. Gather the demonstration materials or draw the phenomenon or situation.

Steps 2–7. Complete steps 2 to 7 as described in the previous *Applying What You Know* student interview activity on heat.

Step 8. Finish the process with a conclusion and a prescription for an appropriate instructional activity on the concept in a short-paper format. Consider the following questions: "What does the student believe (prior knowledge) about the concept or event?" and "How does this belief relate to the scientific view?" As a teacher, what have you learned about this student? How would you start a lesson in this science area for this student?

Include a title page and label the parts of the assignment indicated below.

1. *Concept or generalization*—a description of the concept or generalization and the demonstration materials, or a drawing of the phenomenon or situation.
2. *Script and student background*—a script with the key question and possible follow-up responses you will make to your students.
3. *Reflective journal*—write up the interview events as they occurred in reflective journal form. Identify the student by first name only.
4. *Concluding paper*—write your conclusion and a prescription in a short-paper format.

EXAMPLES OF LEARNING CYCLE LESSON PLANS ON PHYSICAL SCIENCE CONCEPTS

The following learning cycle lessons challenge students' conceptions of a physical science event with a more appropriate explanation. Note the connection of each phase to the students' alternative conceptions addressed in the lesson.

A Learning Cycle Involving Alternative Conceptions about Energy

Alternative Conceptions Addressed by the Lesson Plan:

4. *Energy is not measurable.*
5. *Energy transformations involve only one form of energy at a time and only if they have perceivable effects. For example, transformation of motion energy to heat energy (air friction) is usually not obvious because there is no observable temperature increase.*

Lesson Goal: To allow students to investigate, develop inferences, and differentiate between the concepts of motion energy and heat energy, and the part played by friction in the transformation process.

Grade Level: Grades 4–5.

Prerequisites: Can measure temperature to the nearest 2° with a thermometer.

Exploration

Objective: The students will investigate the effects of motion on an object.

Materials: For each group: two baby food jars one-half filled with sand; two alcohol-type thermometers; newspaper to cover desks or tables; paper towels; paper to make a record and bar graph of results.

Procedure:

A. Tell the students that you are going to give them a thought problem: "You are riding in a car traveling down the interstate highway. The driver takes his foot off of the gas but doesn't put his foot on the brake. The car comes to a stop on the side of the road. Why does the car stop?" Have them discuss and write their answer on a sheet of paper.

B. Place the students in groups of four and assign roles: a materials manager, two timers/recorders, and a helper. All students will also serve as shakers.

C. Describe the materials and instructions needed for groups to carry out the activity of shaking jars containing sand at different rates and times. Discuss safety precautions relating to glass jars and thermometers.

D. *Key question:* What happens to the material inside a jar when you shake it? Draw and describe a jar one-half full of sand after it has been shaken for 5 minutes.

E. Provide each group of students with two baby food jars half-full of sand, a newspaper, and a thermometer. Tell the students to wrap each jar with a piece of paper towel folded over several times to form a strip about 2 inches wide. This will provide insulation to keep the jars from being warmed by their hands.

F. Ask the students to measure and record the temperature of the sand, and examine the contents of the jar. Ask the students to infer what will happen to the contents of the jars if they are shaken for a long time. Have the students record their inferences.

G. Next, ask the students to close each jar tightly and shake each jar for 6 minutes. One jar should be shaken rapidly. The other jar should be shaken moderately. The students in the group can take turns during the shaking process. Each student should shake the jar for 1 minute at a time.

H. After shaking, the students should immediately put thermometers into the jars. After 60 seconds, they should read the thermometers. While waiting, the students can examine the contents of the jar.

I. Ask the groups to report their results to the whole class. Help them communicate the results of their activities using tables and/or bar graphs to justify their conclusions.

Evaluation: Collect the students' responses to the thought problem in step A above. Evaluate them considering their prior knowledge. Evaluate the group's skills by assessing whether all participated equally in the activity.

Invention

Objective: The students will investigate a variety of materials and determine that the heat energy of an object can be changed by transforming motion energy into heat through friction.

Materials: For learning stations: small wood block about the size of an ice cube for each group; ice cube for each group; hammer; a dozen 3-to-4 inch nails; six wood pieces (2 inches × 4 inches × about 1 foot long); wax paper; seven pieces of sandpaper (8 1/2 × 11 inches); paper towels; paper for recording results.

Procedure:

A. Place students in groups of four and assign roles: a materials manager, readers/observers (two students), and a recorder.

B. Have them discuss the key question from the Exploration in their groups. During the discussion, introduce the new idea that the energy of motion from the hand caused the sand particles to move. The motion of the sand particles bumping against each other is called friction. The friction of the sand, stopping the motion of the sand, created heat.

C. Ask each group to perform the following activities at learning stations. Instructions for each station will be given on a laboratory guide available at the station.

Station 1: Quickly slide a small block of wood and an ice cube across a sheet of sandpaper several times. Have each member of the group do the task. Discuss and compare what happened.

Station 2: This station will involve using one large piece of wood, two books, and a piece of wax paper. Put the two books on top of the wood and push the wood along the floor. Then, pile the wood and the two books on top of the wax paper and push it along the floor. Draw, describe, and compare what happened.

Station 3: Take two large pieces of wood and rub them together as hard as possible 15 or more times. Have every member of the group feel both pieces of wood afterwards. Discuss what happened when you carried out the activity and why it happened.

Station 4: For this station, two wood pieces and one piece of sandpaper are needed. Use the sandpaper on just one of the pieces. Rub a piece of sandpaper across one wood piece. Have every group member feel the wood piece. Compare the wood piece that was just rubbed with sandpaper to the wood that was not rubbed with sandpaper.

Next, rub the sandpaper 30 times across the same wood piece. Have every group member feel the wood again. Then, feel a wood piece that has not been rubbed with sandpaper. Compare how both wood pieces feel. Discuss the results.

Station 5: In this station, use a hammer, a nail, and a piece of wood. Put the board on the floor and carefully pound the nail about halfway into it. Discuss safety precautions relating to the use of the hammer. Use the claws of the hammer to pull out the nail. Have every member of the group feel the nail, then discuss how it felt and why.

D. Lead a whole-group discussion concerning motion, friction, transfer of energy, and its real-world effects. Have students give evidence from the learning stations and other experiences they have had with friction. Lead students to draw the conclusions that some of the energy of motion is transformed into heat energy in the objects involved and the greater the amount of friction, the more heat energy is transformed from the energy of motion.

E. As closure, state that the greater the energy of motion, the greater the heat energy produced. The rise in temperature indicates that a transfer of energy took place. The motion energy provided to the grains of sand or wood in the station activities was transformed, as a result of friction, into increased heat energy in each grain of sand and in the wood.

Evaluation: Ask each member of the groups to write out a summary of the actions undertaken and the results obtained by group members at one of the stations. Each member should address a different station.

Expansion

Objective: The students will investigate and describe the chain of events by which motion energy is transformed into heat energy in an everyday situation.

Materials: For problem stations (if possible, students should bring in these items): bicycle pump; bicycle tire; bicycle; shoe; kite; lunch tray; toy car.

Procedure:

A. Provide each group of four students with problems written on 3 × 5 inch cards. Ask each group to perform and, if possible, act out the problem situation. Whether or not they can act out the situation, they are to think about the problem and describe the chain of events by which the energy of motion in the problem becomes transformed into heat energy possessed by the objects involved. Write the key questions on the board. For each situation, draw and describe: "What is moving?" "What becomes warm?" and "How did the energy of motion become heat energy in the object?"

Problem 1: Your group must pump up a bicycle tire for 3 minutes. After 3 minutes, feel the pump and the bicycle tire. Discuss the answers to the key questions.

Problem 2:

You are riding in a car traveling down an interstate highway. The driver takes her foot off the gas pedal but doesn't put her foot on the brake. The car comes to a stop on the side of the road.

Discuss the answer to the key questions. You may use the toy car to act out the problem.

The car's motion caused the tires to move along the road and the parts of the car's drive train to turn and rub against each other. The motion of the tires and drive train creates friction and heat. A car's motion gradually slows because energy of motion is transformed into heat energy.

Problem 3:

A girl is riding a bicycle and stops it using hand brakes.

Discuss the answers to the key questions.

Problem 4:

> A kite is flying in a strong wind. You notice smoke from a fire blowing into the kite. When it passes the kite, the smoke moves more slowly and swirls.

Discuss the answers to the key questions.

Problem 5:

> For lunch today, you put pizza and French fries on your tray and slid the tray on the counter. It came to a stop in front of the cashier.

Discuss the answers to the key questions.

B. Summarize the lesson by stating that when they started the activities, the students may not have been able to tell the difference between the concepts of motion energy and heat energy and the part played by friction in transforming one to the other. The activities with sand in jars, stations, and problems should help them in applying these ideas successfully in their everyday lives. By observing events where something in motion is being heated, they should be able to identify the "source of friction" and apply the terms "motion energy" and "heat energy." Whether they are talking about bicycles or in-line skates, they should be able to use the idea of heat energy being transformed from motion energy.

Evaluation: Ask the students to respond to the following situations:

First, a girl is riding her bicycle and stops by dragging her feet.

Write out your answer to these questions: "What is moving?" "What becomes warm?" and "How did the energy of motion become heat energy in the object?"

Second, you are pushing a brick 6 feet along on a waxed tile floor, an unpainted cement floor, and through dirt on the playground.

"On which of these will more heat be created?"
Write out the answer to this question.

Evaluate the answers to these questions based on their appropriate application of the concepts of motion energy and heat energy, and the part played by friction in the transformation of one to the other. Use a performance checklist such as the one below.

Level of Performance

1. May identify heat as a result of the action and the source of friction in one or both situations. Does not identify energy transformation as the cause of the actions observed.
2. Identifies heat as a result of the action and the source of friction. Identifies the reduction in motion energy and increase in heat energy variables in each situation. Does not identify energy transformation as the cause of the actions observed.
3. Identifies heat as a result of the action and the source of friction. Identifies the reduction in motion energy and increase in heat energy variables in each situation. Identifies the idea of transformation of energy as the source of heat.

See the discussion on this topic in Chapter 1.

Additional activities and information in physical science lessons should relate to the nature of science, as well as the people who participated in creating it and who work in the field today.

Some examples of people who made significant contributions to the physical sciences but have been underrepresented in the mass media are listed in Figure 13-6, along with their major contributions. Additional information can be found in library references such as an encyclopedia. The book *Nobel Prize Women in Science: Their Lives, Struggles, and Mo-*

SCIENTISTS ARE DIVERSE!

Some Who Have Contributed to Our Knowledge of Physical Science

Arnald of Villanova
An alchemist who worked with solutions of solids in alcohol (e.g., tincture of iodine) in Spain.

Callinicus
An Egyptian who explained the nature of combustion.

Har Khorana
An Asian-American from India who invented the first artificial gene.

Tsai Lun
A Chinese scientist who invented paper.

Dorothy Wrinch
An Argentinian who found that the amino acids are where genes have their specific coding.

Benjamin Banneker
An African American who carried out research with honeybees and with a wooden striking clock.

Marie Curie
A Polish woman who discovered radium and polonium and received the Nobel Prize for her work.

Bertha Lamme
An American who worked with the theory and design of motors and generators.

Lewis Latimer
An African American who developed the carbon filament for the electric lightbulb.

Samuel Ting
An Asian American who discovered the J particle in the atom.

FIGURE 13-6   *Underrepresented scientists who have made significant contributions to the physical sciences*

mentous *Discoveries* by S. McGrayne (1993) is a sample resource. An additional Expansion activity to most any physical science lesson is to read a current newspaper item on the contribution of a scientist or use of related physical science concepts by members of the community. Older students can create library research reports and short plays on the contributions of these underrepresented scientists and community members.

Applying What You Know

Planning an Exploration for a Physical Science Lesson

In the third-grade physical science lesson plan on page 384 on the topic of the three states of matter, do the following: (1) identify possible alternative conceptions a student could bring to the lesson (if available, interview a few children); and (2) develop key

(continued)

questions the teacher could use to guide student actions to create a confrontation to students' thinking during the Exploration phase. Use the list, "Sample Alternative Conceptions About the Nature and Structure of Matter Students Bring to Class," described on page 372 as a starting point to identify possible alternative conceptions.

LESSON PLAN

A Learning Cycle Involving Alternative Conceptions about the Nature and Structure of Matter

Lesson Goal: To allow students to investigate, develop inferences, and identify general descriptions for each of the three states of matter: solid, liquid, and gas.

Grade Level: Grade 3.

Prerequisites: The students should have developed an understanding of the concept *property of matter*, grouped matter according to its properties, and made observations using all their senses.

Exploration

Objective: The students will investigate the properties of each state of water (solid, liquid, and gas) by making observations, identifying and classifying examples, and describing properties.

Materials: For the class: Pyrex glass pot or beaker; hot plate; fifteen alcohol-type thermometers; crushed ice; fourteen small jars.

Procedure:

A. Place the students in groups of three. Assign roles: a recorder, a reader/observer, and a materials manager.
B. Describe the materials and instructions needed for the groups to carry out the activity of melting ice. Have students set up a jar, put crushed ice and a thermometer into the jar, and write or draw something every 3 minutes for a 21-minute period (or the time it takes the ice to melt completely into water). A second activity on a side table will be set up with crushed ice and a thermometer in a Pyrex glass pot sitting on a hot plate. Ask students to observe this activity at the beginning, middle, and end of the 21-minute period. Discuss safety precautions related to glass jars, thermometers, and the hot plate.
C. After setting up the crushed ice in the jar on the hot plate for the second activity, ask the observer from each group to come up, make observations, then go back and report the findings to the group. The recorder will list the findings of the observer when he returns. At the same time, ask the materials manager from each group to come to the side table to get the crushed ice in the jar and a thermometer.
D. Ask the key questions before the students begin work. Write them on the board.
E. Following the activity, ask each group to discuss the questions on the board.

Evaluation: Have each student write a list of properties of different "kinds" of material. Address the group's skills by observing whether the group forms quickly and stays together while it is working.

Invention

Objectives:

1. The students will investigate a variety of materials. They will make observations and describe properties of materials as a state of matter: solid, liquid, and gas.
2. The students will identify and classify examples of the three states of matter: solid, liquid, or gas.

Materials: For each learning station: magnifying glasses; paper towels; baby food or other small jars; labels; spoons.
For specific learning stations: dish soap; bar soap; cooking oil; milk; sponge; bottle with an onion juice residue; yogurt; hand lotion; coin; margarine; salt.

Procedure:

A. Ask the students to describe their ideas about the different properties of each kind of matter. As needed, add to their descriptions those general properties of each state of matter that are not mentioned. Introduce the term "matter" for all kinds of material.
B. Ask the students to visit 3 of 12 different discovery stations with different states of matter. As they visit each station, have them write and draw the properties, or characteristics, of the different kinds of matter they see. Students should describe several properties for each item and use all their senses except touch. Examples of properties that may be described include hardness, color, stickiness, ability to pour freely, volume or space taken up, weight, or shape. At the various stations provide liquid dish soap, bar soap, cooking oil, milk, a sponge, a candle, yogurt, an empty bottle, hand lotion, a coin, margarine, and salt. Have the students change their group roles and observe, record, and discuss what they observe.
C. Ask the students to summarize their observations at the stations describing the different properties of each kind of matter they encountered. Next, ask them a series of focus questions about each of the states of matter observed (e.g., "What properties did you observe at station three that led you to decide that the matter was a liquid?")
D. Introduce and explain the terms "solid," "liquid," and "gas." Describe the general properties of each state of matter as it is explained.
E. As closure, ask students to work with you to develop a description of the properties of matter in each state: solid, liquid, and gas. Ask them to record the consensus description for each state of matter in their science notebooks.

Evaluation: Have each student observe and list the properties of three samples of matter. Include samples for each state. Assess the group's skills by noting whether all students in the group identify properties and classify substances and whether evidence is provided to support the ideas when given.

Expansion

Objectives:

1. The students will identify properties and the state of matter (solid, liquid, or gas) of the samples provided.
2. The students will define each of the three states of matter by describing the general properties of each state.

Materials: For each learning station: flour; balloon filled with air; vinegar; baking soda; a mixture of water and cornstarch in a jar; magnifying glasses; paper towels; two baby food jars; spoons.

Procedure:

A. Ask the students to change group roles again and observe, record, and discuss what they observe.
B. Have students describe and identify samples from the collection of materials found on a supply table. For each state of matter identified, ask students to draw and write the properties that make up this state of matter. Materials include flour, air in a balloon, vinegar, baking soda, and a mixture of water and cornstarch.
C. Ask students to summarize the different properties of each state of matter identified. As necessary, elaborate on their answers in order to identify all the general properties of each state.
D. Summarize the lesson by describing each of the activities in the order they were experienced in the lesson. Briefly indicate the main point developed in each activity.

Evaluation: Have each student identify the state, and list the general properties, of five samples of matter. Samples could include Jello, lunch meat, a malted shake, cologne (smelled coming from a bottle), and clay.

A. The possible alternative conceptions a student might bring to the lesson on the three states of matter include (numbers relate to the list of "Sample Alternative Conceptions About the Nature and Structure of Matter Students Bring to Class" described on page 372):
    4. *Everything that is sensed is matter—including heat and light (very young students).*
    5. *Matter does not include gases or things you cannot see (older students).*
    6. *Matter you cannot see (air) is weightless.*
    7. *Matter you cannot see doesn't exist (air is nothing).*
B. Possible key questions to guide student actions during the Exploration, in section D, include:

Ask and write on the board the following key questions before the students begin work: "What did you observe?" and "What changed between observations?" Other key questions, if needed, include: "What are some of the things that you notice about your ice?" "What readings did you see on the thermometer when you noticed things happening to your crushed ice?" and "What evidence do you have for stating that there are 'different kinds of materials, or matter' in these activities?"

SUMMARY

Students develop deep and diverse ideas about the physical environment. They begin to develop complex alternative ideas about the effects of materials, forces, and motion from their experiences with toys and objects in their home environment. It is important to use instructional strategies that help students reconstruct their ideas about the natural world as a daily process when teaching science. Beginning lessons with conceptual discrepancies, when possible, is an effective part of this process. Using the complete learning cycle with the key concepts and generalizations identified in the national standards and state course of study is necessary to help students meaningfully learn about the physical world.

chapter 14

Biological Science Starting Points

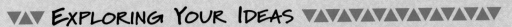

▼▲▼ EXPLORING YOUR IDEAS ▼▲▼▲▼▲▼▲▼▲▼▲▼

"Food and nutrition" are important and very personal areas of knowledge. You can challenge yourself by answering the questions below. To increase the depth of your response, do not use the term "five food groups" or the names of food groups in your answers. If you have difficulty answering the questions, use a resource such as a school textbook or the Internet to find descriptions of basic science ideas related to food and nutrition.

1. List some of the concepts and generalizations in a food and nutrition unit that are appropriate for a primary-age student.
2. What alternative conception do you think a primary-age student in kindergarten or first grade may have about food and nutrition?
3. List some of the concepts and generalizations in a food and nutrition unit that are appropriate for an intermediate-grade student.
4. What alternative conceptions do you expect an older intermediate-grade student may have about food and nutrition?
5. Label your comments in response to questions 1 and 3 with "C" for concept or "G" for generalization. Do you have any facts listed? If so, put an "F" in front of the statement. Remember that, when planning a lesson, the same instructional strategy cannot be used effectively for each type of content.
6. Now, look at the answers suggested below and compare your responses to them. The suggested answers do not include all possible ideas, but these concepts and generalizations should be included in food and nutrition units. *Compare the answers below with your responses and comment on them.*

For questions 1 and 3, possible food and nutrition concepts and generalizations are listed below. Others can be found throughout the next few pages of discussions regarding students' alternative conceptions in food and nutrition. They are also found in state and National Science Education Standards; for example, those of the American Association for the Advancement of Science (1993a). Compare your responses to those suggested below. The "*" indicates examples appropriate at a primary age (K–2). Other examples are introduced in the third and later grades. A focus on the use and transfer of the idea occurs in the fifth and later grades.

Some Possible Concepts Are:

  *food; *natural foods; *processed foods;
    food processing—physical change and chemical change; nutritious food; food energy;
  *natural colors of food; *size of natural foods;
  *food mixtures (e.g., soup); food additives; food labels; five food groups;
    identification and classification of vitamin, mineral, carbohydrate, *seed, *rice, *corn, grain, *apple, fruit, *celery, vegetable, starch, *sugar, *nut, fat, *oil, meat, poultry, fish, *milk, milk group, fiber, and so on.

Some Food and Nutrition Generalizations Include:

*The more a food is processed, the less nutritious it is.

*The darker the color of a natural food (where a range of colors is found), the more nutritious the food.

*The longer it takes to chew a natural food, the more fiber it has.

*The smaller in size and/or the less appearing in a bunch, the more nutrition a fruit or vegetable has (e.g., a Stayman apple is healthier to eat than a hybrid apple bred for large size and a pleasing look).

The food we eat affects our behavior and health.

Our food diet has changed from primitive to modern times and, in the process, it has changed human form and behavior.

Human evolution is related to changes in the human diet.

For questions 2 and 4, examples of alternative conceptions are found in the pages that follow. For question 5, see Chapters 4 and 5 if you are in doubt about whether you have written a fact, concept, or generalization.

Chapter Objectives

1. Describe several examples of students' alternative conceptions in biological science.
2. Interview students on their prior knowledge of ideas in the biological sciences.
3. Given a common alternative conception in biological science, describe a discrepant event activity that would confront students' thinking.
4. Given a biological science lesson plan, identify possible alternative conceptions students might bring to the lesson.
5. Develop one or two key questions a teacher could use to create a "confrontation" and/or a possible student investigation in the Exploration phase of the lesson.

THE BIOLOGICAL SCIENCES

This chapter focuses on identifying and using alternative conceptions in the biological sciences as starting points for designing effective science lessons. There are a number of key areas in the biological sciences in which alternative conceptions create a barrier to learning scientific explanations of concepts and events. These barriers lead teachers to ask the following questions:

- What ideas about biological science do students bring to science lessons?
- What are effective teaching methods that help students understand key ideas in the biological sciences?
- How can I create meaningful learning with hands-on activities in the biological sciences?

The learning cycle is an effective model for teaching students the biological sciences (Lawson, 1988). To demonstrate the learning cycle model for the biological sciences, this chapter presents an overview of the basic content knowledge all students need to learn. As an example, it considers a specific biological science area, "food and nutrition," in depth. The chapter then focuses on students' alternative conceptions in the area of food and nutrition in order to demonstrate elementary and middle school students' specific learning needs. A discussion of alternative conceptions in the more general biological science areas of plants, animals, and functions and structures of living things follows. After

TABLE 14-1   *Examples of key ideas in the general areas of biological science*

Grade Level	Diversity	Regulation and Behavior	Function and Structure of Organisms	Reproduction and Heredity
Primary Age (K–2)	The world has many environments. Organisms can only survive in environments meeting their needs.	An organism's patterns of behavior are related to its environment. Humans change environments in ways that can be beneficial or harmful to themselves and other organisms.	Each organism has different structures that serve different functions in growth, behavior, and reproduction.	Many characteristics of an organism are inherited from the organism's parents.
Intermediate Grade (5–8)	Although millions of plants and animals look very dissimilar, their internal structures and chemical processes are similar.	All organisms obtain and use resources, maintain stable internal conditions, grow, and reproduce.	Living things at all levels of complexity show the complementary nature of structure and function.	Every organism uses a set of instructions specifying its traits. The passage of these instructions from one generation to another is heredity.

Source: Adapted with permission from National Research Council. Copyright 1995 by the National Academy of Sciences. Courtesy of the National Academy Press, Washington, D.C.

the discussion of alternative conceptions, examples of discrepant event activities and learning cycle lesson plans are presented. This chapter is designed to provide a foundation for teachers who wish to effectively plan lessons in the biological sciences that assist students in their learning process.

The **biological sciences** concern life and living processes. They incorporate the disciplines that support and sustain the investigation and understanding of life. The biological sciences include many areas of study: diversity and adaptations of organisms and ecosystems, structure and function in living systems, reproduction and heredity, and regulation and behavior. Biological research is carried out in fields such as botany, zoology, ecology, biochemistry, biomedicine, biomechanics, and bacteriology, among others. The biological sciences grew rapidly during the 20th century. Often, the biological sciences apply knowledge from other basic sciences. The biological sciences are of primary concern to those who are working to achieve a higher quality of life for everyone in the 21st century.

Instructional examples of key ideas covered in some depth in this chapter include diversity of life, regulation and behavior, and the functions and structure of organisms (Table 14–1).

In the biological sciences, food and nutrition are topics covered as a unit of study and indirectly in the elementary and middle school science curriculum.

WHAT SCIENCE KNOWLEDGE IS NEEDED IN THE AREA OF FOOD AND NUTRITION?

Food is an important topic for young students to learn about. **Food** is material taken in by an organism and used to sustain the growth of cells, repair cells, provide energy, and provide materials for other vital processes that maintain a functioning organism. **Nutrition** relates to the process of feeding and the subsequent digestion and assimilation of food material. Some key ideas that should be included in science units involving food and nutrition include the following:

Primary-age students (K–2) should have experience with, and understand, the following:

1. Plants and animals have different food sources and needs.
2. Living things require food, water, and air.
3. Stories on television and in books give plants and animals structures and functions for seeking food they do not possess (such as eyes for plants and human thinking patterns in animals).
4. Both plants and animals need to take in water and air.
5. Animals need to take in food.
6. Animals eat plants and other animals for food.
7. Plants need light to produce their own food.
8. People need food, water, and air, as do other animals.
9. Humans have structures that help them to seek (e.g., eyes and nose), find (e.g., legs), and eat (e.g., hands and teeth) food.
10. Humans need a variety of foods to stay healthy.
11. Some things that humans take into their bodies can hurt them.

Elementary and middle school students (grades 3–8) should have experience with, and understand, the following:

1. A primary difference between plants and animals is that green plants make their own food using the energy of sunlight, carbon dioxide from the air, and water.
2. Plants and animals have a variety of structures and functions that help them make or find food.
3. Living things depend on two connected global food webs: land and ocean. Each web includes plants, the animals that feed on them, and the animals that feed on other animals. In the ocean, the web begins with microscopic ocean plants.
4. Living things, whether they are single-celled or complex organisms, have various structures that serve their needs for food, water, and air.
5. Organisms may interact with one another in the process of making or obtaining food; they may be a producer, consumer, predator, prey, parasite, or host.
6. Almost all kinds of animal food can be traced back to plants that absorb and use energy from sunlight.
7. Some source of energy is needed for all organisms to live.
8. Food supplies the energy and the material for new cell growth or motion for all organisms.
9. If an animal's body is to function well, vitamins and minerals must be present in small amounts.
10. The amount of food an organism requires varies with the size of the organism, its age, activity level, and other natural functions.
11. In plants, light energy is used to make sugars from carbon dioxide and water.

    Carbon dioxide + water yields sugar (sucrose) + oxygen
    $(6CO_2 + 6H_2O \rightarrow C_6H_{12}O_6 + 6O_2)$

12. Food is transformed and stored in both plants and animals.
13. If animals are to use food for energy and growth, the food must be transformed by being digested into usable molecules, absorbed into the blood, and transported to the cells.

14. To release the energy stored in food, both plants and animals deliver oxygen to the cells and remove carbon dioxide from the cells. This process is called *respiration.*

ALTERNATIVE CONCEPTIONS IN FOOD AND NUTRITION

Many school district and state curriculum guides state that third graders can infer that green plants make food from sunlight, water, and carbon dioxide. In reality, many third graders cannot do this. The guidelines also state that fifth-grade students can explain how green plants make food. A great deal of research on students in these grades has found that elementary and middle school children do not typically understand these ideas (Driver, 1995).

Food and nutrition is an area in which children have had a great deal of everyday experience. They have also thought about food and nutrition, heard popular ideas expressed in the media (especially television and in story books), and acquired a lot of common sense beliefs. Every student has developed a deep and extensive knowledge base about food and nutrition that may include many alternative conceptions. When planning and teaching a unit on food and nutrition, an effective teacher needs to be aware of the alternative conceptions that students bring to the unit.

A planned, long-term effort must be made to help students modify commonly-held alternative conceptions of terms and ideas regarding food and nutrition. Alternative conceptions make it difficult for students to understand many key concepts in the biological sciences (e.g., the production and use of food in plants). Researchers have identified 10 common alternative conceptions among students regarding food and nutrition (Conners, 1989; Eaton, Anderson, & Smith, 1983; Sandstead, 1986; Smith & Anderson, 1984a; Underwood, 1986; Wandersee, 1985).

Students' Alternative Conceptions:

1. *Food is anything taken in from the environment by a green plant, including water, minerals, and air.* A more scientifically accurate description of **food** that should be used in science units is: "Foods are materials in the environment taken in by an organism that contain energy such as sucrose, a complex sugar, and starch." Most students identify fertilizer, manure, minerals in the soil, or water as food for green plants. One only has to view a television advertisement on fertilizer or a cartoon about plants to see the commonsense view of plant food (fertilizer) as food for the lawn or to believe that plants take in air and sunlight as food. Although the materials taken in from the environment by green plants are used to create starches through photosynthesis, they are not energy-containing substances.

2. *Green plants get their food from soil. Soil is food.* Green plants bring in no food from their environment. All the food used in green plants is created inside the plant by photosynthesis.

3. *Green plants take food in from the outside.* The materials taken in by a green plant are air, water, and minerals. Air is taken into the leaves through small holes called stomata. Water and minerals are taken into the plant by root hairs attached to the roots of the plant. None of these materials contain energy that can be used by the plant for its functions. Water and carbon dioxide from the air are combined during photosynthesis to create starches that the plant uses as food. It is important to note that only about 1% of the water taken in by the roots is used in photosynthesis. The rest of the water and minerals taken in by the roots either evaporates from the leaves, is used in cell growth or repair, or is stored.

4. *Light is necessary for green plants to live and grow. Sunlight makes green plants healthy. Green plants always need light.* Students with this type of understanding of the function of light believe that green plants need light to live and grow, but this is a partial explanation based only on observation. Light is necessary for green plants to make their own food. Green plants do not take in food; they manufacture it. Light is necessary for the food-making process, *photosynthesis,* to take place. Light doesn't just help the green

plant obtain food from the environment, it is a necessary element in the food-making process. It provides the energy needed to combine materials from the environment—air, water, and minerals—to create starch and sucrose.

Green plants do not always need light. At night, or when seeds germinate in soil, green plants thrive because they use food internally made and stored to create energy for their life processes.

5. *Color differences in green plants are due to disease, death, lack of food, or age of the plant.* The green color in plants is due to a substance called *chlorophyll*. Chlorophyll is found in small bodies within the cell called chloroplasts, which look like little green marbles within the cytoplasm of a green plant cell. They are produced in response to the amount of sunlight a plant receives. A lack of sunlight results in fewer chloroplasts being formed in the cell.

Chlorophyll is not an ingredient in photosynthesis. It is a chemical that aids the transformation of light energy falling onto a leaf into chemical energy that bonds molecules together during photosynthesis. Without chlorophyll, green plants cannot make food. A green plant that has used up its existing stored starch will not have the energy or materials needed for cell repair and cell division. As a result, it cannot grow. It degenerates, often wilting, because it cannot do cell repair.

6. *Food, minerals, and water have the same nutritional benefits for animals. Height and weight of a person are similarly influenced by the amount of food eaten.* Food contains energy and materials that can be used by the body for a variety of functions. These functions include movement, cell repair, cell reproduction, and other vital processes. Food that is taken in or produced by an organism, and not immediately used, is stored. A person's weight is influenced by the amount of excess food taken in.

Other functions of organisms require energy and materials but are not directly related to food intake. Bodily characteristics such as one's height and length of arms are genetically determined. A person's height is an inherited characteristic; therefore, eating food beyond the minimum requirements does not create a taller person. However, having less than the minimum amount of food will not allow the body to create the new cells required for growth. As a result, the person will not grow to the genetically determined height.

7. *Food gives green plants and animals energy directly, with little or no processing by the organism.* Students have difficulty identifying where green plants and animals obtain the energy for movement. They also find it hard to understand that energy is required for all functions of the organism, such as cell reproduction, cell repair, temperature regulation, and movement. Students do not link the processes in cells that obtain energy from food materials in animals to similar processes in plants.

For a green plant or animal to use food for energy and build new cells, the food must first be broken down into molecules that are transported to, and absorbed into, the cell through the cell wall. Oxygen supplied to the cell from outside combines with the food molecules in the cell and releases the energy stored in the food molecule. Carbon dioxide is a waste product that leaves the cell and is expelled by the organism. This process is called *respiration*. The same process occurs in green plants and animals, since respiration occurs in both. In both green plants and animals, respiration is a continuous process during the day and night, liberating energy for use by the organism. The importance of respiration, (combining oxygen and specific chemical compounds resulting from the digestive process to release energy) is not understood by many students.

8. *Fast foods and snack foods have the same nutritional value as the potatoes, meats, and grains out of which they were made.* Highly processed foods such as some cheeses, potato chips, and fruit rolls have been greatly changed from their natural forms. The fibrous content of the original unprocessed food has been greatly reduced, as complex molecules have been turned into simple molecules. For example, complex starches and sugar have become simple starches and sugars. Numerous chemicals in the original have been taken

out. Many additives have been introduced to enhance the taste, smell, texture, and storage characteristics of the food, but not necessarily the nutritional value.

All of these changes during processing reduce the nutritional quality of fast food. Nutritional food should be a regular and necessary part of our diet. By eliminating natural foods, we are forced to eat other foods. For example, to increase our fiber intake, we take high-fiber supplements, or to supplement our diet, we take vitamins. The food processing that eliminates the nutritional value of the food is only partially balanced by additives such as specific vitamins (e.g., "enriched with vitamin C"). Much more is taken out than is added.

9. *The larger the fruit, the better it is. Juice is as good as eating the whole fruit.* Modern agricultural processes have been designed around the look, size, and storage qualities of food. Hybrid forms of fruits, nuts, vegetables, and other natural foods have been bred for these cosmetic qualities. However, the nutritional aspects of these foods have generally been reduced. Buying fruits or vegetables that are naturally darker in color, smaller, and that have fewer fruit to the bunch gives the buyer a generally higher nutritional value. A wild fruit tree near a vacant farmhouse will have fruit that are small, with blemishes, a generally darker color, more nutritional value, and a more pronounced taste than will a hybrid fruit bred for size and extended storage.

10. *Using the food pyramid means eating equal quantities of foods with fats and oils, vegetables and fruits, and grains.* Too often, the food pyramid is displayed in such a way that the food groups at the top of the pyramid appear to be more important (see Figure 14-1). This implies that these food groups should be eaten in quantities similar to the foods at the bottom of the pyramid. At the bottom of the pyramid are grains, which should make up the biggest portion of a human diet (about 50%). The middle portion of the pyramid, the vegetable and fruit group, should be the second largest portion of the human diet. The smallest portion of the human diet, a few percent, should come from the foods at the top of the pyramid, those containing fats, oils, and sugars. Students rank these groups equally or put greater emphasis on the top group—fats, oils, and sugars—when asked to describe a nutritional meal according to the food pyramid. The fats, oils, and sweets group do not

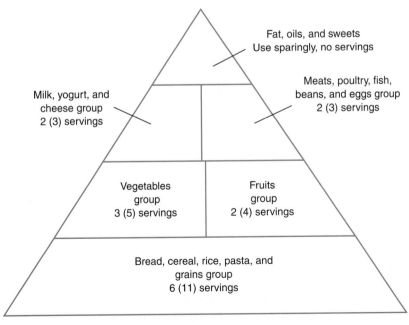

FIGURE 14-1 *Food guide pyramid*

FIGURE 14-2 *A better way to represent the food pyramid*

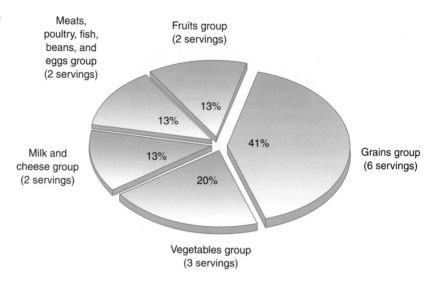

Meats, poultry, fish, beans, and eggs group (2 servings)

Fruits group (2 servings)

Milk and cheese group (2 servings)

Grains group (6 servings)

Vegetables group (3 servings)

13%

13%

13%

41%

20%

represent a serving. They are included in the other food groups. Be careful; don't allow your students to fall into the food pyramid illusion. Other versions besides the food pyramid should be used. One example is the food circle (see Figure 14–2).

DISCREPANT EVENT ACTIVITIES IN FOOD AND NUTRITION

Using students' prior knowledge (often including alternative conceptions) as a starting point, the next step is to write an instructional sequence of student learning experiences. Begin with activities that help the students recall, and become aware of, their prior knowledge of an idea. Awareness is followed by confrontation with a more appropriate understanding. This is the Exploration phase of the learning cycle lesson.

The activities below can be used with one or more alternative conceptions in food and nutrition. The numbers of the alternative conceptions match those given in the list above.

1. **Students' Alternative Conception:** *Food is anything taken in from the environment by a green plant, including water, minerals, and air.*

   Discrepant Activity A: Distribute a pretest during the Exploration phase of a lesson on which students can express their prior knowledge about food. Give them a list of items and ask them to indicate whether or not green plants use each item as food. Ask them to give reasons for all of their choices. Items should include air, water, sugar, starch, soil, fertilizer, sunlight, and minerals such as iron oxide.

   Only sugar and starch are used by green plants as food. The rest of the items are components that green plants use to manufacture food or carry out vital processes.

   Discrepant Activity B: Following the pretest, ask students within each group of three or four to compare their responses and reasons for deciding which of the items are food. Provide the students with a problem sheet including drawings of a small child and a large adult. Below the drawings state the following: A science fiction movie describes the future as one in which people can take a daily vitamin tablet that is so potent that they get all they require. Relate this statement to the drawing above in which the child may have a weight of 40 pounds and the adult a weight of 160 pounds. Can this event in a science fiction movie actually take place? Why or why not?

   Later, during the Invention phase of the lesson, introduce the idea that the total weight of the vitamin tablets would not equal the weight gain nor provide the energy

Where do green plants get their food?

requirements needed by a growing human. Vitamins provide chemicals that facilitate bodily functions. Vitamins do not provide energy to humans. A lack of vitamins causes deficiency diseases because the body cannot adequately carry out the functions those vitamins facilitate. Since the definition of food is material used by an organism that is an energy-containing substance, vitamins cannot be classified as food. The same is true of water and sunlight for both green plants and animals. Minerals taken from the soil by green plants function much as vitamins do for animals.

2. **and 3. Students' Alternative Conception:** *Green plants get their food from the soil. Soil is food. Green plants take food in from the outside.*

Discrepant Activity: Form groups of three or four students. Give each student a problem sheet containing a picture of two trees, each growing in a tub of soil: a young short sapling about 1 foot high, and an older taller tree about 8 feet high with a much larger trunk. Label the sapling as "age: 1 month" and the older tree as "age: 2 years." Below the picture, present the following problem: A young tree is planted in a tub of soil. The tub of soil and the tree weigh 51 pounds. After 2 years, the tree has grown. Now the tub and the tree weigh 81 pounds. During this time, no soil or fertilizer were added nor taken away from the tub. The tree was watered at appropriate times and was sitting in its tub out of doors. Explain where the tree's added weight came from.

Although water does add weight to a tree, if the 2-year-old tree and tub were allowed to dry out completely, the weight of the tub and the tree would still be much greater than the tub and the sapling. The additional weight comes from green plants manufacturing their own food by taking in carbon dioxide from the air, water, and minerals from the soil. Green plants create starch through the process of photosynthesis with energy provided by sunlight. Plant growth, including the creation of new plant cells, occurs through the use of the molecules and energy found in the chemical bonds between the molecules of these stored starches. The increased weight of the tree is due primarily to the added carbon from the starch molecules involved in new cell growth.

4. **Students' Alternative Conception:** *Light is necessary for green plants to live and grow. Sunlight makes green plants healthy. Green plants always need light.*

Discrepant Activity: Organize small groups of four students for a long-term activity: a materials manager, a reporter, an observer, and an illustrator. Do this before the unit on plants begins. These roles should rotate over time. Provide each group with four lima bean seeds, potting soil, and four clear plastic cups. Ask the students to draw what they think both plants grown from the seeds will look like in 10 days. If the students are old enough, ask them to design an experiment to test the effects of light on green plants. Otherwise, give the following instructions: Ask the students to put 2 inches of potting soil into each cup and plant the lima bean seeds about 1 inch below the surface of the soil next to the edge of the cup. Ask them to add 3 tablespoons of water to each cup. Put one cup on the windowsill or in some bright spot in the room and the three other cups on a desk across the room from the window, under a desk on the floor, and in a closet or in a box sealed off from light. Keep a daily diary indicating at least the following observations: the date, a description of the seed or green plant seen under the soil through the plastic wall of the cup, a measure of the height of the plant above the soil, and the number of leaves. Add a little water to each of the plants every day, keeping the soil moist but not wet. The illustrator should sketch the plant each day in a diary. At appropriate points, the group should discuss their results.

The discrepancy here involves the observation that seeds germinate whether or not they are in the presence of light. Once germinated, the plants in the dark grow taller than the plants in the light. However, they are spindly with fewer leaves. If the experiment stops before the plants in the dark die, the students are left with the alternative conception that light is not necessary for plants to live and grow. Therefore, make sure this activity is carried out until the stored food in the seed, the cotyledons, is used up and plants in the dark condition turn brown and die. Follow this discrepancy with an Invention phase during which a clear explanation of the role of light in green plant growth is provided in discussions and other active learning experiences. Light is not required for germination but is required for green plant growth.

5. **Students' Alternative Conception:** *Color differences in green plants are due to disease, death, lack of food, or age of the plant.*

Discrepant Activity A: Organize small groups of three students: a presenter, a discussion moderator, and a recorder. Provide each group with a picture or a drawing of a farmer cutting hay in a field. Part of the field is cut and the other part has hay still standing. Tell the students: "The standing hay is green but the stubble from the cut hay is yellow-brown. Why do you think this happens? How can the different color of the stubble be explained?" Give the groups time to discuss and present their ideas to the class.

The green pigment, chlorophyll, is responsible for the green coloring of the top of the hay plant. In the absence of light, or in light of lower intensity, little or no chlorophyll is produced in the hay plant's stalk or leaf. Since the top of the hay plant is exposed to strong sunlight, it is green. The stubble left after cutting was at the bottom of the plant and was shaded from sunlight in the hay field. A short time after cutting, the stubble turns darker green, with leaf shoots of hay rising up from it as the stubble is exposed to sunlight.

Discrepant Activity B: Organize small groups of four students: a materials manager, a reporter, an observer, and an illustrator. Ask each group to discuss the question, "What will happen to a green plant if only part of it is put in darkness and the rest is in sunlight?" After discussion in groups and a brief presentation of each group's ideas to the whole class, tell the students that they are going to try out their ideas. Provide each group with pieces of black construction paper, scissors, and tape. Select a small tree or bush the class will use near the school building. Preferably, the tree should have large leaves (such as a maple) and branches near the ground so that the students can touch the leaves. Ask the groups to select two leaves but not to pick them off the tree. Tell them to cut out two shapes from the black construction paper (for example, a star and a triangle). The size of these shapes should be smaller than the leaf on the tree. Have them tape one of the shapes to the surface of each leaf. A description of the leaves should be written by the reporter and a drawing made by the illustrator before and after taping. Have the groups return to the tree to inspect their leaves and the area under the taped shapes every day for a few days. Allow time for discussion following the observations and after the last inspection of the leaf. Following the last observation, ask the students to carefully remove the shapes. Come back in a few days and examine the leaves again.

Since many students believe that a lack of green color is due to disease or death, this should be a surprising activity for them. The area under the shape will become less green and, if left long enough, will change color. Chlorophyll is produced in response to the amount of sunlight received. However, the plant is still healthy and it is not dying. The leaf cells still have food stored in the leaf to sustain them. The green color of the affected area will return when the shape is removed.

6. **Students' Alternative Conception:** *Food, minerals, and water have the same nutritional benefits for animals. Height and weight of a person are similarly influenced by the amount of food eaten.*

Discrepant Activity: Organize small groups of four students: a materials manager, a reporter, an observer, and an illustrator. Ask each group to discuss the question, "What will happen to a green plant if it is gently pulled out of the ground, rinsed, and put into a small cup of water for a length of time?" The students should discuss possible results and make a prediction about the plant's health. After students briefly present their ideas to the class, ask them to try out the problem situation. For this activity, each group needs two plants (for example, young lima bean plants a few inches tall, in loose potting soil). Tell the students to loosen the soil around the plants and gently pull them out so that the roots are not damaged. Next, ask them to put the plants into clear plastic cups. The plants can be supported with a toothpick or a stick lying across the top of the cup. Loosely tie the plants to the stick.

Pour distilled water into one cup so that the roots of the plant are covered by the water. In the other cup, add aquarium water or tap water with a little bit of fertilizer (minerals) added. Cover the roots of the second plant with this water.

Ask the student groups to observe, record, and draw their plants over the next week to 10 days until a significant change has occurred in the plant whose roots were covered with distilled water. Afterwards, have the student groups compare their results with their predicted outcomes.

The green plant in the distilled water without minerals will gradually lose its green color and turn brown. The green plant in the water with minerals should flourish as though it is growing in the soil. Water alone is not sufficient to provide the materials for all plant functions.

7. **Students' Alternative Conception:** *Food gives green plants and animals energy directly, with little or no processing by the organism.*

Discrepant Activity: Organize small groups of four students. Give each group a 5-foot piece of shelf paper or manila paper. Ask the groups to choose one member to lie down on the paper, and an outline of this student's body is traced onto the paper. Present the groups with the following problem: Draw and label the complete process of food (such as a carrot) being eaten, down to the production of movement in a muscle in the student's arm. Ask the students to present their drawings and ideas to the class.

The student groups will have difficulty describing what occurs after the food reaches the stomach or intestines. There may be many creative explanations regarding how the food becomes energy in the muscle cells of the arm. During the Invention phase following this discrepant event, use activities and interactive discussion to suggest the idea that food is changed by the action of digestive fluids (mostly enzymes) into dissolved substances such as glucose molecules. The glucose molecules pass through the intestinal wall and are transported to individual cells in the muscle by the circulatory system. This process is called digestion. Oxygen molecules in the lung's air mixture are transported through the circulatory system to the muscle cells. These molecules enter through the cell wall in a process called osmosis, where they are combined in a chemical change in the cell, releasing energy. During this chemical change, called respiration, the new substances of water and carbon dioxide form and energy is released.

8. **Students' Alternative Conception:** *Fast food and snack foods have the same nutritional value as the potatoes, meats, and grains out of which they were made.*

Discrepant Activity A: Organize students in groups of four. Ask students to discuss and record a prediction related to the question: "How does the nutritional value of snack foods and fast food compare to other foods available in a supermarket?" Provide each group with four pairs of nutrition labels from packaged food. In each pair, one label should be from a highly processed or fast food (for example, processed cheese). The other label should be from a less processed or natural form of the food (for example, milk). Additional pairs of labels or nutrition information from cookbooks or other resources can include whole wheat and white bread, raw onions and onion rings, orange juice and orange drink, an apple and applesauce, or whole potatoes and frozen french-fried potatoes. Using a chart, have students compare various nutrients in each pair of labels: the number of calories, the fiber content, salt content, amount of food additives (include preservatives, color agents, vitamins, and minerals), and the complexity of sugars. Glucose and sucrose are simple sugars requiring little body processing while fructose is a complex sugar requiring more processing. Ask the groups to present their findings to the whole class.

Discrepant Activity B: Assign two students in each group to be tasters and two to be recorders. Provide each group of four students with six different types of foods. Ask the students to inspect a set of food samples and group them by the amount of fiber they think each contains. Ask the tasters in the group to eat a small but equal quantity of each of the six foods. The recorders will determine how many chews the tasters use before they swallow each food sample. The food samples can include pieces of oatmeal bread without crust, a few rolled oats, small bits of sugar or candy that easily melt on the tongue, sugarcane or cooked beet, apple, applesauce, potato chips, and raw potato. Ask the groups to discuss their findings, compare them with their predictions, and report the results to the class.

The more a food is processed or changed from its original form, the less fiber content is contained in it. Since fast foods, snacks, and many foods found in grocery stores are highly processed, our diets are usually deficient in fiber. Fiber is important for normal bodily functions such as waste elimination. However, adding fiber to the diet artificially can create other problems in body functioning. For a 2,000 calorie daily diet, 25 grams of dietary fiber are needed. In addition, less than 65 grams of fat, 300 milligrams of cholesterol, and 2,400 milligrams of salt are needed. Helping students become aware of the need for, and to test for, fiber content in foods is an important part of science literacy.

9. **Students' Alternative Conception:** *The larger the fruit, the better it is. Juice is as good as eating the whole fruit.*

Discrepant Activity: For this activity, provide, or ask students to provide through notes to parents, samples of juices, vegetables, and fruits from the grocery store, local gardens, or farm stands. Pair up examples of juice, cosmetic hybrids, and more naturally grown fruits and vegetables. "Cosmetic hybrid" is a term used to mean hybrid fruits or vegetables grown for their commercial success rather than nutritional value or, sometimes, taste. Very large, red, and beautiful apples with a flat taste are one example; include samples such as apple juice, large red "cosmetic hybrid" apples, and a local apple such as Stayman or crabapple; iceberg lettuce and red or romaine lettuce; grape juice, white grapes, and local or concord grapes; and tomato juice, tomato paste, hot house tomato, or a vine-ripened local tomato. Others are possible, but finding a particular set may be limited at different times of the year and in different climatic regions.

Organize students into groups of four. Ask them to discuss and record their inferences related to the following instruction: "Look at the pictures, or samples, of different fruits and vegetables. Decide which sample you would choose to eat from each pair. Describe why you made your choice." Have the groups present their decisions to the whole class.

Provide student groups with two or three paired juices, cosmetic hybrids, and more naturally grown fruits and vegetables. Ask the students to draw and describe the paired sets of fruits and vegetables. Next, have them taste each and describe and record its taste and texture characteristics while eating. Provide the students with nutritional information on each of the paired sets. This should include the calories, fats, dietary fiber, salt, preservatives, and the vitamins and minerals present. This information can be obtained from sources such as healthy-foods cookbooks. One example is a cookbook produced by the American Heart Association, the *Low-Fat, Low-Cholesterol Cookbook* (Grundy & Winston, 1989). Ask students to determine which item in each paired set has the most nutritional value and to present their findings to the class.

Students find that juices have the least total nutritional value, substantially less fiber, and contain many added chemicals that do not relate to nutritional health. The cosmetic hybrid has less nutritional value and often a blander taste when compared to the more naturally grown fruit or vegetable. For example, a raw apple eaten with the skin on provides 2.2 grams of dietary fiber per serving. An apple eaten without the skin provides 1.9 grams of dietary fiber. Apple juice provides only 0.1 grams of dietary fiber.

10. **Students' Alternative Conception:** *Using the food pyramid means eating equal quantities of foods with fats and oils, vegetables and fruits, and grains.*

Discrepant Activity A: Organize small groups of four students: a materials manager, a reporter, an illustrator, and a food diary data gatherer. Ask each group to construct three meals: breakfast, lunch, and dinner, as well as two snacks for one day. Let the students sort through magazines and cut out pictures of foods or draw those they cannot find. They should select foods that, together, create a nutritious set of meals. Next, glue each meal on a paper plate and glue all the snacks for one day on another plate. To assist them in this process, the group may ask one member to describe all the food eaten the day before, or one student from each group may be asked to keep a diary of one day's meals prior to participating in this lesson.

Give each student group a food guide pyramid (for example, one provided by the U.S. Department of Agriculture) that indicates the number of daily servings from each of the food groups (see Figure 14–1). Ask the students to compare the amount of servings in each food group with the foods they chose for their meals and snacks. Ask groups to present the results of their comparison to the whole group.

Discrepant Activity B: Using data provided on the U.S. Department of Agriculture's food pyramid of the basic food groups, ask each group to determine how much food should be eaten from each of the food groups (see Figure 14–1). This can be done graphically or using arithmetic. If done graphically, the students compute the area of each segment on the pyramid and compare the size of each area. For example, the students might cut out the segments representing both the meat and eggs group and the dairy and milk group. Putting those two blocks together, the students should find that they are about the same size as the vegetable group. If arithmetic is used, the students work with the lowest (highest and lowest are usually given) number of servings for each food group and compute the percentage of the total each represents. For instance, 73 percent of all servings eaten during any one day should include vegetables, fruits, and grains; 13 percent of the servings should come from the milk group; and 13 percent should come from the meat and eggs group. For 15 food servings, that's 11 vegetable, fruit, and grain servings; 2 milk group servings; and 2 meat, beans, and eggs servings. For complex foods such as salads, count one serving for vegetables and one for fat in the dressing. For a plain pizza, count one serving each for grain, cheese, and fat for each large piece consumed.

When comparing their actual meals to the food pyramid in Activity A, students often find that they are consistently eating more servings in the groups containing fats or meats, or eating very large servings of 1,000 calories or more, than in other food groups. During the Invention phase of the lesson, provide information to the students about the unhealthy effects of high-fat and high-sugar diets on children and what this might mean for their lives as adults. In Activity B, the students find that mathematics is a useful tool in maintaining a healthy life. Thinking in terms of areas on the food guide pyramid or in the percent of totals they may find when they look at any individual meal or food pattern over the entire day, the students are made more aware of the illusion that is sometimes created in the representation of the food pyramid. The top block on the pyramid does not represent a serving. It represents fats, oils, and sugars that are added to foods and that should be minimal in quantity. The total amount of fatty foods is represented only in the second layer of the pyramid. Their total area represents less than one-fourth of the total daily food calorie intake per day. Some pyramids are drawn in such a way as to suggest that the pyramid is very tall (see Figure 14–3). When students examine these drawings, it appears that the foods with fats in the two top layers of the pyramid have an equal height and thus represent an equal quantity of food as compared to the other food groups. A more accurate representation of a healthy diet uses a flat-topped pyramid with a very small top section and a base much wider than the pyramid's height (see

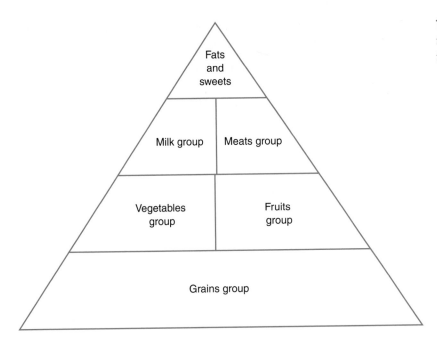

FIGURE 14-3   *Food guide illusion based on distorted illustration*

Figure 14–1). A food wheel is a more accurate representation of the appropriate number of servings or amount of food by area (see Figure 14–2).

IMPLICATIONS FOR CLASSROOM TEACHING OF A UNIT ON FOOD AND NUTRITION

What experiences are helpful in developing students' ideas in the area of food and nutrition? The objectives of a food and nutrition unit should relate to a view of nutrition based on scientific evidence—observation, hypotheses, and generalizations obtained through critical thinking where direct evidence may be difficult to obtain. Beginning a unit with a hands-on lesson considering the key question, "How do the fruits, vegetables, and grains we eat relate to the parts of a plant?" or, for older students, "What is in our food besides the food we expect?" involves identifying and classifying food additives from food labels and is a start in this direction.

Much of the information that students understand about food and nutrition is derived from their own sensory experiences and their social world. They need to distinguish between information derived through various aspects of the physical and the social world and scientific evidence. A great deal of the information students perceive in the everyday world through their senses, television, storybooks, magazines, and adults contains inaccurate, misleading, and partial statements of scientific fact. Even though students may have covered nutrition in classroom units in previous years, much classroom research points to the fact that only a small portion of students learn and use appropriate food and nutrition concepts in their daily lives. It is more typical for students to base their daily nutritional habits on alternative conceptions, or a mix of everyday or commonsense knowledge and school knowledge. An example of this is the students' view that the sun is important for green plants to help them absorb food from the soil. In this case, students separate school knowledge from everyday knowledge; for example, a student might say that green plants make their own food through photosynthesis but still keep the idea that plants obtain food from the soil. Helping students construct conceptions of food and nutrition closely related to scientific evidence is fostered by:

1. Asking small groups of students to talk about their ideas of food and nutrition for green plants and animals and share these ideas with the whole class.
2. Providing numerous experiences before giving explanations of food and nutrition and the relationships of various important factors (see the previous discrepant activities for some ideas):
   a. The use of light by green plants after germination.
   b. The use of light by green plants in making food.
   c. The role of water and minerals from the soil in making food.
   d. The green plant's use of oxygen during the day and night due to respiration.
   e. The green plant's use of carbon dioxide and the liberation of oxygen during photosynthesis.
   f. The role of sunlight in providing energy to make food during photosynthesis.
3. Providing experiences and explanations that help students make a distinction between everyday and scientific uses of the terms "food," "nutrients," "photosynthesis," "chlorophyll," and "respiration."
4. Providing opportunities to compare students' everyday knowledge and experiences with human food and nutrition with scientific fact and theory.
5. Spending a good deal of time experiencing, classifying, and obtaining nutritional information about a wide variety of foods that humans eat and about human nutritional needs (see the previous discrepant activities for some ideas).
6. Giving students ample opportunities to use and apply scientifically accepted ideas about green plants and animal food and nutrition. Students need to work out how to apply these ideas to a wide range of situations. They should begin by relating their theory to experiences that are familiar and lead to the application of the theory in a wider range of situations. These opportunities should involve language activities such as speaking, reading, and writing descriptions of what actually happens to minerals from the soil as they are transported to the leaf, building greenhouses to grow food plants in the winter, and planning and performing experiments to test the difference between competing food and nutrition ideas.

Applying What You Know

Interviewing a Student about Food and Nutrition

Develop an interview question script on the prior knowledge of a primary-age student in one of the 11 food and nutrition areas previously described. In advance, set up a schedule with a classroom teacher that does not interfere with normal class activities. Take notes during and after each interview. Complete a reflective journal entry following the interview. Discuss the results with the teacher and observe the student in daily classroom activities to see if his thinking fits your conclusions. Complete the following steps to accomplish these tasks.

Step 1. Select a discrepant event, phenomenon, or confrontational situation related to a food and nutrition concept or generalization. Use one of the food and nutrition alternative conceptions and activities previously mentioned as an example of the content and format to be used, or construct one using a similar format. Consider the probable prior knowledge of this student as you plan. Gather the demonstration materials or draw the phenomenon or situation.

Step 2. Write a script of one or more key questions and possible follow-up responses you will make. Consider general open-ended questions, problem-solving tasks, garden-path tasks that walk students through the idea, or comprehension tasks. Ask the student to describe his understanding of the event, then ask the student to describe what he thinks about the cause of an event or what he thinks will happen.

Step 3. To start the interview, set the student at ease. Talk to the student about something that will be of interest to him first. Begin the interview with your key question.

Step 4. Find out what ideas the student already has about the phenomenon or situation. What does the student think is happening? For what reasons? What words does the student use to explain or describe it? You are not interested in obtaining the right answer; you are only interested in what the student's answer is and the reasoning that led to the answer.

Step 5. Take the student seriously. Give him the opportunity to discuss or try out ideas by himself.

Step 6. Challenge the student to describe or find evidence for his ideas. Probe the student to get at the deeper understanding of his ideas and follow his line of reasoning.

Step 7. Thank the student for allowing you to listen to his view of the event. After the interview, write up the events as they occurred from steps 1 to 7 in a reflective journal format.

To complete this activity, include a title page and label the parts of the assignment as indicated below, organize them, place them in a folder, and turn in the folder or add it to a portfolio.

1. A description of the concept and the demonstration materials, or a drawing of the phenomenon or situation.
2. A script of the key question and possible follow-up responses you will make to your student.
3. Notes of the interview events and student statements as they occurred written in a reflective journal form. Identify the student by first name only or use a pseudonym.
4. Your concluding comments for the student interviewed written in a short one-page paper. Consider the following questions: "What does the student believe (prior knowledge) about the concept or event?" "Why does he believe this?" and "How does this belief relate to the scientific view?" As a teacher, what have you learned about this student?

A Learning Cycle Example Involving Students' Alternative Conceptions Related to Food and Nutrition

To illustrate the instructional sequence of: (1) identifying students' alternative conceptions, (2) developing a classroom lesson plan, and (3) developing assessment of a specific idea in food and nutrition, an example of a complete lesson and assessment procedure follows.

Alternative Conception Addressed by the Lesson Plan: *Light is necessary for green plants to live and grow. Sunlight makes green plants healthy. Green plants always need light (number 4 on page 393).*

Lesson Goal: To allow students to investigate and develop inferences about the role of sunlight in the nutritional needs of a green plant.

Grade Level: Grades 4–5.

Prerequisites: Can measure height to the nearest millimeter or one-eighth inch.

Exploration

Objective: The students will investigate the effects of sunlight on germinating seeds and young green plants.

Materials: For each group: four lima bean or corn seeds, two full cups of potting soil, and four Styrofoam cups.

Procedure:

A. Organize small groups of four students: a materials manager, a reporter, an observer, and an illustrator.
B. State the key questions: "Is light necessary for plants to live and grow?" "Does sunlight make green plants healthy?" and "Do green plants always need light?" Describe the materials and instructions needed for students to carry out the activity related to the effects of sunlight on growing plants.
C. Provide each group with four lima bean or corn seeds, potting soil, and four Styrofoam cups. Ask the students to design an experiment to test the effects of light on the growth of plants using the lima bean or corn seeds. An example of an experiment has been explained above in number 4 of the discrepant activities in the "Food and Nutrition" section. It includes a description of what was found in the experiment.

   This experiment involves a week to 10 days of plant growth time. Seeds generally require 2 to 3 days to germinate, when they break through the soil, and another week to grow tall enough to have leaves so that the effects of light become evident. Have the illustrator draw the plants at regular intervals. Have the observers record a description of the plant at the same intervals and use it to construct a table or bar graph of plant growth.

D. At appropriate points, have the group discuss the results of the experiment they designed.

Evaluation: Assess the completeness of each group's description of their hypothesis, procedure, data, and results. Assess group skills by observing whether students join their groups quickly when asked and whether the group reviews what needs to be done before starting.

Invention

Objective: The students will describe the effects of sunlight on green plant growth during germination and on green plants after they have broken through the top of the soil (after germination).

Materials: A lima bean seed soaked in water for 24 hours for each student.

Procedure:

A. Have each group present to the whole class its hypothesis, procedure, and the results developed from the Exploration activity. Help students communicate the results of their activities using tables and/or bar graphs to justify their conclusions. Continuously help students compare the results of each group's experiment.
B. Write the key questions from the Exploration on the board. Ask the groups to discuss these questions based on the class discussion of their experiments. Ask them to report their answers to the whole class.

C. Explain the discrepancy involving the observation that seeds germinate whether or not they are in the presence of light. Once germinated, the plants in the dark grow faster than the plants in the light. However, they are spindly with fewer leaves. If the experiment were stopped before the plants in the dark condition die, the students are left with the alternative conception that light is not necessary for plants to live and grow.

D. Provide soaked lima bean seeds and a sheet of paper to all students. In groups, have them take apart the lima bean seeds and tape the parts to the paper. At the bottom of the paper, ask the groups to discuss the function of each part. As an extension, another lesson can involve students in planting these parts to determine which part grows. Have students find these parts: cotyledon(s), seed coat, cover, and an embryo. Tell students that the embryo is the plant and that the cotyledons are food sacs (starch) that the embryo uses to develop roots and a stem with which to reach the soil surface. Corn seeds have only one food sac or cotyledon. The students should have observed this growth during the germination phase of the plant. State that the germination process does not require sunlight, as students have found out through their experiments.

E. Ask students to display the illustrator's pictures of plant growth following germination in dark and light conditions. Explain to the students that even though the plants in the dark grew faster before they started dying, they did not look healthy. They did not have a very green color and they had very few leaves, since sunlight is necessary for the health of green plants in order to make green chlorophyll and additional food. Without this additional food production, the green plant's food sac soon becomes used up and it dies because it lacks the materials and energy that the food provides for growth and maintenance.

F. In closure, light is not necessary for seeds during the germination phase of growth. It is, however, necessary following germination for health and continued growth.

Evaluation: Ask students to create a poem about two plant seeds, one that landed on soil in a field and one that landed on soil in a cavity under a rock or in the woods. Assess students' group skills by observing whether they stay with their group while it is working and pay attention to how much time they have to carry out each activity.

Expansion

Objective: The students will solve everyday problems involving the role of sunlight in green plant growth.

Materials: For each student: a map or drawing of an area with three vegetation zones: deep forest, low shrubs, and meadow (Figure 14–4); a sheet of paper with a 3 x 4 matrix.

Procedure:

A. Provide the following problems and ask groups to discuss their answers and report them to the class. Supportive evidence for each response to the problems should be provided. For problems 1 and 2, give students a map, which may be teacher-drawn, of an area of mixed plant height and foliage. It may have an area of deep forest, an area of small bushes, and a meadow.

   1. In which area will a squash seed planted 3 centimeters below the soil surface reach the soil surface the fastest? (The temperature of the soil is the same in all areas.)

   2. Small squash plants are planted in each area. Draw the plants after 1, 2, 3, and 4 weeks. Provide each group with a 3 × 4 matrix on a whole sheet of paper. Ask students to label the horizontal axis "weeks" and the vertical axis "areas of different plants" (e.g., deep forest, bushes, and meadow).

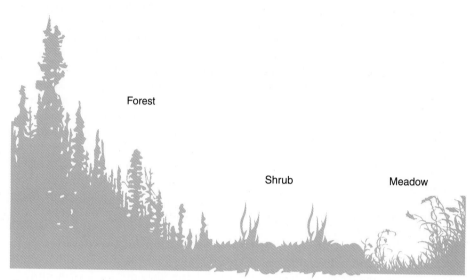

FIGURE 14-4   *Vegetation zones*

3. A farmer purchased an abandoned coal mine to produce mushrooms for sale in grocery stores. The farmer spread lots of horse manure from her stables on the floor of the coal mine. In the complete darkness of the mine, the farmer successfully produced lots of large mushrooms for sale. Explain how this can happen.
   Teacher's note: Mushrooms are part of a class of plants called fungi. This class includes molds, mildew, rusts, and smut. Lacking chlorophyll, they do not produce their own food. Fungi get their food from organic soil materials made from dead plants dissolved in water.

B. Ask students to present their answers to each problem in a report to the class. Discuss the results in an interactive discussion.

C. Summarize the lesson by describing each of the activities in the order in which each was experienced in the lesson. Briefly indicate the main point developed in each activity.

Evaluation: Each student will respond to the following problem. The moon has a day that takes 28 of our Earth days. For 14 Earth days, it is dark at a certain location on the moon, and for 14 Earth days it is light. Describe by illustration and narrative the growth of a lima bean planted on the moon in a protected greenhouse in the middle of the lunar night. Remember that there will be 2 weeks of sunlight followed by 2 weeks of darkness every lunar "day." The lunar "day" is often called a "lunar month" because of its length. The lunar "day" is the origin of Earth's month; there are about 12 in an Earth year. Describe its growth for 2 lunar days. Identify, discuss, and develop inferences about the role of sunlight in the nutritional needs of a green plant on the moon in a protected environment.

EXAMPLES OF ALTERNATIVE CONCEPTIONS IN ADDITIONAL BIOLOGICAL SCIENCE AREAS

Students' alternative conceptions determine what they observe and the meaning they give to these observations, everyday experiences, and information they receive. Since the bio-

logical world is part of students' experiences from the day of birth, they will have preconceived ideas about many of the basic biological science areas. Prior knowledge changes from
year to year with the development of new thought processes and knowledge gained at home
and in school. The following is a sample of basic alternative conceptions commonly held by
students in the areas of biological science. The list demonstrates the depth and breadth of
alternative ideas found in a classroom of students in several basic biological science areas.
This outline includes the areas of plants, animals, and the structure and functions of living
things. Some references for this list are found in several research reports (Bishop & Anderson, 1990; Gallegos, Jerezano, and Flores, 1994; Hergenrather & Rabinowitz, 1991; Leach,
Driver, Scott, & Wood-Robinson, 1992; Mintzes, Trowbridge, Arnaudin, and Wandersee,
1991; Palmer, 1999; Schonfeld, Bases, Quackenbush, Mayne, Morra, & Cicchetti, 2001;
Schonfeld & Quackenbush, 2000; Strommen, 1995; Sunal & Sunal, 1991b, 1991c, 1991e).
Other examples of research are found in the reference section.

Sample Alternative Conceptions about Plants Students Bring to Class

1. A tomato is a vegetable.
2. Trees are not plants.
3. Carrots and lettuce are not plants; they are vegetables.
4. Trees are empty inside (have no internal structure) (younger children).
5. Seedlings are small trees, not young offspring (younger children).
6. Plant growth is seen as a straight-line process, moving from a young plant to an old plant and then dying (there is no idea of a plant being part of an interrelated ecosystem where the environment, including local weather, other plants, and animals, interacts with the plant in the growth process).
7. When part of a leaf loses its green color, that part of the plant is dead.
8. Plants are at the bottom of the food chain because they are small, defenseless, or unable to eat other plants or animals.
9. Plants do not have respiration.
10. Glucose is the end product of photosynthesis.

Sample Alternative Conceptions about Animals Students Bring to Class

1. Only large land animals such as those found in a zoo, farm, or in a home as pets are animals (younger children).
2. Animals have four legs (younger children).
3. Animals are large, bigger than insects, found on land, and furry.
4. If you can't see it breathe, it's not an animal.
5. A living thing can't be both a bird and an animal.
6. Only living things with backbones (vertebrae) are animals.
7. Living things with well-defined limbs and heads are animals (younger children) or vertebrate animals (older children).
8. Living things with soft or long bodies or with shells or exoskeletons are invertebrate animals (older children).
9. The only animals in the ocean are fish and snails.
10. Some young and adult animals are different types of animals; for example, tadpoles and frogs are different animals.
11. The caterpillar and the butterfly are not the same insect (younger children).

12. All animals that fly are birds (does not explain bats and penguins).
13. Animals are not linked to each other as food sources (as in the food chain).
14. Animals are dependent on people to supply them with food and shelter (younger children).
15. The availability of food is not the most important factor in the survival of an animal.
16. Animals can change their food at will according to its availability (similar to human beings going to a supermarket and picking up things they've never eaten).
17. Some animals are numerous in order to fill the needs for food by another population (there are many insects because birds eat them).
18. Germs enter the body through the mouth while eating and leave the body from the mouth.
19. Illness is a result of misbehavior (younger children).
20. People are ill only when someone tells them they are ill, when they have to go to the doctor, or when they have to stay in bed (younger children).
21. Every illness is caused by germs.
22. Drugs kill germs and heal the body immediately.
23. In the long run, health and life span are beyond an organism's control.

Sample Alternative Conceptions about Functions and Structures of Organisms Students Bring to Class

1. Clouds are alive because they move, breathe, reproduce, and die (younger children).
2. Trees are not alive, especially in the winter.
3. Coral and sponge in the ocean are not alive.
4. All living things can be classified as plants or animals.
5. Some living things are not made of cells.
6. Cells perform no useful function.
7. Fluids move freely in and out of cells no matter what type of material is involved (osmosis is not understood).
8. Wilting is a sign of a dead plant (misunderstanding of fluid pressure in cells, turgor).
9. Small animals are filled with liquid or are empty inside (no internal structure) (younger children).
10. The contents of the bodies of large animals and humans are made of food and blood (these are the things that have been seen going into them and coming out of them).
11. The internal organs of animals are not connected, or do not exist as a system (younger children).
12. The brain only controls the parts of the body that we consciously have control over (it does not control digestion or the heart's activity).
13. Blood is a liquid that goes out of the heart but does not return to it.
14. Blood is a simple liquid and is not made of several components.
15. The liquid (plasma) in blood is red.
16. The human heart is solid. The heart is the shape of a valentine. Hearts store or clean blood (young children).
17. Humans have a one-, two-, or three-chambered heart (older children).
18. Human lungs are up near the neck and are small.
19. Plants and animals can change their structures to live successfully in a different habitat (like humans change jobs or wear different clothes).
20. The nonliving environment is made up of air, soil, and water. The nonliving environment, animals, and plants are all made up of different substances and you can't use one in another.
21. Genetic traits are inherited only from the mother (younger children).

22. Genetic traits are inherited from the same sex parent (older children).
23. People only inherit observable features such as hair and eye color, but not liver function.
24. Environmentally produced characteristics can be inherited, such as blindness due to an accident.
25. Organisms develop new (genetic) traits because they need them to survive.
26. Body parts that are not used disappear in offspring.
27. Disabilities are contagious (younger children).
28. All animals in a population will gradually change to form a new version (species) of the animal instead of the survival of the few that have a more successful characteristic.
29. When an environment changes, plants and animals can find a new habitat.
30. Material from dead organisms simply rots and disappears (matter is not converted into other materials and organisms in the environment, matter is not conserved and disappears, decomposing agents such as air and organisms are not needed).
31. Life processes involve creating and destroying matter (there is no cycle of transformation of matter and energy from one form to another).
32. Respiration is breathing.
33. The death of an organism is caused by something external to it.

Applying What You Know

Identifying Possible Alternative Conceptions

Examine one of your biological science lesson plans or a science book chapter and identify possible alternative conceptions related to the content that students might bring to class. If possible, work with a partner on this activity. Answer the questions below:

1. What are the stated or implied concepts and generalizations in the lesson plan or chapter?
2. What are possible alternative conceptions students might bring to class? Check the lesson or chapter concepts and generalizations against the sample lists previously provided. List the possible alternative conceptions you identify.

ACTIVITIES THAT CAN HELP STUDENTS CHANGE THEIR ALTERNATIVE CONCEPTIONS IN BIOLOGICAL SCIENCE

Discrepant events can involve students in the confrontation they need to test out their own conceptions. The activities include discrepant events related to alternative conceptions in biological science. These discrepant events are used in the Exploration phase of a learning cycle lesson.

See the Companion Website that accompanies this text at *http://www.prenhall.com/sunal* for a link to Biology Lessons for Teachers, K-6.

Companion Website

Discrepant Events with Plants

Students' Alternative Conception:
1. *A tomato is a vegetable.*
3. *Carrots and lettuce are not plants; they are vegetables.*
4. *Trees are empty inside (have no internal structure)(younger children).*

Group these foods as fruits or vegetables.

Discrepant Activity: This activity follows a lesson on classifying, naming, and identifying plant parts: roots, stems, leaves, and the parts of a flower. Bring in, or have students' families supply, the following items, or a similar set, for each group: an apple, tomato, carrot, cucumber, parsley, orange, lettuce leaves, beet, celery, squash, grape, kale, potato, pear, and green pepper. Place students in groups of four, assign roles, and ask the materials manager to get one sample of each item. The students are to classify them into groups and describe why they put each item in its group. Ask the students to report the group's decisions. Next, show students how you group the items. Group them as plant parts (fruit or flower, stem, leaf, or root), then pose the question, "Why are there different groupings of the items? Some of you grouped the items like this while others grouped them differently. Some of your groupings are different from mine." Allow students to discuss this question in their groups, then report what they decided to the whole class.

Following the report, ask students to classify their items into two groups: fruits and non-fruits. Ask them to list items in each group and describe why they were put into that group, then ask them to describe or define a fruit.

This activity provides a confrontation to students' ideas about the everyday use of terms associated with plant parts. Most students group tomatoes, cucumbers, squash, lettuce, potatoes, and carrots in a group called "vegetables." The rest of the items are usually grouped by students into a category called "fruits." Having students observe the teacher's alternative way of grouping the items and asking them to classify and define a fruit poses a strong confrontation to the belief of many students regarding what constitutes a fruit. Students associate fruits with sweetness more than anything else. However, an important everyday life understanding of the parts of the plant helps them more adequately assess the variety of foods they are eating. A fruit is the ripened ovary of a flower. It is the reproductive part of the plant that is usually easily detached from the plant. It contains a covering or seed coat, a fleshy part, and seeds. The fruit is designed to foster the germination of seeds by providing nutrients and moisture for growth in the fleshy part. In the Invention phase of the lesson following this discrepant activity, students experience the differences between the characteristics of two sets of food items such as: (1) fruits, including tomatoes, grapes, pears, apples, squash, and string beans; and (2) other items representing the roots, stems, and leaves of plants.

Discrepant Events with Animals

Students' Alternative Conception:
7. *Living things with well-defined limbs and heads are animals (younger children) or vertebrate animals (older children).*
8. *Living things with soft or long bodies or with shells or exoskeletons are invertebrate animals (older children).*

Discrepant Activity: This activity follows a lesson on classifying, naming, and identifying different types of animals. The student groups are provided with 15 to 30 pictures of a variety of animals, such as a fish, frog, deer, elephant, insects of various types, turtle, snake, crayfish, bird, human, mouse, dog, cat, guinea pig, snail, clam, spider, jellyfish, shrimp, whale, and penguin. Ask the students to form two groups with these pictures, those animals that have a backbone (vertebrates) and those animals that do not have a backbone (invertebrates). Have the students record the names of the animals in each group and provide a group report to the whole class. As reports are given, ask the students why there might be differences in each group's results. At this point, provide the students with additional pictures of animal skeletons that may be surprising to them. These pictures can be found in a variety of library resources or on the Internet. They could include pictures of snakes, turtles, fish, frogs, birds, and whale skeletons. Show them a grouping you have made. Ask them to compare their results with this new information and to report what they have concluded to the class.

When teaching a lesson on vertebrates and invertebrates, it is important that the concept to be learned be personally relevant to the student. It must fit into the student's previously developed ideas of the world in order for meaningful learning to occur (Holliday, Helgeson, Blosser, & McGuire, 1985). This discrepant activity can serve two purposes: it can be an introduction to vertebrates and invertebrates, or it can be a clarification of students' alternative conceptions about vertebrates. Studies have indicated that elementary and middle school students of all ages classify animals with well-developed limbs and heads as vertebrates while those with shells or exoskeletons and soft or long bodies are classified as invertebrates. Therefore, snakes, eels, and turtles are generally classified as invertebrates by students, although they are actually vertebrates. Students with alternative conceptions are making classifications based on irrelevant and conflicting information such as body part importance, size, segmentation, and appendages. Although they are invertebrates, many students classify crayfish, crabs, grasshoppers, and spiders as vertebrates because of the inappropriate characteristics they are using for the classification (Trowbridge & Mintzes, 1988).

This discrepant activity deals directly with students' alternative conceptions. It allows students to explain why their view of the concept is correct or incorrect (Holliday et al., 1985). It exposes students to numerous non-examples, as well as examples, of the concept. The activity helps students develop discrimination skills as they make classifications. In the Invention that follows, teachers need to focus students' attention on relevant animal attributes related to the concepts of vertebrate and invertebrate.

This focusing occurs during diverse experiences in which all the senses are utilized (Trowbridge & Mintzes, 1988). Teachers help students understand irrelevant characteristics that should not be used in determining classifications, including the soft or hard appearance of the animal, the importance of recognizable body parts, the size and shape of limbs and body, and the segmentation of body parts. Animal classification requires higher-level thinking in students. Teachers should not introduce this level of classification to students who are very young, such as those in kindergarten or first grade (Simpson & Marek, 1988).

Discrepant Events with Structures and Functions of Living Organisms

Students' Alternative Conception:

30. *Material from dead organisms simply rots and disappears (matter is not converted into other materials and organisms in the environment, matter is not conserved and disappears, decomposing agents such as air and organisms are not needed).*
31. *Life processes involve creating and destroying matter (there is no cycle of transformation of matter and energy from one form to another).*

Discrepant Activity: Prepare, in advance, the following specimen materials: a peach sitting in a jar with its lid on for 3 weeks, another in a jar for 2 weeks, a third in a jar for 1 week, a fresh peach, a jar of peach jam with large pieces of the fruit visible, and a frozen peach or frozen peach slices. If peaches are not in season, apples can be used. Put each of the peach specimens at five stations around the room. At each station, place cards that infer how the fruit got to its present state, including its age and conditions (such as frozen). Ask students the following key question, "Why do you think materials decay?" Have groups of students visit each station and describe their observations at each station. When they have finished their observations, the students should discuss the key question in their groups and report their answer to the whole class. At the beginning of the discussion, repeat the key question, "Why do you think materials decay?" while noting that some of the fruit has decayed and other specimens have not.

This activity provides evidence to confront students' conceptions about why materials decay. Many students in the elementary grades do not understand the roles of temperature, time (age), other organisms, and air in decay. The variety of stations provides different conditions under which the material has or has not decayed. The three peaches sitting in jars have met all the conditions for decay: temperature, time, other organisms, and air. The fresh peach has met all the conditions except time. The frozen peach and heated peach (jam) both have met the time condition. The frozen peach also lacks other organisms because they do not grow, or they grow slowly, in very cold temperatures, even though surrounded by air. The peach jam has been heated and now lacks organisms (they died in the heat) and air. In addition, the sugar inhibits the growth of organisms that get in later.

Applying What You Know

Interviewing a Student about Biological Science

Assess and discuss the prior knowledge of one or more students in a specific conceptual area related to the biological sciences, or assess and discuss the prior knowledge of a student in relation to a biological science unit currently being taught by a teacher in a local school. In advance, set up a schedule with a teacher that will not interfere with his normal class activities. Interview the student. Complete a *reflective* journal entry for each student. Discuss the results with the teacher and observe the student in daily activities to see if the student's thinking fits your conclusions.

Step 1. Select a discrepant event, phenomenon, or confrontational situation related to a biological science concept or generalization. Use the alternative conceptions and discrepant activities above as an example for your student. Consider the background of this student when planning the activity. Gather the demonstration materials or draw the phenomenon or situation.

Complete steps 2 to 7 as described in the previous Applying What You Know feature focusing on a student interview on food and nutrition.

Step 8. Finish the process with a conclusion and a prescription for an appropriate instructional activity on the concept. Consider the following questions: "What does the student believe (prior knowledge) about the concept or belief?" and "How does the belief relate to the scientific view?" As a researcher, answer: "What have you learned about this student?" and "How would you start a lesson in this area for the student?"

Include a title page and label the parts of the assignment indicated below:

1. *Concept or generalization*—a description of the concept or generalization and the demonstration materials, or a drawing of the phenomenon or situation.
2. *Script and student background*—a script with the key question and possible follow-up responses you will make to your student.
3. *Reflective journal*—write up the interview events as they occurred in reflective journal form. Identify the student by first name only or by a pseudonym.
4. *Concluding paper*—write your conclusion and a prescription in a short paper.

EXAMPLES OF LEARNING CYCLES TEACHING BIOLOGICAL SCIENCE CONCEPTS

The following learning cycle lessons challenge students' conceptions of a biological event with a more appropriate scientific explanation. It is important to relate each phase of the learning cycle to the students' prior knowledge.

A Learning Cycle Involving Alternative Conceptions about the Functions and Structures of Organisms

Alternative Conceptions Addressed by the Lesson Plan:

19. *Plants and animals can change their structures to live successfully in a different habitat (like humans change jobs or wear different clothes).*
24. *Environmentally produced characteristics can be inherited, such as blindness due to an accident.*
25. *Organisms develop new (genetic) traits because they need them to survive.*
29. *When an environment changes, plants and animals can find a new habitat.*

Lesson Goal: To allow students to investigate, develop inferences, and differentiate between the concepts of environmentally produced characteristics and genetic characteristics.

*Draw a picture of aquarium fish
and what they do over a short
period of time.*

Grade Level: Grades 2–3.

Prerequisites: Can measure time intervals of a whole and a half-minute.

Exploration

Objective: Students will investigate the observable characteristics of fish over specific time periods.

Materials: For each group: an aquarium filled with a variety of fish, snails, and plants; alternatively, groups can be given two goldfish in a clear plastic container (such as a 2-liter-sized soft drink bottle with the top cut off).

Procedure:

A. Form groups of four students. Assign roles. Tell students you are going to give them a thought problem: "You have just visited a museum that has a large aquarium with fish of different types. Draw a picture of the different fish and what they do. Describe in writing what fish do when you watch them. Discuss your ideas with your group." Have them write their answer on a sheet of paper.

B. Ask each group's reporter to make a brief report to the class on what they have drawn and written.

C. Assign new roles for each student group: a timer/materials manager and three observer/recorders. Describe the materials and instructions needed to carry out the activity of observing fish over specific short time intervals. Tell students they will be drawing and describing fish in an aquarium, observing fish at different times, and comparing how different fish behave and move.

D. Ask the key questions: "What do fish do?" "Do they do the same thing all the time?" "Do they do different things at different times?" and "Do different fish do different things?"

E. Ask the materials managers to get a small aquarium for each group. Tell the students to observe one thing a fish does in a 30-second period. At the end of the 30-second period, have the observer/recorders describe what they saw the fish do, then have them draw this motion on paper and describe the behavior of a particular fish in writing.

F. Ask the students to repeat this procedure three times with 5 or more minutes in between the observing intervals to allow for drawing and discussion. The second observation period involves darkening the environment, perhaps by putting dark paper around the fish containers. The third observation involves fish feeding under normal room-lighting conditions. A small amount of fish food is placed on top of the water. Students label each drawing as time period one—bright, two—dark, or three—feeding. A more effective observation would involve students observing the fish at different times of the day, perhaps in the early morning, around noon, and in the afternoon. The observations are repeated until the students cannot find any additional behavior to observe. Ask the students to staple together their observations for each timed event. Have them add a cover page title, "What Fish Do," followed by the names of the members of the group.

Evaluation: Collect the students' observations from the Exploration. Evaluate them, considering the completeness and specific behaviors drawn or described. Assess the group's skills at letting each person have a chance to share her ideas and listening to each other with interest.

Invention

Objective: Students will investigate the observable characteristics of ocean reef fish over specific time periods.

Materials: A videotape of ocean reef fish with 5 to 10 minutes of action showing a variety of fish, grouping patterns (schooling versus individual swimming), and some extended individual behavior (e.g., Eyewitness Fish, 1994, Dorling Kindersley and BBC Lionheart Television Intl. Inc.).

Procedure:

A. Ask students to report the results of their Exploration activity to the class. Help them communicate the results of their activities by asking them to show their pictures and describe the behavior depicted in the pictures. During the discussion, introduce the idea that fish perform specific motions related to time of day, what's going on around them, and the kind of fish they are.

B. Form groups of four students again. Tell the students they are going to take a trip to the ocean. Near land, in many of the world's oceans, are places where great amounts of fish live. They are going to see a videotape of one of these places. They are to observe what fish do for short time periods as they have before. Ask the students to make observations for 30 seconds, then draw and describe what they saw. They should share their drawings and ideas with their group. At the end of each interval, have the students staple their observation sheets together and label them according to the interval observed.

C. From a preselected section of the videotape, show the students 30 seconds of fish behavior. Select a section showing fish schooling and swimming as individuals. The difference in behavior should be identified as a characteristic by type of fish.

D. For the second time interval, choose a section of the tape related to fish eating. This could show fish pecking, digging into the soil or reef, or investigating a hole in a rock.

E. A third 30-second interval should involve another fish behavior. This could show the relationship of fish to other reef animals or fish being scared or fleeing from a diver or a larger fish.

F. Ask the student groups to discuss their observations and drawings after each time interval. Following the intervals, ask students to briefly report what they have concluded about how fish move. During this discussion, introduce the idea that fish motion and behavior is related to the environment in which they are found and to the type of fish. Try to clearly point out the differences between genetically derived behaviors and behaviors that have been modified or developed by the fish in its environment. The fright behavior of fish and their general pattern of movement, for example, is related to the type of fish, and thus to genetics. Specific behaviors in food hunting and motions of individual fish at a specific time are most likely environmentally related and have been adapted through learning by fish in their habitat. Describe the conditions and limits of learned fish behavior as related to the scientific explanation for the alternative conceptions listed at the beginning of the lesson. As you introduce these ideas, point out student-observed examples and watch a videotaped section again. Allow for as much student interaction in this discussion as possible. Encourage students to point out behaviors on the television screen and how they are different from other fish behaviors.

G. In closure, the discussion should lead the students to draw the conclusions that fish have many types of motion, some related to their environment, and others related to the specific species of fish to which they belong.

Evaluation: Collect the interval observations from each group. Evaluate whether each student reported an observation during each interval. Assess the group's skills of asking for help when needed and listening to everybody's ideas before determining the group's decision.

Expansion

Objective: Students will apply their knowledge of how fish move to a simulation of fish life in an ocean reef to human behavior.

Materials: For each group: a set of four fish puppets. The puppets should have a variety of fish shapes and colors. Two should be identical, and two should differ from these two and each other in shape and color. These will be made by each group. Possible materials are an old sheet, fabric scraps, fabric glue, markers, cloth, paper, and scissors. As a substitute, use heavy paper or thin poster board. Add a back panel to the puppet. The student will insert a hand into this panel so that the puppet moves as the student waves her fingers or the palm of her hand to simulate swimming; a large sheet of paper or butcher paper (2 meters long) for a background scene; scissors; colored markers; tape.

Procedure:

A. Ask each student group to make four fish puppets. The students could also create an ocean scene by coloring in rocks on butcher paper to simulate a reef. This can be taped on a wall.

B. Ask each student group to plan out a play that will simulate fish motion in a reef. Tell them to use the ideas about how and why fish move from earlier in the lesson. Their play will last for 30 seconds. Each group should sketch and describe the behavior their play will demonstrate.

C. After each group puts on its play, ask the students in the audience to describe what they saw the fish do. Following the audience's reporting, ask each group to describe the intended motion and show their drawing. Point out the types of behaviors and the ideas expressed by the students in their discussions. Focus on those instances showing environmentally learned or adapted behavior and those behaviors genetically related to the species of the fish. Construct a chart on the board listing the behaviors under each category that were demonstrated or discussed. Label the categories "Things fish learn to do" and "Things fish always do."

D. Help students apply what they have learned about fish behavior to humans by asking them to participate in a class demonstration. Group the students around you on the floor and ask them to describe behaviors they do during the day that would fall into each of the two types of behaviors. Some examples of things students learn to do might include eating with a fork, writing, reading, and putting on a sock. Examples of things students always do are blinking when somebody claps in front of their face, jumping at a surprise sound, and salivating at the smell of appetizing food.

Evaluation: Ask the students to draw and/or write about the behavior of a pet or neighborhood dog or cat that fits under each of the two categories. For example, dog howling is genetic, as is hiding at a loud noise and pricking up its ears at a new sound. Learned behavior includes jumping in bed with the student at night, doing a trick such as rolling over on command, and coming when its name is called.

Additional activities and information in biological science lessons should relate to the nature of science (see Chapter 1), as well as the people who participated in creating it and who work in the field today. Some examples of people who made significant contributions to the biological sciences but have been underrepresented in the mass media are listed in Figure 14–5, along with their major contributions. Additional information can be found

---

SCIENTISTS ARE DIVERSE!

Scientists Who Have Contributed to the Biological Sciences

Elizabeth Anderson
The first British woman physician.

Avicenna
An Iranian who wrote an encyclopedia on medicine.

Rachel Carson
An American woman who studied the interdependence of plants and animals and the effects of pesticides on the environment.

Manuel Garcia
A Spanish man who invented the larynogoscope.

Michiko Ishimura
A Japanese woman who examined the effects of heavy metal poisoning.

Arnold Maloney
A Trinidadian who examined antidotes for barbituate poisoning.

Lillie Minoka-Hill
A Native American who carried out nutrition research.

Onesimus
A slave in Africa who discovered the inoculation for smallpox.

Gertrude Perlmann
A Czechoslovakian woman who worked on protein chemistry.

Berta Scharrer
A German woman who invented neuroendocrinology.

FIGURE 14-5 *Scientists from typically underrepresented groups who have made significant contributions in the biological sciences* in library references such as an encyclopedia. The book *Women Scientists* by Nancy Veglahn (1991) is a resource example. An added Expansion activity to most any biological science lesson is to read a paragraph about the contribution of a related scientist to make him or her seem more real. Older students can create library research reports and short plays on the contributions of these scientists.

Applying What You Know

Planning an Exploration for a Biological Science Lesson

Using the third-grade biological science lesson plan below on the topic of animals, do the following: (1) identify possible alternative conceptions students could bring to the lesson (if possible, interview a few children), and (2) develop key questions the teacher could use to guide student actions, creating a confrontation to students' thinking during the Exploration phase. Use the list of "Sample Alternative Conceptions About Animals Students Bring to Class" described on page 409 as a starting point to identify possible alternative conceptions.

LESSON PLAN

A Learning Cycle Involving Alternative Conceptions about Animals

Lesson Goal: To allow students to investigate, develop inferences, and identify general descriptions of the growth stages of animals going through metamorphosis.

Grade Level: Grade 3.

Prerequisites: The students should have grouped animals based on their observed characteristics and made observations using all their senses.

Exploration

Objective: Students will investigate the contents of an insect bottle, making observations and stating their inferences.

Materials: For each group: a baby food jar with its lid or a small clear plastic cup with a plastic-wrap lid; oatmeal; ten or more mealworms at different developmental stages: larva, pupa, or adult beetle. Mealworms can be purchased from a bait shop or pet shop. They can be kept in oatmeal in a large aluminum roasting pan. Mealworms need moisture, which is best provided by regularly putting potato or apple slices on the surface of the oatmeal. Adding water to the oatmeal creates mold that kills the mealworms. Mealworms go through 13 moltings of their skin before they form the dormant pupa stage. Adults emerge from the pupa in a few days. The total time for transformation is 5 to 7 weeks; three magnifying glasses; paper towels.

Procedure:

A. Place the students in groups of three. Assign roles: a recorder, a materials manager, and an observer.
B. Provide the groups with the following instructions: They are to observe the mealworms they find in the oatmeal in their container. They should identify, count, and draw the types of mealworms they find.

C. Ask each group's materials manager to get a magnifying glass for each member of their group, a container with mealworms in oatmeal, and a paper towel. The group should begin making observations as soon as they have their materials.

D. After a while, students should discuss the key question presented earlier in the lesson. Ask them to write out their response to the key question.

Evaluation: Evaluate students' group work with regard to the completeness of their counting, drawings, and response to the key question. Assess group skills of staying with the group while working and asking someone to explain their comments.

Invention

Objective: Students will identify and name the stages in the development of a mealworm.

Materials: For each group: eight index cards; drawing materials. For the class: *The Very Hungry Caterpillar* by Eric Carle (1987, NY: Philomel Books).

Procedure:

A. The students will present their results and their responses to the key question to the whole class. Summarize the students' responses in an interactive discussion.

B. Tell the students that you will be reading them a book, *The Very Hungry Caterpillar.* Ask them to start thinking about the mealworms they observed while they listen to the story.

C. After finishing the story, ask the groups to draw each stage of the butterfly on an index card. Each person in the group should draw a different stage. Then ask them to sequence the cards to show how the butterfly developed from its youngest stage to its adult stage. Next, ask them to suggest a similar sequence for the mealworms in the oatmeal. They are to draw the different types of mealworms and sequence them as they did the butterfly.

D. Explain that in some animals, the young are very different in appearance from the adult. Human babies, although small, look very similar to adults. Explain that the process of great change over a short period of time while an animal passes from its young to adult stages is called **metamorphosis**. Explain the name of each stage: egg, larva, pupa or chrysalis (a more specific term for pupa used with some insects), and adult.

E. In closure, animals develop in two basic ways: (1) Many animals are born looking a lot like an adult. As the animal grows up, it changes in some ways but mostly stays the same. (2) Other animals develop through metamorphosis. The young look very different from adults and change quickly.

Evaluation: Ask the students to label the stages of their mealworms' development in their drawings. Have each group staple its drawings together into a "Mealworm Book." Check the books to determine the level of accuracy among the students. Assess group skills of sharing materials and make sure everyone is part of the plan and gets a chance to do her part.

Expansion

Objective: Students will identify and name the stages in the development of animals that go through metamorphosis.

Materials: For each group: one handout per student on the stages of a frog's growth: egg, frog tadpole, frog tadpole with legs, and adult frog; baby food jar with its lid or a small clear plastic cup with a plastic-wrap lid; oatmeal; potato slices; ten or more mealworms at different developmental stages; three magnifying glasses; paper towels.

Procedure:

A. Give the students a handout on which the stages of frog development are drawn in random order: egg, frog tadpole, frog tadpole with legs, and adult frog. Ask them to cut out and sequence them from the youngest to oldest stage of development. Discuss the sequence and have students label the name of each stage.

B. As an extended Expansion activity, have the students observe their mealworm containers daily. The students should put a potato slice in each container to provide moisture for the animals. They should count the individuals and note how many of each stage they have. Over a period of 1 to 2 weeks, they should find a change in the number of mealworms at each stage of development. Their daily observations should be recorded in a "Mealworm Log." At the end of the observation period, the students should report their findings to the whole class. Bar graphs provide a good visual aid for a group's presentation.

C. Summarize the lesson by reviewing the activities and major findings of the various parts of the lesson.

Evaluation: Prepare a handout with pictures of the developmental stages of an insect not included in the lesson, such as the common housefly or mosquito. Ask the students to sequence and label the stages of growth of the insect going through metamorphosis.

A. The possible alternative conceptions a student might bring to a lesson describing the growth stages of animals going through metamorphosis include the following:

10. *Some young and adult animals are different types of animals; for example, tadpoles and frogs are different animals.*

11. *The caterpillar and the butterfly are not the same insect* (younger children).

Young insects and adult insects are different types of insects (this alternative conception was not given in the above lists).

B. Use key questions to guide students' actions during Exploration, section C, including (before the students begin work): "What are some of the things you notice in your container?" Group the mealworms you find. Later, during the Exploration, additional questions are asked: "Are these mealworms the same, similar, or different kinds of insects?" "What is your evidence for deciding whether or not they are the same?" and "Give names to the groups of mealworms you found, tell how many there were, and draw one example of the mealworms you put in each group."

SUMMARY

Students know more about living things than nonliving things because of their personal experiences. They know the most about their own bodies. As a result, students can be expected to have numerous and strong alternative conceptions about living things. It is very important to use instructional strategies that work with conceptual reconstruction when teaching biological science topics, since the students have their own ideas about what will be taught before the lesson begins.

When teaching a lesson in biological science, it is important that the concept be personally relevant to the student. It must fit into the student's previously developed ideas of the world in order for meaningful learning to occur. Students with alternative conceptions make judgments based on irrelevant and conflicting information.

A discrepant event activity deals directly with students' alternative conceptions, asking students to explain why their view of the concept or generalization is correct. It exposes students to numerous non-examples, as well as examples, of the concept. A discrepant event activity can help students develop discrimination skills as well as provide background biological science experiences. In the Invention phase, teachers focus students' attention on relevant attributes related to the concepts or generalizations that are the lesson's goals. This focusing occurs during diverse experiences that utilize all the senses. Teachers then help students become aware of irrelevant characteristics. It is important to provide explanations to students while using experiences. Explanations highlight important characteristics of the concept or generalization being taught. The Expansion phase is important because it allows students to test out their understanding as they transfer it to different contexts.

chapter 15

Earth and Space Science Starting Points

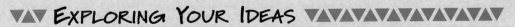

▼▲▼ EXPLORING YOUR IDEAS ▼▲▼▲▼▲▼▲▼▲▼▲▼▲▼

To begin the Starting Points in "Earth and Space Science" unit, answer the questions below:

1. List some of the facts, concepts, and generalizations in an "Earth in space" unit that are appropriate for a primary-age student.
2. What alternative conception(s) do you think a primary-age student in the kindergarten or first grade has about Earth in space?
3. List some of the facts, concepts, and generalizations in an "Earth in space" unit that are appropriate for an intermediate-grade student.
4. What alternative conception(s) will an intermediate-grade student have about Earth in space?
5. Label the statements in questions 1 and 3 with "C" for concept and "G" for generalization. Are there any facts above? If so, put an "F" in front of the statement. When planning a lesson, the same instructional strategy cannot be used effectively for every type of content.
6. Now, look at the suggested answers below and compare your responses to them. The answers do not encompass all possible ideas, but these concepts and generalizations should be included in planning units on Earth in space. *Compare the answers below with your responses and comment.*

For questions 1 and 3, possible Earth in space concepts and generalizations are listed below. Others are found in the next few pages in the discussion of students' alternative conceptions about Earth in space, or in state and national science education standards. Compare your responses to those suggested below. The "*" indicates examples appropriate in primary-age grades (K–2). Other examples are introduced in the third and later grades. A focus on the use and transfer of ideas occurs in the fifth and later grades.

Some Earth in Space Concepts Are:

*observing components of the sky—clouds, birds, sun, moon, stars, and so on; *horizon; *observing shadows; *observing the motion of planes and clouds in the sky; orbit; rotation; revolution; eclipse; clarity of the sky; zenith; cardinal points of the compass; motions of stars, planets, the moon, meteors, and so on in the sky.

Some Earth in Space Generalizations Include:

*The closer an object is to a moving observer, the quicker it will seem to pass.

*The higher the sun is in the sky, the shorter the shadow it will cast.

*The greater the angle between the sun and the moon, the greater the amount of the moon that will be lit by the sun.

*The speed of a planet in orbit around the sun decreases the farther its distance from the sun.

*The greater the tilt of Earth's axis, the greater the difference in seasons.

*The greater the tilt of Earth's axis, the larger the temperature difference between summer and winter.

For questions 2 and 4, examples of alternative conceptions are found in the pages that follow. For question 5, see Chapters 4 and 5 if you are in doubt about whether you have written a fact, concept, or generalization.

Chapter Objectives

1. Give several examples of students' alternative conceptions in Earth and space science.
2. Describe a procedure for interviewing students about their prior knowledge concerning ideas in Earth and space sciences.
3. Given a common alternative conception in Earth and space science, describe a discrepant event activity that confronts students with their alternative conception.
4. Given an Earth and space science lesson plan, identify possible alternative conceptions students might bring to the lesson.
5. Develop one or two key questions to create a "confrontation" and a possible student investigation in the Exploration phase of an Earth and space science lesson.

WHAT IS NEEDED IN THE AREA OF EARTH IN SPACE?

Researchers observing elementary and middle school classrooms have identified numerous areas in Earth and space sciences where students hold alternative conceptions that create a barrier to learning. How do students learn more scientific explanations for Earth and space science events? How should Earth and space science be taught to take advantage of a student's prior knowledge? Starting points are presented in this chapter to demonstrate the learning cycle strategy for Earth sciences. The chapter first presents an overview of the basic content needed by all students. Second, the chapter presents the basic ideas in one area in Earth and space science, Earth in space, for an elementary and middle school science curriculum. Next, selected alternative conceptions in the area of Earth in space are provided to demonstrate specific needs that students have. Specific instructional strategies are discussed for Earth in space difficulties to illustrate general strategies for Earth and space science concepts. These specific alternative conceptions are followed by a discussion of alternative conceptions in the more general Earth and space science areas relating to Earth's oceans and atmosphere, space science, geology, the solar system, stars, and the universe. Following each general Earth and space science alternative conception, examples of discrepant event activities and learning cycle lesson plans are provided. These discussions provide a foundation for teachers who wish to effectively plan lessons that assist students in their learning of Earth and space science concepts.

Earth and space sciences deal with Earth (or any part of it) and Earth's space environment. Earth and space sciences include the disciplines of geology, oceanography, meteorology, and astronomy, among others. They involve the application of both the physical and biological sciences in a study of Earth, the solar system it moves in, and its place in the universe. The rate of knowledge expansion in Earth and space sciences is increasing and is expected to continue to do so throughout the 21st century.

The key ideas in Earth and space sciences involve concepts as diverse as the properties of materials, weather, the dynamic Earth system, aerodynamics, space flight, the solar system, stars, and the universe (see Table 15–1). In Earth and space sciences, Earth in

Table 15–1   *Examples of key ideas in the areas of Earth and space science*

Grade Level	Properties of Materials and Weather	Earth Systems	Aerodynamics and Space Flight	Solar System	Stars and the Universe
Primary Age (K–2)	Weather can be a solid, liquid, or gas as experienced in everyday events.	Many events in nature have a repeating pattern (e.g., weather, Sun movement).	Different objects have different flight patterns.	The Sun provides heat and light. Shadows provide information about the Sun's movement.	Stars can be distinguished by their brightness, location, and patterns.
Intermediate (Grades 3–5)	Earth's materials are solids (rocks and soil), liquids (water), and gases (the atmosphere).	Changes on Earth can take place quickly or over long time periods (e.g., earthquakes and erosion).	The shape of objects can be used to predict their flight characteristics.	The Sun and Moon are seen in repeating patterns due to Earth's spinning on its axis.	Stars have a daily repeating movement due to Earth's turning and a yearly movement due to Earth's orbit around the Sun.
Middle School (Grades 6–8)	Soils have many properties that identify them including texture, color, origin, capacity to retain water, and ability to support plant growth.	Cycling of water in and out of our atmosphere plays an important role in determining climatic patterns.	Motions of objects outside of Earth's atmosphere are related to forces of gravity and thrust produced by the mass of material being expelled by the object or hitting the object.	Due to Earth's turning on an axis that is tilted to the plane of Earth's yearly orbit around the Sun, the Sun is seen to rise higher and take a longer path in the sky during the summer months of the year.	The Sun is a medium-sized star near the edge of a disk-shaped galaxy of stars that can be seen as the Milky Way in the night sky.

space is a topic covered as a unit of study, or indirectly with other ideas in the elementary and middle school science curriculum.

For more information about key Earth and space science ideas, see the link to the National Science Education Standards website on the Companion Website that accompanies this text at *http://www.prenhall.com/sunal*

Companion Website

Basic concepts covered in the units involving Earth in space in the national and state standards, textbooks, state curricula, and teacher-made lessons include the following.

Primary-age students (grades K–2) should have experience with, and understand, the following:

1. Some events in nature appear once, while others have a repeating pattern. The motions of the sun, moon, and stars all have regular patterns.
2. The sun appears in different locations in the daytime sky, which are related to the time of day and the seasons. The location of the sun can be determined by its height in the sky and its direction along the horizon.

3. Sometimes the moon is in the sky at night and sometimes it's in the sky during the day. The moon looks different every day. It gets larger and then smaller and repeats its shape changes month after month. The location of the moon in the sky is also different from day to day. Evidence for its location can be determined from its height in the sky and its place along the horizon.

4. There are more stars in the sky than we can count. They do not all have the same brightness and color. They are scattered throughout the sky unevenly. Stars appear only in the evening sky. Stars appear to move slowly together across the sky each night.

Elementary and middle school students (grades 3–8) should have experience with, and understand, the following:

1. The *sun* is the closest star in the sky. Its motion, if carefully observed, tells us how Earth is moving. The sun's motion, from east to west, gives us evidence that Earth is rotating on its axis from west to east. From month to month, the change in altitude of the sun at noontime is visible. It is evidence for the tilt in the axis of Earth. The tilt causes each part of Earth to be angled closer to the sun in one part of Earth's revolution around the sun and farther away during another part of that revolution.

2. The *moon* revolves around Earth every 28 days. Because of the changing angle of the sun during the year, this revolution causes the shape of the moon to change in a regular cycle. The moon changes from a thin crescent to full and then back to a thin crescent. When the moon is on the opposite side of Earth than the sun, we see a full moon. When the moon appears close to the sun in the sky, it is located between Earth and the sun. At this place in its orbit, just a small part of the moon's surface is lit up, so it appears as a crescent to an observer on Earth. The moon's revolution also causes its location to change each night and from day to day. This motion is in addition to the apparent motion caused by Earth's daily rotation.

3. *Planets* in the sky look similar to stars. Some planets are brighter than any of the stars. The different appearance of a planet and a star can be observed with a telescope or by watching them over a period of time to see if they change their positions among the other stars. Planets change their position but stars remain in the same place when compared to the location of other stars. Earth is one of nine planets in orbit about the sun. All the planets revolve in the same direction (counterclockwise) around the sun. Planets vary in their size, composition, surface features, and distance from the sun. As companions to our sun, planets are the largest of many types of objects that are part of the solar system. Some planets show evidence of geologic activity. Other objects in the solar system include natural satellites, asteroids, comets, flat rings of rock and dust particles orbiting a planet, and other solid, rock-like, nameless objects that range from miles in diameter to specks of dust.

The shape of the solar system is flat. As the planets are observed from Earth, they always appear to be located in a small band of stars encircling Earth. An observer watching from midlatitudes on Earth cannot see planets very far to the north or very far to the south.

4. *Stars* are suns that are so far away that, even though they have motions of their own, to the naked eye each seems to continuously remain stationary in relation to the other stars around it. Stars in the night sky are different distances from Earth, but they are so far away that they all appear to be the same size. The sun is an average star in terms of its physical characteristics. Stars have different sizes, temperatures, compositions, and life histories. The energy a star gives off is created deep in its core through nuclear reactions. It is transported over time to the star's surface, where it is given off in the form of light and other types of radiation.

Patterns in the stars' locations have been given names and are known as *constellations*. In addition to the apparent nightly motion of stars due to Earth's rotation, stars appear to slowly move westward about 1° per day. This apparent motion is due to Earth's orbital motion around the sun. This second apparent motion causes different stars to be seen in different seasons in the night sky.

5. Stars are located in very large groups called *galaxies*. The sun's galaxy can be seen as a glowing band of light that arches across the night sky and is called the Milky Way. Its shape is flattened and encircles Earth and the sun, as evidenced by the glowing band of light. The universe contains many such galaxies, which are organized into large groups separated by relatively few galaxies.

ALTERNATIVE CONCEPTIONS ABOUT EARTH IN SPACE

A specific area of Earth and space science is explored in detail below to provide examples of how students' experiences are used to introduce discrepant events that confront their prior knowledge. Effective lesson plans are then constructed, creating meaningful learning for students that takes into account their prior experiences and ideas.

All people experience Earth and the sky. Students always compare their common-sense view of where they live to the ideas presented in classroom science lessons. When a fourth-grade teacher approaches a chapter in the textbook entitled "Earth in Space" and reads the teacher's guide providing objectives and science vocabulary, concepts such as *globe, planet, orbit, pole, rotation,* and *axis* are found. Students have already developed ideas related to each of these terms. To take advantage of a student's prior knowledge, it is necessary to first provide students with observational and other concrete experiences that relate to the idea being introduced. When these observational experiences are part of an Exploration in a learning cycle format, the teacher confronts the students with an activity that elicits what they know and believe about the idea. Listening to student responses in whole class settings and asking them to listen to peer responses and discuss them in small-group settings provide students and the teacher with the starting points for an effective Earth and space science lesson (Sneider & Ohadi, 1998). These starting points are students' prior knowledge. This knowledge guides students' perceptions about what they have experienced in the real world and what they will learn from your lesson activities.

A long-term effort must be made to help students modify commonly held alternative ideas. Examples of *students' alternative conceptions* about Earth in space include the following six ideas (Bar, Sneider, & Martimbeau, 1997; Baxter, 1989; Cohen & Kagan, 1979; Lightman & Sadler, 1988; Nussbaum, 1979; Nussbaum, 1985a; Philips, 1991; Sadler, 1987; Sneider & Ohadi, 1998; Sneider & Pulos, 1983; Stahly, Krockover, & Shepardson, 1999; Vosniadou, 1991).

1. **Students' Alternative Conception:** *Day and night are caused by the sun going around Earth. Earth rotates in 24 hours.*

Young students often believe that the sun is moving because they have noticed the sun's circular path around the sky. The reverse is actually true; Earth moves around the sun. Yet, when one studies the sky, it is easy to form the perception that the sun is moving around Earth.

Earth rotates on its axis once every 23 hours and 56 minutes. This rotation causes the sun to appear in the same part of the sky once every day. However, it is only roughly in the same spot. Actually, it takes 24 hours and zero minutes for the sun to return to the same spot where it was seen the day before. Earth is rotating 4 minutes faster than this. If we defined a day to be 360° rotation of Earth, the sun would not rise to the same height each day and in 90 days would be on the eastern horizon at noon.

However, more than rotation is occurring. Earth is also revolving, moving in an orbit around the sun. It moves about 1° a day eastward on its 360° path around the sun, thus adding to the rotation angle Earth must make to bring the sun up to the same point in the sky. From noon to noon on consecutive days, Earth must rotate 361°. Earth takes 4 minutes to rotate this extra degree. One degree of extra movement makes a difference; when we look for the sun each day, we see it in exactly the same spot it was 24 hours earlier. These two Earth motions, rotation and revolution, work together to create the appearance of the sun moving through the sky daily on a predictable path of 24 hours and 0 minutes.

2. Students' Alternative Conception: *Earth is flat. Earth is round like a pancake. Earth is round and it is in the sky. Earth is spherical and people live in a flat place on top.* One of the most common alternative conceptions younger students have involves the shape of Earth. Students are told that Earth is round, yet Earth appears flat when we stand on it. Students are asked if they believe that the flat ground they walk on, ride on, and play on actually wraps itself around to form a giant ball. Students are confused by what they actually see and what they are told exists. Therefore, they form alternative conceptions by leaving out some of what is told to them or by mixing what they know with what they have been told.

Students form alternative conceptions because they find it difficult to give up the idea that Earth is flat. To reconcile the concept of a flat Earth with a spherical Earth, some students create an alternative conception that Earth is disk shaped. Others believe that there are two Earths: a round one that is a planet up in the sky and a flat one that people live on. Believing that there are two Earths allows them to keep their flat Earth idea and account for the "official" idea of a spherical Earth. Somewhat older children mix their ideas with school knowledge in a complex way. They create an idea of an Earth that is spherical but has a flat place on top where they actually live. Tied up with these ideas are other barriers to learning. Since gravity pulls things down, students believe living on a flat Earth means that gravity always pulls things in the same direction (down). They mix concepts. For example, if they believe in a spherical Earth with a flat place on top, they construct the belief that gravity in other parts of the world pulls things off of Earth. Therefore, objects thrown upwards in the southern hemisphere, for example, will keep on going up.

3. Students' Alternative Conception: *The moon is stationary; it does not move. The moon is located in a part of the sky that is always dark. The moon goes around Earth in a single day.*

The moon is a satellite of Earth. It revolves slowly around Earth, taking about 28 days for one complete revolution. The moon does not move in its orbit quickly; it only moves about 12° per day. This is determined by dividing 360° by 28 days. The moon is in the day sky for about 14 days and in the night sky for about 14 days. The moon is visible at some place in the sky about 25 of the 28 days it takes to make one revolution. The rest of the time it is too close to the sun to be easily seen.

When viewed in the sky during a clear evening, the moon seems to be suspended and unmoving. If you wait an hour, however, the moon will have moved 15° closer to the western horizon because of Earth's rotation. The moon will set in the west later in the night. If students look for the moon at different times during the same day, they will notice the continued effect of Earth's rotation on the moon. To them, the moon will appear to travel once around in a day because of Earth's rotation.

The next evening, at about the same time, the moon appears to have shifted eastward by 12° compared to its position in the sky 24 hours earlier. This motion is due to the moon's revolution. If the evening moon is compared to its location in the stars an hour before, you will notice a change of one-half degree. One-half degree is equal to the moon's diameter.

4. Students' Alternative Conception: *Earth revolves around the moon. Different countries on Earth see different phases of moon on the same day. Phases of the moon are caused by a shadow from Earth.*

The moon is about 240,000 miles from Earth. At this distance, everyone on the side of Earth facing the moon sees the moon in the same way. The *phases* of the moon occur because, at times, the moon is near the sun, which is the source of light illuminating the moon. At other times, the moon is on the opposite side of Earth from the sun. A small portion of the moon is lit up when it is near the sun in the sky. More of it is lit up as it orbits farther from the sun, so the phase of the moon is different. The only time the moon shows no dark portion is when it is in the full moon. When the sun and moon are on opposite sides of Earth, we see a full moon. The full moon period is the only possible time when the moon could be in Earth's shadow. When the moon does pass in the shadow of Earth, there is a lunar eclipse. The lunar eclipse can only occur during a full moon. Earth's shadow is a small disk because of the great distance the moon is from Earth. Most of the time, the moon misses Earth's shadow during its orbit of Earth.

5. Students' Alternative Conception: *The sun is directly overhead at noon. The daylight is the same length as our local day on any part of Earth. The amount of daylight time increases throughout the summer months.*

For anyone above 23 1/2 degrees north latitude (the Tropic of Cancer), and in every state in the United States except Hawaii, the sun is never directly overhead at noon or at any other time. The sun's path during a single day begins on the eastern horizon. It climbs very high until the sun reaches the south, where it is at its highest point during the day. For people living in tropical regions south of 23 1/2 degrees north latitude (and north of 23 1/2 degrees south latitude), the sun will appear overhead at noon only twice a year. For a person living on the equator, the sun will only be directly overhead at exactly noon on March 21st and September 21st each year. When the sun is directly overhead, we call this being at its zenith. For people living in the United States, the sun at noon on those dates will appear at a medium angle in the southern sky (see Figure 15–1).

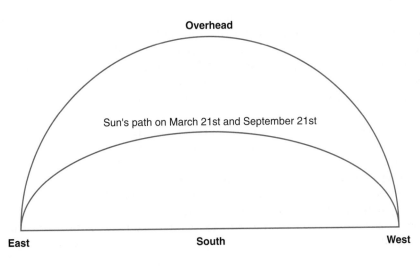

F⟨GURE 15–1 *The sun's path as seen from locations in the United States on March 21st and September 21st each year*

Overhead

Sun's path on March 21st and September 21st

East   South   West

FIGURE 15-2   *The sun seen at noon on the same day from two different locations*

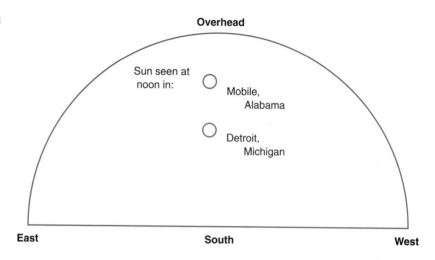

The farther north a person is on Earth, the lower the angle at which the sun will appear in the sky at any time. Try this experiment: Call up a friend who lives a great distance from you directly south or north. Do this near noon on an agreed-upon day. Two people viewing the sun on the same date and measuring the height of the sun at the same time (for example, in Mobile, Alabama, and Detroit, Michigan) will see the sun at different heights in the sky. At noon, the person in Detroit will see the sun 12° lower in the sky, closer to the southern horizon, than will the person in Mobile (see Figure 15–2).

In the summer throughout the 48 contiguous United States, the sun is between 5° and 25° from the point overhead, the zenith, at its highest point during the day. The zenith is at a height of 90° from the horizon. This is the same as saying that it is between 65° (90° − 25°) and 85° (90° − 5°) *altitude* from the southern horizon. The range of degrees is given to show the height of the sun from northern and southern locations in the United States.

In the winter, the sun's highest point is also in the south. However, it is between 57° and 72° from the point overhead. The altitude of the sun at noon in the winter is between 18° and 33° in the continental United States.

Every day following June 21st, the sun will appear to be lower in the sky when looking at it while standing in the same location. Therefore, the sun's height and total path length in the sky above the horizon becomes smaller during the summer months of July and August. They do not increase during the summer months (see Figure 15–3).

Because of the low angle of the sun in the winter as compared to the sun in the summer, the total path of the sun is much shorter. The shorter the time that the sun can be seen, the shorter the length of the day and, proportionately, the longer the night. The sun is lowest in the sky in the northern hemisphere on December 21st; therefore, that is the shortest day in the year everywhere in the northern hemisphere. The sun is highest in the sky in the northern hemisphere on June 21st, so that is the longest day of the year. Between December 21st and June 21st, the sun is a little higher in the sky at noon every day. The rising and setting points of the sun move slightly northward each day. By June 21st, the sun rises in the northeast, moves to a point close to the zenith in the sky, and sets in the northwest. The sun is in the sky much longer than 12 hours on this date; in fact, the sun's path is longest on this date (see Figure 15–4). From June 21st to December 21st, the

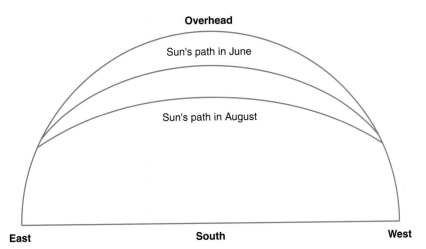

FIGURE 15-3 *The sun's path in two different summer months seen from the same location*

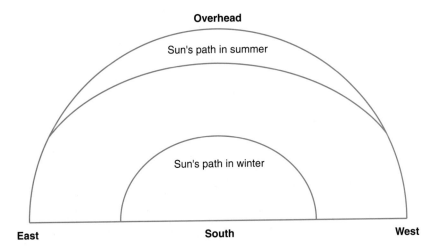

FIGURE 15-4 *The sun's path during different months of the year*

process reverses. The sun gets lower every day, the path of the sun gets shorter, and there are fewer daylight hours (see Figure 15–4). For all of the summer, after June 21st the days are getting shorter.

6. **Students' Alternative Conception:** *The sun revolves around Earth. Earth is in the center of the solar system. The seasons are caused because the Earth is closer to the sun in summer.*

Earth and all the other components of the solar system revolve around the sun. More than 99% of the total mass of the solar system is contained in the sun. Its strong gravitational pull causes the orbits of the planets to be centered on the sun. When seen from the top of the solar system, the remaining mass of the solar system, less than 1%, is moving in the same counterclockwise direction. This remaining mass is mostly made up of the nine planets of the solar system. This mass, including Earth, is not spread evenly around the sun but is strung out in a flat disk-shaped mass centered on the sun. There is almost no material above or below the sun.

Earth is in orbit around the sun in a nearly perfect circle. There is about a 3% variation between the closest and farthest points of its rotation from the sun. Earth is

FIGURE 15–5 *The height of the sun in the sky at noon at various dates*

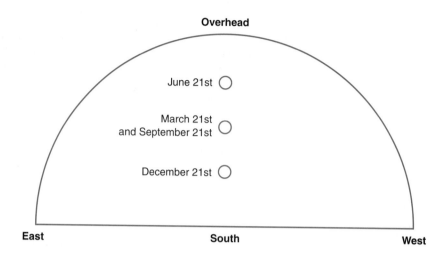

closest to the sun in January and farthest from it in July. This is enough to cause only minor changes in Earth's weather by warming the northern hemisphere slightly in the winter. It is not enough to create seasons on Earth. Evidence for this distance is found by counting the days on a calendar between March 21st and September 21st and comparing this number to the days between September 21st and March 21st. The first time period is longer because Earth is farther from the sun and is moving slower in that half of its orbit.

At the same time as Earth is revolving about the sun, Earth is also rotating; however, its axis is not perpendicular to its orbit. Its axis is tilted 23 1/2 degrees from its orbit. Rotating Earth is spinning in such a way that, like a gyroscope, its axis is always pointing in the same direction towards the same stars in space. As Earth revolves around the sun, its northern axis is at an angle of 23 1/2 degrees, pointing toward the sun for half of its orbit. This occurs during the period from March 21st through September 21st. As seen by a person in Earth's northern hemisphere, the sun appears high in the sky (see Figure 15–5). From September 21st through March 21st, Earth is in the other half of its orbit. Its northern axis is at an angle of 23 1/2 degrees, pointing away from the sun. When this occurs, the sun is directly over some portion of the southern half of Earth. As seen by a person in the northern hemisphere, the sun appears low in the sky (see Figure 15–5). Because the sun is higher in the northern hemisphere in the summer, it shines for more hours; as a result, more heat energy shines on every square meter of the northern hemisphere.

DISCREPANT EVENT ACTIVITIES IN EARTH IN SPACE

After determining the prior knowledge students bring to the classroom about Earth in space, instructional activities are written using their prior knowledge as a starting point. The activities below relate to one or more alternative conceptions about Earth in space. The following are examples of discrepant events appropriate for the Exploration phase of a learning cycle lesson. The numbers of the alternative conceptions indicated below match those given in the previous list.

 1. **Students' Alternative Conception:** *Day and night are caused by the sun going around Earth. Earth rotates in 24 hours.*

Discrepant Activity A: The following activities are done as a school unit with young students, or as an introduction to a unit for older students. With younger students, begin by taking the students outside on a sunny day. Find a tall object like a flagpole, the top of a building, or a tree. Ask the students to outline its shadow on the ground using chalk or string. When they have completed this task, ask them a thought question such as: "Do shadows stay in the same place?" "What causes a shadow?" or "Can you tell me (predict) where the shadow of an object will be at a later time?" After a few minutes, ask the students to observe the shadow that was outlined. Have them compare the original outline with the current position of the shadow. Ask them: "What is happening?" "Why has it happened?"

When working with older students, place them into groups of three. Ask each group to make a prediction and plan a test to check the prediction. The prediction should describe the length of time it takes for the sun to start at one place in the sky and return to the same place on the following day. The students may devise other methods, but a simple one involves outlining the shadow of some tall object outside the classroom on a clear day, noting the exact time, and returning the next day to time the return of the shadow to the original mark. When the students have devised their plan, ask them: "What is a shadow?" "What do shadows tell you about the source of light causing them?" and "Check the outlined shadow and determine its location after ten minutes. Why does the shadow move?"

Discrepant Activity B: It is useful to have students check their beliefs about the motion of objects against reality. This can be done in a thought experiment. Ask the students to imagine sitting in the family car or on a school bus as it rides smoothly down the road. As they look out the side of the car, they may see bridges, houses, or trees moving backwards. Ask the class: "What is happening here?" "What is moving?" and "If you were only allowed to look out the side of your car without knowing whether the vehicle was moving or not, could you tell if the scenery was being moved past you or if you were moving past the scenery?" Focus on the students' statements that report it may not be possible to know whether you are moving or the scenery is moving. What you are seeing is the same no matter which one is moving. This illusion is demonstrated by having the students watch a videotaped clip that shows scenery moving by a window (for example, scenery outside of a train, car, or plane). As students are observing the video clip, ask them to provide evidence indicating which is moving: the scenery or the vehicle from which the scenery is viewed. In the Invention phase of the lesson, relate the discrepant activities provided in the Exploration to the idea that we are standing on a platform called Earth that is moving us past objects viewed in the sky, such as the sun. The students will have discovered in Discrepant Activity A that, within experimental error, the sun's shadow returned to the same spot in 24 hours and zero minutes. The accuracy of their observations is increased by using a tall object. Students may have difficulty determining when the edge of the shadow returns to the same spot because shadows have a fuzzy edge.

Standing on Earth, it is not easy to determine whether the sun is moving or Earth is moving. From what the students discovered about moving objects in the Exploration, they should be able to determine the eastward direction of Earth's motion. For younger students, the sun may appear to move toward a line of trees on the far side of the school. In a car, the scenery appears to be going in the opposite direction from that in which you are traveling. This analogy can be used to determine the direction that Earth is turning past the sun. With older students, the westerly motion of the sun is determined by using a compass. The students are then able to determine the actual direction of Earth's rotation as the opposite of the sun's motion. Earth turns eastward for an observer standing on its surface. This fact does not have to be memorized; students are able to construct it for themselves, since they know that the sun always sets in the west.

2. **Students' Alternative Conception:** *Earth is flat. Earth is round like a pancake. Earth is round and it is in the sky. Earth is spherical and people live in a flat place on top.*

Discrepant Activity: Form groups of three. Ask the groups to discuss and develop a response to the following questions: "What is the shape of Earth?" and "What evidence can you give to convince someone else that your view is correct?" Ask students to draw and write out responses to these questions. Have the students report their responses to the whole class.

Following this discussion, provide each group with a very large round balloon and small toy sailboat, or a cutout drawing of such a toy. The toy should be 2 inches or less in length. Ask the students to blow up the balloon, then have one student in each group press his cheek into the side of the balloon so that his eye is just at its surface. Have the student describe what he sees. Each of the other students in the group should have the same experience.

Have the students repeat the experience. This time, place the toy sailboat near the student's eye and then move it slowly around the balloon. Have each student report what she sees as the sailboat moves away from her eye.

Next, start the sailboat on the side of the balloon and move it toward the student's eye. Ask the student to report what he sees. Repeat this experience with all the students in the group. Ask the students to compare these results with the ideas they had in their earlier discussion about the shape of Earth.

The students should find that placing the side of their face into the balloon creates a flat world with a horizon that forms a ring or disk around their eye. The bottom of the sailboat, as it moves away from the student's eye, gradually disappears, leaving only the top of the sail visible. Eventually, even the top of the sail disappears from view. In the Invention phase, report to the students that sailors today observe this effect when they watch a sailboat through a small telescope or binoculars. This begins to occur at a distance of about 12 miles on a flat surface on Earth, such as the ocean. It also occurs in a desert or on a plain. To the observer, Earth appears to be a disk about 12 miles in radius. Other sources of evidence about Earth's shape are pictures of Earth's shadow on the moon during a lunar eclipse. Have the students discuss and observe the spherical shape of other objects, such as the sun and the moon. They should have access to a number of photographs and videotapes showing Earth from space.

Confrontation activities similar to the ones in the previous discrepant activity are necessary to help students examine their beliefs about the world and replace a more primitive conception of Earth's shape with one closer to reality. The larger the balloon, the more successful the activity will be. Lightman and Sadler (1988) used a weather balloon obtained from a science supply company, and found the activity quite effective in replacing students' alternative conceptions.

3. **Students' Alternative Conception:** *The moon is stationary; it does not move. The moon is located in a part of the sky that is always dark. The moon goes around Earth in a single day.*

Discrepant Activity A: Form groups of three. Ask the groups to discuss and develop a response to the following questions: "Is the moon visible in the sky today?" "What does the moon look like in the sky?" and "When is the moon visible during the day?"

Ask the students to write out their responses and to illustrate their ideas. Have them report their ideas to the class. Ask students to verify their predictions by creating a plan to get evidence to support them; for example, if they predict the moon is visible in the night sky, they should plan to observe the sky that night.

Discrepant Activity B: Use the groups from Discrepant Activity A. Ask them to discuss and develop a response to the following questions: "Does the moon move during the day?" "Can we see its motion? If so, draw how the moon moves when it can be seen in the sky," and for older students, "If it moves, what is the cause of its motion?" Ask the students to write out their responses and to illustrate their ideas.

With the moon visible in the daytime sky, plan a short field trip to the school grounds on a clear day. Ask each student group to make a sketch of the sky and the horizon, including the location of the sun and the moon and the objects visible on the horizon. For elementary school students, this drawing is made in the morning and is repeated during mid-morning, lunch, and in the afternoon. Each field trip will take less than 10 minutes. For middle school students, an observation at the beginning of the period and near the end of the period is possible; an additional observation could be requested of the students during lunch or after school. Following the observations, have the student groups compare their findings with their predictions.

The students in Discrepant Activity A confront their idea of the moon's visibility with reality. The moon is almost always visible. The only time it is not visible is for about 3 days around the new phase. Since it takes 28 days to revolve around Earth, the moon should be visible on any clear day for 25 days of that period. It is seen in the evening sky when its phase is waxing crescent to full. It is seen in the daytime sky between a full moon and a waning crescent. Discrepant Activity B should be planned for a clear day when the moon is in its third quarter phase. At this time, the moon is visible in the sky 90° west of the sun. It is visible in the sky during the day between 6:00 a.m. and 3:00 p.m. Check a calendar for the time of the month when this occurs. During the activity, the students' original ideas are confronted with the noticeably quick motion of the moon. It moves about 15° in an hour, or about 30 moon diameters in a westerly direction.

4. **Students' Alternative Conception:** *Earth revolves around the moon. Different countries on Earth see different phases of the moon on the same day. Phases of the moon are caused by a shadow from Earth.*

Discrepant Activity: Do this activity 2 weeks before a lesson is planned for the phases of the moon. It is best to choose a time when the moon is just past full, visible in the daytime, and appearing early in the morning sky in the east. Repeat the beginning activities in Discrepant Activity B from Students' Alternative Conception number 3. Ask the following questions before groups begin the activity: "Where is the moon in relation to Earth and the sun?" "Draw its location in the sky at the same time over a period of many days. What evidence do you have to support your statement?" "Does the moon have a motion other than that due to Earth's turning (rotation)?" "Do different countries see different phases of the moon on the same day?" and "What causes the phases of the moon?" Devise a plan to get evidence to support the statements just made.

As in Discrepant Activity B above, after students report their plans to the class, begin observing activities with the moon during school hours. These observation activities will be different in that the students observe and record in a pictorial format the daily location and shape of the moon at the same time of day for about 10 days. Ask each group to complete a log entry in a journal for each observation. If some days are cloudy, there may be gaps in the record. Since a weekend will fall during this period, the group may not have records for a Saturday and a Sunday, although home assignments should be given. The observations end when the thin crescent moon is invisible in the bright glare of the sun. Following the observations, have the student groups compare their findings with their original answers to the key questions. When the journal is complete, ask the students to fill in the days where there are gaps in the records due to clouds with an illustration predicting what the moon would look like if it were visible on that day.

During these observations, if they are begun just after a full moon, the moon moves approximately 12° eastward in the sky each day toward the sun. As the moon approaches the sun, its shape turns from a football (gibbous) shape to a crescent shape which is only partially lit up and very close to the sun in the sky. Following this time, the moon passes under or over the sun but, because so little of its visible surface is lit up, and since it is so close to the sun, it will not be visible. In a few days, if the students are instructed to look at the western sky just after sunset, they should be able to see a thin crescent *west* of the sun. With continuing observations, the students will find the moon moving away from the sun each evening and getting larger.

For the Invention phase of the lesson, ask the students to compare their data and answers to their textbook's discussion of moon phases. Give them balls representing Earth, the sun, and the moon, and help them use the balls, in the bright light of an overhead projector, to construct a model showing the Earth, sun, and moon alignment for each of their observations of the moon in the sky.

5. **Students' Alternative Conception:** *The sun is directly overhead at noon. The daylight is the same length as our local day on any part of Earth. The amount of daylight time increases throughout the summer months.*

Discrepant Activity: Form groups of three. Provide the students with a sheet of paper with a large half circle drawn on it (see Figure 15–6). Ask the groups to discuss the following questions and illustrate their answers on the half circle drawing: "Where is the sun at noon today?" and "Where is the sun early in the morning and late in the evening?" Have students draw the path of the sun throughout the entire daytime period. The hours of daylight do not remain the same throughout the year; for example, there are more hours of daylight in the summer than in the winter in

FIGURE 15-6 *Half circle for students to record their observations of the sky*

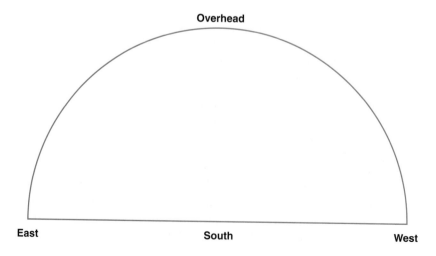

North America. Ask students, "Why does this happen?" When the illustrations and answers are complete, ask students to report their ideas to the whole class. Ask students to verify their predictions by creating a plan to get evidence to support them. For example, if they predict the sun is overhead at noon, they should plan to observe the sun in the sky at noon.

With the sun visible in the daytime sky, plan a short field trip to the school grounds. Give each group an enlarged copy of Figure 15–6. Ask each group to make a sketch of the sky while facing south on its copy of the figure; include the location of the sun and the principal objects visible on the horizon. For elementary school students, this drawing could be made in the morning and repeated hourly throughout the school day. Record all observations on the same drawing. Each drawing created of the sun should include its date and time. A compass should be used by each group to find the local direction of east, south, west, and north. *Warn the students that they are not to look directly at the sun for any length of time.* The sun's rays are so powerful that they will damage retinal cells if any extended direct observations are made. Each field trip will take less than 10 minutes. For middle school students, an observation at the beginning of the period and near the end of the period would work best. Additional observations could be requested of the students during lunch or after school, or as a homework assignment to be done hourly on a Saturday. Following the observations, ask student groups to compare their findings with the predictions they made earlier in response to the key questions.

Students typically make a prediction that the sun will be overhead at noon and rise directly in the east and set in the west. Their observations will not confirm this prediction. For students in the third grade and above, bring a compass outdoors and allow them to determine exactly where on the school grounds south, east, and west are to be found. For younger students, tell them how to stand to view the southern sky.

For a winter sky, students in North America (anywhere in the northern middle latitudes) will find the sun to be less than halfway to its zenith. It will rise in the southeast and set in the southwest. During the school year, the sun will only rise in the northeast and set in the northwest in April and May. For students in the United States and Canada (except Hawaii), the sun is never directly overhead, even during the summer.

6. **Students' Alternative Conception:** *The sun revolves around Earth. Earth is in the center of the solar system. The seasons are caused because Earth is closer to the sun in summer.*

Discrepant Activity: Form groups of three. Provide each group with a current monthly star chart, which can be found in books on astronomy and in *Science and Children*, a publication of the National Science Teachers Association. Ask the groups to find three of the most prominent constellations, name them, and locate the position in which they would be seen in the sky. Next, give each group last month's star chart. Ask students to note the differences in location of the same three constellations. Ask, "In what direction do the constellations seem to be moving during the 2 months—westward or eastward?" Predict where the three constellations will be next month.

When the groups have arrived at their answers, ask them to share their ideas with the rest of the class. There should be some differences in the groups' predictions. Students may be surprised by the answers to the previous questions. Now ask, "Why have the constellations changed their positions from month-to-month in the star charts?" When they have arrived at an answer to this question, give the groups a third sky chart. This chart should show the sky as it appeared last year during the current month (this can be done by taking the current star chart and blanking out references to the current year since the stars will appear in the same location each year over a lifetime). The students should be surprised when they see this new star chart. However, it should fit into an appropriate explanation.

Following these activities, begin the Invention phase of the lesson with a class report from each of the groups regarding why the changes occurred. Make facilitative and informational comments during this reporting period.

The students will find that the constellations they choose move about 30° westward each month. This is a significant change. As an alternative to the previous activity, or in addition to it, ask students to observe and draw on Figure 15-6 a prominent constellation in the night sky on a biweekly basis over a 6-week period. They will note the same effect.

For the in-class activity, the students should have little problem predicting where the constellations they have chosen will be a month from now, since the motion is obvious. The students should be perplexed about the fact that, a year before, stars looked the same as they currently do. It will only make sense to them if they conclude that Earth is in an orbit around the sun and returns to the same spot each year. If we look out from the dark side of Earth into the sky, we should see the same constellation in the same part of the sky. This is like sitting on a merry-go-round looking away from the center at people standing around. Every time we make a complete revolution, we should see the same people standing there if they have not moved. At this point, it is useful to ask the students, "Which way is Earth revolving around the sun?" Ask the students to point out the direction on the star charts in front of them. They should have the previous month's chart on their left side and the current month on their right side. They should have indicated that the stars are moving westward monthly as they've determined by observing the sky at the same time each evening. For this to occur, Earth must be revolving eastward or to the left. Use the analogy of a student walking by rows of chairs in a classroom. If the student is walking toward the back of the room, the chairs appear to be moving toward the front of the room to an observer who is not aware that she is moving. Another analogy is to use a girl looking out of the side window of a car looking at trees and houses moving backwards as the car moves forward. If we know the background is stationary, we can always tell the direction of our motion.

IMPLICATIONS FOR CLASSROOM TEACHING FOR A UNIT ON EARTH IN SPACE

Much of the information students understand about Earth in space is derived from their own sensory experiences and their social world. They need to distinguish between information derived through various aspects of the social world and scientific observation. Part of the information students perceive in the everyday world through their senses, television, storybooks, magazines, and adults contains inaccurate, misleading, and partial statements of scientific fact. Even though students may have covered space topics during classroom units in previous years, research points to the conclusion that only a small portion of students learn and use appropriate space concepts in their daily lives (Driver, Squires, Rushworth, & Wood-Robinson, 1994). More typically, students base their ideas of Earth in space on alternative conceptions or a mix of everyday knowledge and school knowledge. Helping students construct conceptions about Earth in space which are more closely related to scientific fact is fostered by:

1. Providing activities involving daytime and nighttime naked-eye observations and, where possible, through observations with instruments. Experiences with observations of many Earth-related and astronomical events help students develop a basis for the appropriate use of models (e.g., Earth globe, moon in orbit around Earth, and Earth in orbit around the sun). Students using models without background observational experiences generally do not meaningfully learn about the topic.

2. Spending a good deal of time experiencing and obtaining information, classifying, and predicting change in a wide variety of astronomical and Earth-related events (see the previous discrepant activities for some ideas).

3. Providing opportunities for students to compare their everyday knowledge and experiences about Earth in space with models, concepts, and generalizations based on scientific evidence.

4. Giving students many opportunities to use scientifically accepted ideas about Earth in space. Students need to work out how to apply these ideas to a wide range of situations. They begin by relating familiar experiences of observing the sky to star maps and models and then relating the models back to their experiences. They then relate their experiences and the models to theory and then relate theory back to experiences and models. This process leads to the application of theory in a wider range of situations. These opportunities involve the potential for extensive writing, listening, and speaking activities. The activities might include storytelling narratives of observations, such as describing what actually happens to the moon when viewed hourly throughout the evening, telling about an experience of standing at the ocean shore and looking at the horizon while trying to see the curvature of Earth, and planning and carrying out predictions to test the difference between competing ideas.

What experiences are helpful in developing students' ideas in the area of Earth in space? The objectives of an Earth in space unit relate to helping students understand the view of space they have from Earth. They are based on scientific evidence from numerous observations and the accumulation of facts made by other observers. Do this before providing extensive explanations: Ask small groups to share their ideas of space through drawings. They could be asked to "Draw an astronomer," "Draw Earth," "Draw the solar system as you understand it," or "Draw the inside of the sun." Only after such exploration of *their* ideas and many personal observational experiences are students introduced to analogies and models. The limitations of analogies and models should be clearly made. Finally, concepts and generalizations are identified and planned for in later learning cycles that relate to the observations and use of models completed in these earlier, perhaps skills-oriented lessons. Concepts and generalizations are constructed through direct evidence that leads to critical thinking. Begin a unit with a hands-on lesson about a key question, such as, "What does the sun do during the daytime? Draw and explain your drawing." For older students, asking, "How do you know that Earth is a sphere?" or "What evidence would you be able to get to demonstrate that Earth is moving in an orbit?" is a start in this direction. For additional ideas and possible lessons, visit the website of the Eisenhower National Clearinghouse.

For more information about ideas and lessons about Earth, see the link to the Eisenhower National Clearinghouse website on the Companion Website that accompanies this text at *http://www.prenhall.com/sunal*

Companion Website

Applying What You Know

Interviewing a Student about Earth in Space

Assess and discuss the prior knowledge of one or more students in a conceptual area related to Earth in space. In advance, set up a schedule with a teacher that will not interfere with his normal class activities. Take notes during the interview, and later complete a reflective journal entry for each student about the interview. Discuss the results with the teacher and observe the student in her daily activities to see if the student's thinking fits your conclusions. Follow these steps when completing the activity.

Step 1. Select a discrepant event, phenomenon, or confrontational situation related to an Earth in space concept or generalization. Use the previous alternative conceptions and activities as an example of the content and format needed for your student. Consider the probable prior knowledge of this student when planning the activity. Gather the demonstration materials or draw the phenomenon or situation.

Step 2. Write a script of the key question and possible follow-up responses you will make. Consider general open-ended questions, problem-solving tasks, garden-path tasks that walk students through the idea, or comprehension tasks. Ask the student to describe her understanding of the event. Use one of the discrepant activities previously described or construct one using a similar format.

Step 3. To start the interview, set the student at ease. Talk to the student about something of interest. Begin the interview with your key open-ended question.

Step 4. Find out what ideas the student already has about a phenomenon or situation. Ask, "What do you think is happening?" and "For what reasons?" Note the words the student uses to explain or describe it. Focus on the student's response and the reasoning that led to the answer.

Step 5. Take the student seriously. Give her the opportunity to discuss or try out ideas by herself.

Step 6. Challenge the student to describe or find evidence for her own ideas. Probe the student and follow her line of reasoning.

Step 7. Thank the student for allowing you to listen to her view of the event. After the interview, write up the events as they occurred from steps 1 to 7 in a reflective journal form.

To complete this activity, include a title page and label the parts of the assignment as indicated below:

1. A description of the concept or generalization and the demonstration materials or a drawing of the phenomenon or situation.
2. A script of the key question and possible follow-up responses you will make to your student.
3. Notes of the interview events as they occurred written in reflective journal form. Identify the student by first name only or use a pseudonym.
4. Concluding paper—write your conclusion and a prescription in a one-paragraph format. Consider the following questions: "What does the student believe (prior knowledge) about the concept or event?" "Why does she believe this?" "How does this belief relate to the scientific view?" "What have you learned about this student as a teacher?"

A LEARNING CYCLE INVOLVING STUDENTS' ALTERNATIVE CONCEPTIONS RELATED TO EARTH IN SPACE

In order to demonstrate the complete instructional process of: (1) identifying students' alternative conceptions, (2) developing a lesson plan, and (3) developing an assessment for a specific concept of Earth in space, an example of a complete lesson and assessment follows.

Alternative Conception Addressed by the Lesson Plan: *The sun is directly overhead at noon. The daylight is the same length as our local day on any part of Earth. The amount of daylight time increases throughout the summer months* (alternative conception number 5 above).

Lesson Goal: To allow students to investigate and develop inferences about the orientation of Earth in relation to the sun.

Grade Level: Grades 4–5.

Prerequisites: Can measure height to the nearest centimeter. Knows the cardinal points of the compass.

Exploration

Objective: Students will make inferences about the location of the sun in the sky when seen from Earth.

Materials: For each group: one copy of Figure 15-6.

Procedure:

  A. Organize small groups of three students: a materials manager and reporter, an observer, and an illustrator.
  B. Describe the materials and instructions needed to carry out the activity. Provide each group with a sheet of paper on which a large half circle has been drawn (see Figure 15-6). State the key questions, write them on the board, and ask each group to discuss and complete its answers by drawing on the half circle: "Where is the sun at noon today?" and "Where is the sun early in the morning and late in the evening?" Draw the path of the sun throughout the entire daytime period.
  C. When the students have completed their work, ask the reporter from each group to present its results to the entire class.
  D. Ask the groups to discuss the following questions written on the board: "Is the amount of daylight hours the same for all people on Earth today?" "In the winter, there are fewer hours of daylight than in the summer. Why does this happen?" Ask the students to write out their responses and illustrate their ideas. Also, ask the students to devise a plan for providing evidence for their answers to both questions.

Evaluation: Determine whether each group has a complete response to each question and a plan for obtaining evidence to support its answers to each question. Assess the group's skills by observing whether students join their groups quickly when asked and whether the group reviews what needs to be done before starting.

Invention

Objective: Students will investigate and describe the location of the sun and the duration of daylight over different regions of Earth.

Materials: For each group: one copy of Figure 15-6; one globe; a small lump of clay; a toothpick.

Procedure:

A. Have each group present its responses to item D in the Exploration above and its plan for providing evidence for its ideas to the whole class. Help students communicate the results of their discussions using observations to justify their conclusions. Help them compare each group's plan for providing evidence.

B. With the sun visible in the daytime sky, plan a short field trip to the school grounds. Give each group a large copy of Figure 15-6. Ask each student to make a sketch of the sky while facing south and the horizon. Students are to draw in the location of the sun and important objects visible on the horizon from their location on the school grounds. This field trip can be completed in less than 10 minutes. Repeat the activity three to five times throughout the day, twice in the morning, once at noon, and twice in the afternoon. Record all observations on the same drawing, and include the time on each drawing. *Warn the students not to look directly at the sun,* since damage to the eye can occur in just a few seconds.

C. Write the key questions from the Exploration (item B) on the board. Ask the groups to answer these questions based on their observations. Ask them to compare these answers to the answers they inferred during the Exploration. Have them report their comparisons to the class.

D. Elicit and explain the discrepancies between the students' inferences and the observations they just made. It should be clear to the students that their original ideas may not be supported by evidence they have just gathered. During a brief discussion, ask them how they arrived at their ideas about the sun's location and motion in the sky. How different were their original ideas from the observations they made?

   The sun is never directly overhead in the United States. The path of the sun keeps it in the southern part of the sky all day long. During the fall and winter months, the sun rises in the southeast, moves to a high position in the south, and sets in the southwest. As an additional assignment, ask some students to observe the location of sunrise on a weekend morning while others observe the late afternoon sun and a third group observes the sunset. Provide students with a compass to help them with directions.

E. The following activity also requires a clear day with a bright sun. Obtain one Earth globe for each group. The best type of globe to use in this activity is one that is detachable from its stand. Model how students are to use the globe when they go outside. Ask each student group to cut a strip out of poster board 1 inch wide and 1 foot long. Form it into a circle and staple the ends together. Demonstrate how to set up the globe. Take the globe out of its stand and set it on the floor into the base formed by the poster board circle (see Figure 15-7). Put your city or town's location on the exact top of the globe. Point the north pole of the globe toward the direction of north. Instruct the students to do the same with their globes when they go outside. Do this activity outside on a blacktop or on grass to reduce the glare of sunlight on the globe. Tell students that when the sun shines on the globe, it replicates the way Earth looks to an astronaut on the moon. The astronaut would also see parts of Earth lit up by the sun and other parts in shadow. She would see where the day and night come together and the edge of the shadow. The shadow's edge occurs on both sides of Earth.

   To demonstrate a method for students to determine the amount of sunlight any city receives during a day, ask students to find places on Earth at a specific latitude, for example 40° north latitude, that are turning from night into day and day into

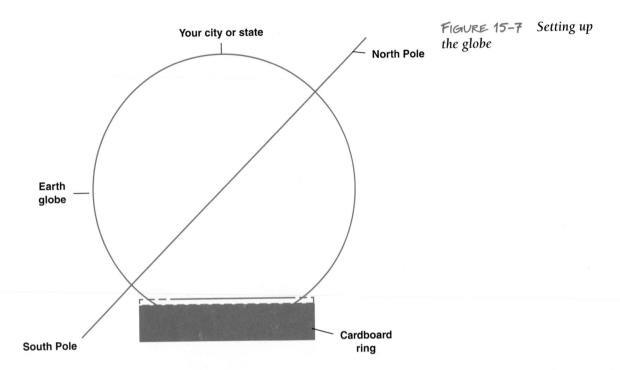

FIGURE 15-7   *Setting up the globe*

Your city or state

North Pole

Earth globe

South Pole

Cardboard ring

night. This is the shadow's edge. Count the number of longitude lines from the shadow's edge on the right side of Earth to the shadow's edge on the left side of Earth. These longitude lines are generally 15° apart. This is how much Earth turns in 1 hour. If there are ten 15° intervals from one shadow's edge to the other, there will be 10 hours of daylight during a 24-hour period at that latitude.

Before taking the students outside, provide each group with a small lump of clay and a toothpick. Then give each group a sheet of paper with the following questions: "Where is the sun overhead right now on Earth?" "How many hours of daylight exist for cities in the following latitudes: 50° north? At the latitude of your town? At the equator? At 40° south of the equator?" Students can stand the toothpick up in the clay and press the clay onto the globe. Shadows cast as the clay and toothpick are moved to different places on the globe provide information useful in answering the first question. The place where no shadow is cast by the toothpick indicates where the sun is overhead. Ask students to explain and illustrate the group's answers to these questions.

F. Return inside and have each group report its findings. Discuss these, adding information as necessary.

G. Closure: The sun is overhead someplace on Earth at any given time. At night, the sun is overhead someplace on the other side of Earth. The sun is never directly overhead of any portion of the United States, except Hawaii. Cities at different latitudes have differing amounts of daylight most days of the year. Only on March 21st and September 21st are daylight hours (12) for every city on Earth the same. This can be seen on a globe outdoors on these days as the shadow's edge lights up half of the Earth so that the shadow cuts exactly through the north and south poles. At other times, the shadow's edge falls to either side of the poles.

Evaluation: Decide whether each group has a complete response to each question and illustrations that provide evidence to support its answers. Assess the students' group skills

Where on Earth is the sun overhead right now?

by observing whether they stay with their group while it is working and pay attention to how much time they have to carry out each activity.

Expansion

Objectives: Students will compare the height of the sun in the sky as seen from different locations on Earth.

> Students will determine that the Arctic and Antarctic are places where the sun will not rise or set.

> Students will determine in what cities on Earth the sun is rising or setting at the time of the lesson.

Materials: For each group: materials from the Invention activity; a 30-centimeter ruler.

> For each student: copies of Figure 15–6; copies of a drawing of the whole Earth.

Procedure:

A. Give the students a handout containing the following directions and information:

> Do this activity outside just as you did the last one using a globe, a small lump of clay, and a toothpick. Set up the Earth globe on the poster-board ring so that your state or town is on top and the north pole points north. The length of the shadow of an object gives information regarding how high the sun is in the sky. Compare the height of the sun from various locations on Earth that are north and south of your town by comparing the length of the toothpick's shadow in various locations. Do this for the

following locations: 0° (equator), plus and minus 30°, plus and minus 60°, and plus and minus 80°. Record this information on the drawing of Earth. Where on Earth today will the sun never rise? Where will it never set? Name two cities where the sun is just setting (in Africa or Europe). Name two cities where the sun is just rising (in Asia or Australia). Record your answers to these questions.

B. As an extended Expansion activity, have the students note the sunset and sunrise times over a 2-week period as reported in the newspaper and comment on the day-to-day changes. Ask the student groups to report their findings to the whole class.

C. Another extended Expansion activity involves students in obtaining the sunrise and sunset times for the town's latitude for an entire year. Ask them to record and graph the length of the daylight period on the first day of each month. Have them report their findings to the whole class.

D. Summarize the lesson by reviewing the activities and major findings of the various parts of the lesson.

Evaluation: Ask students to draw the sun's path on Figure 15-6 during the day from sunrise to sunset. On a drawing of Earth, ask students to circle the area where the sun is overhead at this time. On the same drawing of Earth, ask students to indicate cities where the daylight hours on that day are the greatest and where they are the fewest.

EXAMPLES OF ALTERNATIVE CONCEPTIONS IN ADDITIONAL EARTH AND SPACE SCIENCE AREAS

Students develop alternative conceptions in Earth and space science starting in their primary-grade years. Their observations of the sky and Earth and the representations they see on television (especially in cartoons) provide a source for many alternative conceptions. Although some alternative conceptions may relate to their level of development and can be expected to be modified without much intervention, many ideas about Earth and space sciences developed during the elementary school years will remain with them throughout adulthood unless directly addressed in effective instruction. The following is a brief sample of alternative conceptions commonly found in relation to Earth and space science topics, such as Earth; its structure, history, oceans, and atmosphere; space science; geology; the solar system; and stars and the universe. The list demonstrates the depth and breadth of alternative ideas students bring to class. It also indicates that teachers must be aware of students' alternative ideas in order to plan effective Earth and space science lessons (Bar, Sneider, & Martimbeau (1997); Boyes & Stanisstreet (1997); Driver, Squires, Rushworth, and Wood-Robinson (1994); Gonzalez (1997); Nelson, Aron, & Francek (1992); Philips (1991); Rye, J. A., Strong, & Rubba (2001); Sneider & Ohadi (1998); Stahly, Krockover, & Shepardson (1999); and Taiwo, Ray, Motswiri, & Masene (1999).

Sample Alternative Conceptions about Earth Students Bring to Class

Earth: Its Structure and History

1. The center of Earth is made of black rocks because a man who comes out of a hole is covered with dark dirt (younger students).
2. Thrown objects may fall off Earth when dropped in the southern hemisphere.
3. Earth is sitting on something.
4. Earth is larger than the sun.

5. Molten Earth material comes from the core of Earth.
6. Volcanic eruptions always produce steep-sided cones.
7. Erosion only occurs on steep slopes.

Earth: Its Oceans

1. Coral reefs exist throughout the Gulf of Mexico and the North Atlantic.
2. All rivers flow down from north to south.
3. Materials such as salt or sediment, when dissolved in water, do not change their properties.
4. Oceans stay the same; they don't change.
5. What humans do can't change oceans.
6. When water evaporates, it ceases to exist.
7. When water evaporates, it turns into another visible kind of thing like steam or fog (students do not believe that water can be in the form of a gas, water vapor, which is not visible).
8. Water in all bodies of water on Earth freezes at 0° Celsius or 32° Fahrenheit (due to substances dissolved in rivers and oceans, freezing occurs at lower temperatures).
9. The sea level remains constant.

Earth: Its Atmosphere

1. Rain comes from holes in clouds. Rain comes from colliding clouds. Rain occurs because we need it (younger students).
2. Clouds come from somewhere above the sky.
3. The sun boils the sea to create water vapor.
4. Clouds are made of smoke (younger children).
5. Clouds are made of water (liquid-water filled).
6. Clouds are made of water vapor (older children; however, water vapor is a colorless gas and so it is invisible).
7. Air is not a real substance.
8. Gases make things lighter.
9. Humid air is heavier than dry air so it sinks to the ground.
10. Lightning does not strike the same place twice.
11. The direction of drainage in a sink or bathtub is always in the same direction (older students).

Sample Alternative Conceptions about Geology Students Bring to Class

1. Rocks must be heavy.
2. Rocks cannot float (denser rocks, such as continental rock, float on mantle rock).
3. Very light objects have no weight (examples given are Styrofoam and pumice).
4. Soil must always have been in its present form.
5. There is only one kind of soil.
6. All soil looks, feels, and smells the same. Soil is just dirt.
7. Soil is the same on top as underneath even in undisturbed soil in the forest.
8. Any crystal that scratches glass is a diamond.
9. Washington, D.C., could not be severely damaged in an earthquake in the future.
10. Mountains are created quickly.
11. The continents and oceans of Earth have always remained the same.
12. All radioactivity is made by people.
13. Dinosaurs and cavemen lived at the same time.

When in orbit, are space shuttle astronauts under the influence of gravity?

14. Dinosaurs are the largest animals that ever lived.
15. Crocodiles and alligators are dinosaurs.
16. People are responsible for the extinction of dinosaurs.
17. Dinosaurs lived at the same time as ice-age mammals like the woolly mammoth and the mastodon.

Sample Alternative Conceptions about Space Science Students Bring to Class

1. There is an up and down in space.
2. Gravity cannot exist without air.

3. Gravity requires a material to act through.
4. Rockets in space require a constant rocket thrust or force to continue to move.
5. Gravity acts differently on various materials.
6. Gravity pulls things down (little concept of gravity as directed toward the center of a spherical Earth).
7. Earth's gravitational attraction only extends to the edge of the atmosphere. While in space, the space shuttle astronauts are not under the influence of gravity (gravity still exists; they are weightless due to forces of motion and gravity balancing each other).

Sample Alternative Conceptions about the Solar System Students Bring to Class

1. The sun ceases to exist at night (younger students).
2. The sun is not a star.
3. The sun will never burn out.
4. The moon makes light the same way the sun does.
5. The moon increases and decreases in (physical) size.
6. Different phases of the moon are seen from different locations on Earth on the same day.
7. Phases of the moon are caused by Earth's shadow or by passing clouds.
8. Summer and winter seasons are the direct result of Earth's distance from the sun.
9. Planets appear as a small disk to the naked eye.
10. The solar system appears to us *from Earth* as a set of concentric orbits (circles) revolving around the sun and seen from the top.
11. The sun is smaller than Earth.
12. The solar system is composed of galaxies, stars, and planets.

Examples of Alternative Conceptions about Stars and the Universe

1. The universe is always the same.
2. The universe contains only the planets and stars in our solar system.
3. Stars are all the same distance away.
4. Stars are the same. They are not different in any significant way.
5. Stars are smaller than Earth. Stars are small bodies, much smaller than the sun.
6. Astrology, based on star and planet location, is able to predict the future.

Applying What You Know

Identifying Possible Alternative Conceptions

Evaluate one of your Earth and space science lesson plans, or a science textbook chapter. Determine possible alternative conceptions students may bring to class related to the content to be taught. You may want to evaluate the lesson plan used in the previous Applying What You Know. If possible, work with a partner on this activity. Answer the questions below:

1. What are the stated or implied focus concepts and generalizations in the lesson plan or chapter?

2. What are possible alternative conceptions students might bring to class? Check the lesson's concepts and generalizations against the sample lists provided on the previous page as a beginning. List the alternative conceptions.

ACTIVITIES THAT CAN HELP STUDENTS CHANGE THEIR ALTERNATIVE CONCEPTIONS IN EARTH AND SPACE SCIENCE

Discrepant events provide students with the confrontation they need to test out their prior knowledge. The discrepant events below demonstrate examples from each Earth and space science area. A sample alternative conception is followed by an appropriate discrepant event useful during the Exploration phase of a learning cycle lesson.

Discrepant Events with Earth: Its Oceans

Students' Alternative Conception:
6. *When water evaporates, it ceases to exist.*
7. *When water evaporates, it turns into another visible kind of thing like steam or fog.*

Discrepant Activity: Form groups of three students. Give each group five ice cubes placed as follows: put one ice cube on a plate, a second on a sponge, a third on a piece of construction paper, a fourth on top of potting soil in a Styrofoam cup, and a fifth in a jar with a lid attached. Ask each student group to illustrate and describe its observations. Ask students to discuss and come up with a response to the following questions regarding what happens when ice cubes melt in different locations: "What is happening to each of the ice cubes?" "What happens to the water dripping from the ice cubes?" and "Where did the water go?" Ask students to examine their ice cubes 1 hour later and to respond to each of the questions again. Have the groups report their results and ideas to the class.

This activity elicits student ideas related to ice turning to water and finally disappearing either by absorption into a material or by evaporation into the air. When water evaporates it forms a gas that is invisible (water vapor). Fog and steam are a physical form of water in the liquid state (small water droplets). Water vapor is a gas whose particles are the size of molecules. Neither evaporation nor water vapor can be observed. However, the results of their presence can be seen in the coolness that results when water evaporates, decreased water volume, or the disappearance of wetness in an object that has absorbed water.

Discrepant Events with Earth: Its Atmosphere

Students' Alternative Conception:
3. *The sun boils the sea to create water vapor.*

Discrepant Activity: Form groups of three students. Give each group a tall, straight-walled glass or bottle. Ask each group to fill the container about three-fourths full of water. Then, have students set it on the windowsill or in a location in the room where it will not be disturbed for a few days. Have students mark the level of the water with a marking pen and write the name of their group on it. If the containers are in a sunny location, the results are more quickly seen than if the container is in a darker or cooler location. Ask the students to keep a record of the water level twice a day over the next

3 to 4 days. Each day have one of the groups carefully put a thermometer in its container and measure its temperature. Have the group record the water level, temperature, and the date of each observation on the glass.

The students who expected little to happen should be surprised at the amount of evaporation of water from their open containers. Measuring the temperature confirms that 100° Celsius (212° Fahrenheit) was never achieved in these containers, yet the water disappeared or evaporated from the surface of the water in the container. This consistently happens in the oceans at temperatures far below boiling.

Discrepant Events about Space Science

Students' Alternative Conception:
  7. *Earth's gravitational attraction only extends to the edge of the atmosphere.*

Discrepant Activity: Give each student a sheet of paper with a 10-centimeter (4-inch) diameter Earth circle drawn on it. Ask each to draw where the atmosphere ends (1 millimeter or 1/20th of an inch on this scale) and how far out Earth's gravitational attraction extends. Explain these directions in terms of the students' level of understanding. When they have completed their illustrations, have them write a description of the meaning of the illustrations. Now, ask the students to work in groups of four. Have them describe their answers to each other. Following the discussion, ask each group to discuss and come up with an answer to the following: "The moon is about 400,000 kilometers (240,000 miles) away, or about 30 Earth diameters away (30× 4 inches = 120 inches away on this scale) and revolves around Earth once a month. What keeps it in its orbit around Earth? Compare your answer to this question to the earlier questions."

Older students find their answer to the moon question perplexing. Because of the mass media's emphasis on weightlessness, zero gravity, or microgravity in space-related articles (especially when discussing space shuttle trips), most students believe that gravity ends with the atmosphere. There is gravity everywhere on Earth but none just above the atmosphere for the space shuttle; therefore, gravity ends with the atmosphere.

The moon is held in its orbit by Earth's gravity. If no other forces from other bodies intervened, Earth's force and the effect of gravity would extend infinitely. Gravity becomes weaker with distance. If the distance is doubled, the gravitational force becomes one-fourth as strong. However, the force is still strong enough to affect huge bodies in space, such as the moon. The space shuttle is, on average, only about 250 kilometers (150 miles) above Earth's surface. This is very close to Earth. The shuttle has traveled into space a distance equal to less than 2 percent of Earth's diameter. The moon is 30 times Earth's diameter away. Gravitational attraction at the shuttle's distance from Earth is nearly equal to (about 93 percent) Earth's attraction on its surface. The orbital motion of the space shuttle causes Earth's gravitational force to be balanced by a force due to orbital acceleration. This balance results in weightlessness when orbiting around Earth.

Discrepant Events with Geology

Students' Alternative Conception:
  2. *Rocks cannot float (denser rocks, such as continental rock, float on mantle rock).*

Discrepant Activity: Form groups of three students. Ask the groups to discuss and develop a response to the following questions: "What happens when you pour liquids of different types into the same container?" "What is the evidence that you can give to convince someone else that your view is correct?" "Draw and write out responses to these questions." Have the students report their responses to the whole class.

Following this discussion, provide each group with a tall, narrow container like a cylindrical olive jar or small-diameter juice glass. Ask the group manager to use a marking pen to mark the group's container with two lines one-third of the way up and two-thirds of the way up. Ask the materials managers to take the container to the station marked "cooking oil." Have each fill the container to the first line (one-third full) with cooking oil and take it back to the group so that observations of the first liquid can be made. The group should make and record at least ten observations (for example, its color, odor, quickness of flow, bubbles, size of bubbles, and how fast bubbles move).

Next, the materials manager should go to the station marked "water" and get a 6-ounce drinking cup full of water. Ask the group to make ten observations of the water as the second liquid.

Following the observations, have the materials manager pour the water into the cylindrical container of oil until the second line (two-thirds full) is reached. Ask the group to make ten observations of the pouring process and of what happens after the water is poured.

The materials manager should get a small object from station three. An object that can be used is a one-half inch plastic square cut from the top of a margarine container or other type of thin plastic. After making group observations of the object, the materials manager puts the object into the oil and water container. Ask the group to discuss and answer the following questions: "What happened when the two liquids were put into the same container?" "How does the word 'floating' relate to what you see in the two liquids?" "What happened when you put the object into the two liquids?" "How does the word 'floating' relate to the object?" "Can solids float in a liquid?" and "Can liquids float in liquids?"

Students find the mixing of liquids interesting; for example, most will not have predicted the results of the oil floating on top of the water when the two are put together. Putting the object into the water and oil container enables students to see that the object sinks through the oil and stops at the water boundary, where it floats on the water's surface. These concepts are necessary if students are to be able to make sense of concepts in geology. They relate to molten rock flowing up out of fissures onto land, the continental block of land that makes up North America floating on the denser rock of the mantle, and continents moving over the surface of Earth due to up-welling currents in the mantle (plate tectonics). The Invention for this discrepant event should lead to this concept.

Discrepant Events with the Solar System

Students' Alternative Conception:
8. *Summer and winter seasons are the direct result of Earth's distance from the sun.*

Discrepant Activity: Place students in groups of four. Ask them to discuss and come up with answers to the following questions: "What is the cause of seasons?" and "Why is it warmer in summer and colder in winter?" Have them write and illustrate their responses on a sheet of paper and save them for presentation to the class later.

Give each group a compass, a sheet of paper with a dot for the sun in the middle, and a ruler. Ask students to draw Earth's orbit to scale. Provide them with the approximate distance of the sun from Earth at its maximum of 157,500 kilometers

(94,500,000 miles) and minimum of 152,500 kilometers (91,500,000 miles). Try 30,000 kilometers = 1 centimeter as the scale for the drawing. Students may need help scaling this orbit to the size of the paper. When they are finished, ask them to think about the above questions. Would they like to revise their answers to the questions? If so, ask them to write their second responses below the first ones.

Many of the students will have alternative conceptions about the cause of seasons. Eliciting them and making them public in the Exploration phase of the lesson is important. The circles they draw for orbits should make it obvious to them that the difference in distance between Earth and the sun in various parts of Earth's orbit is insignificant when compared to the average orbital distance from the sun. The Invention leads to the investigation of an explanation of the cause of seasons based on the sun's altitude and length of day in different seasons.

Discrepant Events with Stars and the Universe

Students' Alternative Conception:
3. *Stars are all the same distance away.*
4. *Stars are the same. They are not different in any significant way.*
5. *Stars are smaller than Earth. Stars are small bodies, much smaller than the sun.*

Discrepant Activity: This activity works best following an introduction to stars for grades 5–8. Ask all students to write and illustrate the following: "Draw each of these to the same scale: Earth, sun, North Star, and the star, Betelgeuse, in the constellation of Orion. Describe how these four objects differ from each other." Place students in groups of four and ask them to share their drawings and responses in their groups.

Next, ask each group to complete the following activity. Give each group a copy of Table 15-2 and Figure 15-8. Table 15-2 lists the brightest stars in the constellation of Orion and the important characteristics of each star. Figure 15-8 represents the location of each star in the constellation of Orion. Ask every group to illustrate the size of the sun, Betelgeuse, and Rigel using the information in Table 15-2.

In addition, assign each group a different characteristic of the stars in Orion found in Table 15-2. Each group should make an illustrated presentation to the class of the differences found between stars with this characteristic. The characteristics are brightness (as seen from Earth), companions, color, distance, and brightness compared to the sun. A magnitude 1.0 star is 2.5 times brighter than a magnitude 2.0 star. The letters associated with color are the names given to each color group, so spectrographic classification "B" signifies a *b*luish star.

Most students do not appreciate the differences between stars and what those differences represent. It is important to get students to discuss their own beliefs about stars. At the beginning of the Invention, provide students with the following information about the approximate sizes of the objects they drew earlier.

Earth	8,000 miles in diameter
sun	865,000 miles in diameter
North Star	8,000,000 miles in diameter
Betelgeuse	43,000,000 miles in diameter

Help the student groups develop illustrated presentations of the characteristics of stars using artwork, models, graphs, or overhead transparencies. They should be creative in illustrating each of the characteristics. After the presentations, students' ideas about stars should be challenged.

TABLE 15-2   *Characteristics of stars in the constellation of Orion*

Name	Brightness Seen from Earth (magnitude, 0 = brightest)	Color (OBAFGKM, Blue to Red)	Distance from Earth (light years)	Companion Stars (multiple star)	Size Compared to the Sun (x Sun)
Betelgeuse (Alpha)	0.7	M, reddish	520	1	700
Rigel (Beta)	0.1	B, bluish	900	3	50
Bellatrix (Gamma)	1.6	B, bluish	470	0	4,000
Mintaka (Delta)	2.2	O, bluish-white	1,500	1	20,000
Alnilam (Epsilon)	1.7	B, bluish	1,600	0	40,000
Alnitak (Zeta)	1.8	O, bluish-white	1,600	2	35,000
Saiph (Kappa)	2.1	B, bluish	2,100	0	50,000
Pi-3	3.2	F, yellowish	26	0	3
Lambda	3.4	O, bluish-white	1,800	1	9,000

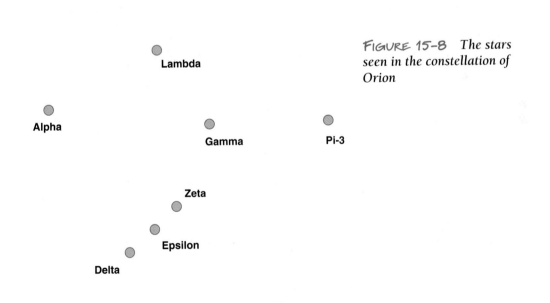

FIGURE 15-8   *The stars seen in the constellation of Orion*

Applying What You Know

Interviewing a Student about Earth in Space

Assess and discuss the prior knowledge of a student in one of the five Earth and space science areas described above. In advance, set up a schedule with a classroom teacher that will not interfere with normal class activities. Take notes during the interview. Later, complete a reflective journal entry for the student. Discuss the results with the teacher and observe the student in daily activities to see if the student's thinking fits your conclusions.

Step 1. Select a discrepant event, phenomenon, or confrontational situation related to a physical science concept or generalization. Use the physical science alternative conceptions and activities above as an example of the format to be used or construct one using a similar format. Consider the probable prior knowledge of this student when planning this activity. Gather the demonstration materials or draw the phenomenon or situation.

Complete Steps 2 to 7 as described in the *Applying What You Know*—Student Interview on Heat in Chapter 13.

To complete this activity, include a title page and label the parts of the assignment indicated below:

1. A description of the concept or generalization and the demonstration materials, or a drawing of the phenomenon or situation.
2. A script of the key question and possible follow-up responses you will make to your students.
3. A report of the interview events as they occurred written in reflective journal form. Identify the student by first name only or a pseudonym.
4. Your conclusion and a prescription written in a short typed paper. Consider the following questions: "What does the student believe (prior knowledge) about the concept or event?" "How does this belief relate to the scientific view?" "What have you learned about this student?" and "How would you start a lesson for this student in this science area?"

EXAMPLES OF LEARNING CYCLES TEACHING EARTH AND SPACE SCIENCE CONCEPTS

The following learning cycle lessons challenge students' conceptions of an Earth and space science event with a more appropriate scientific explanation. Note the connection of each learning cycle phase to the students' alternative conceptions addressed in the lesson.

A Learning Cycle Lesson Plan Involving Alternative Conceptions about Earth: Its Oceans

Alternative Conceptions Addressed by the Lesson Plan:

6. *When water evaporates, it ceases to exist.*
7. *When water evaporates, it turns into another visible kind of thing like steam or fog.*

Lesson Goal: To allow students to investigate, develop inferences, and differentiate between different elements of the water cycle.

Grade Level: Grades 2–3.

Prerequisites: Can measure time intervals of a whole minute. Has experienced activities investigating the properties of matter and the phases of matter—solid, liquid, and gas.

Exploration

Objective: Students will investigate the observable characteristics of evaporation and condensation over specific time periods.

Materials: For each group: a paper plate; a piece of construction paper; a sponge; a Styrofoam cup; a jar with a lid; a small glass; water; potting soil with a spoon for dipping it out of its container; nine ice cubes; container for the ice cubes.

Procedure:

A. Form groups of three students: a materials manager, an observer, and a recorder.
B. Have each materials manager go to the equipment station and pick up the following: a plate, sponge, piece of construction paper, Styrofoam cup which is one-half full of soil, jar with a lid, and a small glass which is one-half full of water.
C. While the groups' materials managers are getting the equipment, ask the other members to make a matrix with six boxes on a piece of paper. Label the boxes as follows: plate, sponge, construction paper, cup with soil, jar with lid, and small glass with water.
D. Ask the materials managers to go to the ice cube station and put nine ice cubes in a container. When they return to their group, the other students place the ice cubes as follows: put one ice cube on a plate, a second on a sponge, a third on a piece of construction paper, a fourth on top of the potting soil in a Styrofoam cup, a fifth in a jar with a lid, and four cubes in a small glass of water.
E. Ask each student group to illustrate and describe its observations as students respond to the following questions on the matrix sheet: "What is happening to each of the ice cubes?" "What happens to the water dripping from the ice cubes?" and "Where did the water go?"
F. Ask the students to examine their ice cubes 1 hour later and respond to each of the questions again.

Evaluation: Collect the students' observations from the Exploration. Evaluate them considering the completeness and specificity of the observations drawn or described. Evaluate the group's skills by assessing whether all students participated equally in the activity and whether individuals offered help and explained ideas or instructions to others in the group.

Invention

Objective: Students will develop inferences about recurring events as related to evaporation, condensation, and precipitation in the water cycle.

Materials: For each group: one Styrofoam cup of hot water; one glass of cold water with an ice cube in it; one copy of Figure 15–9; drawing paper and materials; and a mirror cooled with ice cubes plus one cold mirror for the teacher.

Procedure:

A. Ask students to report the results of their Exploration activity to the class. During the reports, highlight statements made by students that relate to evaporation and

FIGURE 15-9   *A cup and glass water cycle*

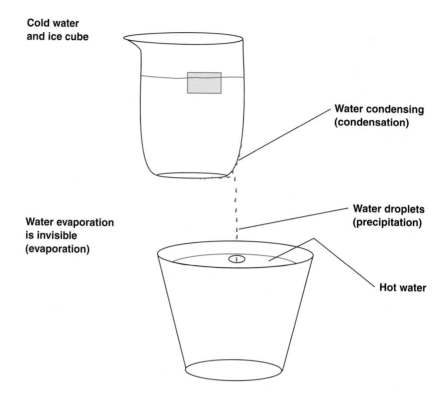

Cold water and ice cube

Water condensing (condensation)

Water evaporation is invisible (evaporation)

Water droplets (precipitation)

Hot water

condensation. Introduce and define the terms at this time using concrete examples from the students' observations. Demonstrate condensation by blowing across a cold mirror and noticing the haze. Give the students cold mirrors and challenge them to do this also.

B. Discuss the three states of matter that water is found in: solid, liquid, and gas. Water can change from one form to another. While in any one form, it can be moved to another location.

C. Have students return to their groups. To illustrate the forms of water and the water cycle, give each group a Styrofoam cup of hot water. Meanwhile, ask each group's materials manager to obtain a paper cup of very cold water with an ice cube in it from a materials station. Ask the observers in each group to hold the glass of cold water just above the hot water and make observations. Ask students to discuss what they see and to record and illustrate their observations.

D. Select a few groups to report their observations to the whole class. They should be able to report the effects of water condensing on the cold glass and dripping back into the glass of cold water. Tell the students that the dripping water is similar to rain. As a result of condensation in nature, precipitation occurs. Precipitation can be in the form of rain (liquid), snow, sleet, or hail (solid). Condensation in nature can be in the form of dew, frost, or fog. Evaporation can occur from rain when it hits the ground and "dries up;" fog when it "disappears" or evaporates; dew on grass when it "disappears;" and lakes, streams and oceans.

E. Challenge the students to observe all three forms of water: gas, liquid, and solid. They cannot observe the gas because water vapor is invisible. We can tell its presence, however, because it condenses on cold glass or metal when the gas brushes against it. Sometimes, we see fog or "steam" around our cup or outside (e.g., in clouds). These

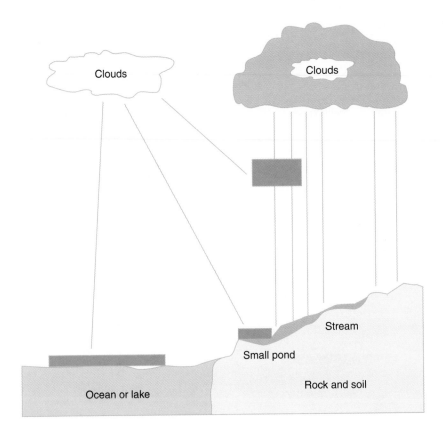

FIGURE 15–10   *A water cycle out-of-doors. Describe what is happening*

are not examples of water as a gas. However, they are examples of water vapor condensing into liquid droplets you can see.

F. Ask the students to illustrate the water cycle where water changes from one form or phase and returns to the original phase again. The students should use their observations of the hot cup of water and the cold glass of water for the illustration. They should use arrows to show the various stages of the water cycle. Ask one group to discuss its drawings with the class. Discuss the cyclic nature of the water cycle: water rises, evaporates from the cup, travels to the glass, condenses on the glass, and drops back into the hot water where it can evaporate again. Although this can happen repeatedly, energy (hot water) must be present to cause water to evaporate. Show the students Figure 15-10 in a transparency.

G. Provide every group with a sheet of paper and marking pens and ask students to illustrate a water cycle that answers this question: "Where does rain that falls on land come from?" Ask students to include a large lake and a flat land area in their drawings. When they have finished, ask two of the groups to present their illustrations to the class. Then, give a copy of Figure 15-10 to each group. Have students compare this drawing with their drawing. Finally, ask one of the groups to explain Figure 15-10. See also Figure 15-11, which provides sample answers.

H. In closure, the discussion leads students to draw the conclusions that the water cycle is a never-ending sequence of events. Water is never used up and never disappears as matter. Water can change form and move to another location where it may change form again, possibly into rain.

FIGURE 15–11 *A water cycle out-of-doors. A sample explanation*

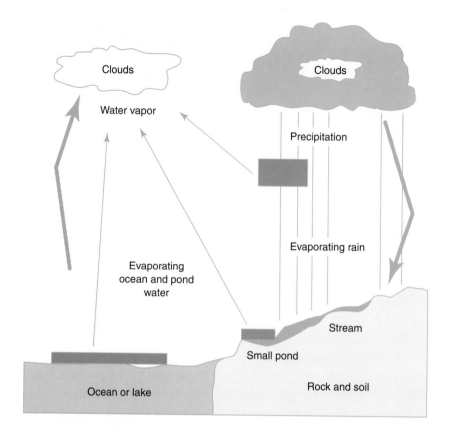

Evaluation: Collect the water cycle drawings and descriptions from each student. Evaluate the completeness and accuracy of each drawing. Evaluate the group's skills by assessing whether the groups review what to do before starting.

Expansion

Objective: Students will apply the concept of the water cycle to recurring events involving evaporation, condensation, and precipitation.

Materials: For each group: three colors of construction paper; scissors; glue; 1-gallon-sized zipper-type plastic bag; one cup of potting soil colored with blue food-coloring dyed water.

Procedure:

A. Ask each group to cut out 1-inch strips of pastel-colored construction paper. There should be three strips per student in each group. Have each student in the group write one term—"evaporation," "condensation," or "precipitation"—on each strip. Have each student glue the strips together to make a paper chain illustrating the water cycle. All students in the group should connect their separate chains to form a continuous, circular chain of water cycles. This helps illustrate the idea that water cycles have no beginning or end but recur over and over again. Ask the students to describe what their chain means.

B. In front of the class, have a student prepare 1 pound of potting soil by adding 2 cups of water with blue food dye in it. Have the materials manager from each group come up and collect a small Styrofoam cup of soil and a 1-gallon-sized zip-closing plastic bag. Ask the other members of the group to put the soil in the plastic bag and zip it tightly closed. Ask the students to predict what might happen if their plastic bag were

---

SCIENTISTS ARE DIVERSE!

Some Who Have Contributed to Our Knowledge of Earth and Space Science

Florence Bascom
A female scientist in the United States studying optical crystallography.

Hisashi Kuno
A Japanese male scientist studying magma.

Matuyama Motonori
A Japanese male scientist studying magnetic field reversals of Earth.

Mela Pomponius
A Spanish male scientist studying climatic regions and doing early geographical work.

Doris Reynolds
An Englishwoman who studied how granite formed.

Shen Kua
A Chinese male who discovered the magnetic compass.

FIGURE 15–12 *Scientists who have made significant contributions in Earth and space sciences*

left in the sun or on their desk overnight. Have students put their plastic baggies near a window with sunshine, if possible. Periodically, during the day and on the next day, ask them to check their predictions by making observations of the plastic baggie. When they make observations, ask them to answer the following questions: "What do they observe?" "What happened to the water in the soil?" "Where did the water go?" "How did the water get from the soil to the top or roof of the bag?" and "What color is the water that is condensed on the top of the bag?"

C. Briefly summarize the main points and sequence of activities during the lesson.

Evaluation: Ask students to draw the water cycle occurring in the plastic baggie. Collect the water cycle drawings and evaluate their completeness and accuracy.

Additional activities and information in Earth and space science lessons should relate to the nature of science (see Chapter 1) and the people who participated in creating it and who work in the field today. Some examples of people who contributed significantly to Earth and space sciences, but have been underrepresented in the mass media, are listed in Figure 15-12 along with their major contributions. Additional information can be found in library references such as an encyclopedia. The books *Women in Science: Antiquity through the Nineteenth Century* by M. B. Ogilvie (1986) and *Random House Webster's Dictionary of Scientists* by Jenkins-Jones (1997) are examples of resources. An Expansion activity to add to most Earth and space science lessons would be to read a paragraph to determine the skills involved in the contribution of a related scientist or to interview a member of the community who uses skills and knowledge from Earth and space sciences in her daily work. The local soil conservation specialist in the community is an example of one such individual whom it may be possible to interview. Ask older students to create research reports and short plays on the contributions of these underrepresented scientists.

Applying What You Know

Planning an Exploration for an Earth in Space Lesson

In the fifth-grade Earth and space science lesson plan below on the topic of soil, do the following: (1) identify possible alternative conceptions a student could bring to the lesson and, if available, interview a few children, and (2) develop key questions the teacher could use to guide students, actions to create a confrontation to their thinking during the Exploration. Use the list of Sample Alternative Conceptions About Geology previously described on page 448 as a starting point to identify the possible alternative conceptions.

A Learning Cycle Lesson Plan Involving Alternative Conceptions about Geology

Lesson Goal: To allow students to investigate, develop inferences, and differentiate between different types of soil.

Grade Level: Grades 3–5.

Prerequisites: Has experienced activities investigating the properties of matter and the phases of matter: solid, liquid, and gas. Has been involved in a lesson on erosion.

Exploration

Objective: The students will investigate the observable characteristics of different types of soil.

Materials: For each group: a cup of water; drawing paper; newspaper or paper towels to cover their desks; four sandwich or quart-sized zipper-type plastic bags; samples of four different types of soil; magnifying lens; two small limestone rocks (usually found along roadsides and in gravel driveways); two small sandstone rocks (usually found in roadside rock outcrops or used as garden rocks); one 30-centimeter ruler.

Procedure:

A. Ask each student to draw a picture of a field with bare soil that a farmer just plowed. Ask them to describe, in writing, the soil that is in the field, then ask the students to describe the soil that is underneath, down deep. When the descriptions and drawings are complete, ask the students to form groups of four and share their descriptions and drawings with each other.

B. The students should help prepare the next activity. Take them out on a short field trip. Give each group four sandwich or quart-sized zipper-type plastic bags. Take the students to different parts of the school grounds to collect different types of soil. Map out the field trips beforehand to note where different soils are located. Check for sand or gravel, mulch around bushes and trees, clay soil on the playground, and topsoil in grassy areas. If many different soils cannot be found, the teacher should provide a small bag of sand, clay, or potting soil from local soils or purchased at a discount store, to add to the diversity of soils the students will collect.

C. Back in the classroom, the groups begin working in the following roles: a materials manager, two observers, and a recorder. The materials managers go to the equipment station and pick up the following: a magnifying lens, old newspapers or paper towels to lay on top of the desks to keep them clean, two roadside or driveway limestone rocks, and two small sandstone rocks (or rocks purchased in bags at a discount store).

D. While the materials manager is getting the equipment, the other team members make a matrix with four boxes on a piece of paper. Each box is labeled with one of the types of soil available, such as potting soil, humus, sand, clay, gravelly soil, and topsoil.

E. Have the students look at the soil in small piles spread out thinly on a sheet of paper and dampened using a little water from a cup. They should use all of their senses except taste when making their observations. The students examine the rocks using a magnifying lens and try to measure grain size.

F. Confront the students with the observation that humus and potting soil are different from clay and sand.

G. Ask each group to illustrate and describe its observations as students respond to the key questions.

Evaluation: Collect students' observations from the Exploration. Evaluate them considering the completeness and specificity of observations drawn or described in response to the key questions. Group skills are addressed by observing whether the group forms quickly and stays together while it is working.

Invention

Objective: Students will make inferences about soil types and where they are found.

Materials: For each group: two limestone rocks and two sandstone rocks from the Exploration activity; two pieces of black construction paper; one magnifying lens; one 30-centimeter ruler; one cup of water; an eyedropper.

Procedure:

A. Ask the student groups to report their findings from the Exploration. Help the students focus on observations made with all their senses, such as the coarseness of grains of soil, the shape of the grains, and the evidence that some soils become wet when water is added while others do not.

B. Ask student groups to take their limestone pieces and hold them over a black sheet of construction paper. They should rub both rocks together until there is a thin coating of limestone dust on the paper. Label this paper "limestone soil." Next, take another sheet of black construction paper, pick up the two sandstone rocks, and repeat the process. Label this paper "sandstone soil."

C. Ask students to gather together as much of the rock soils as possible in a pile on each sheet. Have them make observations of these piles and list the similarities and differences. Measure the thickness of the soil layer (less than a millimeter). Next, add a few drops of water to each of the piles using an eyedropper. Ask the students to compare their results. Add a few more drops of water to the piles. Are there different observations? Instruct each group to use the activity just described to come up with an inference about how soil on Earth forms, how fast different types of soil form, and the different types of soil that might exist.

D. Have a few groups present their ideas to the class. The teacher should add that it takes a long time for soil to form. In some places where the climate is moist and the temperature is hot, it takes thousands of years for a few centimeters of soil to form. In places where it is very cold or in dry desert conditions, it takes soil much longer to form.

   Soil is formed in two ways. One is through weathering: rocks break down because other rocks or water rub or push against them. Soil is also formed through the chemical action of substances dissolved in the water. These are usually weak acids or substances formed from the air and plants. These acids dissolve the rock and carry it away in a solution like sugar water. The teacher should put an outline on the board describing how soil is made: (1) moving air or wind blow away pieces of rock, (2) rain and running water wear down rocks, (3) freezing water in cracks and ice breaks loose rocks, (4) plants and humans break apart rocks, and (5) chemicals dissolved in water decompose rocks. Some soil facts that can be discussed include the fact that in the 1700s the soil in the United States was on average 23 centimeters, or 9 inches, deep. Today, the topsoil covering the United States is 15 centimeters, or 6 inches, deep. In other words, we have lost one-third of our soil from wind and water erosion.

E. In closure, soils are built up very slowly: it takes thousands of years for a few centimeters to be formed. Soils form through the wearing away of rocks either by rubbing or by chemical action. Depending on the type of rock that is weathered and the type of climate, different types of soil will form. Soils have different characteristics including the size of the particles that make them up and their ability to hold water.

Evaluation: Evaluate group reports based on their completeness, specificity, and evidence. Assess group skills at the discovery stations by observing whether all students in the group identify and classify substances and whether evidence is provided to support the ideas when given.

Expansion

Objective: Students will make inferences about soil types and where they are found.

Materials: For each group: one large quart or liter jar with a screw-on lid; a measuring spoon; one cup of sand; one cup of potting soil; one cup of clay.

Procedure:

A. Ask the materials manager from each group to go to the materials station and obtain one jar and one Styrofoam cup each of sand, potting soil, and clay. The other group members should put all of the soils into the jar, tightly close the jar, and shake it up for about 1 minute. The group should then go to a water source in the room and carefully put in enough water to fill the jar two-thirds full and put the jar's lid on tightly again. The jar should then be shaken for about 1 minute.

B. The jar should be placed in the center of the group's worktable and the contents allowed to settle. Students keep a journal noting the time, their observations, and illustrations of their observations. This may take 15 to 20 minutes. The water may not be clear at the end of this time, but the soil will have settled into layers at the bottom of the jar. The groups should present their observations to the class.

C. The teacher should elaborate on students' observations, noting that soil is usually found in layers in areas undisturbed by people such as in forests or near streams. These layers can be seen when areas of soil are exposed in a roadside cut through a hill or a hole dug on the school grounds in an undisturbed area. There are usually four layers, or horizons, in an undisturbed soil profile. The thickness of each layer varies with its location. Not all layers are present everywhere. The topmost layer has a lot of plant material; it looks darker and is usually composed of mostly plant material with a little soil mixed in. A good example is often found in the top layer of leaf litter soil in a forest (see Figure 15-13). The second layer is still fairly dark since it contains some plant material. This is the soil that is usually called "topsoil," which is generally seen in farmer's fields. It has many minerals and nutrients in it. The third soil layer is called the subsoil. It is lighter in color and does not have very much plant

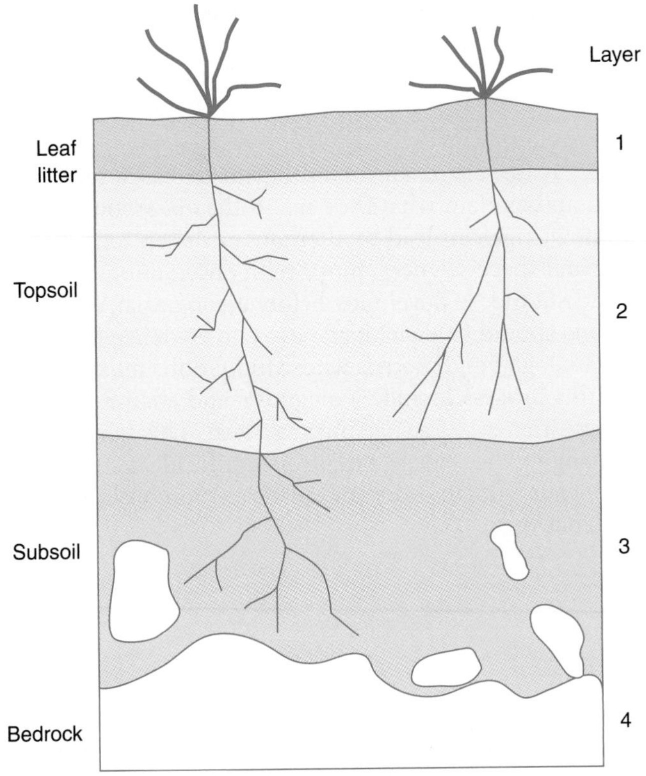

FIGURE 15-13   *Undisturbed soil layers. The depth of each varies with its location*

matter. The subsoil layer is made up almost completely of large rocks and soil that has just broken off of rocks. This layer is on top of the solid rock below it. Beneath this layer is bedrock.

D. If time permits, have students visit a site on the school grounds where soil has not been disturbed and layering is visible. Check this out beforehand. One to three shovelfuls of soil are all that is needed. Ask students to dig a small hole one half to 1 meter (16 to 36 inches) deep. Ask them to draw the variations of color and composition of the soil under the surface. Have them make a comparison of the layers found here using the information on soil layers provided earlier.

E. Briefly summarize the main points and activities of the lesson.

Evaluation: Ask students to describe how soil characteristics vary with depth. Have them illustrate and describe these characteristics, including the nature of the bedrock underneath. Evaluate their completeness and specificity.

Compare your answers with those below.

A. The possible alternative conceptions a student might bring to class regarding soils include the following: 4. *Soil must always have been in its present form. 5. There is only one kind of soil. 6. All soil looks, feels, and smells the same. Soil is just dirt. 7. Soil is the same on top as underneath, even in undisturbed soil in the forest.*

B. Key questions useful in guiding student actions during the Exploration, Section E, include the following: "How many similarities and differences between the soil samples can you find?" "Describe how each soil feels." and "How can you draw or illustrate your observations based on what you hear, touch, and smell?" For Section F, key questions include: "Where do these rocks come from?" and "What types of soils will these types of rocks produce?"

SUMMARY

Students, regardless of how much they read, rely on analogies they make based on familiar objects and events to understand and explain what they see in the classroom. Thus, students' commonsense everyday knowledge can lead to alternative conceptions of science concepts. When teaching Earth and space sciences, purposeful observations and experiences of events are important and should be developed before analogies and models are used. Concepts and generalizations should be developed based on evidence from objects and events and in context with analogies and models whose limitations must be presented. The steps in accomplishing this process include a diagnosis and eliciting of student ideas through experiences, questioning, and demonstrations. This should be followed by a time for testing or challenging these ideas. Finally, scientific ideas supported by evidence should be experienced by students in order to replace a commonsense view developed about Earth and space sciences.

Glossary

Accommodate. Modifying one's mental structures to incorporate new elements encountered in the external world.

Aesthetics. The recognition of beauty and the assignment of value to it.

Alternative conception. Generally, an incomplete or inaccurate view of how the world works.

Analogy. More elaborate and explicit than a simile, this is the idea that if one object or event agrees with another in two or more ways, those objects will probably agree in others.

Assessment. An integral part of the instructional gathering of information for specific purposes.

Assimilate. Incorporating new elements encountered in the external world into existing mental structures without having to modify those structures in order to include the new elements.

Biological sciences. Sciences which concern the study of life or living organisms.

Case studies. Studies which involve students in developing an explanation or conclusion for a specific small set of individuals, objects, or events related to the problem, theme, or issue.

Cause. The manipulated variable in an investigation.

Closed questions. Questions with a narrow focus having either one or a few answers.

Concept. The set of characteristics common to any and all instances of a given type or the characteristics that make certain items examples of a type of thing and that distinguish any and all examples from non-examples.

Concept map and concept web. A process that involves the identification of concepts in a set of materials being studied, and the organization of those concepts into a hierarchical arrangement from the most-general, most-inclusive concept to the least-general, most-specific concept.

Concept name. The labels or terms used to communicate the concept.

Conceptual and inquiry skills focused unit. A unit which combines science concepts and inquiry skills with equal emphasis.

Conceptual bridge. Aspects of a lesson that facilitate students' conceptual change by helping create meaningful links between their experiences and an explanation of those experiences.

Conceptual change. The process of learning that involves making changes in students' knowledge schemas.

Concrete concepts. Those concepts whose meanings can be derived from first-hand experiences with objects or events.

Cooperative learning. An approach and a set of strategies especially designed to encourage student cooperation while learning.

Creative thinking. Using basic thought processes to develop constructive, novel, or aesthetic ideas or products.

Critical thinking. Careful, precise, persistent, and objective analysis of any knowledge claim or belief in order to judge its validity and/or worth.

Descriptive unit. Unit in which content plays the major role.

Discrepant event. Experiences with objects or events, mental or computer (virtual) problems that pose a discrepant challenge, or differences in the interpretation of data discussed between members of a small group of peers.

Disequilibrium. An imbalance occurring when a person encounters an event or object that he is unable to assimilate due to the inadequacy of his cognitive structures. There is a discrepancy or a conflict between the person's schema and the requirements of the experience. This is accompanied by feelings of unease. When faced with a disturbance, the person reacts with responses that attempt to restore an equilibrium.

Evaluation. When the information gathered from assessment is interpreted and used to make judgments and decisions.

Examples. Any and all individual items or events that have the characteristics of a given concept.

Expansion. The part of the lesson that helps students apply and transfer a new idea or skill to different situations.

Exploration. The part of a lesson in which students are involved with a new science idea or skill, make their existing personal knowledge public, and relate old learning to new learning while the teacher diagnoses their existing ideas.

Facts. Statements of observations of objects and events.

Focus questions. Questions that help students make a link with their prior knowledge as well as establish a rationale for studying a unit.

Food. Material taken in by an organism and used to sustain the growth of cells, repair cells, provide energy, and provide materials for other vital processes that maintain a functioning organism.

Formal concepts. These concepts derive their meaning from an established relationship with an assumption, model, or some other hypothetical-deductive system. Meaning is not given to these concepts by information from the senses but through imagination or through developing logical relationships within the system.

Formal definition. Abstract terms used to describe a relationship between observations, forming a concept.

Generalizations. Statements that relate concepts showing how two or more concepts are connected to each other.

Goal. An intended purpose for a unit or lesson.

Heat. Internal energy in the process of transfer.

Heat energy. A measure of how much energy all the particles in an object have lost or gained indicating the total amount of internal energy transferred to or from a specific amount of a substance.

Hypothesis. A statement that attempts to describe the relationship between variables, which is general in the sense that it covers all cases both observed and unobserved.

Inference. A "best guess" statement based on observations that extends beyond those observations.

Inquiry. The method by which students construct meaning and develop generalizations as they learn science.

Inquiry skills-focused unit. A unit in which the specific content learned is less important than the skills to be developed.

Integrated unit approach. Using a focus to interconnect significant and relevant knowledge from various disciplines in a coherent manner.

Invention. The part of a lesson that explains and provides examples of the key new idea or skill leading students to mentally construct new patterns of reasoning.

Issues-focused unit. A unit that attempts to answer a question that is relevant to somebody—an individual, a group of individuals, or society as a whole.

Key question. An open question planned for the Exploration phase of every learning cycle that involves each student in thinking about the main idea of the lesson.

Knowledge. A network of experience and ideas given meaning through an active construction process.

Knowledge schema. A group of experiences and ideas that together form a concept, generalization, thinking skill, or disposition.

KWL. A three-step procedure that gives the teacher some indication of what prior knowledge the students have (K), and what they would like to learn (W) about the science unit topic, and what they did learn (L).

Law. A science regularity that applies to all members of a broad class of phenomena.

Learning. The process of constructing knowledge as sensory data are given meaning in terms of an individual's prior knowledge.

Learning cycle. A set of decision points and criteria that all teachers must address in the planning process to adequately help students learn science.

Learning outcomes. Statements of what the teacher wants the students to learn.

Metamorphosis. The process of great change over a short period of time when an animal is passing from its young to adult stage.

Metaphor. Words or phrases, or figures of thought, where one idea is used in place of another to suggest a likeness between them.

Morals. The standards used to make value decisions; judgments of rightness and wrongness.

Multiple assessment. Using a planned set of different assessments to clarify, provide feedback, and set goals that direct meaningful student science learning activities.

Non-examples. Any and all individual items that may have some, but not all, of the characteristics that make items examples of a given concept.

Nutrition. The process of feeding and the subsequent digestion and assimilation of food material.

Objectives. Statements focusing on what the student will learn and how success can be achieved.

Observation. Using the five senses to gather information from the environment.

Open questions. Questions that, when asked, have many answers.

Operational definitions. Statements used to describe a concept by providing a test for deciding whether an object or event is an example of the concept.

Pedagogical knowledge. Knowledge about appropriate and effective teaching strategies.

Preoperational concepts. Concepts whose meanings are developed through the basic senses.

Principle. A law that is highly general or fundamental and from which other laws are derived.

Problem solving. A thinking strategy that attempts to resolve a difficulty.

Projects. Events which involve students in investigating a problem, theme, or issue in small groups.

Result. The responding variable in an investigation.

Rubric assessment. An ordered sequence of performance levels that students in a class are expected to have at a particular time. These include a listing of actions to be observed during the lesson for individuals or groups of students.

Science. The construction of meaning through systematically using particular ways of observing, thinking, experimenting, and validating to develop interconnected ideas about the physical and biological worlds.

Science assessment. Gathering information on capacities and products viewed as essential in the context where they were learned and are to be used.

Science content knowledge. Knowledge about scientific content.

Science or scientific literacy. An awareness, appreciation, and understanding of key scientific concepts and processes required for personal decision making, participation in civic and cultural affairs, and economic productivity.

Science pedagogical knowledge. Effective use of a number of factors in teaching, including clarity, variety, task orientation, student engagement, questioning, and cooperative learning.

Scientific learning. The understanding of factual information, concepts, and generalizations needed for everyday life; the development of proficiency in using and transferring the content of science into personal decision making; and the acquisition of attitudes and dispositions relating to the appropriate use of science knowledge and the willingness and ability to make informed decisions about the risks and benefits of science and technology in everyday life.

Simile. A figure of speech that compares two unlike things.

Spiral curriculum. Important ideas which are addressed repeatedly over the years in greater depth and more abstractly.

Temperature. A measure of the average rate of motion, or speed, of the smallest particles of matter (atoms and molecules).

Testing. A part of the assessment process in which a tool or instrument is used at widely spaced intervals to measure what a student knows at that time.

Theme. Broad educational ideas; for example, the interactions between materials rather than simply a study of magnets.

Theme-focused units. Units addressing a broad idea, which are often multidisciplinary.

Theory. An explanation of events based on laws, principles, and known consequences of other phenomena.

Total internal energy. The sum of the energy of motion of all of the particles of an object.

Unit. A set of interconnected, related lesson plans that explore, fully invent, and expand a topic.

Unit rationale. A statement describing the rationale for the unit answering these questions: How does the unit affect the future of the *students,* as well as their current individual needs and interests? How does the unit contribute to *societal* issues and help students deal responsibly with them? How is the unit *developmentally appropriate* for the students? How does the unit reflect the spirit and character of inquiry and the nature of science as a *self-learning enterprise* as compared to the view of science as known by someone else as an authority?

Values. Decisions about the worth or importance of something based on a standard we have set.

Wait time. Waiting 3 to 5 seconds before asking a student to respond to your higher-order question and waiting the same time before taking any action to the student's response.

Web. A method to organize the information and ideas from a unit in a graphic design showing interconnections between ideas and skills.

References

Abdi, S. W. (1997). Motivating students to enjoy science. *Science Teacher, 64*(6), 10.

Abraham, M. R., & Renner, J. W. (1986). The sequence of learning cycle activities in high school chemistry. *Journal of Research in Science Teaching, 23*(2), 121–145.

Abraham, R. (1989). Research and teaching: Research on instructional strategies. *Journal of College Science Teaching, 18*(3), 185–187.

Airasian, P. W. (1994). *Classroom assessment.* New York: McGraw Hill, 107–114.

Aldridge, B. (1992). Project on scope, sequence and coordination: A new synthesis for improving science education. *Journal of Science Education and Technology, 1,* 13–21.

Aldridge, B. G. (1994). Anticipating future things: Some thoughts on science education in 2044. *Science and Children, 31*(7), 20–21.

Allen, K. (1992). The effect of a textual reading activity at different phases of the science learning cycle on comprehension of science concepts. *Dissertation Abstracts International, 53,* 9, 3159.

American Association for the Advancement of Science. (1990). *Science for all Americans.* New York: Oxford University Press.

American Association for the Advancement of Science. (1993a). *Benchmarks for science literacy.* New York: Oxford University Press.

Anderson, C., & Smith, E. (1983). *Children's conceptions of light and color: Understanding the concept of unseen rays.* East Lansing, MI: Michigan State University.

Anderson, O. R. (1997). A neurocognitive perspective on current learning theory and science instructional strategies. *Science Education, 81*(1), 67–89.

Atwater, M. (1993). Multicultural science education. *The Science Teacher, 60*(3), 32–37.

Baker, D. R., & Piburn, M. D. (1997). *Constructing science in middle and secondary school classrooms.* Boston, MA: Allyn and Bacon.

Bar, V. (1989). Children's views about the water cycle. *Science Education, 73*(4), 481–500.

Bar, V., Sneider, C., & Martimbeau, N. (1997). Is there gravity in space? *Science and Children, 34*(7), 38–43.

Barell, J. (1991). Reflective teaching for thoughtfulness. In A. Costa (Ed.), *Developing minds: A resource book for teaching,* Revised edition, Volume 1 (pp. 207–210). Alexandria, VA: Association for Supervision and Curriculum Development.

Barman, C. (1989). The learning cycle: Making it work. *Science Scope, 12*(5), 28–31.

Barman, C. (1992). An evaluation of the use of a technique designed to assist prospective elementary teachers in using the learning cycle with science textbooks. *School Science and Mathematics, 92*(2), 59–63.

Barman, C., & Kotar, M. (1989). The learning cycle. *Science and Children, 26*(7), 30–32.

Baxter, J. (1989). Children's understanding of familiar astronomical events. *International Journal of Science Education, 11,* 15–57.

Bednar, A., Cunningham, D., Duffy, T., & Perry, J. (1992). Theory into practice: How do we link? In T. Duffy & D. Jonassen (Eds.), *Constructivism and the technology of instruction* (pp. 17–34). Hillsdale, NJ: Lawrence Erlbaum Associates.

Beisenherz, P. (1991). Explore, invent and apply. *Science and Children, 28*(7), 30–32.

Bell, B. (1981). When is an animal, not an animal? *Journal of Biological Education, 15,* 213–218.

Bell, B., & Barker, M. (1982). Toward a scientific concept of animal. *Journal of Biological Education, 16*(13), 197–200.

Bell, B., & Freyberg, P. (1985). Language in the science classroom. In R. Osborne & P. Freyberg (Eds.), *Learning in science* (pp. 29–40). Auckland, New Zealand: Heinemann.

Bellamy, N. (1994). Bias in the classroom: Are we guilty? *Science Scope, 17*(6), 60–63.

Bereiter, C., & Scardamalia, M. (1993). *Surpassing ourselves: An inquiry into the nature and implications of expertise.* pp. 3–33. Chicago: Open Court.

Berliner, D. (1987a). Knowledge is power: A talk to teachers about a revolution in the teaching profession. In D. Berliner & B. Rosenshine (Eds.), *Talks to teachers.* pp. 93–110. New York: Random House.

Berliner, D. (1987b). Simple views of effective teaching and a simple theory of classroom instruction. In D. Berliner & B. Rosenshine (Eds.), *Talks to teachers.* New York: Random House.

Berliner, D., & Casanova, U. (1987). How do we tackle kids' science misconceptions? *Instructor, 97,* 14–15.

Bernstein, L., Winkler, A., & Zierdt-Warshaw, L. (1998a). *African and African American women of science: Biographies, experiments, and hands-on activities.* Maywood, NJ: The Peoples Publishing Group.

Bernstein, L., Winkler, A., & Zierdt-Warshaw, L. (1998b). *Multicultural women of science: Three centuries of contributions with hands-on experiments and activities for 37 weeks.* Maywood, NJ: The Peoples Publishing Group.

Beyer, B. (1985). Critical thinking: What is it? *Social Education, 49,* 270–276.

Bianchini, J. A. (1998). What's the big idea? *Science and Children, 36*(2), 40–43.

Biehle, J., Motz, L., & West, S. (1999). *NSTA guide to school science facilities.* Arlington, VA: National Science Teachers Association.

Bishop, B., & Anderson, C. (1990). Student conceptions of natural selection and its role in evolution. *Journal of Research in Science Teaching, 27,* 417–427.

Bliss, J., & Osbourne, J. (1985). Children's choices of uses of energy. *European Journal of Science Education, 7,* 195–203.

Blystone, R., & Detting, B. (1990). Visual literacy in science textbooks. In M. B. Rowe (Ed.), *The process of knowing* (pp. 19–40). Washington, D.C.: National Science Teachers Association.

Boyes, E., & Stanisstreet, M. (1997). Children's models of understanding of two major global environmental issues (ozone layer and greenhouse effect). *Research in Science & Technological Education, 15*(1), 19–28.

Bransford, J., Sherwood, R., Kinzer, C., Hasselbring, T., & Williams, S. (1990). Anchored instruction: Why we need it and how technology can help. In D. Nix & R. Spiro (Eds.), *Cognition, education, and multimedia: Exploring ideas in high technology* (pp. 115–142). Hillsdale, NJ: Lawrence Erlbaum Associates.

Brasell, H. M. (1990). Graphs, graphing, and graphers. In M. B. Rowe (Ed.), *The process of knowing* (pp. 69–85). Washington, D.C.: National Science Teachers Association.

Brennon, F. (1997). 5, 4, 3, 2, . . . Thumbs up! *Science and Children, 35*(2), 14–17.

Brody, M., Chipman, E., & Marion, S. (1989). Student knowledge of scientific and natural resource concepts concerning acidic deposition. *Journal of Environmental Education, 20,* 32–41.

Brook, A., & Wells, P. (1988). Conserving the circus: An alternative approach to teaching and learning about energy. *Physics Education, 23,* 80–85.

Brooks, J., & Brooks, M. (1993). *In search of understanding: The case for constructivist classrooms.* Alexandria, VA: Association for Supervision and Curriculum Development.

Brown, D., & Clement, J. (1992). Classroom teaching experiments in mechanics. In R. Duit, F. Goldberg, & H. Niedderer (Eds.), *Research in physics learning: Theoretical issues and empirical studies* (pp. 380–397). Kiel, Germany: Institute for Science Education at the University of Kiel.

Brown, J., & Shavelson, R. (1996). *Assessing hands-on science.* Thousand Oaks, CA: Corwin Press.

Brumby, M. (1979). Problems in learning the concept of natural selection. *Journal of Biological Education, 13,* 119–122.

Brumby, M. (1982). Students' perceptions of the concept of life. *Science Education, 66,* 613–622.

Bruner, J. (1961). The act of discovery. *Harvard Educational Review, 31*(1), 21–32.

Burnett, J. (Fall, 1996). Including students with disabilities in general education classrooms: From policy to practice. *The ERIC Review, 4*(3), Rockville, MD: ACCESS ERIC, 2–11.

Burruss, J. D. (1999). Problem-based learning. *Science Scope, 22,* 6, 46–49.

Butler, G. (1991). Science and thinking: The write connection. *Journal of Science Teacher Education, 5,* 106–110.

Canizo, T. (1997). Mars exploratory vehicles. *Science Scope, 20*(5), 16–19.

Carey, S. (1985). *Conceptual change in childhood.* Cambridge, MA: MIT Press.

Carey, S. (1991). Knowledge acquisition: Enrichment or conceptual change? In S. Carey & R. Gelman (Eds.), *The epigenesis of mind: Essays on biology and cognition* (pp. 257–291). Hillsdale, NJ: Lawrence Erlbaum Associates.

Carle, E. (1987) *The very hungry caterpillar.* New York: Philomel Books.

Carnegie Commission on Science, Technology, and Government. (1991). *In the national interest: The federal government in the reform of K–12 math and science education.* New York: Carnegie Foundation.

Carr, M., & Kirkwood, V. (1988). Teaching and learning about energy in New Zealand secondary school junior science classrooms. *Physics Education, 23,* 86–91.

Champagne, A., Gunstone, R., & Klopfer, L. (1983). Naive knowledge and science learning. *Research in Science and Technological Education, 1*(2), 173–183.

Champagne, A. B. (1990). Assessment and teaching of thinking skills. In G. E. Hein (Ed.), *The assessment of hands-on elementary science programs* (pp. 68–82). Grand Forks, ND: University of North Dakota, Center for Teaching and Learning.

Chi, M., Feltovich, P., & Glaser, R. (1981). Categorization and representation of physics problems by experts and novices. *Cognitive Science, 5*, 121–152.

Children's Defense Fund. (1991). *Leave no child behind.* Washington, D.C.: Children's Defense Fund.

Children's Learning in Science. (1987). *Approaches to teaching the particulate theory of matter.* Leeds, UK: University of Leeds, Centre for Studies in Science and Mathematics Education.

Chittenden, E. (1990). Young children's discussions of science topics. In G. E. Hein (Ed.), *The assessment of hands-on elementary science programs* (pp. 220–247). Grand Forks, ND: University of North Dakota, Center for Teaching and Learning.

Clark, C., & Peterson, P. (1987). Teachers' thought processes. In M. Wittrock (Ed.), *Handbook of Research on Teaching,* 3rd ed. (pp. 225–296), New York: Macmillan.

Clarke, J. H. (1990). *Patterns of thinking, integrating learning skills in content teaching.* Boston, MA: Allyn and Bacon.

Clement, J. (1978). *Mapping a student's causal conception from a problem solving protocol.* Amherst, MA: University of Massachusetts, Department of Physics and Astronomy.

Clough, E. E., & Driver, R. (1986). A study of consistency in the use of students' conceptual frameworks across different task contexts. *Science Education, 70*(4), 473–496.

Cohen, M., & Kagan, M. (1979). Where does the old moon go? *The Science Teacher, 46*(11), 22–23.

Collins, A. (1991). Portfolios for assessing student learning in science: A new name for a familiar idea? In G. Kulm & S. M. Malcolm (Eds.), *Assessment in the service of reform* (pp. 291–300). Washington, D.C.: American Association for the Advancement of Science.

Collins, A. (1997). National science education standards: Looking backward and forward. *Elementary School Journal, 97*(4), 299–313.

Conners, K. (1989). *Feeding the brain: How foods affect children.* New York: Plenum.

Connor, J. V. (1991). Naive conceptions and the school science curriculum. In M. B. Rowe (Ed.), *The process of knowing* (pp. 5–18). Washington, D.C.: National Science Teachers Association.

Costa, A. (1991a). The inquiry strategy. In A. Costa (Ed.), *Developing minds: A resource book for teaching,* Revised edition, Volume 1 (pp. 302–303). Alexandria, VA: Association for Supervision and Curriculum Development.

Costa, A. (1991b). Teacher behaviors that enable student thinking. In A. Costa (Ed.), *Developing minds: A resource book for teaching,* Revised edition, Volume 1 (pp. 194–206). Alexandria, VA: Association for Supervision and Curriculum Development.

Costa, A. (1991c). Teaching for, of, and about thinking. In A. Costa (Ed.), *Developing minds: A resource book for teaching,* Revised edition, Volume 1 (pp. 31–34). Alexandria, VA: Association for Supervision and Curriculum Development.

Crawley, F. E., Barufaldi, J. P., & Salyer, B. A. (1994). Coordinated thematic science in the classroom: A view from pilot teachers. *School Science and Mathematics, 94*(5), 240–247.

Dagher, Z. A. (1994). Does the use of analogies contribute to conceptual change? *Science Education, 78*(6), 601–604.

Dagher, Z. A. (1995a). Analysis of analogies used by science teachers. *Science Education, 32*(3), 259–270.

Dagher, Z. A. (1995b). Review of studies on the effectiveness of instructional analogies in science education. *Science Education, 79*(3), 295–312.

Daisey, P., & Shroyer, M. G. (1995). Parents speak up: Examining parent and teacher roles in elementary science instruction. *Science and Children, 33*(3), 24–29.

de Vos, W., & Verdonk, A. H. (1996). The particulate nature of matter in science education and in science. *Journal of Research in Science Teaching, 33*, 657–664.

Deadman, J., & Kelly, P. (1978). What do secondary school boys understand about evolution and heredity before they are taught the topics? *Journal of Biological Education, 12*, 7–15.

Dempster, F. (1988). The spacing effect: A case study in the failure to apply the results of psychological research. *American Psychologist, 43*(8), 627–634.

Dewey, J. (1904/1962). *The relation of theory to practice in education.* Cedar Falls, IA: Association for Student Teaching.

Dewey, J. (1933). Analysis of reflective thinking. *How we think: A restatement of the relation of reflective thinking to the educative process* (pp. 102–118). Boston: Heath.

Ditchfield, C. (1987). *Better science: working for a multicultural society. Curriculum guide 7.* (ERIC Document Reproduction Service NO. ED 305229.)

Dreyfus, A., & Jungwirth, E. (1989). The pupil and the living cell: A taxonomy of dysfunctional ideas about an abstract idea. *Journal of Biological Education, 23,* 49–55.

Dreyfus, A., Jungwirth, E., & Eliovitch, R. (1990). Applying the cognitive conflict strategy for conceptual change—some implications, difficulties, and problems. *Science Education, 74*(5), 555–569.

Driver, R. (1985). Beyond appearances: The conservation of matter under physical and chemical transformations. In R. Driver, E. Guesne, & A. Tiberghien (Eds.), *Children's ideas in science* (pp. 55–66). Milton Keynes, UK: Open University Press.

Driver, R. (1986). *The pupil as scientist.* Philadelphia, PA: Open University Press.

Driver, R. (1990). Assessing the progress of children's understanding in science: A developmental perspective. In G. E. Hein (Ed.), *The assessment of hands-on elementary science programs* (pp. 204–216). Grand Forks, ND: University of North Dakota, Center for Teaching and Learning.

Driver, R., Guesne, E., & Tiberghien, A. (1985). *Children's ideas in science.* Milton Keynes, UK: Open University Press.

Driver, R., Leach, J., Millar, R., & Scott, P. (1996). *Young people's images of science.* Philadelphia, PA: Open University Press.

Driver, R., & Oldham, V. (1986). A constructivist approach to curriculum development in science. *Studies in Science Education, 13,* 105–122.

Driver, R., Squires, A., Rushworth, P., & Wood-Robinson, V. (1994). *Making sense of secondary science.* New York: Routledge.

Duit, R. (1984). Learning the energy concept in school—empirical results from the Philippines and West Germany. *Physics Education, 19,* 59–66.

Duit, R. (1987). Research on student's alternative frameworks in science—topics, theoretical frameworks, consequences for science teaching. In *Proceedings of the second international seminar: Misconceptions and educational strategies in science and mathematics,* Volume 1 (pp. 151–162). Ithaca, NY: Cornell University.

Dyasi, H. M. (1990). Children's investigations of natural phenomena: A source of data for assessment in elementary school science. In G. E. Hein (Ed.), *The assessment of hands-on elementary science programs* (pp. 248–262). Grand Forks, ND: University of North Dakota, Center for Teaching and Learning.

Dyrli, O., & Kinnaman, D. (1995). Teaching effectively with technology. *Technology and Learning, 15*(6), 52–57.

Eaton, J. F., Anderson, C. W., & Smith, E. L. (1983). When students don't know they don't know. *Science and Children, 20,* 6–9.

Eaton, J. F., Anderson, C. W., & Smith, E. L. (1984). Student's misconceptions interfere with science learning: Case studies of fifth-grade students. *The Elementary School Journal, 84,* 367–379.

Eckhaus, A., & Wolfe, R. (1997). Gathering and interpreting data: An interdisciplinary approach. *Science Scope, 20*(1), 44–47.

Eckstein, S. G., & Shemesh, M. (1993). Development of children's ideas on motion: Impetus, the straight-down belief and the law of support. *School Science and Mathematics, 93,* 299–305.

Eggen, P., & Kauchak, D. (1988). *Strategies for teachers: Teaching content and thinking skills.* Englewood Cliffs, NJ: Prentice Hall.

Eggen, P., Kauchak, D., & Harder, R. (1979). *Strategies for teachers.* Englewood Cliffs, NJ: Prentice Hall.

Emmert, E., Evertson, C., & Anderson, L. (1980). Effective classroom management at the beginning of the school year. *The Elementary School Journal, 80*(5), 219–231.

Ennis, R. (1991). Goals for a critical thinking curriculum. In A. Costa (Ed.), *Developing minds: A resource book for teaching,* Revised edition, Volume 1 (pp. 68–71). Alexandria, VA: Association for Supervision and Curriculum Development.

Erickson, G. (1985). Heat and temperature: An overview of pupil's ideas. In R. Driver, E. Guesne, & A. Tiberghien (Eds.), *Children's ideas in science* (pp. 145–169). Milton Keynes, UK: Open University Press.

Feldkamp-Price, B. (1994). A teacher's guide to choosing the best hands-on activities. *Science and Children, 31*(6), 16–19.

Feldsine, J., Jr. (1987). Distinguishing student misconceptions from alternate conceptual frameworks through the construction of concept mapping. In *Proceedings of the second international seminar: Misconceptions and educational strategies in science and mathematics,* Volume 1 (pp. 177–181). Ithaca, NY: Cornell University.

Fitzsimmons, P. F., & Goldhaber, J. (1997). Siphons, pumps, and missile launchers: Inquiry at the water tables. *Science and Children, 34*(4), 16–19.

Fosnot, C. (1993). Rethinking science education: A defense of Piagetian constructivism. *Journal of Research in Science Teaching, 30*(9), 1189–2201.

Foster, G. W., & Heiting, F. (1994). Embedded assessment. *Science and Children, 32*(2), 30–33.

Foster, G. W., & Penick, J. E. (1985). Creativity in a cooperative group setting. *Journal of Research in Science Teaching, 22*(1), 89–98.

French, J. (1995). Exploring empowering strategies for teaching elementary science methods. *Teacher Education and Practice, 11*(1), 82–98.

Gagne, R. (1965). *The conditions of learning.* New York: Holt, Rinehart, and Winston.

Gallagher, J. J. (1989). Research on secondary school science teacher's practices, knowledge, and beliefs: A basis for restructuring. In M. L. Tobin & B. J. Fraser (Eds.), *Looking into window: Qualitative research in science education.* 78–106. American Association for the Advancement of Science.

Gallegos, L., Jerezano, M. E., & Flores, F. (1994). Preconceptions and relations used by children in the construction of food chains. *Journal of Research in Science Teaching, 31*(3), 259–272.

Gardner, D. H. (1996). Bringing families and science together. *Science and Children, 34*(2), 14–16.

Gellert, E. (1962). Children's conceptions of the content and functions of the human body. *Genetic Psychology Monographs, 65,* 293–305.

Gil-Perez, D., & Carrascosa, J. (1990). What to do about science "misconceptions." *Science Education, 74*(5), 531–540.

Ginsburg, H. P., & Opper, S. (1988). *Piaget's theory of intellectual development.* 3rd ed. Englewood Cliffs, NJ: Prentice Hall.

Glatthorn, A., & Baron, J. (1991). The good thinker. In A. Costa (Ed.), *Developing minds: A resource book for teaching,* Revised edition, Volume 1 (pp. 63–67). Alexandria, VA: Association for Supervision and Curriculum Development.

Glynn, S. M., & Duit, R. (1995). *Learning science in the schools: Research reforming practice.* Mahwah, NJ: Lawrence Erlbaum Associates.

Glynn, S. M., & Muth, K. D. (1994). Reading and writing to learn science: Achieving scientific literacy. *Journal of Research in Science Teaching, 31,* 1057–1073.

Gondree, L., & Doran, D. (1998). Teach me some science. *Science and Children, 38*(3), 44–48.

Gonzalez, F. M. (1997). Diagnosis of Spanish primary students' common alternative science conceptions. *School Science and Mathematics, 97,* 68–74.

Good, T. L., & Brophy, J. E. (1986). *School effects: Occasional paper no. 77.* (ERIC Document Reproduction Service No. ED 264212.)

Greenwood, A. (1996). Science is part of the big picture. *Science and Children, 33*(7), 32–33.

Grundy, S. M., & Winston, M. (Eds.). (1989). *American Heart Association: Low-fat, low-cholesterol cookbook.* New York: Random House.

Guesne, E. (1985). Light. In R. Driver, E. Guesne, & A. Tiberghien (Eds.), *Children's ideas in science* (pp. 10–32). Milton Keynes, UK: Open University Press.

Gunstone, R., & Watts, M. (1985). Force and motion. In R. Driver, E. Guesne, & A. Tiberghien (Eds.), *Children's ideas in science* (pp. 85–104). Milton Keynes, UK: Open University Press.

Gunstone, R., & White, R. (1981). Understanding of gravity. *Science Education, 65,* 291–299.

Guy, M. D., & Wilcox, J. (1998). Science discovery centers. *Science and Children, 36*(3), 50–53.

Hampton, E., & Gallegos, C. (March, 1994). Science for all students. *Science Scope, 17*(6), 5–8.

Hannigan, M. R. (1990). Cooperative learning in elementary school science. *Educational Leadership, 47*(4), 25.

Hardy, G., & Tolman, M. (1997). Rocket investigations. *Science and Children, 34*(5), 8–9.

Harlen, W. (1985a). *Primary science: Taking the plunge.* London: Heinemann.

Harlen, W. (1985b). *Teaching and learning primary science.* New York: Teachers College Press.

Harlen, W. (1991). Performance testing and science education in England and Wales. In G. Kulm & S. Malcom (Eds.), *Science assessment in the service of reform* (pp. 69–102). Washington, D.C.: American Association for the Advancement of Science.

Harmon, M., & Mokros, J. (1990). Assessment in the new NSF elementary science curricula: An emerging role. In G. E. Hein (Ed.), *The assessment of hands-on elementary science programs* (pp. 163–188). Grand Forks, ND: University of North Dakota, Center for Teaching and Learning.

Harms, N. C., & Yager, R. E. (1981). *What research says to the science teacher,* Volume 3. Washington, D.C.: National Science Teachers Association.

Harrison, A. G., & Treagust, D. F. (1994). Science analogies: Avoid misconceptions with this systematic approach. *The Science Teacher, 61*(4), 40–43.

Harter, P., & Gerhke, N. (1989). Integrating curriculum: Kaleidoscope of alternatives. *Educational Horizons, 41,* 12–16.

Haury, D. (1993). *Teaching science through inquiry.* Columbus, OH: ERIC Clearinghouse for Science, Mathematics, and Environmental Education.

Hedgepeth, D. J. (1995). A comparison study of the learning cycle and a traditional instructional sequence in teaching an eighth-grade science topic. *Dissertation Abstracts International, 46,* 142A.

Hein, G. E. (1990a). Assessing assessment. In G. E. Hein (Ed.), *The assessment of hands-on elementary science programs* (pp. 1–17). Grand Forks, ND: University of North Dakota, Center for Teaching and Learning.

Hein, G. E. (1990b). Conclusion. In G. E. Hein (Ed.), *The assessment of hands-on elementary science programs* (pp. 264–279). Grand Forks, ND: University of North Dakota, Center for Teaching and Learning.

Hein, G. E. (1991). Active assessment for active science. In V. Perrone (Ed.), *Expanding student assessment* (p. 106). Washington, D.C.: Association for Supervision and Curriculum Development.

Hein, G. E., & Price, S. (1994). *Active assessment for active science.* London, Heinemann.

Helm, H., & Novak, J. (1983). *Misconceptions in science and mathematics.* Ithaca, NY: Cornell University.

Helm, H., & Novak, J. D. (1992). *Misconceptions and educational strategies in science and mathematics.* Ithaca, NY: Cornell University.

Hergenrather, J., & Rabinowitz, M. (1991). Age-related differences in the organization of children's knowledge of illness. *Developmental Psychology, 27,* 952–959.

Hesse, J. (1989). From naive to knowledgeable. *The Science Teacher, 56,* 55–58.

Hewson, M. G., & Hewson, P. W. (1988). An appropriate conception of teaching science. *Science Education, 72*(5), 597–614.

Hodson, D. (1994). In search of a rationale for multicultural science education. *Science Education, 77*(6), 685–711.

Holliday, W., Helgeson, S., Blosser, P., & McGuire, B. (1985). A summary of research in science education—1983. *Science Education, 69*(3), 275–419.

Holmes Group. (1986). *Tomorrow's teachers: A report of the Holmes groups.* East Lansing, MI: The Holmes Group.

Howe, A. C. (1996). Development of science concepts within a Vygotskian framework. *Science Education, 80*(1), 35–51.

Huntley, M. A. (1999). Theoretical and empirical investigations of integrated mathematics and science education in the middle grades with implications for teacher education. *Journal of Teacher Education, 50*(1), 57–67.

Hynd, C., Alvermann, D., & Qian, G. (1997). Preservice elementary school teachers' conceptual change about projectile motion: Refutation text, demonstration, effective factors, and relevance. *Science Education, 81*(1), 1–28.

Iwasyk, M. (1997). Kids questioning kids: "Experts" sharing. *Science and Children, 35*(1), 42–46.

Jacobowitz, R. (1997). 30 tips for effective teaching. *Science Scope, 21*(4), 22–25.

Jenkins-Jones, A. (Ed.). (1997). *Random house Webster's dictionary of scientists.* New York: Random House.

Johnson, C., & Wellman, H. (1982). Children's developing conceptions of the mind and brain. *Child Development, 53*(1), 222–234.

Johnson, D., Johnson, R., & Holubec, E. (1990a). *Circles of learning: Cooperation in the Classroom.* Edina, MN: Interaction Book Company, 8, 129–136.

Johnson, D. W., & Johnson, R. T. (1978). Cooperative, competitive, and individualistic learning. *Journal of Research and Development in Education, 12*(1), 3–15.

Johnson, D. W., & Johnson, R. T. (1991). Group assessment as an aid to science instruction. In G. Kulm & S. Malcom (Eds.), *Science assessment in the service of reform* (pp. 281–289). Washington, D.C.: American Association for the Advancement of Science.

Johnson, M. (1987). *The body in the mind: The bodily basis of meaning, imagination, and reason.* Chicago, IL: The University of Chicago Press.

Johnson, R. T., & Johnson, D. W. (1986). Action research: Cooperative learning in the science classroom. *Science and Children, 24*(2), 31–32.

Jonassen, D. (1995). Supporting communities of learners with technologies: A vision for integrating technology with learning in schools. *Educational Technology, 35*(4), 60–63.

Jones, M. G. (1994). Assessment potpourri. *Science and Children, 32*(2), 14–17.

Jones, M. G., Carter, G., & Rua, M. J. (2000). Exploring the development of conceptual ecologies: Communities of concepts related to convection and heat. *Journal of Research in Science Teaching, 37,* 139–159.

Joyce, B., & Weil, M. (1992). *Models of teaching.* Englewood Cliffs, NJ: Prentice Hall.

Jungwirth, E. (1975). Preconceived adaptation and inverted evolution (a case study of distorted concept formation in high school biology). *Australian Science Teacher Journal, 21,* 95–100.

Kahle, J. (1989). *Images of scientists: Gender issues in science classrooms. What research says to the science and mathematics teacher, No. 4.* Perth, Western Australia: Curtin University of Technology.

Kalchman, M. (1998). Storytelling and astronomy. *Science and Children, 36*(3), 28–31, 70.

Kargbo, D., Hobbs, E., & Erickson, G. (1980). Children's beliefs about inherited characteristics. *Journal of Biological Education, 14,* 137–146.

Karplus, R. (1979). Teaching for the development of reasoning. In A. E. Lawson (Ed.), *1980 AETS yearbook: The psychology of teaching for thinking and creativity.* Columbus, OH: ERIC/SMEAC.

Kass-Simon, G., & Farnes, P. (1990). *Women of science: Righting the record.* Bloomington: Indiana University Press.

Keil, F. (1989). *Concepts, kinds, and cognitive development.* Cambridge, MA: MIT Press.

Kesidou, S. (1990). *Scheulervorstellungen zur irreversibilitaet.* Kiel, Germany: Institute for Science Education at the University of Kiel.

Kesidou, S., & Duit, R. (1993). Students' conceptions of the second law of thermodynamics: An interpretive study. *Journal of Research in Science Teaching, 30,* 85–106.

Kindersley, D. & BBC Lionheart Television Intl. (1994). *Eyewitness fish.* London, UK: BBC Lionheart Television Intl.

King, A., & Rosenshine, B. (1993). Effects of guided cooperative questioning on children's knowledge construction. *Journal of Experimental Education, 61*(2), 127–148.

Klausmeier, H., Ghatala, E., & Frayer, D. (1974). *Conceptual learning and development: A cognitive view.* Orlando, FL: Academic Press.

Kleinheider, J. (1996). Assessment matters. *Science and Children, 33*(4), 22–25.

Klumb, K. (1992). *Generic consideration in adjusting curriculum and instruction for at-risk students.* Lucerne, CA: Lucerne Valley Unified School District. (ERIC Document Reproduction Service No. ED 342 141.)

Kounin, J. (1970). Discipline and group management in classrooms. Huntington, NY: R. E. Kreiger.

Kulm, G. E. (1991). The control of assessment. In G. Kulm & S. Malcom (Eds.), *Science assessment in the service of reform* (pp. 55–70). Washington, D.C.: American Association for the Advancement of Science.

Kulm, G. E., & Stuessy, C. (1991). Assessment in science and mathematics education reform. In G. Kulm & S. Malcom (Eds.), *Science assessment in the service of reform* (pp. 71–87). Washington, D.C.: American Association for the Advancement of Science.

Kyle, W. C. (1986). An implementation study: An analysis of elementary student and teacher attitudes toward science in process-approach vs. traditional science classes. (Report No. SE 047 523.) (ERIC Document Reproduction Service No. ED 275 540.)

Kysilko, D. (Ed.). (1995). *Winners all: A call for inclusive schools.* Alexandria, VA: National Association of Boards of Education.

Langley, D., Ronen, M., & Eylon, B. (1977). Light propagation and visual patterns: Preinstruction learners' conceptions. *Journal of Research in Science Teaching, 34*(4), 399–424.

Laubenthal, G. (1999). Web of life connections: Learning about the interdependence of life. *Science and Children, 36*(4), 20–23.

Lawson, A. (1995). *Science teaching and the development of thinking.* Belmont, CA: Wadsworth.

Lawson, A. E. (1988). A better way to teach biology. *American Biology Teacher, 50,* 266–278.

Lawson, A. E., Abraham, M. R., & Renner, J. W. (1989). *A theory of instruction: Using the learning cycle to teach concepts and thinking skills.* Atlanta, GA: National Association for Research in Science Technology, Monograph #1.

Layman, J. (1996). *Inquiry and learning: Realizing science standards in the classroom.* New York: The College Entrance Examination Board.

Leach, J., Driver, R., Scott, P., & Wood-Robinson, C. (1992). *Progression in understanding of ecological concepts by pupils aged 5 to 16.* Leeds, UK: The University of Leeds, Centre for Studies in Science and Mathematics Education.

Lee, O., Eichinger, C., Anderson, C., Berkheimer, G., & Blakeslee, T. (1993). Changing middle school students' conceptions of matter and molecules. *Journal of Research in Science Teaching, 30,* 249–270.

Lehman, J. (October, 1994). Assessment for preservice teachers. *Science and Children, 32*(2), 48–49.

Lehrer, R., & Schauble, L. (1998). Reasoning about structure and function: Children's conceptions of gears. *Journal of Research in Science Teaching, 35,* 3–25.

Lepscky, I. (1992). *Marie Curie.* Hauppauge, NY: Barron's Educational Series.

Leyden, M. B. (1991). *Discrepant events.* Teaching K–8, 21(5), 25–28.

Lightman, A., & Sadler, P. (1988). The Earth is round? Who are you kidding? *Science and Children, 25*(5), 24–26.

Linn, R. L. (1991). *How American teachers teach science in kindergarten and first grade.* Urbana, IL: Center for the Study of Reading.

Lopez-Freeman, M. A. (February, 1995). Invited papers. *The Science Teacher, 62*(2), 10.

Loving, C. (1998). Young people's images of science. *Science Education, 82*(6), 706–710.

Lowery, L. F. (1996). Pathways to the science standards. *Guidelines for moving the vision into practice,* Elementary school edition. Arlington, VA: National Science Teachers Association.

Lowery, L. F. (1997). *NSTA Pathways to the science standards—elementary school edition.* Arlington, VA: National Science Teachers Association.

MacKinnon, G. R. (1998). Soap and science. *Science and Children, 35*(5), 28–31.

Madrazo, G. M., & Rhoton, J. (1999). Classroom meets real world. *Science Scope, 22*(4), 26–28.

Magnusson, S. J., & Palinscar, A. S. (1995). The learning environment as a site of science education reform. *Theory into Practice, 34*(1), 43–50.

Manganus, V., Rottkamp, K. M., & Koch, J. (1999). Science is about not knowing, but trying to find out. *Science and Children, 36*(5), 38–41.

Marker, G. (1996). Social studies and the internet: developing a school policy. *Social Studies, 84*(6), 244–249.

Martens, M. (1990). Getting a grip on groups. *Science and Children, 27*(5), 18–19.

Martens, M. L. (1992). Inhibitors to implementing a problem solving approach to teaching elementary science: A case study of a teacher in charge. *School Science and Mathematics, 92*(3), 153.

Martin, D. J. (1997). *Elementary science methods: A constructivist approach.* Albany, NY: Delmar.

Martin, R. E., Jr., Sexton, C., Wagner, K., & Gerlovich, J. (1994). *Teaching science for all children.* Boston, MA: Allyn and Bacon.

Martin, R. E., Jr., Sexton, C., Wagner, K., & Gerlovich, J. (1997). *Teaching science for all children,* 2nd edition. Boston, MA: Allyn and Bacon.

Martin-Kniep, G. O., Feige, D. M., & Soodak, L. C. (1995). Curriculum integration: An expanded view of an abused idea. *Journal of Curriculum and Supervision, 10*(3), 227–249.

Marx, R. W., Blumenfeld, P. C., Krajcik, J. S., & Soloway, E. (1997). Enacting project-based science. *Elementary School Journal, 97*(4), 341–358.

Mayer, D. A. (1995). How can we best use children's literature in teaching science concepts? *Science and Children, 32*(6), 16–19, 43.

Mayer, V. J. (1995). Using the Earth system for integrating the science curriculum. *Science Education, 79*(4), 375–391.

McElroy, K. B. (1989). A taste of cooperativeness within an elementary school. *Pointer, 33*(2), 34–35.

McGrayne, S. (1993). *Nobel Prize Women in Science: Their lives, struggles, and momentous discoveries.* New York: Birch Lane Press.

McLaughlin, D. W. (1997). School to school partnerships. *Science and Children, 34*(5), 26–29.

Mead, M., & Metraux, R. (1957). Image of the scientist among high-school students: A pilot study. *Science, 126:* 384–390.

Meng, E., & Doran, R. L. (1990). What research says . . . about appropriate methods of assessment. *Science and Children, 56*(1), 42–45.

Meng, E., & Doran, R. L. (1993). *Improving instruction and learning through evaluation: Elementary school science.* Columbus, OH: ERIC Clearinghouse for Science and Mathematics Education, 11–94, 128–130.

Millar, R., & Driver, R. (1987). Beyond processes. *Studies in Science Education, 14,* 33–62.

Miller, K. W., Steiner, S. F., & Larson, C. D. (1996). Strategies for science learning. *Science and Children, 33*(6), 24–27, 61.

Minstrell, J. (1992). Facets of students knowledge and relevant instruction. In R. Duit, F. Goldberg, & H. Niedderer (Eds.), *Research in physics learning: Theoretical issues and empirical studies* (pp. 129–149). Kiel, Germany: Institute for Science Education at the University of Kiel.

Mintzes, J., Trowbridge, J., Arnaudin, M., & Wandersee, J. (1991). Children's biology: Studies on conceptual development in the life sciences. In S. Glynn, R. Yeany, & B. Britton (Eds.), *The psychology of learning science* (pp. 179–202). Hillsdale, NJ: Lawrence Erlbaum Associates.

Mitchell-Powell, B. (1995). More than just a pretty interface: access, content, and relevance in computer technology. *Social Studies and the Young Learner, 4*(3), 11–13.

Morrison, D., & Collins, J. (1995). Epistemic fluency and constructivist learning environments. *Educational Technology, 35*(4), 60–63.

Mullins, I., & Jenkins, L. (1988). *The science report card: Elements of risk and recovery.* Princeton, NJ: Educational Testing Service.

Murphy, P. (1990). What has been learned about assessment from the work of the APU science project? In G. E. Hein (Ed.), *The assessment of hands-on elementary science programs* (pp. 148–179). Grand Forks, ND: University of North Dakota, Center for Teaching and Learning.

Musheno, B. V., & Lawson, A. E. (1999). Effects of learning cycle and traditional text on comprehension of science concepts by students at differing reasoning levels. *Journal of Research in Science Teaching, 36*(1), 23–37.

Nagy, M. H. (1953). The representation of "germs" by children. *Journal of Genetic Psychology, 83,* 227–240.

Nakhleh, M. B., & Samarapungavan, A. (1999). Elementary school children's beliefs about matter. *Journal of Research in Science Teaching, 36,* 777–805.

National Aeronautics and Space Administration. (1992). *NASA's strategic plan for education, a strategy for change: 1993–1998,* 1st ed. Washington, D.C.: NASA.

National Council of Teachers of Mathematics. (1989). *Curriculum and evaluation standards for school mathematics.* Reston, VA: The National Council of Teachers of Mathematics, Inc.

National Education Association. (1993). *Student portfolios.* West Haven, CT: National Education Association Professional Library.

National Research Council. (1996). *National science education standards.* Washington, D.C.: National Academy Press.

National Science Teachers Association. (1993). *Science for all cultures: A collection of articles from NASA's journals* (S. J. Carey, Compiler). Arlington, VA: National Science Teachers Association.

National Science Teachers Association. (1994). *Everyday science: An enrichment calendar.* Arlington, VA: National Science Teachers Association.

Nelson, B. D., Aron, R. H., & Francek, M. A. (1992). Clarification of selected misconceptions in physical geography. *Journal of Geography, 91,* 76–80.

Nelson, G. D. (1999). Back to basics: Thoughts on improving U.S. science curriculum. *The Science Teacher, 66*(1), 54–57.

Nicaise, M., & Barnes, D. (1996). The union of technology, constructivism, and teacher education. *Journal of Teacher Education, 47*(3), 205–212.

Nichols, J. W. (1996). Family nature walks. *Science and Children, 34*(2), 42–43.

Novak, J. D. (1995). *Concept maps help teachers learn.* New York: Cornell University.

Novak, J. D., Gowin, D. B., & Johansen, G. T. (1983). The use of concept mapping and knowledge vee mapping with junior high school students. *Science Education, 67,* 625–645.

Nussbaum, J. (1979). Children's conceptions of the Earth as a cosmic body: A cross-age study. *Science Education, 58*(2), 21–23.

Nussbaum, J. (1985a). The earth as a cosmic body. In R. Driver, E. Guesne, & A. Tiberghien (Eds.), *Children's ideas in science* (pp. 170–192). Milton Keynes, UK: Open University Press.

Nussbaum, J. (1985b). The particulate nature of matter in the gaseous phase. In R. Duit, F. Goldberg, & H. Niedderer (Eds.), *Research in physics learning: Theoretical issues and empirical studies* (pp. 124–144). Kiel, Germany: Institute for Science Education at the University of Kiel.

Nussbaum, J., & Novick, S. (1982). Alternative frameworks, conceptual conflict and accommodation: Toward a principled teaching strategy. *Instructional Science, 11,* 183–200.

Ogborn, J. (1985). Understanding students' understandings: An example from dynamics. *European Journal of Science Education, 7,* 141–150.

Ogilvie, M. B. (1986). *Women in science—antiquity through the nineteenth century.* Cambridge, MA: MIT Press.

O'Reilly, K. (1991). Infusing critical thinking into United States history courses. In A. Costa (Ed.), *Developing minds: A resource book for teaching,* Revised edition, Volume 1 (pp. 164–168).

Alexandria, VA: Association for Supervision and Curriculum Development.

Osborne, R., & Freyberg, P. (1985a). Children's science. In R. Osborne & P. Freyberg (Eds.), *Learning in science* (pp. 5–14). Auckland, New Zealand: Heinemann.

Osborne, R., & Freyberg, P. (1985b). *Learning in science.* Auckland, New Zealand: Heinemann.

Osbourne, J. (1996). Beyond constructivism. *Science Education, 80*(1), 53–82.

Osbourne, J., & Wittrock, M. C. (1983). Learning science: A generative process. *Science Education, 67*(4), 489–508.

O'Sullivan, C. Y., Reese, C. M., & Mazzeo, J. (1997). *NAEP 1996 science report card for the nation and the states: Findings from the national assessment of educational progress.* Washington, D.C.: Office of Educational Research and Improvement, U.S. Department of Education.

Padilla, M. J., & Pyle, E. J. (1996). Observing and inferring promotes science learning. *Science and Children, 33*(8), 22–25.

Palmer, D. (1999). Exploring the link between students' scientific and nonscientific conceptions. *Science Education, 83,* 639–653.

Patton, J. R., & Polloway, E. A. (1987). Analyzing college courses. *Academic Therapy, 22*(3), 273–80.

Paul, R. (1991). Teaching critical thinking in the strong sense. In A. Costa (Ed.), *Developing minds: A resource book for teaching,* Revised edition, Volume 1 (pp. 77–84). Alexandria, VA: Association for Supervision and Curriculum Development.

Peck, G. (1989). Facilitating cooperative learning: A forgotten tool gets it started. *Science and Children, 28*(1), 17–20.

Penick, J. E. (1996). Questions are the answers. *Science Teacher, 63*(1), 26–29.

Perie, M. (1997). *Time spent teaching core academic subjects in elementary schools. Comparisons across community, school, teacher, and student characteristics. Statistical analysis report.* Washington, D.C.: American Institutes for Research in the Behavioral Sciences.

Perkins, D. (1992). Technology meets constructivism: Do they make a marriage? In T. M. Duffy & D. Jonassen (Eds.), *Constructivism and the technology of instruction* (pp. 45–55). Hillsdale, NJ: Lawrence Erlbaum Associates.

Perkins, D., & Blythe, T. (1994). Putting understanding up front. *Educational Leadership, 51*(5), 4–7.

Perkins, D., & Salomon, G. (1991). Teaching for transfer. In D. Costa (Ed.), *Developing minds: A resource book for teaching thinking,* Revised edition, Volume 1 (pp. 215–223). Alexandria, VA:

Association for Supervision and Curriculum Development.

Perkins, D. N. (1994). Creativity by design. *Educational Leadership, 42*(1), 18–24.

Philips, W. C. (1991). Earth and space science misconceptions. *The Science Teacher, 58,* 21–23.

Piaget, J. (1950). *The psychology of intelligence.* London: Routledge and Kegan Paul.

Piaget, J. (1963). *Origins of intelligence in children.* New York: Norton.

Piaget, J. (Forward to Hans G. Furth.) (1969). *Piaget and knowledge: Theoretical foundations.* Englewood Cliffs, NJ: Prentice Hall.

Piaget, J. (1970a). *The child's conception of movement and speed.* New York: Ballantine Books.

Piaget, J. (1970b). *The grasp of consciousness: Action and concept in the young child.* Cambridge, MA: Harvard University Press.

Piaget, J. (1970c). *The science of education and the psychology of the child.* New York: Orion Press.

Piaget, J. (1977). *The essential Piaget.* New York: Basic Books.

Piaget, J. (1978). *Success and understanding.* Cambridge, MA: Harvard University Press.

Posner, G., Strike, K., Hewson, P., & Gertzog, W. (1982). Accommodation of a scientific conception: Toward a theory of conceptual change. *Science Education, 6*(2), 211–227.

Potari, D., & Spiliotopoulou, V. (1996). Children's approaches to the concept of volume. *Science Education, 80*(3), 341–360.

Presst, B. (1976). Science education—a reappraisal, Part 1. *School Science Review, 57,* 201, 628–634.

Price, S., & Hein, G. (1994). Scoring active assessments. *Science and Children, 32*(2), 26–29.

Putnam, J. (1993). *Cooperative learning and strategies for inclusion: Celebrating diversity in the classroom.* Baltimore, MD: Paul H. Brookes Publishing Company.

Quality of Education for Minorities Report. (1990). *Education that works: An action plan for the education of minorities.* Cambridge, MA: MIT Press.

Quinn, M. E., & George, K. D. (1975). Teaching hypothesis formation. *Science Education, 59,* 289–296.

Rakow, S. J. (ed.). (1998). *NSTA pathways to the science standards. Middle school edition: Guidelines for moving the vision into practice.* Arlington, VA: National Science Teachers Association.

Ramadas, J., & Driver, R. (1989). *Aspects of secondary students' ideas about light.* Leeds, UK: University of Leeds, Centre for Studies in Science and Mathematics Education.

Reichel, A. G. (1994). Performance assessment: Five practical approaches. *Science and Children, 32*(2), 21–25.

Renner, J. W., Abraham, M. R., & Birnie, H. H. (1985). The importance of form of student acquisition of data in physics learning cycles. *Journal of Research in Science Teaching, 22*(4), 303–326.

Renner, J. W., Abraham, M. R., & Birnie, H. H. (1988). The necessity of each phase in the learning cycle in teaching high school physics. *Journal of Research in Science Teaching, 25*(1), 39–58.

Renner, J. W., & Marek, E. A. (1988). *The learning cycle and elementary school science teaching.* Portsmouth, NH: Heinemann.

Renner, J. W., & Marek, E. A. (1990). An educational theory base for science teaching. *Journal of Research in Science Teaching, 27,* 241–246.

Renner, J. W., Stafford, D. G., Lawson, A. E., McKinnon, J. W., Friot, E., & Kellog, D. H. (1976). *Research teaching and learning with the Piaget model.* Norman, OK: University of Oklahoma Press.

Richmond, G. (1994). An integrated approach. *Science Teacher, 61*(7), 42–45.

Riley, G. (1999). Elementary teachers' use of desktop publishing software. Unpublished doctoral dissertation. Tuscaloosa, AL: The University of Alabama.

Roach, V., Ascroft, J., & Stamp, A. (1995). *Winning ways: Creating inclusive schools, classrooms and communities.* Alexandria, VA: National Association of Boards of Education.

Ross, M. (1997). Scientists at play. *Science and Children, 34*(8), 35–38.

Rossman, A. D. (1993). Managing hands-on inquiry. *Science and Children, 31*(1), 35–37.

Roth, K., Anderson, C., & Smith, E. (1986). *Curriculum materials, teacher talk, and student learning: Case studies in fifth-grade science teaching.* East Lansing, MI: Michigan State University, The Institute for Research on Teaching.

Roth, W. -M. (1996). Teacher questioning in an open-inquiry environment: Interactions of context, content, and student responses. *Journal of Research in Science Teaching, 33,* 709–736.

Roth, W. -M. (1997). Interactional structures during a grade 4–5 open-design engineering unit. *Journal of Research in Science Teaching, 34,* 273–302.

Roueche, W. L., Sorensen, N., & Roueche, C. (1988). Strategies to verify the essential elements in secondary science. *The Clearing House, 62,* 65–71.

Rowe, M. B. (1987). Wait-time: Slowing down may be a way of speeding up. *American Educator, 11*(1), 38–47.

Rowe, M. B. (1991). Assessment implications of the new science curricula. In G. Kulm & S. Malcom (Eds.), *Science assessment in the service of reform* (pp. 89–96). Washington, D.C.: American Association for the Advancement of Science.

Rowe, M. B. (1996). Science, silence, and sanctions. *Science and Children, 34*(1), 35–37.

Rowe, M. B., & Holland, C. (1992). The uncommon sense of science. In M. B. Rowe (Ed.), *The process of knowing* (pp. 87–97). Washington, D.C.: National Science Teachers Association.

Ruggiero, S., Cartelli, A., Dupre, F., & Vincentini-Missoni, M. (1985). Weight, gravity, and air pressure: Mental representations by Italian middle-school students. *European Journal of Science Education, 7,* 181–194.

Rutherford, F. J., & Ahlgren, A. (1990). *Science for all Americans.* New York: Oxford University Press.

Ryan, J. (1996). Writing to learn math and science. *Teaching PreK–8, 27*(1), 78, 81.

Rye, J. A., & Rubba, P. A. (1998). An exploration of the concept map as an interview tool to facilitate the externalization of students' understandings about global atmospheric change. *Journal of Research in Science Teaching, 35*(5), 521–546.

Rye, J. A., Strong, D. D., & Rubba, P. A. (2001). Global warming and ozone layer depletion: STS issues for social studies classrooms. *Social Education, 65*(2), 90–95.

Saavi, P., & Allison, A. (Eds.). (1996). *Scientists.* New York: U.X., an imprint of Gale Publishing.

Sadler, P. (1987). Misconceptions in astronomy. In J. Novak (Ed.), *Proceedings of the second international seminar: Misconceptions and educational strategies in science and mathematics,* Volume III (pp. 422–425). Ithaca, NY: Cornell University.

Sandstead, H. (1986). Nutrition and brain function: Trace elements. *Nutrition Review, 44,* 37–41.

Sanger, M. J., & Greenbowe, T. J. (1997). Common misconceptions in electrochemistry: Galvanic, electrolytic, and concentration cells. *Journal of Research in Science Teaching, 34*(4), 377–398.

Saunders, W. L. (1992). The constructivist perspective: Implications for teaching strategies for science. *School Science and Mathematics, 92*(3) 138.

Schafer, L. E. (1994). *Behind the methods class door: Educating elementary and middle school teachers.* Columbus, OH: ERIC Clearinghouse for Science, Mathematics, and Environmental Education.

Scharman, L., Hampton, C., & Orth, C. (1995). Cooperative learning and preservice elementary teacher science self-efficacy. *Journal of Science Teacher Education, 6*(3), 125–133.

Schon, D. (1987). *The reflective practitioner.* New York: Basic Books.

Schonfeld, D. J., Bases, H., Quackenbush, M., Mayne, S., Morra, M., & Cicchetti, D. (2001). Pilot-testing a cancer education curriculum for grades K–6. *Journal of School Health, 71*(2), 61–65.

Schonfeld, D. J., & Quackenbush, M. (2000). Fixing children's worst misconceptions about AIDS. *Educational Digest, 66*(1), 57–60.

Schrag, J., & Burnett, J. (1993–1994). Inclusive schools. *Research Roundup, 10*(2), Alexandria, VA: The National Association of Elementary School Principals. (ERIC Document Reproduction Service No. ED 367 077.)

Schwab, J. (1974). The concept of the structure of a discipline. In E. Eisner & E. Vallance (Eds.), *Conflicting conceptions of curriculum.* Berkeley, CA: McCutchan.

Scribner-Maclean, M. (1996). Science at home. *Science and Children, 34*(2), 44–46.

Seiger-Ehrenberg, S. (1991). Concept development. In A. Costa (Ed.), *Developing minds: A resource book for teaching,* Revised edition, Volume 1 (pp. 290–294). Alexandria, VA: Association for Supervision and Curriculum Development.

Sexton, U. (1998). Each day is an opportunity: Reflections from the 1998 Shell awardee. *Science and Children, 36*(1), 40–42.

Shapiro, B. L. (1996). A case study of change in elementary student teaching thinking during an independent investigation in science: Learning about the "face of science that does not yet know." *Science Education, 80*(5), 535–560.

Shaw, E. L., & Hatfield, M. M. (1996). A survey of the use of science manipulatives in elementary schools. Paper presented at the annual meeting of the Mid-South Educational Research Association. (ERIC Document Reproduction Service No. ED 404160.)

Simpson, W., & Marek, E. (1988). Understandings and misconceptions of biology students: Concepts held by students attending small high schools and students attending large high schools. *Journal of Research in Science Teaching, 25*(5), 361–374.

Simsek, A. (1993). The effects of learner control and group composition in computer-based cooperative learning. *Proceedings of selected research and development presentations at the convention of the association for educational communications and technology sponsored by the research and theory division.* New Orleans, LA: Association for Educational Communications and Technology, 1–39. (ERIC Document Reproduction Service No. ED 362 205.)

Simsek, A., & Simon, H. (1992). The effects of cooperative versus individual videodisc learning on student performance and attitudes. *International Journal of Instructional Media, 19*(3), 209–218.

Slavin, R. E. (1989). Research on cooperative learning: Consensus and controversy. *Educational Leadership, 47*(4), 52–54.

Slavin, R. E. (1995). *Educational psychology,* 4th ed. Needham Heights, MA: Simon & Schuster.

Small, L., & Petrek, J. (1992). Teamwork testing. *Science Scope, 15*(6), 29–30.

Smith, E., & Anderson, C. (1984a). Plants as producers: A case study of elementary science teaching. *Journal of Research in Science Teaching, 21,* 685–698.

Smith, E., & Anderson, C. (1984b). *The planning and teaching of intermediate science: Final report.* East Lansing, MI: Michigan State University, The Institute for Research on Teaching.

Smith, E., & Anderson, C. (April, 1986). Alternative conceptions of matter cycling in ecosystems. Paper presented at the annual meeting of the National Association for Research in Science Teaching, San Francisco, CA.

Smith, E. L. (1990). Implications of teachers' conceptions of science teaching and learning. In M. B. Rowe (Ed.), *The process of knowing.* 41–54. Washington, D.C.: National Science Teachers Association.

Sneider, C. I., & Ohadi, M. M. (1998). Unraveling students' misconceptions about the Earth's shape and gravity. *Science Education, 82,* 265–284.

Sneider, C. I., & Pulos, S. (1983). Children's cosmographies: Understanding the Earth's shape and gravity. *Science Education, 67,* 205–221.

Snyder, Tom (1997). *Science Court.* [Computer software]. Watertown, MA: Tom Snyder Productions.

Solomon, J. (1985). Teaching the conservation of energy. *Physics Education, 20,* 165–170.

Solomon, J. (1986). When should we start teaching physics? *Physics Education, 21,* 152–154.

Songer, N. B., & Linn, M. C. (1991). How do students' views of science influence knowledge integration? *Journal of Research in Science Teaching, 28*(10), 761–784.

South Central Bell. (1994). *Black achievers in science.* Birmingham, AL: South Central Bell.

Spargo, P. E., & Enderstein, L. G. (1997). What questions do they ask? Ausubel rephrased. *Science and Children, 34*(6), 43–45.

Stahl, R. J. (1992). A context for "higher order knowledge": An information-constructivist (IC) perspective with implications for curriculum and instruction. *Journal of Structural Learning, 11*(3), 189–218.

Stahly, L. L., Krockover, G. H., & Shepardson, D. P. (1999). Third grade students' ideas about the lunar phases. *Journal of Research in Science Teaching, 36,* 159–177.

Stanley, G., & Brickhouse, N. (1994). Multiculturalism, universalism, and science education. *Science Education, 78*(4), 387–398.

Stavy, R. (1991a). Children's conceptions of changes in the state of matter: From liquid (or solid) to gas. *Journal of Research in Science Teaching, 27,* 247–266.

Stavy, R. (1991b). Children's ideas about matter. *School Science and Mathematics, 91,* 240–244.

Stavy, R., Eisen, Y., & Yakobi, D. (1987). How students aged 13–15 understand photosynthesis. *International Journal of Science Education, 9,* 105–115.

Stead, B. (1980). *Energy, learning in science project, working paper no. 17.* Hamilton, New Zealand: University of Waikato.

Stefanich, G. P. (1992). Reflections on elementary school science. *Journal of Elementary Science Education, 4*(2), 13–22.

Stein, M. (1997). Lightly stepping into science. *Science and Children, 34*(5), 18–21.

Stepans, J. I., Beiswenger, R. E., & Dyche, S. (1986). Misconceptions die hard. *The Science Teacher, 53,* 65–69.

Stepans, J. I., & Kuehn, C. (1985). What research says: Childrens' conception of weather. *Science and Children, 23,* 44–47.

Strommen, E. (1995). Lions and tigers and bears, oh my! Children's conceptions of forests and their inhabitants. *Journal of Research in Science Teaching, 32,* 683–698.

Suares, M., Pias, R., Membiela, P., & Dapia, D. (1998). Classroom environment in the implementation of an innovative curriculum project in science education. *Journal of Research in Science Teaching, 35*(6), 673–696.

Sunal, C. (1994). Conceptual reconstruction among elementary school children. *Proceedings of the Russian–American Symposium.* Manhattan, KS: 14–29.

Sunal, C., & Haas, M. (1993). *Social studies for the elementary/middle school student.* Ft. Worth, TX: Harcourt Brace Jovanovich.

Sunal, C., & Sunal, D. (1983). Adapting science for the hearing impaired. *Resources in Education.* (ERIC Document Reproduction Service ED No. 273 177.)

Sunal, C., Sunal, D., Smith, C., & Britt, J. (1996). Using the Internet: Preservice teacher experiences.

Paper presented at the annual meeting of Mid South Educational Research Association, Tuscaloosa, AL.

Sunal, C., Sunal, D., Smith, C., & Britt, J. (1998). Using the Internet to create meaningful instruction. *The Social Studies, 89*(1), 13–18.

Sunal, D., & Sunal, C. (1982). Teachers' guide for science for the hearing impaired. *Resources in Education.* (ERIC Document Reproduction Service ED No. 213 176.)

Sunal, D., & Sunal, C. (1998). Semiconductive science. *Science Scope, 22*(1), 22–26.

Sunal, D. W., & Burry, J. (1992). Context-related characteristics of expert science teaching. Paper presented at the annual meeting of the National Association for Research in Science Teaching. Boston, MA.

Sunal, D. W., & Sunal, C. S. (1990). Helping young children appreciate beauty in natural areas. *Day Care and Early Education, 18*(1), 26–29.

Sunal, D. W., & Sunal, C. S. (1991a). Backyard aesthetics. *Science Scope, 15*(1), 25–29.

Sunal, D. W., & Sunal, C. S. (1991b). Balance in the forest. *Day Care and Early Education, 18*(3), 22–25.

Sunal, D. W., & Sunal, C. S. (1991c). Tree growth rings: What they tell us. *Science Activities, 28*(2), 19–28.

Sunal, D. W., & Sunal, C. S. (1991d). Woodland aesthetics. *Science Scope, 15*(1), 8–12.

Sunal, D. W., & Sunal, C. S. (1991e). Young children learn to restructure personal ideas about growth in trees. *School Science and Mathematics, 91*(7), 314–317.

Sunal, D. W., & Sunal, C. S. (1994a). *Soils and Plant Growth.* Parsons, WV: U.S. Forest Service.

Sunal, D. W., & Sunal, C. S. (1994b). *The water cycle.* Tuscaloosa, AL: University of Alabama printing.

Sunburst Technology. (1998). *The factory deluxe.* [Computer software]. Pleasantville, NY: Sunburst Technology.

Sutman, F. X. (1995). Instructional strategies in three scenarios. *Science and Children, 32*(5), 30–33.

Sutton, C. (1992). *Words, science, and learning.* Philadelphia, PA: Open University Press.

Taiwo, A. A., Ray, H., Motswiri, M. F., & Masene, R. (1999). Perceptions of the water cycle among primary school children in Botswana. *International Journal of Science Education, 21*, 413–429.

Teague, W. (1995). *Alabama course of study—science.* Bulletin 1995, No. 4. Montgomery, AL: Alabama State Department of Education.

Tennyson, R., & Cocchiarella, M. (1986). An empirically based instructional design theory for teaching concepts. *Review of Educational Research, 56*, 40–71.

Texley, A. (1996). *NSTA pathways to the science standards.* Arlington, VA: National Science Teachers Association.

Thagard, P. (1992). Analogy, explanation, and education. *Journal of Research in Science Teaching, 29*(6), 537–544.

Thelen, L. J. (1983). Values and valuing in science. *Science Education, 67*(2), 185–192.

Tiberghien, A. (1983). Critical review of the research aimed at elucidating the sense that notions of temperature and heat have for students aged 10 to 16 years. In *Proceedings of the first international workshop research on physics education* (pp. 73–90). Paris: Editions du CNRS.

Tippins, D., & Dana, N. (1993). Culturally relevant alternative assessment. *Science for all cultures.* Arlington, VA: National Science Teachers Association.

Tobin, K. (1988). Alternative perspectives of effective science teaching. *Science Education, 72*(4), 433–451.

Tobin, K., & Fraser, B. J. (1987). A comparison of exemplary and non-exemplary teachers of science and mathematics. In K. Tobin & B. J. Fraser (Eds.), *Exemplary practice in science and mathematics education.* Perth: Curtin University of Technology.

Tobin, K., & McRobbie, C. (1996). The significance of cultural fit to the performance in science of Asian Americans. Paper presented at the annual meeting of the American Educational Research Association, New York.

Tolman, M. N., & Hardy, G. R. (1995). *Discovering elementary science: Method, content, and problem-solving activities.* Boston, MA: Allyn and Bacon.

Tressel, G. W. (1988). A strategy for improving science education. Paper presented at the annual meeting of the American Educational Research Association, New Orleans.

Trowbridge, J., & Mintzes, J. (1985). Students' alternative conceptions of animals and animal classification. *School Science and Mathematics, 85*, 304–316.

Trowbridge, J., & Mintzes, J. (1988). Alternative conceptions in animal classification: A cross age study. *Journal of Research in Science Teaching, 25*(7), 547–571.

Underwood, B. (1986). Evaluating the nutritional status of individuals: A critique of approaches. *Nutrition Review, 44*, 213–224.

U.S. Department of Education. (1989). Eleventh annual report to Congress on the implementation of the Education of the Handicapped Act. Washington, D.C.: U.S. Government Printing Office.

Vandercook, T., York, J., & Forest, M. (1989). The McGill action planning system (MAPS): A strategy for building the vision. *Journal of the Association for Persons with Severe Handicaps, 14*(3), 205–215.

Veglahn, N. (1991). *Women scientists.* New York: Facts on File.

Viennot, L. (1979). Spontaneous learning in elementary dynamics. *European Journal of Science Education, 1,* 205–221.

Vockell, E., & Schwartz, E. (1992). *The computer in the classroom.* Watsonville, CA: Mitchell McGraw Hill.

Vosniadou, S. (1991). Designing curricula for conceptual restructuring: Lessons from the study of knowledge acquisition in astronomy. *Journal of Curriculum Studies, 23,*(3) 219–237.

Vygotsky, L. (1978). *Mind in Society.* Cambridge, MA: Harvard University Press.

Vygotsky, L. S. (1962). *Thought and language.* Cambridge, MA: MIT Press.

Wandersee, J. H. (1985). Can the history of science help science educators anticipate students' misconception? *Journal of Research in Science Teaching, 23,* 581–597.

Wang, M. C., & Zollers, N. J. (1990). Adaptive instruction: An alternative service delivery approach. *Remedial and Special Education (RASE), 11*(1), 7–21.

Watts, D. (1983). Some alternative views of energy. *Physics Education, 18,* 213–217.

Watts, D. M., & Gilbert, J. K. (1983). Enigmas in school science: Students' conceptions for scientifically associated words. *Research in Science and Technological Education, 1*(2), 161–171.

Watts, M. (1983). A study of school children's alternative frameworks of the concept of force. *European Journal of Science Education, 5,* 217–230.

Watts, M. (1986). The differentiation of heat and temperature: An evaluation of the effect of microcomputer teaching on students' misconceptions. Technical report. Cambridge, MA: Harvard Graduate School of Education.

Weber, M. C., & Renner, J. W. (1972). How effective is the SCIS program? *School Science and Mathematics, 72*(4), 10–12.

Wiser, M. (1986). The differentiation of heat and temperature: An evaluation of the effect of microcomputer teaching on students' misconceptions. Technical report. Cambridge, MA: Harvard Graduate School of Education.

Wolf, D. (1989). Portfolio assessment: Sampling student work. *Educational Leadership, 46*(7), 35–39.

Yager, R. E. (1988). What science should contribute to cultural literacy. *The Clearing House, 62,* 297–301.

Yager, R. E., Hidayat, E. M., & Penick, J. E. (1988). Features which separate least effective from most effective science teachers. *Journal in Research in Science Teaching, 25*(3), 165–177.

Yager, R. E., & Lutz, M. V. (1994). Integrated science: The importance of "how" versus "what." *School Science and Mathematics, 94*(7), 338–346.

Name Index